꓿ THE EAST-WEST CENTER—officially known as the Center for Cultural and Technical Interchange Between East and West—is a national educational institution established in Hawaii by the U.S. Congress in 1960 to promote better relations and understanding between the United States and the nations of Asia and the Pacific through cooperative study, training, and research. The Center is administered by a public, nonprofit corporation whose international Board of Governors consists of distinguished scholars, business leaders, and public servants.

Each year more than 1,500 men and women from many nations and cultures participate in Center programs that seek cooperative solutions to problems of mutual consequence to East and West. Working with the Center's multidisciplinary and multicultural staff, participants include visiting scholars and researchers; leaders and professionals from the academic, government, and business communities; and graduate degree students, most of whom are enrolled at the University of Hawaii. For each Center participant from the United States, two participants are sought from the Asian and Pacific area.

Center programs are conducted by institutes addressing problems of communication, culture learning, environment and policy, population, and resource systems. A limited number of "open" grants are available to degree scholars and research fellows whose academic interests are not encompassed by institute programs.

The U.S. Congress provides basic funding for Center programs and a variety of awards to participants. Because of the cooperative nature of Center programs, financial support and cost-sharing are also provided by Asian and Pacific governments, regional agencies, private enterprise and foundations. The Center is on land adjacent to and provided by the University of Hawaii.

East-West Center Books are published by The University Press of Hawaii to further the Center's aims and programs.

PROPAGANDA AND COMMUNICATION
IN WORLD HISTORY

PROPAGANDA AND COMMUNICATION IN WORLD HISTORY

VOLUME II

Emergence of Public Opinion
in the West

edited by

Harold D. Lasswell
Daniel Lerner
Hans Speier

AN EAST-WEST CENTER BOOK ⚘
Published for the East-West Center by
The University Press of Hawaii
Honolulu

Library of Congress Cataloging in Publication Data
Main entry under title:

Emergence of public opinion in the West.

   (Propaganda and communication in world history ; v. 2)
   "An East-West Center book."
   Includes index.
    1. Public opinion—History. 2. Propaganda—History.
3. Communication in politics—History. 4. Social
movements—History. I. Lasswell, Harold Dwight,
1902–   II. Lerner, Daniel. III. Speier, Hans,
1905–   IV. Series.
HM258.P74   vol. 2 [HM261]   301.14s   [301.15'4'09]
  ISBN 0-8248-0504-6   79–18790

These three volumes are dedicated to
        JEAN LERNER
our indispensable collaborator
who, with insight, skill, and good cheer,
did whatever needed to be done
through the years of these studies

CONTENTS

Contents

PREFACE

In the world history of communication, the rise of Western civilization can be dated from the invention of the printing press in the mid-fifteenth century. William Bouwsma's opening chapter shows that preparation for print began in the thirteenth century. The great Renaissance contribution to public, rather than elite, communication then shaped the development of print from the fifteenth through the seventeenth century. Maritime exploration and global colonization—in America conventionally dated from Columbus' voyage in 1492 to the landing of the Pilgrims in 1619—carried people from Europe around the world. They brought printed European messages with them.

The phases of communication history fit nicely with general historical periodization, which usually dates the rise of modern Western civilization with the transition from medievalism to the Renaissance in Europe. Accordingly, volume I ended with the Middle Ages and volume II begins with the Renaissance, focusing on the subsequent emergence of public opinion in the West. This sequence contributed to the transformation of stateways, thoughtways, and lifeways in the modern world.

Among the far-reaching reforms of the Renaissance and the Reformation was a shift from the Universal Latin of medievalism (a "universal" language shared by only a small elite in a few countries) to the "national" languages of the people. Much

of secular Renaissance literature was written in the vernacular.
The Bible was translated into national languages everywhere;
sermons were preached in German, French, English, and so
forth; Luther's ninety-five theses were written in German. So
effective was the New Word spread by the Reformation that the
Catholic church soon followed suit by transforming much of its
own communications into the vernacular. This process, which
has continued from the Counter-Reformation to the present
time, exemplifies a major communication strategy that has
been characterized by Lasswell as "restriction by partial incorporation."

The Enlightenment took the history of communication in a
new direction—to the secular "city of God" created by the
philosophes of the eighteenth century. Their etiquette was
French, but their ideas were deployed everywhere on the Old
Continent and in the New World (Jefferson was their heritor
and *The Federalist Papers* the fruit of their seed). If some of the
new philosophers were deist, many of them were atheist and
others were virulently antichurch. If they refrained from attacking religion, it was probably on the view attributed to Voltaire
—that piety was good for "the common people" because it
kept *vox populi* quiet. Themselves a cosmopolitan elite, the
philosophes were cautious in politics and, as Peter Gay writes,
indulged only in "gingerly treatment of the masses."

This was to change radically in the populist politics of the
French Revolution. Even pre-Revolutionary Europe, as Hans
Speier makes clear, was already promoting the rise of public
opinion in many countries. In the post-Revolutionary century,
roughly from the Congress of Vienna to World War I, radical
politics in the form of secular (even "scientific") socialism
claimed a large share of attention in Western communication.
The successive chapters in the second part of this volume clarify
the propaganda components of the historical process which hastened the spread of radical ideologies, both millenarian and
Marxist. The global eruption of the latter in the Bolshevik Revolution, and its aftermath, are analyzed in chapters by Padover,
Griffith, Speier, and Whaley.

A new era of crisis politics was inaugurated in Europe after
World War I: dynasties fell; empires crumbled; and the coercive
ideologues, whose "politics of the street" was amplified by the

mass media of print and radio, reached for and often grasped the reins of power. Communism in Russia was followed by Fascism in Italy, by Nazism in Germany, by Falangism in Spain, and by dozens of antidemocratic movements elsewhere.

The process of crisis politics was accelerated after World War II, when the European empires virtually disappeared and new nations emerged on the world stage. These changing arenas involved an arduous, and often violent, quest for new identities, national and personal, as discussed by Harold Isaacs. The aspirations and demands of the new nations are clarified by Lucian Pye. The world communication network was reshaped in significant ways, as described by Oscar Schachter, when the United Nations became the world forum for communication between the new nations and the old.

Over these struggles for terrestrial power hung the enigma of nuclear power: would it multiply the sources of energy that could benefit mankind, or would it destroy the human race? The three chapters assembled in our "nuclear colloquy" deal with this momentous question.

THE ENLARGING SYMBOLIC
OF THE MODERN WEST

1

THE RENAISSANCE AND THE BROADENING OF COMMUNICATION

WILLIAM BOUWSMA

The historical significance of the Renaissance, whether this term is taken to signify a cluster of cultural movements or a period of time variously defined for Italy and for northern Europe, has long been one of the classical problems of historical discussion. Much of this has been inconclusive, largely because it has been couched in excessively general terms. But recent scholarship has tended to focus on increasingly specific issues, with the result that scholars are more successful now than in the past in identifying particular areas of important innovation. Thus it has recently become apparent that the Renaissance occupies a crucial position in the development of theories about human communication and in the practical uses of communication for the promotion of concrete political and social goals. Behind these changes lay major transformations in political and social life, and at the same time they must be seen within the larger context of new values and attitudes toward human existence in general.

The importance of this development can be grasped only in the light of conceptions dominant in medieval culture. Two aspects of the situation at the beginning of the fourteenth century must be emphasized: that its vision of man and his relations with the world was largely appropriate to a fragmented agrarian society, and that it interpreted man's destiny in Christian terms and proposed to coordinate all earthly matters to man's ultimate end.

For most men, the agricultural basis of life, with its dependence on the seasons and the eternal round of biological nature, had supplied some foundation in experience for a perception of reality as dependable regularity. Interruptions in the patterns of life, irregularity and disorder, were experienced as intrusions rather than as the normal condition of existence; they were literally perceived as special acts of God. At the same time the constant and trivial changes in the almost infinitely articulated mosaic of the feudal world, which lacked strong and relatively stable centers of political organization, stood in the way of any conception of linear and significant political development. Under these conditions earthly change seemed meaningless and, in the nature of things, unresponsive to deliberate efforts at transformation by men.

The high degree of abstraction in much of medieval thought corresponded, then, to a world in which experience displayed a high degree of regularity, so that man could generalize about it and identify reality as a set of objective and eternal verities relieved of the need for empirical verification. This vision of the world also fitted a conception of man, inherited from Greek philosophy rather than from the Judaeo-Christian past, that identified man's essence with his rational intellect, which in turn was understood to have a direct access and correspondence to an external reality created by God for man's edification and use. Thus the order man discerned in the universe was assigned an objective existence, and the supreme function of the intellect was seen as the identification of the abstract pattern underlying all reality, and the elaboration and development of its ultimate implications by the rigorous application of logic. The characteristic products of such intellectual activity were the comprehensive and utterly consistent systems of scholastic thought resting on a metaphysical base and corresponding in both method and substance (if not identical) with the equally systematic and objective truths of theology.

This conception of intellectual activity made scholastic thought fundamentally passive in relation to the world. Thought was directed, at its highest level, to contemplation rather than to worldly action; by the same token, the primary function of communication was to convey a species of ultimate, systematic, objective, and rational wisdom for human admiration. The world, on the other hand, appeared worthy of attention only when it obstructed the elaboration and dissemination of this ultimate wisdom or seemed incongruent with it. The world then needed to be reminded of the ideal structure of reality to which it was obligated to conform, and on occasion it also needed to be disciplined. Other types of communication, such as were required to hold together even a relatively simple society, commanded only minimal attention and little esteem.

These conceptions found further support in a characteristic social structure, and especially in the social role assumed by the clergy. Society was itself conceived of as an order, descending from God himself through a hierarchy of social ranks, that was also an expression of the central principles of order inherent in all reality. Wisdom therefore was to be proclaimed, and conformity to its prescriptions enforced from above. Its supreme representative in this world was, of course, the pope; those entrusted with the discovery, elaboration, preservation, and transmission of wisdom were primarily members of the clergy, a specialized group of intellectuals, generally university men and members of religious orders under the special protection of the pope, who were conceived to be closer to ultimate truth precisely because of their separation from and superiority to the world. The abstract, technical, and esoteric language they employed served to emphasize both the subtlety and sublimity of wisdom and their own superior status, on which all other men were presumed to depend.

I

But even as this ideal model was achieving its fullest articulation in the thirteenth century, it was being undermined by forces of political and social change already long at work. In major parts of Europe the feudal mosaic had been giving way in a slow process of centralization that was eventually to culminate with the emergence of city states and powerful monarchies, as well as other types of territorial states, that had increasingly clear geographical definition, a relatively long life, and individual patterns of development that appeared to refute the assumptions that change is meaningless and that only the abstract and general is real. And as these entities claimed an equality of status despite obvious inequalities of power, their existence tended to dissolve the notion that reality is necessarily organized hierarchically.

For men whose attitudes were defined in this new atmosphere, the real world was more and more the absorbing world of their own daily experience, not—as it now often appeared—the coldly impersonal and rigid world of scholastic abstraction. Experience presented itself to them not as dependable regularity based on the universal and objective order of things, but as a series of unpredictable and novel events. From this perspective, scholastic systems seemed not so much false as merely irrelevant; the real world was not, after all, intellectually apprehensible in the old manner but fraught with contradiction and even moral ambiguity. It could be made to yield a kind of sense only in more modest personal ways, in the context of individual needs and particular situations. Truth itself now looked different and required new, more concrete, and more flexible forms of expression.

Furthermore the problem had a serious practical dimension. Survival in the arena of politics and commerce depended above all on adaptation to novelty, on flexibility and improvisation; any insistence on the universal application of general principles threatened these practical virtues. In social life itself the notion of hierarchy was less and less compelling as men, driven by profit or ambition, sought to rise in the world through their own talents. In addition, towns and other secular-political organizations were dominated by laymen, whose authority, dignity, and thus political effectiveness were threatened by claims of clerical superiority. Increasingly well educated, self-conscious, and assertive, such men required a new culture of which they would themselves be the major representatives. This new culture, in contrast to the old, would need to deal directly with the concrete world of common experience in all its color, variety, and change. It would be required, too, to serve practical needs; and because these were increasingly perceived as relative to time and place, it would no longer be expected to reflect the sublime consistency of the older patterns. And among its other obligations, it would have to serve the needs of social control in a new climate in which reliable guidance could no longer be accepted from above.

These stipulations were generally met by the culture of the Renaissance, with its antipathy to abstract system building, its compartmentalization of life, its secularism (though this should by no means be interpreted as a hostility to religion, which Renaissance thought chose rather to define in its own way), its tendencies to naturalism, its relativism and skepticism. Integrally related to all of these was a set of novel views about the nature and uses of communication, which was now conceived to be no longer primarily a means of conveying an ultimate wisdom, but rather the essential bond among men in society. The significance of the Renaissance here lies first of all in its changing sense of what is communicable, but equally in its conception of the uses of communication to meet the needs of social existence. For the new age, communication could no longer transmit ultimate truths, for these—as experience demonstrated—seemed beyond all human comprehension. It had, if it would communicate anything, to deal with lesser things, base itself on the familiar world of concrete experience apprehensible to ordinary men, speak in a common language they could understand, and attempt to serve their various and changing needs.

II

This is the general significance of Renaissance humanism, with its repudiation of scholastic discourse and its effort to revive and adapt to contemporary uses the rhetorical theory and practice of antiquity. If humanism is defined simply as the study of the classics, it must be acknowledged that medieval culture also included a strong humanistic element. Vergil and Cicero, in addition to Aristotle, were widely read in earlier centuries; the *Summa Theologica* and the *Divine Comedy* bear witness in different ways to the seriousness with which the literature and the insights of antiquity were regarded. But such uses of the antique past as one encounters in Thomas Aquinas and Dante were quite different from those of the Renaissance. For such medieval thinkers the classics were primarily guides in the pursuit of a perennial philosophy ultimately independent of any particular culture. Once identified, this philosophy was to be fused with the equally perennial revelations of the Christian faith into a single, universally valid system of eternal truth. Seen in this way classical literature was of small value for itself, as a splendid creation of men; it was likewise of small importance to examine it in its integrity, as a communication out of the past based on the common humanity of mankind. Renaissance humanism was a novelty because it approached the classics in a different spirit. It disclaimed the reduction of classical themes to a system of final wisdom and sought instead to appropriate the works of ancient literature in all their human individuality.

The characteristic medieval preoccupation with the expression of ultimate truth had been reflected in an emphasis within the medieval arts curriculum that was to make education one of the major areas of conflict between Renaissance humanists and schoolmen. Based on the traditional division of learning into the seven liberal arts, which in turn were grouped in the literary *trivium* (grammar, logic, rhetoric) and the quantitative *quadrivium* (arithmetic, geometry, astronomy, music), this curriculum had developed a decided preference for logic in the course of the thirteenth century. There was a corresponding distaste for rhetoric (except in sermons) as a sophistical technique likely to falsify truth under the influence of human interests and sinful passions; grammar was largely a tool for getting at the meaning of texts for logical evaluation. Only logic seemed useful to get at the truth. This emphasis led, within the classical corpus, to a preference for the ancient philosophers, whose distrust of poetry was shared by their medieval followers. The humanists of the Renaissance, on the other hand, often identified themselves as poets, that is, as artists of verbal expression.

Nevertheless Renaissance humanism, as it first emerged in fourteenth-century Italy, owed much to medieval classicism, from which it inherited a body of classical texts and an initial respect for antiquity itself. The needs that humanism met also had developed only gradually. The precocious urbanization of northern and central Italy had been gathering force since at least the tenth century, in a process that required novel and increasingly complex social organization, and with it the less tangible bonds of community. Italian towns needed governments capable of maintaining the support of their inhabitants; agencies to maintain order, levy taxes, correspond with other governments, and keep records; lawyers and notaries to meet the needs of both private and public business. Under such conditions talent for both oral and written expression was essential; thus in 1284 a public official in Reggio had to be dismissed because of a speech defect.[1] Expressive gifts were especially required among notaries, representing the traditional *ars dictaminis,* who prepared documents and wrote letters for a variety of clients,[2] and among lawyers, who represented them in the courts. The importance of these occupations in both the backgrounds and the development of humanism is, indeed, only now widely recognized. It is significant that the famous law school at Bologna originated as an academy of rhetoric, that law was the favorite discipline of Italian students, and that lawyers were in a unique position to perceive the value of eloquence for practical life; lawyers and notaries, organized in a single guild, were also unusually prominent in public affairs.[3] Meanwhile, as town chanceries became increasingly active, their officials were more and more concerned with the effectiveness of literary style. Collections of their correspondence began to circulate as stylistic models before the end of the thirteenth century.[4]

Renaissance humanism was a product of the combination of this practical development with an interest in the classics, which had previously been more lively in northern Europe, especially in France, than in Italy. Two features of the Italian scene made Italy unusually receptive to classicism. One was the fact that scholastic culture had relatively shallow roots in Italy, where it was introduced, chiefly in the schools of the religious orders, only toward the end of the thirteenth century. In addition the history and geography of Italy suggested that Italians were the legitimate heirs of ancient, and in particular of Latin, culture; the fact that ancient literature had met the needs of a society based on cities did not escape attention. Indeed, classical interests of a very different sort from those exhibited by the schoolmen were already manifesting themselves in Italy before the end of the thirteenth century, notably in Padua and Florence, where public officials had begun to imitate Latin models in composing letters and orations.

In Padua this interest produced the first prominent humanist of a Renaissance type in Albertino Mussato (1262–1329), a notary who defended poetry as a source of wisdom against the exclusive claims of philosophy and theology; exhibited a novel concern with the changing world of human affairs by writing history modeled on Livy, Caesar, and Sallust, and a Latin tragedy attacking tyranny; and influenced chancery style and education in Venice as well as in his native city.[5] In Florence the early fusion of classical and civic interests was represented by Brunetto Latini (about 1220–1294), who studied the rhetoric of Cicero in order to teach his contemporaries, in the words of the chronicler Giovanni Villani, "how to speak well, and how to guide and rule our republic according to policy."[6]

These interests were much stimulated by fourteenth-century Italian contacts with France, especially through Avignon during the long papal residence there. Study of the classics, though submerged by scholastic emphasis on logic, had never disappeared in France, and works of ancient literature were more readily available there than in Italy. They were especially numerous in the papal library at Avignon, which was therefore a center for copying manuscripts and of trade in books.[7] These resources were notably exploited by Francesco Petrarca, known as Petrarch (1304–1374), greatest of the fourteenth-century Italian humanists, who was soon to be regarded as the father of the humanist movement.

Petrarch anticipated most of the themes that were to make Renaissance humanism into a movement of major historical importance. He attacked the schoolmen of his day for their unintelligibility and for an abstract intellectuality irrelevant to the moral and political needs of men.[8] But his sense of these needs led him to seek a remedy. Regarding his own time as peculiarly wretched, and thus animated by a nostalgic admiration for antiquity as a happier age, he attempted to master Latin literature as a whole. In this interest he collected manuscripts, improved texts, and modeled his own style on the ancients, with marked benefits for the clarity and—as his interests were both broad and lively, touching on many aspects of human experience and the world—for the range of both Latin prose and Italian lyric verse.

Language, under Petrarch's influence, became a more flexible and effective instrument, and what it could communicate was vastly enlarged. Thus his classicism was also related to a new conception of the uses of human discourse. Words, for Petrarch, realized their highest potentiality not in the revelation of an ultimate wisdom, for he was largely skeptical of man's ability to penetrate into such matters, but in their use as a tool for a variety of concrete human purposes. He had himself taken occasional service with princes, undertaking diplomatic missions on which he delivered official orations; he was also a reformer and moralist, and valued language for its ability to persuade men to virtue.

With these preoccupations, he discovered the rhetorical doctrines of Cicero and employed them to meet the needs of the new social and political order. For Cicero rhetoric had been the supreme art, supreme in the first place because it drew on every other art and every branch of knowledge, so that it also implied the broadest possible education, in contrast to the narrowness of the schools. This pointed ultimately to a new cultural ideal; the universal man of the Renaissance is foreshadowed in the Ciceronian idea of the orator. But above all, rhetoric was supreme for Cicero because, unlike abstract philosophy, it conceived of man as not merely or even primarily an intellectual being; and because it appealed to other dimensions of his personality as well, rhetoric alone could advance truth to its full realization in action. The Ciceronian subordination of wisdom to action evidently pointed to a view of truth and of man's access to final knowledge quite different from that of the schoolmen; it also pointed to a different audience.

For in the world of action, communication had to be directed generally to the understanding of ordinary men and thus to employ their language rather than an esoteric technical vocabulary; it remained incomplete if it was apprehensible only to a specialized elite. As Cicero had written in his *De oratore,* "Whereas in all other arts that is most excellent which is farthest removed from the understanding and mental capacity of the untrained, in oratory the cardinal sin is to depart from the language of everyday life, and the usage approved by the sense of the community." Whereas the humanists had begun by writing chiefly in Latin, this revived Ciceronian position would eventually compel Latin to give way before the various vernaculars of Europe. In addition, as the common man and his community had variable and changing needs, these doctrines implied that communication, as an informative and persuasive act, should be capable of assuming many forms and of pointing in various directions that might not assume, as a whole, any consistent pattern. Thus wisdom itself tended to assume a practical and relative character; it became a function of social needs.[9]

All of this was conveyed by Petrarch to his contemporaries,

although its full appreciation took several generations. In addition Petrarch was largely responsible for a new quality of historical perspective that involved what might be described as an ability to communicate with the past as the past. For from the contrast between his own time and the age of Cicero, between which he saw that there had intervened a Dark Age, he perceived the profound disjunction between the present and the past. No longer could the pronouncements of ancient worthies be regarded as expressions of a perennial truth applicable to all men in any period, so that one could regard Cicero as an oracle for every age. The ancients had to be regarded as products of a different time and different conditions, and to understand them required not simply intellectual effort but a strenuous act of imagination working on the authentic sources thrown up from the past. This insight may not have been altogether consistent with Petrarch's insistence on the relevance of Cicero, but it was based on a new and fruitful recognition of the reality of change and the individuality of particular cultures. It meant that figures of the past could now be approached as complex human beings in all their concreteness rather than as abstract types.[10] It also facilitated the development of a new type of discourse, based on the importance of change, that was to culminate in the later Renaissance with the great histories of Machiavelli, Guicciardini, and Paolo Sarpi.

The fourteenth century, however, was still ambivalent in the presence of these novel conceptions, which were in such radical conflict with traditional values. In addition the peculiar uncertainties of later fourteenth-century life, the demographic catastrophes initiated by the Black Death in 1348, prolonged economic depression, internal disorders, and foreign wars, made the public world whose needs humanism was calculated to meet appear singularly unattractive, and the security afforded by the older patterns of thought constantly alluring.[11] Petrarch himself shared in this ambivalence, often giving expression to the attractions of a life of solitude devoted to the pursuit of a reliable abstract wisdom. Similar uncertainties may be discerned in his followers of the generation after his death. In Florence, which was destined eventually to give particular expression to Petrarch's more profound influence, his immediate followers were often the partisans of a merely academic classicism in which the

Petrarchan love of antiquity was detached from contemporary life and converted into narrow philological scholarship.[12]

But the most important figure of this period, Coluccio Salutati, although he wavered between the attractions of the contemplative life and civic responsibility, nevertheless served Florence well through a series of crises. A professional notary in various towns before coming to Florence, he was chancellor of the city from 1375 till his death in 1406; in this important post, despite his moments of doubt about the values of this world, he applied the humanism of Petrarch directly to civil life. The eloquence of his official correspondence, which reflected his wide knowledge of classical authors, made a profound impression on contemporaries. For perhaps the first time in European history, the pen seemed mightier than the sword; the tyrant of Milan is reported to have said that Salutati's writings were worth more than a thousand horsemen. Against the challenge to Florence from this ruler he wrote persuasively of the city he served as the heir to republican Rome in the defense of civic freedom, which he praised as the necessary condition of human virtue and high culture.

In a famous tract Salutati praised law above medicine because laws are directed to "the conservation of society, the common good and political felicity," a more important end than the systematic knowledge of nature on which medicine was based. Against this background he elaborated on the function and importance of rhetoric as the source of eloquence. This art alone, he declared, made it possible "to control the motions of the mind, to turn your hearer where you will, and to lead him back to the place from which you moved him, pleasantly and with love."[13] Only speech made it possible for one man to help another; to it therefore were owed all the benefits of society. Such sentiments did not prevent him from expressing quite different views on other occasions, so that the identification of his own convictions has been the source of some controversy; but such adaptability to a variety of audiences or even to one's own changing moods was at the heart of rhetoric, as it was not with the logic of the schoolmen.

In Florence, the uncertainties that had characterized the fourteenth century in the presence of the new culture of humanism were resolved only in the course of the prolonged crisis of Florentine independence provoked by the aggressive expansionism of Milan in the years before and after 1400, together with a similar danger from Naples some years later. In this period Salutati was succeeded as the major figure in the humanist movement by an even greater humanist, Leonardo Bruni, under whose leadership humanism was at last largely accepted as the basis of the new culture required by citizenship in a free and independent republic. In 1414 Bruni became chancellor of Florence, and in this position he both applied in practice the Ciceronian rhetorical theory of Petrarch and Salutati and developed some of its deeper implications. Above all, in the course of defending the values represented by Florence, he celebrated the moral effects of the civic life of free communities, in which he discerned a uniquely favorable environment for the release of human energy and the realization of man's potentialities. In Florence, he proclaimed in one of his most famous orations, a typical expression of the rhetorician's art:

Equal liberty exists for all . . . ; the hope of winning public honors and ascending is the same for all, provided they possess industry and natural gifts and lead a serious-minded and respected way of life; for our commonwealth requires virtue and probity in its citizens. Whoever has these qualifications is thought to be of sufficiently noble birth to participate in the government of the republic. . . . This, then, is true liberty, this equality in a commonwealth: not to have to fear violence or wrong-doing from anybody, and to enjoy equality among citizens before the law and in the participation in public office. . . . But now it is marvellous to see how powerful this access to public office, once it is offered to a free people, proves to be in awakening the talents of the citizens. For where men are given the hope of attaining honor in the state, they take courage and raise themselves to a higher plane; where they are deprived of that hope, they grow idle and lose their strength. Therefore, since such hope and opportunity are held out in our commonwealth, we need not be surprised that talent and industry distinguish themselves in the highest degree.

The amiable sentiments conveyed in this passage illustrate nicely, however, the ease with which the new humanist rhetoric could be converted to the uses of political propaganda. And meanwhile other humanists were employed by the tyrants of the age, for example Conversino (1343–1408) at Padua and Decembrio (1392–1477) at the Visconti court in Milan. Predictably, such men praised not liberty but the security, prosperity, and efficiency that were allegedly guaranteed by despotic rule, under which most men would be freed of all public responsibility and could therefore devote themselves to merely private concerns. The ideal for human life implied here suggests that such uses of rhetoric were in the long run subversive of rhetoric itself, understood as public communication for social ends. So too does the fact that arguments for autocracy tended to be inserted into a framework of traditional conceptions such as God's monarchy over the universe, the ultimate model, to which, as it was maintained, princely rule alone conformed.

Thus humanism under the patronage of despots could not bring out the full implications of the rhetorical tradition. It pointed ultimately to the imposition of a stable order from above in which, in the end, rhetorical appeal would presumably become superfluous. Only in the more open society supplied by a republic could humanism take on its full significance.[14] For Bruni the freedom of Florence made her the center of a new culture, nourished by the revival of classical letters and based on the needs and capacities of citizens to communicate with one another, for the rest of Italy (and by implication, perhaps the rest of the world) to imitate. That Bruni was right is suggested by the fact that Florence, rather than Milan, was the major center of Renaissance culture.

These values and attitudes shaped Bruni's major work, his *History of the Florentine People,* composed between 1415 and 1429, which, as a *history,* reflected both the new historical perspective and the concreteness, the concern with the changing world of human affairs, and the flexibility of the new humanist culture. It had a practical and patriotic purpose; Bruni stated immediately his intention "to write down the deeds of the Florentine people, their weighty struggles at home and abroad, their renowned deeds in peace and in war." At the same time, the work is notable for its concern with truth (a matter of major importance if a history is to provide useful guidance to its readers), its critical rigor, and its psychological insight and expository skill, qualities that reflect both rhetorical training and a practical sense of the interconnection of all events and their human actors that may be seen as the fruit of Bruni's own political experience. Bruni's *History of the Florentine People* is the first great work of modern historiography.[15]

The political meaning of humanism is further revealed in Bruni's anticipations of Machiavelli. His work did not merely glorify, in a general way, the pluralistic values he associated with the freedom of Florence. It also celebrated specifically the relativistic political ends with which the new rhetorical culture was associated. "I confess," Bruni wrote, "that I am moved by what men think good: to exend one's borders, to increase one's power, to extol the splendor and glory of the city, to look after its utility and security."[16] Like Machiavelli, he eschewed any consideration of ultimate values; his moralism depends only on the welfare and survival of the state. It was primarily in this context that rhetoric could flourish.

Two other figures, who were less closely identified with political life and therefore perhaps in a better position to consider other dimensions of rhetorical culture, will deepen this sketch of the implications of Italian humanism. Vittorino da Feltre sought to embody the ideals of humanistic culture in a new educational ideal, and Lorenzo Valla, the most penetrating thinker among the humanists of the Italian Renaissance, expounded its more profound implications.

One of the major expressions and vehicles of humanist influence was a new model for education that aimed, through classical study, to mold men into well-rounded, articulate, and therefore generally effective personalities for life in the world; and many humanists served as teachers in schools and universities or as private tutors. Traditional education was largely defective, from the standpoint of the new culture, because it was excessively specialized and professional and failed to meet general social needs. Before the end of the fourteenth century, Pier Paolo Vergerio, a professor at Padua, had advanced a new ideal of education in his treatise *Of Virtuous Life,* which proposed a curriculum based on the study of classical moral philosophy as the theory of virtue, history as its illustration through practical example, and rhetoric as the art of moving other men to virtue. Shortly afterward, these suggestions were strengthened with the translation into Latin of Plutarch's essay on education, and above all with the discovery of Quintilian's *Education of an Orator,* which, with Cicero on the same subject, was long regarded as the supreme authority on education.

One of the earliest efforts to put these conceptions into practice was the school opened in 1423 by Vittorino da Feltre for the education of children at the court of Mantua. Vittorino was clear about the general aims of his instruction. "Not everyone," he declared, "is called to be a lawyer, a physician, a philosopher, to live in the public eye, nor has everyone outstanding gifts of natural capacity, but all of us are created for the life of social duty, all are responsible for the personal influence which goes forth from us." The curriculum he devised largely followed the conceptions of Vergerio. He focused on the Latin classics for the moral instruction of his younger students, adding Greek ethical philosophy as they became more advanced; he gave marked attention to ancient history as ethics teaching by example; and he gave a notable emphasis to rhetoric as the art by which moral principles can be made active in the world. His concern with the formation of the entire personality for a useful life in society also led him to pay a novel attention to physical education. Vittorino's influential example assisted in the spread of the humanist ideal of a general education based on the classics that would be standard among the ruling groups in Europe for several centuries.[17]

The achievement of Lorenzo Valla (1405–1457) reveals how philological scholarship, long associated with humanism in its concern with the meaning and power of words and the reconstruction of authentic classical texts, could, if more rigorously pursued, produce results of which earlier humanists had scarcely dreamed. A more systematic scholar and a more acute critic of scholastic method than the Florentines, who had never clearly reconciled their interest in the imitation of classical models with the growing realization that culture is bound to particular conditions of time and place, Valla undertook the exact restoration of ancient Latin on scientific principles in his *Elegancies of the Latin Language* (1444). The ultimate consequence of this achievement was to reduce Latin to a historical artifact, to the considerable shock of those humanists who still yearned for a perennial authority in the antique past. Valla did much the same in his application of more careful philological scholarship to Roman law, whose relevance to the conditions of modern life seemed doubtful once it was analyzed in terms of its concrete meaning to its own time. And the same talents revealed that important documents long relied on for understanding the Christian past, or, as in his treatment of the Donation of Constantine, for supporting the material claims of the church, were spurious. Thus a fuller appreciation of historical change and its application even to language, which meant in effect turning humanist theory upon itself, had the most radical implications for a wide range of cherished beliefs. Indeed, Valla went even further toward the dissolution of the certainties of the new humanist culture. In *On Pleasure* he suggested that the moral philosophy of the ancients had no value as preparation for the Christian life; in this celebrated (and to contemporaries scandalous) dialogue, he implied that neither Stoicism nor Epicureanism was consistent with Christianity, which had to rest entirely on faith. Yet this position was also turned to the advantage of rhetoric. Because Valla saw Christianity as based on the will rather than on the understanding, religion too depended on oratory rather than on philosophy, for only oratory could speak to the heart, galvanize the will, and transform lives. Valla's influence was chiefly technical, but he is useful in revealing the radical implications in the humanist view of language.[18]

The concrete possibilities in the humanist movement may be illustrated finally with another celebrated figure, Eneas Silvius Piccolomini (1405–1464), who in 1458 became Pope Pius II, largely in recognition of the value of humanist attainments even in so traditional an institution as the papacy. For churchmen too required secretaries skilled in the new rhetoric; and as a government of a special kind, the papacy, like other governments, found the art of oratory indispensable. Born near Siena, Eneas received a classical education there and achieved some fame as a poet. He then served as secretary—a normal employment for a young humanist—to a number of cardinals at the Council of Basel, eventually becoming secretary to the council itself; meanwhile he performed numerous diplomatic missions. In due time he passed into the service of the emperor in Vienna in a similar capacity, and finally, after a reconciliation with the pope, he was appointed to a secretarial post at the Curia in Rome. His engaging commentaries, dictated toward the end of his life and themselves a notable example of rhetorical art, describe a career of increasing success as an orator and diplomat, which found its ultimate recognition in his election to the highest post in Christendom. From this lofty position he employed his persuasive powers to stimulate Europe to wage a general crusade against the infidel. He was not a thoughtful man, and he was indifferent to those broader implications of humanist culture that were so antithetical to the old order of which the papacy was apex and guardian. But he makes clear that, as the art of effective communication, rhetoric had many uses.[19]

Humanism provoked vast enthusiasm in Italy during the first half of the fifteenth century, above all because it corresponded both to a new vision of man in the world and to a variety of political and social needs. But in the latter part of the century the conditions to which it corresponded were changing, especially in Florence, the capital of early humanist culture. Although the forms of republican government were preserved, the veiled despotism of the Medici steadily reduced the actual participation of citizens in Florentine political life. Before the end of the century, Italy as a whole had been converted into a battleground for the armies of France and Spain, great powers with which the smaller Italian states felt helpless to cope. By 1530 Italy, with Spain triumphant, had largely fallen under Habsburg domination; in the following decades the papacy of the Counter-Reformation embarked on an increasingly emphatic reassertion of the traditional principles against which humanism had been directed, principles that generations of insecurity had made to seem more and more attractive.[20]

Thus, although oratory retained its value for diplomacy and propaganda, the public communication that rhetoric had facilitated steadily declined in significance. The eloquent sermons of Savonarola, which mingled civic and religious sentiment in their appeal to the people of Florence, and the republican enthusiasm, the concern with civic virtue, and the historicism of Machiavelli, suggest that the new values were slow to die.[21] But Italians (with the partial exception of Venice) felt more and more helpless to control their own fate; they were clearly subjects again rather than free citizens, compelled to live in a world ruled only by power. And power seemed largely indifferent to eloquence. Under such circumstances humanism in Italy turned in other directions.

Valla's reduction of the classical past to a mere historical interest pointed in one direction. Denied a part in public life, humanists buried themselves in scholarship, adding an increasingly expert knowledge of Greek to their Latin learning. In Rome classical studies were notably supplemented with archaeological investigation, and by the first decade of the sixteenth century, collections of ancient objects were being enthusiastically assembled in the major centers of Italy.[22] Some humanistic scholars entered the service of the new printing industry, improving texts for new standard editions. Thus in Venice Ermolao Barbaro (1453–1493) edited authentic Greek texts of Aristotle, previously available chiefly through Latin translations from medieval Arabic versions and, as this complicated and indirect transmission would suggest, remarkably corrupt.

It now became possible for the first time to attempt to identify the precise meaning of Aristotle, and eventually of other authors whose texts were similarly improved. The result was greatly to improve philosophical discussion based on classical philosophical problems.[23] But the most distinguished classical scholar of the later fifteenth century was the Florentine Poliziano (1454–1494), a man of great critical and esthetic gifts. An excellent textual critic and Greek scholar, he was also the first to appreciate late classical writings: writings, it may be observed, that also reflected a postrepublican world. He had by no means lost touch with the earlier humanists' interest in literary style, but he focused it, in both his literary doctrines and his own poetry, on esthetic satisfaction rather than social utility. The result, however, was further to broaden the expressive powers of language.[24]

Meanwhile other men were employing the broader acquaintance with ancient texts made possible by humanistic scholarship for the construction of new philosophical systems that somewhat resembled, in their renewed universalism, their pursuit of absolutes and, in their abstractness, the scholastic systems that humanism had largely repudiated. This enterprise had been facilitated by the revival of Greek learning, which not only gave a fresh impetus to Aristotelianism but also made possible for the first time in Western Europe the systematic study of Plato. Florence again led the way, above all with the labors of Marsilio Ficino (1433–1499).

Under the patronage of the Medici, Ficino employed Plato as

a guide in the philosophical interpretation of Christianity, much as the schoolmen had used Aristotle. His tendency to syncretism was carried a good deal farther by his younger disciple, Giovanni Pico della Mirandola (1463–1494), who tried to combine Arabic, Hebrew, and even more exotic types of wisdom, with that of the Greeks and Romans, into a comprehensive system of truth that was intended to be both universal and Christian. Although both men retained something from their humanist predecessors, above all a high esteem for the freedom and the creative powers of man, their values once again were intellectual rather than active and social, and neither had a high regard for the rhetorical skills that seemed largely irrelevant to the contemplative life.

The most important form of communication again was the transmission of an abstract truth for which a technical language inaccessible to the masses of men was generally appropriate; eloquence once more presented itself as a distraction from the pursuit of philosophical certainty. This development was of special importance for the future because northern Europeans were coming into increasing contact with Italian thought in the later fifteenth century, when the rhetorical emphasis of Renaissance humanism had lost its early vigor.[25]

Still another development in later Italian humanism facilitated its transmission northward. From its beginnings, as we have seen, humanistic rhetorical techniques had been as useful to princes as to republics, even though the latter more fully corresponded to the deeper values of the ancient rhetorical tradition; thus humanists early found patrons among the despots of Italy. And as Italy was increasingly a place of princely courts, humanism became acclimated to a new environment. Although a concern with rhetoric as an essential instrument for responsible citizenship virtually disappeared from the Italian scene, the increasing refinement of humanist expression was more and more appropriate for an aristocratic society consisting of the courtiers surrounding princes.

As Baldassare Castiglione's *Book of the Courtier* (1510) so gracefully illustrates, the concern of humanist education with the formation of all aspects of the personality and the production of a generally effective human being became the basis of a new lifestyle: a style, however, still appropriate to life in society, although the society of the court was in major respects rather different from that of a republic. Thus the ideals of the Renaissance in Italy, as Denys Hay has suggested, were transposed "to a key in which they could be appreciated in northern Europe."[26]

III

Yet the notion that the culture of the Renaissance originated in Italy and simply spread across the Alps no longer can be maintained. It is true that much of northern Europe was less urbanized than Italy and that even in the Low Countries, where townsmen were both numerous and prosperous, a traditional aristocratic and ecclesiastical culture retained a dominance that it had perhaps never possessed in Italy. The consequence was that classical interests outside of Italy were more likely to be pursued within a religious framework; indeed it may be that the contact of English, French, and German scholars with the circle of Ficino made Italian interests seem more consonant with their own concerns than the rhetorical emphasis of an earlier generation of Italian humanists would have struck them.

But the differences even between earlier Italy and the rest of Europe were not absolute. The movement known as the *Devotio Moderna,* which spread from the Low Countries into much of northern Europe in the fifteenth century, suggests that everywhere townsmen were discontented with the specialized and inaccessible subtleties of scholastic discourse and craved a spiritual and moral guidance that spoke directly to their condition in a language they could understand; this need found prominent expression in the *Imitation of Christ* by Thomas à Kempis. The schoolmasters of this movement, the Brethren of the Common Life, showed an interest in classical texts that paralleled that of the humanists in Italy.[27] And although northern humanism was for some time associated rather with schools and universities than with public life and courts, the developing monarchies outside of Italy eventually discovered the value of rhetorical skills for many of the same purposes they had earlier served in Italy.

This discovery, nevertheless, came only after a considerable delay. On this point the early history of humanism in France is particularly instructive because France had been the center of both twelfth-century classicism and of the scholastic movement thereafter.[28] French classical study, however, though overshadowed by scholasticism, had never disappeared altogether; and, as we have noted, early Italian humanists, including Petrarch, had found both ancient texts and congenial company in France, notably at Avignon, which was a meeting ground for French and Italian scholars through the fourteenth century.

But it was characteristic of French humanists during the entire period of the Renaissance to reject the notion of any Italian cultural leadership. Early French humanism was more concerned with moral and religious problems than with philology and rhetoric, although this did not prevent some interest among the secretaries of the royal chancery in the imitation of classical style in the manner of Petrarch. But without roots in a community seeking expression in a new culture, this interest disappeared during the middle decades of the fifteenth century; humanist activity did not reappear in Paris until the latter part of the century. It was only in 1472 that Guillaume Fichet introduced the teaching of rhetoric at the University of Paris, but from this time onward humanistic learning became an increasingly important component of French culture.

Yet its larger implications were for a long while hidden by its subordination to religious purposes. Although a circle of enthusiastic humanists gathered around Robert Gaguin (1433–1501), who was an ardent Ciceronian, its ideal was largely the fusion of eloquence with knowledge for the promotion of a thoroughly traditional Christianity. This religious concern was deepened under the influence of Jacques Lefèvre d'Etaples (1450?–1536), who applied the Platonism and the philological concerns of later fifteenth-century Italy to deepen and reform contemporary religious life.[29]

Early English humanism presents much the same picture. A few English scholars and aristocratic patrons had earlier interested themselves in classical study and the acquisition of manuscripts, but only at the end of the fifteenth century did such concerns begin to emerge as an effective movement under the leadership of John Colet (about 1466–1519). Deeply influenced by the Florentine Platonists in the course of an extended trip to Italy, Colet returned to England and in 1496 at Oxford began a series of lectures on St. Paul that ignored the scholastic commentaries on the sacred texts in favor of a direct encounter, from the sacred texts alone, with the message and personality of Paul. His concern for the propagation of humanist learning as a foundation for Christian piety also was reflected in his establishment of St. Paul's School in 1510. Meanwhile Italian humanists had begun to teach at Oxford and Cambridge, and the early Tudor court had recognized the value of rhetorical skills in political life; Henry VII established the post of Latin secretary, which he filled with an Italian rhetorician. But, as in France, the larger resonance of humanism was felt only in a later generation.[30]

Although they displayed many of the tendencies we have observed in France and England, humanistic interests had developed somewhat earlier in Germany, perhaps in the absence of a dominant courtly center that kept chivalric culture alive. Classical study, largely under Italian influence, was widespread in the fifteenth century.[31] At the same time early German humanism generally had a more academic flavor than the humanism of Italy; it was focused rather on education than on immediate public needs, although the imperial chancery had been a center for rhetorical activity as early as the mid-fourteenth century and continued to employ humanists as secretaries, among them Eneas Silvius. A distinguishing characteristic of German humanism was also its association with patriotic sentiment. As Rudolph Agricola (1444–1485), sometimes considered the father of German humanism, made the point: "I have the brightest hope that we shall one day wrest from haughty Italy the reputation for classical expression which it has nearly monopolized, so to speak, and lay claim to it ourselves, and free ourselves from the reproach of ignorance and being called unlearned and inarticulate barbarians; and that our Germany will be so cultured and literate that Latium itself will not know Latin any better."[32]

But, as elsewhere outside of Italy, humanism in Germany presented itself especially as a movement of religious renewal, an interest in which the nourishment supplied by the *Devotio Moderna* was supplemented toward the end of the fifteenth century by contact with the circle of Ficino in Florence. Agricola, like many other German humanists, had been educated by the Brethren of the Common Life as well as in the universities of

Germany; after this he had spent a decade in Italy, where he developed his enthusiasm for rhetoric. Yet the reform he envisaged as the result of its application to religious life was superficial; his Christianity was still conventional and medieval.

Under the leadership of Conrad Celtis (1459–1508), German humanism became a more coherent movement in which national patriotism, esteem for the broad culture of the rhetorician, and concern for the deepening of piety were fused into an increasingly self-conscious and aggressive opposition to scholastic culture as a primary obstacle to human improvement. Among the most prominent of the German humanists was also Johann Reuchlin (1455–1522), another admirer of the later Florentines and the leading Hebrew scholar of his age. For Reuchlin, Hebrew was the language God had chosen for communication with mankind, the language par excellence, therefore, for the transmission of religious truth and the reform of the faith. Renaissance preoccupation with the linguistic instruments of communication thus found a new and deeper level of application.

On first inspection, northern humanism may appear to contrast strikingly with the humanism of Italy. Yet it may be observed that the adaptation of humanistic techniques to religious purposes in France, England, and Germany also reflected, if in a somewhat different way, the concern, typical of all Renaissance humanists, with the concrete actualities of the world, a dissatisfaction with traditional cultural forms because of their failure to communicate useful illumination to the masses of men, and their resultant inability to transform a lamentably defective society. The Christian humanists of the north, and to some degree even the humanists of the later Italian Renaissance, also proposed, like Petrarch and his successors in the earlier Renaissance, to move men by means of an educational program based on the renewal of ancient languages and literature, and by an appeal developed with all the resources of the rhetorical art and directed not simply to the intellectual dimension of the human personality but to the whole man. For Lefèvre and Colet as for Celtis and Reuchlin, broad communication was the only hope for a world in crisis. But their ambitions were somewhat more grand; they aspired to move men not only with words but with the Word.

All of these tendencies may be discerned in the leading humanist of the earlier sixteenth century, Desiderius Erasmus of Rotterdam (1466–1536).[33] Educated by the Brethren of the Common Life, Erasmus reflected their distaste for scholastic discourse and their preference for the Bible; but he also developed an early admiration for Italian philology and especially for the rigorous critical method of Valla, in which he saw hope for the recovery of ancient oratory. Converted to a deeper piety by Colet during a visit to England, he devoted the rest of his life to making more widely available the texts of both classical and Christian antiquity and to the reform of secular and the deepening of religious life, an enterprise in which he exhibited a high degree of rhetorical skill. Much of his scholarly activity was directed to disseminating the texts of the Gospel.

In 1516 he published the first Greek edition of the New Testament, a work that expressed humanist emphasis on the importance of direct communication through the original language of a text. In addition he produced a new Latin translation of the New Testament as well as various paraphrases of its particular books for an even wider audience, stimulated by his confidence that immediate contact with the Scriptures would stimulate a true piety of the heart. His own conception of the Christian life was conveyed above all in his *Enchiridion Militis Christiani* (1504), which stressed the inwardness of faith and at the same time insisted on the value of classical studies for kindling Christian fervor. Meanwhile a series of colloquies—typical humanist dialogues—attacked superstition and abuses in the church, and his *Praise of Folly* (1511) held up to ridicule all aspects (among other matters the irrelevance of scholastic speculation) of a world in sad disarray. His numerous eloquent writings and his enormous correspondence with the intellectual and political leaders of Europe made him a peculiarly influential figure during the first third of the sixteenth century. Thus Erasmus's facility in the handling of words was made to implement his conviction of the practical and reforming power of the Word.

A second generation of sixteenth-century humanists, particularly in the service of the English and French courts, made northern humanism more obviously like the humanism of the earlier Italian Renaissance. An aristocracy whose traditional political and social role was being steadily reduced under the pressure of expanding royal authority found some comfort in Italian ideals of citizenship associated with civic humanism; a new species of aristocratic education, based on the classics, increasingly stressed the duties of service to community and prince and defined "true" nobility, following Italian precedent, in terms of virtuous achievement.[34] This conception was elaborated in such works as Sir John Elyot's *Boke named the Gouvernour* (1531) in England, where members of Colet's circle, like Thomas More, moved into the arena of public affairs. More's *Utopia* (1516) opened with a discussion of the active life reminiscent of the great Florentines of a century before, and during much of his reign Henry VIII was surrounded by humanists who not only prepared his correspondence, orations, and tracts, but also supplied him with political advice.

But in some respects France during the later Renaissance was even more clearly the heir to the political culture of the Italian Renaissance. The outstanding example of this movement at the French court was Guillaume Budé (1468–1544), who was as fervently attached to his own country as the German humanists had been to theirs. He was also devoted to philological study as an instrument of general reform. "Once an ornament," he wrote, "philology is today the means of revival and restoration." Thus his impressive scholarship was directed to practical ends, according to his view that "vast knowledge, if dissociated from practical prudence and the art of social behavior, may make the sage useless to himself and society." This sentiment would be repeated by generations of French scholars. And Budé's scholarship was regularly animated by a profound historical sense, reflecting the influence of Valla, that associated eloquence with periods of vigor in the lives of political communities. He applied this historicism particularly to legal study, with the aim of initiating legal and institutional reform by exposing the pristine sources of contemporary practice. And to train the scholars who would be able to carry on so admirable a work, he persuaded Francis I to establish a group of lectureships, primarily in ancient languages, that became the nucleus of the Collège de France. Until the end of the sixteenth century the ideals of Budé were shared by a large proportion of the major officials and jurists of France, who believed with him that power over words, developed through classical studies, would give power over the conditions of social life.[35]

IV

Renaissance humanism was, however, specifically based on the study of *classical* languages and literatures, and the eloquence it aimed to develop was in the first instance an eloquence in Latin. In this respect its ability to communicate with large groups of men was limited. Indeed the tendency, especially among later humanists, to insist on the classical purity of Latin and on the elimination of those subsequent modifications—considered corruptions—that had kept Latin a flexible instrument of communication through the Middle Ages now threatened to make of it a truly dead language. The same tendency was also implicit, perhaps, in the growing historical perspective with which antiquity was increasingly regarded; the classical past, too, presented itself now as long dead. Yet the humanistic principle that language is above all social and that its highest use is in public communication pointed in a different direction. And while some humanist scholars seemed to be presiding over the final interment of Latin, other humanists were applying this principle to the benefit of the vernacular languages. For the perfection of vernaculars in the age of the Renaissance and the flourishing of a singularly brilliant and expressive vernacular literature in the major European languages was a phenomenon not altogether independent of the humanist movement.

The traditional notion that Italian humanism was essentially hostile to the vernacular therefore no longer can be maintained. Not only did major humanists, from Petrarch to Poliziano, owe much of their literary reputation to their Italian works. In addition, the republican patriotism represented by Bruni made a good deal of the fact that the cultural distinction of Florence had already found major expression in a distinguished vernacular literature that included the writings of Dante and Boccaccio.

First in Bruni, and then among other humanists of the fifteenth and sixteenth centuries, even though much of their own literary production was still in Latin, the conviction grew that Florence possessed a vernacular literature as great as that of antiquity, and more generally that every language was equally capable of supporting a distinguished literature. In his own *Vite di Dante e di Petrarca* (1436) Bruni dealt in Italian with such subjects, previously reserved for Latin, as esthetics and history.

For Bruni's historical sense allowed him to grasp the implications of the fact that Greek and Latin once had been vernacular languages too, products of the concrete historical experience of particular peoples rather than predestined vehicles for the communication of an ultimate and unchanging wisdom. This insight was to be the starting point for the dispute about the relative merits of the ancients and moderns, and thus of the modern idea of progress.[36]

Among the humanists who contributed to the new prestige of the vernacular was also Leon Battista Alberti (1404–1472), who defended the expressive utility of Italian in his treatise *Della famiglia,* a major vernacular composition of great interest for its depiction of contemporary social and economic life, matters unusually suited to treatment in Italian. Alberti also sought to broaden the range of Italian poetry by the use of classical forms; in addition he was probably the author of the first grammar of the Tuscan vernacular, the *Regole della Lingua Fiorentina,* which made its regularities explicit.[37]

This effort was completed early in the next century by the Venetian Pietro Bembo. Although a purist in his attitude to Latin, in his *Prose della volgar lingua* (1525) Bembo attacked the alleged superiority of classical languages, promoted the Tuscan dialect as standard Italian, and established its grammatical principles. The popularity and applicability of this position elsewhere may be illustrated by the *Deffence et Illustration de la Langue françoyse* (1549) of Joachim Du Bellay, which transferred the arguments on behalf of Italian to support the use of French.[38]

Aided by this development, the vernaculars penetrated into all fields of writing in the sixteenth century, although Latin was by no means displaced. Indeed the antique classics remained of fundamental importance to this development and were employed as models for the perfecting of vernacular expression, for example in the great historical compositions of Machiavelli and Guicciardini, the modern epics of Ariosto and Tasso, and a host of works in French, Spanish, German, and English. Thus Renaissance humanism prepared the way for the great classical literatures of the seventeenth and eighteenth centuries, in which ancient example contributed to the clarity and elegance of expression in modern languages.

V

Meanwhile, just as Renaissance humanism was supplying a justification in principle for broader communication, Europe saw
the birth of a major new technological instrument that was to
make it immensely easier. This was the development of printing
with movable type, an achievement that produced another sort
of revolution in communication. The early history of the printing press was, in fact, closely bound to the humanist movement. Humanistic enthusiasms contributed to the growing demand for books, which made printing economically feasible
and assisted its rapid diffusion throughout Europe; a significant
proportion of the earliest works to be printed were editions of
the classics, and many early publishers were themselves men
with classical interests. The scholarly tendencies in later humanism can be explained in part by the needs of the printing industry for good, standard texts. By the same token, the prominence
of classical interests in Venice in the later fifteenth and sixteenth
centuries, when Venice began to supplant Florence as the
Italian capital of the movement, was largely the result of the
fact that Venice was the center of book production in Italy. It
was at Venice that scholars like Merula, employed by printers,
standardized orthography and edited texts with a new methodi-
cal rigor.[39] Ermolao Barbaro's new Greek Aristotle owed its influence largely to its availability in editions he prepared for the
press.

But there were also other elements in the growing demand
for books during the centuries preceding the development of
the printing press. The numbers of literate Europeans had been
growing steadily, and their interests had been expanding. They
required school books of every description, a broad variety of
pious literature, calendars, practical manuals, romances for
amusement, as well as scholarly texts. The laborious and expensive processes of manuscript-book production, even when rationally organized in large shops, had long failed hopelessly to
meet the demand.

Meanwhile other conditions were ripe for the development of
a new method of producing written materials in quantity.
Paper, introduced into Europe from the Orient as early as the
twelfth century and for some time used in making hand-copied

books, began to be produced in Italy in the fourteenth century; cheaper and lighter than parchment, its manufacture spread rapidly. In this period too the artists of the Low Countries developed oil-based paints that required only slight modification for the production of inks that would stick to metal typefaces. A device for exerting pressure had long been available in the screw-press used to squeeze grapes and olives, and it had already been employed to stamp designs on cloth, to press the water from paper, to make covers for manuscript books, and even to print block-pages. Again, the processes for cutting or casting small metal objects had been highly refined by medalists and goldsmiths. Like other complex machines, the modern printing press was developed through the combination of a number of simpler processes. What still was required was a method of producing types accurately and of a standard size so that they could be assembled, would hold together under pressure, and could be torn down again after use, to be reassembled for another job. The accomplishment of the fifteenth century lay primarily in the development of such a method.

The question of priority has long been debated, and the assignment of credit to Johann Gutenberg of Mainz sometime after 1440 is largely conjectural. Given the general circumstances described above, one would expect to find various groups attempting to develop a practical method of printing in a number of places, and efforts along these lines have been noted in the Low Countries and Avignon. What is clear, nevertheless, is that the Rhineland was the source from which printing spread into the rest of Europe, and that this happened very rapidly. The earliest printed material that can be dated with any certainty is a form for the granting of an indulgence in 1454 to those who contributed money to fight the Turks; printed by the firm of Fust and Schoeffer in Mainz, it consisted of a printed description of the indulgence with blank spaces for the name of the donor and other details. The so-called Gutenberg Bible, which was not dated but had appeared by 1456, was probably also the work of this firm, which expanded rapidly; by 1465 it had agencies in several cities, including Paris. From the Rhineland the new process was quickly carried to the rest of Europe, largely by itinerant German printers. A printing press had been set up near Rome by 1463, for example, and by 1477 a dozen printing establishments were at work in Rome itself. In 1470 three German printers set up the first press in Paris, in the basement of the Sorbonne. The printing press reached Poland in 1474, Spain in 1475, England in 1476. And from these early presses poured a deluge of books: some thirty thousand works or editions by 1501.[40] In Venice alone it has been estimated that some two million books had been printed by this date.

Contemporaries were quick to notice the importance of the new invention. Celtis celebrated it in verse as an achievement of the German fatherland,[41] and its uses for propaganda also were promptly recognized. Thus the presumably unique possession of the printing press by Christian Europe was given providential explanation: printing was an instrument sent by God for the spread of Christianity over the entire world. The French orientalist Guillaume Postel (1510–1581) suggested, for example, that "merely from the printing of the Arabic language" the religious unity of the world was at last in sight.[42] For more secular minds printing was one of several technological devices that proved the superiority of the moderns to the ancients. Francis Bacon was only citing a standard argument when he wrote, in the *Novum Organum:* "We should note the force, effect, and consequences of inventions which are nowhere more conspicuous than in those three which were unknown to the ancients, namely, printing, gunpowder, and the compass. For these three have changed the appearance and state of the whole world."[43] In any case the sense of vast new possibilities for human communication opened up by the printing press was a significant element in the more expansive European mood of the sixteenth century.

Nor, in retrospect, does this immediate conviction of the importance of printing seem misplaced, although in a modern perspective it may be seen to rest on somewhat different grounds. Printing transformed many aspects of the world. It made the Renaissance revival of learning permanent, as no earlier revival had been; never again would the classical heritage be lost, nor would it again need to be rediscovered. Indeed, all data could henceforth be preserved, and the steady accumulation of knowledge could proceed without such interruptions as had occurred in the past; in addition, as books could be easily produced and rapidly transported anywhere, knowledge could now advance simultaneously in many places rather than in a few scattered centers.

For society in general the availability of books (and notably of the Bible) lessened the dependence of laymen on clerical intellectuals and thus speeded up a process already evident in humanist culture. For governments the printing press vastly facilitated communication with subjects and their own officers; official edicts now could be multiplied rapidly in a standard form, and printed statute books made legal administration more uniform. In these ways, as well as by the standardization of vernaculars, national communities grew more centralized and better unified. The broad uses of publicity also now became apparent, as in the case of Pietro Aretino (1492–1556), a kind of early and often scurrilous journalist in Venice, who was known as "the scourge of princes," a title that suggests the new power of the printed word. And at a deeper level it may be that the cumulative experience with the standardized printed page gradually produced a collective mentality characterized by a new love of regularity and order.[44]

VI

Yet, although the significance of the Renaissance for our subject lies chiefly in the adaptation of communication to a new and larger audience, for new purposes, and with new techniques, the picture presented by the age as a whole is still somewhat ambiguous. For even as communication was being broadened to meet wider social needs, a reaction was under way. Part of it was connected with a reassertion of the traditional view of truth as a system of absolutes largely accessible only through the mediation of clerical intellectuals. A source of reassurance in a world that seemed to be changing with frightening speed, this vision again was being aggressively promoted by the Papacy after it had clearly survived the challenge of Conciliarism, and well before the Protestant Reformation. The *Index of Forbidden Books* would testify to the fear of public communication in this tradition, as well as to the power of the printing press; and it was paralleled by secular censorship.

In addition, some groups of lay intellectuals, isolated and turned inward as governments became increasingly despotic and the opportunites and responsibilities of citizenship declined, developed new theories of private and esoteric communication. These supplied a variety of satisfactions. They appealed to a new set of eternal verities based on some of the exotic sources made available by humanist scholarship in a time when, for many learned men, traditional orthodoxy had been discredited beyond any rehabilitation; thus they also offered security in a troubled world. In some forms they also promised power over the mysterious forces of the universe, whether for personal aggrandizement or the benefit of mankind. Moreover, they regularly appeared as a source of personal distinction in a period that—in frequent contrast to the earlier Renaissance—was increasingly fearful and contemptuous of the masses of men.

Some of these tendencies already were implicit in the thought of earlier humanists as they considered ancient mythology and the function of poetry. Petrarch had regarded poetry as superior to philosophy for the communication of ultimate truth, and Boccaccio had viewed it as equal to theology and indeed as performing somewhat the same function. The task of the poet, from this standpoint, was to penetrate through the veil of appearances to the ineffable reality hidden from the multitude; the poet therefore was a kind of priest. For Salutati anthropomorphic representations of God in Christian discourse were no more than inadequate hints of his true nature, and thus comparable to the myths of pagan poetry. Religious truth could not be communicated in ordinary language, but the poet might provide intimations of it for those whose sensibilities were sufficiently refined.[45]

But this suggestion of an esoteric and elitist intellectuality was overshadowed in the earlier period by more public concerns, and it did not emerge as a major tendency of thought until the later fifteenth century, when it constituted an important strain in Florentine Platonism. It was nourished by Plato's own perceptions of philosophy as a mystical initiation for a gifted elite, as well as by growing knowledge of the esoteric strands in the thought of the hellenistic world. Thus, in describing a projected work of his own, Pico Della Mirandola declared, ''It was the opinion of the ancient theologians that divine subjects and the secret Mysteries must not be rashly divulged. . . . That is why the Egyptians had sculptures of sphynxes in all their temples, to indicate that divine knowledge, if committed to writing at all, must be covered with enigmatic veils and poetic dissimulation. . . . How that was done . . . by Latin and Greek poets we shall explain in the book of our Poetic Theology.''

From his cabalistic studies he absorbed the gnostic notion of an esoteric truth that paralleled the vulgar revelation adapted to the capacities of the masses; he pointed with disdain to ''the tailors, cooks, butchers, shepherds, servants, maids, to all of whom the written law was given.'' Then, he asked rhetorically, ''Would these have been able to carry the burden of the entire Mosaic or divine understanding? Moses, however, on the height of the mountain, comparable to that mountain on which the Lord often spoke to his Disciples, was so illumined by the rays of the divine sun, that his whole face shone in a miraculous manner; but because the people with their dim and owlish eyes could not bear the light, he addressed them with his face veiled.'' Thus secrecy and restriction, based on a sense of the disparity between the written word and truth, as well as on a growing belief in the inequalities of human spirituality, became a new source of authority.[46]

The most concrete expression of this tendency was the diffusion of the so-called Hermetic Books, for which Pico's master, Ficino, was largely responsible. Hermetism drew its name from Hermes Trismegistus (Thrice-Great), the legendary source of that Egyptian wisdom referred to by Pico above, under whose name a large body of occult writings had circulated between about A.D. 100 and 300. Typical examples of Hellenistic syncretism, these works mingled Neoplatonic, Stoic, Jewish, Persian, and perhaps even native Egyptian elements; but for Renaissance thinkers they were the pristine source of all later forms of wisdom.

Their first direct contact with this tradition came after the arrival of a manuscript of the *Hermetica* in Florence about 1460. Cosimo de' Medici set Ficino to translate it immediately, even ahead of Plato, as it was considered an earlier form of the wisdom Plato had transmitted. Ficino's translation, entitled *Pimander* from its first book, was widely reproduced, and the vogue of Hermetism was soon reflected in a large body of other works and commentaries. Notable in this literature was a concern with the creative and mystical (rather than the social and broadly communicative) value of the Logos and of words in general, the association of holiness with remoteness in time, an astrological framework coordinating man with nature, and a radical intellectual elitism.[47]

For many of the devotees of such wisdom, esoteric communication conveyed only private insights and values. But for others it merged into a species of magic in which words were combined with ritual acts for the manipulation of the occult properties of nature—another peculiarly Renaissance use of communication (and a testimony to the sense of its enormous power) that has remote connections with the origins of science. Thus the esoteric sage became at times a magician, whose secret insights into the mysterious relations and properties of the universal order of the world could be converted into a fearful power for good or evil. As Francis Bacon, who owed something to this tradition, was to say of the scientist, the magus was "master and possessor of Nature."[48] The medical theory of Paracelsus, the philosophical speculations of Giordano Bruno, and the enterprises of a host of intellectual alchemists and astrologers of the later Renaissance were all dependent on such views.

On the other hand mystery was useless unless its keeper could convey some hint of what he possessed to others, if only to leave an impression of his own distinction. Hence men like Pico consciously cultivated cryptic modes of expression that would, tantalizingly, both communicate and refuse to communicate. Yet precisely this element in the esoteric attitude to communication also made it fruitful both for poetry and for painting, as it justified an attempt to hint at far more than could be made explicit. This chapter has largely ignored nonverbal communication; but at least it should be recalled that the Renaissance was one of the great ages in Western history for painting and the plastic arts.

As instruments of communication, these can be seen to exhibit much the same expressive concerns and transformations that we have observed in attitudes to verbal communication, from the representation of the ultimate values of the Gothic world through the humanized and public art of the early Renaissance to the often mysterious and puzzling works of the later fifteenth- and early sixteenth-century Italians. Like literary compositions of Platonic or Hermetic inspiration, such masterpieces as Botticelli's *Primavera* and *Birth of Venus,* Raphael's

Graces, Titian's *Sacred and Profane Love,* and Michelangelo's *Bacchus* make a paradoxical effort to convey mystery without revealing and thus destroying it. Yet it is to this effort that they owe their haunting allusiveness, and perhaps one can only conclude that a theory that led nowhere as a basis for discursive communication had demonstrable validity for the simultaneity that characterizes visual expression.[49]

For the notion of esoteric communication, which came close to being a contradiction in terms, proved a dead end. By the beginning of the seventeenth century it had largely run its course, though the perennial impulse behind it continued to find isolated expression in a variety of occult and theosophical groups. The future was to lie with the movement toward broader, more flexible, steadily more accessible forms of communication that had been given so original and fruitful a theoretical basis by Renaissance humanism, and such a massive impetus through the development of printing.

NOTES

1. Daniel Waley, *The Italian City-Republics* (London, 1969), pp. 72–73.

2. On the *ars dictaminis* in the background of Renaissance humanism, see Paul Oskar Kristeller, *Renaissance Thought: The Classic, Scholastic, and Humanist Strains* (New York, 1961), pp. 11ff., 100ff.

3. Jerrold E. Seigel, *Rhetoric and Philosophy in Renaissance Humanism: Ciceronian Elements in Early Quattrocento Thought and Their Historical Setting* (Princeton, 1968), pp. 69–70. On the general point, see also Myron P. Gilmore, *Humanists and Jurists: Six Studies in the Renaissance* (Cambridge, Mass., 1963), and Lauro Martines, *Lawyers and Statecraft in Renaissance Florence* (Princeton, 1968).

4. See Peter Herde, "Politik und Rhetorik in Florenz am Vorabend der Renaissance," *Archiv für Kulturgeschichte* 47 (1965).

5. Roberto Weiss, *The Spread of Italian Humanism* (London, 1964), pp. 14–17.

6. Quoted by Marvin B. Becker, *Florence in Transition* (Baltimore, 1967–1969), vol. 1, p. 42.

7. B. L. Ullman, "Some Aspects of the Origin of Italian Humanism," *Philological Quarterly* 20 (1941):20–31; Franco Simone, *The French Renaissance,* trans. H. Gaston Hall (New York, 1970), pp. 46ff.

8. Especially in *De sui ipsius et multorum ignorantia,* trans. Hans Nachod,

in Ernst Cassirer et al., eds., *The Renaissance Philosophy of Man* (Chicago, 1948), pp. 47–133.

9. Siegel, pp. 3ff.; for the quotation from Cicero, p. 7. See also the fine essay of Hanna H. Gray, "Renaissance Humanism: The Pursuit of Eloquence," *Journal of the History of Ideas* 24 (1963):497–514.

10. T. E. Mommsen, "Petrarch's Conception of the Dark Ages," *Speculum* 18 (1942): 226–242.

11. Cf. Millard Meiss, *Painting in Florence and Sienna after the Black Death: The Arts, Religion and Society in the Mid-Fourteenth Century* (Princeton, 1951).

12. On this point and much else in the present chapter, see the by now classic work of Hans Baron, *The Crisis of the Early Italian Renaissance*, rev. ed. (Princeton, 1966), pp. 291ff.

13. Quoted in Siegel, pp. 76–77. On Salutati, see also B. L. Ullman, *The Humanism of Coluccio Salutati* (Padua, 1963); Ronald G. Witt, "The *De Tyranno* and Coluccio Salutati's View of Politics and Roman History," *Nuova Rivista Storica* 53 (1969):434–474; and Eugenio Garin, "I cancellieri umanisti della Republica Fiorentina da Coluccio Salutati a Bartolomeo Scala," *Revisita Storica Italiana* 71 (1959):185–208.

14. From the funeral oration on Nanni degli Strozzi, quoted by Baron, p. 419.

15. In addition to Baron, see Donald J. Wilcox, *The Development of Florentine Humanist Historiography in the Fifteenth Century* (Cambridge, Mass., 1969).

16. Quoted by Wilcox, pp. 88–89.

17. William H. Woodward, *Vittorino da Feltre and Other Humanist Educators* (Cambridge, 1897).

18. On Valla, see, in addition to Seigel, Donald R. Kelley, *Foundations of Modern Historical Scholarship: Language, Law, and History in the French Renaissance* (New York, 1969), pp. 19ff.; and Hanna H. Gray, "Valla's *Encomium of St. Thomas Aquinas* and the Humanist Conception of Christian Antiquity," in *Essays in History and Literature Presented to Stanley Pargellis* (Chicago, 1965), pp. 37–51.

19. The most recent studies of this figure are Berthe Widmer, *Enea Silvio Piccolomini, Papst Pius II* (Basle, 1961), and R. J. Mitchell, *The Laurels and the Tiara: Pope Pius II* (London, 1962). For the *Commentaries*, see G. Bernetti, "Ricerche e problemi nei Commentarii di E. S. Piccolomini," *La Rinascita* 2 (1939):449–475.

20. Rudolph von Albertini, *Das florentinische Staatsbewusstsein im Übergang von der Republik zum Principat* (Bern, 1955); William J. Bouwsma, *Venice and the Defense of Republican Liberty: Renaissance Values in the Age of the Counter Reformation* (Berkeley, 1968).

21. Donald Weinstein, *Savonarola and Florence: Prophecy and Patriotism*

in the Italian Renaissance (Princeton, 1970); Felix Gilbert, *Machiavelli and Guicciardini: Politics and History in Sixteenth Century Florence* (Princeton, 1965).

22. Roberto Weiss, *The Renaissance Discovery of Classical Antiquity* (Oxford, 1969).

23. W. Theodor Elwert, *Studi di letteratura veneziana* (Venice, 1958), pp. 11ff.; Vittore Branca, "Ermolao Barbaro e l'umanesimo veneziano," *Umanesimo europeo e umanesimo veneziano* (Venice, 1963), pp. 193–212.

24. Aldo Scaglione, "The Humanist as Scholar and Politian's Conception of the *Grammaticus*," *Studies in the Renaissance* 8 (1961):49–70.

25. Eugene F. Rice, *The Renaissance Idea of Wisdom* (Cambridge, Mass., 1958), pp. 49ff.; Ernst Cassirer, *The Individual and the Cosmos in Renaissance Philosophy,* trans. Mario Domandi (New York, 1964), p. 61; George Holmes, *The Florentine Enlightenment (1400-1450)* (London, 1969), p. 243; Quirinus Breen, "Giovanni Pico Della Mirandola on the Conflict between Philosophy and Rhetoric," *Journal of the History of Ideas* 13 (1952): 384–426.

26. In the *New Cambridge Modern History,* vol. 2 (Cambridge, 1958), p. 377.

27. Hans Baron, *New Cambridge Modern History,* vol. 1 (Cambridge, 1957), p. 55ff.

28. For what follows, see Simone, pp. 39ff.

29. On Lefèvre, see Augustin Renaudet, *Préréforme et l'humanisme à Paris pendant les premières guerres d'Italie (1494-1517)* (Paris, 1916).

30. Roberto Weiss, *Humanism in England during the Fifteenth Century* (Oxford, 1941); Baron, *New Cambridge Modern History,* vol. 1, pp. 55–56.

31. For what follows, see Lewis W. Spitz, *The Religious Renaissance of the German Humanists* (Cambridge, Mass., 1963).

32. Quoted by Spitz, p. 25.

33. For Erasmus, see Augustine Renaudet, *Études érasmiennes* (Paris, 1939); and, more recently, Roland Bainton, *Erasmus of Rotterdam* (New York, 1969).

34. Cf. Michael Walzer, *The Millennium of the Saints: A Study in the Origins of Radical Politics* (Cambridge, Mass.), p. 237.

35. Hans Baron, "Secularization of Wisdom and Political Humanism in the Renaissance," *Journal of the History of Ideas* 21 (1960):131–150; Kelley, pp. 53ff.

36. Cf. Baron, *Crisis,* esp. pp. 273ff., 338ff., 438–439; and his "*Querelle* of Ancients and Moderns," *Journal of the History of Ideas* 20 (1959):3–22.

37. Joan Gadol, *Leon Battista Alberti: Universal Man of the Renaissance* (Chicago, 1969), pp. 217ff.

38. Hay, *New Cambridge Modern History,* vol. 2, pp. 377–378.

39. On this figure, see Pier Giorgio Ricci, "Umanesimo filologico in

Toscana e nel Veneto," *Umanesimo europeo e umanesimo veneziano* (Venice, 1963), pp. 169–170.

40. Douglas C. McMurtrie, *The Book* (New York, 1937); Lucien Febvre and H. J. Martin, *L'apparition du livre* (Paris, 1958).

41. Spitz, p. 84.

42. William J. Bouwsma, *Concordia Mundi: The Career and Thought of Guillaume Postel* (Cambridge, Mass., 1957), pp. 240–241.

43. Quoted by Elizabeth L. Eisenstein, "Some Conjectures about the Impact of Printing on Western Society and Thought," *Journal of Modern History* 40 (1968):1.

44. In addition to the work just cited, see, by the same author, "The Advent of Printing and the Problem of the Renaissance," *Past and Present* 45 (1969):19–89.

45. Becker, vol. 2, pp. 8–10; Baron, *Crisis,* p. 296.

46. Edgar Wind, *Pagan Mysteries of the Renaissance* (New Haven, 1958), pp. 18–26; for the quotations from Pico, p. 24, 25.

47. Frances Yates, *Giordano Bruno and the Hermetic Tradition* (London, 1963), pp. 2ff.

48. Charles G. Nauert, *Agrippa and the Crisis of Renaissance Thought* (Urbana, 1965), pp. 234–238; see also Paolo Rossi, *Francis Bacon: From Magic into Science,* trans. Sacha Rabinovitch (London, 1968).

49. See, in general, the work of Wind cited above.

2

THE IMPACT OF THE REFORMATION ERA ON COMMUNICATION AND PROPAGANDA

Nancy L. Roelker

THE REFORMATIONS OF THE SIXTEENTH CENTURY

Sixteenth-century Europe experienced a series of upheavals in religious belief, practice, and institutions which, because they were inextricably linked with fundamental changes in secular spheres, made the Reformation era a watershed in European history. The age-old notion of Western Christendom under a single church persisted, periodically animating new attempts to revive it, but it lost historical reality in the middle decades of the sixteenth century when several rival establishments came into existence, thus replacing a theoretical if loose religious unity with an actual, structured diversity.

This first and most basic change did not soon bring about religious toleration for dissenting groups or individuals—quite the reverse, as will be seen. A very fundamental change had nevertheless occurred: before the breakup of the "universal" Roman Catholic hegemony such dissenters, "heretics," were always condemned to a position of dangerous isolation comparable to that of outcasts from a tribe; afterward there existed alternative options, at least for some people in some places, and the way had been opened for further challenges, other new formulations of Christian doctrine and other ways of organizing Christian society. From the beginning there was a proliferation

of small independent groups, usually radical in both the religious and the secular spheres, and in the intervening centuries
the fragmentation process has continued with a seemingly endless diversity, until we find in the second half of the twentieth
century more than three hundred kinds of organized Protestantism recognized in the world.

These now exist, however, in a basically secular society, which
has come into being in the last two hundred years; the spiritual
and intellectual climate of the twentieth century should not be
projected into the sixteenth. Similar caution should be exercised with regard to the extrareligious factors in the Reformation revolution, such as the nation-state, the capitalist
economy, and the individualistic orientation of culture in the
modern world, all of which began to take shape in the sixteenth
century. Some historians have been so impressed by these new
factors from which our "modern" society and culture have
since evolved, that they have overlooked or neglected the persistent remnants of earlier patterns; others, in their anxiety to redress the balance, have swept aside the new and insisted that
modernity can be meaningfully defined only in such terms as
the triumph of science or industrialism. This historiographical
controversy has embraced both the Renaissance and the Reformation, which were virtually simultaneous—and inseparable—
in northwestern Europe.[1]

Attempts to put neat labels on the Reformation era as a
whole in terms of medieval versus modern distort the complex
reality. Old patterns were entirely destroyed or basically altered
in some places; new ones developed rapidly here, slowly there;
some Reformation phenomena took root, became institutionalized, and have changed relatively little since, as in Spain or
Scotland; others have since been greatly modified or lost their
vitality. Yet when all necessary qualifications have been made,
the Reformation era still can be seen as truly revolutionary and
"modern" in some respects. If the beginning of rival church establishments is the first of these, the impact on education, communication, and propaganda is surely the second, for the very
existence of rival confessions created competition for members
and heightened the importance of persuasion, argument, literacy, and publicity.

Hindsight after four hundred years inclines twentieth-century minds to regard the Reformation as a single if many-faceted phenomenon, with more explicit links between religious and secular factors than appeared to sixteenth-century minds, whose vocabulary and conceptual scheme were predominantly religious. Sixteenth-century Europeans thought as Christians; they sought to reform the contemporary church and restore Christianity to its pure and uncorrupted state, believed to have existed in the "primitive church" of the earliest generations, from Jesus' lifetime through the era of the "Church Fathers." In historical terms this means the late Roman Empire and early Middle Ages, approximately the first six hundred years of the Christian era, prior to the rise of a centralized church organization under the direction of the papacy.[2]

The idea of reform was not new in the sixteenth century. There had been recurrent reform movements in the medieval church; some led by the popes themselves, like the struggle of Gregory VII against the lay investiture of bishops in the eleventh century; others by lesser religious leaders like the abbots of Cluny in the twelfth century; still others by private individuals more concerned with the spiritual life of every Christian than with institutions, like the Italian Francis of Assisi in the thirteenth century, the Englishman John Wycliffe in the fourteenth, and the Czech John Huss in the fifteenth. Reforms whose leaders were highly placed in the power structure generally were successful, at least in part, whereas reforms from below usually failed to modify the church in any important way except to provoke repressive measures and bring about increased rigidity and more elaborate machinery for control. Reforms that failed were consigned to the category of heresy and often became important continuing movements in themselves, like those of the Lollards in England and the Hussites in Bohemia.

The history of the Franciscan movement after the death of its founder provides an instructive case history in the complex relationship between heresy and reform in the later Middle Ages. Owing to the statesmanship of Pope Innocent III, the order had been incorporated into the structure of the Roman church and the friars accorded priestly functions, but success in official terms and the ensuing prosperity created tensions within the order. Those who felt that the original spiritual thrust had been blunted or lost sought in successive generations to revive it, with

the result that they often ended up as "heretics." A significant
number of the earliest sixteenth-century reformers, especially in
Italy, had been associated with dissident Franciscan groups.[3]

Conversely, it may be said that central doctrines of all important medieval heresies implied reform of some kind in the contemporary church, if only to modify the relations or lessen the
differences between the priesthood and the laity, a theme common to them all. Indeed, the specific content of Martin
Luther's original reform program repeats and summarizes the
criticisms and goals of earlier reformers to a striking degree. Belief in the Bible as the sole authority for Christians, with concomitant attacks on the powers and claims of the papacy, the
special powers of priests, and the sacramental system are among
the most important.

These continuities are significant, yet they should not obscure the fact that the sixteenth-century movement was so different in scope and outcome that it differs from all others, not
merely in degree but in kind. To account for this, or to explain
why it became a full-scale (and largely successful) revolution
that changed European history instead of one more item in a
long line of abortive movements, one must consider the context
in which it occurred, its "causes."

The point has already been made that the movement was primarily religious, and it cannot be repeated too often as a re-
minder to skeptical moderns that in the sixteenth century, religious issues were "real," that is, always taken seriously, usually
given priority, and seldom used as a cover for other matters such
as economic status or political power. These were also regarded
as real, of course, in their different, lesser sphere. The religious
causes of the Reformation, basic to the men of the sixteenth
century, can be classified in two categories, "negative" and
"positive."

A very large proportion of the propaganda to be considered
in this chapter reflects the negative religious causes, that is, conscious criticism of the existing church and documentation of its
defects and lapses from the "pure" primitive church. There is a
long catalogue of evils to be eliminated. Some are usually described as "abuses," such as the sale of indulgences, by which
the time of souls in purgatory was supposed to be shortened;[4]
the commercial exploitation of saintly relics and places of pil-

grimage; the plurality of benefices held by bishops, who thus had the use of vast revenues and sometimes did not perform their spiritual duties; inadequate qualifications in both character and training of much of the lower clergy—the list is long and all too familiar. These dishonorable abuses outraged all conscientious Christians, including the most orthodox. More significant is their longevity. They had been the staple of medieval satirical literature in every European country—one has only to remember Chaucer's *Canterbury Tales*—and the great Renaissance satirists like Erasmus and Rabelais carried the genre to perfection. Chronic opposition to the abuses had neither diminished them nor caused a revolutionary upheaval.

The same is true of an even larger and less clear-cut category of beliefs, practices, and institutions developed in the course of the Middle Ages that may be called "encrustations." In the Gospels one finds no privileged priesthood distinct from the laity, no sacramental system on which the priestly status depends, no bishops, no pope, no purgatory, no saints, no relics—one finds, in fact, only Jesus and his disciples, living and praying according to a few fundamental teachings, concerned with doing God's work in the communities of which they were a part. Perhaps the most important means by which the Renaissance (as an intellectual movement) gave rise to the Reformation was that increased familiarity with the text of the New Testament, first among the educated and then filtering down through all classes, greatly heightened perception of differences between apostolic Christianity and the contemporary Roman church, so that many practices formerly taken for granted came to be seen as man-made additions, or adulterations of God's word.

Even with the desire to remove the encrustations added to the outcry against abuses, these "negative" factors did not by themselves cause the sixteenth-century reform movement, although they provided most of its fuel. More powerful were the "positive" religious forces, stronger than in earlier times, together with certain secular forces that favored religious change and helped to implement it.

The positive religious cause par excellence is described as "lay piety." Beginning in the fifteenth century, there were numerous manifestations of and impressive spiritual revival among the laity of northern Europe. One can note especially, first, the humanist revival of Biblical texts in the original languages and later in the vernacular translations; second, the *Devotio Moderna,* which combined an emphasis on inner spirituality with practical Christ-like morality, spread by the Brethren of the Common Life through their schools in the Netherlands and the Rhine Valley, whose students included Erasmus, Luther, and many less-known men whose lives and works bore the mark of the Brethren.[5] Finally, there was a marked spiritual concern in the princely courts and nobility, especially conspicuous among noblewomen. This third thrust usually was combined with the humanist one in its outstanding representatives, such as Marguerite de Navarre, sister of François I of France and a leading patron of the humanist reformers. The characters of her *Heptameron* begin and end each day with scripture reading and prayer, and a high moral tone marks their conversations, in keeping with the "Christian humanism" of the north and in contrast to the characters in Marguerite's Italian models, Castiglione's *Courtier,* and Boccaccio's *Decameron.*[6]

Among the secular forces that successfully exploited the desire for religious reform and fostered the new culture, the most important was the drive of secular rulers to gain control over subjects whom they could not reach because of clerical immunities and privileges, especially in fiscal matters. This was matched on the part of their subjects by a sharp rise in national feeling, that is, an increasing tendency to identify themselves with a government and culture transcending their locality but excluding fellow Europeans whose allegiance was given to a different government and culture. This was a major factor in the spread of Lutheranism ("Germans" against "Rome") early in the century and in the identification of Protestantism with their independence from Catholic Spain by Englishmen and Dutchmen later in the century.

In addition, new groups in the middle and lower classes, especially urban merchants, lawyers, and artisans, found their personal and professional goals more in harmony with the morality and practices of one of the new Christian confessions than with Roman Catholicism. An increase in geographical and social mobility and the pressures of demographic and economic change caused tension and discontent, as well as rising expectations. We shall see that representatives of many different social and professional groups responded to the new ideas, from one end of Europe to the other.

The diversity in causes of the religious upheavals was matched by the variety of religious doctrines and ecclesiastical institutions they produced. Of the several reformations, those which developed new, rival churches are collectively described as "Protestant,"[7] whereas the Roman church itself experienced two phases of reform. Each wave of reformation showed the influence of its predecessors, and its leaders were obliged to differentiate sharply the issues that separated them from others, a necessity that greatly stimulated both debating and propaganda techniques as well as scholarly documentation and argument. Each new Christian formulation made its appeal to particular groups of believers in particular regions, and its institutional development reflected regional or national political, socioeconomic, and cultural patterns.

Three major new confessions were implanted and institutionalized in the middle third of the century: Lutheranism in northern Germany and Scandinavia, Calvinism in parts of the Continent and Scotland, and the Church of England. While differing markedly from each other, they share the characteristics of a centralized ecclesiastical organization with administrative, regulatory, and judicial powers and with some kind of relationship to the secular state. One scholar therefore has described them as "magisterial," in contrast to the various manifestations of the "Radical Reformation," none of which share these characteristics.[8]

Although Martin Luther began as a rebel challenging the old church, and the earliest explosion in communication and propaganda to be explored belongs to that phrase of his movement, the Lutheran church when fully institutionalized was the most conservative of the new confessions, with an episcopal hierarchy of its own and rigid theological doctrines enforced in an authoritarian manner. The founder's insistence that the priesthood should have power only in spiritual matters, leaving administration, even of church property, in the hands of secular rulers whose authority also came from God, made it possible for the Lutheran princes to gain control of the church.[9]

Some of the reformed churches that followed the lead of John Calvin, on the other hand, became associated with limitations on secular authority in the name of individual spiritual rights, although the original Calvinist theology is a much more tightly structured and authoritarian system than Luther's.[10] This double paradox stems from historical circumstances: Lutheranism was adopted by the north German princes who held the real power in their states and could use Lutheranism as a support for that power, whereas Calvinism was the religion of minority groups in France and the Netherlands (and later in England), forced to defend their right to exist against secular rulers in a position to repress them. Thus authoritarian Calvinism spawned civil rights theories for dissenters and constitutional theories of government—material for another surge of propaganda—while the church launched with the slogan "every man his own priest" sometimes became the bastion of and apologist for absolute government.

The nature of the Church of England was also partly determined by secular factors inherent in its context. England's earlier native reformist heresy, Lollardy, stemming from Wycliffe, had prepared the soil for later reform in certain areas and social groups, but the official break with Rome was accomplished by Henry VIII for political reasons.[11] He subsequently confiscated the wealth of the monasteries, but the Henrician church retained the doctrines of the old church—minus the special powers of the "Bishop of Rome." Not until after his death did this national church become Protestant in doctrine; that is, allowing the cup to the laity, abolishing celibacy for and denying miraculous powers to the clergy, and shifting the emphasis from the sacraments to the Bible, especially to preaching "the Word." This moderate Protestantism, a "middle way," challenged from the right by Roman Catholics and from the left by Calvinists (especially during the "Puritan" revolution of the seventeenth century), survived all the successive crises and has maintained itself down the centuries as a peculiarly English institution. From the beginning the Anglican church has been a department of the state, under crown and Parliament, supported by taxation. It is one of the more conservative Protestant confessions but with a considerably greater degree of internal flexibility than the Lutheran.[12] Although each of the Tudor monarchs imposed a particular religious settlement on the country, we shall see that Englishmen too exploited every avenue of communication and produced floods of polemical literature. Propaganda from the opponents of Anglicanism at either extreme of the religious spectrum was countered by official propaganda skillfully promulgated by the crown and its ministers.[13]

Whereas secular forces in the regions of their appeal often favored the establishment and consolidation of the three magisterial confessions, the reverse was true of the "Radicals," a term that embraces a wide variety of splinter groups ranging from Dutch and German Anabaptists to Italian "Free Spirits," whose diversity is matched by their originality and ingenuity.[14] They can be grouped together only as dissident, nonmagisterial (repudiating centralized church institutions and any sharing of functions between church and state), and radical in the true etymological sense of the word, going to the root of a matter. Thus the Anabaptists rejected the very notion of a church coterminous with society, which is implied by infant baptism, and insisted on personal commitment by each individual at the time of baptism, when he is old enough to assume and understand his Christian responsibility, while the more sophisticated and better-educated Radicals, like Michael Servetus, repudiated doctrines like the Trinity.[15] Whereas the Italians tended to be radical only in religious and philosophical spheres, the Germans often held radical views in the secular sphere also, specifically the repudiation of established authority and private property. This explains the last of the common characteristics that can be attributed to all the Radicals: they held the distinction of being consistently and savagely persecuted by the magisterial Protestant churches as well as by Rome, usually with devastating success.

Since they were few in number and lacked the resources of political and economic power, the Radicals suffered grave disadvantages in the competition for the instruments of communication and propaganda, with the result that their pamphlets and manifestoes, turned out by clandestine printers often under assumed names and always on the run, were produced in small editions and were exceptionally vulnerable to censorship and even total destruction by the persecuting authorities. The Radicals were necessarily more dependent on personal contact and oral communication, but what has survived is rich in interest.

The old church too called upon every force available, especially in the latter part of the century when it mobilized the most impressive of all systems to promulgate its doctrines—redefined and newly formulated at the Council of Trent—control its members, and suppress dissent. Its major instruments in this "Counter-Reformation" phase, which followed the failure of a liberal reform movement, were the preaching and missionary activities of the Society of Jesus, the Inquisition, and the *Index*. Where it had the support of the secular authorities, the Roman church was brilliantly successful in reinforcing orthodoxy and putting an iron curtain between the protected regions and the dangerous outside world that had gone over to heresy.[16] Leaders of all the rival confessions tried every means to convince people of their own version of the truth and developed ingenious ways of discrediting that of others.

COMMUNICATION

Some means of persuasion that had been used for centuries not only persisted into the Reformation era but were refined and elaborated to increase their effectiveness. Since many people could not read and hand-written materials were always scarce and expensive, communication in earlier centuries had been primarily oral. This continued to be the case in the sixteenth century, especially in some regions, and the advent of the most revolutionary means of communication in history prior to broadcasting—the printing press—served in many ways to stimulate such oral means as preaching and teaching. The most important spheres of oral communication in the Reformation era, where a good many new developments can be discerned, were religion, education, entertainment, commerce, and migration.

The religious sphere itself is particularly rich in new oral techniques. Protestants everywhere, from Martin Luther to the Anglican bishops, believed that the core of Christianity was the Word, that is, the teachings of Jesus; they held that to proclaim it was the prime function of the ministry. Sermons took the central position in church services, and the shock troops of each succeeding wave of reform were self-proclaimed interpreters of the Word. Even the newer access to it, in private Bible reading made possible by the mass production of vernacular Bibles and rising literacy, resulted in large part from its publicizing by

preachers who emphasized "the idea that the Holy Spirit speaks
directly to whom it will from the pages of the sacred book . . .
and as it happened their effort . . . fell in with the great advance of the popular language as the chief instrument of information and of printing and the book trade."[17]

This linkage between preaching and the printed Word distin-
guishes the various Protestant reformations from the Catholic,
where the failure to encourage biblical humanism by the Council of Trent is described by one scholar as "the great refusal of
1546," which had permanent effects; " . . . in no field did
fear of Protestantism leave deeper marks on the development of
the Catholic religion."[18] The chief argument of the Domini-
cans who blocked the liberal Catholic move to favor lay reading
of the Bible in the vernacular was that it would mean victory for
the Protestants.

In England Hugh Latimer was the most influential preacher
of the early Reformation, "the prime evangelist of the book."
He began under Henry VIII like an ancient prophet denouncing
the spiritual decadence of the times and eventually attacked the
mass itself, during a career that saw him ride high in royal favor
under Edward VI and die a martyr's death under Mary. The
standard plan of Protestant sermons was simple: the application
of a scriptural text to particular concerns of the congregation
present. The effectiveness of the Reformation preacher is
brought out by William Haller in his study of Foxe's *Book of
Martyrs:*

> [He] taught people to see themselves, their own predicaments, the
> predicaments of their time, mirrored in the scriptural saga of
> spiritual striving. He demonstrated . . . the way of escape from
> frustration, doubt and confusion. . . . The preacher set forth an
> enthralling drama of self-examination leading to the resolution of
> uncertainties and inhibitions and so to a life of positive endeavour
> and a sense of achievement. . . . There could be no question but
> that salvation was written plain in the Bible for all to read about
> and hope for, and what men hope for ardently enough, they do not
> as a rule expect to be denied.[19]

Secular rulers committed to some form of Protestantism, like
the Lutheran princes, the town councils of many Swiss and German cities, or Queen Elizabeth, were dependent on their

preachers to support their regime and stand for law and order. In the case of Elizabeth, whose reign began with the threat of a civil war when she succeeded her half-sister Mary who had restored Catholicism, "she had not been many days on the throne" before her astute advisor, William Cecil, "was drawing up lists of preachers having the strongest personal reasons for loyalty to the new regime, many of them returned exiles, to be called to address the people at Paul's Cross." On all significant occasions there was preaching from this most important of all English pulpits, but it took place also at court, in Parliament, in the Inns of Court and on market days and days of assizes throughout the country. The leaders "made haste to ordain and license as many recruits as they could find capable of preaching, and if a man lacked academic learning, it could be enough if he knew his Bible and had the gift of expounding it. Study groups known as 'prophesyings' were presently formed in various places for the discussion of scripture texts and the training of such persons in the art of the pulpit."[20]

Eventually the prophesyings of more radical Protestants—Puritans—were to create problems for the Anglican crown and hierarchy, for this was an instrument of communication not confined to the Establishment, though its resources made fuller exploitation possible than for dissidents. Where the authorities were bent on suppressing heresy, there was widespread incidence of clandestine preaching, outside the towns and often at night. In the Netherlands in the 1560s, when the government of Philip II was determined to stamp out reformed ideas, the authorities were unable to eliminate what was called "hedge-preaching" by unauthorized persons in unlawful gatherings.[21]

In France, the reformed congregations met at night in private houses. One of the first important events in the history of French Protestantism occurred when one such meeting was discovered and disrupted by the authorities, with the consequent arrest of about one hundred and thirty persons, including thirty-seven women; this was *l'affaire de la rue St. Jacques,* in the Latin quarter of Paris on 5 September 1557. Many of the provincial churches originated with secret nocturnal preaching, such as that of Poitiers, founded in this manner by John Calvin himself before he fled to Geneva. After he had established himself as the spiritual leader in that city he sent a steady stream of pastors into France to serve the multiplying French reformed congregations.[22] In addition, we know that large numbers of humble people in the countryside and in some trades gathered together in secret to listen to the Bible read aloud, as the great enamelist Bernard Palissy reports in Poitou; and in England, illiterate Lollards memorized long biblical passages that they recited to each other.[23]

Music also was used in new ways by the reformed groups. Luther's hymns, while fitting into the medieval German tradition of choral singing, provided a new medium for reformed expression, and wherever the Calvinist movement spread there arose the practice of singing the Psalms as a central feature of worship. The Psalms had been translated into French by Clément Marot in the first phase of the evangelical movement. The Lyonnais printer, Antoine Vincent, then built up a flourishing business by publishing successive editions in that city and later in Geneva. The printing workers of Lyon, to give but one example, were noted for assembling in large groups to sing the Psalms. Many of them were foreigners or transients, and this activity provided them with "a feeling of warmth and acceptance." The Psalms were "their badge and also their invitation to the unlettered"; they "made their music propaganda—'to attract others to their damnable sect' "—as it was put by one who feared it. The considerable success of the Psalms as instruments of conversion and builders of morale has been widely recognized, and it was to remain a notable feature of Huguenot life, in their worship and in moments of crisis: "The Psalms were powerful agents of conversion, they inspired the soldiers of Coligny to attack and later those of the Béarnais" [Henry IV].[24]

In addition to the revolutionary effects of vernacular printing, education was deeply affected by the Reformation through oral communication. The establishment of presses near universities like Wittenberg, Paris, and Cambridge meant that students and teachers fraternized with booksellers anxious to sell their wares. As we shall see, this was a milieu intimately connected with the reform. The graduates later would become teachers in *collèges* (secondary schools) usually in another part of the country, which often then became centers of religious ferment and sometimes of violent upheaval. Barthélemy Aneau, regent of the Collège de la Trinité in Lyon, headed a professorial staff deeply penetrated by the new ideas in the 1550s. The authorities were disturbed and tried to check the trend by such means as requiring attendance at mass three times a week and banning the teaching or use of any books containing doctrines that "cast doubt on the authority of our Holy Mother Church." The heretical reputation of the institution was such that when a Catholic procession turned into an anti-Protestant riot in June 1561, the crowd forced its way into the *collège,* dragged Aneau into the street, and murdered him. Schools in Dijon, Tournon, and Nîmes also were disseminators of heresy in their respective towns, and there were many others. The prominence of high-ranking university men in the English Reformation is well known. Many of the Marian exiles who returned to lead the Anglican establishment under Elizabeth had been converted in their student days at Cambridge, where certain colleges were known as "Little Germany." This had also been the case of prominent martyrs, including Hugh Latimer himself.[25]

Any large gathering of people was a seedbed for the communication of religious messages. Religious processions might erupt into violence against unpopular dissidents, as in Lyon, or they might be used to reinforce Catholic loyalty and intimidate potential heretics. Examples could be drawn from every Catholic city in Europe, with Paris almost certainly in the lead. The volatile population of the French capital was repeatedly aroused to emotional expression of ultra-Catholic sentiment, especially at the height of the Holy League, the French arm of the Counter-Reformation, which assassinated Henry III, last of the Valois kings, in 1589, and refused to recognize his successor for four years because he was a Calvinist.[26]

Theatrical productions, especially those of itinerant performers in marketplaces and town squares, offered a fertile field for oral communication. In Germany, reformist ideas would be ad-libbed into medieval morality plays and traditional dramas performed at carnival time, satirizing the pope and the clergy and contrasting their behavior (notably in sexual and financial matters) with that of simple illiterates who followed the Gospels. In one example, a cardinal is calculating how to increase his revenues, a bishop thinks of nothing but rich food and fine clothes, a parish priest curses his parishioners for quoting the New Testament while his concubine curses the bishop for laying taxes on their illegitimate children, a monk mocks his vows of celibacy, and a noble castigates his ancestors for having endowed churches and monasteries instead of leaving their money to the family. In later scenes the simple piety and gullibility of illiterates who respond to a crusading appeal are exploited by papal agents, and the spirits of St. Peter and St. Paul denounce the temporal power of the pope, disclaiming any connection with the alleged successor of Peter, whose real name, they say, is Antichrist. Old Testament scenes also were frequently dramatized in such a way as to contrast simple piety with contemporary Catholicism. In the England of Mary Tudor, the government resorted to suppression of all stage plays for some months toward the end of the reign because so many had attacked both the church and the queen.[27]

In the commercial centers of northwest Europe that experienced an explosive growth in the sixteenth century, London, Antwerp, Amsterdam, and all the Atlantic ports, men of widely differing origins and languages mingled on the docks and in the taverns, exchanging views on religious (as well as other) matters, arguing and often coming to blows. Taverns commonly served as meeting places for suppressed groups and as key points on the transmission belts for forbidden books. Itinerant peddlers carried small devotional books under bundles of cloth or household wares from German and Swiss cities, especially Geneva, into France and through the Alpine valleys into northern Italy. Some were conscious carriers of the faith and died as martyrs if they were caught. In other cases they revealed under questioning that they had been paid for their dangerous work, and begged leniency on the grounds that their poverty compelled them to accept such missions because they would otherwise starve. Still others claimed no knowledge of the contraband goods, which they declared to have been planted in their baggage. Rumors with a propagandistic intent were also carried this way, some false, such as the "news" of 1549 that the Republic of Venice was about to give financial and military aid to the Lutheran princes in Germany. This undoubtedly was the work of papal agents seeking to discredit the Venetians, who were always ready to flout the will of the Holy See.[28]

Other itinerant carriers of the Word included the shepherds of southwestern France. The upsurge of heresy in that region in the second quarter of the century can be traced on a map along their routes between the plateaux of Gascony where they wintered to the high mountains of Béarn and Spanish Navarre to which they led their flocks each summer.[29] Most important of all the oral carriers of reformist heresy were of course the refugees, who fled from persecution and formed migrant communities elsewhere, German Anabaptists in eastern Europe, Italian radicals in Switzerland or England and eventually in Poland, French Huguenots in England or the Netherlands—and seventeenth-century English Puritans in North America.

The Word carried by refugees was communication with serious intent, proselytizing, but scurrilous or obscene jokes and irreverent popular songs about the mass and the clergy also abounded. As Henry VIII said in a proclamation to Parliament in 1545, "The most priceless jewel, the Word of God, is disputed, rhymed, sung and jangled in every alehouse and tavern."[30]

The overlap between oral and printed communication and the interplay of personal contact with the new book culture were considerable in this period of fluctuating opinion that every faction wished to capture. One amusing anecdote, from southeastern France in the 1530s, must suffice as an example. A certain M. Aloat, a notary of Sisteron, was deeply impressed by the arguments of his cousin, the reformer Guillaume Farel, during a visit of the latter on one of his frequent journeys between France and Switzerland. The whole Aloat family seemed well on the way to conversion. In his enthusiasm the notary bought a copy of Léfèvre d'Etaples's translation of the New Testament and carried it conspicuously upon emerging from the bookstore. Within a few minutes, however, a passerby told him it was heretical, whereupon he returned to the bookstore and exchanged it for a copy of a standard medieval work, *The Shepherd's Calendar*.[31]

However great the sixteenth-century increase in evangelical preaching, commerce, and geographical mobility, the concurrence of the religious upheavals with the full development of the new technology of printing was responsible for the quantum leap in communication and propaganda represented by the Reformation era in comparison with all the previous centuries. Protestants naturally felt that the press was providential, invented by God's inspiration to facilitate the promulgation of the Word, and their characteristic emphasis on literacy and education meant that they would exploit it fully. The Roman church, even at the height of the Catholic revival in the late sixteenth and early seventeenth centuries, failed to take maximum advantage of the new medium through opposition to lay Bible reading. The very basis of the Protestant printing explosion—to bring the Word directly to every Christian and demystify the role of the clergy—was the basis for the Catholic opposition. Persecuted Protestants like Anabaptists, Huguenots, and Puritans were particularly ingenious and prolific. As the dangers of oral communication increased and as repression prevented open assembly and preaching, the printed Word became ever more important because it was easier to transmit in secret or to keep anonymous, and harder to trace. Materials in print have possibilities of exactitude and permanence lacking in oral or handwritten ones, and the reproductive process endows them with the advantages (and sometimes disadvantages) of speed and quantity in dissemination. If the printing industry played a determining role in the creation of our modern culture, characterized by "mass literacy, mass education, mass government and mass participation in a highly organized economy," it is to some extent, as one historian puts it, "a consequence of certain peculiarities in the Christian religion that have dominated the western ethos," specifically its emphasis on the Word.[32]

Printers therefore operated at the core of every heretical movement, scarcely less central than the religious leaders themselves and largely responsible for the range and impact of the latter's influence. Inevitably printers, at least the masters, were literate and their principal clientele would consist of educated people. In the context of the Renaissance, this meant chiefly members of the clergy, lay scholars and their patrons, lawyers, and businessmen.

Within a few years of the actual invention in Germany, presses were founded near the University of Paris, traditionally the training ground of clerical scholars from all over Europe. By 1500 there were 181 Parisian print shops and 95 in Lyon, the great commercial and banking center of southeastern France. This was a generation before the incidence of printed heresy would so alarm the authorities that constraints would be put on French use of the revolutionary invention. During this time families of scholar-printers were creating in northern cities successful businesses similar to those long characteristic of Italian cities, especially Venice. The Frobens of Basel, the Estiennes of Paris and Geneva, and the Plantins of Antwerp were outstanding examples. Along with the humanist-printer, there appears the printer who is personally connected with reformers, like Thomas Aushelm of Tübingen (a friend of the great German humanist Johannes Reuchlin), his son-in-law Setzer (a friend of Reuchlin's nephew Philip Melanchthon, sometimes called the "humanist of the Reformation"), or the leaders of the Geneva printing industry who were close associates of Calvin and Beza.

The fact that printing was usually a family business, with marked generational continuity, reinforced both the ideological commitment and the business incentive—failure of the movement could mean loss of the family fortune and possibly persecution. An important study of printing as a historical force underlines the special vulnerability of printers arising from their connections with reformers. "The first to read the manuscripts, they were often the first to be converted and the first to fight for the ideas."[33] The scholar-printers have their own special martyr in Etienne Dolet, burned at the stake in 1546 for heresy, though his concerns were philosophical and scholarly rather than directly religious.

Princely patrons like Marguerite de Navarre supported the printers along with the scholars whose work was to be printed. Thus in 1529, Simon du Bois moved his press from the Latin quarter of Paris to the Norman town of Alençon, one of Marguerite's domains. There, in the following five years, he printed twenty-eight clandestine publications in French, destined *pour les simples et les rudes* which included eight books of scripture and twenty small "manuals of Christian devotion," among which were translated excerpts of Luther, Erasmus, and Lorenzo Valla and two editions of Marguerite's own contribution to evangelical literature, *The Mirror of the Sinful Soul*.[34]

The fact that this book, from the pen of the king's own sister, was condemned as heretical and that she was obliged to stop writing in this vein is an indication of the risks incurred by less highly placed disseminators of the reform. Du Bois himself dropped out of sight after 1534 and scholars have found no trace of his whereabouts, while Clément Marot, translator of the

Psalms who had been a member of Marguerite's household, and her protégé John Calvin—among others—were forced to flee France entirely. Twenty years later, at least seven printers figure among the Marian exiles from England.[35]

The religious leaders themselves were highly conscious of the value of the printers and their products to the cause. Even before it had become certain that the church would not reform as he wished and that the emperor would support the church, Luther embraced the printing press as his most valuable ally. In a very short space of time he wrote several enormously influential pamphlets that mark the crossing of his personal Rubicon in that they were incontrovertibly heretical. *The Address to the Christian Nobility of the German Nation,* for example, called on the territorial princes to reform the church in their lands; *The Babylonian Captivity* attacked the sacramental system; *On Monastic Vows* denounced the regular clergy and the whole notion of celibacy. While a refugee in the Wartburg, after his condemnation by the Diet at Worms and rescue by the Elector of Saxony (1521), Luther began his translation of the Bible that virtually created the modern German language and has profoundly influenced German culture.

As early as 1520 Luther was the most widely read German author and had produced thirty devotional works, including slim editions of the Ten Commandments and the Lord's Prayer. The Wittenberg presses turned out more than six hundred works between 1518 and 1523, including fifteen editions of *The Address to the German Nobility* (the first edition of four thousand was sold out within a week). Meanwhile his enemies were not idle, and some of his would-be followers went off at tangents of their own. Hundreds of pamphlets poured from the presses of fifty German cities. Vernacular publications in 1524 numbered about nine hundred, as compared with one hundred and fifty in 1518. One scholar says that in his anxiety to spread the truth and correct misinterpretations Luther "organized a veritable press bureau." He sought out and attracted to Wittenberg the ablest pamphleteers and propagandists. By carefully studying both the content and the stylistic and polemical devices of his opponents he was able to outbid them with the most important groups of readers by his own vigorous argument, forceful style, and colorful language. One result was that he became a new authority throughout Germany, "the Pope of Wittenberg," taking the place of the old authority. This influenced the future development of the movement in ways not predictable at the outset that might not have occurred if the controversies, both religious and political, had not been blown up and carried to every German-speaking area by the printing press. It is to be noted that this flood of German pamphlets receded abruptly after 1525, when the peasant uprisings were repressed by the princes, with Luther's support, and they gained control of the movement for all practical purposes.[36]

In England the phenomenon is even more striking in that it continued in ever-increasing volume from the 1530s through the Puritan revolution of the mid-seventeenth century, and embraced every religious current. At the height of the Marian persecutions, Nicholas Ridley, bishop of London, who was a prisoner in the Tower, devoted his energies to writing and securing the publication of a number of tracts on the sacraments, on church-state relations, and on persecution and martyrdom. Although the Protestant leaders were in prison, the government was unable to prevent these from being published in Protestant continental cities like Strasbourg, Frankfurt, and Geneva, because of the existence of an extensive and efficient network of sympathizers both in England and abroad who risked their lives to transmit the manuscripts and the resulting books. Mary's proclamation against sedition reflects the situation accurately. It condemned those who took it upon themselves

> to preach and to interpret the word of God after their own brain in churches and in other places both public and private, and also . . . by printing of false-found books, ballads, rhymes and other treatises in the English tongue . . . touching the high points and mysteries of the Christian religion, which . . . are chiefly by the printers and stationers set out to sale to her grace's subjects of an evil zeal for lucre and covetous of vile gain.[37]

The martyrdoms of the three bishops in the Tower, Latimer, Ridley, and Cranmer, with those of numerous lesser men and women, were to be enshrined in the reign of Queen Elizabeth in a book considered so important that in 1570 a copy was placed in every church beside the Bible, and so influential in English history that it has been compared to English seapower.

This was John Foxe's *Book of Martyrs,* to use the abbreviated title. The Foxe phenomenon owes its unique importance to its usefulness to the Elizabethan regime, but the English Cardinal William Allen was no less ready to use the press as his chief instrument against Elizabeth, and Puritan publications number in the thousands.[38]

Geneva was the spiritual home of English dissenters, although the more radical of them would not have been tolerated there, and from the Genevan presses came the flood of publications that sustained the reform movements in France, Scotland, and the Netherlands. Leading Parisian printers like the Estiennes, and Lyonnais like Pierre de Vingle and Jean de Tournes moved some part of their business to "the Protestant Rome" when forced to flee France. With the exception of Robert and Henri Estienne, whose publications were primarily classical, these presses were devoted to serving the Reform militant.

The largest publishing business in Geneva was that of Laurent de Normandie, a childhood friend of Calvin's in Noyon, who has been called the Calvinist "minister of propaganda." He owned four printing shops in Geneva but also provided work for other presses. At his death in 1569 his estate contained twenty-five thousand plates, including ten thousand of the works of Calvin. His accounts show about two hundred distributors in his employ, operating in a large number of northern cities. Although most of them were booksellers by profession, the roll also includes ministers, merchants, artisans, and some nobles.[39]

The list of Laurent de Normandie's outlets and customers is one indication of a significant factor in the impact of the Reformation on communication: by mid-century the enterprising printers had created a single European market for their goods, with a regular and efficient system for transacting business, and Frankfurt am Main, with its annual book fair, was its hub. Writers, booksellers, printers, and businessmen of all kinds flocked to Frankfurt from every corner of Europe each autumn. For some it was a convention, professionally essential; for others, who might be called tourists, it was a distraction, a sight to be seen. Deals of all sorts were negotiated and production for the next year planned. The occasion was also a great generator of rumors and news.[40]

Because of its location and the entanglement of the book trade with the reform, the Frankfurt fair was an important source of and outlet for Protestant propaganda. In a country like France, where by mid-century heresy was severely repressed, the printers had another, subordinate and clandestine, means of communication, described by one authority on the subject as ''a veritable network of subversion.'' Its headquarters were a Parisian bookshop called L'Ecu de Bâle because it had originated with the printer-sellers of Basel. As early as 1483 the Basel booksellers had a permanent agent in Lyon; by 1500 there were agents also in Strasbourg, Avignon, Toulouse, Châlons, and Paris. The Paris branch grew in importance and the bookstore known as L'Ecu de Bâle was established in 1516. It did a flourishing business in reform literature until the repression of the late 1520s, printing some works on the spot and importing others. In 1519, for example, six thousand copies of Luther's works were imported and sold. The joint censorship of the crown and the Sorbonne obliged the owners to give up printing heretical works in Paris, but they continued to import and sell them at considerable risk to themselves.[41]

In Paris the book trade was right under the eyes of the authorities and it was bound to be seriously crippled, but Lyon was far from Paris and near Geneva. Moreover, many Lyonnais printers were natives of or had connections with Germany and Switzerland, while an upper-class Protestant clientele created a demand for Protestant works. Lyon therefore became the center of French intellectual activity, of reform propaganda, and of the printing industry in France.[42]

It would be a mistake to attribute the persistence of printing and bookselling in situations made dangerous by persecution exclusively to religious zeal or a taste for martyrdom, though these undoubtedly existed. The new book-oriented culture and especially the religious revival made it a very promising business, and one may assume that economic motives quite honestly predominated with a considerable proportion of businessmen in the sixteenth as in any other century.

The London book trade was organized for the first time in 1557 when the crown established the Company of Stationers, granting its members certain privileges, imposing regulations, and claiming a share of the profits. Two years later when the

Marian exiles returned, they were prepared to apply techniques they had learned in Frankfurt and Geneva, while English Catholics, exiles in their turn, began plying their compatriots with books printed abroad or secretly at home. "The result was that book-production in England soon became not only a flourishing trade but in its effects a major factor and a major problem in public life." John Day, who had been excluded from the Company of Stationers by Mary as the printer of Latimer's sermons and other subversive works, became the leading Establishment printer, with Archbishop Parker as his patron and John Foxe as his editor. Among his religious publications were the works of Ridley, sermons, letters and manifestoes of the martyrs, and, of course, Foxe's *Book of Martyrs* itself. He also held exclusive rights to the English service book and ABC books.[43]

Reformation publications can be classified in a number of ways. Bibles, editions of the church fathers, theological treatises, sermons, and letters of religious leaders and martyrs constitute the most impressive category. For our purposes, other publications can be described as either directly and explicitly polemical or indirectly polemical, that is, those that ostensibly inform or instruct the reader in some secular subject, or entertain him, in such a way as to persuade him to adopt a particular religious position.

Purely religious works of devotional instruction, *livres de piété,* were produced in the greatest volume by Protestant presses everywhere and scholars are unanimous in emphasizing their influence. Issued in small format, easy to transport and conceal, inexpensive, they carried the lessons of personal piety into the homes and workshops of the middle and lower classes. "Expositions" of the Lord's Prayer, the Sermon on the Mount, the Parables, and the Ten Commandments were typical subjects. Another approach was to offer a Protestant substitute for some rejected Roman practice. An anonymous pamphlet of forty pages, called *Brève instruction pour soy confesser,* printed by Simon du Bois, is a good example. After proving that confession and penance in the Catholic manner are man-made innovations, that is, they are not found in the Gospels, it goes on to expound the doctrine of justification by faith, with the corollary that only God's grace can procure forgiveness for the truly repentant Christian. Advice and comfort for the persecuted constitute another theme, as in du Bois's clandestine publication, *Le Combat Chrestien,* where the various kinds of battle to be fought by the Christian against particular dangers are catalogued and prescribed for from the Epistles of St. Paul.[44]

Pamphlets, or *libelles,* were similar in form to devotional books and almost as numerous, but their content is better described as ecclesiastical or political than as spiritual, even if they deal with religious matters. Luther's famous pamphlets mentioned above are good examples, as are the Huguenot pamphlets of the wars of religion, at least three of which are considered of major importance to the development of constitutional theory: François Hotman's *Franco-Gallia,* Theodore Beza's *Du Droit des magistrats sur leurs sujets,* and the *Vindiciae contra Tyrannos,* of disputed authorship but now generally attributed to Philippe DuPlessis-Mornay. All three were written and published after the Massacre of St. Bartholomew (1572) and addressed themselves to relations between church and state, and the issues of religious toleration and right of resistance, which were of great importance to French Protestants at the time—and later to Catholics when the Calvinist Henry IV became king. A striking feature of the political theory of the Reformation era is the use of identical arguments by Protestants in some circumstances and by Catholics in others, each claiming the right to resist when they were persecuted and advocating obedience when the government was on their side.[45] More ephemeral polemical publications included manifestoes, proclamations of governments and opposition parties, and broadsides or handbills. These were constantly pouring from the press throughout the Reformation era and some had considerable historical importance. The appearance of placards attacking the mass (and asserting that the administration of the sacraments was a commemoration) in France in October 1534 marked the end of the relatively tolerant phase of François I's policy toward the reform and the beginning of severe repression. In the light of developments later in the century, it is seen as a turning point in the fate of Protestantism in France.[46]

A characteristic of much polemical writing in the sixteenth century was dissimulation, the use of fictitious names and false places of publication to avoid detection, or of outright deceit by the attribution of opinions to a person or group, distorting or even directly contradictory to their true opinions, to serve the purposes of the real—as opposed to the alleged—author. The French were particularly gifted in this respect. The printer-bookseller Pierre de Vingle, whose publications include the famous placards, was an outstanding practitioner of the art, and the unscrambling of some of his aliases and imaginary presses required extensive detective work by an expert. Productions of this kind, often satirical or obscene, reached a peak in the struggles of the Holy League against Henry IV in the 1590s. A priceless collection made by the Parisian diarist Pierre de l'Estoile can be found in the fourth volume of the complete edition of his *Mémoires-Journaux.*[47]

An interesting case of serious false attribution to a well-known person on a religious theme is *La Confession de M. Noel Béda,* also printed by Pierre de Vingle. The real Noel Béda was the spokesman of the ultra-Catholic faculty of theology at the University of Paris and chief persecutor of the humanist-reformers in the 1520s. Having overstepped the bounds of propriety and incurred the wrath of the king, he was in disgrace in the early 1530s. The confession of the false Béda is a statement of pure reformed doctrine, denouncing the sacraments and clergy of the Roman church—an ostensible plea for pardon for the error of the real Béda's known ways. This particular example was so flagrantly out of character that it was quickly detected as false and heretical, but the volume and popularity of such works demonstrate two significant features of the Reformation era: great familiarity with the Bible and the church tradition, and "the intense desire of religious publicists to bring about the triumph of their own version of the faith, by no matter what means. Conscious of the importance of spreading the Word in print, they devoted their full energies to [doing so] without respect to persons . . . even without scruples, one might say."[48] There were always violent denunciations and repudiations by the person or group misrepresented, but the method continued to be popular and effective with all the sects, and the perpetrator's defense was always the same: any means toward the end of God's truth is justified.

A good many scholarly works of the Reformation era are indirectly polemical, presenting serious argument or accurate information with a certain interpretation that it is hoped the reader will adopt. National histories were an especially suitable vehicle, as can be seen from the great Tudor chronicles of Camden, Stowe, and Holinshed, and from Foxe's *Book of Martyrs* in the later, expanded editions, as well as the works of the French Huguenot historians during the wars of religion. With the notable exception of Foxe's book, these were less accessible because scarcer and more expensive than the other kinds of polemical literature, and their impact was more likely to be restricted to the educated classes.

By contrast, most of the indirect polemical literature was popular, addressed to the man in the street, small in format, inexpensive, and simplistic in style and argument. Its purpose tended to be information, instruction, or entertainment. Almanacs and calendars were very popular. The Reformation input was to replace Catholic, or merely superstitious or astrological, ''days,'' practices, biblical verses, and parables. The same new trend is to be found in the Books of Hours and emblem-books made for the aristocracy. The overriding purpose of all is to lead the reader to the scriptures. A good example is the *Almanach spirituel et perpetuel, nécessaire à tout homme sensuel et temporel,* printed by du Bois in Alençon, probably in 1531, which shows the influence of several German writings inspired by Luther. Fragments of the Old Testament and the Gospels are inserted in the usual subject matter, such as the dates of new and full moons, eclipses, and important fairs.[49]

Manuals of instruction in everyday activities like ploughing, planting, and harvesting also were used by reform publicists, but the most significant instructional use was in alphabet books and primers. One that met with great success has been traced to the pen of Robert Olivétan, Calvin's cousin and translator-editor of the Huguenot Bible. It is entitled *L'instruction des enfants cou tenant la matière de prononcer et écrire en françois,* and printed by Pierre de Vingle in Geneva in 1533. It teaches the alphabet, grammar, the use of accents, and simple arithmetic, but also the basic articles of the reformed faith.[50]

An example from Lyon later in the century bears the title ALPHABET OU INSTRUCTION/ *chrestienne, pour les petits enfans/nouvellement reveue et augmentée/ de plusieurs choses/ MAT. X/ Laissez les petis enfans venir à moy, et ne/ les empeschez, car à tels est le/ Royaume de Dieu/ EPHES. VI/*

Père, nourrisez vos enfans en la discipline et correction de nostre Seigneur. The first section takes up the Ten Commandments, followed by some Psalms, in Marot's versification, and then come prayers for every hour of the day and every activity of the child's life, but none of them is addressed to the saints or the Virgin. Heavy emphasis is placed on God the Father and obedience to the child's father as His deputy. Prayers are included for the conversion of secular rulers to the true faith and for its protection against the ''ravenous wolves'' who would devour it. A leading scholar of the French Reformation remarks, ''Here is a little book, very inoffensive in appearance, a simple primer designed for children; the peddler who transports it can easily conceal it, the teacher can slip it into his pupil's hand without attracting attention. Yet this little booklet is an awe-inspiring weapon of war, it is a résumé in brief and popularized form of Calvin's *Institutes*—it is the whole religious revolution ready to explode in the classroom.''[51]

The penetration of reformed ideas into popular drama has already been mentioned, and the oral impact here undoubtedly was more important, especially with those who could not read. But the volume of popular reform literature produced and sold indicates that literacy was more prevalent in the lower classes, at least in some areas, than is commonly supposed, and it was increasing rapidly under the pressure of reformed teaching and emphasis on the Bible, even as vernacular writings multiplied.[52] Poetry and fiction were infiltrated by Reformation polemics, especially in Germany, were allegorical subject matter in metrical verse to be recited or sung grew naturally out of a strong medieval tradition. One popular poem, called *The Triumph of Virtue,* is is in reality a long commentary on the engraving that serves as its frontispiece, showing Luther, ''the nightingale of Wittenberg,'' with his allies standing before the throne of God. His enemies are on the other side. Appropriate praise for the former and condemnation of the latter are set forth in the text, much of it put in the mouths of Old Testament prophets or Christian martyrs. The identification of Luther with the nightingale, who gives the signal that night is over and dawn about to break, stems from a famous allegorical drawing of Hans Sachs. The nightingale is singing in the branches of a huge tree; the moon has not yet faded from the sky and the wolves are still devouring innocent lambs under cover of the darkness, but one lamb toward the east bears the cross and the malicious animals all show fear. The accompanying text makes sure that the reader will get the point. The opening verse bids him awake, and further on he is enjoined, "Know that the blessed nightingale who hails the dawn is Dr. Martin Luther, Augustin of Wittenberg, who draws us out of the night where we have been led astray by the moon [Roman Catholicism] and become prey to the lion [Pope Leo X] and other evil creatures [the clergy]; he will give us instead the lamb [Gospel]."[53]

With few exceptions, principally the masterpieces of Albrecht Dürer, the illustrations in Reformation books are more important as propaganda than as art. Yet the *livres de piété* put out by the Lyonnais printers were as much sought after for their illustrations as for their texts, and Haller remarks the "reportorial effectiveness" of the woodcuts in Foxe's *Book of Martyrs,* which were "designed . . . to illustrate a memorable scene and to score a point off the adversary in the manner of a satirical cartoon." In the 1570 edition, greatly enlarged, volume I ends with twelve full-page illustrations of the decline and corruption of the papacy, including one of King John humiliated, kneeling before the pope, as he is forced to accept his kingdom as a papal fief. This contrasts strikingly with one in the second volume, where Henry VIII sits in council holding his sceptre, his foot on the neck of Clement VII, while Cranmer hands him the Bible. Haller comments, "The latter picture expressed the dominant theme of the work from this point on. Everywhere . . . in its account . . . up to this point has been planned to lead up to Henry VIII. Everything on was intended to lead to Elizabeth."[54] The *Book of Martyrs* is thus a prime example of the mobilization of every means of communication in the service of the Reformation and its affiliated political regime, combining Renaissance development in language and learning with religious fervor to bring the desired message to every reader.

PROPAGANDA

So many different messages were transmitted that one needs some general guidelines to avoid being overwhelmed and bewildered by the conflicting streams of Reformation propaganda on the one hand or long study of the various movements on the other. Despite their many divergences, two generalizations can be applied to all the Protestant movements: first, their propaganda had two objects, a negative one, to exploit sources of discontent with the old religious order, and a positive one, to build on desires, aspirations, and expectations by associating their fulfillment with a new religious order. Second, their propaganda, like their motives, includes both spiritual and secular elements.

Little as the Church of England and the Kirk of Scotland appear to have in common with each other or the Radicals, their propaganda shares many themes of the negative sort that reflect widespread resentment against the Roman Catholic church of the sixteenth century. Every form of polemical writing and graphic illustration of the Protestant sects drew heavily on the "abuses." The papacy was attacked not only for its worldliness, wealth, and ostentation, but for having usurped authority and substituted itself for the true authority of the Gospels, and for creating a temporal state with a fiscal bureaucracy. The entire clergy was attacked for lack of spirituality and for temporal preoccupations, the priests especially for ignorance and the monks, most virulently of all, for immorality and as parasites on society. The very notions of the privileged priesthood and the sacramental system were denounced and celibacy universally rejected. Practices like the sale of indulgences and doctrines like the intercession of saints were only the most conspicuous of those attacked.

The entire secular order of government and society was at least indirectly implicated because the officers, privileges, and institutions of the church were so deeply embedded in it. Rulers like the German princes and powerful nobles everywhere responded to these themes on the level of their interests—desire to consolidate power and secure revenues—and, in many cases, on the spiritual level also, as devout Christians seriously persuaded that the church had gone astray. The educated classes were deeply penetrated by the Christian humanist doctrine that the essence of Christianity lay exclusively in the Gospels and all else was false, superstition, or mercenary exploitation. In addition, their business or profession involved them with the secular powers; they served as officers in the growing bureaucracies or depended on the state for markets and other business advantages.

Artisans who often were the victims of clerical exploitation might be attached to old industries or trades suffering from competition, dislocation, unemployment, or inflation, or to new ones like printing and metallurgy, which required patronage and protection from the newly aggressive secular rulers. Unskilled workers, peasants, and the underprivileged generally resented centuries-old injustices that seemed less tolerable in an age of rising geographical mobility and economic opportunity, when persuasive voices were proclaiming that although all men might be fully equal only in the sight of God, they were not therefore required to accept particular traditional forms of inequality in the sight of man.

These negative factors could stir up repeated unrest, even in some circumstances rebellion, but only the promise or prospect of fulfillment of men's positive aspirations could lay the foundation of a new order that would capture the imagination, command allegiance from all classes, and provide a new cohesion to replace that which was felt to be lost. There was a conscious need for personal commitment in religion and for participation at the level where it really counts. The old church, even though many clerics from village priests to cardinals were devout, was so overburdened with institutional complexities that the layman felt impotent, unimportant, a mere follower, trapped by the rules and requirements.

The initial phase of lay piety had been a response to the German mystics and the *Devotio Moderna,* a conception of religion that was simple and personal, strongly emotional but at the same time practical in its application to daily life. The new thrust of sixteenth-century piety responded to the evocation of the pure apostolic age combined with the intellectual appeal of straightforward doctrine, cut to the bone, which did not strain the bounds of reason. The Renaissance had flowered with the maxim "back to the sources," and the new religious leaders confined their teachings—at least at first—to the ancient texts purified of all additions. One was required to take on faith only the Gospels and the Epistles of St. Paul. The living Word was thought to speak directly to each Christian soul providing only that he had faith, though his access would be more complete, and more satisfactory to him, if he could read it for himself in his own language. Solace for every burden and predicament lay as close as the nearest New Testament.

Moreover, in the most dynamic of the new forms of Christianity, that of Calvin, the Christian was in large part relieved of responsibility for his personal salvation, which was in God's hands. He was given instead a responsibility he could really assume and nobody else could take his place: a direct share in God's work, in "the world," either in his present place and activity or in one he could attain through his own efforts. Every kind of constructive work was regarded as part of the Lord's Plan, so that the peasant at his plough, the artisan at his bench, the merchant in his shop, the housewife in the kitchen, and the child in the schoolroom each had a "calling" with a spiritual dimension, and could feel that his work was sanctified because it was done for the glory of God and in obedience to His will. Every man was in this sense a priest. If, through hard work, education, or the grasping of opportunity he could "rise in the world," this was approved as a proper use of his talents and pleasing to God. Resignation was an appropriate response to suffering sent by God, including persecution, for this is how faith is tested, but in earthly matters work to help or improve oneself was the sign of the true believer (although "works" in the traditional Catholic sense were repudiated).

The theme of restoration, or "back to the Gospel," was the single most powerful unifying theme of all the Protestant reformations. As soon as it became necessary to institutionalize new beliefs and practices, to go beyond the assertion of faith and the Word, they inevitably became divided into the "magisterial" forms and, for those who rejected these, into the various radical groups.

A second positive theme was very powerful in some areas, depending on secular historical circumstances. This was the rise of consciously formulated new allegiances resulting from identification with a territorial or national government and culture. "Christendom," which had been the political counterpart of the universal Roman church, was no longer realistically united, and the small localities where most men lived all their lives had been or were becoming absorbed in larger units with a character of their own, usually centered around a ruling dynasty and a common language. *Res christiana* faded into memory, leaving *cuius regio eius religio* as the compelling reality.[55]

By its very nature this theme created new cohesion within

each of the new centers of allegiance but heightened differences between them. There certainly were greater differences (and greater consciousness of difference) between the subjects of Queen Elizabeth and those of Henry IV than between Englishmen and Frenchmen a century earlier, although then they had recently waged war against each other for several generations (the Hundred Years War). For the great majority in either nation who were not associated with the levers of power, this greater consciousness stemmed from an increasingly differentiated culture and national history. The particular religious doctrines and institutions adopted by each in the Reformation era became embedded in the national culture. In Germany, Lutheranism stimulated the growth of a unified culture but it was not accompanied by political unification, and "the Germanies" remained fragmented until the nineteenth century. The national character of the Scots was institutionalized by the Kirk of Scotland, and the United Provinces of the Netherlands came to birth as a nation in this era through a struggle that was both religious and national.

The propaganda formulated by the victorious parties in the Reformation era has colored their respective national histories and self-images for four hundred years. There also exist some minority images, the heritage of the losers, such as English Catholics and French Protestants. England is the most clear-cut case for the dominant view, possibly because national religion and culture were indigenous and developed together, whereas in France the ultimately triumphant religion was after all doctrinally Catholic, and the variants of Gallicanism involve areas of administration that overlap with the secular power rather than spiritual issues.

The fact that Henry VIII carried out the establishment of a national church quite rapidly, through acts of Parliament, and that the only rebellion of his reign was confined to one area and was short-lived, had led historians to underestimate the opposition, according to Geoffrey Elton, the leading twentieth-century constitutional historian of the reign. In a recent book, *Policy and Police,* he has set the record straight with abundant documentation of the extent and various manifestations of opposition, followed by a detailed analysis of the means by which Thomas Cromwell, the king's chief minister, overcame it. Elton believes that to Cromwell's "propaganda staff," especially Richard Morison, a gifted pamphleteer, belongs much credit for persuading the nation to accept Henry's divorce, the break from Rome, and the subsequent Henrician settlement.[56]

In a pair of particularly effective pamphlets of 1539, Morison produced "a mixture of Protestant religion and patriotic fervor" that was to become characteristic of English polemics. *An Invective against the great and detestable vice of treason* attacks prominent Catholics who oppose Henry and concludes that they and the pope are bound to fail "because the King has seen the light [of Protestantism]." *An Exhortation to stir all Englishmen to the defence of their country* predicts defeat of the wicked bishop of Rome and his allies; with the Lord's help English hands and English hearts will win even if they are outnumbered. The ad hoc purpose of these pamphlets was to make preparations for war against the French more palatable, but the long-range message was England's good fortune and the dangers threatening her through Catholicism. The conclusion was that all Englishmen should rally to support the king who had broken the yoke of Rome and would make England's future safer and even more glorious than her past.[57]

When the Marian exiles returned at the beginning of Elizabeth's reign, this theme of England's special position and virtue assumed its fullest and most exalted expression in Foxe's *Book of Martyrs,* through an extension of the Christian philosophy of history formulated by St. Augustine in the fifth century. The great determining events are the Creation, the Fall, and the life of Christ, whose resurrection carries the promise of redemption for believers. But that promise will not be fulfilled until the Last Judgment, and in the meantime human history is the story of the struggle of the City of God against His enemies. The Hebrew notion of the Chosen People is thus transferred to Christians. The sixteenth-century reformers, especially Calvin, who was much influenced by the Old Testament, elaborated the concept of the "elect," those predestined by God for salvation, and the Radicals also held the millennium to be their goal.

The idea of the elect as peculiarly English was first articulated by John Bale, who saw history as "the age-long contention of English rulers and people against intruders forever seeking to subvert the English state and corrupt the English church by open violence or by false doctrine." The story began when Joseph of Arimethea brought the pure Gospel to Britain. In later centuries agents of Rome and the Normans corrupted it, but there were always some good native kings and spiritual teachers to keep the true faith alive even in the darkest times.[58]

John Aylmer, writing in 1559, by dramatizing Elizabeth's sufferings and exemplary behavior during Mary's reign, established her as the latest and greatest of the godly rulers who defended His chosen realm. Englishmen should thank God that they were not born Italian, French, or any other nationality because not only does England abound in all good things, such as beef, beer, and wool, but "God and His angels fight on her side against all enemies." "God is English," the writer exclaims in the margin. Haller points out that Aylmer "spoke for a highly articulate group of intellectuals with a common grievance, a common purpose, a common body of ideas, a common vocabulary for making their ideas known, and a vital stake in the security of Elizabeth's person and the success of her regime."[59]

Such is the context in which Foxe took up the theme and perfected it, in successive editions of the *Book of Martyrs,* each with richer detail from past centuries and recent decades concerning "the Elect Nation." Where earlier editions had covered the history of England before Wycliffe in one hundred pages, the 1570 edition has five hundred, and the increase of space devoted to contemporary history is even greater. The significance of this expansion and incorporation of legends about the national past can hardly be exaggerated, according to Haller:

> It was for its own time and for several succeeding generations a com prehensive history of England based upon a conception of human nature and of the meaning and course of history which few of its readers were in any state of mind to do anything but accept as universally true.[60]

Simultaneously, English chroniclers like Camden, Stowe, and Holinshed were creating a secular national legend that made the English people "aware of themselves as a people having a common past full of meaning for the present."[61] And indeed for the future as well. Down to the twentieth century, Englishmen have carried this special sense of righteousness and moral mission as they traded, colonized, and conquered in every corner of the world. Transplanted Englishmen adapted it to their new nation in North America, alleged to be even more elect because it was free from the taints of the old, with a manifest destiny to fulfill.[62]

A third positive theme in Protestant propaganda is the thirst for justice, supposed to be the business of rulers, for which they are accountable to God. This is a complex theme with many components. In addition to the obligation of governments to protect the true faith and suppress heresy, it embraces the idea of greater equality—matching the spiritual liberation of the laity—the claim to rights, beginning with those of conscience and broadened by some into a whole series of civil rights, and consequently in many cases a demand for autonomy. Lutheran princes, French Huguenot nobles, Dutch provincials, and English Puritans are among those who expressed some of these aspirations during the Reformation era. The striking initiative of women in the Protestant reformations may be an expression of their (unconscious) feeling that where the laity was on a par with the ministry they would be less completely subordinated to men than in the predominantly male Roman church. (Their conscious motives were wholly spiritual and moral, however.)

We know for certain that the peasants in Germany rose in rebellion in the 1520s believing that if Luther proclaimed every man his own priest, he would support their challenge to the lesser, secular authority. We also know how bitterly disappointed they were, and that he lost much peasant support even as he consolidated his following among the nobles and the princes—whose aspirations against the emperor and the pope he had encouraged. The German situation is a good example of a typical pattern: where social aspirations or demands for rights suited the secular powers they were achieved, at least in part; otherwise they were largely frustrated. Anabaptists who wanted a real social revolution were doomed to fail, while Cambridge intellectuals who were willing to identify their cause with the stability of Elizabeth's regime succeeded. Catherine de Medici would grant to Huguenot members of the great nobility a degree of religious autonomy denied to their humbler coreligionists, unless they had powerful protection. Seventeenth-century Puritans in New England (Massachusetts Bay) had defied the king and left their homeland in the name of religious liberty, but refused to grant it to Independents in Plymouth or Rhode Island.

The egalitarian message of the reform thus often aroused expectations and demands beyond what those who proclaimed it or their powerful supporters were ready to concede, a pattern not unusual in revolutions, as can be seen from the ultimate results of the two great liberal revolutions of the late eighteenth century in America and France.

Students of the Reformation era have struggled in vain to distinguish neatly between religious and secular elements in sixteenth-century propaganda. Sometimes when one thinks a particular case is clearly pinned down to an obvious secular motive, such as peasants' resentment of landlords and desire for their own land, or the demands of printing workers on their masters, one is forced to qualify it by the discovery that much of the social criticism in popular English literature "ends up in criticism of the church," or that their economic conflict did not prevent Protestant *compagnons* from closing ranks on religious issues with their Protestant masters in Lyon.[63]

By attempting to separate religious and secular concerns in the sixteenth century too sharply, historians often have been trapped into contradictions or mired in confusion. This happens especially when they are simultaneously trying to label the period as "medieval," when religion is alleged to have predominated, or "modern" and secular. This is a false dilemma, based on erroneous assumptions. In a perceptive and influential essay entitled "Factors in Modern History," J. H. Hexter suggests that the century is best understood in terms of "polarpairs" between which "there is tension, the issue is *never* one of either-or; it is *always* more-or-less." Elaborating the point farther on, he says, "[O]nce we realize that the religious and the secular, though polar to one another, *can* both at once rise to higher levels of intensity, we will recognize that they both *did* so rise in the sixteenth century."[64] Moreover, it should always be remembered that the natural idiom of the times was religious, unlike the Western world of the twentieth century, although the continuation of confessional bitterness in Northern Ireland to the point of civil war should remind us that some sixteenth-century patterns persist today as did medieval ones in the early modern period.

The Catholic Reformers obviously could not use any of the three positive themes in precisely the same way as did Protestants. Roman propagandists had to resort to counterarguments in each case. They countered the appeal to the Gospels and the primitive church by emphasizing the venerable and continuous Roman tradition. Against national aspirations they set the universality of the one true church, heightening its splendor and glorifying its uniqueness. The desire for justice presented the greatest difficulties, because the Tridentine Church Council was not prepared to modify the hierarchical principle, as we have seen in the test case of lay access to and interpretation of the Bible. Despite the educational successes of the Jesuits, the Roman church could win the educational competition with Protestants only where the contest was made unequal through repression of Protestantism by the secular authorities. Fear of subversion often led the church to oppose scientific or medical advances and social change, so that in the four hundred years between the Council of Trent and Vatican II the religious life of Catholics was increasingly compartmentalized and set apart from their secular lives.

One weapon was handed to the Roman propagandists by the Protestants themselves—their ever-proliferating divisions. The ablest Catholic polemicists used it very effectively, ridiculing the hair-splitting doctrinal differences among Protestants and pouring scorn on the presumption of man-in-the-street authority substituted for the accumulated wisdom of the vicars of Christ, successors of St. Peter, whose power was delegated by Jesus himself. The church also developed a unique weapon of its own in the exploitation of the visual arts. Protestants of every stripe deplored the characteristic decoration of Catholic churches with painting and sculpture, and the use of rich vestments and vessels. All but Anglicans and Lutherans condemned what they called "images," and the Radicals often attacked them physically. Music also was banned in many of the new churches. By contrast, a conspicuous feature of the Catholic Reformation at its height was an artistic flowering, often called the baroque, that ranks among the greatest in modern history. Although scholars do not agree about the extent to which religion inspired such works as the paintings of Caravaggio or the architectural style known as "Jesuit," some use of the arts was demonstrably propagandistic, like the frescoes of the Massacre of St.

Bartholomew in the Vatican by Vasari, commissioned by Pope
Gregory XIII.[65]

The unprecedented impact of the Reformation era on propaganda resulted, on the one hand, from the intensity of religious
sentiment and, on the other, from the competition for converts
between religious and political leaders of rival factions who
knew how to use new forces of language, learning, and technology. In isolation any one of the waves of reform might have effected only limited changes, but all of them together made a
revolution that affected every sphere of Western European society by a sort of chain reaction through the communication networks, oral, visual, and in print.

In the chapter in this volume on Renaissance communication, William Bouwsma points to the change from a medieval
conception of reality as universal, objective, and relatively unchanging, above man's earthly life, to a conception oriented to
everyday experience, "a series of unpredictable and novel
events . . . dominated by laymen . . . increasingly well educated and assertive." The new culture such men brought to
birth, he demonstrates, made more practical demands on communication, which "became an essential bond among men in
society," requiring greater flexibility of language.[66] The Reformation sprang directly out of this new culture, inspired in its
spiritual content by the revived ancient languages, especially
the Greek of the New Testament, and then transmitted its message through the developing vernacular languages and the
printing press. The Reformation impact on the conception of
reality went beyond that of the Renaissance in that the reformers' concern with ultimate Christian truth required the redefinition of transcendent, eternal reality and some new explanation
of its relationship to earthly experience. The post-Reformation
era thus inherited a conception embracing three quite different
spheres, one eternal-Christian, much revised as compared to the
medieval, another from the classical world as revived by the Renaissance, in addition to that of practical experience.

Knowledge also had to be redefined: it was necessary to differentiate the kind of knowledge man could aspire to, concerning matters of faith, from information that could be demonstrated by reason or tested by experience. The simultaneous
appearance of so many new conceptions of eternal truth—

Christianity—with the explosion of worldly knowledge in many areas explains some of the contradictions of the era that led to the futile attempts, already mentioned, to decide whether it was ''medieval'' or ''modern,'' an aspect of the Renaissance or a reaction against it.

If the Reformation is judged by Puritan echoes of Old Testament prophets, Anabaptist iconoclastic violence, and the aridity of much Protestant thought, it appears to be a movement directly in conflict with the Renaissance—an effective, though largely temporary, setback to the flowering of the human spirit. But if one also looks at the constitutional bulwarks against tyranny and the (ultimate) achievement of individual dignity through civil rights, or the extraordinary incidence of spirituality and courage in every group from the Anabaptists to the Jesuits, or the works of genius it inspired in men like Dürer and Milton, the Reformation is seen as a particular expression of the Renaissance—the Christian Renaissance.

As such, it was probably the most widely influential of all the various manifestations of the Renaissance. It certainly reached more people in more places, especially in the lower classes, than did the scholarly and artistic works of the fifteenth-century Italians. And it affected them on a fundamental level, restructuring their self-image and conception of the meaning of life. The ideas and institutions produced by the several reformations have shown an astounding durability and, in some cases, flexibility, proving themselves historically functional by meeting the needs of pluralistic Western society. The effective use of communication and propaganda was the central and indispensable instrument in this achievement.

NOTES

1. Space does not permit even minimal bibliography; the interested reader can find preliminary guidance in historiographical aids prepared for students: R. Dannenfeldt, ed., *The Renaissance, Medieval or Modern?* (Heath series, Problems in European History, Boston); W. Stanford Reid, ed., *The Reformation, Revival or Revolution?* (Holt, Rinehart and Winston, European Problem series, 1968). Both contain excerpts of important interpretations and good bibliographical suggestions from recent historical literature.

2. The first pope who could exercise real authority over all other Western bishops was Gregory I (the Great, 590–604); the full machinery of the papal

monarchy dates from Innocent III (1198-1216). Certain influential theologians of the eastern Roman Empire are known as the Greek Fathers; the major "Latin" Fathers were St. Ambrose, St. Jerome, editor of the Roman Catholic Bible *(Vulgate),* and St. Augustine, author of *The City of God,* who died in A.D. 430. The influence of the latter was especially important in the Reformation era.

3. See, for instance, Gordon Leff, *Heresy in the Later Middle Ages: The Relation of Heterodoxy to Dissent* (Manchester, 1965), and John R. H. Moorman, *A History of the Franciscan Order from Its Origins to 1517* (Oxford, 1968).

4. For the background and historical development of the indulgence controversy, see standard histories of Lutheranism (note 9), and for definitions of doctrinal and ecclesiastical terms consult F. L. Cross, ed., *The Oxford Dictionary of the Christian Church* (Oxford, 1957).

5. Wallace K. Ferguson, *Europe in Transition* (Boston, 1962); chaps. 11 and 15, give an excellent general account of the *Devotio Moderna* and the Brethren. For more detail, see Albert Hyman, *The Brethren of the Common Life* (Grand Rapids, 1950), and *The Christian Renaissance* (Hamden, Conn., 1960).

6. Unfortunately there is no biography of Marguerite in English. The standard work is Pierre Jourda, *Marguerite d'Angoulême,* 2 vols. (Paris, 1930). Brief discussion in Nancy L. Roelker, *Queen of Navarre: Jeanne d'Albret, 1528-1572* (Cambridge, Mass., 1968), pp. 11-15. On French noblewomen, see Nancy L. Roelker, "The Role of Noblewomen in the French Reformation," in *Archive for Reformation History,* Autumn 1972, and "The Appeal of Calvinism to French Noblewomen in the Sixteenth Century," in *Journal of Interdisciplinary History,* Spring 1972. On German women: Roland Bainton, *Women of the Reformation* (Minneapolis, 1971); on English noblewomen: D. K. McConica, *English Humanists and Reformation Politics* (Oxford, 1965), chap. 7.

7. When the Emperor Charles V tried to reassert his authority over the German princes who had converted to Lutheranism in 1529, they drew up a protest declaring that they could not be compelled in matters of conscience. This is the origin of the term Protestant, later extended to all non-Roman Catholics in the West.

8. George H. Williams, leading authority on the Radicals and author of several books and articles. See especially, *The Radical Reformation* (Philadelphia, 1962).

9. Two good general introductions that have helpful bibliographies on each of the major reform movements are recommended: Roland H. Bainton, *The Reformation of the Sixteenth Century* (Boston, 1966); A. G. Dickens, *Reformation and Society in Sixteenth-Century Europe* (London, 1966).

10. In addition to works on Calvinism in Bainton and Dickens, see, for a

fuller account, John T. McNeil, *The History and Character of Calvinism* (New York, 1954).

11. The best general introductory work is A. G. Dickens, *The English Reformation* (London, 1965).

12. Some English Protestants preferred a more conservative service, with vestments, chanting, and a sacramental emphasis. Their interpretation of communion was also similar to the Roman Catholic, although denying the miraculous power of the priest to transform the bread and wine into the body and blood of Christ (Transubstantiation). This tendency within the Anglican church came to be called "high." "Low-church" Anglican services resemble those of other Protestant sects in their simplicity; their interpretation of communion is commemorative and the sermon is the core of their worship. The Prayer Book prescribed for all in Elizabeth's Act of Uniformity allows for either alternative.

13. See two excellent studies: Geoffrey R. Elton, *Policy and Police: The Enforcement of the Reformation in the Age of Thomas Cromwell* (Cambridge, 1972); and William Haller, *The Elect Nation: The Meaning and Relevance of Foxe's Book of Martyrs* (New York,1963).

14. Williams's *Radical Reformation* is the outstanding work; see also Bainton, *Reformation of the Sixteenth Century,* chaps. 7, 11.

15. Williams, *Radical Reformation,* chap. 23, section 4 and passim; Roland H. Bainton, *Hunted Heretic: The Life of Michael Servetus* (Boston, 1953) is a readable biography.

16. On the Catholic Reformation, see A. G. Dickens, *The Counter Reformation* (London, 1969); H. O. Evenett, *The Spirit of the Counter Reformation,* ed. J. Bossy (Cambridge, 1968).

17. Haller, p. 50.

18. Dickens, *Counter Reformation,* p. 115.

19. On Latimer, Haller, pp. 26–27; on preaching, Haller, p. 97.

20. Haller, pp. 92, 103.

21. No study of this movement exists in English. Like all Netherlands phenomena it must be examined in each province. For Utrecht, I am indebted to the doctoral dissertation of Sherrin Wyntjes, "The Lesser Nobility in the Netherlands Revolt in Utrecht" (Tufts University, 1972).

22. The sources (French) for the *affaire* are listed in the article cited in note 6, by Roelker, in *Archive for Reformation History;* Robert M. Kingdon, *Geneva and the Coming of the Wars of Religion in France* (Geneva, 1956).

23. Henri Hauser, *Etudes sur la Réforme française* (Paris, 1909), pp. 91–93; Dickens, *English Reformation,* p. 13.

24. Eugénie Droz, "Antoine Vincent: la propagande par le Psautier," in *Aspects de la propagande religieuse,* ed. H. Meylan (Geneva, 1957), no. 28 of *Travaux d'Humanisme et Renaissance* (hereafter cited as *Aspects*), pp. 276–293; Natalie Z. Davis, "The Protestant Printing-Workers of Lyon in

1551," *Aspects,* pp. 247–257; Henri Hauser, *La Naissance du protestantisme,* 2d ed. (Paris 1962), p. 61.

25. Georgette Brasart-de Groër, "Le Collège, agent d'infiltration de la Réforme," *Aspects,* pp. 167–175; Dickens, *English Reformation,* p. 79.

26. For a lively account of the climate of opinion in Paris, see Nancy L. Roelker, ed., *The Paris of Henry of Navarre: The Mémoires-Journaux of Pierre de L'Estoile* (Cambridge, Mass., 1958).

27. Maurice Gravier, *Luther et l'opinion publique* (Paris, 1942), pp. 175–190; Dickens, *English Reformation,* p. 273.

28. On the taverns and other places of business or trade as agents of reform propaganda, see *Hérésies et sociétés dans l'Europe pré-industriel, du 11ième au 18ième siècles* (a symposium of the VIe Section of the Ecole des Hautes Etudes, Paris, 1968), pp. 278–285, 401–405; on the spread of the reform among the common people in France, see Hauser, *Etudes,* pp. 83–103; on the reform carriers to northern Italy, see Edouard Pommier, "Propagande protestante dans la République de Venise," *Aspects,* pp. 240–246.

29. Charles Dartigue, *Le Vicomté de Béarn sous le règne d'Henri d'Albret* (Paris, 1934), pp. 478–480.

30. A. G. Dickens, *English Reformation,* p. 190; for examples, see p. 28.

31. Eugénie Droz, "Pierre de Vingle, imprimeur de Farel," *Aspects,* pp. 38–78.

32. On the importance of printing to the Reformation in general, see Elizabeth L. Eisenstein, "L'Avénement de l'imprimerie et la Réforme," in *Annales; Economies, Sociétés, Civilisations* (1971), pp. 1355–1382, which has many valuable references as well; A. Tricard, "La Propagande évangélique en France," *Aspects,* pp. 1–37; Robert M. Kingdon, "The Business Activities of Printers Henri and François Estienne," *Aspects,* pp. 258–275; Robert M. Kingdon, "Patronage, Piety and Printing in Sixteenth-Century Europe," in D. H. Pinkney and T. Ropp, eds., *Festschrift for Frederick B. Artz* (Durham, N.C., 1964), pp. 19–36, citation, p. 26; Lucien Febvre and Henri-Jean Martin, *L'Apparition du Livre* (Paris, 1958), passim.

33. Febvre and Martin, pp. 28–29.

34. Tricard.

35. On Marguerite, see the references in note 6; on the Marian exile printers, see Dickens, *English Reformation,* p. 283.

36. Louise W. Holborn, "Printing and the Growth of a Protestant Movement in Germany, 1517–1524," *Church History* 11 (1942):123–137; Gravier, pp. 217–221; Henri-Jean Martin, *Le Livre et la civilisation écrite* (Paris, 1968), pp. 162–163.

37. Haller, pp. 39–40; Mary's Proclamation, Haller, p. 24.

38. Haller, p. 14, citing Gordon Rupp, "Foxe's *Book* counted in English history as much as Drake's drum"; on Cardinal Allen's use of the press, see Garrett Mattingly, "William Allen and Catholic Propaganda in England,"

Aspects, pp. 325–339, and Thomas B. Clancy, *Papist Pamphleteers: The Allen-Persons Party and the Political Thought of the Counter-Reformation in England, 1572–1615* (Chicago, 1964); Robert M. Kingdon, "William Allen's Use of Protestant Political Argument," in C. H. Carter, ed., *From the Renaissance to the Counter Reformation: Essays in Honor of Garrett Mattingly* (New York, 1965), pp. 164–178. Muriam Chrisman, of the University of Massachusetts, Amherst, has analyzed all Strasbourg publications of the Reformation era, as yet unpublished.

39. Heidi-Lucie Schlaepper, "Laurent de Normandie," *Aspects,* pp. 179–230; Kingdon, "Patronage, Piety and Printing."

40. Kingdon, "Business Activity"; James W. Thompson, *The Frankfort Book Fair* (Chicago: Caxton Club, 1911).

41. Martin, *Le Livre,* pp. 164–165. Peter G. Bietenholz, *Basle and France in the Sixteenth Century: The Basel Humanists and Printers in Their Contacts with Francophone Culture* (Geneva, 1971).

42. Droz, "Pierre de Vingle"; the forthcoming major study of the Lyon printing workers by Natalie Z. Davis, *Strikes and Salvation* (Stanford University Press) deals with this subject extensively.

43. On English book production, Haller, p. 111; on John Day, Haller, pp. 114–115.

44. Tricard, pp. 24–25, 29–33.

45. These have been translated and edited by Julian H. Franklin, *Constitutionalism and Resistance in the Sixteenth Century* (New York, 1969). See also William F. Church, *Constitutional Thought in Sixteenth-Century France* (Cambridge, Mass., 1941).

46. Robert Hari, "Les Placards de 1534," *Aspects,* pp. 79–142.

47. Droz, "Pierre de Vingle," p. 56; Brunet et al., eds., *Mémoires-Journaux de Pierre de l'Estoile,* 12 vols. (Paris, 1888–1896).

48. Gabrielle Berthoud, "Livres Pseudo-catholiques de contenu protestant," *Aspects,* pp. 143–154, citation, p. 153.

49. Tricard, pp. 33–37.

50. Droz, "Pierre de Vingle," pp. 66–67.

51. Hauser, *Etudes,* pp. 274–286; citation, p. 281.

52. Holborn, "Printing," pp. 136–137.

53. Gravier, pp. 191–192: Martin, *Le Livre,* p. 146.

54. The illustrations of Lyon analyzed in Martin, *Le Livre,* pp. 156–159; citation in Haller, pp. 123, 173.

55. The formula "to whatever prince one is subject one belongs also to his religion" was adopted by the Lutheran princes; at the Peace of Augsburg (1555), which ended the religious war in Germany, it was embodied in the settlement. This was a victory for Luther's idea and a defeat for the Holy Roman emperor, but Catholic princes also could exploit it to their own advantage.

56. Elton, *Policy and Police*.

57. Ibid., pp. 202–210.

58. Haller, p. 69

59. Ibid., pp. 87–88; citation, p. 88.

60. Ibid., p. 142.

61. Ibid., p. 149.

62. The French have a considerably older and more complex sense of themselves as an elect nation, dating from the Middle Ages, which has assumed many (secular) forms in modern history. It is not discussed here because it is not a product of the Reformation era, though some aspects of the argument appear in both Huguenot and Ligueur propaganda. See Joseph R. Strayer, "France: The Holy Land, the Chosen People and the Most Christian King," in Theodore K. Rabb and Jerold E. Seegal, eds., *Action and Conviction in Modern Europe: Essays in Honor of E. H. Harbison* (Princeton, 1969), pp. 3–16; Miriam Yardeni, *La Conscience nationale en France pendant les guerres de religion, 1559–1598* (Paris, 1970).

63. Helen C. White, *Social Criticism in Popular Religious Literature of the Sixteenth Century*, 2d ed. (New York, 1965), pp. 31–35; Davis, *Strikes and Salvation,* chaps. 7, 8.

64. J. H. Hexter, *Reappraisals in History* (New York, 1961), pp. 26–44; citations from pp. 34, 42. Other "polar-pairs" include church-state; court-country; dynasty-region; and Catholic-Protestant. The last is atypical in that it called for "mutual exclusion, indeed, mutual extermination."

65. Dickens, *Counter Reformation,* pp. 165–170, especially the illustrations. See also Carl J. Friedrich, *The Age of the Baroque* (New York, 1952).

66. See chapter 1 in the present volume.

3

THE ENLIGHTENMENT AS A
COMMUNICATION UNIVERSE

Peter Gay

THE LITTLE FLOCK OF PHILOSOPHES
I

There were many philosophes in the eighteenth century, but
there was only one Enlightenment. A loose, informal, wholly
unorganized coalition of cultural critics, religious skeptics, and
political reformers from Edinburgh to Naples, Paris to Berlin,
Boston to Philadelphia, the philosophes made up a clamorous
chorus, and there were some discordant voices among them, but
what is striking is their general harmony, not their occasional
discord. The men of the Enlightenment united on a vastly ambitious program, a program of secularism, humanity, cosmo-
politanism, and freedom, above all, freedom in its many forms
—freedom from arbitrary power, freedom of speech, freedom of
trade, freedom to realize one's talents, freedom of aesthetic response, freedom, in a word, of moral man to make his own way
in the world. In 1784, when the Enlightenment had done most
of its work, Kant defined it as man's emergence from his self-
imposed tutelage, and offered as its motto *Sapere aude*—
"Dare to know": take the risk of discovery, exercise the right of
unfettered criticism, accept the loneliness of autonomy.[1] Like
the other philosophes—for Kant only articulated what the
others had long suggested in their polemics—Kant saw the Enlightenment as man's claim to be recognized as an adult, responsible being. It is the concord of the philosophes in staking

this claim, as much as the claim itself, that makes the Enlightenment such a momentous event in the history of the Western mind.

Unity did not mean unanimity. The philosophic coalition was marked, and sometimes endangered, by disparities of philosophical and political convictions. A few—a very few—of the philosophes held tenaciously to vestiges of their Christian schooling, while others ventured into atheism and materialism; a handful remained loyal to dynastic authority, while radicals developed democratic ideas. The French took perverse pleasure in the opposition of church and state to their campaigns for free speech and a humane penal code, and to their polemics against "superstition." British men of letters, on the other hand, were relatively content with their political and social institutions. The German *Aufklärer* were isolated, impotent, and almost wholly unpolitical. As Georg Christoph Lichtenberg, essayist, wit, physicist, and skeptic, wrote in the privacy of his notebooks: "A heavy tax rests, at least in Germany, on the windows of the Enlightenment."[2] In those Italian states that were touched by the new ideas, chiefly Lombardy and Tuscany, the reformers had an appreciative public and found a sympathetic hearing from the authorities. The British had had their revolution, the French were creating conditions for a revolution, the Germans did not permit themselves to dream of a revolution, and the Italians were making a quiet revolution with the aid of the state. Thus the variety of political experience produced an Enlightenment with distinct branches; the philosophes were neither a disciplined phalanx nor a rigid school of thought. If they composed anything at all, it was something rather looser than that: a family.[3]

But while the philosophes were a family, they were a stormy one. They were allies and often friends, but second only to their pleasure in promoting the common cause was the pleasure in criticizing a comrade-in-arms. They carried on an unending debate with one another, and some of their exchanges were anything but polite. Many of the charges later leveled against the Enlightenment—naïve optimism, pretentious rationalism, unphilosophical philosophizing—were first made by one philosophe against another. Even some of the misinterpretations that have become commonplace since their time were originated by philosophes: Voltaire launched the canard about Rousseau's primitivism, Diderot and Wieland repeated it; Hume was among the first to misread Voltaire's elegant wit as sprightly irresponsibility.

To the delight of their enemies, the philosophes generated a highly charged atmosphere in which friendships were emotional, quarrels noisy, reconciliations tearful, and private affairs public. Diderot, generous to everyone's faults except Rousseau's, found it hard to forgive d'Alembert's prudent desertion of the *Encyclopédie*. Voltaire, fondest of those who did not threaten him with their talent gave Diderot uneasy and uncomprehending respect, and collaborated on an *Encyclopédie* in which he never really believed; in return, Diderot paid awkward tributes to the literary dictator of the age. He honored Voltaire, he told Sophie Volland, despite his bizarre behavior: "Someone gives him a shocking page which Rousseau, citizen of Geneva, has just scribbled against him. He gets furious, he loses his temper, he calls him villain, he foams with rage; he wants to have the miserable fellow beaten to death. 'Look,' says someone there, 'I have it on good authority that he's going to ask you for asylum, today, tomorrow, perhaps the day after tomorrow. What would you do?' 'What would I do?' replies Voltaire, gnashing his teeth, 'What would I do? I'd take him by the hand, lead him to my room, and say to him, 'Look, here's my bed, the best in the house, sleep there, sleep there for the rest of your life, and be happy.' ''[4] There is something a little uneasy beneath this charming fable: Diderot thought well of Voltaire's writings and Voltaire's humane generosity, but he somehow never quite trusted him, and the two men did not meet until 1778, when Voltaire came back to Paris to die. For their part, the Germans, like Lessing, had distant, correct, or faintly unpleasant relations with the French: they admired them judiciously and from afar. Rousseau, at first indulged by all, came to reject and to be rejected by all, even by David Hume. Only Hume, corpulent, free from envy and, in society, cheerfully unskeptical, seems to have been universally popular, a favorite uncle in the philosophic family.

The metaphor of a philosophic family is not my invention. The philosophes used it themselves. They thought of themselves as a *petite troupe,* with common loyalties and a common world view. This sense survived all their high-spirited quarrels: the philosophes did not have a party line, but they were a party. Some of the harshest recriminations remained in the family, and when they did become public, they were usually sweetened by large doses of polite appreciation. Moreover, harassment or the fear of harassment drove the philosophes to remember what they had in common and forget what divided them. The report of a book burned, a radical writer imprisoned, a heterodox passage censured, was enough. Then, quarrelsome officers faced with sudden battle, they closed ranks: the tempest that burst over Helvétius's *De l'esprit* in 1758 and the prohibition issued against Diderot's *Encyclopédie* in the following year did more to weld the philosophes into a party than Voltaire's most hysterical calls for unity. Critics trying to destroy the movement only strengthened it. In 1757 the journalist Fréron denounced Diderot to the chief censor, Malesherbes, as the "ringleader of a large company; he is at the head of a numerous society which pullulates, and multiplies itself every day by means of intrigues,"[5] but Malesherbes continued to protect the philosophes to the best of his considerable ability. In 1760, Palissot, a clever journalist with good political sense but doubtful taste, wrote a meager comedy entitled *Les philosophes,* in which he lampooned Rousseau as an apelike savage and brutally satirized Helvétius, Diderot, and Duclos as an unprincipled gang of hypocrites who exploit idle, gullible society ladies with pretentious schemes. Palissot took it for granted that "everybody knows that there is an offensive and defensive league among these *philosophic* potentates."[6] Obviously, the potentates survived this assault: Horace Walpole, who did not like them, had no hesitation in identifying the little flock when he reached Paris in 1765. "The *philosophes,*" he wrote to Thomas Gray, "are insupportable, superficial, overbearing, and fanatic: they preach incessantly. . . ."[7]

Walpole's characterization is too bilious to be just. In fact, the philosophes tolerated a wider range of opinions than fanatical preachers could have: Voltaire was happy to admit that while atheism is misguided and potentially dangerous, a world filled with Holbachs would be palatable, far more palatable than a world filled with Christians, and Holbach, who thought little of deism, returned the compliment. There was one case, to be

sure, that seems to shatter the unity of the movement: the philosophes' persecution of Rousseau. But the persecutors did not
see it that way. They rationalized their ruthlessness by arguing
that Rousseau had read himself out of the family to become that
most despicable of beings, an ex-philosophe. "No, my dear,"
wrote Diderot reassuringly to his Sophie Volland in July 1762,
shortly after Rousseau's *Émile* had been condemned and
burned, "no, the Rousseau business will have no consequences.
He has the devout party on his side. He owes their interest in
him to the bad things he says about philosophes. Since they
hate us a thousand times more than they love their God, it matters little to them that he has dragged Christ in the mud—as
long as he is not one of us. They keep hoping that he will be
converted; they're sure that a deserter from our camp must
sooner or later pass over into theirs."[8] While, in general, arguments among philosophes were conducted in the tones Voltaire
used about Holbach rather than the tones used by Diderot
about Rousseau, Diderot's rhetoric in this letter—"we" against
"they," the military metaphors, and the virulent hatred of the
opposition—reveals at once the anxiety concealed behind the
confident façade and the cohesion achieved by the men of the
Enlightenment by the 1760s.

The Enlightenment, then, was a single army with a single
banner, with a large central corps, a right and left wing, daring
scouts, and lame stragglers. And it enlisted soldiers who did not
call themselves philosophes but who were their teachers, intimates, or disciples. The philosophic family was drawn together
by the demands of political strategy, by the hostility of church
and state, and by the struggle to enhance the prestige and increase the income of literary men. But the cohesion among the
philosophes went deeper than this: behind their tactical alliances and personal fellowship there stood a common experience
from which they constructed a coherent philosophy. This experience—which marked each of the philosophes with greater or
lesser intensity, but which marked them all—was the dialectical
interplay of their appeal to antiquity, their tension with Christianity, and their pursuit of modernity. This dialectic defines
the philosophes and sets them apart from other enlightened
men of their age: they, unlike the others, used their classical
learning to free themselves from their Christian heritage, and

then, having done with the ancients, turned their face toward a modern world view. The Enlightenment was a volatile mixture of classicism, impiety, and science; the philosophes, in a phrase, were modern pagans.

II

To call the Enlightenment pagan is to conjure up the most delightfully irresponsible sexual license: a lazy, sun-drenched summer afternoon, fauns and nymphs cavorting to sensual music, and lascivious painting, preferably by Boucher. There is some reality in this fantasy: the philosophes argued for a positive appreciation of sensuality and despised asceticism. But these preachers of libertinism were far less self-indulgent, far more restrained in their habits, than their pronouncements would lead us to believe. Rousseau had masochistic tastes which he apparently never gratified; Hume had an affair in France; young Benjamin Franklin "fell into intrigues with low women" and fathered an illegitimate son; Diderot wrote a pornographic novel to keep a mistress in the style to which she hoped to become accustomed; La Mettrie, a glutton, died at the Prussian court shortly after eating a spoiled game pie, thus giving rise to the delicious rumor that he had eaten himself to death; Voltaire had a passionate, prolonged affair with his niece—one of the few well-kept secrets of the eighteenth century. But this rather scanty list almost exhausts salacious gossip about the Enlightenment. Generally, the philosophes worked hard—made, in fact, a cult of work—ate moderately, and knew the joys of faithful affection, although rarely with their wives. When Diderot found his Sophie Volland in middle age, he found the passion of his life. His disdain of prostitutes or "loose women," which is such a curious theme in his correspondence, was not motivated by mean fear of venereal disease: it was the cheerful acceptance of obligation, the self-imposed bond of the free man. David Hume testified in 1763 that the French "Men of Letters" were all "Men of the World, living in entire or almost entire Harmony among themselves, and quite irreproachable in their Morals."[9] As a group, the philosophes were a solid, respectable clan of revolutionaries, with their mission continually before them.

In speaking of the Enlightenment as pagan, therefore, I am

referring not to sensuality but to the affinity of the Enlightenment to classical thought.[10] Words other than pagan—Augustan, Classical, Humanist—have served as epithets to capture this
affinity, but they are all circumscribed by specific associations:
they illuminate segments of the Enlightenment but not the
whole. "Augustan" suggests the link between two ages of
literary excellence, mannered refinement, and political corruption. "Classical" brings to mind Roman temples, Ciceronian
gravity, and Greek myths translated into French couplets. "Humanist" recalls the debt of the Enlightenment to Renaissance
scholarship, and a philosophy that places man in the center of
things. Yet I do not think that any of these terms makes, as it
were, enough demands on the Enlightenment; they have about
them subtle suggestions of parochialism and anemia of the
emotions: "Augustan" properly applies to Great Britain in the
first half of the eighteenth century; "Classical" is the name for
a noble, artificial literary style and for a preference for antique
subject matter; "Humanism" in all its confusing history has
come to include an educated piety. The Enlightenment was
richer and more radical than any of these terms suggest: Diderot's plays, Voltaire's stories, Hume's epistemology, Lessing's
polemics, Kant's Critiques—which all belong to the core of the
Enlightenment—escape through their meshes.

III

For Walpole or Palissot, as for most historians since their time, a
philosophe was a Frenchman. But *philosophe* is a French word
for an international type, and that is how I shall use it in these
pages. To be sure, it is right that the word should be French, for
in France the encounter of the Enlightenment with the Establishment was the most dramatic: in eighteenth-century France,
abuses were glaring enough to invite the most scathing criticism, while the machinery of repression was inefficient enough
to permit critics adequate room for maneuver. France therefore
fostered the type that has ever since been taken as *the*
philosophe: the facile, articulate, doctrinaire, sociable, secular
man of letters. The French philosophe, being the most belligerent, was the purest specimen.

Besides, Paris was the headquarters and French the lingua
franca of European intellectuals, and philosophes of all nations

were the declared disciples of French writers. In Naples, Gaetano Filangieri, the radical legal reformer, acknowledged that he had received the impetus for writing his *Scienza della Legislazione* from Montesquieu. Beccaria, Filangieri's Milanese counterpart, told his French translator, Morellet, that he owed his "conversion to philosophy" to Montesquieu's *Lettres persanes,* and that d'Alembert, Diderot, Helvétius, Buffon—and Hume—were his "constant reading matter," every day and "in the silence of night."[11] Hume and Gibbon attributed much of their historical consciousness, Adam Ferguson and Jean-Jacques Rousseau, most of their sociological understanding, to their delighted discovery and avid reading of Montesquieu's works. D'Alembert's *Discours préliminaire* to the *Encyclopédie* was widely read in Scotland and on the Continent. Adam Smith, without being a physiocrat himself, learned much from the physiocrats during his French visit from 1764 to 1766. Bentham derived his utilitarianism partly from Helvétius; Kant discovered his respect for the common man by reading Rousseau; while Voltaire's campaigns against *l'infâme* and on behalf of the victims of the French legal system had echoes all over Europe. Even Lessing, in rebellion against the French neoclassical drama of Corneille, Racine, and Voltaire, assailed it with weapons supplied to him by Diderot. And it is significant that monarchs like Catherine of Russia and Frederick of Prussia, who forced themselves on a movement to whose ideals their policies owed little, incessantly proclaimed their indebtedness to French models.

But while Paris was the modern Athens, the preceptor of Europe, it was the pupil as well. French philosophes were the great popularizers, transmitting in graceful language the discoveries of English natural philosophers and Dutch physicians. As early as 1706, Lord Shaftesbury wrote to Jean Le Clerc: "There is a mighty light which spreads itself over the world, especially in those two free nations of England and Holland, on whom the affairs of all Europe now turn."[12] Shaftesbury himself, with his optimistic, worldly, aesthetic, almost feminine Platonism, exercised immense power over his readers: over the young Diderot; over Moses Mendelssohn, Wieland, and Kant; over Thomas Jefferson; all in search of a philosophy of nature less hostile to the things of this world than traditional Christian doctrine. The propagandists of the Enlightenment were French, but its patron saints and pioneers were British: Bacon, Newton, and Locke had such splendid reputations on the Continent that they quite overshadowed the revolutionary ideas of a Descartes or a Fontenelle, and it became not only tactically useful but intellectually respectable in eighteenth-century France to attribute to British savants ideas they may well have learned from Frenchmen. In an *Essai sur les études en Russie,* probably by Grimm, we are told that ever since the revival of letters, enlightenment had been generated in Protestant rather than Catholic countries: "Without the English, reason and philosophy would still be in the most despicable infancy in France," and Montesquieu and Voltaire, the two French pioneers, "were the pupils and followers of England's philosophers and great men."[13]

Among scientists, poets, and philosophers on the Continent, this admiration for England became so fashionable that its detractors coined a derisive epithet—Anglomania—which its devotees applied, a little self-consciously, to themselves. Skeptics like Diderot and Holbach, who ventured at mid-century to find some fault with British institutions, were a distinct minority. In the German-speaking world the poets Hagedorn and Klopstock and the physicist Lichtenberg confessed to *Englandsehnsucht,* while Lessing discovered Shakespeare and patterned his first bourgeois tragedy, *Miss Sara Sampson,* on an English model. In the Italian states, reformers idealized the English constitution and the English genius for philosophy: Beccaria's friends could think of no more affectionate and admiring nickname for him than *Newtoncino*—little Newton. But *Anglomanie* was practiced most persistently and most systematically in France. Montesquieu constructed a fanciful but influential model of the British government for other, less favored nations to imitate; Voltaire, well prepared by his early reading, came back in 1728 from his long English visit a serious deist and firm Newtonian and in general a lifelong worshipper of England: "A thousand people," he wrote in 1764, "rise up and declaim against 'Anglomania.' . . . If, by chance, these orators want to make the desire to study, observe, philosophize like the English into a crime, they would be very much in the wrong."[14]

For all of Voltaire's earnest claims, it must be admitted that this cosmopolitan dialogue was not always conducted on the highest level. Hume's influence on the French and the Germans is a study in missed opportunities. Kant, for all his much-advertised debt to Hume, seems never to have read the *Treatise of Human Nature*. Except perhaps for d'Alembert and Turgot, the Parisian philosophes, whom Hume greatly liked and who gave him a rousing reception during his stay in the 1760s, neither shared nor fully understood his skepticism; Voltaire, who told an English visitor in his quaint accent that "I am hees great admeerer; he is a very great onor to Ingland, and abofe all to Ecosse,"[15] appears to have been as ignorant of Hume's epistemology as he was amused by Hume's quarrel with Rousseau. Still, not all philosophic intercourse was gossip and triviality. British empiricism transformed French rationalism; French scientific and political propaganda transformed Europe.

The philosophe was a cosmopolitan by conviction as well as by training. Like the ancient Stoic, he would exalt the interest of mankind above the interest of country or clan: as Diderot told Hume in an outburst of spontaneous good feeling, "My dear David, you belong to all nations, and you'll never ask an unhappy man for his birth-certificate. I flatter myself that I am, like you, citizen of the great city of the world."[16] Rousseau's intense patriotism was exceptional. Wieland, with all his pessimism, still thought *Weltbürgertum* a noble ideal: "Only the true cosmopolitan can be a good citizen"; only he can "do the great work to which we have been called: to cultivate, enlighten, and ennoble the human race."[17] Gibbon explained in his magisterial tones that "it is the duty of a patriot to prefer and promote the exclusive interest and glory of his native country; but a philosopher may be permitted to enlarge his views, and to consider Europe as a great republic, whose various inhabitants have attained almost the same level of politeness and cultivation."[18] As products of the best schools, with a solid grip on classical culture, the philosophes, the most privileged citizens in Gibbon's great republic, spoke the same language—literally and figuratively.

The typical philosophe, then, was a cultivated man, a respectable scholar and scientific amateur. The most distinguished among the little flock were academics like Kant, Lichtenberg, and Adam Smith, or men of letters like Diderot and Lessing and Galiani, who possessed an erudition a professor might envy. Some of the philosophes were in fact more than amateurs in natural philosophy. Franklin, d'Alembert, Maupertuis, Lichtenberg, and Buffon first achieved reputations as scientists before they acquired notoriety as philosophes. Others, like Voltaire, advanced the cause of scientific civilization with their skillful popularizations of Newton's discoveries.

At the same time, learned as they were, the philosophes were rarely ponderous and generally superbly articulate. It was the philosophe Buffon who coined the celebrated maxim, *Le style est l'homme même;* the philosophe Lessing who helped to make German into a literary language; the philosophe Hume who wrote the most elegant of essays as well as the most technical of epistemological treatises. Rigorous Christians found it a source of chagrin that practically all the best writers belonged to the philosophic family. Even men who detested Voltaire's opinions rushed to the bookseller for his latest production. This concern with style was linked to an old-fashioned versatility. The philosophes remained men of letters, at times playwrights, at times journalists, at times scholars, always wits. Adam Smith was not merely an economist, but a moralist and political theorist—a philosopher in the most comprehensive sense. Diderot was, with almost equal competence, translator, editor, playwright, psychologist, art critic and theorist, novelist, classical scholar, and educational and ethical reformer. David Hume has often been accused of betraying his philosophical vocation for turning in his later years from epistemology to history and polite essays. But this accusation mistakes Hume's conception of his place in the world: he was exercising his prerogative as a man of letters qualified to pronounce on most aspects of human experience, and writing for a cultivated public in which he was consumer as well as producer.

Such a type could flourish only in the city, and in fact the typical philosophe was eminently, defiantly, incurably urban. The city was his soil; it nourished his mind and transmitted his message. His well-publicized visits to monarchs were more glittering than the life of the coffeehouse, the editor's office, or the salon, which was often little more than a gathering of congenial intellectuals. But they were also less productive. The philosophe belonged to the city, by birth or adoption: if he was born in the country he drifted to the city as his proper habitat. "The

Town," observed David Hume in his autobiography, is "the true Scene for a man of Letters."[19] What would Kant have been without Königsberg, Franklin without Philadelphia, Rousseau without Geneva, Beccaria without Milan, Diderot without Paris, or for that matter, Gibbon without Rome? When the philosophe traveled, he moved from urban society to urban society in a pleasant glow of cosmopolitan communication. When he retired to the country, as he often did with protestations of his love for the simple life, he took the city with him: he invited like-minded men of letters to share his solitude, he escaped rural boredom by producing plays, he lined his walls with books, and he kept up with literary gossip through his correspondents in town—his letters were almost like little newspapers. For many years Holbach gathered an international company around his dinner table: Diderot and Raynal were regular visitors, joined from time to time by Horace Walpole, David Hume, the abbé Galiani, and other distinguished foreigners who would sit and talk endlessly about religion, about politics, about all the great forbidden subjects. In Milan, Beccaria, the Verri brothers, and other like-minded *illuministi* founded a newspaper, *Il Caffè;* it was short-lived, but its very existence documents the alliance of sociability and reformism in the Enlightenment everywhere. The leaders of the Scottish Enlightenment—a most distinguished society—were personal as well as intellectual intimates: Adam Smith, David Hume, Adam Ferguson, William Robertson, Lord Home—political economists, aestheticians, moralists, historians, philosophers and philosophes all—held continuous convivial discussions during the day and often through the night in libraries, clubs, coffeehouses, and when these closed, in taverns. Voltaire presided over a literary government-in-exile at Ferney. He stayed away from Paris for twenty-eight years in succession, but that did not matter: where he was, *there* was Paris. The best of the urban spirit—experimental, mobile, irreverent—was in the philosophes' bones.

But this urbanity was colored and sometimes marred by a sense of mission. The philosophes were threatening the most powerful institutions of their day, and they were troubled by the nagging anxiety that they were battling resourceful enemies—for one, a church (as Voltaire said ruefully) that was truly built on a rock. That is why the philosophes were both witty and humorless: the wit was demanded by their profession, the humorlessness imposed on them by their belligerent status. Obsessed by enemies, not all of whom were imaginary, they were likely to treat criticism as libel and jokes as blasphemy. They were touchy in the extreme; Diderot's correspondence and Rousseau's *Confessions* record bickerings over matters not worth a moment of a grown man's attention. David Hume, who saw through the press a polemical pamphlet directed against himself, was quite uncharacteristic; far more typical were d'Alembert, who petitioned the censors to stifle his critics, or Lessing, who pursued scholars of opposing views and inferior capacities with his relentless, savage learning. This is what Goethe had in mind when he called the Berlin *Aufklärer* Nicolai a "Jesuitenfresser"; and this is why Horace Walpole observed in 1779 that "the *philosophes,* except Buffon, are solemn, arrogant, dictatorial coxcombs—I need not say superlatively disagreeable."[20] No doubt Walpole, the fastidious spectator of life, saw the philosophes clearly, but what he did not see is that this intensity and self-assurance (which often make men disagreeable) are occupational hazards which reformers find hard to avoid.

IV

In drawing this collective portrait, I have indiscriminately taken evidence from the entire eighteenth century, from Montesquieu to Kant. This procedure has its advantages: it underlines the family resemblance among the little flock. But it may obscure the fact that the Enlightenment had a history. Its end was not like its beginning precisely because the last generation of philosophes could draw on the work of its predecessors.

It has been traditional to delimit the Enlightenment within a hundred-year span beginning with the English Revolution and ending with the French Revolution. These are convenient and evocative dates: Montesquieu was born in 1689 and Holbach died in 1789. To be sure, these limits are not absolute, and there have been repeated attempts to move the boundaries, to demote the Enlightenment by calling it the last act of the Renaissance, or to expand it by including Bayle, or even Descartes, among the philosophes. But while these attempts have thrown much light on the prehistory of eighteenth-century polemics, I intend to stay with the traditional dates: I shall argue that while characteristic Enlightenment ideas existed long before, they achieved their revolutionary force only in the eighteenth century. Hobbes, and even Bayle, lived and wrote in a world markedly different from the world of Holbach or Hume.

The Enlightenment, then, was the work of three overlapping, closely associated generations. The first of these, dominated by Montesquieu and the long-lived Voltaire, long set the tone for the other two; it grew up while the writings of Locke and Newton were still fresh and controversial, and did most of its great work before 1750. The second generation reached maturity in mid-century: Franklin was born in 1706, Buffon in 1707, Hume in 1711, Rousseau in 1712, Diderot in 1713, Condillac in 1714, Helvétius in 1715, and d'Alembert in 1717. It was these writers who fused the fashionable anticlericalism and scientific speculations of the first generation into a coherent modern view of the world. The third generation, the generation of Holbach and Beccaria, of Lessing and Jefferson, of Wieland, Kant, and Turgot, was close enough to the second, and to the survivors of the first, to be applauded, encouraged, and irritated by both. It moved into scientific mythology and materialist metaphysics, political economy, legal reform, and practical politics. Criticism progressed by criticising itself and its own works.

So the Enlightenment displays not merely coherence but a distinct evolution, a continuity in styles of thinking as well as a growing radicalism. The foundations of the philosophes' ideas did not change significantly: between the young Montesquieu's essay on ancient Rome and the aging Diderot's defense of Seneca there is a lapse of half a century, and interest in ancient architecture and sculpture had risen markedly during the interval; yet for the two philosophes, the uses of antiquity remained the same. Similarly, the devotion to modern science and the hostility to Christianity that were characteristic of the late Enlightenment as well. The dialectic which defined the philosophes did not change; what changed was the balance of forces within the philosophic coalition: as writer succeeded writer and polemic succeeded polemic, criticism became deeper and wider, more far-reaching, more uncompromising. In the first half of the century, the leading philosophes had been deists and had used the vocabulary of natural law; in the second half, the leaders were atheists and used the vocabulary of utility. In Enlightenment aesthetics, in close conjunction with the decay of natural law, the neoclassical search for the objective laws of beauty gave way to subjectivity and the exaltation of taste, and especially in France, timid and often trivial political ideas were shouldered aside by an aggressive radicalism. Yet the scandal the later books caused was no greater than that caused by the pioneering efforts: had Montesquieu's *Lettres persanes* been published in 1770, the year of Holbach's *Système de la nature,* rather than in 1721, it would have seemed tame beside that materialist tract, and would have offered nothing new to a world long since hardened to cultural criticism.

One reason the educated world of eighteenth-century Europe and America had come to accept these polemics, or at least to read them without flinching, was that the hard core of the Enlightenment was surrounded by an ever-growing penumbra of associates. The dozen-odd captains of the movement, whose names must bulk large in any history of the European mind, were abetted by a host of lieutenants. Some of these, little read today, had a considerable reputation in their time. They were men like the abbé de Mably, precursor of socialism and propagandist of the American cause in France; Jean-François Marmontel, fashionable, mediocre playwright, careerist protégé of Voltaire and d'Alembert, elected to the Académie française and chosen Royal Historiographer despite his participation in the *Encyclopédie* and his pronounced views in favor of toleration; Charles Duclos, brilliant and widely respected observer of the social scene, novelist, and historian; the abbé Raynal, ex-priest turned radical historian, whose *Histoire philosophique et politique des établissements et du commerce des Européens dans les deux Indes,* first published in 1770, and immediately proscribed, went through several editions, each more radical than its predecessor; the abbé Galiani, a Neapolitan wit who became an ornament of the Parisian salons and a serious political economist; Moses Mendelssohn, Lessing's friend and Kant's correspondent, aesthetician, epistemologist, and advocate of Jewish emancipation; Baron Grimm, who made a good living purveying the new ideas to monarchs and aristocrats rich enough to afford his private news service; Louis-Jean-Marie Daubenton, a distinguished naturalist whose contributions to science were eclipsed by Buffon, with whom he collaborated; Freiherr von Sonnenfels, a humane political economist, professor at the University of Vienna and, for all his advanced ideas, advisor to the Hapsburgs; Nicolas-Antoine Boulanger, who died young, but left behind him two unorthodox scientific treatises on the origins of religion for his friend Holbach to publish. These men were philosophes of the second rank. Beyond them were the privates of the movement, the hangers-on, consumers and distributors rather than producers of ideas: men like Étienne-Noël Damilaville, Voltaire's correspondent in Paris, who basked in borrowed prestige or secondhand notoriety by running humanitarian errands, smuggling subversive literature through the mails, hiring theatrical claques, or offering disinterested friendship in a harsh world. As the century progressed, these aides grew in number and influence: to embattled Christians, they appeared to be everywhere, in strategic positions—in publishers' offices, in government posts, in exclusive salons, in influential university chairs, near royal persons, and even in the august Académie française. By the 1770s and 1780s, precisely when the philosophes had grown intensely radical in their program, they had also achieved a respectable place in their society.

APPEARANCES AND REALITIES
I

In 1784, in the essay in which he tried to define the Enlightenment, Kant expressed some skepticism about his century. "If someone asks," he observed, "are we living in an enlightened age today? the answer would be, No." But, he immediately added, "we are living in an Age of Enlightenment."[21]

Kant's observation is penetrating and important. Even late in the eighteenth century, for all their influence and palpable successes, the philosophes had reasons for uncertainty and occasional gloom. Voltaire, down to his last days, insisted that his age was an age of cultural decline, and other philosphes deplored what they considered the public's willful resistance to them, its greatest benefactors. "People talk a lot about Enlightenment and ask for more light," Lichtenberg wrote. "But my God, what good is all that light, if people either have no eyes, or if those who do have eyes, resolutely keep them shut?"[22] Diderot, in a moment of depression, exclaimed to Hume: "Ah, my dear philosopher! Let us weep and wail over the lot of philosophy. We preach wisdom to the deaf, and we are still far indeed from the age of reason."[23] And David Hume himself thought that beyond the world of Enlightenment and its cultivated supporters, there lay a large desert of darkness, of stubborn indifference, of illiteracy and superstition, a realm he described with obvious distaste as the realm of "Stupidity, Christianity & Ignorance."[24]

But then—and this was the other side of Kant's Delphic pronouncement—in their optimistic moods the philosophes liked to think of themselves as the potential masters of Europe. Surveying the cultural scene from Königsberg, Kant discerned a "revolt against superstition" among the civilized countries and civilized classes, and called this revolt the *Aufklärung* and its leaders the *Aufklärer*. The British did not naturalize the name "Enlightenment" until the nineteenth century, but even in the eighteenth, British philosophes thought that they were living in, and dominating, a civilized, philosophical age. The French philosophes liked to speak of a *siècle des lumières* and were sure that they were the men who were bringing light to others; with sublime self-satisfaction (for what can be more self-satisfied than to name a century after yourself?) they praised their age as an Age of Philosophy.

Both of these moods were grounded in reality, but there was more ground for hope than for despair. The Enlightenment of the philosophes was embedded in an enlightened atmosphere, a pervasive and congenial cultural style which supplied them with some of their ideas and much of their vocabulary. At once the gadflies and the representatives of their age, the philosophes preached to a Europe half prepared to listen to them.

Evidence for this enlightened climate is profuse. In 1759—to offer but one instance—Samuel Johnson's *Rasselas* appeared nearly simultaneously with Voltaire's *Candide,* and Johnson himself, Boswell reports, remarked on the resemblance between these two Stoic tracts: had they "not been published so closely one after the other that there was not time for imitation, it would have been in vain to deny that the scheme of that which came latest was taken from the other."[25] Boswell insisted, sensibly enough, that the intentions of the two authors had not been the same, but the crosscurrents of the eighteenth century made this famous conjunction into something more than a coincidence. Samuel Johnson called Voltaire a villain, Voltaire called Samuel Johnson a superstitious dog, but the political, literary, and even philosophical ideas of these two bore a striking resemblance. Voltaire took pride in the culture he was trying in his witty way to improve out of all recognition, while Johnson, who detested the philosophes as unprincipled infidels, accepted much of their program: he had the Enlightenment style. Antiphilosophe and archphilosophe were yoked together as improbable and unwitting allies. All manner of men—even clergymen—claimed to possess light. Even Berkeley, it seems, advanced his outrageous epistemological paradoxes in the name of good sense. William Magee, archbishop of Dublin, voiced his concern over the pernicious influence of Hume's writings on even "the most enlightened"—that is, on modern Christians like himself.[26] And when Johnson and Boswell visited the Hebrides, a Scottish divine proudly told his visitors that the world was wrong to take the local clergy to be "credulous men in a remote corner. We'll show them that we are more enlightened than they think."[27] It is in this sense that the age of Montesquieu was also the age of Pope, the age of Hume also the age of Mozart.

The philosophes discovered influential friends everywhere. A king who tried to abolish the financial privileges of the clergy, a duke who expelled the Jesuits, a censor who winked at materialist tracts, an Anglican bishop who taught that good will was enough to get a Christian into heaven or a Tuscan bishop who prohibited pilgrimages and closed roadside shrines, an aristocrat who protected a proscribed atheist, a scrupulous or sensitive believer (like Albrecht von Haller, say, or Samuel Johnson) who was haunted by religious doubts, and perhaps best of all, a devout scholar who discredited religious mysteries with his philological or historical criticisms—none of these accepted all of the philosophes' program, or even much of it, but each of them was doing the philosophes' work. One of the most significant social facts of the eighteenth century, a priceless gift from the enlightened style to the Enlightenment of the philosophes, was the invasion of theology by rationalism: Jesuits gave fair and even generous hearing to scientific ideas, Protestant divines threw doubt upon the miraculous foundations of their creed, and churches everywhere tepidly resisted the philosophy of the philosophes with their own bland version of modern theology.

This treason of the clerks had its secular counterparts. Revolutionary innovations in science, psychology, economic and social ideas, education, and politics, most of them produced by serious and often by devout Christians, by men like Haller and Euler and Hartley and Priestley, aided the efforts, and consolidated the advanced positions, of the radical Enlightenment. So did the activities—the very mental style—of solid citizens who endowed schools and hospitals, supported humane causes, railed against superstition, and denounced enthusiasm. Ideas and attitudes generally associated with subversive, atheistic philosophes—the disdain for Gothic architecture and for Dante, the condemnation of feudal institutions, the rejection of metaphysics and of Scholasticism—were the common property of most educated men in the eighteenth century. The philosophes did not lack courage, and their place in history is secure, but the war they fought was half won before they joined it.

II

These brilliant prospects, linked to their belligerent status and bellicose ideology—their uneasy coexistence with their world—obscured for the philosophes the complexity of their situation. Much like other combatants before and after them, the philosophes found it convenient to simplify the welter of their experience, to see their adversaries too starkly, and to dramatize their age as an age of unremitting warfare between the forces of unbelief and the forces of credulity—that is, between good and evil. Diderot's facile separation of the men of his century into philosophers and "enemies of philosophy"[28] was characteristic, but, in truth, both parties were made up of coalitions, both had affectionate ties with their adversary—the course of battle was beclouded by unstable treaties, cowardly retreats, inadequate intelligence of the enemy's strength and movements, moments of low morale, and treason within the ranks. The philosophes themselves were divided by differences over modes of religious thought and political tactics; there was never an end to debate within the little flock, and the triumph of the materialists and utilitarians was never complete. And on the other side, Anglicans, Lutherans, Catholics, were often hostile to one another. And so at times the philosophes, linked to their culture by their cultivation, were friendlier with Christians than with one another.

In their moments of calm reflection, when they discarded the naïve dichotomies that usually served them so admirably, the philosophes did recognize their age as something other than a perpetual bout between critics and Christians. Diderot amicably corresponded with père Berthier, the editor of the Jesuit *Journal de Trévoux;* Hume noted that Bishop Butler, the formidable apologist of Anglican Christianity, had recommended his essays; and even Voltaire, who publicly denounced the Jesuits as power-mad, sly, and as a lot, revolting pederasts, privately conceded that his old Jesuit teachers had been decent men and respectable scholars. But such moments were rare, partly because there were many times of real crisis when the philosophes stood against the rest, when the faithful squared off against unbelievers; besides, in the long run the issues between the secular world the philosophes wanted and the religious world in which they lived could not be compromised. But for all that, the philosophes were tied to their civilization—at least to the enlightened segment of it—by sutble, fine-spun ties. It is ironic to see the philosophes, as overworked ideologists, reluctant to acknowledge these ties: devoted though they were to piercing the veils of appearance, they often took appearances for realities. They were right to think of themselves as modern, secular philosophers, wrong to claim that they owed their Christian culture nothing.

In politics, their false consciousness took rather a different form. Far from dividing their age into two hostile camps, the philosophes cultivated their connections with power, and their cozy fraternizing with the enemy cost them heavily. It distorted their tactics, long circumscribed their freedom of action, sometimes seduced them into intellectual dishonesty, and blurred their radicalism, not only for others but for themselves as well. True, not all their protestations of innocuousness need be taken seriously: they knew they were more subversive than they admitted to being—their constant evasions testify to that. They were too familiar with the history of martyrs to wish to join them. At the same time, it is clear that the philosophes often misread the drift of their age and the consequences of their ideas. Voltaire's insensitive reading of Rousseau's *Contrat social* and Diderot's equally insensitive reading of Rousseau's *Émile* are symptomatic: here are two of the most intelligent men of the century face to face with two of its prophetic masterpieces— books that came out of the philosophes' world and took some of the philosophes' ideas to their logical conclusion. The intellectual revolution over which the Enlightenment presided pointed to the abolition of hierarchy as much as to the abolition of God. But most of the philosophes found much to cherish in the existing order. It is revealing that Rousseau (and we must always come back to Rousseau when we wish to emphasize the complexity of the Enlightenment), perhaps the only Encyclopedist with moods in which he totally rejected his civilization, was treated as a madman by other philosophes long before his clinical symptoms became obtrusive.

All this does not mean that the philosophes were merely opportunists. They were radicals, even if they were not nihilists: for all the pretentious philosophizing the marquis de Sade injected into his tedious novels, he was never more than a caricature of the Enlightenment whose heir he claimed to be. The philosophes' comfortable sense that they belonged to the Establishment and the Enlightenment at the same time was not solely a symptom of self-deception: there was no conflict in their dual allegiance—not even in France, where the tension was strongest and the rhetoric most extreme. The philosophe Voltaire was royal historiographer and was succeeded in that post by the philosophe Duclos. The philosophe Buffon, aristocratic and self-protective, was the distinguished curator of the *Jardin du Roi.* Turgot cut short his career by preaching toleration of Protestants and by infuriating vested interests with his free-trade policies, but he always considered himself a conscientious servant of the French state. Even d'Alembert, who lived modestly and gave away half he earned, was not wholly detached from the old order: in a letter in which Hume praises his independence he adds that d'Alembert "has five pensions: one from the King of Prussia, one from the French King, one as member of the Academy of Sciences, one as member of the French Academy, and one from his own family."[29] Such a man, and others like him, were hardly alienated revolutionaries. After all, they prized wit, admired elegance, and craved the leisure essential to the cultivated life. When they denounced civilization, they did so urbanely: even Rousseau confessed that he had adopted his bearish mode of conduct only because he was too awkward to practice the manners of good society. Seeking to distinguish themselves, the philosophes had little desire to level all distinctions; seeking to be respected, they had no intention of destroying respectability. Their gingerly treatment of the masses, which became less patronizing as the century went on, reveals their attachment to the old order and their fear of too drastic an upheaval.

It is at this critical point of contact—between philosophe on the one hand and the "lower orders" on the other—that the problem of communication arises in its most acute form. The men of the Enlightenment found no difficulty communicating with the elite except perhaps that of offending the powerful and the vindictive. They masked blasphemy and carefully avoided insulting a minister's mistress. Their principal difficulty in communicating with the middle levels of society—with small merchants, lesser officials, or literate craftsmen—was purely a tactical one: the philosophe who, in Diderot's famous formulation, wished to "change the general way of thinking," had to be blunt enough to make his point, not blunt enough to arouse the vigilance of censors. But what of the workman or the illiterate peasant? In their complacent (though, for their century, perfectly comprehensible) liberalism, the philosophes were inclined to treat the poor as objects of concern rather than as full-fledged participants in the political public. In short, the men of the Enlightenment spoke for the masses, not to them.

In drawing the traditional Platonic analogy between society and the individual, the philosophes cast the poor in the role of unchecked and unmanageable passion; the "lower orders" were, in this analysis, incapable of steady conduct, deliberate choice, rational decision. Far from being simply incapable of receiving the philosophes' message, the poor and the ignorant were thought likely to misread and misuse it. This pessimistic view was at the heart of Voltaire's injunction to keep the truth, especially the truth of religion, from the *canaille:* once a mere artisan learned that there is no eternal vengeance in heaven, he was likely to feel no compunction in launching into a career of crime. "We have never pretended to enlighten shoemakers and servants," Voltaire wrote, rather flippantly, to d'Alembert. "That is the job of the apostles." It is no accident that it should have been the philosophes who impressively advanced the study of political manipulation: from Montesquieu to Hume, from Voltaire to Gibbon, the men of the Enlightenment took a vigorous interest in the arcana of government and in the popular uses of religious threats and religious promises. They studied, with interesting results, the way that the ancient Romans withheld or distorted information for the sake of rule.

The stories exemplifying this disdain are familiar, though many of them are the malicious inventions of later critics. Yet, as Voltaire's comment to d'Alembert makes plain, not all of these stories were fictions. "The populace who have only their arms by which to live," were, in Voltaire's considered judgment, unfit to think, and hence unworthy of receiving any but the most rudimentary communications from those who were ostensibly, and actually, devoting themselves to making society a more reasonable, more humane place—for everyone, including the poor. Yet at the same time the liberalism of the Enlightenment contained within it elements that allowed it to expand its aims and widen its political base. The central ideal of the Enlightenment, after all, was improvement through education, and, as the century progressed, the philosophes increasingly recognized the possibility that the circle of effective communication could profitably be enlarged. They all wrote clearly in any event; they came to write yet more clearly for the sake of reaching the new audience that was lurking in the wings of politics. Voltaire, the greatest master of communication the eighteenth century possessed, in his later years deliberately repeated his arguments, gave his abstract reasoning a popular touch with well-chosen anecdotes, and kept up the interest of his readers with his biting wit. Others followed his lead.

The younger generation of philosophes, in particular the group centered around the materialist Holbach, were perfectly ready to address anyone who could conceivably listen. Holbach and his friends were certain that there is never any justification for lying to the masses—inventing, say, a God who sees all and avenges all. And in the 1760s even the most celebrated practitioner of disdain, Voltaire himself, came to discriminate in his judgments of the populace and to moderate his aristocratic liberalism. In May 1767, after he had enjoyed close intercourse with all manner of Genevans—with local patricians, merchants, and artisans—he wrote a significant reply to Linguet, who had told him that once the *peuple* learns that it, too, is intelligent, the social order is lost. Voltaire answered:

> In what you call *people,* let us distinguish the professions that demand a respectable education from those that only demand manual labor and daily toil. The latter class is the more numerous. All it will ever want to do for relaxation and pleasure will be to go to High Mass or to the tavern—there is singing there, and it too can sing. But the more skilled artisans who are forced by their very profession to think a great deal, to perfect their taste, to extend their knowledge, are beginning to read all over Europe. . . . The Parisians would be astonished if they saw in several Swiss towns, and above all in Geneva, almost all those who are employed in manufacture spending in reading all the time that they cannot devote to work. No, monsieur, all is not lost when one puts the people in a state to see that it has intelligence. On the contrary, all is lost when one treats it like a herd of cattle, for sooner or later it will gore you with its horns.[30]

The causes that prompted Voltaire's extraordinary shift to the left are too complex to be explored fully here; they included his willingness to learn from experience, and his experience with Genevans, especially of the disfranchised, articulate, responsible artisans, was very instructive indeed. It helped him to recognize that he, and with him the other philosophes, might safely cast their net more widely than they had thought possible in the early years of their campaigns, and to make allies with groups in the populace who had, in the 1740s and even the 1750s, seemed beyond the pale of rational and candid communication.

In this fluid situation, in which neither collaboration nor enmity appeared irrevocable, philosophes and the forces in power made frequent alliances. Montesquieu defended the French *parlements* against the king; Voltaire later defended the king against the *parlements.* This forced Montesquieu into a common front with the Jansenists, who deplored his deism, and Voltaire into a common front with chancellor Maupeou, who hated all philosophes. On the other side, Malesherbes, in charge of censorship from 1750 to 1763, often acted like an agent of the little flock rather than like a repressive government official; and the Parisian attorney and diarist Barbier, who was no philosophe, was still anticlerical enough to seek out prohibited secular propaganda and applaud Voltaire's efforts in behalf of Louis XV's program to tax the clergy. Barbier, as his intelligent diary shows, was more articulate than many of his fellow attorneys, but he was typical of educated men all over Western Europe, alert and critical beneficiaries of their social order, ready to be titillated and half converted by radical propaganda. There were many men like Barbier, nominal Christians who quoted the *Dictionnaire philosophique,* cried over the *Nouvelle Héloïse,* objected to the imprisonment of Diderot, welcomed Lessing's Masonic writings, applauded the banishment of the Jesuits, practiced the new empiricism, embraced the new critical spirit, and in general found something attractive in the philosophes' paganism and something exciting in the philosophes' hopes. Thus, the philosophes were simultaneously at peace and at war with their civilization, and much of their revolutionary ideology was pushed forward by men who were hostile to its spokesmen and blind to its implications.

The philosophes, then, lived in a world at once exhilarating and bewildering, and they moved in it with a mixture of confidence and apprehensiveness, of shrewd understanding and ideological myopia. They never wholly discarded that final, most stubborn illusion that bedevils realists—the illusion that they were free from illusions. This distorted their perception and gave many of their judgments a certain shallowness. But it also lent them the aggressor's *élan* at a time when the defense was paralyzed by self-doubt, inner divisions, and costly concessions: as usual, the price the defense paid for misreading its situation was far greater than the price paid by its radical adversaries. Kant had admitted that his was not an enlightened age, but he could claim, after all, and with justice, that his was an age of Enlightenment. History was on the philosophes' side: it was a good thing to know.

NOTES

1. "Beantwortung der Frage: Was Ist Aufklärung?" *Werke,* vol. 4, p. 169.
2. Aphorism L 88. *Aphorismen, 1793–1799,* ed. Albert Leitzmann (1908), p. 26.
3. Since I have already used, and shall continue to use, the word "philo-

sophe'' as a synonym for the men of the Enlightenment all over the Western world, I have naturalized it and dropped the awkward italics.

4. 27 January 1766. *Correspondance*, vol. 6, p. 34.

5. 21 March 1757. Quoted in Diderot, *Correspondance*, vol. 1, p. 239.

6. Quoted in F. C. Green, *Jean-Jacques Rousseau: A Study of His Life and Writings* (1955), p. 115.

7. 19 November 1765. *Letters*, ed. Mrs. Paget Toynbee, 16 vols. (1904–1905), vol. 6, p. 352.

8. 18 July 1762. *Correspondance*, vol. 4, p. 55. Another, rather less tragic case involved Beccaria. After he had acquired a European reputation in the mid-1760s with his treatise *Dei Delitti e Delle Pene*, his good friends the Verri brothers, who had encouraged Beccaria (often indolent and depressed) to write it, began to gossip about him from sheer envy. But later there was a reconciliation.

9. Hume to Hugh Blair (? December 1763). *Letters*, vol. 1, p. 419.

10. It is worth emphasizing that the philosophes did not lay claim to all possible varieties of paganism. Before the eighteenth century was over, the philosophes were under severe pressure from a Germanic ideology, a strange mixture of Roman Catholic, primitive Greek, and folkish Germanic notions—a kind of Teutonic paganism. Its inspiration was the *Nibelungenlied*, not Vergil's *Aeneid;* German folk songs, not Horace's *Odes*. Sometimes the benevolent critic, more often the implacable adversary of the Enlightenment, this Teutonic paganism (quite as much as traditional Christian doctrine) was to become a formidable rival to the Mediterranean paganism of the philosophes.

11. Beccaria to Morellet (26 January 1766). *Illuministi Italiani*, ed. Franco Venturi (1958), vol. 3, p. 203. In return, the young Montesquieu had greatly admired, and hoped to emulate, the Neapolitan historian Pietro Giannone.

12. 6 March 1706. *Life, Unpublished Letters, and Philophical Regimen*, ed. Benjamin Rand (1900), p. 353.

13. In Diderot, *Oeuvres*, vol. 3, p. 416.

14. "To the *Gazette littéraire*" (14 November 1764). *Oeuvres*, vol. 25, pp. 219–220.

15. Ernest C. Mossner, *The Life of David Hume* (1954), p. 487.

16. 22 February 1768. *Correspondance*, vol. 8, p. 16.

17. *Gespräche unter vier Augen*, in *Werke*, vol. 42, pp. 127–128.

18. *Decline and Fall of the Roman Empire*, vol. 4, p. 163.

19. *My Own Life*, in *Works*, vol. 3, p. 4.

20. Walpole to Horace Mann (7 July 1779). *Letters*, vol. 10, p. 441.

21. "Beantwortung der Frage: Was Ist Aufklärung?" *Werke*, vol. 4, p. 174.

22. Aphorism L 469. *Aphorismen, 1793-1799*, p. 90.

23. 17 March 1769. *Correspondance*, vol. 9, p. 40.

24. Hume to Hugh Blair and others (6 April 1765). *Letters,* vol. 1, p. 498.

25. *Life of Johnson* (under 1759), vol. 1, p. 342.

26. John Rae, *The Life of Adam Smith* (1895), p. 429.

27. James Boswell, *Journal of a Tour to the Hebrides with Samuel Johnson, 1773,* ed. Frederick A. Pottle and Charles H. Bennett (1961), p. 189.

28. Diderot to d'Alembert (about 10 May 1765). *Correspondance,* vol. 5, p. 32.

29. Hume to Horace Walpole (20 November 1766). *Letters,* vol. 2, p. 110.

30. I have explored this issue in considerable detail in *Voltaire's Politics: The Poet as Realist* (1959), chap. 4. For the quotations I have used here, see esp. pp. 222–223.

4

THE MODERN HISTORY
OF POLITICAL FANATICISM:
A SEARCH FOR THE ROOTS

ZEV BARBU

Since both *modern history* and *political fanaticism* are expressions with a highly elastic connotation, it would be profitable, even at the risk of appearing pedantic, to introduce the subject matter of the present chapter by discussing some problems of definition and classification. This is all the more necessary as some events under consideration have been and are taking place under our eyes.

Fanatic is a term that is being applied equally to individual and group behavior. Our concern here is mainly with the latter use of the term. In this sense it connotes a type of political action and an organization (a party, a movement, or goal-oriented group) rooted in or motivated by strong feelings and rigid convictions. This type of group may exhibit one or more of the following three features. First, the participants may share in common a general conception, a project of society, or a certain political program that they experience and represent not only as the sole and ultimate purpose of their political activities but also as a supreme value for their community as a whole. This admittedly is best illustrated by revolutionary groups or social movements dedicated to the idea of a new society or a social order in the making. But it may equally apply to political organizations and movements dedicated to an existing and past social order; fanatic conservatism nowadays is not as rare a phenomenon as it may appear at first sight. Second, the participants may experience feelings of admiration and devotion to their leader or their organization as such, feelings that they express by unconditional obedience and total involvement. This applies to a great variety of political behavior motivated by beliefs in the charisma of an individual leader, a ruling group, a movement, or a party. Third, the participants may experience strong feelings and compulsive needs for (political) action and demonstration *tout court* within a loose and spasmodic form of organization, and with a vague, if any, long-range purpose. The mystique of action is a subtle but nonetheless distinctive form of political fanaticism.

Brief as it is, the above characterization provides some basic insights into the meaning of the phenomenon under consideration. One is dealing with an overmotivated form of action and organization analogous to a religious type of action and organization in that a series of terms such as intemperate zeal or enthusiasm, credulity, bigotry, intolerance, can be applied to both. Moreover the analogy is not only a formal one; a whole range of phenomena dealt with in the following pages seems to be both political and religious in character. In political form, these organizations display such features as belief in the supernatural origin and prophetic gifts of their leader and the sacred nature of their mission, as well as strong needs for perfection, purity, and salvation motivating their participants. One hastens to add, however, that fanatic political action can be purely secular and even antireligious in intention. As the relationship between political and religious phenomena is a complex and subtle one, it suffices for the moment to emphasize the general idea that in certain specific social and psychological circumstances political fanaticism is closely associated with dissacralizing attitudes and intentions, which is the very opposite of religious fanaticism.

Another notion frequently occurring in this context is that of irrationality. As applied to political behavior and action, this has a variety of meanings. At this early stage it should be enough to refer briefly to Weber's distinction between a rational and a nonrational type of action, on the obvious assumption that political fanaticism belongs to the latter. As is well known, Weber is strongly inclined to an instrumentalist definition of rationality, that is, rationality as fitness between ends and means. This is obviously an ideal type of definition, meaning that a concrete instance of action, individual or collective, is rational when it fulfills in various degrees the following main conditions: (1) It is carried out at the conscious level; more precisely the actor or the actors involved are conscious of the goals of their action as well as the means by which to achieve it. (2) It is a deliberative type of action, meaning that the actors are free, both to choose from the available means those that are more suitable to the achievement of their goal, and able to adjust their goals, at least temporarily, to the means available. In addition—and this is admittedly a somewhat free interpretation of Weber's definition—one can say that this is what has more recently been described as action at the reality level, or simply a realistic type of action in the specific sense that the actors are able to take into account, to assess, combine, and even to compromise over, a great variety (Weber would be inclined to say the totality) of conditions affecting their situation. Now, as political fanaticism lies at the very opposite of this, it is tempting to compare it with other major types of social action defined by Weber—notably with affective action or with a subdivision of rational action, namely, value-oriented action. The exercise, however, may be less rewarding than it would appear at first sight, for the main reason that the notion of political fanaticism includes a series of phenomena cutting across Weber's categories of social action. Nonetheless, before leaving Weber it would be useful to make a general remark regarding the opposition between a rational and a fanatic type of action, namely, the former can be described as a goal-oriented, whereas the latter is a goal-glued, type of action. As to the nature of the goal pursued by the two types of action, one can hardly say anything definite at this stage. The dichotomy of rationality versus nonrationality has only a limited classificatory value. One can easily find instances not only of fanatic action perpetrated on behalf of reason but also of political groups and organizations fighting fanatically for what they describe as, and appears to be, the very embodiment of reason in human society. Weber is only dimly aware of the irrational ingredients of rational organization and of bureaucracy in particular. In this respect we seem to know better. It is not only that pure science, the epitome of rational knowledge, has its fans, but that the scientific organization and control of human action, including political action, have become a dominant creed in our contemporary civilization. A distinction between rationality and rationalization would be perhaps useful in this context. But more about this later.

One last point about the concept of political fanaticism: namely, its relationship with the concept of (political) democracy and especially political liberalism. This is all the more relevant as the connotation of the two concepts is normally established in dichotomic terms. In contrast to the former, the latter refers to a type of action and organization that can be described as flexible and deliberative, and tolerant of ambiguity of purpose and diversity of points of view. But, needless to say, neat as it is, a theoretical distinction such as this has in our case only a limited operational value. It should be enough to mention the word *Montagnard* in order to realize that some phenomena falling within the scope of the present inquiry may display in various proportions and at various levels both democratic and fanatic features. Later on it may be necessary to accommodate, modify, or refine our conceptualizations. In the meantime, we can proceed to the discussion of the most important aspects and stages in the recent history of political fanaticism. For reasons which we hope will become gradually apparent, we shall focus the present inquiry mainly on the formative stage of the phenomenon. In doing so, however, our purpose will be a twofold one, first, to trace the common roots, and second, to point out the mainstreams in the more recent development of political fanaticism, such as, fanaticism of the left, fanaticism of the right, and the fanaticism of actions characterizing contemporary student movements.

THE HISTORICAL CONTEXT OF POLITICAL FANATICISM

In a certain essential sense, modernization means secularization, that is, transition from a social order based on tradition and consecrated by religious beliefs to a social order based on, or adjustable to rules and principles derived from, human experience and reason. As far as the political aspect of social life is concerned, this implies separation of politics from religion, or to use more fashionable terms, dissacralization of authority and power in society. A bold expression of this broad and diffuse process can be found in Machiavelli's thought, another one in the political ideas of the Enlightenment and of the philosophes in particular. According to the former, politics, like science, has and should have nothing to do with religion: power and authority, that is, in the capacity and the right to rule, are secular virtues, skills resting on a more or less flexible constellation of psychological traits, such as cunning, intelligence, ambition, generosity, determination, and toughness, to mention only the most obvious ones. Although full of inconsistencies in their political thought, the philosophes were in fundamental agreement on the main idea that "the prince derives from his subjects the authority he holds over them, and this authority is limited by the laws of nature and of state";[1] in other words, that the only legitimate authority was the authority of the law, which needless to say was an expression of human reason. Admittedly Machiavelli's prince could easily give way to his emotions and feelings, be they appetite for power or love of glory. But however far he might go in this direction, he could not be a fanatic. He could be a crafty cynic, even an impulsive, cruel "lion," but not a fanatic. Fanaticism would have been a disqualifying attitude for a kind of role in which success depended so much on cool reasoning and subtle calculation. This qualification applies even more to the political man conceived by the philosophes, who could be even a despot provided that he was an enlightened one, that is, open-minded or, in the language of the period, guided and limited in his decisions and actions by the universal rules of human reason or by a set of principles shared and consented to by the majority of his subjects. That this excludes fanaticism hardly needs explaining. And yet political fanaticism is essentially a modern phenomenon.

This situation is not only because fanaticism appeared more frequently and at an increasing rate during the modern period of our history, but also because it was closely related, embedded, one would say, in a secular humanistic civilization of the type developed in Europe since the Renaissance. Although this may appear to be a paradox, the main reasons for it are relatively easy to grasp. There was first the separation of politics from religion, the differentiation of political roles in society, and above all the gradual autonomy of political values. One could say that Machiavelli gave an early expression to the process by formulating the ideal type of political man with his own hierarchy of values, *raison d'etat* at the top, the implication being that the political action has or should have a structure of its own requiring specific skills and interests as well as goals and values of its own that under certain circumstances may create in their possessors a state of mind of total involvement and personal identification. But this alone cannot explain such a complex phenomenon as political fanaticism. For this purpose one has to take into account two other main outcomes or concomitants of the process of secularization, humanism and rationalism.

Unlike the ancient Greek and Chinese humanism and rationalism, modern humanism and rationalism were structurally bound with what may be called a radically anthropocentric vision of the world. Whereas the classical Greek and Confucian humanism and rationalism had obvious ethical roots (the personal and communal spheres of human existence were never rigidly divided), modern humanism and rationalism had such a decisive individualistic and subjective orientation that community, ethical or political, was almost entirely constructed out of the individual's mind as a categorical imperative, as a quantitative majority or a qualitative entity, that is, the people or the nation. Furthermore, Greek humanism and rationalism were intrinsically bound with an epic vision of human life in that man perceived himself not only at the center, but also, and primarily, as a part of the world, of "the great design," of the great "rhythm of life" that included nature and the gods. On the other hand, modern humanism and rationalism were essentially dramatic in character, that is, rooted in and contributive to a world view according to which man's awareness of himself, and indeed his self-realization, was so closely related to his differentiation and separation from the world that the process led inevitably to a stage at which he felt trapped into his unique destiny as *unum contra mundum*. Although the social and cultural expression of this tense relationship between man and the world is unusually rich, it can be seen as gravitating around two dialectically related themes underlying the development of Western civilization, namely, the Faust theme (confidence, dominance, and acquisition) and the alienation theme (anxiety and withdrawal).

For our present interest, namely, the formative context of political fanaticism, the following more specific points are relevant. There is, first of all, the historical fact that in Western Europe the development of a humanistic and rationalist culture was almost equivalent with secularization. This is not the place to discuss the many and varied circumstances contributing to this development. It is enough to stress the idea that in no other civilization known so far has the death of God constituted such a necessary condition for the assertion of human values and of human reason in particular. Although there is much to be said about the significance of the Promethean motif in ancient Greek civilization, it would be relatively easy to demonstrate that in this particular case a prolonged conflict between man and the gods resulted in a progressive humanization and rationalization of the latter. In modern Europe, the conflict soon developed into a total war, or, to use a more appropriate analogy, a liberation war in which man had to prove himself not only strong enough to drive God out of the world but also to rule in his absence. The extent to which he was successful is a moot point. What really matters is that the enterprise itself—and here the analogy with a war of liberation is particularly suggestive —contained the seed of new forms of fanaticism, political fanaticism included.

As this complex and often paradoxical psychohistorical phenomenon constitutes the chief concern of the present study, its meaning has to be revealed gradually. To grasp its rationale, however, it is necessary to outline a prototype situation in which it occurred. That secularization in Europe required and stimulated a rapid increase in man's awareness of and confidence in himself as a natural being is a self-evident truth. Withdrawal of God meant the advance of man, and every particular act of dissacralization was allowed and indeed performed by an act of humanization. Thus human reason began to chase the divine agencies from the realm of nature; the authority of the law, of man-made rules, and the prestige of talent and personal achievement were gradually replacing divine authority and sacred tradition in the sphere of political and social life. Even in the sphere of religious life, rational living, and personal effort and worth were contending for priority in matters of salvation, and human initiative began to challenge divine guidance in earnest. But the point is that one should make a distinction between actions, motives, and intentions on one side, and goals, ideals, and values on the other. No revolution, however violent it may be, has the slightest chance of succeeding unless and until it generates its own morality, that is, its own values and norms, which are as a rule more rigid and severe than those it destroyed. This was precisely what had happened in the case of secularization, the only revolution that fully deserves to be called a Copernican revolution.

As man's ambitions had to be justified and his growing self-reliance bolstered up, new values and beliefs emerged that for a certain period were even more fascinating and sacrosanct than the traditional religious values and beliefs had ever been. To give an example, "nature," a vague notion defined in opposition to everything that was however remotely related to the so-called supernatural order, including the traditional order of society, became the source of all values, the basic frame of reference for human life. To put it bluntly, what was natural was good, true, and beautiful; what was unnatural was bad, false, and ugly. This should suffice to grasp the emotional potential and hence the irresistible appeal of such a notion, but there was much more to it. Nature was a vague, mainly negative concept and for this reason likely to be employed as a sheer value concept. Indeed, this was the case with the main representatives of the Enlightenment. More precisely, starting in their social, philosophical, and scientific thought from the feeling—a sort of primary intuition—that the order of existing society was neither natural nor rational, they built up an idea of nature that included approximately everything that in their opinion was missing but desirable in their society, culture, and perhaps personal lives. Thus nature was rational and orderly, yet the epitome of spontaneity and freedom; it was savage and at the same time noble, mysteriously complex and yet shining through its simplicity. The point is admirably made by P. Hazard when he writes:

> Nature was too rich in its composition, too complex in its attributes, too potent in its effects to be imprisoned in a formula and the formula gave way under the strain. Despite all their efforts to elucidate it by analysis, to get possession of it through science, to reduce it to some easily intelligible concept, those same wise and learned men

who should have been basking in the warmth of certitude, still went
on giving the world all manner of different and sometimes directly
contradictory interpretations. Conscious of all this, they began to
behold in Nature the reappearance of that Mystery which they were
bent on banishing from the world.[2]

Mystery is certainly the right word, for soon after, that is, during
the French Revolution, nature acquired sacred and even cultic
connotations. Thus, owing to its inner dynamics, the process of
secularization had reached a stage at which feelings, beliefs, and
myths were more important than reasoning for its maintenance.
This is yet another way of saying that ''man as a rational being''
was to a certain extent a projection of belief.

Now, we do not want to dwell on the obvious. The
eighteenth-century secular rationalists were unique in that they
combined in their intellectual activities the role of abstract
thinkers with that of social analysts and social reformers. They
were, or at least they wanted to be, both interpreters and
makers of their society and of human history. That man was
born free and that society was the result of conscious rational arrangements between free individuals were for them not simply
theoretical, but also political statements. Even highly abstract
concepts, such as reason, rationality, materialism, theism, and
atheism, let alone human perfectability, were in essence program ideas, the assumption being that ignorance, prejudice,
reliance on established authority and divine intervention, constituted the main obstacles against social progress. As to the
question whether the philosophes were fanatics, the answer cannot be either a simple or a single one. They certainly believed in
human freedom and human reason as fanatically as their opponents believed in the absolute authority of the king or in divine
providence. But in saying this it is necessary to distinguish between fanaticism of ideas and fanaticism of action. Granted, the
philosophes were highly committed intellectuals. Furthermore,
they were conscious in a high degree of the unity of their group
and so cohesive and conspiratorial in their activities that they
were often compared to a religious sect. But even when they
invested their ideas with moral and social imperatives, they believed that such imperatives were essentially rational and rationality was a natural condition of man. Intolerance and oppres-

sion were so closely associated in their minds with the society in which they lived that it would be hard to imagine Diderot or Rousseau terrorizing people to make them free or to accelerate the work of reason in society. And yet the cultural climate in which they lived and which they helped create produced the first example, an almost ideal type, of modern political fanaticism. What the philosophes allowed themselves to do only in dream, Robespierre and Saint-Just did in reality.

THE PATHOS OF FREEDOM AND REASON: THE TWIN SOURCES OF MODERN POLITICAL FANATICISM

The Regime of Terror is commonly considered a highly if not the most significant and, at the same time, incongruous episode in the French Revolution. The more one knows about it the more one becomes aware not only of its complex nature but also and above all of the infinite variety of accidental, emotional, and irrational factors entering into its compositon. If an expression such as "total fact" or "total event" has any warranty, this is the place to use it. What follows is a brief examination of the most salient features of this event in terms of political fanaticism.

The first and most general point refers to the obvious connection between revolutionary zeal and political fanaticism. The Montagnards were a product of the Revolution, that is, a more or less voluntary association of people or self-recruiting group organized and functioning (a) in opposition to an anti-social background, and (b) in conflict with other revolutionary organizations and groups. One could say therefore that an initial commitment to the aims of the Revolution and a growing involvement in the revolutionary process constituted their raison d'être. But although a constellation of circumstances such as this may throw considerable light on the nature of political fanaticism, it does not explain the Montagnard phenomenon. After all, the same or similar circumstances gave birth to many other revolutionary groups and factions. The revolutionary zeal of the Girondins, not to mention the *enragés* or the *sans culottes,* a loosely organized but clearly oriented group, was not less real than that of the Montagnards. To grasp the specific nature of the Montagnard phenomenon it is therefore necessary to make a distinction between revolutionary zeal and political fanaticism. By comparison with the former, the latter type of behavior and action requires a more enduring motivational structure, a more articulate and better-integrated belief and cognitive system, and, needless to say, a high degree of compatibility between motivational structure and belief system. Now, the suggestion is that the Montagnards, at least their leaders, Robespierre and Saint-Just, came very near to fulfilling this requirement. Lest someone is inclined to believe that the *enragés* came even nearer, it would be useful to specify that despite, or because of, their left-wing radicalism their belief and cognitive framework was neither coherent enough nor compatible or integrated enough with their motivational system. They were predominantly angry people and because of this inclined to be spasmodic and fragmentary in their revolutionary project and political action in general. This applied even more to the *sans culottes*. Granted they were strongly motivated people, but in the context of the Revolution their motives were both diffuse and relatively nonspecific. Their economic aspirations were too vague and subjective to provide them with a coherent project of political action. If the term *fanatic* could be mentioned in this context—and a case could be made for the *enragés*—this means fanaticism of action. However, more about this later.

Although the Montagnards shared many features with other revolutionary groups, they distinguished themselves through their consistency and single-mindedness. This was not only because they were strongly motivated people in terms of revolutionary action, but rather and above all because they identified themselves as individuals and as a group with an ideational structure—the word *ideology* was coined a few decades later —which was not only consistent with their motives but appeared at least for a certain period to give a coherent expression to the revolutionary situation as a whole. This was the ideational structure of the Enlightenment. As a result of this, the Montagnard leaders and notably Robespierre and Saint-Just were able not only to legitimize their position in terms of a relatively coherent system of beliefs and ideas but also to rationalize their personal inclinations to a degree verging on the absurd. Space allows for but a brief and selective illustration of this curious process, which could truly be called the fanaticism of reason.

Robespierre and Saint-Just had been pushed into political prominence in the winter of 1792 by a double set of circumstances, reverses of war and intensified internal conflicts. This was, therefore, a typical situation that objectively speaking demanded urgent and strong measures and above all unity of command. In this respect most revolutionary activists would have reacted in a similar manner. But the Montagnards did something more. Not only did they establish order and authority, but in a relatively short time they managed to create such a degree of cohesion in the revolutionary situation and, to a certain extent, in the country at large that every individual event, every concrete political item, every member of society, could be and exclusively was seen and assessed in terms of a relatively simple structure of meanings or constellation of symbols, such as, for example, fatherland, the Revolution, reason, liberty. As to the ideological proclivity of the Montagnards, it is important to emphasize that it was not sheer exegetic exercise but a many-sided process growing less and less articulate from a firm base of symbolic interpretation of reality through political action into an institutional framework. But as the latter stage, the much talked about Institution was far away in the future, if ever to come; all that was achieved was an excessively fluid and malleable situation, that is, a present dominated by the future, social reality dominated by a dream.

The first revealing situation for the political behavior of the Montagnards was supplied by the circumstances surrounding the fate of the monarchy and the final trial of the king in 1792. To be sure Robespierre and Saint-Just always had held radical views regarding the nature of revolutionary authority, which they believed should rest entirely with the people. "I have always held," wrote Robespierre, "that equality of rights belongs to all the members of the State."[3] It is, therefore, reasonable to assume that their unequivocal rejection of the monarchy and their uncompromising attitude during the trial of the king was consistent with their inclination to identify the Revolution with the people and in doing so to identify themselves with the people. But however strong their inclination might have been, it could not sufficiently account for their language and particularly their reasoning in the circumstances, which was highly revealing for their subsequent political development. One point stands out in this respect, namely, most of what they say and think sounds glaringly evident, a sort of impeccable conclusion drawn from obvious premises. For instance, when, following the insurrection of August 1792 the Convention considered it necessary to decide once and for all the fate of the king, Robespierre presented the case by making the following staggering points: he reminded the delegates that the king was not on trial, that the insurrection of August 1792 had already decided his fate, and consequently, the candidates were not his judges. While both Robespierre and Saint-Just stated the case categorically, that is, Louis was king and France was a republic, the latter added the significant point that the king was no longer a citizen but an enemy and that the duty to punish him was implicit in the right to dethrone him. In other words, deliberation and judgment, the very meaning of the trial, were replaced by evident rights and duties.

This was only the beginning, the foundation stone of one of the most grandiose masterpieces of Gothic imagination in modern politics. In the months to come, Saint-Just continued to argue that the king was condemned, not for any particular crime he or his ministers had committed in the past, but simply because he was a king and monarchy, moreover the ancien régime in itself, was a crime. This marked the first major stage in the development of Montagnard fanaticism, that is, their total rejection of the past, of anybody and anything representing it, including libraries, streets, and place-names. The process reached a peak toward the end of 1792 with the de-Christianization movement and the new calendar according to which September 22 (the proclamation of the Republic) was the beginning of a new era.

A difference between Robespierre and Saint-Just may be suggested here. While the former tended to take, at least as far as de-Christianization was concerned, a more tactical view, in other words, to preserve for the time being and for political reasons certain aspects of religion, the latter condemned the past in toto, not only because the past was evil but also and mainly because it was the source of injustice and corruption in the present. Here Saint-Just forcefully expressed a characteristic common to all sectarians, namely, the perception of the present as unbearable and the consequent identification with the future. "Believe me everything that exists around us must change and come to an end, because everything around us is unjust.'' Then Saint-Just symptomatically continues, ''Obliged to *isolate himself from the world and from himself,* man drops his anchor in the future and presses to his heart the posterity which bears no blame for the evils of the present.''[4]

But as a visionary is not necessarily a fanatic, the question arises of how to explain that Saint-Just and Robespierre can be described as such? The shortest and the most common type of answer to this question is a situational one. That is, the Montagnards were driven by the very logic of a deteriorating political situation into a dictatorial position that was a combination of authoritarian emotionalism (politics of despair) and authoritarian strategy of the kind used, a century and a half later, by Stalin with his recurrent reference to the threat presented by the class enemy, inside and abroad. But although there is a great deal to be said about this type of approach, it has one important limitation. As just suggested, it accounts mainly for the authoritarian features of the Montagnards. More precisely, it explains political terrorism rather than political fanaticism, and in doing so it makes little of the fact that some of the most successful terrorist regimes were the work of political cynics rather than of political fanatics.

Another type of answer given to the question of the Montagnard fanaticism is a psychological one. As is well known, a great deal has been said about Robespierre's quasi-pietistic background, his narrow prudential morality, and, above all, his obsessional paranoid personality. Similarly, frequent references have been made to Saint-Just's adolescent moral rigor, his identification with an ideal ego structure, and his exalted quasi-manic personal traits. However, while admitting the usefulness of such an approach, it is necessary to note that much more research is needed before something definite can be said about personality structure and above all about forms of abnormality and madness in eighteenth-century France.[5] In addition, for reasons that will become apparent at a later stage, the thesis put forward in the present chapter is that political fanaticism is essentially a cultural phenomenon. To demonstrate this it is necessary to go back to a point made earlier regarding the relationship between the Montagnards and the Enlightenment.

One thing should be made clear from the very outset. It concerns the intellectual status of the Montagnards and of their leaders in particular. That most revolutionary clubs were intellectually active and that the ideological awareness of their members, including those of humble origin, was astonishingly high is an undeniable fact.[6] But not less undeniable is another fact, namely, that Robespierre and Saint-Just were and wanted to be political activists and their concern with the political writings of the philosophes and of Rousseau in particular was basically determined by this. In saying this the intention is, to be sure, not to minimize the ultimate impact of the Enlightenment on the political thought of the Montagnards but rather to establish a point of analytical priority, that is, a vantage point from which one can see the main outline of their political vision.

To start with, it was in their capacity as political activists that Robespierre and Saint-Just fully grasped the relevance of Marat's intuitive formula, "it takes an absolute regime to overthrow another absolute regime," which became in fact a cornerstone of their political praxis. We are introducing rather abruptly the term *praxis* to delineate as quickly as possible an area of phenomena that occupies an intermediary position between political thought and political action, and that has a particular analytical value in the present context. To remain within the same example, any close examination of the principle involved in Marat's formula shows that it cannot be meaningfully related to or derived from the political thought of the Enlightenment, no matter how radically and at times emotionally toned this might have been. A formula such as "il faut tout examiner, tout remuer, sans exception et sans menagement . . ." should not obscure the basic assumptions and tenets of this thought, such as reliance on human reason, and man's natural inclination and ability to assert his moral, political, and even inner freedom as an individual. At the beginning of his political career, Robespierre himself defended the freedom of the press, and opposed the death penalty as well as censorship in the theater. Nor could Marat's formula be compatible with the basic requirements of political action, on account of its irrationally destructive implications. (The "total war" phase of Hitler's regime ceased to be a political action despite the fact that it is sometimes referred to as the "scorched earth policy.") But the same formula made perfect sense as a link, a mediator between political theory, or simply ideology, and political action. It made sense to the extent that it referred to and combined an action-patterning type of theory and a value-patterning type of action, to use an ad hoc definition of the term *praxis*. A century and a half later, but in a similar context, the communists used the expression "living dialectics," that is, an interpretive or rather heuristic device by which Marxist political doctrine was considered as little more than a code, a system of signs and meanings that could and should be adjusted and derived from the concrete circumstances and requirements of political action, and, conversely, the meaning of political action should be derived from the Marxist doctrine so interpreted. This is, of course, praxis in an advanced form, and the reason for mentioning it here is to bring into focus the general principle underlying the function fulfilled by the Montagnard leaders within the context of the French Revolution. One has to bear in mind, however, that we are dealing here with an incipient if not rudimentary form of an historical process. More precisely, at a later stage, the so-called praxis had become a more consciously organized process. Following Lenin's example, communists all over the world claim that the relationship between (political) ideology and action is a matter of scientific knowledge and technical expertise. This may be an exaggeration; on the other hand it is difficult to deny the emergence of specific institutions and organizations as well as differentiated roles—whether they be called party men, ideologues, or technocrats—fulfilling this function.

There is nothing farther from the truth than to describe Robespierre and Saint-Just as political technocrats, and yet their role position was basically the same. As political activists working in a revolutionary situation their most significant task was to code political action in terms of ideology and decode ideology in terms of political action. It is only that their role style was remarkably different from that of the so-called political technocrats. Briefly, Robespierre and Saint-Just can be truly called the "primitives" of political praxis, in that not only did they play their roles mainly by ear, but there was no specific institution in their environment, no systematic theory of revolutionary action, not even an established structure of experience to supply a stable frame of reference for their political insights and action.

To grasp this one should bear in mind that the question is of the real beginning of political modernization, or more precisely the first modern revolution in Europe. In addition, the Montagnards were a deliberating society rather than a political, let alone revolutionary, party, and so were all other revolutionary and counterrevolutionary groups and factions. "Debating" is in fact a suggestive unifying verbal symbol for a political situation dominated by an assembly type of decision making and very often of political action too. The revolutionary leaders and notably the Montagnards were prototypical in this respect, and often found themselves in a situation analogous to that of ancient Greek demagogues relying mainly on their rhetoric and even more so on their personal enthusiasm and power of persuasion as a means by which to sustain a course of action and legitimize their position. Paradoxically enough, while the spirit of the age was becoming increasingly dominated by reason, political authority was becoming increasingly a matter of belief and make-believe. The paradox lies at the very core of Montagnard fanaticism.

The purer expression of Montagnard fanaticism was not the Regime of Terror as such, but the rationalization of terror, or simply terror conceived as the most adequate means for the achievement of a rational social order. This ought to be stressed because terror as a political means can be and often is an expression of cynicism. Moreover, terrorist regimes are normally self-maintaining and self-propelling systems in that terror produces more terror.[7] As this seems to be to a lesser degree true of the Montagnards and particularly the Thermidorian regime, it is necessary to discuss briefly the specific manner in which this regime rose and developed. This is all the more relevant as we may be able to throw light on some important problems of communication involved in this type of political fanaticism.

It should be remembered that the Montagnards came into the limelight of political life at a time (winter 1792) when the three-year-old Revolution was on the brink of total collapse. Add to this the chronic weakness of the revolutionary regime, that is, its instability and factionalism, and one can easily understand why Robespierre perceived the situation in terms of "now or never" and consequently projected himself and the Montagnards into the role of savior. Theoretically speaking one can distinguish between two main routes leading to the Regime of Terror, corresponding on the whole to two types of situations and two types of reactions characterizing the Montagnard leaders. Let us romanticize the issue—perhaps not altogether inappropriately—and call them the route of the heart and the route of the head. The first refers to situations of mass gatherings, crowds, and popular demonstrations as well as to the corresponding aspects of more formal gatherings, such as assemblies, clubs, committees, and many other forms of encounter eliciting an emotional, direct, and, in this case, symbolic type of communication. To be sure, eloquence and rhetoric were the order of the day. Nor was there a shortage of outstanding public figures and political leaders. Nonetheless the case easily could be made for the superiority of the Montagnard leaders, not so much on account of their rhetoric—although Saint-Just outshone most other revolutionary leaders in this respect—as on account of their deep awareness of the main features of the situation and their more systematic exploitation of it. In a period in which the main emphasis seemed to be put on spontaneity, affluence, and novelty of expressions—behavioral, linguistic, and symbolic—the Montagnard leaders excelled through their systematic and manipulatory grasp of the situation. First of all, they showed an astonishingly clear awareness of the basic principles characterizing human reaction to situations of stress, that is, the tendency to see the world in black and white, to perceive things and feel about most situations in dichotomic terms: good-bad, love-hate, safe-dangerous, friendly-inimical, all this superimposed on the dichotomy "us-them." The manner in which the Montagnard leaders reacted to this kind of situation supplies us with an almost classical example of communication in terms of emotional logic. To start with they were extremely alert and persistent in handling and reinforcing the feeling aroused by the imminent danger facing the Revolution. And needless to say they did this not in general rhetorical terms but by pointing out, identifying, and defining the enemies (individual or groups) of their supporters and of "the people." In this respect Robespierre presents a fascinating case that deserves a study of its own. To say that he had a suspicious mind or a paranoid disposition is to confuse the real issue, for what really matters in this respect is the specific manner in which he reacted to and manipulated circumstances presented to him. Even at an early stage of his career, at the outbreak of the war, he, unlike most other leaders, examined the situation lucidly and in detail to identify not only the obvious external but particularly the internal, as yet not visible enemy, that is, the counterrevolutionary danger involved in such an adventure.

No wonder that the first major setback in the conduct of the war (winter 1792) brought him into political prominence, for, to put it crudely, in his opinion, which later on was shared by many others, this was entirely the result of the fact that the power as well as the subtlety of the enemy had been underestimated. From this early stage to the end of his life, one of the principal tasks of Robespierre, closely seconded by Saint-Just, consisted of identifying and sometimes inventing the enemies of the Revolution. As mentioned earlier, this had been carried out under various and subtle forms starting from the person of the king and growing in larger and larger circles to include monarchy and the idea of monarchy, from the traditional ruling class to the ancien régime as a whole, from clergy and the church to religion and God, from the odious past to the corrupted present. Granted this may look like a *catalogue raisonne* of the enemies of the Revolution, but Robespierre went far beyond it into the dark, often inarticulate world of human feelings, private and collective, relentlessly unmasking and denouncing any hesitation and weakness, any form of deviation even in his closest associates, so as to make sure at every particular moment who were the enemies and who were the friends of the Revolution.

FROM PATHOS TO ETHOS

This basic polarization was reinforced at various levels and finally shaped into a veritable Manichaean vision of the world. First came the moral level, at which the Montagnard leaders projected themselves and their followers as models of virtue, and in so doing they worked out and imposed one of the most rigid codes of sectarian ethics ever known. As this is one of the best-known aspects of the Thermidorian regime, it should be enough to point out some of its most subtle and original features. The famous Weberian thesis regarding the origins of ethic may be relevant here, as the Montagnard leaders endea-

vored and succeeded in doing something more than just identify themselves with an idea of virtue and morality defined in
conventional terms, such as industry, dedication, conscientious-
ness, honesty, and incorruptibility, to use some of their favorite
terms. They redefined the idea, moreover, and created a new
morality in terms of prevailing feelings, beliefs, goals, and aspirations. One kind of evidence, perhaps the most direct one, can
be drawn from a series of semantic processes characteristic of the
time. Take, for instance, the growing association and final
amalgamation of the notion of virtuous man with the notion of
dutiful citizen, or citizen *tout court*. Granted, the intellectual
origins of the process can be traced back to the Enlightenment,
and notably to Rousseau's writings. On the other hand it would
be difficult to imagine how a series of abstract notions, such as
"Spartan," "patriot," or "citizen" could have acquired a concrete moral connotation had it not been for the climate of opinion created by the Montagnard regime, or for the living examples set up by Robespierre and Saint-Just. Briefly, what the
Montagnards did was to politicize morality in the sense that
they superimposed, and almost reduced it to, a normative system of behavior strictly derived from revolutionary praxis, or,
according to an earlier definition of the term *praxis,* from a dynamic contextual interpretation of the goals of the Revolution.
Thus, virtue or, simply, being moral came to connote the fulfillment of the demands placed on you by your community in
its effort to attain the goal of the Revolution.

To go back to Weber's thesis, the emergence of a new ethic
was intrinsically bound with the rise of a new prestige group, or
elite. As Robespierre and Saint-Just were almost ideal types in
this respect, it would be helpful to point out the most salient
features of their referential belief and value system, for this may
supply us with a first insight into the nature of the phenomenon. As mentioned earlier, Robespierre consistently identified
the Revolution with the people and in so doing identified himself with the people. One can say, therefore, that at least as the
formative stage is concerned the new elite group can usefully be
compared with what has lately been defined as populist elites,
that is, a more or less cohesive group of people who claim and
obtain prestige and authority on the basis of their dedication to
and identification with "the people" or the community at

large. To grasp the point one has to bear in mind the specific manner in which the vague notion of "the people" was worked out and its meaning reinforced by clustering with two other emotion-laden words "nation" and "fatherland," all this being closely associated with the key concepts of democracy, such as freedom, liberty, fraternity, equality, justice, and many others. This strong concentration of *idées forcées,* dream words, or *mots d'illusion,* as Brunot very aptly puts it, reveals a basic aspect of the new elite.[8] Briefly, they consisted of a group of people bound together through their love of the nation, a sentiment that in their own as well as in the opinion of many others justified their claim for superiority.

Although it may seem slightly contrived to mention the word *charisma* in a historical context such as this, one can hardly fail to notice that some essential features of the situation are highly suggestive in this sense. After all, the Montagnards came to power in a situation of crisis that affected not only the fate of the Revolution but also, and in a far more visible sense, the future and survival of the nation as a whole. This should be enough to understand why concepts such as fatherland, nation, and even liberty had acquired new meanings and an incantational resonance that only objects of veneration usually have. Brunot speaks in this context about the sacralization of such notions by their persistent association with biblical words, such as *évangile, credo, martyrologe, Bonne Nouvelle dea liberté.* However, as we are still concerned with a specific aspect in the political development of the Montagnards, the position can briefly be described as follows: in their struggle to attain the goal of the Revolution, that is, a rational democratic social order, a number of political activists underwent a process of radical change amounting to a conversion. Whether this can be accounted for in terms of their inner dispositions or external circumstances, or both, is for the moment a moot point. The important fact is that they reached a stage at which they perceived themselves and were perceived by some other members of society as exceptional people, singled out by *nature,* which bestowed upon them the great mission of saving their nation and fatherland. That this has a great deal to do with Montagnard fanaticism is self-evident. But the Montagnards present us with another problem that is considerably more characteristic of modern political fanaticism. To grasp this we have to turn our attention to the other route to the Regime of Terror followed by the Montagnard leaders, the route of the head.

The Montagnards were highly dedicated revolutionaries who pledged themselves to the task of creating a new society modeled on the ideas of the main representatives of the Enlightenment. Reason, individualized reason in a Cartesian sense, occupied a key position in their conception of man and society. Reason was the source of freedom, tolerance, and equality, the supreme guarantee of the new democratic society. How can one then account for their fanaticism?

The first type of answer, and one which is frequently voiced, refers to their intellectual background. For reasons that will become apparent presently, it is convenient to examine the question under two aspects, one concerning the Enlightenment in general, the other, the special position occupied in this respect by Rousseau. With regard to the first aspect it is generally held that while the philosophes expressed the need, moreover, totalized the multiple aspirations of the masses for a drastic change in their society, they themselves were not revolutionaries; more precisely, they were inclined to believe that such a change could be achieved consensually as a result of progressive enlightenment. In other words, the philosophes would not and did not allow human reason to overstep itself by becoming impatient and overconfident, hence turning into its very opposite. Now, although this is true, there is another side of the Enlightenment that ought to be borne in mind when trying to assess its impact on the Revolution and the Montagnards' leaders in particular.

The philosophes, and indeed most representatives of the Enlightenment in France, filled a complex, non- or rather pre-differentiated cultural role normally referred to as men of letters. This included practically all forms of expressive, interpretative, and creative activities falling between the extreme of abstract systematic thinking, on one side, and that of imaginative, purely fictional writing, on the other. But the main point is that this constituted a coherent whole, and that the French men of letters in the eighteenth century perceived themselves and were perceived by others as an identifiable occupational group fulfilling a well-defined role. Moreover, most of them were aware that diversity of interest and performance was a basic requisite for the fulfillment of such a role. Although they hated the word "system," there is little doubt that Diderot and Rousseau, to give two outstanding examples, were almost obsessionally concerned with the same kind of problems and fought the same battle in all their major works, philosophical, political, literary, and even autobiographical. Further, it would be reasonable to maintain that impressive as it might have been, their diversity of interests and activities was not as much a matter of natural endowment—Diderot's literary talents were moderate —as of an explicit need and determination to express their role fully, to say everything they had to say, and to say it variedly and emphatically.

Of paramount importance is the part played by the literary writings of the men of letters in relation to their work as a whole. Without a clear understanding of this it is difficult to make a balanced and adequate judgment on their historical significance. To go back to a point made earlier regarding their impact on the Revolution, it is true that in their theoretical writings the philosophes and the men of letters in general were daringly and even aggressively progressive without being revolutionary, that is, without pleading for radical and violent changes in their society. Most of them expressed views according to which the desired changes could take place within the existing system. Thus, like Montesquieu, Voltaire expressed his faith in an "enlightened absolutism and constitutional monarch," and even in "traditional aristocracy." While pleading for freedom and equality, and while thundering against the evils of ignorance and prejudice, including religion, Helvetius and Holbach sincerely believed that all the desired changes could be brought about by the monarch within the framework of conventional morality: they were explicitly against involving the people in such an enterprise. Diderot refrained from encouraging anyone to break the laws, even the bad laws, "because this may authorize everyone else to break the good ones."[9] The examples can easily be multiplied, but the more one does so the more one feels the need to raise the following critical questions: How and to what extent does this express their perception of themselves, their role image, and, finally, their conception of man, society, and history? Where does the other side of their intellectual activity come in?

In tackling the above questions it is not enough to take into account that the people referred to included the authors of famous fictional works, such as *La Nouvelle Héloïse, La Religieuse, Les Bijoux indiscrets, Le Neveau de Rameau, Supplément au Voyage de Bougainville,* to mention only a few. Equally essential is that they lived in, and to a certain extent represented, a period and a sociocultural climate in which the so-called *littérature licencieuse* reached a peak, and which produced or inspired the work of Chaderlos de Laclos and de Sade as well as the beginning of the so-called *roman intérieur*. Briefly, before anything definite is said about the historical significance of the men of letters, it is necessary to consider their fictional vision of man in general and of society in particular. Although the point has a more general application, we have to confine ourselves to a brief, mainly illustrative discussion of Diderot's literary work. Apart from being one of the most if not the most outstanding representatives of the period, Diderot also was highly aware of the substantial unity of his work.

Diderot's persistent preoccupation as an author and critic with *la littérature licencieuse* can be interpreted in a great variety of ways, that is, as an expression of a slightly abnormal trait in his personality, as a disguised manifestation of a quasi-scientific interest, of a unique insightfulness into the lower depth of the human mind, or simply as a contribution to a fashionable if not dominant literary trend. But useful as they may be, these and other similar kinds of interpretations touch only the surface of the question with which we are concerned here, which is one of meaning rather than origins. For this reason it is necessary to place Diderot's *littérature licencieuse* in the totality of his work, and derive its meaning from the general intention of his intellectual activities and the specific manner in which he perceived his role as a man of letters. This is admittedly a difficult task, but fortunately Diderot himself supplies us with a first insight. He confesses that whenever he saw someone, and particularly a member of the upper classes, buying his *Bijoux indiscrets,* he had the feeling that he had caught him red-handed, the feeling that in dropping the mask of conventional sexual morality the purchaser was on the way to freeing himself from all conventions and becoming a man like all others. There is, therefore, little doubt that *la littérature licencieuse* was for him neither a form of entertainment nor a therapeutic exercise, but a constituent part of his strategy as a man of letters, a powerful weapon in his total war of liberation. As in his philosophical and political writings he led a systematic campaign against any form of oppression, so did he, in his literary writing, fight against any form of repression, prejudice, and convention, in a word, anything that prevented the individual from a genuine contact with his inner self.

But while the campaign was the same, the tactics and particularly the achievements were considerably different, and in this lies the specific significance, historical and existential, of Diderot's fictional writings, which we in the twentieth century have only just begun to realize. In his philosophical and political works Diderot was vigorously critical, cynical, and fearless in his attack, but he would not and could not use the "knock out" technique. To be sure he had little doubt that in order to demolish the existing social order and to build a new one it was necessary to be free. But, at the same time, he distinctly felt that in this case freedom should operate within a definite, normally moral framework, that social change should be guided by common sense, by reason and persuasion rather than by force. Like Holbach and many other representatives of the period, Diderot was inclined to conceive of reason ontologically, as a powerful autonomous agency that cures the evils of the world and finally establishes the reign of liberty. In the realm of social life, freedom, reason, and ethos should go hand in hand.

The position is considerably different when one looks at Diderot's literary vision of the world, and particularly of human existence. Here spontaneity and freedom reign absolutely. Moreover, one can confidently say that Diderot was one of the greatest iconoclasts of all times, the first fully fledged modern artist, that is, one who felt and hammered home his feeling that art should be and is a direct manifestiation of man's inner life, the most authentic—Diderot used the word "honest"—contact that an individual could have with himself. In art as in dream, man makes himself whatever he wishes to be. The term *whatever* is used deliberately to underline this surprisingly modern, almost Pirandellian, aspect of Diderot, namely, his awareness that beneath the mask of convention and social identity there lies in each individual a series of other, far more authentic identities. Consider, for example, his reaction to his own portrait by Michael van Loo, "Mais que diront mes petits enfants, lorsqu'ils viendront à comparer mes tristes ouvrages avec ce riant, mignon, efféminé, vieux coquet-là? Mes enfants, je vous préviens que ce n'est pas moi. J'avais en une journée cent physionomies diverses selon la chose dont j'étais affecté. . . . J'ai un masque qui trompe l'artiste."[10]

So much for the literary side of Diderot's work. The main points emerging from what has been said so far may be formulated briefly as follows: in his theoretical writings, Diderot was not a revolutionary either in a Montagnard sense or in the sense in which a writer such as Marx was. The main reason for this was that he did not and could not establish a close, unmediated, unreflexive, and compulsive connection between radical criticism and vision, on the one hand, and radical action, on the other. His notion of revolutionary praxis remained undistinguishable from the notion of human action, moreover, of human nature in general. Nature, morality, and action constituted an existential trinity. However, the same Diderot may and does appear considerably different if one takes into account the view of the world and man emerging from his literary writings. What a contemporary apostle of revolution, Jean-Paul Sartre, considers to be the hallmark of eighteenth-century literature as a whole is glaringly true of Diderot's fictional work: it does indeed constitute a model of "protest literature," a fact that enhances the historical significance of his work as a whole.[11] In the present context the following two points are exceptionally relevant: First, in his literary work, Diderot presents a revolutionary image of man in that most of his characters lead an endless battle not only against the conventions and institutions of their society but also against the encroachment of society in general. The kind of freedom they aspire to is the freedom "to sleep with their own mother and kill their own father." Second, and this should be regarded as a necessary positive conclusion from the first point, in these writings Diderot makes a bold attempt to establish the value of the individual's inner life, of his interiority. To be sure this has a multiplicity of aspects, not all of them clearly articulated in Diderot's writing. But what clearly emerges from these writings is his effort to show not only that the individual has the ability as well as the right to pull off the mask put on him by society and thus establish his true identity from within, but also, and above all, that consultation with oneself, self-consent or, as the existentialists would have it, coincidence with oneself constitutes the safest basis for any authoritative decision regarding one's own existence, personal or social.

The extent to which Diderot and other representatives of the Enlightenment had succeeded in legitimizing the value of interiority, to translate inner freedom in terms of social freedom, is a big question that cannot be discussed here. We suggest, however, that this aspect of their view of man had a great deal to do with the Revolution. In brief, Diderot contributed to the creation of a cultural climate that enabled Robespierre and Saint-Just to form the conviction that their own ideas, intuitions, and aspirations constituted in themselves sufficient guidance for their (revolutionary) action, moreover, that their conscience constituted a supreme authority. To be sure, the process involved here was one of diffuse cultural refraction rather than one of direct influence. Although we have reasons to believe that the Montagnard leaders were highly introspective—Robespierre had conspicuous artistic inclinations—the manner in which they perceived and dealt with their inner life differed considerably from that of Diderot's characters. Whereas the latter were inclined to accept, and sometimes to identify with their inner drives and feelings, the former tended to control them, unconsciously, of course, by projecting them onto the external world, onto dominant values, ideas, and cultural symbols in general. As will be shown presently, they were strongly inclined to equate pathos, that is, inner mobilization and consultation, with ethos. In the meantime, however, it is necessary to examine another aspect of their cultural background.

Both Robespierre and Saint-Just took Rousseau as their first model, and consequently they were strongly inclined to a romantic conception of human reason. Particularly relevant is Rousseau's concept of "the general will," a mysterious notion or, rather, assumption according to which the individual members of a community can, under certain circumstances, make political decisions that are not only self-evident but also morally binding for everyone and in equal measure. Moreover, as expressions of universal reason such decisions are not only accessible but evident to the legislator. This clumsy equation between human nature, reason, and political society, which has sometimes been described as an early expression of a totalitarian form of democracy, can certainly be considered an important ingredient in the political outlook of the Montagnards. Their identification with the people and their firm belief that they were acting on behalf of the people as an abstract monolith testify to this. But in saying this there still remains a formidable question to be faced. Rousseau was a theoretician, and as such he could hardly conceive of the problems with which the political activists would be faced. To put it bluntly, how could the Montagnards act upon the assumption that there was a general will, a rational, and hence evident, formula for the interests of all, when all the appearances were to the contrary? More precisely, when and how did they arrive at the conclusion that they were the right interpreters of the general will and consequently the representatives of the people *tout court?*

While laying no claims for possessing a definite answer we should like to conclude the present chapter by discussing the main issues involved in, and the main types of approach made to, such questions.

The argument put forward here has on the whole been organized around two main points, one referring to the sociocultural features characterizing the period under consideration, the other to the specific nature of a revolutionary situation. Regarding the first, one can briefly state that the Montagnards belonged to a period of incipient nationalism and of confident, even virulent, rationalism. As to the historical significance of the phenomenon, it suffices to point out that we are dealing with the formative stage of what was soon to become one of the most powerful sociocultural trends in modern history and one that found its most adequate expression in the so-called romantic period and, notably, the philosophical thought of Hegel and Herder. Now, the main contention of the present chapter is that the Montagnards constituted an early, mainly political expression of this particular sociocultural cluster. Furthermore, we suggest that their political fanaticism can be seen as an ideological and behavioral syndrome of a period and sociocultural climate characterized by incipient nationalism and virulent rationalism.

As the part played by the so-called nationalistic motif in the political behavior of the Montagnards has been discussed at some length elsewhere, it can briefly be summed up as follows: as the Montagnard leaders perceived themselves as patriots, impeccable and sacrosanct patriots, it is reasonable to assume that in this respect they represent an early but nonetheless distinct articulation of demotic nationalism with both messianic and nativistic features. Saint-Just's dichotomic conception of morality —self-centeredness as the source of all evil and community-centeredness as the source of all good—as well as his romantic imagery about rural agrarian society and style of life, contains a strong element of what may be called fanaticism of the right.

Not so obvious was the other side of Montagnard fanaticism, which was closely related to the main tenets of late eighteenth-century rationalist thought and particularly to the impact that this had on Robespierre's and Saint-Just's views of man and of themselves as political activists. As much of what was said at an earlier stage when we discussed the relationship between the Montagnards and the Enlightenment bears on this, it remains only to conclude the argument by making a series of points of a more specific character. A point of emphasis should come first, namely, the conception of reason as a moral and social force. Although the idea can be found, implicitly or explicitly, in many writers of the Enlightenment, Robespierre and Saint-Just stand nearer a romantic, especially Hegelian and early Marxian, version of this basic theme in modern rationalist thought. Sometimes this seems to be so obvious that it would be hardly an exaggeration to consider them as a prefiguration of the romantic concept of totality, that is, a human condition of perfect unity between reason, will, and feeling, between knowledge, morality, and politics. But in saying ''prefiguration'' an important point of qualification should be made at once. For one thing, there is the objective fact that Robespierre and Saint-Just lived before such a vision of man was conceptualized by Hegel and, shortly after, by Marx. But even more significant in the present context is that they were neither abstract thinkers nor visionaries in a romantic sense of the word, the implication being that they had arrived at and expressed this view of man neither conceptually nor simply intuitively, but in a more concrete way, through their style of life, or, to use another existentialist expression, through their chosen mode of being. As this is obviously both a complex formulation and a complex phenomenon, we suggest that, if for analytical purposes one factor has to be isolated, that factor should be the role structure and style of the two Montagnard leaders. The reason for this is twofold: first, this aspect of their existence expresses in the most concrete manner possible their chosen mode of being, and second, it throws direct light on their inclination to perceive ideas in terms of rights and duties, to believe that what is rational is equally desirable and realizable, and, consequently, to conceive of man as a maker of history.

Of the many and varied ways in which the above view of man was expressed by the Montagnard leaders, only those will be mentioned here that have a direct bearing on their political fanaticism. Most revealing in this respect was their anxiety to achieve and maintain that state of inner cohesion and total harmony on the (unconscious) assumption that totality means inner totality *tout court*. We confess that owing primarily to lack of more detailed empirical study in this area, we are unable to deal adequately with this phenomenon. All we can do is outline a manner of approach that may be rewarding for future research. One aspect that commands particular attention in this context is Robespierre's famous ''withdrawals'' on the eve of important decisions, such as before the liquidation of the Hebertists and Dantonists (February 1794), and just before the fate of the Terror and consequently his own fate was decided (July 1794).[12] These ritualistic inner consultations constituted so many efforts toward reaching a state of perfect consensus between his judgment, feeling, and will, and consequently to arrive at an unambiguous formulation of his position. A series of useful insights can be gained if one compares the case with other, better-known experiences of this sort, such as, for instance, the retreats of early Christians, medieval mystics, seventeenth-century pietists and puritans, not to mention a well-known case in contemporary history, that of Hitler. The most obvious characteristic of this type of situation briefly can be described as a mental state of total mobilization, a heightening of inner life to the degree of eliminating any resistance, from within or from without, of superseding all contradictions, all doubts and hesitations. The normal outcome is that inner spark, that state of certitude and confidence that are unmistakable signs of a ceaseless drive toward the autonomy of inner life and, often, total internalization of reality. As a result of this kind of experience, Jacob Böhme found out that God dwelt inside the soul of man, more precisely, inside himself, or, to paraphrase Angelus Silesius, that God without him cannot exist for a moment. In his "Psychologie des Deutschen Pietismus," H. R. Günther makes this point particularly clearly.[13] In their anxiety to relate their wishes to the will of God, the minds of the Pietists moved in smaller and smaller circles until the two points, their wish and God's will, met. The result was that God often agreed with their wish. Similarly Robespierre often came to the conclusion that his reasons were reason itself.

One point of qualification is necessary. It is not suggested here that increased inner awareness and extension of the boundaries of the self are and necessarily should be related to the practice of seclusion and inner examination. It is quite possible, and the case of Saint-Just may be suggestive in this respect, to reach a similar state of intense contact with others, by (collective) situations of interstimulation, as Durkheim would have it. At any rate it was this kind of mental condition, this permanent inner mobilization that accounted to a great extent for Robespierre's and Saint-Just's voluntarism, or, if the above analogy can stand the strain, for their feeling that since one wills it is willed. As to the question who or what the *it* was, the Montagnard leaders had more than one answer, or rather a colorful variation that included "the people," fatherland, man, humanity, reason, and, above all, the Revolution with its obvious connotation of posterity and history.

What has just been said sheds light on another cluster of psychocultural traits characteristic of the Montagnard leaders that more than anything else may account for their political fanaticism. For lack of a better expression we call it the "activist cluster," its origins lying, obviously, in the same condition of permanent inner mobilization referred to above. One expression of this consisted in their readiness to equate passivity, neutrality, and indifference with guilt. Another one consisted of their all too obvious tendency to equate freedom with order, or, better said, freedom with control, for in this way we point to the very root, the deep motivation of the feeling and vision of order in human existence, namely, control over the self. That the Spartan ideal of man is relevant here hardly needs mentioning. Equally familiar is Robespierre's compulsive manner of justifying the Regime of Terror, that is, the despotism of freedom. On this point Saint-Just presents us with a broader, more imaginative, and for this reason a more symptomatic expression of the situation and of the human condition involved in it. Even his notion of terror appears more punctuated than that of Robespierre: "We rule by iron those who cannot be ruled by justice," with more paternalistic rather than sheerly repressive connotations, and on the whole more distinctively future-oriented. His well-known concern with institutions, which he conceived of as an alternative to terror, bears witness to this. As he aptly put it, "They [institutions] are the substitution of the power of morals for the power of men," or, in another place, "They make man what he wishes to be."[14] One can hardly doubt that by alternative he meant rational control and inner authority as opposed to coercion.

It is this broad vision of revolutionary task that places Saint-Just in a category of his own. His emotional ethic, his exalted vision of future society, and, above all, his bucolic imagery of rural life, "la volupté d'une cabane, d'un champs fertile cultivé par vos mains, une charrue, un champ, une chaumière . . . voila le bonheur"—all this makes it sometimes difficult to brand him a fanatic. On the other hand, dream makes reality unbearable; nothing can more readily justify man's impatience, intolerance, and repression of present reality than his dream of a free and happy future. As an old French proverb says, "Par requirre de trop grande franchise et libertés chet-on en trop grand serveigne." Saint-Just's fanaticism even more than that of Robespierre was the fanaticism of Freedom. No one had a deeper understanding of this paradox than Hegel when he saw in the French Revolution an expression—*incarnation* would be a better word—of man's tragic vision of the world, and in Saint-Just the quintessence of a tragic hero. The springboard of tragedy lay in his abstract concept of freedom, that is, in that inner dreamlike vision of human freedom that could not and would not compromise with the concrete circumstances of life, with history. And here lay also the very source of Saint-Just's fanaticism, for, as Hegel says, "fanaticism is the voice of abstraction and the refusal of structuration . . . a blind claim of liberty."[15] Saint-Just casts a long shadow over our own time.

NOTES

1. From the article "Autorité politique," *Encyclopédie.*

2. *European Thought in The Eighteenth Century* (London, 1954).

3. *Textes choisis,* ed. Jean Popereu (Paris, 1956), vol. 1, pp. 89–94.

4. *Oeuvres,* vol. 2, p. 494. Italics mine.

5. For a recent, highly valuable contribution, see F. Weinstein and G. M. Platt, *The Wish To Be Free: Society, Psyche and Value Change* (Berkeley and Los Angeles, 1969). For an earlier, similar treatment of the subject, see Z. Barbu, *Dictatorship and Democracy* (London and New York, 1956), pp. 55–56; *Problems of Historical Psychology* (London and New York, 1960), esp. pp. 205–218; and "The New Intelligentsia," in J. Cruikshank, ed., *French Literature in Its Background* (Oxford, 1968), vol. 3.

6. George Rude, *Crowds in History* (New York and London, 1964).

7. This point has been developed in some detail by E. G. Walter, *Terror and Resistance* (New York and Oxford, 1969).

8. F. Brunot, *Histoire de la langue française,* vol. 9, p. 623.

9. *Supplement au voyage de Bougainville,* ed. Dieckmann (1955), p. 65.

10. *Essais sur la peinture* (posthumously published in 1795).

11. Sartre, *What Is Literature?* (New York, 1965).

12. In the same order of ideas it is relevant to note that, during the period immediately preceding his decision to increase the pressure of the Terror, Robespierre was preoccupied with the introduction of the cult of the Supreme Being and arrangements for the great fête of 8 June 1794.

13. In *Persönlichkeit und Geschichte* (1947).

14. *Oeuvres,* vol. 2, p. 422.

15. "Introduction," *Philosophy of Right.*

THE SYMBOLIC IN WORLD
REVOLUTIONARY PROCESSES

5

THE RISE OF PUBLIC OPINION

HANS SPEIER

I

Public opinion is often regarded as opinion disclosed to others or at least noted by others, so that opinions that are hidden or concealed from other persons may be called either private or clandestine opinions. The criterion for distinguishing between private and public opinion thus appears to lie in the realm of communication. In expressions like "public good," "public ownership," "public law," however, our point of reference is not communication but rather a matter of general concern, more precisely, *res publica*. This political meaning of the word is older than the meaning we customarily associate with the term "public opinion."

Thomas Hobbes, for example, distinguishing public worship from private worship, observed that public is the worship that a commonwealth performs "as one person."[1] According to this usage, the distinctive mark of private worship need not be secrecy; it might rather be heresy. Hobbes mentions indeed that private worship may be performed in "the sight of the multitude," which is an old-fashioned, if more concrete, way of saying "in public." Private worship performed in public he regarded as constrained either by the laws or by the "opinion of men." Correspondingly, in considering the nature of heresy, Hobbes remarked that it "signifies no more than private opinion."[2] If we follow the lead Hobbes gives us, we may arrive at an understanding of public opinion that makes political sense and is useful for the purposes of this historical review.

Let us understand by public opinion, opinions on matters of concern to the nation freely and publicly expressed by men outside the government who claim as a right that their opinions should influence or determine the actions, personnel, or structure of their government. In its most attenuated form this right asserts itself as the expectation that the government will publicly reveal and explain its decisions in order to enable people outside the government to think and talk about these decisions or, to put it in terms of democratic amenities, in order to assure "the success" of the government's policy.

Public opinion, so understood, is primarily a communication from the citizens to their government and only secondarily a communication among the citizens. Further, if a government effectively denies the claim that the opinion of the citizens on public matters be relevant, in one form or another, for policy making or if it prevents the free and public expression of such opinions, public opinion does not exist. There is no public opinion in autocratic regimes; there can only be suppressed, clandestine opinion, no matter how ingenious or careful the government may be in permitting an organized semblance of truly public opinion for the sake of democratic appearances. By way of illustration, no German public opinion existed in occupied Germany after the Second World War under the rule of military governments, despite the speedy liberalization of press and radio in the Western zones, and despite the expression of many opinions in public. This was because the Germans were neither free to act politically according to their own decision, having been deprived of sovereignty, nor free to criticize the actions of the military governments or of the Allied Control Council.

Finally, for public opinion to function, there must be access to information on the issues with which public opinon is concerned. This means, above all, that the actions of the government must not be kept secret. Thus, Jeremy Bentham demanded full publicity for all official acts so that what he called "the tribunal of public opinion" could prevent misrule and suggest legislative reforms. Public communication of governmental acts

(Oeffentlichkeit) was demanded by the political philosophers of enlightenment. The practice of submitting a budget to popular representatives, if not to the public at large, was established in England by the time of the revolution in 1688 and in France at the time of the French Revolution of 1789. The more democracy progresses and the more intensely public opinion is cherished as a safeguard of morality in politics, the louder become the demands for the abolition of secrecy in foreign policy as well. After the First World War such demands led to the so-called new diplomacy. Under the system of the League, international treaties had to be registered so as to prevent the inclusion of secret clauses.[3]

If public opinion be regarded primarily as a public communication from citizens *to their government,* it may be distinguished from policy counseling by policy advisers or governmental staff members, which is one of the processes of communication bearing on decision making *within the government* (whether it is democratic or not). Public opinion is also distinguished from diplomacy, which may be regarded as communication *among governments.* Finally, one may speak of governmental information and propaganda activities as communications *from a government* to its own citizens, other governmental personnel, or foreign audiences in general.

Public opinion can of course be studied also with a view to what I have called its secondary communications process, that is, with respect to the communications it involves *among the citizens.* In this context questions of the relations between opinion leaders and followers arise, as do problems of the size and anonymity of the public, the competence and representativeness of its organs, the direction and intensity of the interest taken in matters of public concern, the level and organization of public discussions, and so on. On many of these aspects of public opinion our historical knowledge is limited. In the history of public opinion the most conspicuous landmarks are the dates when governments ceased to censor the public expression of political dissent. In France, free communication of thought and opinion was proclaimed as ''one of the most valuable of the rights of men'' during the Revolution of 1789. In England, censorship in the form of licensing was abolished with less fanfare about a century earlier (1695).

II

Older discussions of our subject do not differ much from modern writings in estimating the influence popular opinions exert upon the actions of men; they differ in assessing the influence popular opinions have or should have upon the actions of statesmen and philosophers. It was common knowledge among older writers that opinions hold sway over the success, conduct, and morals of men. Shakespeare called opinion a mistress of success, and Pascal regarded it as the queen of the world. John Locke pointed out that men judge the rectitude of their actions according to three laws, namely, the divine law, the civil law, and the law of opinion or reputation, which he also called the law of passion or private censure. He attributed overwhelming power to the third law, the law of opinion, because man fears the inexorable operation of its sanctions. Dislike, "ill opinion," contempt, and disgrace, which violators of the law of censure must suffer, force men to conform. When Locke was attacked for his allegedly cynical view of morality, he defended himself by saying that he was not laying down any moral rules but was "enumerating the rules men make use of in moral relations, whether these rules are true or false. . . . I only report as a matter of fact what *others* call virtue and vice."[4]

Locke did not advance the view, however, that popular opinion should govern the actions of government. Characteristically, he used the phrase "the law of *private* censure" as a synonym for "the law of opinion." Moreover, he described the law of opinion "to be nothing else but the consent of private men, *who have not authority enough to make a law.*"[5]

Locke did not say that he shared popular opinions about morality. He knew that independent minds examine such opinions, although they cannot lightheartedly provoke the censure of others in whose company they live by showing disregard for what others consider to be right and wrong; the philosophers would otherwise "commit the fault of stubbornness," as Montaigne charmingly put it.[6]

Sir William Temple's essay *On the Original and Nature of Government,* written in 1672, has often been cited as an early discussion of public opinion. Temple observed that it cannot be that "when vast numbers of men submit their lives and fortunes absolutely to the will of one, it should be want of heart, but must be force of custom, or opinion, the true ground and foundation of all government, and that which subjects power to authority. . . . Authority rises from the opinion of wisdom, goodness, and valour in the persons who possess it."[7]

But Temple did not speak of public opinion. He spoke of opinion or "general opinion." In fact, he used the old term "vulgar opinion" when he wished to designate opinions critical of authority. "Nothing is so easily cheated," he said in his essay *Of Popular Discontents,* "nor so commonly mistaken, as vulgar opinion."[8] Temple's concern was with the nature and stability of government. He opposed the contractual theories of government, no matter whether they advanced a sociable or a bellicose view of man in the state of nature. If men were like sheep, he once wrote, he did not know why they needed any government; if they were like wolves, how they could suffer it. Contending that political authority developed out of habits and feelings formed in relation to the father of the family, he regarded opinion as a conserving force that helped the few to govern the many. The word "public," however, he reserved for the common good or the common interest of the nation: the "heats of humours of vulgar minds" would do little harm if governments observed the public good and if they avoided "all councils or designs of innovation."[9] It was precisely such innovation with which public opinion was concerned when it came to be called "public opinion" in the eighteenth century.

Even Rousseau, who put public opinion in its modern political place, demanding that law should spring from the general will, still spoke of opinions also in the traditional, predemocratic way. In his *Nouvelle Héloïse* he equated "public opinion" with vain prejudices and contrasted them with the eternal truths of morality; and in his *Considerations about the Government of Poland* he said: "Whoever makes it his business to give laws to a people must know how to sway opinions and through them govern the passions of men."[10]

The discussions of popular opinions up to the eve of the French Revolution lay much stress upon the power of opinions as means of restricting freedom, upon their prejudicial character, their changeability as to both time and place; they also indicate that men of judgment, whether philosophers or statesmen, deal prudently with popular opinion. Especially during the eighteenth century there are discussions to the effect that governments should take account of popular opinion instead of merely imposing their laws on the people. Finally, in the traditional views popular opinion was seen in close relation to imagination and passions rather than to intelligence and knowledge. Jacques Necker, who was the first writer to popularize the notion and the term "public opinion" throughout Europe at the eve of the French Revolution, still spoke of "imagination and hope" as "the precious precursors of the opinion of men."[11]

It did not occur to older writers that the "multitude" should know more about government than a good ruler, an experienced counselor, or a political philosopher. Only when economic and social inequalities were reduced and the rising elements in the population became unwilling to put up with political inequality could the claim be advanced that the government should make concessions to public opinion. Public opinion is a phenomenon of middle-class civilization. At the end of the ancien régime in France, Count Vergennes, one of M. Necker's colleagues, wrote in a confidential report to the king: "If M. Necker's public opinion were to gain ascendancy, Your Majesty would have to be prepared to see those command who otherwise obey and to see those obey who otherwise command."[12] With reference to Locke's remark about "the law of opinion" one might say that Count Vergennes warned the king of public opinion, because the people who formed it had gained enough authority to make a law.

III

In his fierce criticism of Edmund Burke's ideas on the French Revolution, Thomas Paine remarked that "the mind of the nation had changed beforehand, and the new order of things has naturally followed the new order of thoughts."[13] The observation that the habits of Frenchmen had become republican while their institutions were still monarchical is well sustained by modern research, although it should be borne in mind that it was a numerically small class that had slowly changed its habits.

Lord Acton attributed the growing influence of public opinion in eighteenth-century France to the rise of national debts and the increasing importance of the public creditor.[14] It is curi-

ous that this important insight into the origin of public opinion
has not led to more detailed research by the historians of public
opinion. The history of public opinion has been written primarily with reference to channels of communication, for example,
the marketplace in ancient Greece; the theater in Imperial
Rome; the sermons, letters, ballads, and travels in the Middle
Ages; pamphlets, newspapers, books and lectures, telegraph,
radio, film and television in modern times. We know more
about the history of literacy, the press, the law of sedition, and
censorship than about the relationship between the struggle for
budgetary control and the history of public opinion or about
the emergence of social institutions, other than the press, which
were instrumental in the political rise of public opinion.

In some older sources the close interconnection between public finance and public opinion is fully recognized. In the French
ancien régime publicists and financiers no less than the middle
classes at large condemned public loans. Bankruptcy was demanded by courts of justice and by political philosophers like
Montesquieu. "It was a reaction against these proposals of
bankruptcy that the French constitutions at the end of the eighteenth century proclaimed that the public debt was sacred."[15]

Jacques Necker had occasion to observe as minister of finance
that his contemporaries were much concerned with his fiscal
policies. He, in turn, regarded it as the "dear object" of his ambition to acquire the good opinion of the public. He contrasted
the "extensive horizon" of the public with the court at Versailles, the place of ambition and intrigue, and made the interesting observation that the minister of finance could not consider the court as a "suitable theatre" for himself; Versailles, he
said, was a place appropriate perhaps for ministers of war, the
navy, and foreign affairs, "because all the ideas of military and
political glory are more connected with the pageantry of mag-
nificence and power."[16] By contrast, the minister of finance
"stands most in need of the good opinion of the people."
Necker recommended that fiscal policies should be pursued in
"frankness and publicity" and that the finance minister "associate the nation, as it were, in his plans, in his operations, and
even in the obstacles that he must surmount."[17] Necker's great
contribution to the history of public opinion was not so much
what he wrote about its power but rather his important innova-

tion of publishing fiscal statements *(compte rendu)* so that the merits and faults of governmental policy in this field could be appraised in public. He did so "to calm the public which began to distrust the administration of finances and feared that the income of the treasury would not offer any security to the capital and interests of its creditors."[18] Mme de Staël, Necker's daughter, regarded this innovation as an important means for pacifying public opinion. The government, she observed, was forced by its need for public credit not to neglect public opinion; but Necker did not yet hold the view that the general will of the public should take the place of the government. He represents a transitional phase between the predemocratic and the revolutionary-democratic views of public opinion.

The institutional changes that preceded the restriction of absolutist rule and contributed to the rise of public opinion can be stated in this historical sketch only in bare outline. Gains in economic power of the middle class and the gradual spread of literacy are merely two aspects of this process.

The first impetus toward increasing literacy was given by the Reformation, which created a broad reading public seeking edification without the mediation of priests in religious literature written in the vernacular. As Sören Kierkegaard noted with extraordinary perspicacity about Luther, he "unseated the Pope —and put 'the public' on the throne."[19] During the eighteenth century, popular religious literature gradually was replaced by secular reading materials. Content and style of fiction changed in the process. The novel of manners and the epistolary novel, both primarily addressed to women, made their appearance, and the moral concern of the readers was shared by their authors. It became possible for them to earn a livelihood by writing. The professionalization of writing was furthered by the breakdown of the patronage system and its replacement by the collective patronage of the anonymous public.[20]

Parallel with the formation of a broader literary public, the middle classes transformed musical life. Public concerts to which an anonymous audience paid admission fees took the place of concerts given by the personal orchestras at the courts of European rulers and in the luxurious residences of distinguished aristocrats.

The expansion of the reading public was accompanied by the

development of related social institutions such as reading societies, reading clubs, circulating libraries, and secondhand bookstores. The establishment of the first circulating library in London coincided with the publication of Richardson's *Pamela*. Secondhand bookstores appeared in London during the last third of the eighteenth century. European reading societies were influenced by the model of the American subscription libraries, the earliest of which was founded by Franklin in Philadelphia in 1732. Thirty years later there were several *cabinets de lecture* in France, and the first German reading circle seems to have been established in 1772.[21] In addition to fiction—the favorite literature of the ladies—books on history, belles-lettres, natural history (that is, science), and statistics were read in these circles. But the favorite reading matter was political journals and scholarly magazines. In fact, the reading societies of the eighteenth century must be considered as the collective patrons of the moral weeklies that contributed so much to the articulation of middle-class opinion on matters of moral concern.

In German social history one looks in vain for the social institutions that contributed powerfully to the formation of public opinion in England and France, the coffeehouse and the salon, respectively. Germany's middle classes lacked the commercial strength that made the coffeehouse so important in England. In Europe, coffeehouses date back to the middle of the seventeenth century; they became popular as centers of news gathering and news dissemination, political debate, and literary criticism. In the early part of the eighteenth century, London is said to have had no fewer than two thousand coffeehouses. Addison wanted to have it said of him that he had brought philosophy out of closets and libraries "to dwell in clubs and assemblies, at tea tables and in coffee houses."[22] The English middle classes began to accomplish their own education in the coffeehouses.

Like the history of the coffeehouse in England, that of the French salon goes back to the seventeenth century and even farther to the Italian courts of the Renaissance. In the history of public opinion the French eighteenth-century salons were important because they were the gathering places of intellectually distinguished men and women who cherished conversation, applauded critical sense, and did not regard free thought or irreverent ideas as shocking unless they were advanced pedantically.

During the second half of the eighteenth century the salons governed opinion in Paris more effectively than the court. Men of letters were received regardless of their social origin and met on terms of equality with the most enlightened members of society. The salon, a place where talent could expect to outshine ancient titles, was an experiment in equality that assumed paradigmatic importance within a hierarchically organized society.[23] As d'Alembert said in his *Essay upon the Alliance betwixt Learned Men and the Great,* ''the man of quality, whose ancestors are his only merit, is of no more consequence in the eye of reason, than an old man returned to infancy, who once performed great things.''[24]

In Germany the salon never exercised the influence on the dignity and the literary style of authors or on the manners and opinions of their public that it did in France. Germany was a poor, divided, and in part overmilitarized country; it had neither a Versailles nor a Paris. The social institutions that helped to pave the way toward the social recognition of the ideas of enlightenment in Germany were the predominantly aristocratic language orders of the seventeenth century and the stolid moral and patriotic societies of the eighteenth century in which civil servants played an important role. Both of them may be regarded as forerunners of the Masonic lodges in Germany. They practiced egalitarian rituals, opposed the conventional customs of the courtier, extolled merit and virtue as the new principles of prestige, read and discussed John Locke, and cultivated mutual confidence as a bulwark against the dangerous intrigues in politics.

These institutional changes in European society that led to the emergence of public opinion as a prominent factor in politics may be summed up without regard to national differences as follows. A closed, restricted public gradually developed into an open one, enlarging both its size and its social scope as illiteracy receded. This movement ran its full course only during the nineteenth century. It extended to the lower classes much later than the late eighteenth-century attempts to parade the Third Estate as the nation would make us believe. From the end of the eighteenth century we have glowing accounts of the widespread eagerness of people to read and to learn, but illiteracy was still widespread. It has been estimated that about 57 percent of the men and 27 percent of the women could read and write in France at the time.[25]

Geographically, the process of diffusion spread out from urban centers, with the United States, England, and Germany taking the lead over France, where printing presses as well as the socially influential circles were concentrated in Paris.

The economic and technical landmarks of this process of diffusion are reflected in the cost of mass communication to the poorer classes of society. Here again progress was made more rapidly during the nineteenth century than the eighteenth century. Taxes on newspapers and advertisements were fairly high until 1836 and partly until 1845; the poor could not afford to buy them. Even postal service was not readily available to them until 1839, when penny postage was introduced. Harriet Martineau said at the time that the poor now can ''at last write to one another as if they were all M.P.'s.''[26]

As regards the men of letters and the publicist, the prerequisite of their wider influence was the recognition of merit as a criterion of social status, so that authors could climb the social ladder regardless of origin merely on the strength of performance. It might be added that the rise of public opinion presupposed a redefinition of scholarship and a program of its missionary diffusion to laymen, a process in which ''the world'' took the place of ''the school'' and education became a technique for the establishment of a classless society.

One of the earliest and most radical instances illustrating this missionary zeal can be found in Christian Thomasius' *Einleitung zur Vernunftlehre,* published in 1691. Thomasius believed that it was the result only of differences in social status that not everybody arrived at wisdom; science ought to be the common property of all mankind. Everybody was capable of becoming learned, and the scholar should disseminate rather than attain knowledge.[27] It has been said that Thomasius repeated ''the Lutheran teaching of general priesthood in the secularized form of general scholarship.''[28]

Thomasius' notion of scholarship is close to Condorcet's doctrine of education or Sieyès' views of public opinion. Condorcet's aim was to render it impossible through education to use the masses as ''docile instruments in adroit hands'' and to enable them to avoid the ''philosophic errors'' on which he be-

lieved "all errors in government and in society are based."[29]
And Sieyès wrote: "Reason does not like secrets; it is effective
only through expansion. Only if it hits everywhere, does it hit
right, because only then will be formed that power of public
opinion, to which one may perhaps ascribe most of the changes
which are truly advantageous to mankind."[30]

IV

The elimination of prejudice, ignorance, and arbitrary government that the advocates of enlightenment wrote upon their
banner in order to base the commonwealth upon reason and
civic virtue is frequently regarded as a rationalistic program in
which no cognizance was taken of the so-called irrational factors
of human nature. For this reason, propaganda has often been
presented as a counterpart to the process of public opinion. It is
erroneous, however, to believe that the advocates of enlightenment neglected or overlooked the emotional facets of life.

The advocates of enlightenment themselves proposed the
equation of government with adult education. They suggested,
for example, that the government should engage orators for political instruction as it paid priests for religious service (Weck-
herlin); that attendance of courses on the nature of society
should be made obligatory for the acquisition of citizenship
(Mercier de la Rivière); that the government should control and
publish newspapers to increase loyalty to the sovereign (Ques-
nay); and that historical works should be written to increase patriotism and national pride (Voss).

Perhaps even more important than these suggestions of political indoctrination were the proposals for the organization of
public spectacles and celebrations in order to evoke enthusiasm
for common causes and enlist the sentiments of those who did
not think. Dupont de Nemours in *Des Spectacles nationaux*
developed a theory of national celebrations based on the idea
that the desire for pleasure is the driving force of mankind. The
people should be brought to develop their patriotic virtues by
way of exaltation over public celebrations in which they were to
participate—an idea, one might say, that was realized in both
the institutionalized public celebrations of the French Revolution and in the Nuremberg festivals of the Nazis or in May Day
celebrations. Other writers who pointed to the educational

function of national festivals and public plays were Diderot, Condorcet, and Rousseau, and, in Germany, among others, Stephani, Voss, and Zachariä.

In view of these facts it cannot be maintained without qualification that the modern advocates and practitioners of totalitarian government propaganda have superseded the theory and practices of the reformers who helped public opinion on its way to political prominence. It would be more correct to say that the participation of large masses of the population in public affairs, characteristic of both government by public opinion and modern tyranny, is spurious in character under totalitarian regimes in that it is demonstrative rather than determinative of governmental action. It may also be said that in totalitarian regimes mass participation in politics is regarded by the intellectuals as a design to conceal the truth about power processes, whereas in the eighteenth century such participation was considered as a measure toward the ultimate elimination of the irksomeness of power, if not of power itself.

It was believed that man guided by reason and inspired by rectitude would reduce politics to a calculation in happiness and do away with war. Nevertheless, the French Revolution gave rise to war and to war propaganda, and it lifted many restrictions on warfare. It created what William Pitt called "armed opinions" and Jomini "wars of opinion." Liberty, equality, and fraternity were not merely the aims of Frenchmen; they were held to be rights of man regardless of political and national affiliation. The French revolutionary armies did not wage war against other countries but for the liberation of man from old, oppressive governments.[31] Foreign exiles in sympathy with the new regime were admitted to the French clubs, the national guard, and the public departments. They could be found even in the Ministry for Foreign Affairs.[32] They were organized in foreign legions fighting the battle for France. Indeed, the foreigners fighting on the side of the French for the ideas of the French Revolution may be regarded as the prototype of the armed contingents that, hailed by their respective "governments-in-exile," joined the British, American, and Soviet Russian forces of World War II in "the crusade" to end Hitler's tyrannical rule. Similarly, the Girondists imagined that foreign nations in their desire to be delivered from the tyranny of their rulers and priests would rally in support of revolutionary principles. Robespierre's program of 24 April 1793 envisaged a universal republic in which all citizens in all countries would unite against the aristocrats and the tyrants.[33] As Burke pointed out, before the time of the French Revolution there had been no instance "of this spirit of general political factions, separated from religion, pervading several countries, and forming a principle of union between the partisans in each."[34]

It was not only the conquest of foreign territory and the subsequent provisioning of the French armies by plunder, but also revolutionary, cosmopolitan enthusiasm and the leveling of social inequalities that enabled twenty-five million Frenchmen to defeat a coalition of seventy-four million enemies. The royalist adversaries put twice the number of soldiers in the field as did the young republic. But although the French armies lost two-thirds of their nine thousand royalist officers through defection, the *levée en masse* mobilized hitherto untapped human resources for war. As the Committee of Public Safety decreed in 1793:

> The young men will go to battle; the married men will forego arms and transport food; the women will make the tents, garments, and help in the hospitals; the children will cut old rags into strips; the old men will place themselves in the public squares to influence the courage of the warriors, incite hatred against the kings, and recommend the unity of the Republic.[35]

The most important change in military tactics brought on by revolutionary enthusiasm was the emergence of the *tirailleurs,* marksmen, who aimed their shots at a target instead of relying on volleys, as the disciplined armies of the ancien régime had done. The new tactic was known only from the American War of Independence and, in Europe, from the fighting of the notoriously cruel Pandours of Croatia. Advocates of the old Frederician tactics regarded the behavior of the *tirailleurs* as "militarily superfluous," "politically odious,"[36] and indicative of "the scoundrel hidden in every man."[37] Indeed the new tactic was adopted by the conservative enemies only after their defeat, in Austria (1806) and in Prussia (1809 and 1812).

The leveling of social distinctions in the French nation also affected the status of officers and had repercussions in the logistics of war. In Prussia every lieutenant had two horses, one for riding and one for his baggage; captains could not do without three to five baggage horses each. In the French revolutionary armies no such luxury existed. Privates had to shift without tents, whereas no less than sixty pack horses carrying tents followed each Prussian regiment.[38] In 1806, the French baggage train was one-eighth to one-tenth that of the Prussians.[39]

In the international turmoil following the French Revolution, the enemies of France were incapable of restricting the war to its former, military dimensions. They responded to the ideological challenge. In October 1793, His Majesty's Government sent a declaration to the commanders of the British forces in which France was accused of attacks on "the fundamental principles by which mankind is united in the bond of civil society."[40] And William Pitt found the most eloquent expression for the ideological issue raised by the French Revolution. On 7 June 1799 he spoke in the House of Commons, moving that the sum of £825,000 be granted to His Majesty to enable him to fulfill his engagements with Russia. Pitt pointed out that this subsidy would be used for the deliverance of Europe. In reply Mr. Tierney contended that the funds were to be used against the power of France "not merely to repel her within her ancient limits, but to drive her back from her present to her ancient opinion." Mr. Pitt rose once more and said, among other things:

> It is not so. We are not in arms against the opinions of the closet, nor the speculations of the school. We are at war with armed opinion; we are at war with those opinions which the thought of audacious, unprincipled and impious innovations seeks to propagate amidst the ruins of empires, the demolition of the altars of all religion, the destruction of every venerable, and good, and liberal institution, under whatever forms of policy they have been raised; and this, in spite of the dissenting reason of men, in contempt of that lawful authority which, in the settled order, superior talent and superior virtue attain, crying out to them not to enter on holy ground nor to pollute the stream of eternal justice; admonishing them of their danger, whilst, like the genius of evil, they mimic their voice, and, having succeeded in drawing upon them the ridicule of the vulgar, close their day of wickedness and savage triumph with the massacre and waste of whatever is amiable, learned, and pious, in the districts they have overrun.[41]

V

After the Congress of Vienna the utilization of public opinion in international affairs became, as it were, respectable also among statesmen who did not pursue any revolutionary cause. Once the importance of public opinion was discovered as a new factor in international relations, it became tempting on moral as well as on expediential grounds to utilize it. Neither Canning, who believed that public opinion should be invoked in the pursuit of British foreign policy, nor Palmerston, who held that public opinion founded on truth and justice would prevail against the force of armies, realized that they were continuing to revolutionize European diplomacy by their actions. A diplomat of the old school like Metternich was appalled by Canning's enthusiasm and could see only preposterous folly in the Englishman's notion of public opinion as "a power more tremendous than was perhaps ever yet brought into action in the history of mankind."[42]

The art of arousing public opinion nevertheless became a valued skill during the nineteenth century even of statesmen like Bismarck, who failed to respect public opinion, remained indifferent to its moral claims, and made no attempt to raise its level of competence. Bismarck condemned policies inspired by sentiments or moods. He regarded public opinion as dependent, to a large extent, on mood and sentiment, incapable of the calm calculations that had to precede political decisions. Nor did he believe in the political insight of public opinion. "As a rule," he said, "public opinion realizes the mistakes that have been committed in foreign policy only when it is able to review in retrospect the history of a generation."[43] Given the political constitution of Prussia and the Reich, Bismarck could afford to make foreign policy against public opinion, if he regarded such action as necessary and if he had the confidence of his monarch. Thus, in 1866 he waged war against the will of almost all Prussians, but he also refused to risk war against Russia by interfering in Bulgaria, a course rashly sponsored by the liberal press. Similarly, in the Boer War, Chancellor von Bülow disregarded German public opinion, which strongly favored interference, in the well-considered interest of the country.

The scope of governmental influence upon public opinion

was limited throughout the nineteenth century and, if compared with recent activities in this regard, had an almost patrimonial character. In nineteenth-century Europe public opinion was a synonym of opinions expressed by the political representatives of the electorate, by newspapers, and by prominent members or organizations of the middle class. In England their faith in the beneficial effects of discussion and the persuasiveness of liberal opinion upon conduct of domestic affairs grew particularly under the influence of Bentham and his followers.[44] Toward the end of the nineteenth century, Lord Bryce pointed out that in England the landowners and "the higher walks of commerce" not only form the class which furnish the majority of members of both houses but also express what is called public opinion. He held that in Germany, Italy, and France as well public opinion was "substantially the opinion of the class which wears black coats and lives in good houses."[45] He contrasted these conditions with those prevailing in the United States, where he believed government by public opinion to exist, because "the wishes and views of the people prevail even before they have been conveyed through the regular law-appointed organs."[46]

Like de Tocqueville and other nineteenth-century writers,[47] Lord Bryce recognized the decisive importance of class distinctions in limiting participation in public opinion, although he failed to appreciate the limiting influence upon public opinion exercised by pressure groups in the United States. He also lacked the perspicacity of de Tocqueville, who detected the threats to freedom of thought that public opinion in conditions of social equality presents. Reactionaries, romantics, Saint-Simonians, and Marxists attacked liberal convictions and threw doubt upon the morality, distinterestedness, and representativeness of middle-class opinions in the nineteenth century. They were not concerned, however, with freedom of thought; they contributed, in fact, to its modern decline. De Tocqueville, however, clearly saw that in "ages of equality" the liberation of the people from ignorance and prejudice by enlightenment may be purchased at the price of equalizing thought.

> There is, and I cannot repeat it too often, there is here matter for profound reflection to those who look upon freedom of thought as a holy thing and who hate not only the despot, but despotism. For

myself, when I feel the hand of power lie heavy on my brow, I care but little to know who oppresses me; and I am not the more disposed to pass beneath the yoke because it is held out to me by the arms of millions of men.[48]

Perhaps the most wrathful condemnation of public opinion and its architects, the journalists, was advanced by Sören Kierkegaard. It shocked him deeply that a single person should be able every week or every day to get forty thousand or fifty thousand readers to speak or think like him.[49] His shock might have been cushioned, had he known that the ways men act—to judge by political elections in nineteenth-century Europe as well as twentieth-century America—do not necessarily reflect the preferences of the press they read.

NOTES

This chapter is a revised and enlarged version of "The Historical Development of Public Opinion" (1950), reprinted in *Social Order and the Risks of War*, paperback (Cambridge: The M.I.T. Press, 1969), chap. 24.

1. Thomas Hobbes, *Leviathan,* vol. 2, p. 31.

2. Ibid., vol. 1, p. 11.

3. For a discussion of secrecy in international negotiations versus secrecy of international agreements, see Harold Nicolson, *Diplomacy* (London, 1939), and *Peacemaking 1919* (New York, 1939), pp. 123ff.

4. John Locke, "The Epistle to the Reader" in *An Essay concerning Human Understanding,* ed. A. C. Fraser (Oxford, 1894), vol. 1, p. 18. The italics are Locke's.

5. Ibid., bk. 2, chap. 28, section 12. My italics.

6. Montaigne, *Essays,* bk. 3, chap. 8.

7. *The Works of Sir William Temple: A New Edition* (London, 1814), vol. 1, pp. 6–7.

8. Ibid., vol. 3, p. 39.

9. Ibid., p. 44.

10. Rousseau regarded public opinion as "the standard of free society," but as questionable from a "transpolitical point of view." See Leo Strauss, "On the Intention of Rousseau," *Social Research* 14 (December 1947):473.

11. J. Necker, *A Treatise on the Administration of the Finances of France,* 3rd ed. (London, 1787), vol. 1, p. 17. The two best expositions of the treatment of "opinion" and "public opinion" by political theorists are Paul A. Palmer, "The Concept of Public Opinion in Political Theory" in *Essays in History and Political Theory in Honor of Charles H. McIlwain* (Cambridge, Mass., 1936), and Hermann Oncken, "Politik, Geschichtsschreibung und öf-

fentliche Meinung,'' in *Historisch-politische Aufsätze und Reden* (Berlin and Munich, 1914), vol. 1, pp. 203–244. See also Wilhem Hennis, ''Zum Begriff der öffentlichen Meinung,'' in *Politik als praktische Wissenschaft* (Munich, 1968), pp. 36–48.

12. Cited from Soulavie's *Mémoires historiques* in Ferdinand Tönnies, *Kritik der öffentlichen Meinung* (Berlin, 1922), p. 385.

13. Thomas Paine, *Rights of Men,* Modern Library ed., p. 141.

14. Lord Acton, ''The Background of the French Revolution,'' reprinted in *Essays on Freedom and Power,* ed. Gertrude Himmelfarb (Boston, 1948), p. 267.

15. Gaston Jèze, ''Public Debt,'' in *Encyclopaedia of the Social Sciences,* vol. 12, p. 602. Cf. Thomas Paine's remark: ''The French nation, in effect, endeavored to render the late government insolvent for the purpose of taking government into its own hands: and it reversed its means for the support of the new government.'' Paine, p. 175.

16. Necker, p. 54.

17. Ibid., p. 73.

18. August Wilhelm Rehberg, *Über die Staatsverwaltung deutscher Länder* (Hanover, 1809), p. 58.

19. Sören Kierkegaard, *Die Tagebücher,* selected and translated by Theodor Haecker (Innsbruck, 1923), vol. 2, p. 340.

20. See Charlotte E. Morgan, *The Rise of the English Novel of Manners* (New York, 1911); Leo Lowenthal, *Literature, Popular Culture and Society* (Englewood Cliffs, N.J., 1961); Martin Greiner, *Die Entstehung der modernen Unterhaltungsliteratur: Studien zum Trivialroman des 18. Jahrhunderts* (Hamburg, 1964).

21. Walter Götze, *Die Begründung der Volksbildung in der Aufklärungsbewegung* (Berlin and Leipzig, 1932), p. 64.

22. On the history of coffeehouses in England, see E. F. Robinson, *The Early History of Coffee Houses in England* (London, 1893); Ralph Nevill, *London Clubs: Their History and Treasures* (London, 1911); Hermann Westerfrölke, *Englische Kaffeehäuser als Sammelpunkte der literarischen Welt im Zeitalter von Dryden und Addison* (Jena, 1924).

23. See Helen Clergue, *The Salon: A Story of French Society and Personalities in the Eighteenth Century* (New York and London, 1907); Erich Auerbach, *Das französische Publikum des XVII. Jahrhunderts* (Munich, 1933); Chauncey B. Tinker, *The Salon and English Letters* (New York, 1915); Conférences du Musée Carnavalet, *Les grands salons littéraires* (Paris, 1928).

24. Jean d'Alembert, *Miscellaneous Pieces in Literature, History and Philosophy* (London, 1764), p. 149.

25. As Aulard has pointed out, ''It was by the political song, sung in the theatre, in the cafés and in the street, that the Royalists and Republicans succeeded, principally at Paris, in influencing the people,'' during the French Revolution. Quoted by Cornwall B. Rogers, *The Spirit of Revolution in 1789*

(Princeton, N.J., 1949), p. 26. This book is a monographic study of the propagandistic importance of oral communication, especially lyrics, during the French Revolution.

26. Quoted by Howard Robinson, *The British Post Office* (Princeton, 1948), p. 302.

27. In chapter 13, Thomasius discussed the origin of error, distinguishing between the "prejudice of human authority" and "the prejudice of precipitation." See the reprint of this chapter as well as the equally relevant chap. 1 of Thomasius' *Ausübung der Sittenlehre* (1696), in F. Brüggemann, ed., *Aus der Frühzeit der deutschen Aufklärung,* Deutsche Literatur, Sammlung literarischer Kunst- und Kulturdenkmäler, Reihe Aufklärung, vol. 1 (Berlin and Leipzig, 1928). For the relation between prejudice and the demand for enlightening education, cf. especially Thomas Hobbes, *Elements of Law,* ed. Ferdinand Tönnies (London, 1889): "The immediate cause . . . of indocibility is prejudice; and of prejudice, false opinion of our own knowledge" (I, 10, section 8), and *Leviathan,* chaps. 13 and 15.

28. Götze, p. 20.

29. For a convenient summary of Condorcet's views on education contained in his "Report on Education," presented to the Legislative Assembly on 20–21 April 1792, see Salwyn Schapiro, *Condorcet* (New York, 1934), chap. 11, pp. 196–214. On the educational views of leading writers in the eighteenth century, see F. de la Fontainerie, ed., *French Liberalism and Education in the Eighteenth Century* (New York, 1932).

30. Sieyès, *The Third Estate,* chap. 6.

31. According to Alexis de Tocqueville, the Revolution "a considéré le citoyen d'une façon abstraite, en dehors de toutes les sociétés particulières, de même que les réligions considèrent l'homme en général indépendamment du pays et du temps." *L'Ancien Régime et la Révolution,* 8th ed. (Paris, 1877), p. 18.

32. Albert Mathiez, *The French Revolution* (New York, 1928), p. 217.

33. Corneliu S. Blaga, *L'Évolution de la technique diplomatique au dix-huitième siècle* (Paris, 1937), p. 421.

34. Edmund Burke, "Thoughts on French Affairs," in *Reflections on the French Revolution and Other Essays,* Everyman's Library ed., p. 289.

35. Quoted in Shelby C. Davis, *The French War Machine,* p. 100.

36. Max Lehmann, *Scharnhorst* (Leipzig, 1886), vol. 1, p. 323.

37. Hans Delbrück, *Geschichte der Kriegskunst* (Berlin, 1920), vol. 4, p. 469.

38. Ibid., p. 461.

39. Ibid., p. 479.

40. Quoted in W. Allison Hillet and Arthur H. Reede, *Neutrality,* vol. 2: *The Napoleonic Period* (New York, 1936), p. 8.

41. *British Historical and Political Orations from the 12th to the 20th Century,* Everyman's Library ed., pp. 146–148.

42. Nicolson, p. 73.

43. Bismarck, *Memoirs,* vol. 3, p. 157.

44. The Benthamites did not share the belief in natural rights. Bentham had deplored the Declaration of Rights in France because he regarded them as metaphysical and did not believe that political science was far enough advanced for such declarations. Cf. A. V. Dicey, *Law and Opinion in England* (New York, 1930), p. 145, n. 1.

45. Lord Bryce, *The American Commonwealth* (New York, 1919), vol. 2, p. 260.

46. Ibid., p. 257.

47. Thus Bluntschli in his *Staatswörterbuch* (1862), said of public opinion that ''it is predominantly the opinion of the large middle class.'' This notion was predicated upon the conviction that public opinion was a matter of free judgment. ''Without training of the reasoning power and the capacity to judge there is, therefore, no public opinion.'' For the same reason, Bluntschli observed that public opinion is possible in political matters but alien to religious piety *(Ergriffenheit).* Cf. Oncken, pp. 229ff.

48. Alexis de Tocqueville, *Democracy in America* (New York, 1948), vol. 2, pp. 11–12.

49. Kierkegaard in 1849; cf. Kierkegaard, vol. 2, p. 37.

6

MILLENARIANISM AS A REVOLUTIONARY FORCE

GUENTER LEWY

The phenomenon of revolution is not new. The term *revolution* itself, borrowed from astronomy, has been in use only in modern times, but the occurrence of basic political change, the introduction of a new political order, is as old as written history and probably older. Aristotle discussed at length the causes of sedition *(stasis),* including the desire to bring the existing order in line with a different conception of justice, and he distinguished between what today we call rebellion—the endeavor of a seditious party "to get the administration into the hands of its members" while continuing "to maintain the system of government"—and revolution—sedition "directed against the existing constitution" with the intent "to change its nature."[1] Numerous premodern revolutionary movements have sought radical change in this sense of the term.

The fact that many ancient visions of a new and better society involved a return to a Golden Age of the past does not in our view establish the unrevolutionary nature of these dreams. They must be judged against the existing situation, Lawrence Stone has correctly insisted, and then "it makes no difference whatever whether the idealized Golden Age is in the past or in the future. All that matters is the degree to which the vision differs from the reality of the present."[2] Moreover, many of these conceptions of a perfect age to come involved a radical break with the past and conjured up a vision of something entirely new. The militant Jewish apocalyptics battling Roman overlordship of the first Christian century, for example, looked forward to a new condition of the world, a messianic age of bliss, that did not repeat anything that had ever been and involved something totally new. Likewise, the "new heaven and new earth" predicted by the author of the Christian Book of Revelation represented a dream of radical renewal, one that continued to have a powerful appeal to the downtrodden and underprivileged all through the medieval period. To deny mass movements such as the Bohemian Taborites of the fifteenth century, for example, the epithet "revolutionary" would appear to fly in the face of common sense, and if today we call many of these upheavals rebellions rather than revolutions, this is due not so much to the alleged restricted scope of their goals and programs but rather to the fact that they were defeated and failed. Similar revolutionary mass movements, inspired by eschatological religious visions, can be found in other major and minor religions of the world.[3]

In the discussion that follows we seek to elucidate the characteristics and causes of revolutionary millenarianism—social movements in which religion has played the role of a revolutionary ideology inspiring or at least legitimizing political revolt. Among the main characteristics of these revolutionary movements indeed have been their ambitious and wide-ranging goals; they sought not merely the redress of grievances or a new set of political and social institutions but expected and strove to achieve an age of eternal happiness, the end of human travail once and for all. We consider these movements to be a part or subdivision of the larger category *millenarianism,* or chiliasm, a term which, following the increasingly accepted usage of anthropologists and sociologists, we employ not in its literal and strictly historical sense, referring to the Kindom of God of one thousand years duration in the Judaic-Christian tradition (the Latin word *millennium* and the Greek equivalent *chilias* mean a thousand years), but rather use figuratively and typologically.

The phenomenon of revolutionary millenarianism casts light on and illustrates the manifold ways of symbolic mobilization for revolutionary action. The fact that the modern communication media greatly facilitate the recruitment of large masses of people for active political involvement is, of course, undisputed. But the ability of many revolutionary millenarian movements to mobilize vast numbers of men for a radical attack upon the existing political and social order shows that reliance upon the modern media is not the only way of accomplishing this end. Spellbinding oratory, the working of "miracles," collective prayer, religious prophecy, made in face-to-face contact as well as with the help of sacred texts, are some of the means that millenarian leaders have utilized to create in the popular consciousness a powerful demand for revolutionary change and develop a spirit of heroic fervor for a struggle that would end all struggles.

CHARACTERISTICS

Revolutionary millenarianism, summarily described, involves religiously inspired mass movements that seek imminent, total, ultimate, this-worldly collective salvation, to be achieved through human action but with the help of a supernatural or superhuman agency.[4] The salvation sought is imminent for it is to come soon if not immediately; it is total for it will radically and completely transform human life and usher in perfection itself; it is ultimate for it will bring the last and final redemption; it is this-worldly for it is to be realized here on earth rather than in some otherworldly heaven; it is collective for it is to redeem not just chosen individuals but an organized group of faithful if not humanity itself. Lastly, this terrestrial salvation will come to pass as a result of human desire or effort but will also require intervention by supernatural or superhuman forces.

Certain mass movements of modern times, such as revolutionary Marxism and Bolshevism, share many of the characteristics of revolutionary millenarianism and they, therefore, have often been called secular religions or movements of secularized millenarianism. However, there is one all-important difference. Missing from these political movements with millenarian overtones is the supernatural element; the Marxist conception of history involves determinism, but, despite certain metaphysical qualities, it rests ultimately on a rationalistic conception of human nature and the worth of human action. Revolutionary millenarianism must also be distinguished from Christian millenarian sects like the various branches of the Adventist movement or Jehovah's Witnesses. These religious bodies believe in the early second coming of Christ and the establishment of a millenarian kingdom on earth, but this expectation for them is a matter of passive waiting and does not lead to specific actions.[5] They are religious sects but not social movements, they view human society as corrupt and evil but do not actively seek to change the social or political order. The seventeenth-century Jewish Sabbatean movement, too, was nonpolitical and nonrevolutionary. Sometimes a millenarian movement begins as essentially quietistic and nonpolitical and later becomes radicalized. The opposite path of development, that is, deradicalization, can also be observed. We will return to this pattern of change, often involving rather fluid dividing lines, below.

Apart from these basic features—the search for imminent, total, ultimate, this-worldly, collective salvation requiring both human action and supernatural intervention—the goals and characteristics of revolutionary millenarian movements exhibit much diversity that reflects their anchorage in different cultural settings. They all look forward to a radically new and perfect age to come, but their vision of this future age of eternal happiness includes varying amounts of traditional ideas. Different answers are given to such questions as how soon the perfect age will begin, what will be the correct "mix" between human action and divine intervention necessary for the onset of the millennium, whether violence is admissible to bring it about, what role will be played by prophets or messianic figures. We will next look at some of these different manifestations of millenarianism as well as at certain recurring themes and traits that transcend specific cultural and historic conditions.

Charismatic Leadership

Leadership in millenarian movements in practically all cases is of the charismatic type. The authority of the charismatic leader, as Max Weber explained in his well-known elucidation of the term, is accepted because of his followers' "belief in the extraordinary quality of the specific *person.*"[6] On account of the way in which the leader's personality is perceived and valued by his followers, this person "is set apart from ordinary men and treated as endowed with supernatural, superhuman, or at least specifically exceptional powers or qualities. These are such as are not accessible to the ordinary person, but are regarded as of divine origin or as exemplary, and on the basis of them the individual concerned is treated as a leader."[7]

Given the radical aims of revolutionary millenarian movements, which seek a complete change in the organization of society, and in view of the intense and total commitment required of their members, it is, of course, not surprising that these social movements will have charismatic leaders. The receptivity of most people to what is wholly new is limited; for an extraordinary action men must have extraordinary justification. Hence in a milieu dominated by religion—the typical setting of millenarianism—the mobilization for drastically new goals will require supernatural sanction, and the charismatic leader provides just that. He is the link between God (or the gods or spirits) and man, he provides the legitimation for the radical attack upon the existing order, his mandate reassures his followers and enables him to pronounce: "It is written—but I say unto you . . ."

The messianic stature of Jesus of Nazareth and his prophecy of the coming of the kingdom of God are shrouded in ambivalence, but most leaders of millenarian movements have made unambiguous messianic claims. The head of the Jewish revolt against Rome in the second century of the Christian era, Bar Kochba; numerous Chinese rebels appearing as Maitreya, the returned Buddha; the king of the Anabaptist saints in Münster, John of Leyden; the Sudanese Mahdi as well as the Heavenly King of the Taiping Rebellion in the nineteenth century— these and many other millenarian leaders acted as human-divine saviors of their people or of God's elect. In some instances as in the case of the black messiah André Matswa in the French Congo, the messianic title was bestowed upon the leader posthumously, whereas other millenarian movements have prophets acting as precursors of the messiah or messiahs (as in the Melanesian cargo cults where the spirits of the dead ancestors often function as multiple messiahs). The figure of the leader of the movement and the figure of the messiah may be entirely distinct, and in a few cases messiahs play no role whatever. In some of the cargo cults, Japanese or American soldiers were the agents of liberation and even mechanical devices like flying saucers can be expected to trigger the age of bliss. Although the great majority of millenarian movements are also messianic movements, there thus is no necessary connection between the two.[8]

The leader of the millenarian movement need not be a messianic figure, but he practically always enjoys the aura of charisma. This charismatic leadership can take many different forms. In the case of Jewish, Christian, Islamic, or Buddhist messiahs or God-ordained redeemers, the supernatural mandate, focused upon one person, is most pronounced and so is the element of charisma. In primitive societies a similar role is played by ancestor spirits or culture heroes who are expected to return and usher in an age of plenty. All of these messianic types are outstanding figures with great achievements or special gifts. On the other hand, some leaders are not particularly distinguished individuals. "In some regions," notes Yonina Talmon, "millenarianism is an endemic force, and when it reaches a flash-point it may seize upon any available figure. The initiative in such cases comes primarily from believers who sometimes almost impose the leadership position on their leader. Some of the leaders are in fact pale and insignificant. Their elevation to such a position seems to be accidental—they happen to be there and fulfill the urgent need for a prophet."[9] This pattern of charisma being bestowed rather than emerging as a result of self-selection confirmed by a following is especially frequent in the Melanesian cargo cults. Another difference between messianic figures and prophets can be seen in the fact that whereas the messiah usually is a mediator between the human and the divine, with close kinship ties to the deity, the prophet announces the good tidings by virtue of a mission he claims to have received from God or the gods.[10] He himself remains a mere human.

Whether a messianic figure or prophet, the charismatic leader of a revolutionary millenarian movement offers the vision of a new society and leads his followers toward this goal. Social psychologists and sociologists studying the phenomenon of leadership have been unable to find personality traits common to all leaders, and instead, taking a "situational" approach, they see the leader as one who fits the needs of a particular group in a specific situation.[11] Charismatic leadership, in particular, depends upon the attitudes and perceptions of followers, and since these will be different in different societies (and in the same society at different times) it should follow that there can be no universal charismatic types.[12] Still, it appears possible to note certain characteristics that commonly help establish a charismatic relationship. The charismatic leader very often is a person with a high energy level and considerable vitality, he exhibits coolness in the face of danger or crisis, he has fanatical faith in his cause, and he is able to evoke devotion, enthusiasm, and self-sacrifice from his followers. The charismatic leader also usually is an effective orator and his charismatic appeal often is further enhanced by the dramatic solution of a major crisis or by the performance of miraculous acts like healing the sick. As part of their personal magnetism many charismatic leaders are credited with extraordinary eyes.[13]

The charismatic leader of a revolutionary millenarian movement proposes to transform his society, he looks toward the future. Yet to find a following he must also communicate a sense of continuity between himself and the values, myths, and heroes of the past. His message must be appropriate to the social climate in which he operates and his acceptance as a charismatic leader depends decisively upon the reactions of his would-be followers. In other words, as Max Weber repeatedly emphasized, a leader's charisma is anchored in and validated by the perceptions of the people he leads. It is not so much what a leader is but how he is regarded by those subject to his authority that is decisive for the existence and strength of his charisma.[14] For a charismatic relationship to develop, the leader's personality and actions must be recognized and valued by his followers. Once such a charismatic appeal has been established even failure and death will not easily shake the believers' faith in their prophet. Indeed, martyrdom often serves to enhance charisma. The African prophets Simon Kimbangu and André Matswa, for example, became more rather than less popular as a result of their imprisonment and death.

CONCEPTIONS OF TIME, HISTORY, AND CONFLICT

Revolutionary millenarian movements look forward to a radically new social order on earth that will represent the consummation of history. They seek not an amelioration of the human condition but an end to history as such. Humanity will be freed from pain and unhappiness and an age of eternal bliss will set in. In many cases it is believed that such a redemption will be preceded by a great catastrophe. The world as we know it will be destroyed before the new and perfect order can begin. Even if this apocalyptic view does not include an eschatological event of cosmic proportions, there often prevails the belief that the time just before the moment of redemption will be one of special stress and great suffering. God's people, the Jewish Book of Daniel prophesied, will be delivered at the moment of greatest need, and similar expectations of "messianic woes"—unprecedented upheavals and calamities as signs of the beginning of the end—can be found in other millenarian movements. Seen psychologically, as Mühlmann notes, the situation is, of course, exactly reversed. Because the present is felt to be a time of terrible and unbearable afflictions, millenarianism creates the escapist view of a terrestrial state of perfection to come. The conception of the messianic woes reflects a feeling of extreme alienation from life as it is and the need to escape from history.[15]

Salvation on earth, the millenarians believe, cannot come to pass without divine intervention. Yet, in practically all cases we also find a definite commitment to human action. The believers must employ certain measures such as prayer and cleansing to ensure their prepared condition for the great event, and, more importantly, they must act to hasten the moment of redemption. Indeed, the main difference between millenarian sects and revolutionary millenarian movements is precisely the latter's resolve to engage in revolutionary activity against the powers that be, to help end the present state of corruption. Imbued with the conviction that the end of human travail is near and that the elect are working in accordance with the divine plan of redemption, these millenarian groups create a spirit of heroic action and extreme dedication. Their followers pit themselves against the forces of evil and in one final and catastrophic struggle expect to usher in the new and yet timeless age of perfection. Such an ideology of holy and total war can be observed in the Jewish Zealots' fight against Rome, among the Bohemian Taborites, in the German peasants' uprising led by Thomas Müntzer, among the radical Anabaptists, the Fifth Monarchy Men in the Puritan Revolution, the Taipings in nineteenth-century China, the Sudanese Mahdia, and in some of the Melanesian cargo cults and African messianic movements.

Conflict with the surrounding world often is the result of the very essence of the millenarian movement. The unwillingness to participate in ordinary human affairs and the rejection of earthly authority many times provoke rulers into a violent reaction; at times a pattern of hostility is thus created without any deliberate plan on the part of the millenarians. In other cases, the willingness to use violence to bring about the age of nonviolence and peace is there from the very beginning. Whether a millenarian movement will be reluctantly violent or violent by design appears to depend on the religious and cultural setting in which it develops, on the chances for victory in a violent conflict, and on the nature of the leadership—all factors to which we will return at a later point in our discussion.

Millenarian groups consider themselves a religious elite, they often compensate for their lowly status in this world by the claim of being God's elect who can do no wrong. This elitism and the accompanying sense of mission account in good measure for the ruthlessness and brutality of millenarian revolts. The enthusiasm that characterizes these groups, the spirit of total dedication to a cause of overriding importance, the conviction of doing God's will, often cause a dehumanization of the opponent, who is conceived as all-evil and all-depraved. The Taipings called their enemies outright demons. Originally noble impulses thus often get transformed into a reality of hatred and violence.[16]

The same logic of religious enthusiasm also explains the frequent occurrence of internal strife. The bitter factional disputes among the defenders of Jerusalem in the Jewish war against Rome, for example, can be traced in part to the desire of men engaged in a holy war to institute a reign of virtue and meticulously to obey God's will—the indispensable condition of divine intervention that would lead to the rout of God's enemies. As mere humans usually develop different readings of God's will, the insistence of the true believer on divine inspiration and ideological unity almost necessarily leads to splits and conflicts among the leadership. The charismatic leader cannot tolerate diversity; any divergence from his view of truth is heresy that must be extirpated. The attraction that millenarian movements, engaged in rebellion against authority, probably hold for non-conformist and contentious people may further deepen the tendency of such groups for fissions.[17]

Millenarianism is future-oriented and often is accompanied by a breaking of traditional norms, taboos, and religious symbols. This iconoclasm sometimes is a result of the conscious desire to emphasize the distinctiveness of the millenarian group. The Taipings, for example, destroyed Taoist, Buddhist, and Confucian temples and statues in part to establish the radically new character of their religion. The wish to break completely with the past also can lead to the ritualized violation of old taboos, especially sexual conventions. In this way a new morality is asserted, the members of the group are bound together in common guilt, and internal cohesion and solidarity are strengthened. In Melanesia and South Africa, it would appear, millenarians sought to prove to themselves and to the spirits complete confidence in their charismatic leaders and in the imminence of redemption, and they therefore engaged in the wholesale destruction of pigs, cows, crops, and other treasured material objects. In the siege of Jerusalem by the Romans in the Great Jewish War the defenders may have burnt the granaries for the same reason—to demonstrate their complete trust in God and in his imminent saving intervention.

Some millenarian movements are characterized by highly emotional displays of trances, mass possessions, and motor phenomena such as shaking, twitching, and convulsions. These phenomena are especially widespread in Africa and among the Melanesian cargo cults where they may be tied to prevailing mores. The same connection probably was at work in the resort to sorcery by some of the Hakka leaders of the Taiping Rebellion. On the other hand, more general factors also may account for these outbursts of emotional fervor. Hysterical phenomena can be caused by strong feelings of deprivation, frustration, and strain for which certain kinds of motor behavior may provide relief. Also, as noted by H. Richard Niebuhr, emotional fervor is a common mark of the religion of the untutored and less privileged. "Where the power of abstract thought has not been highly developed and where inhibitions on emotional expression have not been set up by a system of polite conventions, religion must and will express itself in emotional terms."[18] The informality and spontaneity of religious expression also may enable the faithful to obtain a foretaste of the complete liberation that is vouchsafed them in the millenarian era.[19]

Despite the pronounced forward-looking tendency of millenarian movements, their vision of the future usually contains traditional elements. Indeed, as Yonina Talmon has emphasized, "it is precisely this combination of a radical revolutionary position with traditionalism which accounts for the widespread appeal of these movements."[20] Thus, for example, much of the attraction of the Taiping Rebellion can be traced to its promise of an imminent heavenly kingdom of peace, a concept that adroitly combined traditional and innovative goals. The emphasis on restoring a former alleged condition of bliss is usually strongest in the case of cultural disruption, as when people subjected to the foreign customs of a colonial power seek to revive certain features of their traditional culture. Anthropologists call such movements "restorative" or "nativistic".[21] Basically, however, all millenarian movements partake of both restorative and innovative elements, they are past- and future-oriented at the same time.

CAUSES

Fundamentally, millenarian movements simply express man's dissatisfaction with the human condition, the yearning for a happier existence than life on earth makes possible. As no society throughout history has been able to provide a life free of hardships and sorrows, it is hardly surprising that the dream of escaping history and reaching an age of perfection, a land without evil, or regaining the lost paradise, has been so widespread among men at almost all times.

And yet, universal as are the difficulties of human life, millenarianism has not been the only response of man to adversity. Whole societies have suffered dumbly, others have sought to change their lot by means of reform or political or social revolution. The question, therefore, arises, what specifically causes the millenarian variant of revolutionary movements? Why do some people at certain times engage in the pursuit of the millenarian dream, the search for total and ultimate redemption on earth? We suggest that such millenarian movements develop (1) in situations of distress or disorientation, the roots of which are not clearly perceived or appear immune to ordinary and available remedies, (2) when a society or group is deeply attached to religious ways of thinking about the world and when the religion of that society attaches importance to millenarian ideas, (3) when a man or men obsessed with salvationist fantasies succeed in establishing their charismatic leadership over a social movement.

It should be borne in mind that these causes must be present together, and indeed they usually are interrelated. The causative factor "distress," for example, as we will see in more detail soon, does not represent an objective fact, corresponding to a specific empirical reality, but depends very decisively on how individuals or groups of men *perceive* reality. Leaders, and especially charismatic ones, through their teachings often cause in their followers a strong sense of dissatisfaction and deprivation that may not develop otherwise. Conversely, a certain kind of person will be accepted as charismatic leader only in very specific situations of stress. Many religious ideas, too, have ambiguous meanings and will be interpreted differently at different times and places, depending on the social setting of the moment and the political leanings of believers and leaders. The Christian idea of the "Kingdom of God" or the Confucian "Mandate of Heaven" are obvious cases in point. Lastly, there remains the element of historical accident that further complicates any causal analysis. If Hung Hsiu-ch'üan had passed his examinations or if Oliver Cromwell had followed his inclination in the early 1630s to emigrate to America, the course of two revolutionary millenarian movements might have taken a completely different route or they might never even have begun. The most that we are able to say, therefore, is that in certain situations and given the appearance of certain ideas and men, the emergence of revolutionary millenarianism is a likely occurrence.

Distress, Deprivation, and Disorientation
Dissatisfaction with the prevailing social, economic, religious, or political order strong enough to drive people into revolutionary action can be caused by factors external or internal to the society in question. Resentment following the loss of national independence to a foreign conqueror is an example of such

externally caused distress; severe hardships resulting from a natural catastrophe or from oppression by a native ruling class are internally caused. In either case the longing for millenarian delivery can develop when the sense of distress is very acute and ordinary remedies seem unavailable.

Subjection to a foreign power will be felt as especially humiliating when the people who have lost their independence considered themselves as divinely favored or when a dethroned ruler also functioned as head of the native religion. The ancient Israelites saw themselves as God's chosen people who had been vouchsafed victory over all of their enemies through a special covenant. The destruction of the first temple and the loss of independence successively to the Persians, Syrians, and Romans therefore were regarded as particularly devastating blows for which the Jews were ill-prepared and which they considered preludes to the inevitable appearance of the messianic deliverer who would make good God's promises of redemption. Similarly, following the British conquest of Burma in 1885–1886, the Buddhist people of this subjugated country lost not only their native king but the traditional head and protector of their religion as well. The resultant sense of bitterness and distress eventually exploded in the millenarian Saya San rebellion of 1930–1931 that promised the liberation of Burma from the heathen English and the inauguration of a Golden Age under an ideal Buddhist ruler.

A millenarian response to foreign rule is also likely when the alien power seeks to suppress or seriously interfere with the religion of the colonized people. The decrees of the Roman emperor Hadrian forbidding the practice of circumcision, the recitation at public services of the most important Jewish prayer, the Shema, and the decision in the year A.D. 130 to erect a pagan temple in the holy city of Jerusalem probably were the precipitating causes of the messianic rebellion against Roman rule led by Bar Kochba. In the nineteenth-century Sudan, the Mahdi's cause profited not only from the attempts of the Egyptian rulers to stamp out the economically profitable slave trade but also from their insistence on promoting a more orthodox form of Islam. In twentieth-century Africa, too, the emergence of revolutionary millenarian movements has been encouraged by the simultaneous occurrence of political, cultural, and religious

distress. African messianism has arisen in a setting of colonial
rule, racial discrimination, and forced acculturation that has in-
terfered with political and social as well as religious aspirations.
Millenarianism there at times has functioned as a kind of
"sacred nationalism," a struggle against the inferiority imposed by both colonial administrators and missionaries.

Endogenously caused distress leading to revolutionary millenarianism also has been frequent. In late medieval Europe such
movements arose in areas of swift social change where trade and
industry were developing, where the population was increasing
rapidly and traditional group ties were being disrupted. Norman Cohn points out:

> Revolutionary millenarianism drew its strength from a population
> living on the margin of society—peasants without land or with too
> little land even for subsistence; journeymen and unskilled workers
> living under the continuous threat of unemployment; beggars and
> vagabonds—in fact from the amorphous mass of people who were
> not simply poor but who could find no assured and recognized
> place in society at all. These people lacked the material and emo-
> tional support afforded by traditional social groups; their kinship-
> groups had disintegrated and they were not effectively organized in
> village communities or in guilds; for them there existed no regular,
> institutionalized methods of voicing their grievances or pressing
> their claims. [22]

For such groups of oppressed and disinherited, the idea of
Christ's return to earth to establish a reign of perfect justice and
well-being had an obvious appeal. The precipitating events for
such outbursts often were plagues, long droughts, devastating
fires, and similar calamities that drastically aggravated a situation of endemic deprivation. [23]

Economic and social distress, it should be added, are not the
only sources of millenarian fantasy. During the age of the
Reformation the spirit of religious renewal, excitement, and
biblicism, combined with the suffering of the early reformed
believers, produced a climate of widespread eschatological expectations in which hope for the second coming of Christ was
strong. Many of the Anabaptists, in particular, severely persecuted by both Catholics and Protestants, interpreted their suf-

fering in apocalyptic terms as the messianic woes, and as a prelude to the day of reckoning when they would overthrow the godless and help establish the kingdom of God on earth. For these radical sectarians both the papacy, which Luther himself had called the Antichrist, and the major reformers had lost all spiritual authority and legitimacy; the search for more immediate and authentic methods of redemption than the hierarchical churches were able to offer eventually led them into the path of revolutionary millenarianism. Resentment of the worldliness of the clergy and doubt about the ability of ostentatiously living prelates to help man to attain salvation had had a similar effect in medieval times. Religious deprivation, too, thus can be a cause of millenarian revolt, and its impact will be especially strong when it becomes combined with other sources of distress. The fact that the economic situation in Holland and northwest Germany during the early 1530s had been very bad facilitated the rise of the millenarian prophet John Matthys of Amsterdam and helped him establish the New Jerusalem at Münster.

A subjective awareness of distress shared by a group or society is crucial in all these different types of severe dissatisfaction. As students of mass movements have recognized for some time, it is not so much the severity of deprivation that provides the motive force for revolutionary outbursts as the discrepancy between legitimate expectations and the means of their satisfaction, a subjective state known as "relative deprivation." Such a discrepancy can be created either by a drastic worsening of conditions or by new and expanded horizons or a combination of both.[24] Thus revolutionary millenarianism in medieval Europe developed during a time of rapid social change when poverty and hardships were no longer taken for granted, when new wants had been created amid a widening gap between rich and poor. A militant Jewish messianism, as we have noted above, emerged as a result of severely disappointed hope, the contrast between the promises made by God to his chosen people, and the harsh reality of foreign rule and oppression. In the colonized countries of Asia and Africa, too, relative deprivation held the explanatory key to anti-European agitation. Since the time of World War I, in particular, people under colonial rule had become increasingly aware of the economic and social gap between their own underdeveloped condition and that of their European colonizers. The resultant spirit of severe resentment, when more direct political remedies were out of reach, led to millenarian agitation. The fact that frustrated expectations rather than actual suffering cause such movements of protest can be seen from the example of the cargo cults in the east-central highlands of New Guinea. Here the white man had not yet even entered the secluded habitat of these aboriginals and their material or social condition had not changed at all when, as a result of hearsay, they developed an intense desire for the goods of the white man. Such changed expectations and the acute frustration that followed the inability to satisfy these new wants eventually led to the emergence of a cargo cult.[25]

The development of new expectations that have remained unfulfilled also has been an important factor in the rise of African messianic movements. As a result of reading the Bible, which had been translated into their own languages, and exposure to the biblical ideas of equality, justice, and fairness, African Christian converts began to perceive the discrepancy between biblical Christianity and the discriminatory and patronizing ways of the European missionaries and colonial rulers. These religious writings and the prophetic strain contained in them thrust into the popular consciousness a powerful revolutionary dynamic; they created a strong sense of religious and eventually political deprivation that helped generate revolutionary millenarian movements.

In many cases of millenarian agitation it is not so much economic deprivation on the part of the lower classes in a stratified society as the experience by an entire colonized people of disorientation and anomie that causes such movements. The impact of a powerful and totally different culture, the transition from a relatively stable village community to the fast-changing and impersonal ways of urban life—all these different aspects of the modernization process can have a highly unsettling effect and create considerable anxiety and existential dread. In this situation, a crisis comparable to the identity crisis of the individual may occur in an entire community,[26] and a new religious cult may arise that seeks to allay these anxieties and create a secure sense of identity. The emergence of several thousand separatist churches in twentieth-century Africa can be traced in part to this function, and many of these independent churches have developed into revolutionary millenarian movements.

Distress, deprivation, and disorientation can create precondi-

tions for revolutionary unrest, but it will take the form of millenarianism only in a certain cultural and religious context. An
examination of the nature of this religious setting is our next
task.

Millenarian Beliefs

Revolutionary millenarian movements have arisen only in countries or among groups in which religion determines and domi-
nates the total world outlook. In such a milieu any challenge to
the prevailing value system has to be couched in religious
language, and leadership tends to be of the charismatic type.
This was the situation in medieval Europe and has been the case
in many of the developing nations where education has had only limited reach and the nature of the problems confronting
these societies often is not clearly perceived. In most countries
of Europe and America, on the other hand, intellectual modernization, beginning with the skeptical mentality and the
scientific discoveries of the sixteenth and seventeenth centuries,
has created a situation in which traditional religious ideas no
longer permeate the ethos of society. Social problems now can
be and are attacked frontally, and revolutionary movements follow a more secular model, emphasizing political action rather
than reliance upon supernatural assistance. In such a setting we
can still find millenarian sects, attracting individuals of fundamentalist religious temperament, but most of those seeking a
remedy for severe economic, political, or social distress will support secular revolutionary movements.

Messianic ideas can be found in most cultures and religions.
They were present in Egypt in the seventh century B.C. and perhaps earlier; they were also to be found in Babylon at about the
same time.[27] A strong millenarian tradition developed for the
first time in Persian Zoroastrianism, linked to the eschatological
myth of an end of the world by fire. This event, from which the
good will escape unharmed, it was believed, will bring "a new
world, free from old age, death, decomposition and corruption" and "the world shall be perfectly renewed."[28] From Per-
sia this new conception of time and history, breaking with the
view of practically all traditional societies that man's existence is
caught in an infinite repetition of cosmic cycles and promising
him an end to suffering, found its way into Judaism and from
there into Christianity and Islam. The Book of Daniel, com-

posed at the height of the Maccabean revolt about 165 B.C., is the first great apocalyptic work of Judaism and has been the prototype of all later works of eschatology. Written at a time of terrible hardships for the Jewish people suffering under Syrian rule, the Book of Daniel has most of the elements of millenarian hope—deliverance by God at the moment of greatest need, the imminent coming of an everlasting kingdom of God that will be the final stage of history, the resurrection of the dead. Many other such apocalyptic works originated during the time of Roman lordship over Palestine, and early Christianity, too, despite the ambivalent teachings of Jesus of Nazareth himself about the coming kingdom of God, had a pronounced millenarian character. The Apocalypse of John (or the Book of Revelation), probably composed during a time of severe persecution in the last two decades of the first Christian century, is the most famous Christian apocalyptic work. Its prophecy of a return of Christ to establish his messianic kingdom on earth for a thousand years, an interregnum to be followed by "a new heaven and a new earth" where there will be neither death nor pain, has had a powerful influence upon later centuries.

Both Judaism and Christianity, and later Islam, too, have a teleological conception of history, leading toward the fulfillment of God's plan and the final redemption of mankind in a state of universal happiness. Not surprisingly it has been this linear view of history that has provided the most fertile setting for a variety of millenarian traditions and movements. Revolutionary chiliasm, Norman Cohn has observed, thrives best "where history is imagined as having an inherent purpose which is preordained to be realized on earth in a single, final consummation."[29] It is more difficult to construct a millenarian belief system when the world is seen as caught in an endlessly repeated cycle of death and regeneration, and the majority of millenarian movements are indeed linked to the Judaic-Christian tradition. Because of its extensive missionary activity all over the world, Christianity, in particular, has provided the most frequent underpinning for millenarianism. Despite the fact that orthodox Christianity has repudiated the idea of a terrestrial kingdom of abundance and happiness and instead, following St. Augustine, has stressed the promise of the spiritual delivery of the individual soul in heaven, the millenarian tradition has always retained a foothold in Christianity. Indeed,

wherever Christian missionaries have gone to work, the millenarian promise of an eternal earthly paradise has had a strong
appeal for new converts.

In modern times it has been Protestantism with its tradition
of individual interpretation of scripture, and especially millenarian branches like the Seventh Day Adventists and the
Watchtower movement, that have been the most important carriers for the spread of millenarian ideas. In a few instances millenarian movements have appeared in a Catholic setting. The
sect of the Antonians in the Congo of the early eighteenth century, the Lazzaretti movement in Italy in 1870, a revival of the
medieval Joachite heresy, or the followers of the Brazilian messiah, Antonio Conselheiro, in the late nineteenth century are
cases in point.[30] But the hierarchically organized and disciplined Catholic church by and large has succeeded in discourag-
ing millenarian tendencies. A decree of the Sacred Congregation of the Holy Office issued on 21 July 1944 once again
reaffirmed the inadmissibility of teaching the millenarian doctrine of the return of Jesus Christ to preside over a visible terrestrial kingdom.[31] In Africa and Melanesia, millenarian movements, in practically all cases, have emerged out of a Protestant
climate, especially the unrestricted access to the Bible and the
prophetic message contained therein. In some cases we can even
trace the influence of specific millenarian elements. The
favorite book in the Bible of Te Va, the leader of the Hauhau
movement among the Maori people of New Zealand in 1862,
was the Book of Revelation.[32]

Although the linear conception of history of the Judaic-
Christian–Islamic tradition has been conducive to the development of millenarian ideas, the great religions of Asia—
Hinduism, Buddhism, and Taoism—have not entirely lacked
such tendencies. Hindus look forward to the reappearance of
Vishnu as Kalki, who will usher in an age of abundance; Buddhism teaches the coming of Maitreya, the future Buddha, who
will introduce a life of peace and plenty; Taoism has the notion
of a perfect ruler who will transform life on earth and guarantee
man's immortality. However, these messianic strains have not
always led to millenarian movements. In India, for example,
the millenarian myth of Kalki has aroused only feeble interest
in the popular imagination. This may have been the result of
the enormous lengths of the eternally recurring cycles of Hindu

cosmology which puts the coming of the redeemer so far away into the future as to take away all hope of relief in any humanly forseeable time. Moreover, as Hinduism knows no end of history and the coming of Kalki was believed to repeat itself at the end of each of these huge time periods, the figure of the savior lacked the unique status of the messiah in the Judaic-Christian tradition. The help offered by the Hindu redeemer is not final, he cannot create a new heaven and earth or arise above the perpetual flux of history.[33] There is no promise of an ultimate triumph of the good or the vindication of the righteous. Lastly, Hinduism's understanding of human history as part of a cyclical cosmic process, moving according to inexorable laws, that leaves little if any room for man's history-making ability;[34] the otherworldly orientation of Hinduism with its devaluation of earthly success; the absence of egalitarian ideas and the acceptance of the rigid caste system; and the fact that Hindu religion has brought forth only what Max Weber called "exemplary prophets," men who provided a model for a way of life of personal virtue[35]—seem further to have discouraged the spread of millenarian ideas.

In the case of Theravada Buddhism, prevalent in Ceylon, Burma, Indochina, and India, the cyclical conception of history with its immense stretches of time and the absence of either a beginning or an end of the world also appears to have discouraged hope for the final salvation of mankind. The Theravada, the "teaching of the elders," knows the idea of Maitreya, the future Buddha, but this messianic figure by and large has not inspired revolutionary millenarianism. His coming is not expected in the foreseeable future and even then his role is limited mainly to that of helping man to achieve spiritual liberation. The fact that kings, many of whom were anything but benefactors of their people, often claimed the title of future Buddha further weakened the concept's revolutionary significance. During the numerous armed clashes that preceded the conquest and pacification of Burma by the British in the nineteenth and early twentieth centuries the titles of universal monarch and Maitreya were claimed by rebel leaders, some of them monks, seeking to restore Buddhism to its former position of eminence. Even after the achievement of independence the coming of such a righteous king continued to be expected by what one observer has called a "messianic Buddhist association."[36] An uprising in

Thailand around the turn of the century is said to have begun
with the prophecy of the coming of a "noble righteous ruler"
with great merit who would rule the world.[37] But these appear
to be phenomena arising in special circumstances, exceptions to
the rule. Theravada Buddhism generally has not encouraged
millenarian agitation. The belief in Maitreya in Ceylon, for example, involves the the notion of a god granting favors to his
devotees rather than that of a savior,[38] and in Burma, too, the
so-called messianic associations have remained "semi- subterranean personalized cults without impact on Buddhism or on the
majority of its followers."[39]

Mahayana Buddhism, on the other hand, recognizes *bodhi-
sattvas* (literally, "beings of enlightenment"), who are believed
to have stayed in this world to help others to reach enlightenment, and some Chinese Buddhist sects worshipped these
saviors as messianic figures who would relieve suffering and provide happiness and prosperity. Often a minority religion,
Chinese Buddhism consequently has frequently played a revolutionary role. Almost from the time of the introduction of
Buddhism to China in the first century of the Christian era,
various Buddhist sects and secret societies have led millenarian
revolts of the peasantry, promising delivery from turmoil and
poverty. Various subsects of Taoism also were occasionally involved in rebellion. Messianic hope here centered on a perfect
emperor who would realize the vision of the deified Lao Tzu. In
a situation where the Confucian orthodoxy often failed to meet
both the spiritual and material needs of the Chinese people,
heterodox movements promising relief from spiritual emptiness
and everyday misery could never be completely eliminated.
Thus despite the fact that orthodox Chinese Buddhism and
Taoism have few elements conducive to messianism, unorthodox branches of both religions have often been involved in millenarian movements. The fact that, once successful, these rebel
movements restored and continued the traditional sociopolitical
order rather than introduce basic changes does not change the
revolutionary character and appeal of these heterodox sects.

Messianic, eschatological, and millenarian ideas and movements also can be found outside the major religions, in primitive societies without contact with Christianity or any other developed religious system. Many preliterate societies know the
concept of a returning hero or god. One such redeemer, known

as Mansren, who was expected to inaugurate an age of plenty and resurrect the dead, figured prominently in several native myths of New Guinea that later fused with the Western-inspired cargo cults. The case of the Guarani Indians of Amazonian Brazil is another example of a millenarian movement that apparently arose in an entirely independent fashion without cultural contact. Expecting an end of the world, these Indians engaged in periodic migrations to the sea from where they hoped to reach the "land without evil" and escape the coming cosmic catastrophe. As much as we can tell, these migrations, involving fights against hostile Indians and whites on the way, were not prompted by population pressure, famine, or war, nor by contact with the Portuguese conquerors. To escape from the Europeans the Guaranis could have moved just into the next valley in the vast underpopulated regions of the Amazonian interior. It would appear indeed that we are dealing here with a messianic movement caused entirely by religious motives, perhaps rooted in existential dread—a projection of fears of the death of the human body. That the desire to live in a pure and beautiful world may have been intensified by the shock of the Portuguese conquest cannot be ruled out though it seems clear that the idea of the "land without evil" itself predates the coming of the Europeans.[40]

Revolutionary millenarianism, we can conclude, can be motivated by a great variety of messianic beliefs. The Judaic-Christian type is undoubtedly the most widespread of these messianic ideas, but it is not the only one. It is "fatuously and absurdly ethnocentric to suppose," writes an American student of these phenomena, "that every native messiah is necessarily patterned on a European Christ. The fact is not so much that all native messiahs derive historically from the only genuine messiah, as that Christ himself is one example of a culturally very common type."[41] Certain religious belief systems more than others are conducive to the emergence of messianic ideas, but sometimes millenarian movements can develop even in the framework of a cyclical and world-renouncing cosmology.

Prophets

Social movements require leadership, but the leader is not necessarily one of the causes of such movements. In the case of revolutionary millenarianism, on the other hand, leaders usually are indeed just that. Impelled by motives that combine sincere altruism, selfish aims, religiosity, and, often, madness in uneasy coexistence, they act as causative factors and help bring a millenarian movement into being.

The leader of a revolutionary millenarian movement is the bearer of the chiliastic prophecy. Unlike the mystic, the prophet actively seeks a following for his ethical and political message;[42] he is a charismatic type whose inspiration usually derives from some special episode or experience in his life history. Sometimes the future prophet has hallucinatory and salvationist fantasies for months if not years without finding a following, without becoming the leader of a group. In other instances the prophet's personal religious experience and the birth of a movement are almost simultaneous. In either case the charismatic prophet is not a mere "reflection" of certain social processes. As Max Weber has argued forcefully, the bearer of charisma is an innovative force who often changes the course of history. There was nothing inevitable about the emergence of prophet figures like Mohammed Ahmed, the mystic leader of the Mahdia of the Sudan, or Hung Hsiu-ch'üan, the crazed heavenly king of the Taiping Rebellion. Each of these men left his special imprint upon the fate of his people. Their prophecy, even though anchored in part in the cultural heritage of their society, sprang from their own very personal religious experience, and this prophecy became a causative factor in a powerful social movement. Even where messianic expectations are rampant, as in the time of Jesus of Nazareth, the objective situation that may encourage the bestowal of charisma does not determine the nature of the prophetic message. The charismatic leader, therefore, always is an initiator, his vision creates the new ideology of a movement.[43]

The leadership role played by the charismatic prophet has been termed the catalyst of the millenarian movement, his function is "to make a latent conflict conscious, to give form to a preexisting movement, to impart direction to its energies, and to help it focus on definite ends." As in the case of immersing in a chemical solution a catalyst that will activate and actualize the elements already there, the effect of the leader is said to be determined by the situation in which he acts; "without the right substances and setting his intervention would be entirely without avail.''[44] The analogy between chemical change and a revolutionary social process stresses the dynamic interactions between certain social conditions and the role of the leader. As we have argued above, there can be no millenarian movement without the factor of perceived distress or disorientation. But the charismatic leader does not merely reflect distress or precipitate and activate ideas already in existence; he does not only champion felt needs. Although in a basic sense it is true that the leader, no matter how gifted, cannot conjure a social movement out of a void, the charismatic leader may create or increase the expectations and dissatisfactions that make for a revolutionary situation.[45]

The millenarian prophecy carried and spread by the charismatic leader often functions as such a source of revolutionary sentiments and ideas. A common pattern there is the linkup between the apocalyptic fantasies of an individual with extraordinary leadership ability and an ongoing social upheaval. The prophecy of total redemption injected by Thomas Müntzer into the German Peasant Movement, by John of Leyden into the attempts of the merchants and artisans of Münster to oppose the economic policies of their bishop-sovereign, by Hung Hsiu-ch'üan into the search of the bandit-ridden peasants of Kwangsi province for security in nineteenth-century China, transformed in each of these cases a movement of limited aims into a revolutionary attack upon the political and social order. It was the millenarian prophecy pronounced by the charismatic figure that created a revolutionary mass movement where previously there had existed only a demand for the reform of certain concrete grievances. On the strength of supernatural revelations the conflict was described as a cataclysm that would transform the world once and for all. The ideology of these revolutionary millenarian movements, as Norman Cohn speaking of European medieval examples emphasizes, ''in each case corresponded not to the objective social situation and the possibilities it offered but to the salvationist fantasies of a handful of freelance preachers; and they were accordingly boundless.''[46] That, too, of course, is one of the main reasons why all of them failed.

By pointing out the connection between overreaching aims and failure we do not want to suggest a pattern of historical inevitability. Although millenarian movements so far have always been unsuccessful in their great design—the new world of peace and perfection has eluded them—in many instances these movements have scored impressive victories and achievements and were finally defeated only at great cost. To be sure, in the process of consolidating earthly successes a millenarian movement often loses much of its apocalyptic fervor. The victorious Mahdist regime in the Sudan, for example, gradually took on the features of a traditional sultanate, and the building of a workable state by the Khalifa, the successor to the Mahdi, necessitated the abandoning of the principles of millenarian theocracy. But to the extent that a revolutionary millenarian movement thus becomes more "realistic" its chances of success grow, and it is at this point that the availability of able leadership can make the difference between victory and defeat. Thus an ambitious Chinese Buddhist monk leading a rebellion of the millenarian Maitreya sect in 1368 succeeded in deposing the Yüan and became the founder of the Ming dynasty. The movement of the Fifth Monarchy Men during the Puritan Revolution, on the other hand, was handicapped by the lack of forceful and sufficiently charismatic leaders, and their plots, therefore, probably were doomed from the very start. Even in a situation of intense millenarian excitement, as was the Puritan Revolution, the quality of leadership is still crucially important.

Do charismatic leaders emerge in certain social settings more than in others? Basically, of course, the culture of a society must sanction the kind of leader-follower relationship that is involved in the phenomenon of charismatic leadership. Several leading figures of the Taiping Rebellion were able to establish their credentials as charismatic leaders through the practice of sorcery, a commonly accepted activity among the Hakka people of southern China where the Taipings originated. Such a validation of charisma would seem out of place in an atheistic society like Communist China today or in an essentially secular society committed to rationality like the present-day United States. Some segments of the counterculture here, disillusioned with science and technology, may find solace in magic and rituals of satanism but these are obviously marginal phenomena.[47] It has also been suggested by many writers, including Max Weber, that charismatics will be the natural leaders "in times of psychic, physical, economic, ethical, religious, political distress."[48]

The fact that in such a milieu of perceived deprivation charismatic leadership is often transferred with considerable ease from one person to another—the succession of John Matthys by John Bockelson as prophet-king of the Anabaptist New Jerusalem in Münster is a good example—indicates the persistent demand for charisma in certain circumstances.[49] In stressing the importance of the charismatic milieu we must, of course, bear in mind that, as indicated above, the prophet often is himself an active agent whose revolutionary message helps crystallize the crisis that gives rise to the call for charismatic leadership. Stated succinctly: "The point to be made is that the actions of the leader may help define the situation that is stipulated as a prerequisite or precondition of his emergence."[50] The prophet not only reflects an objective situation, the world as it is, but his ambitious and challenging vision of what the world ought to be decisively shapes the environment in which he operates. There exists a pattern of dynamic interaction between leader and situation in which the message of the prophet is more than just a response to collective needs in a time of trouble. He, too, is a cause.

The finding that prophet figures are most frequent in time of crisis and disorder may also help us understand the process of religious conversion that often precedes the emergence of such a prophet. Many of the great religious prophets of mankind as well as many of the charismatic leaders of millenarian movements have been described as men suffering from various mental disorders. St. Paul, Mohammed, and most of the Jewish prophets like Hosea, Isaiah, and Jeremiah are said to have exhibited signs of psychotic behavior—visions, hallucinatory experiences, ecstatic states, and trances. The ecstasy of the preexile prophets, writes Max Weber, "was accompanied or preceded by a variety of pathological states and acts."[51] Similar behavior patterns have been reported about many of the minor prophets leading millenarian episodes. Indeed, several of these men were obviously deranged. Hung Hsiu-ch'üan, John of Leyden, Sabbatai Zevi, Mohammed Ibn 'Abd Allah (known as the mad Mullah), and Antonio Conselheiro are some of the better-known millenarian leaders about whose mental illness there can be little doubt. However, all of these men were able to function as charismatic leaders of social movements; they turned their erratic mental behavior into a special asset, and in many cases an experience of religious conversion functioned as a therapeutic process facilitating this constructive use of internal conflicts.

The great majority of reported cases of religious conversion involve adolescents.[52] For such young people, as William James observed, conversion may be a perfectly normal phenomenon, "incidental to the passage from the child's small universe to the wider intellectual and spiritual life of maturity."[53] A study of the youthful members of a Swedish revivalist church revealed that almost all of them had been brought up in religious homes and their conversion was merely "a detail in a larger socialization process."[54] On the other hand, the experience of religious conversion by adult prophet figures usually has pathological roots, it represents a way of overcoming severe mental stress, and such religious conversion is therefore often only a pseudo-solution.[55]

Mental strain can be caused by severely traumatic experiences in a person's life history. The repeated failure of Hung Hsiu-ch'üan to pass his civil service examinations is a good example of how frustrated ambition and humiliation can lead to mental disturbance. A state of serious social disorganization, interfering with the normal processes of maturation and the formation of a secure sense of personal identity, also may create mental stress. In seventeenth-century England, it has been suggested, large numbers of men became Puritan "saints" in order to escape social disorder and personal anxiety.[56] Whatever the source of personal strain, religious conversion may serve as a way of release from such severe mental tension.

Practically all reported cases of adult religious conversion are preceded by a history of suffering. "Whether it be the experience of illness, mutilation, imprisonment, or hunger, or some domestic misfortune, or moral perturbation," notes one student of this psychological phenomenon, "it is indisputable that every true conversion has suffering for its antecedent."[57] There is helplessness, anxiety, and a sense of oppression and nervousness.[58] Prior to the conversion experience many persons display symptoms of inactivity, an extreme sense of guilt and depression. The actual experience of religious conversion is usually an acute hallucinatory episode of brief duration that results in an observable change in subsequent behavior. Stress and tension are reduced if not alleviated, feelings of escape from sin, happiness, and exaltation are expressed and a new sense of identity emerges. A fresh psychic systematization, a "reintegration of the ego,"[59] has taken place as a result of which the convert is said to be "twice-born."

The precise physiological mechanisms of this dramatic therapeutic experience are not clear. The anthropologist A. F. C. Wallace has described religious conversion as "mazeway synthesis," a reorganization of the brain's codified archive of perceptions of the external world and its values. At a critical point of mazeway disorder, Wallace argues, a convulsive effort takes place to overcome the severe stress experienced, a new value system is created that is linked to the existence of supernatural beings, and internal biopsychic equilibrium is restored. As an example of such prophetic revelation and religious inspiration, Wallace uses the conversion of an Indian named Handsome Lake among the Seneca tribe of New York State in 1799 that led to the creation of a new Indian religion.[60] Needless to say, this explanation of the physiology of religious conversion remains highly speculative.

Some men who have gone through the experience of religious conversion become strong personalities and leaders, capable of inspiring enthusiasm and devotion to a cause.[61] Social support, in turn, tends to have a stabilizing impact on the personality of the prophet. The eccentricities of George Fox, the founder of Quakerism, it has been noted, became less marked as large numbers of people responded to his message.[62] For other men, however, the therapeutic value of conversion is incomplete. If ego strength is insufficient to handle the "combined unconscious and conscious conflicts," according to a psychiatrist studying the phenomenon of religious conversion, a loss of reality testing and the development of a delusional system may result.[63] Behavior may then be marked by irrational, hysterical, and destructive actions. Many of the wonder-working saviors of medieval Europe are described by Norman Cohn as such paranoid megalomaniacs who "saw themselves as incarnate gods or at least as vessels of divinity [and] really believed that through their coming all things would be made new."[64] Clinicians are well familiar with this disorder, called "reformatory or religious paranoia." Patients afflicted with this disease feel "called upon to reform society and bring about a new state of paradise on earth, or preach a new gospel.''[65] In situations of social distress such a messianic conviction can easily communicate itself to a multitude of followers. Indeed, sometimes the yearning for such deliverers is so great that crude imposters manage to pass themselves off as saviors of their people. Given our limited knowledge of human motivation and beliefs, the quest whether someone is a sincere fanatic or an imposter or a mixture of both is usually difficult to answer. That many such men, whatever their precise psychic makeup, have had a tremendous influence in history is clear.

OUTCOMES

All revolutionary millenarian movements in history so far have failed to accomplish their central objective—the attainment of heaven on earth. The millennium has not come and, as one would expect, this failure of the prophecy of redemption usually has created serious problems for such movements. Most of them have indeed been relatively short-lived. The promise of imminent and total delivery at first is a source of strength, attracting followers eager to participate in the final struggle for justice and plenty, but when setbacks set in and divine assistance fails to materialize the movement commonly fails to survive this disappointment and it disintegrates.

Millenarian movements have reacted to defeats and dashed hopes in several different ways. For some of them a cushioning effect to initial failure was provided by the concept of the ''messianic woes.'' According to this idea, first found in the Book of Daniel, God will redeem his people at the moment of greatest need and only after a prolonged period of severe suffering. It was reliance upon this prophecy that hardened the resistance of the Jews defending Jerusalem against the Romans in the Great Jewish War and inspired them to fight on ferociously until the very end of the long siege. Altogether it is probably true that the promise of total redemption and divine assistance makes people accept supreme sacrifices with great willingness and acts as a counterforce to the rational calculation of the chances of success.

In the case of some Christian millenarian sects, disconfirmation of a dated prophecy of the second coming of Christ has been followed not by an immediate dispersion of the disappointed members but instead has led to increased proselytizing. Thus the American Second Adventists or Millerites, for example, tried to resolve the cognitive dissonance induced by the failure of Jesus to appear in the year 1840, predicted for his return, by stepping up their missionary activity. Similar reactions have been reported about a more recent flying saucer cult. In the words of the investigators of this seemingly paradoxical phenomenon: "If more and more people can be persuaded that the system of belief is correct, then clearly it must, after all, be correct."[66] They add that there is a limit, however, beyond which belief cannot withstand disconfirmation. The Millerites survived several disappointments, but after another date set for the return of Christ, 22 October 1844, had proved incorrect, the sect finally collapsed. In the case of revolutionary millenarian movements the impact of disappointed hope is severely magnified by the heavy casualties that a suppressed revolt usually entails. Few of them therefore, have been able to maintain their enthusiasm for any length of time after a number of serious defeats.

A more typical response to repeated rout is the adjustment of the doctrine that originally provided the impulse for the revolutionary movement. Jewish Messianism, after three catastrophic defeats at the hands of the Romans, was transformed from a militant creed of eschatological war against pagan enemies into a doctrine of passive waiting for delivery by God, a redemption that would take place in the indefinite future and could not and should not be hurried. A similar change in doctrine can be observed in the case of Jehovah's Witnesses. After prophetic failures in 1878, 1881, and 1914, explained retrospectively as a result of the fallibility of human judgment, the sect for some years refrained from any dated prophesying of the second coming of Christ while at the same time it asserted that certain supernatural "events," constituting symbolic proof of the millenarian prophecy and not open to disconfirmation, actually had transpired. The more recently heard predictions tied to the middle of the 1970s are couched in sufficiently vague language to minimize the danger of falsification by empirical counter-evidence.[67]

The substitution of a diffuse and spongy prophecy for a specific prediction involving a precise date, time, and place repre-

sents a possible course of action for millenarian sects committed
to passive waiting for God's saving action. It probably has less
usefulness for a revolutionary millenarian movement that cannot so easily manipulate the zeal and enthusiasm of its supporters anxious to have a part in the cosmic drama. In the case
of the latter, therefore, decisive defeat usually has led to a radical change in the character and ideology of the movement. Thus
after the Taborites had finally been crushed at the battle of
Lipan in 1434, the doctrine of chiliastic total war gave way to
the preaching of nonviolence as a sacred principle. The intellectual descendants of the bloodthirsty Taborites, the Bohemian or
Moravian Brethren, were dedicated pacifists. Similarly, following the disaster of Münster the Anabaptists returned to the political quietism of the founders of the sect. Known as Menno-
nites, the Dutch Anabaptists again conceived of the coming
kingdom of God as an entirely spiritual entity. Various off-
shoots of Anabaptism survive to this day as communities of
mutual aid and brotherhood who have withdrawn from a world
they failed to convert to their ways.

Sometimes when the chance of scoring a military upset over
the oppressors appears completely unrealistic, a millenarian
movement may develop a commitment to nonviolence from the
very beginning. Thus in the late 1880s, after the end of the Indian wars, the prophets of the Ghost Dance religion among the
North American Plains Indians predicted that after a series of
disastrous earthquakes, storms, and floods a happy millennium
would follow in which the Indians would enjoy boundless prai-
ries covered with wild grass and filled with great herds of buf-
falo and other game. Most of the prophets of this rapidly
spreading cult warned against fighting and preached amity with
the white man. The battle of Wounded Knee on 29 December
1890 was the result of an unfortunate incident and certainly was
not intended by the Sioux who suffered so horribly in this
massacre.[68]

If decisive military defeat usually spells the end of a revolutionary millenarian movement, so does success. Such deradicalization caused by the acquisition of a large organizational structure, a mass constituency, and a recognized place in society is,
of course, a phenomenon well known from the experience of
various modern radical political movements,[69] as well as from
the field of religion. The histories of Zorastrianism, Christiani-

ty, Islam, and the Baha'i faith provide examples of the transformation of a millenarian creed into an institutionalized religion.[70] The natural process of the passage of time often appears to lead to changes in structure and doctrine. By its very nature, H. Richard Niebuhr has argued, the sectarian type of organization has difficulty surviving the arrival of children born to the voluntary members of the first generation. The sect must then "take on the character of an educational and disciplinary institution, with the purpose of bringing the new generation into conformity with the ideals and customs which have become traditional. Rarely does a second generation hold the convictions it has inherited with a fervor equal to that of its fathers, who fashioned these convictions in the heat of conflict and at the risk of martyrdom. As generation succeeds generation, the isolation of the community from the world becomes more difficult."[71] Such a change in the basic character of a religion or movement usually is the result of mutually reinforcing factors at work. Thus the fact that the illegal Kimbanguist cult in the Congo after World War II had gradually abandoned political protest probably was one of the reasons for its rapid expansion. The deradicalization of the former militant antiwhite movement led the Belgian authorities to grant legal recognition to "The Church of Jesus Christ on Earth by Simon Kimbangu," and this legalization in turn contributed to the further rapid growth of the church and reinforced the trend of deradicalization. The relationship between success and deradicalization is thus one of dynamic interaction.

A similar pattern of unintended consequences is at work when a sect thrives economically as a result of religious discipline. As H. Richard Niebuhr observed in his study of the origins of denominationalism, "wealth frequently increases when the sect subjects itself to the discipline of asceticism in work and expenditure,"[72] and such worldly success contributes to the attenuation of the revolutionary impulse. Thus the peasant members of the erstwhile revolutionary millenarian sect of the Lazzarettiani today are more than averagely well-off and include many men of substance.[73] Needless to say, a movement that has prospered will find it difficult to maintain its original sense of alienation from the world; it "acquires a stake in the stability of the order in which this success has been won."[74]

Another frequent trend of development, especially in many

of the developing nations, is the transformation of revolutionary millenarianism into secular political radicalism and nationalism. For this reason many students consider political millenarianism in primitive societies an essentially prepolitical phenomenon that occurs mainly in periods of transition. Millenarianism, suggests Yonina Talmon, "does not appear in areas largely untouched by modernization, and it appears only rarely in areas in which modernization has reached an advanced stage. It occurs mainly during the intermediate, 'neither here nor there' stages of modernization."[75] Millenarian movements here often play a unifying role, bringing together previously isolated or even hostile groups in a new unity transcending kinship and local loyalties. Millenarianism thus is a precursor of political awakening, and functions as a "rudimentary nationalism"[76] that sooner or later is "followed by movements of a more rational kind."[77]

Both in Africa and Melanesia millenarian movements have indeed often served as a kind of preparatory school for nationalists and revolutionaries. Worsley has shown that as the natives of Melanesia become more familiar with the ways of the white man and better educated, their cargo cults often yield to secular forms of political organization. In Africa, too, millenarianism has functioned as a kind of "sacred nationalism." And yet, many of these movements are tribal rather than pantribal in their political aspirations and the preoccupation with religious concerns often can lead to quietism and thus delay the development of secular politics. After the achievement of independence, movements like the Lumpa Church of Zambia can become a pronounced hindrance to national integration. Last but not least, we must beware of a mechanical, evolutionary interpretation of millenarianism. Although the most frequent sequence of development in these emerging nations indeed is from religion to politics, the opposite trend also can be observed. In the case of André Matswa in the former French Congo, for example, a political movement with purely secular aims changed into a messianic cult,[78] albeit with pronounced political content, and a similar pattern held for the Hauhau movement of the Maori people of New Zealand in 1862.[79]

In the advanced societies of the West, millenarianism has largely become the preserve of fundamentalist sects, and revolu-

tionary impulses have found secular outlets. This is probably
the result, on one hand, of the fact that these societies are no
longer dominated by a religious ethos and, on the other, of the
slim chance of success for a rebellion led by a small group of
militants. Secular insurrectionist movements like the Blanquists
and the revolutionary anarchists for the same reason have been
superseded by class parties emphasizing political organization
and political action. In such a setting millenarian sects like Jehovah's Witnesses or the Adventists are nonpolitical and paci-
fist. As Worsley notes, these sects "blame the world's evils not
on the rulers of society, on a dominant Church, or on a foreign
government, but on the people themselves as worldly sinners.
Their sins are the root of evil; salvation can come only by recognition of guilt and by self-purification, not by war against the
ungodly Establishment."[80] The saints are still expected to inherit the earth, but their triumph depends on God and not on
human action. Our knowledge of the social composition of
these sects is rather limited, but it would seem that they appeal
primarily not to the very poor but to the lonely, to people with
limited education or in the backwaters of a society overwhelmingly committed to rationality, science, and the belief in progress.[81] Many of the converts to the millenarian Doomsday
Cult, studied by John Lofland, has been raised in small towns
and rural communities and all of them "retained a general pro-
pensity to impose religious meaning on events."[82]

The United States of America, being a largely Protestant
country, has always provided a fertile setting for sectarians of all
kinds, including the millenarian strain. Adventist speculation,
observes one student of sectarianism, became especially rife in
the nineteenth century. "In the uncertain conditions of a new
country, literal biblicism was a substitute for the standards of
order that had been imposed in England by a settled church,
monarchy, aristocracy, gentry and the magistracy and government. Needing, as had the Puritans before them, a model for
social organization, they, too, identified themselves as a covenant people. With the Bible as the basis for interpreting their
destiny they were, in troubled times, easily led to millennial
speculation."[83] Within the framework of an open and pluralistic society and in a cultural setting stressing optimism and
growth, these millenarian sects were not likely to turn in a revo-

lutionary direction; it was in part a reflection of the strength of the democratic ethos in America that even underprivileged racial minorities like the Indians and the blacks did not generate movements of revolutionary millenarianism.

In recent years the explosive mixture of status improvement, rising expectations, and continuing discriminatory practices, experienced primarily by Northern urban blacks, has somewhat changed this situation. Black militancy today openly challenges peaceful change, gradualism, and integration; yet while we find religious bodies like the Black Muslims emphasizing racial pride and black identity, there still are no revolutionary millenarian movements. In a situation where radical political action, including the resort to violence, has been productive of results, innovative black Christian theologians like Albert B. Cleage, the pastor of the Shrine of the Black Madonna in Detroit, explicitly warn against religious escapism and reliance upon divine intervention. Black Christians suffering oppression in a white man's land, he argues, must recapture the spirit of the Old Testament prophets and of Jesus who is pictured as ''a revolutionary black leader.'' Black Christians must repudiate ''the individualistic and other-worldly doctrines of Paul and the white man,'' they must come together as black people and reinterpret the Christian message ''in terms of the needs of the Black Revolution.''[84] In the spirit of a kind of black ''theology of revolution,'' Cleage writes:

> We no longer feel helpless as black people. We do not feel that we must sit and wait for God to intervene and settle our problems for us. We waited for four hundred years and he didn't do much of anything, so for the next four hundred years we're going to be fighting to change conditions for ourselves. . . . We have come to understand how God works in the world. Now we know that God is going to give us strength for our struggle. As black preachers we must tell our people that we are God's chosen people and that God is fighting with us as we fight. When we march, when we take it to the streets in open conflict, we must understand that in the stamping feet and the thunder of violence we can hear the voice of God.[85]

The fact that the radical religious impulse here finds an outlet in the political demand for black power rather than in the idea of a black millennium would seem to support the point made above that millenarian movements develop primarily in situations of deprivation where no ordinary remedies seem available. In the contemporary United States, political action and even playing at revolution are usable tactics and this fact tends to undercut the attraction of revolutionary millenarianism.

Revolutionary millenarian movements have largely disappeared from the advanced societies of Europe and America, but this does not mean the eclipse of the millenarian impulse. Indeed it can be argued that starting with the eighteenth-century Enlightenment, millenarianism has simply been secularized and, thus refashioned, has reappeared in certain types of radical political revolutionism. The point of transition in this secularization of an old religious doctrine, as E. L. Tuveson has convincingly demonstrated, was the eighteenth-century idea of progress—"the notion of history as a process generally moving upwards by a series of majestic stages, culminating *inevitably* in some great, transforming event which is to solve the dilemmas of society."[86] As a result of the merger of the concept of providence with that of natural law, there was born a new secular salvation.

The millenarian theme can be clearly seen in the revolutionary thought of Marx and Engels.[87] History, replacing God, now becomes the force that moves mankind to the inevitable day of judgment when the mighty are cast down and the lowly exalted, when the expropriators are expropriated. There follows the reign of the saints, the dictatorship of the proletariat, and lastly the kingdom of heaven, the egalitarian classless and stateless society, the realm of love, free of conflict and compulsion. Only then, Marx and Engels believed, would man fully become man. Human history truly begins at the moment when the laws governing all previous history finally have been overcome and transcended. The escape from history is then complete.

According to Marxism, the great transformation, the victory of the proletarian revolution holding promise of eternal salvation, will come about necessarily as a result of severe contradictions in bourgeois society, but not without human effort. "The consummation of time is guaranteed by history," writes an astute observer, "but history is not justified by faith alone, but by works." It is the rigor of Marxism's deterministic creed that "arouses in the believers the most resolute and patient action and thus their acts confirm the faith, and the faith the acts."[88]

The same synthesis of determinism and revolutionary assertion, a secular apocalyptic activism, can be found in anarchism. The dying world of the bourgeoisie has had its day, declared the Russian anarchist Sergei Nechaev: "Its end is inevitable, we must act to hasten that end."[89]

In the case of Leninist Communism and Maoism, often called secular religions, an element of prophecy has been added: the promise of necessary delivery is vouchsafed by a line of prophets who are invoked as authoritative figures and cited as in earlier times was the Bible. The founders of the creed, Marx and Engels, have been joined by the great interpreters—Lenin, Stalin, Mao. The exalted status of these men has been downgraded by the current unpopularity of the cult of the personality in the Soviet Union, whereas the personal adulation rendered Chairman Mao in Communist China hardly knows bounds and at times approaches true deification. Apocalyptic elements are also strong in the contemporary New Left, whose enthusiastic members, endowed with the zeal of the true believer, a recent writer has appropriately called the "Anabaptists of the Welfare State."[90]

NOTES

1. *The Politics of Aristotle,* trans. Ernest Barker (New York, 1958), bk. 5, chap. 1, p. 204.

2. Lawrence Stone, "The English Revolution," in Robert Forster and Jack P. Greene, eds., *Preconditions of Revolution in Early Modern Europe* (Baltimore, 1970), p. 60.

3. Hannah Arendt is one of many recent writers who restricts the phenomenon and the very idea of revolution to modern times. In her view, the notion "that an entirely new story, a story never known or told before, is about to unfold, was unknown prior to the two great revolutions of the eighteenth century." *On Revolution* (New York, 1965), p. 21. We regard this observation as empirically false.

4. Our characterization of revolutionary millenarianism is derived from the definition of millenarian movements developed by Norman Cohn in "Medieval Millenarianism: Its Bearing on the Comparative Study of Millenarian Movements," in Sylvia L. Thrupp, ed., *Millennial Dreams in Action* (The Hague, 1962), p. 31 (hereafter cited as Cohn, "Medieval Millenarianism"). See also Yonina Talmon, "Millenarian Movements." *Archives Européennes*

de Sociologie 7 (1966):159 (hereafter cited as Talmon, "Millenarian Movements").

5. Cf. Bryan A. Wilson, "Millennialism in Comparative Perspective," *Comparative Studies in Society and History* 6 (1963):97.

6. *From Max Weber: Essays in Sociology,* trans. H. H. Gerth and C. Wright Mills (New York, 1958), p. 295.

7. Max Weber, *The Theory of Social and Economic Organization,* trans. A. M. Henderson and Talcott Parsons (New York, 1964), pp. 358–359.

8. Talmon, "Millenarian Movements," p. 169; Wilson, p. 100; Wilhelm E. Mühlmann, *Chiliasmus und Nativismus* (Berlin, 1961), pp. 306–307; Peter Worsley, *The Trumpet Shall Sound,* 2d ed. (London, 1968), p. 12.

9. Talmon, "Millenarian Movements," p. 170.

10. Henri Desroche, *Dieux d'hommes: Dictionnaire des messianismes et millenarismes de l'ere Chrétienne* (Paris, 1969), p. 7.

11. Cf. Luigi Petrullo and Bernard M. Bass, eds., *Leadership and Interpersonal Behavior* (New York, 1961); Alvin W. Gouldner, ed., *Studies in Leadership* (New York, 1950).

12. Ann Ruth Willner and Dorothy Willner, "The Rise and Role of Charismatic Leaders," *Annals of the American Academy of Political and Social Science* 358 (March 1965):84.

13. Ann Ruth Willner, *Charismatic Political Leadership: A Theory,* Center of International Studies Research Monograph no. 32 (Princeton, 1968), pp. 63–69 (hereafter cited was Willner, *Charismatic Leadership*). See also Eric Hoffer, *The True Believer* (New York, 1964), pp. 105–106.

14. Willner and Willner, p. 79; T. K. Oomen, "Charisma, Social Structure and Social Change," *Comparative Studies in Society and History* 10 (1967):85. Reinhard Bendix has pointed that the modern totalitarian dictatorship, controlling all channels of communication, can easily simulate the attributes of charismatic leadership and thus create a widespread belief in the charisma of the leader. "Reflections on Charismatic Leadership," in Bendix, ed., *State and Society: A Reader in Comparative Political Sociology* (Boston, 1968), p. 625.

15. Mühlmann, pp. 282–283; Talmon, "Millenarian Movements," pp. 174–175.

16 Cf. Hoffer, p. 94.

17. Yonina Talmon, "Pursuit of the Millennium: The Relation between Religion and Social Change," *European Journal of Sociology* 3 (1962): 134–135 (hereafter cited as Talmon, "Pursuit of Millennium").

18. H. Richard Niebuhr, *The Social Sources of Denominationalism* (New York, 1965), p. 30.

19. Vittorio Lanternari, *The Religions of the Oppressed: A Study of Modern Messianic Cults,* trans. Lisa Sergio (New York, 1965), p. 249.

20. Talmon, "Pursuit of Millennium," p. 147.

21. Cf. Ralph Linton, "Nativistic Movements," *American Anthropologist* 45 (1943):230–240.

22. Norman Cohn, *The Pursuit of the Millennium,* 2d rev. ed. (New York, 1970), p. 282 (hereafter cited as Cohn, *Pursuit of Millennium*). As medievalists like Gordon Leff and J. B. Russell have pointed out, Norman Cohn in some of his writings overstates the class factor in medieval heresy.

23. Talmon, "Millenarian Movements," p. 181.

24. The concept of relative deprivation was for the first time given a central role by S. A. Stouffer et al., *The American Soldier* (Princeton, 1949). Cf. the detailed discussion by Robert K. Merton, *Social Theory and Social Structure,* rev. ed. (New York, 1957), chap. 8. See also W. G. Runciman, *Relative Deprivation and Social Justice* (London, 1966), p. 3; David F. Aberle *The Peyote Religion among the Navaho* (Chicago, 1966), pp. 323–329; Charles Y. Glock and Rodney Stark, *Religion and Society in Tension* (Chicago, 1965), p. 246.

25. Worsley, p. 243.

26. Cf. Anthony F. C. Wallace, *Religion: An Anthropological View* (New York, 1966), pp. 157–158.

27. Wilson D. Wallis, *Messiahs: Their Role in Civilization* (Washington, D.C., 1943), p. 187.

28. *Yasht,* vol. 19, pp. 14, 89, cited by Mircea Eliade, *The Myth of the Eternal Return,* trans. Willard R. Trask (New York, 1965), p. 124, See also Gerardus van der Leeuw, "Primordial Time and Final Time," in Joseph Campbell, ed., *Man and Time,* Bollingen Series, 30 (New York, 1957), pp. 324–350.

29. Cohn, *Pursuit of Millennium,* p. 307.

30. For the Antonians, see Louis Jadin, *Le Congo et la secte des Antoniens* (Brussels, 1961). For a brief discussion of the Lazzarettiani, see E. J. Hobsbawm, *Primitive Rebels* (New York, 1965), pp. 68–73. A detailed treatment of the insurgency led by Antonio Conselheiro is the Brazilian classic of Euclides da Cunha, *Rebellion in the Backlands,* trans. Samuel Putnam (Chicago, 1944).

31. Cf. *Acta Apostolicae Sedis,* 36 (1944), p. 212; and, for the background of this decree, G. Gilleman, S.J., "Condamnation de millénarisme mitigé," *Nouvelle Revue Theologique* 67 (1945):847–849.

32. Kenelm Burridge, *New Heaven, New Earth: A Study of Millenarian Activities* (Oxford, 1969), p. 16.

33. Emil Abegg, *Der Messiasglaube in Indien und Iran* (Berlin, 1928), pp. 143–144; Charles Eliot, *Hinduism and Buddhism: An Historical Sketch* (London, 1962), vol. 1, pp. 46–47.

34. S. J. Samartha, *The Hindu View of History: Classical and Modern* (Bangalore, 1959), pp. 7, 15.

35. Max Weber, *The Sociology of Religion,* trans. Ephraim Fischoff (Boston, 1964), pp. 55–56.

36. Cf. E. Michael Mendelson, "A Messianic Buddhist Association in Up-

per Burma," *Bulletin of the School of Oriental and African Studies,* University of London, 24 (1961):560–580.

37. Cf. Charles F. Keyes, "Millennialism, Theravada Buddhism and Thai Society," paper delivered at the 24th annual meeting of the Association of Asian Studies, in New York, 29 March 1972.

38. Gananath Obeyesekere, "The Buddhist Pantheon in Ceylon and Its Extensions," in Manning Nash, ed., *Anthropological Studies in Theravada Buddhism* (New Haven, 1966), p. 10.

39. Manning Nash, "Buddhist Revitalization in the Nation State: The Burmese Experience," in Robert F. Spencer, ed., *Religion and Change in Contemporary Asia* (Minneapolis, 1971), p. 116. Melford E. Spiro reports that overtones of a millennial Buddhism—"the conjunction of the Buddhist notion of a Universal Emperor and a Future Buddha with the Burmese notions of a Future King, *weikzahood* [magicianship] and occult power"—continued to reverberate in Burma during his research there in 1961–1962 (*Buddhism and Society* [New York, 1970], p. 172), but even he admits that membership in messianic sects involves no more than "a tiny percentage of the population" and that "belief in savior gods is, for the most part, nonexistent" (pp. 186, 132).

40. Weston La Barre, *The Ghost Dance: Origins of Religion* (Garden City, 1970), p. 313; Alfred Metraux, "Messiahs of South America," *Inter-American Quarterly* no. 2 (April 1941):53–60; Maria Isaura Pereira de Queiroz, "Indianische Messiasbewegungen in Brasilien," trans. Hans Schreen, *Staden-Jahrbuch* 11–12 (1963–1964):31–44; Mircea Eliade, "Paradise and Utopia: Mythical Geography and Eschatology," in Frank E. Manuel, ed., *Utopias and Utopian Thought* (Boston, 1966), pp. 260–280. René Ribeiro, "Brazilian Messianic Movements," in Thrupp, p. 56.

41. La Barre, p. 268.

42. Cf. Isidor Thorner, "Prophetic and Mystic Experience: Comparison and Consequences," *Journal for the Scientific Study of Religion* 5 (1965):84.

43. This stress on the innovative role played by the charismatic leaders of revolutionary millenarian movements is not meant to contradict the observation of Edward Shils that "charisma not only disrupts social order, but it also maintains or conserves it." "Charisma, Order and Status," *American Sociological Review* 30 (1965):200.

44. Werner Stark, *The Sociology of Religion: A Study of Christendom* (London, 1967), vol. 2, p. 48.

45. This point is well made by Willner, *Charismatic Leadership,* p. 45, who uses Gandhi as the example of a leader who taught his people how depressed they were.

46. Cohn, "Medieval Millenarianism," p. 38.

47. See the suggestive article by Andrew M. Greeley, "Superstition, Ecstasy and Tribal Consciousness," *Social Research* 38 (1970):203–211.

48. *From Max Weber,* p. 245.

49. Wilson, p. 103.

50. Willner, *Charismatic Leadership,* p. 45.

51. Max Weber, *Ancient Judaism,* trans. Hans H. Gerth and Don Martindale (Glencoe, Ill., 1952), p. 286.

52. Carl W. Christensen, "Religious Conversion," *Archives of General Psychiatry* 9 (1963):210.

53. William James, *The Varieties of Religious Experience* (New York, 1958), p. 164.

54. Hans L. Zetterberg, "Religious Conversion as a Change of Social Roles," *Sociology and Social Research* 36 (1952):166.

55. Cf. Leon Salzman, "The Psychology of Religious and Ideological Conversion," *Psychiatry* 16 (1953):179.

56. Michael Walzer, *The Revolution of the Saints* (Cambridge, Mass., 1965), pp. 308–309.

57. Sante de Sanctis, *Religious Conversion: A Bio-Psychological Study,* trans. Helen Augur (London, 1927), p. 46.

58. Edward S. Ames, *The Psychology of Religious Experience* (Boston, 1910), chap. 14.

59. Christensen, p. 212. See also W. Lawson Jones, *A Psychological Study of Religious Conversion* (London, 1937), p. 227.

60. Anthony F. C. Wallace, "Mazeway Resynthesis: A Bio-Cultural Theory of Religious Inspiration," *Transactions of the New York Academy of Sciences* 18 (1956):635.

61. Dorothy Emmett, "Prophets and Their Societies," *Journal of the Royal Anthropological Institute* 86 (1956):17.

62. Anton T. Boisen, *The Exploration of the Inner World: A Study of Mental Disorder and Religious Experience* (Chicago, 1936), p. 66.

63. Gerda E. Allison, "Psychiatric Implications of Religious Conversion," *Canadian Psychiatric Association Journal* 13 (1967):60.

64. Cohn, *Pursuit of Millennium,* p. 85.

65. H. I. Schou, *Religion and Morbid Mental States,* trans. W. Worster (New York, 1926), pp. 87–88.

66. Leon Festinger et al., *When Prophecy Fails* (Minneapolis, 1956), p. 28.

67. Cf. Joseph F. Zygmunt, "Prophetic Failure and Chiliastic Identity: The Case of Jehovah's Witnesses," *American Journal of Sociology* 75 (1970):926–948.

68. Burridge, pp. 76–83. For an older and more detailed account, see James Mooney, *The Ghost Dance Religion and the Sioux Outbreak of 1890,* A. F. C. Wallace, ed. (Chicago, 1965).

69. See the perceptive essay of Robert C. Tucker on the deradicalization of Marxist movements in his *The Marxian Revolutionary Idea* (New York, 1969). The inverse relationship between organizational strength and the preservation of radicalism was first stressed by Robert Michels in his classic *Political Parties.*

70. Mühlmann, pp. 275–276.

71. Niebuhr, pp. 19–20. As Bryan Wilson and others have shown, Niebuhr somewhat overstated the inherent tendency of sects to turn into denominations and churches.

72. Ibid., p. 20.

73. Hobsbawm, p. 71.

74. Tucker, p. 187.

75. Talmon, "Millenarian Movements," p. 184.

76. Guglielmo Guariglia, *Prophetismus und Heilserwartungs-Bewegungen als Völkerkundliches und Religionsgeschichtliches Problem* (Vienna, 1959), p. 268.

77. "Prophetic Movements as an Expression of Social Protest," *Internationales Archiv für Ethnographie* 49 (1960):154.

78. Cf. Betty R. Scharf, *The Sociological Study of Religion* (London, 1970), p. 69.

79. Burridge, pp. 15–22.

80. Worsley, p. 232.

81. Cf. Herbert H. Stroup, *The Jehovah's Witnesses* (New York, 1945); William J. Whalen, *Armageddon Around the Corner: A Report on Jehovah's Witnesses* (New York, 1962); Alan Rogerson, *Millions Now Living Will Never Die: A Study of Jehovah's Witnesses* (London, 1969).

82. John Lofland and Rodney Stark, "Becoming a World Saver: A Theory of Conversion to a Deviant Perspective, *American Sociological Review* 30 (1965):868. See also John Lofland, *Doomsday Cult* (Englewood Cliffs, N.J., 1966).

83. Bryan Wilson, *Religious Sects: A Sociological Study* (London, 1970), p. 96.

84. Albert B. Cleage, *The Black Messiah* (New York, 1968), pp. 4, 6.

85. Ibid., p. 6.

86. Ernest Lee Tuveson, *Millennium and Utopia: A Study in the Background of the Idea of Progress* (New York, 1964), p. 75. See also Rosemary Radford Ruether, *The Radical Kingdom: The Western Experience of Messianic Hope* (New York, 1970), pp. 38–43.

87. Tucker, p. 183. See also Raymond Aron, *The Opium of the Intellectuals,* trans. Terence Kilmartin (London, 1957), p. 66.

88. Donald G. Macrae, "The Bolshevik Ideology: The Intellectual and Emotional Factors in Communist Affiliation," *Cambridge Journal* 3 (1954):167. See also W. Banning, *Der Kommunismus als politisch-soziale Weltreligion* (Berlin, 1953).

89. Quoted in Franco Venturi, *The Roots of Revolution* (London, 1960), p. 383.

90. Erwin Scheuch, *Wiedertäufer der Wohlstandsgesellschaft* (Cologne, 1968). The close similarity between the Radical Reformation and the New Left is argued by Arthur G. Gisch, *The New Left and Christian Radicalism* (Grand Rapids, Mich., 1970), chap. 2.

7

KARL MARX—THE PROPAGANDIST AS PROPHET

SAUL K. PADOVER

Of the three men whose theories have had the greatest impact on the world in the last century—Einstein, Freud, and Marx—only Marx was steadily committed to a cause beyond his scholarly ("scientific") writings. Einstein and Freud operated in the traditional mode of the scientist—formulating and validating theory, leaving implications and consequences to teleologists and assorted practitioners and believers. Marx, on the other hand, was himself a teleologist and a practitioner—a revolutionary activist—writing his books, brochures, and articles with the deliberate intent of achieving particular purposes, of helping to change opinion for the purpose of overthrowing existing institutions.

In the light of Marx's redoubtable reputation as a theorist and thinker today, it is interesting to note that he was by profession a journalist, and not an *Akademiker,* although he was the proud possessor of a well-earned doctorate in philosophy.[1] His career as an active journalist extended over a period of two decades: from 1842, when at the age of twenty-four, he became contributor to and editor of the Cologne *Rheinische Zeitung,*[2] to 1862, when at the age of forty-four, he wrote his last article as the London correspondent of the *New York Daily Tribune*[3] and the Vienna *Presse.*[4] Thereafter, until he died twenty-one years later,[5] he pursued no other calling than the one with which he had started, namely journalism, although his newspaper articles were now published only sporadically.

To understand, at least in part, the polemical nature of Marx's writings, one has to keep in mind that in his day, journalism was not a neutral occupation. On the European continent, where Marx made his debut as a newspaperman, journalism could not possibly be objective. In a Europe ruled by absolutist monarchs and oligarchs, the press was tolerated only insofar as it conformed to the rules and restrictions of the widely prevailing censorships. A newspaper desiring to be other than a mouthpiece for the authorities was, almost by definition, in actual or potential conflict with the censorship. Editors and journalists had only two choices. They could defend, or refrain from criticizing, the status quo, in which case they were likely to be rewarded with money and other favors; or they could attack it, a course that was certain to expose them to harassment, prosecution, and, in the end, even exile. Marx, by temperament and conviction a rebel determined to rearrange the universe, chose the latter alternative. Predictably, he ran afoul of the censorship, which closed his *Rheinische Zeitung* in 1843 and his *Neue Rheinische Zeitung* in 1849, and he was finally driven out of Prussia. Marx spent the rest of his life as a stateless exile in London.

Contentiousness was a congenial role that Marx played with zest. He felt most at home as a polemicist, for he was often angry and wrote from passion. In a sense, his writings illustrated the Hegelian dialectic, one of his major intellectual instruments: state a proposition; knock it (or its opponents) down; suggest your alternative. From the very first, Marx was an embattled writer, driven by wrath. In a revealing letter, written in June 1844, his adoring wife, Jenny, whom he had married the previous year,[6] pleaded with him:

> But don't write too bitterly and angrily. . . . Write either factually and politely or humorously and lightly. Please, dear Heart, let your pen glide over the paper, and if it should occasionally stumble and trip over a sentence—still, your ideas stand like the Grenadiers of the Old Guard, so honorable and firm, and like them, they can say, *elle meurt mais elle ne se rend pas.* . . .[7] Loosen the harness, undo the cravat, and raise the shako—let the participles run free and place the words as they themselves would like to be placed. . . . And your troops are after all already in the field. Good luck to the commander-in-chief, my swarthy lord!

Marx never ceased to be a combatant. Even his economic writings, with their immense erudition, were designed to serve a cause. For Marx was dedicated to a special vision, fed by a seemingly nondepletable supply of indignation. He was easily aroused to anger over all kinds of injustices—to American slaves, Belgian miners, French prostitutes, German tailors, Irish rebels, London cabbies, Polish patriots, Prussian forest-poachers, Russian serfs, Silesian weavers, Spanish strikers, and all other conceivable victims of the "bourgeois" world. Injustice, indeed, was rife everywhere, and Marx, an inveterate reader of newspapers in many languages, was likely to react to it at all times. Thus in his writings, including his economic writings, he was, to use the words of his favorite foreign language, *un homme enragé,* as well as *engagé.* This, of course, has imbued his works with a scintillation and passion that go far to explain his perduring and worldwide appeal.

But Marx was no ordinary radical or wearisome agitator. He was an overpoweringly learned man, with an easy mastery of history, the social sciences (such as they were in his time), and mathematics.[8] His mind was honed by a knowledge of the profundities and subtleties of all known philosophers from Aristotle to Zeno. As a student at the University of Berlin, 1836–1841, he had not only mastered Hegel and all other European thinkers, but had also read, and made voluminous extracts from, the medieval scholastics, theologians, and jurists. Even as a young man, his philosophic erudition was already impressive. After meeting the twenty-three-year-old Marx in Cologne in 1841, the German socialist philosopher Moses Hess wrote to a friend that in Marx's presence he felt like a "clumsy bungler" in philosophy: "Dr. Marx, this is the name of my idol . . . he combines the deepest philosophical seriousness with the most cutting wit; think of Rousseau, Voltaire, d'Holbach, Lessing, Heine and Hegel united in one person; I say *united,* not tossed together—and you have Dr. Marx."

Marx was also a linguist. He knew Dutch from his mother, who was born and raised in Holland and whose relatives he often visited there. In school he learned French, Greek, and Latin, in all of which he acquired high proficiency. Indeed, he wrote his first book, *La Misère de la philosophie* (1847) in French, and not in German. In later years he taught himself

other European languages, including Rumanian. He learned
Spanish so as to read Calderon and Cervantes, as well as Iberian
newspapers in preparation for his articles on the revolutions in
Spain.[9] It took Marx six months to learn Russian, which he did
at the age of fifty, in order not only to enjoy Gogol and Pushkin
in their native tongues but also to read historians and economists, such as N. Flerovsky[10] and Maxim Kovalevsky,[11] then not
available in Western languages. Marx, indeed, came to possess a
collection of Russian works, which he referred to as *"russisches*
on my book shelf.'' He used to say: ''A foreign language is a
weapon in the struggle of life.''

Altogether, Marx was intellectually the most formidably
equipped revolutionist in recorded history. Never before had so
much sheer brain power and knowledge, such a gift of abstract
reasoning, so sharp an articulation, such deep hatred, and so
single-minded a dedication been combined in such a concentrated effort to change the thinking, and alter or overthrow the
institutions, of a whole historical epoch.

His mental force and passionate convictions—a sort of charisma—were conveyed in his appearance and mode of expression.
A contemporary, the liberal Russian writer and landowner Annenkov, who became friends with Marx in Brussels, was impressed by his drive and will to dominate. Annenkov described
Marx—the hirsute, vigorous, and arrogant German exile—as
having the qualities of a dictator:

> Thick black mane; hands covered with hair; the coat buttoned awry
> —still, he had the appearance of a man who had the right and the
> authority to demand respect, even though his looks and acts rarely
> enough warranted it. His gestures were angular but bold and sure,
> his manners ran counter to the usual social behavior. He was proud,
> with a tinge of contempt, and his sharp voice which rang like metal,
> coincided remarkably with his radical judgments of men and
> things. He spoke in nothing but imperatives, tolerating no contra-
> diction, his words penetrating everything by his painfully sharp
> tone. . . . To me, he appeared the personification of a democratic
> dictator.

Marx did not start his professional life as a communist or socialist—words then loosely, often interchangeably, used and ill-
defined.[12] He was, at first, merely another radical German in-

tellectual, in opposition to the existing institutions of church and state. He pictured himself then as a man engaged in "ruthless criticism of all that exists," but without any systematic political philosophy. In his first essay on the subject of communism, written in the *Rheinische Zeitung* on the day he took over as editor,[13] Marx stated: "The *Rheinische Zeitung,* which cannot concede the theoretical reality of communist ideas even in their present form, and can even less wish or consider possible their practical realization, will submit these ideas to a thorough scrutiny."

But communist-socialist theories, primarily those of the French utopians, were prevalent even in Germany, where they were made respectable in a scholarly work by a Hegelian professor (at Kiel), Lorenz von Stein, in his *Der Sozialismus und Communismus des heutigen Frankreich.*[14] In the autumn of 1842, Marx began studying contemporary French writers. The utopian authors, including the followers of Saint-Simon,[15] did not convert Marx to their doctrines, with which, indeed, he was to be at unremitting war in later years,[16] but they helped him cross the long bridge between the speculative universe of Hegelian abstraction and the hard world of material reality.

Marx's road to economics led through communism, which, in turn, was to be strengthened by his economics. He did not embrace communism, or what then passed for this ideology, or undertake any serious study of economics, until he moved to Paris in October 1843, when he was twenty-five years old, to become copublisher of the *Deutsch-Französische Jahrbücher.* He wrote to his coeditor, the Hegelian Arnold Ruge, that he was not in favor of communism or utopianism and that he was opposed to any "ready-made" system. He considered the contemporary writers in the field too dogmatic and one-sided for his taste:

> I am, therefore, not in favor of raising a dogmatic flag; quite the contrary. We should try to help the dogmatists to clarify their ideas. Thus communism, in particular, is a dogmatic abstraction, and by this I do not mean some fanciful or possible communism, but the real existing communism, as Cabet, Dézamy, Weitling,[17] etc., teach and conceive it. This communism is itself separate from the humanist principle, being merely a phenomenon affected by its opposite: private existence.

Marx's residence in Paris, from October 1843 to February 1845, proved to be a turning point in his life. He and his strikingly beautiful bride moved into a house[18] that was a kind of "communist community" occupied by German intellectuals. Marx's circle soon included a brilliant lot of foreigners, among them the German poets Heine and Herwegh, and such Russian exiles as Bakunin. "There was," Mrs. Marx recalled later in her *Reminiscences,* "a lot of gossip and quarrels over bagatelles." One such quarrel—over communism, with which Marx was beginning to sympathize—was with Arnold Ruge; it ended both the publication of the *Deutsch-Französische Jahrbücher*[19] and the friendship between the two men. Ruge's opinion of Marx in Paris provides some insight into the latter's character. "He reads very much," Ruge wrote to Ludwig Feuerbach; "he works with uncommon intensity and has a critical talent that occasionally degenerates into dialectical arrogance, but he finishes nothing, he always breaks off and plunges anew into an ocean of books." Ruge, himself a writer and editor, added that Marx was "born to be a scholar and author" but, as such, "absolutely spoiled" for a journalist.

For Marx, coming out of parochial, small-town Germany, which had no national cultural or political center and which he considered a land dreary in its conformity and cowardly in its submission to authority,[20] Paris was a heady experience. The glittering city was then the center of a galaxy of writers whose appeal extended far beyond the borders of France. But, above all, Paris provided Marx with the first opportunity of getting to know real proletarian communists and socialists, not just theorizers like Proudhon, whom he met in July 1844. Contact with radicals in Paris was provided by a circle of German intellectuals centered around Moses Hess, Marx's friend and admirer from Cologne. Hess, now in Paris, devoted himself exclusively, as he wrote to Auerbach, "to philosophic projects of communism." This whole new crop of German refugee radicals greatly impressed the poet Heine, who had been living in exile in Paris since 1831. He wrote in his *Geständnisse* (Confessions):

The more or less secret leaders of the German communists are great logicians, the strongest of whom have come out of the Hegelian school and they are beyond doubt Germany's ablest heads and most energetic characters. These Doctors of Revolution and their relentlessly determined followers are the only men in Germany who have life in them, and, I fear, the future belongs to them.

Paris had a colony of about ten thousand German artisans and journeymen—"shoemaker" was then virtually synonymous with "German"—with strong communist leanings. In the Faubourg St. Antoine, there were often violent street clashes between the German workers, who spoke no French, and the Parisian proletarians, who resented them for undercutting their own wages. Marx was introduced to the German artisans by a refugee physician, August Hermann Ewerbeck, who was a member of the *Bund der Kommunisten* (League of Communists) and head of the secret society *Bund der Gerechten* (League of the Just). Marx attended their meetings and learned something about "class conflict." He likewise came in contact with French communist workers. A police spy (Paris was then full of them) reported that in the summer of 1844 he often saw Marx attend secret meetings of French communist societies in the Barrière du Trône, on the rue de Vincennes. The French workers impressed Marx enormously with their intelligence, energy, and idealism. "In the meetings of the communist artisans," he wrote, "brotherhood is not a phrase but the truth, and nobility shines from the labor-hardened faces." He expressed the same idea in a letter to Ludwig Feuerbach in Germany: "You have to attend one of the meetings of the French *ouvriers* to realize the virginal freshness and nobility that is generated among these workingmen."

Marx was always to have a special interest in, and perhaps romantic illusion about, the French proletariat, as can be seen in his later writings, particularly *The Class Struggles in France, 1848-50* (1850)[21] and *The Civil War in France* (1871).[22] Two of his daughters were to marry French socialists.[23] Although Marx joined neither secret French societies nor any German *Bunds*, it is certain that by the summer of 1844 he was already a convinced communist.

This was also the period when he began seriously to study economics, a field that, with many interruptions, was to become a lifelong pursuit. A strong impetus to Marx's economic studies was provided by Frederick Engels, who was then working in his father's textile business, which he hated, in Manchester, England. Engels sent to Paris two lengthy articles, which Marx, as coeditor, published in the *Deutsch-Französische Jahrbücher.* Both were vintage Engels. One, "The Condition of England," was a review of Thomas Carlyle's *Past and Present* (London, 1843), which Engels lauded for its serious exposure of English ruling-class values and its criticism of the prevailing ideals of "competition and demand," and "supply and mammon." The other Engels article, "Outlines of a Critique of Political Economy," was more directly influential on Marx. It dealt with the development of modern capitalism, from mercantilism to the contemporary English factory system, England being, Engels wrote, of "immeasurable importance for history and for all other countries." The article highlighted commerce, competition, value, ground rents, capital, and labor.[24] It was a sweeping review of a subject, modern capitalism, about which Engels knew a great deal and Marx as yet very little. The article had strong moral overtones, for Engels was then already a communist. In his concluding sentence, he wrote: "For the rest, I hope soon to have the opportunity of developing in detail the abominable immorality of this [factory] system and of exposing pitilessly the hypocrisy of the economists which appears here in its full glitter."[25] Engels's tone of moral indignation obviously appealed to Marx, who was always full of it himself. Later, in his preface to his own *Critique of Political Economy,* he praised Engels for his "brilliant essay on the critique of economic categories."

Marx's espousal of communism crystallized in the summer of 1844, when Engels stopped off in Paris on the way from Manchester to his natal Barmen, Germany. He visited Marx, and the two young Germans—Marx was twenty-six and Engels twenty-four—spent ten days together, discovering each other's minds and discussing the whole range of philosophic and social problems, particularly as they related to European radicalism. They found themselves, to quote Engels, "in accord in all theoretical fields," and they decided then and there to collaborate in their future work.

In character, Marx and Engels presented striking similarities and contrasts. Both were brash and witty, lovers of books and ideas. Each was brilliant and blunt, often bawdy and even vul-

gar, possessing special gifts for barbed and not infrequently malicious polemicism. Engels was the more intuitive of the two; he
saw ideas and situations in a flash. He was also the more practical and earthy. Marx, on the other hand, needed a great
amount of reading and exhaustive research before writing. More
important, he was the profounder thinker, as the unpretentious
Engels himself always realized and candidly admitted.

The earliest Marx-Engels collaboration, dating from the period when Marx was beginning his economic studies, took the
form of two books, which were philosophical-polemical rather
than economic. *The Holy Family,* written from September to
November of 1844, in Paris, was published in Frankfurt in
1845. *The German Ideology,* written in Brussels in 1845–1846,
was not published in full until 1932.[26] Both of these collabora-
tive books, together with the *Communist Manifesto,* which
Marx and Engels wrote at the end of 1847, constituted mile-
stones in the thinking of the two founders of "Marxism," in
that they cleared away Hegelianism and philosophic Idealism,
as if they were debris cluttering up the intellectual landscape, to
make room for the materialist theories of society, history, and
economics—theories in whose development and propagation
Marx and Engels were to collaborate for the rest of their lives.

Marx undertook his systematic studies of economics, or political economy, as it then was called, at the end of 1843 with a
survey of the leading English and French theorists. He made extensive extracts (they run into nineteen printed pages) of James
Mill's *Elements of Political Economy* (London, 1821), a "great
work." He also studied other classic English economists, most
notably Ricardo and Smith, who made a lasting impression on
him as can be seen from numerous references in his own later
economic writings and from the voluminous extracts from and
critical comments on them in the so-called volume IV of
Capital.[27]

Between April and August of 1844, Marx wrote down his
thoughts on political economy and its interconnection with
"the state, law, ethics, civil life, etc." These notes, now known
as *Economic and Philosophic Manuscripts of 1844,*[28] formed in
effect the last link between Hegel and Adam Smith. The
Manuscripts contain more philosophy than economics, but the
thrust is definitely in the direction of political economy. Marx

here uses some genuine economic categories, such as capital, private property, ground rent, and labor ("alienated labor"), topics that later he was to explore with such amplitude in *Capital.*

Marx's great opportunity to pursue economic studies came when he settled in London, after having been exiled from Paris in 1849. The preface to his *Critique* states: "The enormous amount of material relating to the history of Political Economy assembled in the British Museum, the fact that London is a convenient vantage point for the observation of bourgeois society, and finally the new stage of development which this society seemed to have entered with the discovery of gold in California and Australia, induced me to start again from the beginning and to work carefully through the new material."

Marx wrote what was to be his first published work on economics, *Zur Kritik der Politischen Oekonomie,* between August 1858 and January 1859. It was a relatively short book of about 145 printed pages,[29] dealing with commodities, theory of value, and money. There was, in this, an irony that did not escape Marx. When he finished the little manuscript, he had no money to pay for postage to the Berlin publisher. As usual, he asked Engels for help: "The hapless manuscript is ready, but cannot be sent out, as I do not have a farthing to mail or insure it. The latter is necessary, since I do not have a copy. . . . If you could send me £2, it would be very welcome. . . . [30] I do not believe that anyone has ever written about 'money' and suffered such a lack of it. Most authors on the subject have been in profound peace with the subject of their researches."

Zur Kritik has special importance because of its preface, which contains, in capsule form, the basic "Marxist" idea of "economic determinism." In essence, he wrote, economic foundations and what he called "relationships of production," rather than the human mind or will, shape social institutions and determine behavior. On the real foundations of society, the economic structure, there arises "a legal and political superstructure." The totality of the economic relationship, Marx stated, conditions the "general process of social, political, and intellectual life." When economic conditions change, as they are always bound to, so do the relationships and the whole superstructure—legal, religious, artistic, and philosophic. Then begins the era of social revolution, transforming everything; and men, becoming aware of those changes, fight them out. Thereafter, a new stage of development begins. This process of transformation, Marx wrote, can be studied ''with the precision of natural science.'' The ''science'' in question was political economy. As the anatomy of civil society, including the processes of revolutionary change, had to be found in political economy, Marx claimed, it was logical for him to seek—and, of course, find—the truth of his ideas in that all-encompassing field.

Marx was convinced, or tried to convince himself, that his approach to economics was that of a scientist, and not that of an agitator like Weitling or utopian like Proudhon. He claimed that he did not invent conditions and the inevitable changes flowing from them, any more than he invented the class struggle. He saw himself as only a ''scientist,'' reporting the stark historic forces and actual realities as they manifested themselves —that is, as inexorable nature created them—regardless of the ''interested prejudices of the ruling classes.'' He, in his own eyes of course, had no prejudices. At the entrance to science, as at the entrance to hell, Marx concluded in his preface, the motto must be, in the words of Dante's *Divine Comedy:*

Qui si convien lasciare ogni sospetto
Ogni viltà convien che qui sia morta.[31]

Marx's ''science'' was to be used to achieve communism. The first step, he believed, was to demolish the foundations of the prevailing European socialist theories of men like Proudhon and other ''false brothers,'' as he called them; the second, to lay the ''scientific'' foundations of communism, that is, ''Marxism.'' To do so, it was necessary that his ideas become known among radicals through a distribution of his written work. On 1 February 1859 he wrote to his communist friend, Joseph Weydemeyer, who then lived in Milwaukee, Wisconsin: ''I hope to gain a scientific victory for our party. But the party itself must now show whether its membership is numerous enough to buy enough copies to ease the publisher's 'scruples of conscience.' The continuation of the project depends on the sale of the first parts [of the book].''

It did not work out as Marx expected. The publisher, Duncker, printed one thousand copies, but there was no market for the book in Germany and hence no conduit for Marx's ideas. Even socialists were disappointed, for they had expected a book on socialism and, instead, got a learned dissertation on economic categories. *Zur Kritik* was not even a *succès d'estime,* as Germany's political economists did not bother to review it. As Marx put it, ''not a single rooster has crowed over the thing.'' Being thus ignored was one more psychological rejection by his native country. Marx was wounded and angry. To Lassalle, the flamboyantly successful Berlin lawyer and socialist leader who had persuaded Duncker to publish the book, Marx wrote: ''You are mistaken, however, if you think that I expected laudatory recognition from the German press or that I give a farthing for it. I expected attacks or criticisms, but not complete disregard, which must also hurt the sales. They had so thoroughly reviled my communism on various occasions that it was to be expected that they would let loose their wisdom on its theoretical foundations. Professional economic journals do, after all, exist in Germany.''

Marx was convinced that the silence about *Zur Kritik* was the result was the result of a conspiracy against him. If his enemies, the ''German literary rabble,'' find that abuse is not enough, they ''honor'' him, he said, with a ''conspiracy of silence.'' His previous books, *The Poverty of Philosophy* and *The Eighteenth Brumaire of Louis Bonaparte*[32] had also been ignored in Germany. The failure of *Zur Kritik* was a fiasco from which the whole Marx family suffered. At Christmas time in 1859, Mrs. Marx wrote to Engels about the ''pettiest miseries'' of the indigent household, adding: ''This has been aggravated by the shameful *conspiration de silence* on the part of the Germans over Karl's book, on which he had quietly pinned long-cherished hopes—a conspiracy broken only by a few wretched belletristic feuilletons which dealt only with the Preface and not with the content.''

Duncker, bound by his contract, was reluctantly prepared to bring out the second *Heft* of *Zur Kritik,* but Marx did not manage to finish it. He was in the throes of a severe persecution complex, passionately convinced that the whole intellectual world of Germany had ganged up on him and his ideas. His suspicions were so inflamed that he came to view virtually all his

German friends as enemies, among them the consistently loyal supporter Ferdinand Lassalle in Berlin, the faithful socialist follower Wilhelm Liebknecht in Leipzig, and the helpful poet Ferdinand Freiligrath in London. Marx considered them either part of the conspiracy against him or at least its passive supporters.

In this state of mind Marx became involved in an acrimonious, raging squabble with an obscure German pedant named Karl Vogt, whom he accused of calumny against him. Striking out at one visible target at least, Marx sued the Augsburg *Allgemeine Zeitung,* which had printed a Vogt brochure containing a few passages he considered offensive. In the tangle of widening charges and countercharges, Marx set into operation an overwrought anti-Vogt campaign, collecting materials from everywhere, accusing Vogt of being a Bonapartist spy, and suing two more newspapers, the Berlin *National Zeitung* and the *London Daily Telegraph,* which, he said, published some of the Vogt "crap" against him. The Vogt affair, lasting through the year 1860, was not Marx's finest hour. It cannot be said to have enhanced Marx's reputation for good judgment, sense of proportion, or priorities. It was an exercise in meaningless rage, sapping his health, wasting his talents, and consuming his meager resources. For at least one year he did little serious work on economics.

After the failure of *Zur Kritik,* Marx recast his plan of work. Instead of bringing out separate *Heften,* as originally planned, he would organize a structure along different lines. The new work, to which he and his family were constantly to refer as *"das Buch"* would be large and comprehensive. It would also be brought out by a new publisher, Meissner in Hamburg.[33] Marx's final plan resulted in *Das Kapital,* which carried the old title in the subtitle.[34] The whole work was to consist of three volumes.

Marx worked on *Capital* four or five years, but there were long lacunae, partly of his own choosing and partly as a result of wretched personal circumstances. In September 1864 he involved himself in the organization of the International Working Men's Association in London—the so-called First International[35]—and for the next eight years he was its active de facto leader, draftsman, champion, and mentor. This may have been a psychological escape for Marx, as one modern scholarly critic claims.[36] The First International, many of whose sessions were held in Marx's own home, consumed much of his time and energy, particularly as he was so prone to engage in squabbles with those he considered opponents, whose number was legion, and thus further postponed completion of the first volume of *Capital*. Indeed, the last four years of the First International, which Marx angrily liquidated in Europe in 1872, were so stormy that they drained his energies and emotions, and thus contributed to the noncompletion of the last two volumes of *Capital*.

In addition, Marx was plagued by poverty and depressed by unending debts. Constantly dunned by creditors, he was also threatened with eviction. His economic woes were such that it is surprising he was able to work at all and achieve as much as he did. On 19 January 1867, at a time when he was trying to put the finishing touches to the first volume of *Capital*, he wrote Engels:

> My circumstances . . . are becoming worse daily and everything threatens to collapse over my head. The baker alone demands £20, and all the devils of butchers, grocers, taxes, etc. To top everything, some time ago I received a letter . . . demanding, first, the rent for which I am in arrears for the last quarter and, second, asking whether I intended to renew [the lease] . . . I did not answer. Whereupon I received a second letter yesterday, stating that I must declare myself, otherwise his 'agent' would take steps to rent the house to others. So in a fix.[37]

Engels, as always, came to his friend's relief. He sent Marx £20, sufficient momentarily to appease some of the creditors, including the landlord, whose agent was hanging around the house, waiting to collect. Marx remarked that vis-à-vis the dunning agent, he had to play the ironic role of Mercadet in Balzac's *Comédie Humaine.* He was then reading Balzac's *Le Chef d'Oeuvre Inconnu* and *Melmoth Réconcilié,* which he called "two little masterpieces, full of delicious irony."

Irony was Marx's sometime philosophic refuge from economic and somatic misery. A few days before his fiftieth birthday, he took stock of his chronic indigence and commented, in a letter to Engels (30 April 1868): "In a few days I will be 50. As that Prussian lieutenant once said to you: 'Twenty years in the service and I am still a lieutenant,' so I can say: Half a century on my back and still a pauper! How right my mother was! If only Karell[38] had made capital instead of [writing about it], etc.!''

Poverty-induced anxieties stimulated chronic illnesses, further delaying completion of *Capital.* Some of the afflictions, such as frequent headaches and sleeplessness, were psychological, as Marx himself realized. He was, like Job, a truly afflicted man, but without the surcease of a personal dialogue with God. Marx suffered from a continuing series of ailments—lung abscesses, liver disorder (from which, he said, his father had died and which he thought was hereditary), eye infections, toothaches, bronchitis, pleurisies, and hemorrhoids, among others—that would have broken the spirit of a less fierce and embattled man. The iatric woes were aggravated by an unbalanced and careless diet, spiced foods for example, and excessive cigar smoking, which did his tubercular lungs not a bit of good. After publication of *Capital,* Marx said that the income from the book did not pay for the cigars he smoked while writing it.

Worst of all the torments were the carbuncles and furuncles, which periodically invaded his body and which harassed him almost beyond endurance. They were sometimes treated surgically, but more often with arsenic, which, Marx said, dulled his brain. His whole torso became scarred. Once the pain was so excruciating that Marx seized a razor and sliced open the pus-infected carbuncles on a delicate part of his body. In the period when he was at work on *Capital,* carbuncles were ravaging him chronically from shoulder to scrotum, so that he could neither sit nor lie comfortably. The boils kept on bursting out in various and unexpected spots. To do any writing, he said, ''I must at least be able to *sit.*'' And when he had finished correcting the next to last batch of proofs of *Capital,* he wrote to Engels, ''I hope the bourgeoisie will remember my carbuncles all the rest of their lives.''

He kept on doggedly, driven by the ''daemon'' that his father had detected in Marx's boyhood. In this instance, the daemon was directed against the bourgeoisie, whom he liked to call *Schweinehunde* (filthy pigs). He saw himself, as he said, ''engaged in the most bitter conflict with the world,'' and *Capital* was to be his great weapon. In 1864 he told a communist friend, Carl Klings, that he hoped his book would ''deliver the

bourgeoisie a theoretical blow from which it will never re-
cover.''

At the end of March, 1867, Marx finished polishing *Capital*.
To prevent what he thought might be a repetition of a German
publishing conspiracy against him, as he was sure had been the
case with *Zur Kritik,* he decided to take the manuscript personally to Meissner in Hamburg. For the trip, he needed financial
help from Engels, to whom he wrote on 2 April 1867: ''Now I
must first redeem my clothing and watch from the pawnshop.
And also I can hardly leave my family in the present condition,
where it is without a sou and the creditors become daily more
insolent.'' Engels replied 4 April 1867: ''Hurrah! The exclama-
tion was irrepressible when I finally saw in black and white that
Volume One *is* ready and that you want to go with it to Hamburg. So that you do not lack *Nervus Rerum* [the sinews of life],
I am enclosing seven half-Pound notes, a total of £35 [*sic*], the
second half to be sent immediately upon receipt of the usual
telegram.''

Marx with his manuscript sailed from London on 12 April
1867, arriving in Hamburg two days later after a stormy passage. As soon as he landed, at noon, he went to see Meissner,
who was not in, and the impatient Marx left his card. That
evening the two men—the author unrestrainedly hirsute and
the publisher elegantly bearded but bald—had what Marx
called a *''pourparler''* (palaver). Marx decided that Meissner
was ''all right.'' The manuscript of *Capital* was put in the publisher's safe, Meissner promising that printing would begin
within a few days and then proceed quickly. Marx reported to
Engels on 13 April 1867: ''We began to tipple, and he told me
of his great 'delight' in making my worthy acquaintance. He
told me he now wants the book to appear in *three volumes. . . .*
At all events, *we* now have in Meissner a man entirely at our disposal; he has great contempt for the whole *Lumpenliteraten-
pack* [pack of literary rascals].''

Meissner was as good as his word. Four days after he received
the manuscript of *Capital,* he sent it to the printers.[39] Marx then
went to Hanover, where for nearly a month he was the pam-
pered guest of Dr. Ludwig Kugelmann, a locally prominent gy-
necologist and, as Marx informed Engels, ''a fanatical follower
of our doctrine and both our persons.'' Fussed over by the

whole Kugelmann family, Marx felt carefree and happy. He was charming and entertaining, went to the theater and to parties, and had at least one flirtation, with a Frau Tenge, wife of a Westphalian *Gusbesitzer* (landowner). Now that *Capital* was at last in the hands of the printers, Marx felt a sense of triumphant achievement after so many years of torment, doubt, and illness. On 30 April 1867, while waiting for the first proofs to arrive, he wrote a revealing letter to Sigfrid Meyer, a communist friend who had emigrated to New York:

> Why did I not write you for such a long time? Because I have been constantly suspended over the edge of the grave. I had to utilize EVERY possible moment in which I was capable of working, in order to complete my work, for which I have sacrificed health, happiness, and family. . . . I laugh at the so-called 'practical' men and their wisdom. If one wants to be an ox, then one can, of course, turn one's back on man's torments and tend only to one's own skin. But I would really have considered myself *impractical* if I had croaked without having finished my book, at least in manuscript.

The first proofs came on Marx's birthday, 5 May. A few days later he returned to London, dreading the prospect. What awaited him at home, he confided to Engels, was nothing but "Manichaeans," clamoring for the payment of debts, and the usual *"Familienjammer* (family woes), inner collisions, rat race." On 25 July, Marx wrote the preface to *Capital,* explaining the purpose and direction of the work, and about three weeks later he completed the final proofs of the whole book. At two o'clock in the morning 16 August he penned a brief note to Engels, expressing his infinite gratitude: "Dear Fred: Have just finished correcting the *last sheet* (59) of the book. . . . Preface ditto corrected and returned yesterday. So *this volume is finished.* Only YOU alone I have to thank for making this possible! Without your self-sacrifice on my behalf I could never possibly have done the enormous work for the three volumes. I embrace you, full of thanks."[40]

Capital, volume I, came out on 14 September 1867, in an edition of one thousand copies, selling at 3 taler and 10 groschen. The work was the culmination of nearly a quarter of a century of intermittent research and writing. It was to be Marx's last book in his lifetime. Stresses, distresses, and carbuncles conspired to prevent the completion of the other volumes of *Capital,* although Marx lived on for another sixteen ailing years after the publication of volume I. It is, of course, the masterpiece on which Marx's worldwide reputation rests. Into the preparation of this, as well as the posthumously published volumes, went an immense variety of sources, including government reports, amounting to about fifteen hundred titles. Volume I, described on the title page as "The Process of Capitalist Production," dealt with commodities, surplus value, and the accumulation of capital. But it was more than just another book on political economy. In the preface Marx claimed, as he had also done in *Zur Kritik,* a special universality for it. He stated that he had discovered "natural laws," which were, by definition, inevitable, and that the ultimate aim of the work was "to lay bare the economic laws of motion of modern society."

Capital has a perduring appeal also because it is a literary *chef d'oeuvre,* and not a dry-as-dust piece of economics. It has an unmistakable personal style. Marx himself, referring to the book's construction, rightly called it a "work of art." Underlying the factory reports, the labor statistics, the financial data, and other economic components, are deep convictions and intellectual brilliance, illuminated by sardonic flashes. Here, for example, is an ironic passage on the accumulation of capital:

> This primitive accumulation plays in Political Economy approximately the same role as original sin in theology. Adam bit into the apple, and thereupon sin came upon the human race. Its origin is supposed to be explained as an anecdote of the past. In times long past, there was, on the one side, an industrious, intelligent, and, above all, a frugal elite; and, on the other, lazy ones, spending their substance, and more, in dissipation. The legend of the theological original sin tells us, to be sure, how man came to be condemned to eat his bread by the sweat of his brow; but the history of economic original sin reveals to us why there are people to whom this is by no means necessary. Never mind! So it came to pass that the former sort accumulated wealth, and the latter sort in the end had nothing to sell except their own skin. And from this original sin dates the poverty of the great mass that, despite all its labor, still has nothing to sell but itself, and the wealth of the few that increases constantly, although they have long ceased to work.[41]

Capital is both a work of immense scholarship and an original literary creation. Its qualities of style, irony, moral judgment, and social relevance[42] help to explain why, in the words of Paul A. Samuelson (not an admirer of Marx), *Capital* is a book that has "changed the course of history."[43]

Marx's philosophy of determinism in human affairs did not extend to the propagation of *Capital*. With the fiasco of *Zer Kritik* always painful in his memory, he was determined not to permit the world, especially the German world, to ignore his work this time. Now he would fight the expected "conspiracy of silence" by organizing a systematic propaganda campaign to make *Capital* known to the public. This was hardly in line with the aloofness he professed in the last paragraph of the preface to *Capital:* "Every judgment of scientific criticism I welcome. Vis-à-vis the prejudices of so-called public opinion, to which I have never made concessions, I apply, as ever before, the slogan of the great Florentine: *Segui il tuo corso, e lascia dir le genti!*"[44]

On 13 September 1867, one day before the official publication of *Capital,* Marx and his prospective son-in-law, Paul Lafargue, went to Manchester to plan with Engels a campaign to publicize the book. The three set up a fairly elaborate publicity machinery. The basic plan was to mobilize friends and acquaintances in Germany and on the rest of the Continent to push the book.

In essence, the publicity campaign consisted of three parts: distribution of copies to key people and publications likely to be interested; goading fellow-radicals to publicize the work and, wherever possible, to print extracts from it in the socialist and communist press; and, finally, reviews written by Engels—with Marx's occasional help—for free distribution among journals, preferably the "bourgeois" press. Engels in Manchester and Kugelmann in Hanover were to be the prime movers in the campaign.

Among the copies of *Capital* that were distributed, two went to Englishmen, the historian Edward Spencer Beesly and the journalist Peter Fox (André), both of whom were fellow members of the First International.[45] But all efforts to make *Capital* known in England were largely wasted. An interesting sidelight is provided by the letter that Charles Darwin wrote Marx on 1 October 1873 in acknowledgment of the receipt of the second German edition (1872):

I thank you for the honour which you have done me by sending me your great work on Capital; and I heartily wish that I was more worthy to receive it, by understanding more of the deep and important subject of political economy. Though our studies have been so different, I believe that we both earnestly desire the extension of knowledge, and that this in the long run is sure to add to the happiness of Mankind.[46]

In general, the English, then or later, were not interested in Marx's writings, whether economic or political. The British Labour party, for example, unlike Continental, Asian, and Latin American socialist parties, has never been Marxist. There was no review of *Capital* in the English press, nor an English translation of it during Marx's lifetime. A critique that Engels wrote for *The Fortnightly Review* in mid-1868 was rejected with the comment that it was "too scientific for the English magazine-reading public." One of the rare notices of *Capital* appeared in the *Saturday Review* (25 January, 1868), a conservative London weekly, which, in a discussion of several other books, commented on Marx: "The author's views may be as pernicious as we conceive them to be, but there can be no question as to the plausibility of his logic, the vigour of his rhetoric, and the charm with which he invests the driest problems of Political Economy." To which Marx's comment was: "Ouff!"

Copies of *Capital* were sent to a number of influential Europeans, among them the poet Ferdinand Freilighausen in London, the anarchist theoretician Jean-Jacques-Elisée Reclus in Paris, and the academic economist Karl Wilhelm Contzen in Leipzig. A copy to Michael Bakunin, Marx's anarchist enemy-friend (who, in 1868, began to translate *Capital* into Russian but never completed the task) went unacknowledged.

The pressures of Engels and Kugelmann on their German friends and acquaintances to publicize *Capital* were not altogether wasted but they were not greatly successful, either. For a long time, there was only one professional review, written by Eugen Dühring, a *Privatdozent* (Lecturer) at the University of Berlin.[47] Marx, grateful for any attention, thought that despite Dühring's misunderstanding of much in *Capital* the review was nevertheless "very decent." Engels, on the other hand, was not pleased. He felt that Dühring showed embarrassment and anxiety when confronted with a work like *Capital.* "The vulgar economist," he commented to Marx, "is cut to the quick and does not know what to say except that one would be able to pass judgment on the first volume only after the third has appeared." A decade later, Engels was to castigate the "vulgar economist" in a famous polemic known as *Anti-Dühring*.[48]

By the end of 1867, only a handful of German publications had bothered to notice *Capital* or print any extracts from its preface.[49] Marx was upset, and came down with another severe attack of carbuncles. To be consistently ignored even by German workers, for whom he believed he had sacrificed so many years of labor and effort, was, in the words of his wife, a "torment." Engels appealed to Kugelman in Hanover to do something—anything—to get notices in the German press: "The main thing is that the book be discussed again and again. And since Marx cannot act freely in this matter, and also feels embarrassed like a virgin, we others must do it. Be so kind as to let me know what success you have had in this thing up to now and which papers you believe can still be used. In this, to use the words of our old friend Jesus Christ, we must act as innocent as doves and be as cunning as serpents." The worst thing, Engels continued, was to be ignored. He told Kugelmann that even unfriendly reviews, including attacks on *Capital,* would be welcome. If *Capital* were mentioned in fifteen or twenty newspapers, Engels stated, notice would be taken of the work "simply as an important phenomenon that deserves consideration." Then the "whole gang" of nonradical economists would begin to "howl" and be *compelled* to pay attention to *Capital.*

Marx himself, however, drew the line at publicity in certain publications. He thoroughly despised those that had a mass appeal as "vulgar." When Kugelmann suggested that an advertisement of *Capital* be placed in *Gartenlaube,* an illustrated weekly "family paper," Marx urged him "definitely to give up this joke." He thought that appearing in publications designed for the common masses was "*beneath* the character of a scholarly man." By way of example, he told Kugelmann that when *Meyers Konversationslexikon* had asked him for a biographical note about himself, he ignored it: "I did not even answer the letter. Everybody must attain salvation in his own way."

Engels' campaign strategy did not quite work out as he expected. The reviews he wrote and sent to the press were published in eight papers, none of them of consequence.[50] Marx, in

London, anxiously scanned the German press for mentions or reviews. These were scant, indeed, amounting altogether to around a dozen.[51] To Marx's chagrin, the important German dailies paid no attention whatever to *Capital.* Marx commented: "The great bourgeois and reactionary papers carefully keep their mouths shut."

The German academic and professional economists also were mostly silent. In addition to Dühring's, there seem to have been only two reviews in the first several years after the publication of *Capital.* Marx thought both of them ridiculous. One, published anonymously, claimed that Marx was a pupil of the French economist Frédéric Bastiat, an advocate of class "harmonies" instead of class struggles. Marx considered the review a "farce" and called the editor of the journal, the economist Julius Faucher, "*Mannequin Pisse* Faucher"—a reference to the famous statue of the urinating boy in a public fountain in Brussels.

The other professional review appeared two years later, in *Jahrbücher für Nationalökonomie und Statistik,*[52] written by Karl Friedrich Rösler, an economist who indulged in what Marx called bourgeois "drivel" in lieu of hard economic categories or realities. In a letter to Engels (20 July, 1870), Marx described Rösler's review as "*philosophic* twaddle worthy of Moses Mendelssohn, smart-assing, peevish, know-it-all, nit-picking." The whole thing, he wrote, made him laugh: "My physical condition hardly predisposes me to merriment, but I have cried with laughter over this essay, bona fide tears of mirth."

Ignored by what is today called the Establishment, Marx's ideas made their way but slowly in Germany. They began to spread only with the steady growth of the Social Democratic party, which came under Marxist influence in the 1870s and 1880s. A second German edition of *Capital,* revised by Marx, appeared in 1872; this time, Meissner printed three thousand copies. After Marx's death, Engels prepared a third edition, which came out in 1883, and a fourth in 1890. Engels also brought out volumes II (1885) and III (1894) of *Capital,* from the hardly legible chapters, notes, and tables, all of the latter factually inaccurate,[53] which Marx had left behind. By that time, *Capital* was selling fairly steadily in Germany, at the rate of several hundred copies a year.[54]

Elsewhere, *Capital* made quicker headway. It is of historical significance that the first foreign translation of the work was not into English or French, but into Russian. In an episode that forms a fascinating footnote in the history of human communications, *Capital* was passed by the Czarist censorship in a manner that was hardly a tribute to its efficiency or farsightedness. The Russian censors cleared the book on the ground that, being scientific, it would not be available to the common people and hence, presumably, no threat to Czarism. The censor's report stated: "Although the author is, according to his convictions, a thoroughgoing socialist and the whole book bears the stamp of a fully socialist character, nevertheless, out of consideration for the fact that the presentation is such that it can in no way be accessible just to anybody, but does, on the contrary, possess strictly mathematical and scientific proofs, the committee declares that prosecution of this book before a court of justice would be impossible."

The Russian translation of *Capital*,[55] which came out in 1872, was an immediate success. Of an edition of three thousand copies, about nine hundred were sold within the first month, something of a record in a country with a relatively small circle of educated people. The book was widely discussed by intellectuals and professional economists. "Most journals and newspapers," Danielson, one of the translators, informed the delighted Marx, "have carried reviews. All of them—with one exception—have been very laudatory."[56] In 1873 and 1874, rioting radical students in big Russian cities quoted from *Capital* in their propaganda. The work was still being debated in important Russian journals as late as 1879, the year both Stalin and Trotsky were born. Marx was pleasantly surprised. In 1880, he wrote to a friend that in Russia, a country he generally despised as barbaric, he was "more read and appreciated than anywhere else." His influence on Russian radicalism, if not on the science of economics,[57] was to be continuous, through the Russian Revolution of 1917 and into our own time.

Marx was particularly anxious to have a French translation of *Capital*, for Paris was still the intellectual pacesetter of Europe. As Marx's daughter Eleanor, echoing "Papa's" thoughts, wrote to Danielson on 23 January 1872, "I hope very much that as soon as a French edition has come out, an English one will follow—the English are aping everything the French do; only

when something comes from *Paris* does it have success here.''
After years of effort and negotiation, primarily with various
translators, a French publisher[58] brought out a first installment
of *Capital* in an edition of ten thousand copies, which were
quickly sold. The whole book, translated by at least two men[59]
but in the end thoroughly corrected and revised by Marx himself, came out three years later, in 1875.

An English translation of *Capital* was long in coming. It did
not appear until 1887, two decades after the first German edition and four years after Marx's death. One problem involved in
the delay was linguistic expertise. A translation of some chapters by the English socialist Henry Mayers Hyndman[60] was exposed by Engels as completely inaccurate.[61] He wrote: ''Marx is
one of the most forceful, most terse and most exact writers of
our time. To convey his meaning properly, one has to be master
not only of the German but also of the English language.''
There were apparently few such masters to be found in England. The English translation was finally made by two friends
of Marx and Engels, the lawyer Samuel Moore and the journalist
Edward Aveling. Both Engels and Eleanor Marx, who lived with
Aveling, supervised and helped with the translation, for which
Engels wrote a preface in 1886.

The English translation[62] was more a labor of love and prestige than a fulfillment of demand. There were few sales[63] of
Capital, and only one review.[64] The royalties amounted to
£12.3.9 for 1887–1888, and to a mere £1.3.1 for 1893–1894.
The English obviously were not greatly interested in Marxism.

Capital did better in America.[65] In 1890, a Barnum-type
publisher in New York, seeing that the volume contained a section entitled ''The Accumulation of Capital,'' cunningly printed a circular stating that in this learned tome by a German
scholar one can learn ''how to accumulate capital,'' and sent it
to all the bank officials in the United States. The greedy money-
men, eager to make a killing, quickly sent in their orders for the
book. An edition of five thousand copies of *Capital* thus was
sold out. Marx, with his sardonic sense of the ridiculous, would
have roared with laughter to find himself a ''best seller'' in the
United States, a country that he called ''the most modern form
of bourgeois society.''[66]

Capital, as well as Marx's other socioeconomic writings, made their way gradually around the world.[67] What is known as "Marxism" has had, and is having, a strong appeal in less developed countries where substantial numbers of the population have economic and social grievances. The Marxist appeal has been both to the heart and to the mind, invoking, as it does, certitudes of hope based on "science." That Marx's socialism is not, as he claimed it was, "scientific" in any meaningful sense of the word, and that his economics has only a coincidental relationship to "science," has little relevance in the realm of the communication of ideas. His economic writings constitute the scriptures of, and the learned authority for, communism. Marx is, in brief, a latter-day prophet—an angry prophet, to boot—who used the tools and data of political economy to propound his vision.

NOTES

1. Marx's dissertation, for which he received his Ph.D. at Jena University in 1841, was based on extensive original Greek and Latin sources and was entitled *Differenz der demokritischen und epikureischen Naturphilosophie* [Difference between the Democritean and Epicurean philosophy of nature].

2. Marx was editor from 15 October 1842 to 17 March 1843, when he resigned "because of the censorship."

3. Marx was the *Tribune*'s correspondent for a decade; his last article in that paper, "The Mexican Imbroglio," appeared on 10 March 1862.

4. Marx was correspondent of the *Presse* from 25 October 1861 to 4 December 1862.

5. Marx died on 14 March 1883.

6. Marx married Jenny von Westphalen on 19 June 1843.

7. The Old Guard "dies but does not surrender"—a famous phrase attributed to the Napoleonic general at Waterloo, Pierre Cambronne, who denied that he ever uttered it.

8. In his later years in London, when unable to work because of recurring illnesses, Marx read science and mathematics for relaxation. Thus, at the end of 1878, Marx perused Descartes' mathematical works as well as Otto Caspari's *Leibniz' Philosophie vom Gesichtspunkt der physikalischen Grundbegriffe von Kraft und Stoff* [Leibniz's philosophy from the point of view of the basic physical concepts of energy and matter] (Leipzig, 1870), and Emil Du Bois-Reymond's *Leibnizsche Gedanken in der neueren Naturwissenschaft* [Leibniz's ideas in recent natural science] (Berlin, 1871).

9. For Marx's articles on Spain, see Saul K. Padover, ed., *On Revolution,* vol. 1 of The Karl Marx Library (New York, 1971), pp. 541–640.

10. Flerovsky was the pseudonym of Vassily Vassilyevich Bervy, author of *Poloshenye Rabotshevo Klassa v Rossyi* [The condition of the working class in Russia] (St. Petersburg, 1869), a book that greatly impressed Marx.

11. Maxim Maximovich Kovalevsky, a Russian sociologist and historian, sent Marx his book *Obshchinnoye Zyemlyeva-dennye, Pritsinny, Chod Y Posledstvya Yevo Raslozhennyia* (Moscow, 1879).

12. As late as 13 February 1894, Frederick Engels wrote to Karl Kautsky, the Marxist theorist: "The expression *Communism* I do not consider today as *generally* applicable, but rather I reserve it for use in cases where *more specific* definition is necessary, and even then I demand an explanation, since for 30 years the word has not been in practical use."

13. "Der Kommunismus und die Augsburger *Allgemeine Zietung*" [Communism and the Augsburg *Allgemeine Zeitung*], in *Rheinische Zeitung,* 16 October 1842; for text, see Padover, pp. 3–6.

14. [Socialism and communism in contemporary France] (Leipzig, 1842).

15. Claude de Saint-Simon, *L'Industrie* (Paris, 1817); *Du Système industriel* (Paris, 1821); *Catéchisme des industriels* (Paris, 1823–1824); *Nouveau Christianisme* (Paris, 1825).

16. Marx came to consider utopianism muddle-headed nonsense, inimical to real socialism. On 19 October 1877, he wrote to Friedrich Adolph Sorge, a German-born American radical: ". . . *utopian* socialism, the chimerical game played with the future structure of society, is again raging [in Germany]. . . . It is natural that utopianism, which *before* the era of materialist-critical socialism concealed the latter within itself *in nuce* [kernel], coming now *post festum* [after the event], can only be silly, stale, and basically reactionary."

17. Wilhelm Weitling, *Garantien der Harmonie und Freiheit* (Vivis, 1842).

18. No. 41, Rue Vaneau, Faubourg St. Germain.

19. In March 1844 the journal suspended publication after one double issue, which came out at the end of February. Despite its title, *Deutsch-Französische Jahrbücher* contained no French contributors.

20. Marx excepted German workers from his strictures on Germany. In "Critical Marginal Notes on the Article 'The King of Prussia and Social Reform,' " *Vorwärts,* 7 August 1844, he praised the intelligence, education, and talent of the German proletariat; for text, see Padover, pp. 7–22.

21. For text, see Padover, pp. 154–242.

22. Ibid., pp. 332–372.

23. Laura Marx married Paul Lafargue in 1868, and Jenny Marx married Charles Longuet in 1872.

24. In his review, Engels wrote about the English working poor: "In 1842,

England and Wales had 1,430,000 paupers, of whom 222,000 were incarcerated in work-houses—the people call them poor-law Bastilles. Thanks to the humanity of the Whigs! Scotland has no poor-law, but a mass of poor. Ireland, by the way, can boast of 2,300,000 paupers.''

25. Engels developed these ideas in his first book, *Die Lage der arbeitenden Klasse in England* [The condition of the working class in England] (Leipzig, 1845).

26. The Moscow Institute of Marxism-Leninism brought out the first full German edition in 1932 and a Russian one in 1933. An English translation by R. Dixon was published by Foreign Languages Publishing House, Moscow, in 1956.

27. Progress Publishers, Moscow, brought out in English translation the so-called volume IV of *Capital* under the title *Theories of Surplus Value,* pt. 1, 1963; pt. 2, 1968; pt. 3, 1971. The material in these volumes consists mainly of notes and comments, which Marx had not integrated into a book before his death.

28. First published in full by the Institute of Marxism-Leninism, Moscow, 1932. The first English translation, by Martin Milligan, was published by Progress Publishers, Moscow, in 1959.

29. A lengthy introduction (about twenty-five printed pages), which Marx wrote in August and September, 1857, was not included in the book; it was published in *Die Neue Zeit* in 1903.

30. Engels, as always, complied. On 26 January 1859, Marx wrote him: "The £2 duly received; the manuscript mailed.''

31. Here all distrust must be abandoned;
    Here all cowardice must be dead.

32. It was originally published under the title *The Eighteenth Brumaire of Louis Napoleon* in the New York City German-language monthly *Die Revolution,* December 1851 to February 1852. When it came out as a book in German, the title was changed to *The Eighteenth Brumaire of Louis Bonaparte* Hamburg, 1869).

33. Meissner also had an American outlet, L. S. Schmidt, New York City.

34. *Das Kapital. Kritik der politischen Oekonomie.*

35. For Marx's role, see Saul K. Padover, ed., *On the First International,* vol. 3 of The Karl Marx Library (New York, 1973).

36. See the comprehensive psychological study by Arnold Künzli, *Karl Marx: Eine Psychographie* (Vienna, 1966).

37. The last sentence was in English.

38. Marx's Dutch-born mother, née Henriette Presborg (or Presburg), who never fully mastered the German language, pronounced her son's name as "Karell.''

39. Otto Wigand, in Leipzig.

40. The last sentence was in English.

41. Translated by Saul K. Padover from the 4th German edition of *Das Kapital* (Hamburg, 1890), vol. I, chap. 24, section 1. In the English translation of 1887, this passage is found in chapter 26.

42. Robert Heilbroner: "Why then bother with Marxian economics when, as virtually every economist will tell you, it is 'wrong'? The reason is that, unlike neoclassical analysis, which is 'right,' the Marxian model has in surfeit the quality of social relevance that is so egregiously lacking in the other"; quoted in Saul K. Padover, "Marx Redivivus," *New School Bulletin*, 31 March 1969.

43. Samuelson, "Marx's *'Das Kapital,' "* in *Newsweek*, 16 October 1967.

44. Follow thy own course, and let people say what they will! Dante, *Divine Comedy*, "Purgatory."

45. At the third General Congress of the International, held in Brussels, 6–13 September 1868, the German delegates proposed a resolution praising Marx for his "scientific" socialism and suggesting that *Capital*, soon to be published and which they obviously had not read, be translated into foreign languages.

46. In 1880, when Marx asked the greatly admired Darwin for permission to dedicate to him volume II of *Capital*, on which he was still working, the famous scientist politely refused, among other things on the ground that he did not wish to hurt his family's religious sensibilities.

47. Dühring's review appeared in *Ergänzungsblätter zur Kenntniss der Gegenwart* (Hildburghausen, 1867), vol. 3, pp. 182–186.

48. Engels, *Herrn Eugen Dührings Umwälzung der Wissenschaft* [Herr Eugen Dühring's revolution in science] (Leipzig, 1878).

49. In the year 1867, notices of publication of part of the preface of *Capital* appeared in: *Der Beobachter* (Stuttgart daily), 7 September; *Der Vorbote* (Geneva monthly), September, October, November; *Courrier Français* (Paris weekly), 1 October; *La Liberté* (Brussels daily), 13 October; *Libertà e Giustizia* (Naples weekly), 27 October. An English notice appeared in *The Bee-Hive Newspaper* (London weekly organ of the First International), 7 September.

50. In 1867: *Die Zukunft* (Berlin daily), 30 October; *Elberfelder Zeitung* (daily), 2 November; *Düsseldorfer Zeitung* (daily), 17 November; *Barmer Zeitung* (daily), 19 December; *Der Beobachter* (Stuttgart daily), 27 December; *Staats-Anzeiger Für Württemberg* (Stuttgart daily), 27 December. In 1868: *Neue Badische Landeszeitung* (Mannheim daily), 21 January; *Demokratisches Wochenblatt* (Leipzig weekly), 21 and 28 March.

51. Among the other reviews were a series of twelve articles, "Das Werk von Carl [sic] Marx," in *Der Social-Demokrat* (a labor publication appearing three times weekly in Berlin), 22 January to 6 May 1868; *Börsenhalle für Deutschland* (Hamburg daily), 14 February 1868; *Literarisches Centralblatt für Deutschland* (Leipzig), 4 July 1868.

52. Published by the economist and statistician Bruno Hildebrand, Jena, 1870.

53. Engels to Marx's daughter Laura Lafargue, 11 April 1864: "I am frightfully busy, am stuck deep in Ground Rents, which gives me great trouble, since Mohr's [Marx's nickname among intimates] tables almost without exception contain errors in calculation—you know what a genius he was with figures!—and I have to recalculate everything anew."

54. The royalties from *Capital* in Germany were: £130 (2,600 marks) in 1886, £43 in 1889, £45 in 1890, £38 in 1892, thus showing a small but constant sale.

55. The translators were the economic writer Nicolai Frantzevich Danielson and the liberal landowner German Alexandrovich Lopatin. The publisher was Nicolai Petrovich Polyakov, in St. Petersburg.

56. One review that Marx greatly appreciated was by a St. Petersburg University professor, Illarion Ignatzievich Kauffmann, "Karl Marx's Point of View in Political Economic Criticism," in *Vestnik Evropy,* May 1872.

57. A Russian economist, Ludwig Slonimski, in his book *Attempt at a Critique of Karl Marx's Economic Theories* (German translation, Berlin, 1899), concluded: "In the history of the . . . labor movement Marx's work plays a significant role; but he did not advance economic science by a single step!"

58. Maurice Lachâtre (La Châtre), a radical Paris journalist and Communard.

59. The translation was begun by Joseph Roy and completed by Charles Keller, but neither of them really satisfied Marx.

60. Hyndman, writing under the pseudonym John Broadhouse, published the first of his seven translated chapters of *Capital* in the October 1885 issue of *To-day,* a monthly of which he was editor.

61. Engels, "How Marx Should Not Be Translated," in *The Commonweal,* November 1885.

62. The London publisher was Swan Sonnenschein & Co.

63. The price of the book was 30 shillings in 1887 and 10 shillings 6 pence in 1889.

64. An anonymous one in *The Athenaeum,* 5 March 1887.

65. In 1906 Charles H. Kerr Co. of Chicago brought out a "revised and amplified" translation by Ernest Untermann; it was no great improvement on the Moore-Aveling one.

66. For Marx's opinions on America and American capitalism, see Saul K. Padover, ed., *On America and the Civil War,* vol. 2 of The Karl Marx Library (New York, 1972).

67. The censorship prevailing in countries like Italy, Poland, Portugal, and Spain slowed up translations of *Capital* but did not finally prevent them. Italian and Spanish translations came out in 1886 and a Polish one (in Leipzig) in 1890. There was also a Dutch translation in 1885 and a complete translation in Dutch in 1894.

8

COMMUNIST PROPAGANDA

WILLIAM E. GRIFFITH

THE HERITAGE OF MARXISM

The personality, career, and ideology of Karl Marx placed a permanent stamp on communist propaganda. Marx was an émigré most of his life and could do little but write and propagandize. He was a prophet and a preacher—as Edmund Wilson called him, "the great secular rabbi of our century." He was an intellectual and quite naturally saw intellectuals as the torchbearers of communism. Most important, his ideology predisposed the communist movement toward a high priority for propaganda. Marx's "scientific socialism" took over from Hegel, with so much else, the doctrine that knowledge is the key to reality, that only full consciousness can bring full perception of reality. The task of communist revolutionaries, therefore, is primarily to achieve consciousness themselves and transmit it via education (that is, propaganda) to the proletariat. Thus the Marxist sense of certainty, its passion for conversion, and its emphasis on educating the masses predisposed its followers toward regarding propaganda as one of its most important tasks.

Marxist ideology thus inclined its propaganda toward elitism and manipulation of the masses. The communists were an elite, bearers of knowledge to the proletariat. Moreover, according to Marxist doctrine, true knowledge cannot be achieved by the process of cognition alone, but only by a combination of cognition and revolutionary activity—praxis. In other words, the philosopher must be a revolutionary and the revolutionary a philosopher. Furthermore, Marx relativized morality and ethics, and his ideology therefore made it easy for Lenin and his successors to justify the thesis that the end—the revolution and the consolidation of socialism—justifies the means: a further justification for elitism and manipulation. Finally, the Marxian doctrine of scientific socialism justified its political legitimacy by the monopoly of its "guardians," the communists, on scientific truth, that is, on the understanding of and ability to predict history according to the universally valid laws of scientific socialism. Thus, in theory, once one understood the class relationships in a society, the policies required to bring about socialism could and should be automatically deduced from them. Policy proposals that non-Marxists would regard as normative decisions are thus in Marxist ideology couched in analytical forms, what may be called the "indicative imperative." (For example, the Soviet press will say "the world proletariat is rallying ever more closely around the CPSU" when it means that "it should.") These indicative-imperative statements are justified in terms of quotations from the ideology of Marx (or Lenin or Stalin or Mao or Castro.) Because in a communist polity the professional Marxist propagandists have a monopoly of the interpretation of this ideology, as a priestly caste does in a religion, they are also the official public proclaimers, as opposed to shapers, of policy.

COMMUNIST PROPAGANDA AS A DEVELOPMENTAL MECHANISM

Marx believed that socialism could come only in a highly developed industrial society. But in fact, with the exception of East Germany and the Czech lands it has come in underdeveloped societies. Communist propaganda there has played a major role in political and economic development and in mass mobilization for these purposes. To do so, its organizational mechanism has been structurally integrated with the Communist party organization itself. Its strategies and tactics have varied according to the stages of political and economic development. The less developed the society, the more communist propaganda has concentrated on face-to-face communication as opposed to the printed or spoken word. Its function, as Liu has pointed out, has been to create the infrastructure for what did not exist in preindustrial societies: a national mass communication system, geographical unification (normally by transportation), a national language (for example, Russian or Mandarin), and mass literacy. All these have been the preconditions for mass political and social mobilization, for rapid economic development, and for centrally directed propaganda indoctrination.

LENIN AND PROPAGANDA

Disillusioned by the lack of revolutionary consciousness and activism in the working class of Europe, which had turned toward reform rather than revolution, Lenin became much more of an elitist than Marx. For him revolutionary consciousness could be brought to the working class only from outside, by the Communist party, which he defined as a small disciplined band of trained revolutionary fanatics. As he, like Marx, spent long years in exile, where he had to concentrate on propaganda activities, Lenin emphasized propaganda even more than did Marx himself. Because of his elitism, Lenin added coercion to persuasion to make up that special mix, "coercive persuasion," which has since characterized propaganda in most communist societies. Lenin was convinced that to prevent the working class from falling prey to false opinions and to allow maxiumum opportunity for the communists to impose their revolutionary consciousness on it, the Communist party must control all means of communication. It must lead, not follow, public opinion. Its propaganda must be exhaustive, differentiated, and entirely controlled by a centralized propaganda apparatus. Lenin was a voluntarist, far more so than Marx: he believed that the consciousness of the masses could be and must be manipulated. Finally, Lenin originated the use of propaganda declarations for policy purposes, what is now known as "esoteric communication."

LENINIST ESOTERIC COMMUNICATION

The Marxist-Leninist ideological tradition, which obtains its legitimacy from commonly held, unquestionable "scientific" doctrine, requires that this doctrine be officially and unanimously adopted and supported. Yet once Marxist-Leninists come to power, they suffer from the same conflicts, struggles among interest groups, and bureaucratic rivalries that characterize all polities. Therefore, to maintain the myth of unanimity while at the same time communicating among the elite and using elite communications in these struggles and conflicts, the public expression of them came to be in the form of ideological pronouncements directed in theory against deviationists (that is, secular heretics) but in fact intended as weapons in power struggles. Moreover, as the legitimization of Marxist-Leninist ideology arises in large part from its "sacred texts"—the works of Marx, Lenin, Mao, and so on—as the near-interminable length and variety of these works can provide ample textual justification for various policy points of view, the propagandists of various factions support their views by citing the appropriate "sacred" Marxist-Leninist texts. Finally, the traditional authoritarianism and ritualization of supreme authority in the Russian and Chinese empires stamped these characteristics on Russian and Chinese Marxism, so that their propaganda is often carried on in a ritualistic as well as in the more purely ideological manner.

In communist states, therefore, esoteric elite communication —particularly as an expression of struggles among factions—is normally carried on not only to transmit policy guidance to party cadres but also to influence the outcome of factional struggles. Its propaganda cloak, ideological language, guarantees that the secrecy of these struggles will be maintained against the masses of the population and all except a few specialists in the noncommunist world. Typically, this variety of communist propaganda—intra-elite struggles—is carried on in terms of ideological polemics against alleged deviationists and also in ritualistic and symbolic forms: appointments, dismissals, changes in rank, order in listing and photographs, frequency of citation, and so on. The more personalized such statements and the more they are cloaked in the authority of the highest communist levels of leadership, the more authoritative they are. Thus statements by Brezhnev are much more authoritative than those by his subordinates. Statements in *Pravda* are more authoritative than those, say, in a Soviet journal on international affairs. Anonymous editorials are more authoritative than signed ones, unless the signator is of very high rank. Esoteric polemics often are carried on in a historical framework, for example, in the changing attitude toward Stalin.

THE PROPAGANDA OF DICTATORSHIP AND PERSONALITY CHANGE

In the case of communist leaders who have become total dictators, propaganda is frequently used to develop an overwhelming cult of personality and thus to create or strengthen a charismatic leader. Moreover, in the case of massive and bloody purges, propaganda creates such fear—by violent denunciation of "enemies" who then confess or are "liquidated"—that the society is largely atomized and the rule of the dictator, based primarily on the monopoly of terror, is further strengthened. This was the case with Stalin and also has been so with Mao and Castro. In the cases of Stalin and Mao, the propaganda adulation has gone to unprecedented heights and perhaps, at least after the former's death, even to counterproductive heights.

The most extreme category of communist propaganda is found in the attempt to bring about actual transformation in human personalities. This has been particularly the case with Maoist and Fidelista propaganda. This phenomenon will be discussed later in some detail. Suffice it here to say that this variety of communist propaganda has been a major component of such developments as the Cultural Revolution in China and the guerrilla mystique of the Cuban Revolution.

THE ORGANIZATION, STRATEGY, AND TACTICS OF COMMUNIST PROPAGANDA

Leninist propaganda, as I have said, is totalistic. It is intended to dominate and control not only all means of elite and mass communication but also all history, social science, literature, art, and music. Indeed, under Stalin and Mao it came to dominate natural science as well. This has been so because the instrumentalist view of education and propaganda characteristic of the Leninist tradition requires not only that there be nothing in communication media or any other intellectual output contrary to the Communist party line, but in addition that they be positively harnessed to the implementation of that line. As the propaganda line is directed not only to the elite but to the masses as well, and as the Leninist concept of the gradual transformation from bourgeois to socialist consciousness requires total mobilization of all means of communication, the concept, for example, of *l'art pour l'art* is foreign to the Leninist tradition. Lenin himself was prepared to allow in literature and art a certain amount of autonomy in style, although not in content, but since his death "socialist realism" generally has characterized communist cultural activities.

The negative aspect of communist propaganda, that is, its prevention of the expression of any views contrary to the party line, is normally implemented by censorship. Its positive aspect, the active implementation of the party line, is embodied in the direction of the elite and mass communication media and all cultural activities toward positive propaganda content. Both are under the supervision of the agitation and propaganda section of the Central Committee of the Communist Party (the "Agitprop"). The Agitprop controls the central communication media directly through its issuance of propaganda guidelines for implementation of the party line and negatively by its directives to the censorship prohibiting them from approving certain categories of political content and bias. The Agitprop also provides the ideological language in which policy decisions are set forth. It also originates propaganda campaigns against ideological deviationists, for education of party activists, for agitation among the noncommunist population, and for propaganda to foreign countries, socialist and nonsocialist. (Lenin made the distinction between propaganda, directed toward the communist elite, and agitation, directed toward the masses. In fact, however, most communist propaganda tends to be agitation. Only recently, as will be seen below, have efforts been made, notably in the Soviet Union, to strengthen the purely propaganda aspect. For the purposes of this chapter, however, I shall use propaganda to refer to both). The Agitprop operates through subordinate agitprop sections of lower-level Communist party organizations, over which it exercises staff supervision and control. It also controls the various so-called front organizations, which ostensibly represent and express the views of occupational, cultural, or other sectors of the population, but are in fact used as "transmission belts" for the implementation of Agitprop propaganda lines. (These front organizations are particularly important for propaganda to noncommunist areas).

COMMUNIST INTERNATIONAL PROPAGANDA

Communist ideology in theory has always been oriented toward "the world revolution of socialism." After communism came to power in major countries, however, notably the Soviet Union and China, it predictably became increasingly oriented toward the growth of the international power and influence of these countries. It is important to understand, however, that communists, whether ideologists or not, have not consciously seen a contradiction in the Marxist-Leninist ideological imperative for world revolution and the spread of Soviet or Chinese state influence—any more than the ideologists of American imperialism, for example, in the period of Theodore Roosevelt, saw a contradiction between spreading American ideology and American imperial influence. By now, therefore, Russian, Chinese, or Cuban national policy tends to give more emphasis to national influence than to ideology, but the two remain organically linked in the consciousness of their proponents.

It follows, therefore, that as there are substantial communist movements and groups of communist or Marxist sympathizers in countries in the developed and the underdeveloped world who are assets in terms of spreading both communist ideology and a favorable image of, for example, the Soviet Union, China, or Cuba, communist governments have been deeply involved in propaganda on the international level. Communist international propaganda has been extensively developed through press, radio, television, tourism, and the use of economic and military aid for propaganda purposes. Like domestic communist propaganda, it is centrally administered by the Agitprop. It is directed toward both communist and noncommunist sectors of the populations, as well as, notably in terms of economic and military aid and commerce, toward rightist groups, which have reasons of *Realpolitik* for sympathy toward or alliance with the Soviet Union or China.

The themes of communist international propaganda toward the developed world have been primarily anti-American, anti-German, and anti-Japanese. It has particularly concentrated on the issue of peace, through various front organizations and through constant propaganda stress on the theme that communist countries are for peace while their capitalist opponents are for war. With respect to the underdeveloped countries, the theme of peace has been less emphasized than those of anticolonialism and anticapitalism. Positively, communist propaganda toward the underdeveloped world has specialized in support of the various national liberation movements and in demonstrating that the Soviet Union, China, or Cuba is actively aiding them; in portraying the United States as the chief fortress and perpetuator of world imperialism; in demonstration of economic and military aid, notably to certain areas of strategic interest to the Soviet Union or China, such as the United Arab Republic and India for the Soviet Union and East Africa for China; and, finally, in the more general themes of peace and anti-Westernism. With respect to the control and implementation of communist objectives in international propaganda, the role of international or semi-international propaganda organs and of radio broadcasting in foreign languages is especially important. This is notably true of such officially international but actually Soviet-controlled propaganda organs as the *World Marxist Review*, or, under Stalin, the Cominform journal. Organizationally, it is true of such organizations as the World Peace Council, the World Federation of Trade Unions, the Afro-Asian People's Solidarity Organization, and so on. The Chinese have used the *Peking Review* and Radio Peking as international as well as national instruments, while Castro has formed and used such officially international organizations as the Latin American People's Solidarity Organization.

PROPAGANDA CREDIBILITY

Credibility is probably the most important key to the effectiveness of any propaganda, communist or otherwise. It is particularly important, it seems to me, for communist propaganda, since in the communist world, ideology, as expressed in propaganda declarations, is uniquely the legitimizing factor. It is often endangered by factional struggles—for example, between Khrushchev and Malenkov in the Soviet Union, or between Mao and Liu Shao-chi and later Lin Piao in China—and by sharp changes in propaganda line such as the Soviet-Nazi Pact and the Nixon visit to Peking. Finally, when periods of liberalization have occurred, as in Khrushchev's destalinization program, the propaganda attacks against a previous dictatorial ruler like Stalin created, as will be seen below, serious crises, particularly among revisionist intellectuals. I shall discuss in the conclusion to this chapter some current problems of communist propaganda credibility.

RECENT AND CURRENT SOVIET PROPAGANDA DEVELOPMENTS

Under Stalin, particularly in his later years, Soviet propaganda, like all other aspects of the Soviet political system, had become ossified and fanaticized. The USSR was in the grip of Stalin's terrorist dictatorship in which he used the secret police rather than the Communist party as his main instrument of domination and rule. The very extremism of Stalinist propaganda, not only against the West but even more against Tito and Zionism, tended to discredit it abroad and at home as well, as became clear after his death. Indeed, Marxist-Leninist ideology, like the CPSU itself, had lost most of its vitality as a result of its reduction by Stalin to a sycophantic instrument of his terrorist rule. Khrushchev was determined to revitalize the Communist party as the chief instrument of political rule. This required the revitalization of Marxist-Leninist ideology and of the effectiveness and credibility of propaganda. This was all the more necessary, Khrushchev felt, because his policy of peaceful coexistence, that is, East-West détente vis-à-vis the West and particularly the United States, required intensification of the ideological struggle within the socialist world, which otherwise might become dangerously undermined by Western influence. Post-1953 domestic destalinization did result in a massive decline in police terror and a major readjustment of propaganda policies toward material and ideological incentives rather than terror. Khrushchev's attempt to revitalize communist ideology centered around his implementation of the CPSU line on the transition to communism, which resulted in many books and hundreds of articles sketching in great detail what a pure communist society would be. At the same time, in foreign propaganda Khrushchev strongly stressed not only the peace issue but also, particularly using Sputnik, the applicability and attractiveness to the underdeveloped world of the Soviet model of rapid forced industrialization of a previously underdeveloped country, and the political and propaganda goal of surpassing the United States in

GNP. Khrushchev had some success in revitalizing Soviet propaganda, notably by combining it with such appealing themes as space travel and rocketry, but the crises in eastern Europe and above all the Sino-Soviet split confronted him with new propaganda problems and ideological difficulties that he was far from mastering when he was removed in 1964.

Under Brezhnev and Kosygin, the tendency already noticeable under Stalin and even more under Khrushchev of emphasizing Soviet strength and technological progress, was carried much farther. Conversely, Khrushchev's attempt to revitalize communist ideology by concentrating on the utopian vision of the transition to communism was abandoned by his successors, who devoted much more attention in propaganda and other aspects of their policies to material incentives and to pushing forward the scientific-technological revolution. Not that Brezhnev and Kosygin were consequential modernizers or liberalizers. Their insistence on maintaining and, indeed with respect to culture, for example, intensifying party control brought a halt to destalinization, prevented genuine rationalization of the backward Soviet agriculture, stood in the path of rational decentralization of the Soviet economy, and led to increased cultural repression. But fundamentally they have seen themselves as modernizers, inter alia in propaganda.

In their reforms of Soviet propaganda, they have stressed specificity of function, that is, attention to particular audiences toward which specific varieties of propaganda should be directed; rational and universalistic norms of conduct; and, finally, considerations of achievement, particularly in science and technology, rather than exclusive emphasis on political and moral incentives. These Soviet reforms have resulted in recent years in greater attention to propaganda as opposed to agitation, in respect of themes, institutionalization, and centralization at the agitprop level in Moscow, as well as considerable decentralization of mass agitation activities. In the area of universalistic and rational policies, Soviet propaganda now makes much more use than in the past of survey research, social psychology, and such achievement criteria as planning, coordination, supervision, assessment, and rewards.

These recent reforms have been part of the general process of modernizing and increasing the education of Communist party members. In particular, they have resulted in the development of a new category of more educated propaganda officials, the so-called politinformators who appeal to specific groups of the Soviet intelligentsia and who are, therefore, expected to have some competence in the professional fields of those whom they propagandize. Although, of course, survey data are lacking or at least are unavailable in the West by which one can judge the effectiveness of these reforms in Soviet propaganda, I think it probable that they have made it more successful than it was under Stalin and Khrushchev. On the other hand, however, the growth of the movement of intellectual dissent in the Soviet Union and the regime's ambivalence about suppressing it probably have discredited Soviet propaganda among the critical Soviet intelligentsia, notably propaganda treatment of sanctions against dissenters, more than propaganda reforms have improved it.

CHINESE COMMUNIST PROPAGANDA

Chinese communist propaganda has also been a mixture of the Marxist-Leninist propaganda tradition with the influence of a specific history and culture. It has been and still is profoundly influenced by the personality of Mao Tse-tung, notably in terms of his dedication to anti-intellectualism, conflict, social manipulation, total politicization, and extreme radicalism. Chinese communism has had a peasant base and has been strongly nationalistic and populist in character. It is not surprising, therefore, that it has taken over from traditional Chinese culture what the Chinese communists call "thought reform," nor that emphasis on coercive persuasion is much stronger than in the Soviet Union. The populist characteristics of Chinese communism are reflected in Mao's emphasis on the "mass line"—on keeping in constant close touch with and drawing inspiration from the Chinese masses. This plus his extreme politicization and radicalism often have led him to come down on the side of politicization and radicalism rather than rational bureaucracy, occupational differentiation, and expertise—in short, to prefer red to expert. Emphasis on thought reform and coercive persuasion has been characteristic of Chinese communism in its moderate and radical phases. Chinese propaganda reflects the personal experience of Mao and his closest associates: physical

isolation during the long guerrilla struggle, emphasis on individual combat, peasant mobilization, a united front with non-
communists (a political and propaganda line characteristic of
anticolonial struggles), and emphasis on such principles of mass
persuasion as insulation, emotional arousement, extreme simplification, and radical politicization. For example, in the 1950s
the Maoist concept of the "people's democratic dictatorship"
placed greater emphasis on coercive persuasion instead of on
violence than had been the case after the Bolshevik Revolution
in the Soviet Union. The radicalization of the Cultural Revolution in the 1960s, on the other hand, although it also placed
emphasis on coercive persuasion, made the element of coercion
far greater. Chinese thought reform has emphasized reading
Marxist classics, notably "The Thoughts of Chairman Mao,"
group discussion, and physical labor. It is explicitly intended to
change the individual and collective personality of the Chinese
so as to produce conflict rather than Confucian harmony, emphasis on collectivity rather than on the family, liberation of
women, and extreme radical politicization.

Because China is so underdeveloped, Chinese communist
propaganda, as in other underdeveloped communist countries,
has also been engaged in developmental activities. It has emphasized the achievement of mass literacy, the establishment of
centralized control over regional propaganda media, the use of
such techniques as big character posters *(tatzepao)*, wired radio,
and small group discussions—all instrumentalities with low capital and high labor costs.

Chinese thought reform, as we know from the studies of Lifton and Schein, has been characterized by ideological totalism,
coercive persuasion, and a passion for unanimity: totally controlled personality and environment. Through its demand for
ideological purity, through its deliberate creation of a milieu of
guilt and shame on the part of those against whom it is directed, through its obsession with confession and purging,
through its combination of extreme coercion and exhortation, it
has attempted literally to change human personalities, by a process that Schein calls "unfreezing, changing, and refreezing."
This process reached its height with respect to the Chinese
masses in the Cultural Revolution of the mid-1960s. Mao always
had believed in mass persuasion, done primarily by amateurs

rather than professionals and carried out through word of mouth. He was convinced that if this were done properly and radically enough, it would precipitate a genuine change in individual and group consciousness. Furthermore, Mao was convinced that the bureaucratism inevitable in the consolidation of any revolution, communist or not, could be overcome only by periodic, radical application of these propaganda techniques. Finally, he became convinced that the party bureaucracy headed by Liu Shao-chi, and indeed the propaganda apparatus itself, were so bureaucratized that they were unable and unwilling to carry out the Cultural Revolution. Therefore he destroyed the party and propaganda apparatus and turned to the army and the youthful Red Guards for support. Through the combination of armed force, massive coercive persuasion, and mobilization of youthful enthusiasm, Mao greatly raised the level of politicization and made Chinese communist propaganda operations much more extreme and radical. Communication became more communalized, Mao's works were institutionalized as a kind of Chinese Protestant ethic, and remarkable uniformity was for a time obtained. Yet the traditional Chinese combination of outward conformism and patience in waiting until the wind changes is such that we can hardly know the long-term effectiveness of Cultural Revolution propaganda, and are probably well advised to be somewhat sceptical about it. No matter how effective, however, it has been the most extensive and intensive propaganda operation in the history of communism, and insofar that it has been directed against bureaucracy, it probably achieved considerable popularity, particularly among the youth. But its extremism and Mao's subsequent crushing of this extremism, that is, the purge of not only Liu Shiao-chi and his associates but subsequently of Lin Piao and his, probably have had many of the same effects that Stalin's great purges did: one can imagine that, particularly among the Chinese intelligentsia, the credibility of Mao's propaganda must have suffered considerably in the process.

CUBAN COMMUNIST PROPAGANDA

Little academic research has been done on Cuban propaganda. What I have to say about it here represents primarily my own impression. Fidelism shares with Maoism a guerrilla mystique;

an emphasis on youth, on a charismatic leader (for Fidel is essentially a radical Latin American Caudillo), on moral rather than material incentives; and, finally, a penchant for massive, fanatical campaigns such as Castro's ill-fated attempt to harvest ten million tons of sugar. Castro is probably the most effective demagogue orator since Hitler, and his propaganda is more personalized than has been the case with any other communist leader. It has also been concerned extensively with foreign propaganda, for Castro regards himself as the second Simon Bolívar. He feels that Cuba is much too small for him and sees himself therefore as the leader of a radical anti-U.S. revolution throughout Latin America. Furthermore, Fidel has been an attractive model, at least until recently, to much of the European and American New Left and has tried to utilize this propagandistically for his own benefit. Yet the current economic crisis in Cuba, the failure of Castro's attempts to lead guerrilla violence in Latin America, and his recent harassment of communist intellectuals (the Padilla affair) have all tended to discredit his propaganda abroad and probably to some extent at home. Yet Castro's revolution so emphasizes modernization, national independence, and anti-U.S. (that is, anticolonial) mentality that its popularity among youth, students, and the economically lowest third of the population in Cuba must still be considerable. This particularly would seem to be the case, as he, uniquely among communists, has exported most of his strongest opponents to the United States via the air lift to Miami, and as Cuba is still in the initial phase of the revolution.

MARXIST REVISIONISM AND COMMUNIST PROPAGANDA

Ever since Lenin, communist propaganda has concentrated inter alia on combatting ideological revisionism. This was the case against the Workers Opposition, Bukharin, and Trotsky in the interwar period. It has been even more the case in the post-Stalin period, as reflected in Soviet and Chinese struggles against revisionism in Eastern Europe, intellectual dissent in the Soviet Union, and bureaucratism and intellectual discontent in China. The main causes of communist revisionism in postwar eastern Europe were moral revulsion of intellectuals against the crimes of Stalinism and his disregard and humiliation of eastern

European nationalism. Revisionism in Poland and Hungary in 1956, in Czechoslovakia in 1968, and in Croatia in 1971 was particularly strong among writers and journalists, who achieved considerable albeit brief control over some or all means of elite and mass communication, and thus for a short time were able to demoralize the Agitprop and propagandize the masses for their revisionist views. Indeed, the collapse of the Agitprop and of censorship was such a great challenge to Moscow and the local communist leaders that it was in large part responsible, for example, for the Soviet invasion of Czechoslovakia in 1968 and for Tito's crackdown in Croatia in 1971. East European revisionism was particularly politically effective, as in Poland in 1956, Czechoslovakia in 1968, and Croatia in 1971, when it was widespread in the party apparat, notably in the Agitprop. Its brief successes demonstrated how vital to the maintenance of the Communist party's power is the negative control function of the Agitprop, and how determined the Soviets (and Tito) are to preserve it.

Mao was horrified by the revisionism revealed during the Hundred Flowers period, which he immediately crushed. Since then genuine revisionism in China has not appeared in public.

The New Left in the developed countries has been at least as much cultural as political and at least as much influenced by Freud and Wilhelm Reich as by Marx. It has been strongly anarchist in tendency and hostile to ideological and organizational discipline. Furthermore, its initial models, Mao and Castro, have been somewhat discredited: the former by his rapprochement with the United States, and the latter by his rapprochement with the Soviet Union, the failure of guerrilla activities in Latin America, the economic crisis in Cuba, and his persecution of conformist intellectuals. The New Left also has become a propaganda target for orthodox communist ideologists.

More generally, communist revisionism, beginning with Eduard Bernstein, has presented a challenge to Marxist-Leninist orthodoxy in the areas of ethics (the revival of neo-Kantianism), economic decentralization, cultural autonomy, and national autonomy from control by Moscow or Peking. Finally, the growth, beginning with György Lukács, of what has come to be known as "western Marxism" has been seen by orthodox Marxist-Leninist ideologists as another challenge to their ideology. It is not surprising, therefore, particularly when one considers the problems the Soviet Union had in 1956 with revisionism in Poland and Hungary and in 1968 in Czechoslovakia, and the shock Mao received from the Hundred Flowers revisionism in China, that both Moscow and Peking during the last two decades have spent much of their propaganda efforts in combatting revisionism. This has been done primarily within the communist world although there also has been some attention paid toward combatting it in Soviet and Chinese international propaganda directed outside of it. The most effective weapon that the Agitprop has used against revisionism has been political control via the censorship and purges of the staffs of communication media.

One recent case of antirevisionist propaganda has been in Croatia, where in 1971 Tito led a purge of the Croatian Communist party of nationalists and revisionist. This seems to have been a case in which the two trends were generally combined but in which Croatian ethnic nationalism provided what Tito saw as the most dangerous challenge to the existence of the state of Yugoslavia as well as to the political restrictions that he still feels it necessary to maintain. The purge was particularly strong in the communication media and is an example, as are the recurrent purges of writers and journalists in the Soviet minority republics and in Slovakia, of the particularly dangerous dynamic that arises from the combination of nationalism and ideological revisionism.

INTERPARTY POLEMICS: THE SINO–SOVIET DISPUTE

Propaganda polemics within the communist world have been recurrent ever since the Bolshevik Revolution. Stalin propagandized both at home and abroad against Trotsky, Bukharin, and others of his opponents. The Soviet-Yugoslav dispute from 1948 to 1953 and in 1958–1959 was characterized by violent propaganda polemics on both sides. The continuing polemics against revisionism, discussed above, are another example. Certainly the most extensive and intensive interparty polemics in recent years, however, have been those that arose as a result of the Sino-Soviet dispute.

This is not the place to attempt even the briefest summary of the dispute. Suffice it to say that in my view its causes have been primarily geopolitical and organizational rather than ideological. But the fact that the polemics of the dispute have been conducted by propagandists in terms of Marxist-Leninist ideology has given the dispute certain special characteristics. The initially still binding and implicitly agreed rule not to divulge communist difference in public led to delay in the public surfacing of explicit polemics and their initial expression, particularly from 1958 to 1962, on a very esoteric plane. As the dispute continued and developed into a split, it led to an increasingly complex, factionalized struggle, not only between the Soviet Union and China but also within and among various neutralist and revisionist Communist parties. The dispute has tended further to distort and to empty of any credible content the common ideology and increasingly to become concentrated on national and geopolitical rather than ideological arguments. Basically, it has led not so much to polycentralism as to pluralism, that is to say, political diversity among most communist states and parties. This has inevitably produced increasing differentiation in propaganda lines. Since then the domestic factor in propaganda has made the study and analysis of communist propaganda far more difficult than before. As the dispute developed, it appeared, in terms of overt propaganda, to be taking an essentially cyclical course, first worsening then improving. But in fact the general tendency has been one of deterioration, with the appearance of improvement being primarily tactical on the part of the Soviets and the Chinese, intended to appeal to other Communist parties more than to reflect genuine political positions.

Propaganda in the dispute may be categorized in a series of escalatory steps that can be summarized as follows in the ascending order of worsening of state and party relations: (1) implicitly diverging ideological lines, but without reference by one side to the other (1958–1959); (2) polemics against historical deviationists who in fact are used as surrogates for the other side; (3) polemics directed against ostensibly anonymous opponents, that is, the Chinese polemics against "modern revisionists" and the Soviet polemics against "dogmatists"; (4) polemics against surrogate but explicitly identified foes other than the two main contestants—the Chinese against Yugoslavia and the Soviets against Albania; (5) the reprinting of explicit polemics by other Communist parties; and finally, since about July 1963, (6) completely explicit polemics, first still on the ideological level and then later, particularly at the height of the Sino-Soviet border conflicts in 1969 and as a result of the Sino-American rapprochement of 1971, explicit polemics primarily of a nationalistic rather than an ideological nature. These nationalist polemics also have involved attempts by propaganda to interfere in factional struggle on both sides, the Chinese in the Soviet Union and the Soviet Union in China.

The violence of the Sino-Soviet polemics has had a profoundly disillusioning effect, particularly among foreign communists, for it has so completely exposed as a myth the Marxist doctrine of proletarian internationalism. This recently has become even more the case, as the Soviet Union now explicitly regards China as a greater enemy than the United States and China feels the same about the Soviet Union.

CURRENT COMMUNIST PROPAGANDA ADVANTAGES

One should not conclude an analysis of the current state of communist propaganda on such a one-sided, negative note. The problems of Western society present new opportunities for communist propaganda. The ineffectiveness or, as many of its opponents maintain, the immorality of American policy in Vietnam; the drug problem; the increased attention given in the Western world to problems of poverty in advanced industrial societies; the psychological alienation characteristic of much of the university youth of developed countries; the declining concern of the United States with the Third World; the relative decline of Western and particularly American economic and military power as compared with that of the Soviet Union—all these are effectively utilized by the Soviet and Chinese propaganda.

THE FUTURE OF COMMUNIST PROPAGANDA

Probably in post–Cultural Revolution China, certainly in the Soviet Union and eastern Europe, and probably eventually even in Cuba, propaganda reforms such as Brezhnev has carried out are likely to continue and intensify. The appeals of communist propaganda will become more nationalistic, more concerned with power, science, and technology—in short, with power and modernization. Yet the challenge of ideological revisionism, the superiority of Western science and technology over that of the communist states, the Sino-Soviet split, and the development of an essentially balance-of-power relationship among the Soviet Union, China, and the United States that disregards ideological differences will be continuing problems for communist propaganda. However, communist rule in the Soviet Union and China as well as in eastern Europe, North Korea, North Vietnam, and Cuba seems as of this writing (1972) likely to continue for a prolonged period. Propaganda will remain a major part of this rule, for the communist commitment to a totality of positive and negative propaganda control remains essentially unchanged. Propaganda is seen as essential both for retention of power by the communist bureaucratic elite and also for modernization and political and social integration of communist societies. That its tactics, even its strategy, will change seems likely. That its essence will continue seems almost certain.

SELECT BIBLIOGRAPHY

Barghoorn, Frederick C. *The Soviet Cultural Offensive.* Princeton: Princeton University Press, 1960.

——. *Soviet Foreign Propaganda.* Princeton: Princeton University Press, 1964.

Benn, David Wedgwood. "New Thinking in Soviet Propaganda." *Soviet Studies* 21 (1969):52–63.

Buzek, Antony. *How the Communist Press Works.* New York: Praeger, 1964.

Clews, John C. *Communist Propaganda Techniques.* New York: Praeger, 1964.

Griffith, William E. "Communist Esoteric Communications: *Explication de Texte." Studies in Comparative Communism* (January 1970).

Hopkins, Mark W. *Mass Media in the Soviet Union.* New York: Pegasus, 1970.

Inkeles, Alex. *Public Opinion in Soviet Russia.* Cambridge, Mass.: Harvard University Press, 1950.

König, Helmut. "Der sowjetisch-chinesische Rundfunkkrieg." *Osteuropa* (August 1969):561–574.

Lifton, Robert Jay. *Thought Reform and the Psychology of Totalism.* New York: Norton, 1961.

Liu, Alan P. *Communications and National Integration in Communist China.* Los Angeles and Berkeley: University of California Press, 1971.

Mickiewicz, Ellen. "The Modernization of Party Propaganda in the USSR."
    Slavic Review (June 1971).

Pye, Lucian W., ed. *Communications and Political Development*. Princeton:
    Princeton University Press, 1963.

Schein, Edgar J., with Inge Schneier and Curtis Barker. *Coercive Persuasion*.
    New York: Norton, 1961.

Unger, Aryeh L. "Static in Agitprop." *Problems of Communism* 19
    (September-October 1970).

Yu, Frederick T. C. *Mass Persuasion in Communist China*. New York:
    Praeger, 1964.

SYMBOL MANAGEMENT
IN THE CONTINUING SPREAD
OF CRISIS POLITICS

9

THE COMMUNICATION
OF HIDDEN MEANING

Hans Speier

OVERT AND COVERT MEANING

Many communications have a simple structure: a communicator
(C) transmits a message (m) with an overt meaning (M_o) to a recipient (R). If R is ignorant, prejudiced, or superstitious and C
is knowledgeable, R acquires knowledge from C by learning M_o
and is consequently enlightened. If C's message concerns beliefs
or designs to shape the future, R may (or may not) be persuaded
to adopt the beliefs or support the policies C champions. Despite weighty differences between these two types of communications they can be represented by the same schema:

Schema 1 $C \rightarrow m \rightarrow M_o \rightarrow R$

In informative or propagandistic statements the intended
meaning is clearly apparent, lying, as it were, on the surface,
whether C says "2 + 2= 4," "Paris is the capital of France,"
"God created the world," "Black is beautiful," or "To preserve peace we must arm."

The intended sense of a statement is not necessarily its literal
meaning. A recipient who confuses the two meanings in the
event of a conflict between them is either foolish or may, to
make us laugh, pretend to be so. If someone is told "Go jump
in the lake," he is not expected to dive into the nearest body of
water. Cicero commented at length on the fact that ambiguity

in the meaning of words, allegorical phraseology, metaphorical language, and ironical statements may be sources of jests.[1] In all these cases the joke springs from double meaning. Schema 1 is not readily applicable to communications in which language is used playfully or serves aesthetic rather than enlightening or propagandistic ends. Strictly speaking, the metaphorical aspects of language—in the widest sense of the term "metaphorical"— are *bound to* impede the pertinence of schema 1, and relatively few communications are entirely free of metaphors. By way of illustration it may be noted that the words "bound to" in the preceding sentence (in lieu of, say, "inevitably") are derived from "binding," an image under which life and the working of fate were interpreted in ancient Hebrew, Babylonian, Vedic, Roman, Greek, Celtic, Norse, and Slav thought.[2] One of the functions of metaphors is to make it possible to live with the dreadfully incomprehensible by inventing verisimilitudes to something that is comprehended.

When a communicator uses metaphors to convey an intended meaning "graphically," we do not suspect him of double-talk. But everyday speech gives us many clues to the common awareness of the fact that meaning in a given communication is neither necessarily overt nor, for that matter, necessarily intended by C and, conversely, that C indeed may wish and manage to convey more than one meaning in the same message.

We say that somebody is speaking with "tongue in cheek" when we want to express the opinion that he means more than he appears to be saying. We are aware that something may have to be taken "with a grain of salt"; for example, an obsequious salutation—*deus* for emperor (in Rome), governor for mister, officer for policeman—means less than what is being said. In either case the "message" has not only an open meaning but also a second one. This covert meaning (M_c) lies below the surface. Similarly, the Japanese refer to a man who says one thing but means something else as somebody using *haragei, hara* signifying "stomach"—in this case "mind" or "intention"—and *gei* designating "art." We speak of "reading or writing between the lines" when we want to convey the notion that an esoteric communication has a covert or esoteric meaning in addition to its surface sense. The expression is derived from the medieval practice of writing short glosses between the lines of a manuscript. In regard to certain jokes and other forms of allusive communication we speak of "double entendre," and everyone has encountered "double-talk," "flattery," "irony," and other forms of intended ambiguity in discourse.

When the bitter truth is offered to us as a "sugar-coated pill" —an expression widespread in older literature[3]—we are not supposed to take the coating for the substance. Often we say that someone expressed himself "diplomatically"; we mean that he spoke cautiously. Although we may be only dimly aware of the many possible reasons for such caution in a given case, we can easily see that diplomatic caution is a response to risk and to uncertainties regarding the future, the adversary's intentions, and one's own willingness to seek, accept, or withdraw from growing conflict. We also know that diplomatic caution may "keep the adversary guessing," "save his or one's own face," "stall for time," and so on. Our knowledge stems from experience: diplomatic language is used not only in international affairs but in all intelligently conducted negotiations, whether among businessmen, between labor and management, with criminals, between lawyers, with one's superior, and in other adversary relationships.

In illiberal regimes common words may be used to convey covert meanings according to advance agreements so that "insiders" may protect themselves against dangerous "outsiders." Needs of closeness and solidarity alone tend to foster the use of insider-language. If fear of detection and persecution are added, clandestine communication or, in the event that public discourse is unavoidable, the incorporation of covert meanings into everyday speech may become a matter of survival. Examples of such improvised *codes* in correspondence or telephone conversations to mislead eavesdroppers abound. Lali Horstman reports about Nazi Germany that in her circle of anti-Nazis, "Sybil" was used for England, "Pit" for Russia. "The patient's health is unchanged, worse, or hopeless, was the expression we agreed on to describe the state of German defence."[4] Another, more farcical, instance of an impromptu code can be found in the transcript of a meeting that John W. Dean III and Bob Haldeman had with President Nixon on 21 March 1973. Dean reported that he telephoned John Mitchell at his home to inquire as to whether he had been able to raise money to pay Mr.

Hunt, a Watergate defendant. Dean said Mitchell "was at home, and Martha [Mrs. Mitchell] picked up the phone, so it was all in code. I said, 'Have you talked to the Greek [Mr. Pappas]?' And he said, 'Yes, I have.' I said, 'Is the Greek bearing gifts?' He said, 'Well, I call you tomorrow on that.' "[5]

The term *Aesopic language* has gained currency. It perhaps was introduced by Saltykov-Shchedrin, the author of *The Golovyov Family* (1876) and *Fables* (1885), works in which the author attacked by way of circumlocution government officials, backward landowners, and greedy capitalists. Lenin as well used the terms Aesopic language and *slave language* to characterize the practice of the revolutionaries prior to the October Revolution of employing euphemisms in public print in order to hide their radical ideas from the censor. For example, the word "constitution" was understood by properly predisposed readers to mean "revolution." Even in Russia, however, the use of Aesopic language is older than either the Bolsheviks or Shchedrin. In the 1820s the participation of writers in political conspiracies and Pushkin's sympathy and that of other writers with the Decembrists led the censors to suspect literature of being the cause of uprisings everywhere. When the journal *The European* was forbidden in 1832, and its editor placed under police surveillance, the censors issued a "notification" in which an objectionable contribution to the journal was characterized as follows: "Although the author says that he does not talk about politics, but about literature, he thinks something entirely different. The word 'enlightenment' he understands as 'liberty.' 'Activity of the mind' means to him 'the revolution,' and the 'carefully found medium' can only mean 'constitution.' "[6] Although the term Aesopic language does not appear in the notification, it was precisely this cunning form of political communication that aroused the censor's suspicion.

Nor is the term Aesopic language felicitous, as it is not always fables that are used to convey hidden meanings. Anthropologists following Sir James George Frazer refer to the avoidance and adoption of certain forms of communication in preliterate societies as *"guarded speech."* More recently, Nathan Leites and Elsa Bernaut in their examination of the Moscow Trials have analyzed in great detail the grammar and syntax of the "veiled language" in which the Bolshevik defendants expressed themselves in order to communicate with other leaders without revealing themselves to the masses.[7] We shall speak of "esoteric communication" not only when an exclusive group—age group, sex group, profession, or secret society—uses a special vocabulary but also when the covert meaning conveyed to insiders is concealed from outsiders despite the use of a common, exoteric vocabulary.

Of course, the ruling groups as well as rebels and critics may resort to euphemisms and other devices of esoteric communication. The word for genocide used among Nazi leaders was "final solution." When there is contempt for or fear of the masses, the ruling elite may resort to esoteric communication among themselves. As long as the masses are illiterate and no right to education and active participation in politics is recognized, the need for communication between the rulers and the ruled is small. Many modern dictatorships, however, insist on adherence by the masses to official ideologies. If in these circumstances the ruling elite considers it important to keep the masses in a state of ignorance about conflicts and struggles for power among the rulers, it may become desirable for them to use exoteric communications with the masses while conveying at the same time esoteric meanings to the sub-elites. In the political analysis of the Soviet regime and its policies, the understanding of communist esoteric communications has engaged the attention of many scholars.[8]

Not only political communication may convey esoteric meaning, but philosophical discourse as well. In our time, Leo Strauss reflected more than any other man on the art of philosophical writing in times when those who speak the truth run the risk of persecution. The danger to which they are exposed lies not only with the authorities but, more generally, with those who are ignorant, or, to use the older term, with the vulgar; and the authorities may be among them. Strauss pointed out that "premodern philosophers were more timid . . . than modern philosophers": being convinced that "philosophy as such was suspect to, and hated by, the majority of men" they eschewed popularization and concluded "that public communication of the philosophic or scientific truth was impossible or undesirable."[9]

But today the most common awareness of hidden meaning is

unquestionably the result of the popularity of Sigmund Freud's teaching. In a letter to Fliess dated 12 March 1897, Freud observed, "It is a pity that one always keeps one's mouth shut about the most intimate things."[10] Lecturing to law students in 1906 on psychoanalysis and the ascertaining of truth in courts of law, Freud presented "an analogy between the criminal and the hysteric. . . . In both, we are concerned with a secret, with something hidden." He continued that the secret of the hysteric, different from that of the criminal who knows his secret and hides it from the judge, is "a secret he himself does not know."[11] According to Freud, the indicators of "hidden meaning," that is, in this instance, of secrets hidden from the self, are certain typical features of the patient's communication by which he betrays himself involuntarily. These features include hesitation and stops "in his flow of ideas," "even the smallest digressions from the ordinary form of expression," and discrepancies in repeated accounts of the same recollection.[12] Thus the meaning is transmitted by C, the patient, to R, the analyst, *without* the former's intention and knowledge; it is nevertheless contained in his communication and perceived by the analyst as covert meaning (M_c).

In brief, in preliterate and literate societies, and particularly, though not exclusively, in illiberal regimes; among those who wield power as well as those who live under its sway; among victims, critics, and detached observers—in all of these circumstances and all of these groups we encounter efforts to convey hidden meaning to certain recipients. Correspondingly, in everyday nonpolitical and political discourse as well as in the exegesis of sacred texts, the understanding of myths, allegories, parables, and poetic imagery, the interpretation of philosophical writings, the critical appreciation of paintings and literature —in all of these contexts we encounter efforts to find the way from an overt sense to a deeper "real" meaning intended by the communicator.

ALLEGORICAL INTERPRETATION

Sometimes, the search is not for one specific covert meaning, for example, the theological meaning of Herman Melville's *Billy Budd,* the philosophical sense of Jonathan Swift's *Gulliver's Travels,* or the political teaching of George Orwell's *Animal*

Farm, but for several meanings in addition to the overt one. To cite but one famous opinion, that of Dante:

> Books can be understood and ought to be explained in four principal senses. One is called *literal*, and this it is which goes no further than the letter, such as the simple narration of the thing of which you treat. . . .
>
> The second is called *allegorical*, and this is the meaning hidden under the cloak of fables, and is a truth concealed beneath a fair fiction; as when Ovid says, Orpheus with his lute tamed wild beasts, and moved trees and rocks; which means that the wise man, with the instrument of his voice, softens and humbles cruel hearts, and moves at his will those who live neither for science nor for art, and those who, having no rational life whatever are almost like stones. . . .
>
> The third sense is called *moral* and this readers should carefully gather from all writings, for the benefit of themselves and their descendants; it is such as we may gather from the Gospel, when Christ went up into the mountain to be transfigured, and of the twelve apostles took with him but three; which in the moral sense may be understood thus, that in most secret things we should have few companions.
>
> The fourth sense is called *anagogical* (or mystical), that is, beyond sense; and this is when a book is spiritually expounded, which, although (a narration) in its literal sense, by the things signified refers to the supernal things of the eternal glory; as we may see in that psalm of the Prophet, where he says that when Israel went out of Egypt Judaea became holy and free. Which, although manifestly true according to the letter, is nevertheless true also in its spiritual meaning,—that the soul, in forsaking its sins, becomes holy and free in its powers.[13]

As regards allegorical interpretation, Dante is merely a link in a long history, which went back to the Church Fathers and further to Philo. In the Jewish tradition no verse in scripture, whether narrative or law, had to be taken literally but was subject to free interpretation.[14] Philo also was conversant from Greek philosophical literature with the practice of assimilating certain elements of the Greek myths by understanding them as allegories.[15] Such attempts at accommodating a venerated heritage to new thought is a frequent occurrence in the history of in-

terpretation. The Chinese used Confucian ethics to justify the
introduction of European innovations. In general, allegorizing
means interpreting a text "in terms of something else, irrespec-
tive of what that something else is"—"book learning . . . practical wisdom . . . speculative meditation . . . urging necessi-
ties of changed conditions of life," and so on.[16] Sometimes,
allegorical interpretations also were used "to defeat the crude
literalism of fanatical heresies; or to reconcile the teachings of
philosophy with the truths of the Gospel."[17]

In the many centuries in which the allegorical interpretation
of sacred texts, whether Jewish, Christian, or Mohammedan,
dominated exegesis, the legitimacy of the method was not questioned, although there were controversies about the number of
meanings to be discovered, the rules and methods that were to
govern the interpretation, and the correctness of specific instances of exegesis.

In dealing with hidden meaning critically it is necessary to
distinguish works written by authors like Maimonides or
Rabelais who explicitly state that meaning is concealed in their
writings, from writings like the Homeric poems or sacred texts,
in regard to which the assertions of hidden meaning stem exclusively from the interpreters. The gods in Homer and Hesiod are
not allegories, but to the Stoics Zeus meant *logos,* Ares war,
Hermes reason, and so on. Many centuries later, John of Salisbury elaborated earlier allegorical interpretations of Virgil and
taught that the truths of philosophy were expressed in the
Aeneid under the guise of a legend. Origen and St. Augustine,
following a kindred Talmudic tradition, held that the Song of
Songs signified Christ and the Church, although the text itself
allows such interpretation only if certain rules of allegoresis are
accepted. Philo had laid down the rule "that no anthropomorphic expression about God is to be taken literally"; he assumed
that such expressions were "introduced for the instruction of
the many."[18] St. Augustine taught that "whatever in Holy
Writ cannot properly be said to be concerned either with
morality or with the faith must be recognized as allegorical."[19]

The fact that Dante subscribed to the scholastic teaching of
the four meanings allows us then to presume that *The Divine
Comedy* is to be taken as a work in which indeed four meanings
can be discovered, because they were intended by the author. In

other instances, however, the author's instruction to search for hidden sense is less obvious than in Dante's case and can be established only by very careful inquiry, if at all. In still others it cannot be proved and, if claimed, must be regarded as an invention of the interpreter. In the latter category belongs, for example, the cabalistic methods of gematria.

Assuming first that a given text conveys the four meanings mentioned by Dante, it stands to reason that not all readers will "receive" all of them. For example, a child (R_1) may understand only (some of) the literal meaning (M_{li}), say, of *The Divine Comedy;* other readers (R_2) may derive from (M_{li}) the moral meaning (M_m); a still smaller (R_3) group may be learned enough to understand the allegorical meaning (M_{al}) as well as (M_{li}) and (M_m). Finally, a few interpreters (R_4) of the text may ascend to the height of anagogical meaning (M_{an}), which all other readers fail to comprehend. Thus, schema 1 has to be changed to accommodate not only four different meanings but also four different groups of recipients, as follows:

Schema 2a $\quad C \rightarrow m$
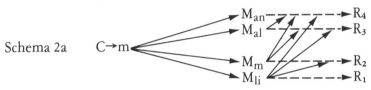

Inasmuch as it is not always certain that C intends to convey several meanings in his message, it is possible that some of them are *read into* the message by the interpreters of the text. This possibility was not in Dante's mind: it is rather a modern thought, having to do with the discrediting of allegoresis by the Protestant Reformation, if not with the modern inclination to favor living readers over dead authors. To Dante meaning was given in the texts to which he referred for illustration. The notion that meanings might have been invented, that is, merely read into the scriptures or Ovid, without being intended by God, the Evangelist, or the Poet, would have been alien to him. Indeed, it would have been as absurd to him as the assertion that the Gospel according to St. John opened with the words: "In the beginning there was human Reason."

If we assume now that the various hidden meanings of a given text are *invented* by the interpreter rather than discovered by him as lying within the author's intention, schema 2a takes the form of

Schema 2b $C \rightarrow m \rightarrow M_o$

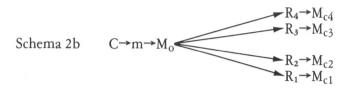

$$R_4 \rightarrow M_{c4}$$
$$R_3 \rightarrow M_{c3}$$
$$R_2 \rightarrow M_{c2}$$
$$R_1 \rightarrow M_{c1}$$

In this instance, the covert meanings are due not to the communicator's but to the recipient's intention. Whereas according to schema 1, only one meaning was conveyed, 2a and 2b represent communications with multiple meanings; in addition, whereas schema 1 refers to communications with a homogeneous audience, both versions of schema 2 envision a heterogeneous audience: each of the four recipients represented in either 2a or 2b has a different understanding. Thus schemata 1 and 2 may be said to stand for opposite extremes of communication, schema 1 being primarily, though not exclusively, the paradigm of enlightenment, schema 2 that of communications requiring or representing exegesis.

Evidently, the two schemata do not represent all facets of the universe of communications. The intentions of the communicator, the diversity of meanings, and the differences among various recipients are more complex and numerous than appears from the two schemata. In the following discussion an approach to the complex maze of communications will be taken that may help in the search for the communicator's skill in conveying esoteric meanings.

DISCLOSING AND WITHHOLDING

The realm of communication will now be viewed as a continuum bounded by the two extremes of full disclosure and total withholding of that which is in the communicator's mind. In every transaction the communicator discloses *and* withholds. The specific mixture of the two efforts, that is, the location of any given communication on the continuum, varies; but it does not vary at random. It depends, among other things, on the context in which the communicator and his audiences are placed and—within it—on the relationship between the communicator and the recipients. In the following discussion special attention will be paid to this context and to this relationship.

Any communicator may be more or less secretive, but this trait of his personality will not be discussed, although like other personality traits, such as a strong need to confide in others, it may affect his habits of communication. Nor shall we deal with inadvertent disclosure and withholding. Hesitation, stammer, blanching, slips of the tongue, the pen, the eye, or the ear—and other phenomena to which Freud has alerted us—will be disregarded. We shall focus on deliberately intended meanings.

Negatively stated, we shall not view all communication outside of propaganda as a more or less successful effort of enlightenment. The object of communication is not necessarily to inform and obtain understanding. The object may be indeed not to spread knowledge to a given ignoramus but to maintain his ignorance; not to profess feelings but to hide or feign them; to lead astray rather than to guide the perplexed; to give not the best advice but the next best; not to enlighten but to obscure, to explain inadequately, to oversimplify, to slant, to popularize; to tell only part of the truth, to mask it, or simply to lie.

Aside from all that, a person often renders the same subject in quite specifically circumscribed terms when talking to different persons. Observe a physician speaking about an illness to his colleague and then to his suffering patient, or a father conversing about God with his child in the morning and his priest at noon. Matters kept secret from laymen can be expressed precisely in technical language to experts. If this communication is "translated" into popular terms for purposes of communicating with a larger audience, precision is inevitably lost. In his hearing before the Personnel Security Board, J. Robert Oppenheimer testified,

> I know of no case where I misrepresented or distorted the technical situation in reporting it to my superiors or those to whom I was bound to give advice and counsel. The nearest thing to it that I know is that in the public version of the Acheson-Lilienthal report, we somewhat overstated what would be accomplished by denaturing. I believe this was not anything else than in translating from a technical and therefore secret statement into a public and therefore

codified statement, we lost some of the precision which should have gone into it, and some of the caution which should have gone into it.[20]

Role-differentiated discourse about the same subject will appear elusive to those observers who expect every communication to be a full disclosure of that which is on the speaker's mind. Similarly, those observers may easily overlook the fact that a person may not only deliberately delete from his speech information concerning the subject he dwells on, but also deliberately say something to indicate that he is withholding something else.

Although often everything is disclosed and nothing withheld, there are many other communications in which something remains unsaid. The message is curtailed, as it were, like an incomplete confession or a prestidigitator's performance that makes us take illusion for reality; from the vantage point of the recipient, the communication may resemble a view that is partially veiled or a tune reaching him only in fragments from afar. Finally, there are communications in which withholding is indeed total: evasive answers, lies, deliberate obscurities, loquacious flooding of the channels with socially acceptable nonsense, and so on.

It might be objected that the view of communication as a continuum bounded by full disclosure and complete withholding is a misanthropic one, as it seems to assume that man is essentially secretive, if not deceitful or at least uninterested in enlightening his fellowmen. No such opinion of man's nature is meant to be implied.

Let us recall, first of all, Hugo Grotius's distinction between negative and positive stratagems. In negative stratagems we conceal all or part of what we know, as in diplomatic silence or in the withholding of some information available to us when we otherwise speak the truth. This negative stratagem is dissimulation. In positive stratagems or in simulation we do not speak truthfully. The doctor who does not tell his patient that he is going to die, although he expects his death, dissimulates; if he tells the patient that he is going to live, he uses a positive stratagem.

This illustration suggests that the use of stratagems is not necessarily reprehensible from a moral point of view and cannot be readily equated with lying. Which stratagems are permissible or indeed mandatory from a moral point of view depends altogether upon the intention with which the stratagem is used and upon circumstances. Grotius cites the instance of King Solomon, who proposed that the contested child be divided and thereby induced the true mother to reveal herself—a permissible stratagem used in the pursuit of justice. Similarly he agrees with Quintilian that children can be taught many useful truths in the dress of fiction. And there are other situations, such as self-defense against an enemy, or occasions in which conventional rather than "sincere" conduct is generally expected, where concealment of sentiment, simulation of knowledge or intent, and even feigned respect for values constitute deviations from the truth that leave no moral blemish.

Man communicates for good and evil purposes. Unless he is ill, he knows that not everyone is his enemy to be met with tight lips or lies, and yet only a blabbing fool treats everyone like a trusted friend. Furthermore, just as concealment no less than disclosure may serve a good purpose, so disclosure like concealment may do harm in certain circumstances. Even in talking to a friend concern or curiosity may be curbed out of respect for his privacy, just as sad tidings may be withheld from him so as to spare his feelings. Conversely, in certain circumstances we conceal nothing from our enemy and give him a full account of our strength—especially if we judge it to be overpowering—and of our good or ill will toward him. In short, although the general view of communication that is being suggested here enables the observer to take account of the fact that the political nature of the social universe impinges upon communication, it does not postulate man to be either angelically straight or fiendishly crooked. Man walks upright, but he can bend.

Before proceeding we may dispose of another possible initial objection. If it be admitted that communication is mixed disclosing and withholding, the extreme case of full disclosure is more plausible than the opposite extreme of a communicator withholding everything he knows, believes, wants, or feels. For cannot total withholding rather easily be accomplished by silence instead of communication? The argument is fallacious. Neither silence nor the explicit refusal to say anything is neces-

sarily sufficient to avoid disclosure. Silence itself may be communicative. For example, it may express consent or dissent, as
the case may be. An audience may be able not only to understand its meaning but to force it upon the silent person, so that
he must speak to escape such dictates. Literally or figuratively
speaking, a correspondent may receive the message, "If I do not
hear from you, I shall assume that you agree with me." Similarly, in a manipulated mass meeting silence at a prescribed moment of cheer or applause is tantamount to a demonstrative act
of defiance, as is the silence of a heretic under pressure to re-
cant. In such cases, the communicator cannot remain passive.
He has to use words, gestures, or actions, if he wishes to avoid
disclosing something he does not want to say by remaining
silent.

When the significance of silence is not tightly controlled by
others, many different meanings may yet be imputed to it,
which is often true of statements, gestures, and actions as well.
Only an additional communication may prevent the listener
from ascribing that particular meaning to silence which "the
silent speaker" wants to withhold. For example, although silence may indicate that a person is shy, defiant, indifferent, or
proud, the listener may take it to mean that he feels guilty, a
meaning that the silent person may have good reason to deny or
be anxious to conceal. In either case he must speak up, much as
in doing so he must swallow his pride which prompted him to
be silent at first. Silence among men is always alive. Paradoxically, it is most alive when there is "a dead silence." In short,
like other means of communication, silence is a way of disclosing and withholding, although it sometimes lacks the ruthlessness of the "outspoken." Silence in writing on certain subjects
also can be used by an author to express an intended meaning
obliquely, for example, that he considers these subjects to be
unimportant or commonly held views on them to be mistaken.[21]

Silence and a high incidence of withholding in communication need not be stratagems in efforts to gain advantages over
others or safeguards against disadvantages possibly to be incurred by disclosure. Instead, such "reticence" may stem from
the conviction that everyday language fails to serve because it is
blunted by abuse. Modern literature provides ample comment

on such despair in contemporary civilization. Indeed, when we listen attentively to what we hear today most of the time, then over the distance of half a century the quiet voice of Hans Karl Buehl, the most modern character in Hofmannsthal's plays, touches us to the quick: "But everything one says is indecent. The simple fact that one says something is indecent."[22]

Perhaps this feeling for the "indecency" of all speech reveals a refined sentiment bordering on decadence, but perhaps there reverberates in it the older, profounder, conceit of the romantic and the mystic that ordinary speech cannot reach the truth. The opposing view was most forcefully stated by Hegel in the preface to his *Phenomenology*. Impatient with Jacobi and the romantics, with Schlegel and Schleiermacher, whose "intensity without content" he equated with "superficiality" and "dreams," he thundered: *"Die Kraft des Geistes ist nur so gross als ihre Äusserung. . . ."* The power of the mind is only as great as the power of expression.[23]

HETEROGENEOUS AUDIENCES

The view of communication as disclosure and withholding is taken from the vantage point of the communicator. In role-differentiated discourse he changes the specific "mixture" of disclosure and withholding according to his intention toward the recipient and according to the latter's known or presumed predisposition (for example, child versus priest, patient versus colleague). We may therefore distinguish between role-adequate and role-inadequate discourse. An exposition of Leibniz's monadology to a butler is role-inadequate; so is an aerodynamic explanation of flight to a babe.

Although the effort at role-adequacy presents no extraordinary difficulties to the communicator who addresses a recipient he knows well, a partner, a friend, or a homogeneous group of recipients, the matter becomes considerably more difficult—and possibly hazardous—for the communicator who faces a recipient whose predisposition he does not know or who addresses a *heterogeneous* audience.

Consider the statesman who must reckon with the fact that both allies and adversaries of his country as well as neutrals hear what he says in public. On 6 September 1946 Secretary of State Byrnes gave a speech in Stuttgart on American policy toward

Germany. While its unusually conciliatory tone so soon after the termination of World War II brought tears to the eyes of some German listeners, it annoyed the French because of their adamant distrust of their neighbors to the east. Byrnes's speech was not "role-adequate" with regard to the French; they were not directly addressed but "overheard" what had been said. From the vantage point of Byrnes, the French may have been "unwanted recipients" (R_u) and only the Germans "intended recipients" (R_i). In this case, schema 1 would have to be replaced by:

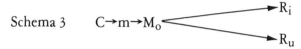

Schema 3 $C \rightarrow m \rightarrow M_o \begin{cases} R_i \\ R_u \end{cases}$

In diplomatic discourse, it happens often—indeed it is almost normal—that the response to a public message is diversified, as the international "community" is a heterogeneous audience. The French therefore can be regarded as "unintended recipients" only if Byrnes failed to take their political predispositions into account. More to the point of schema 3 is an incident involving Secretary of State Henry Kissinger. On 11 March 1974 he remarked to an audience of congressmen's wives that since World War I there had been "very rarely fully legitimate governments in any European country." The secretary learned too late that "the press office [of the State Department] had invited some newsmen to cover his remarks from an enclosed booth to the side of the auditorium."[24] To cushion the shock he had caused abroad, Kissinger subsequently issued an apology ruefully stating that he seemed to get into trouble when ladies and the press were present. Thus he managed to put the blame in part on others without admitting that he had rashly yielded to the temptation to be brilliant rather than prudent in public.

Strictly speaking, for communication to a heterogeneous audience to be fully role-adequate, the same message would have to have multivarious meanings. This requirement is met, of course, only in exceptional cases. Sometimes, it is possible by way of a second, corrective communication to convey once more the meaning that part of the audience missed in the first instance. Thus a teacher may repeat a lesson for inattentive students or amplify for the slow-witted what his bright students had fully understood in the first, brief rendition.

The class of cases, however, that is of particular interest to this discussion is that in which the communicator wishes to be understood only by selected members of his audience—"the intended recipient"—while wishing not to be understood by others—"the unwanted recipient" of the message. Put differently, he endeavors to disclose what is on his mind to R_i while withholding it from R_u. If such a communication is successful, R_i gets the message and its meaning while R_u may hear only noise or nonsense (N). Thus,

Schema 4

Even a dog may play the role of R_u when its master speaking to R_i, for example his servant, avoids pronouncing a word that the dog "understands." By spelling it—"o-u-t" for "out"—he may succeed in communicating with the servant without cueing the dog (until it has learned the new cue "o-u-t"). Whispering a message to R_i so that R_u cannot get its meaning follows the same pattern. So do the "asides" on the stage, which establish an understanding with the audience in the theater from which other actors on the stage are presumed to be excluded. By the same token, Turgenev wrote some of his letters to Pauline Viardot (R_i) in German, because Louis Viardot, her husband (R_u), did not understand German. Turgenev had availed himself of what Gibbon once referred to as "the obscurity of a learned language."[25] Resorting to a foreign language may enable parents to convey to each other a meaning that they want to withhold from their children. These may reciprocate by conversing in a contrived "secret" language, which adults are supposed not to understand.

It is possible that the nonsense the unwanted listeners hear may appear to them as a secret (S) shared by the communicator and his equals, whereas the latter in turn may indeed use a special language whose secret meanings (M_s) are intelligible only to them. The special language is an instrument of solidarity, social exclusiveness, religious privilege, or power over those who fail to understand the secret. Because in this case the unwanted recipients are definitely meant to understand the fact that secrets are being passed between C and R_i as a privilege from which the unwanted recipients are excluded, schema 4 changes to

Schema 5

The communicator discloses to some recipients (R_i) what is on his mind and to others (R_u) the fact that he, the communicator, and R_i are in possession of mysterious secrets; but he withholds the content of the secrets from these outsiders.

The most important examples of this class of messages are communications transacted in liturgical languages, like Greek, Old Slavonic, Armenian, and Coptic, and the Latin of scholars in Medieval Europe.[26] Similarly, in the old Indian drama, "Sanscrit was the language of gods, kings, princes, brahmans, ministers, chamberlains, dancing masters and other men in superior positions and of a very few women of special religious importance, while Prakrit was spoken by men of an inferior class, like shopkeepers, law officers, aldermen, bathmen, fishermen and policemen and by nearly all women."[27]

Secret languages—as distinguished from codes—are contrived by children in many societies (including that of the Maoris of New Zealand), but there is also at least one instance of a secret language designed by a grammarian. In the fifth century A.D., the grammarian Virgilius Maro based *berba na filed* ("the poet's language"), which was long held in high repute in Irish schools, upon distortion of current words by reduplication, amputation, and displacement of syllables. The result was a "slang" containing words from Latin, Greek, and Hebrew, native archaic words, and distorted common words, which "was preserved by tradition in the schools as a secret language."[28]

We have said that in a heterogeneous audience certain recipients may either fail to understand or misunderstand the communicator. In the second, more complicated case, R_u does not hear noise or nonsense; nor does he know and accept the fact that secrets are being withheld from him. Instead, he understands a meaning, but it differs from that received by the intended recipient. Of course, such misunderstanding occurs very frequently. For example, in a classroom a few students understand the teacher, others fail to understand, and still others misunderstand. As this outcome is not intended by the teacher, it may be regarded as a mishap.

More interesting, and more relevant to this discussion is the case of the communicator who *wants to be misunderstood* by certain unwanted recipients in a heterogeneous audience. The communicator manages to transmit a message that has *two* meanings, an overt one (M_o) and a covert one (M_c). He discloses M_c to the intended recipient (R_i) but withholds it at the same time from R_u by inducing R_u to think that the only meaning he intends to convey is M_o. The intended recipient, whom the communicator wants to receive M_c, understands both M_o and M_c, is able to discriminate between them, and realizes that the overt meaning is meant to preoccupy the unwanted other recipient (R_u), thereby keeping him from noticing the covert meaning. It should be noted that this rather complicated transaction presupposes a common bond between C and R_i as a result of shared feeling, experience, belief, or purpose. Conversely, the fact that the unwanted recipient of the message is a stranger or outsider and as such not bound together with the communicator, accounts for his naiveté in assuming that M_o is the sole meaning in C's message. Thus,

Schema 6

Stendhal's *Lucien Leuwen* contains an amusing illustration of such a communication. Young Lucien visits for the first time the Countess de Chasteller whom he loves, but the unexpected presence of a stranger in the room, Miss Bérard, who happens to be a malicious gossip, bewilders him. Although tongue-tied at first, Lucien at last has "a miserable little inspiration." He would be very happy, he says in the presence of both ladies, if he were to succeed in becoming a good officer in the cavalry for it seems that heaven had not chosen him ever to be an eloquent political deputy. At this point Miss Bérard pricks up her ears because she thinks that Lucien is talking about politics. He continues that as a deputy he would not be capable of presenting in the Chamber matters of deep concern to him. Away from the rostrum he would be plagued by the vivacity of the feelings that inflamed his heart. But were he to open his mouth in front of that highest and stern judge whose displeasure would make him tremble, he could only say, "Look at my diffidence, you fill my whole heart, which lacks even the strength to reveal itself to you." By this time, Countess de Chasteller's initial pleasure has given way to unease; she fears her female companion. Lucien's words appear "too transparent" to her. Hastily she asks him whether he really had any prospects of being elected a deputy.[29]

Let us consider this episode somewhat more closely. Lucien evidently assumed that the countess would not betray the covert meaning of his speech to Miss Bérard, and the countess in her turn felt that Lucien was expecting her not to betray it. We may therefore say that C and R_i *trust* each other, whereas both of them *distrust* R_u. The awareness of this mutual trust becomes a delicate token of their love, which incidentally neither of them had ever before openly professed in the novel: the bond between them, as well as the hidden meaning of Lucien's speech, is a secret. Had the countess told Miss Bérard what Lucien "really" meant, she would have disclosed to her not only the hidden meaning but also various other things: to Miss Bérard she would have revealed that Lucien loved her, but that she did not love him; and to Lucien her brutal response would have told him in addition that she cared so little for his love as to make it and her rejection of it public. It is questionable whether his feelings of shame would have allowed him to protest dissemblingly that she had evidently misunderstood what he had said: he had meant precisely what he had said (M_o). In any event, the reader is inclined to feel that only an unashamedly public profession of love on Lucien's part (in the presence of Miss Bérard) would have deserved so cold and brutal a rejection by the countess: vulgarity would have been answered by disdain. Everything would have been different in the absence of Miss Bérard: the countess might have rejected Lucien's open declaration of love, but then she might have only dissembled her feelings, and Lucien would have known that she had not necessarily spoken her last word.

The Misses Bérard, that is, the listeners who do not understand covert meanings, are always felt to be ludicrous, as they suffer from a defect: like dull-witted censors they fail to comprehend what is going on, and dupes are comical characters par excellence.

Another very fine illustration of schema 6 may be found in Molière's *The School for Husbands* when Isabella and Valère declare their love for each other. They do so in the presence of Isabella's guardian, Sganarel, and for this reason are obliged to express themselves in skillfully ambiguous language. As a result, and to the audience's delight, Sganarel misunderstands the discourse and believes that Isabella faithfully loves him, addressing Valère in indignation at his advances to her.[30]

Nor is such allusive talk about love confined to Western literature and life. In the sixteenth-century Chinese novel *Chin P'in Mei,* the son-in-law of Hsi Men, master of the household and hero of the novel, has a clandestine love affair with Golden Lotus, Hsi Men's fifth wife. Once he sends her a letter in which he assures her of his devotion and of his hope to overcome all opposition to the consummation of their love. The author comments, "The writer had expressed himself in deliberately obscure phrases, which any other member of the household would hardly have been able to decipher"; but Golden Lotus was "much gratified."[31]

Choosing a broader perspective, every *roman de clef* has an overt meaning that is accessible to all readers, but conveys at the same time a covert meaning to a limited number of insiders who detect the identity of the living persons the author wished to portray in the guise of fictional characters.[32] It is of course also possible to model one particular character in a work of fiction after a person famous in real life. Again, illustrations abound. Particularly noteworthy achievements in modern literature are the satirical portraits of Gerhart Hauptmann as Pepperkorn in Thomas Mann's *Magic Mountain* and of Walther Rathenau as Dr. Arnheim in Robert Musil's *The Man Without Characteristics.*

THE AUDIENCE SEEKING MEANING

In all instances thus far adduced, except for schema 2b, it has been C who availed himself of the context in which covert meaning became intelligible, because he shared dispositions, experiences, or interests of the intended recipients. It is possible, however, that meaning springs to life *seemingly without the intention of the communicator.* The message appears to acquire meaning merely in consequence of the fact that it fits certain predispositions of the audience. We may describe this situation, somewhat boldly, as one in which *the audience seeks the meaning* that it needs.

In the years when Hitler ruled Germany, Ernst Jünger wrote a book, *On the Marble Cliffs,* which was widely read in Germany. The author used fantastic imagery to depict certain aspects of modern tyrannical regimes. The main figure in his book was a "Chief Forester." Later, in May 1945, Jünger noted in his diary that in times of censorship "the imagination of the reader cooperates exegetically—much more powerfully than the author wishes. The 'Chief Forester' was understood to be now Hitler, now Göring, now Stalin. This sort of thing I had foreseen, to be sure, but not intended."[33]

There is much evidence to support the contention that whenever freedom of expression is suppressed, the sensitivity to allusions increases. Another German writer said about the Nazi regime that "not only in reading but also in conversation the slightest allusion was understood. Everywhere one smelled a reference to current politics, even when no such reference was made. A conferencier complained to me that his audience was so super-keen of hearing as to interpret politically any joke he was telling."[34]

In 1953, Helmut Thielicke, the theologian, published a book of sermons on the Lord's Prayer.[35] He had given the first eight of the eleven sermons in Stuttgart toward the end of World War II, while the city was subject to severe bombing raids. Professor Thielicke told me in 1953 that he recalled the feeling of political audacity he had had when giving these sermons, although they contained no single overt political reference. He added that in reading proof in the early fifties, he could no longer discover which specific passages in his sermons had made him feel that way. By the same token, he said, he had experienced after the war that when speaking in a church in Communist East Berlin one only had to whisper what in West Germany required, as it were, the sound of trumpets to be understood. Several other German authors with whom I talked after the war about their experiences in writing and talking between the lines during the Nazi period, spontaneously testified in the same way to the heightened sensitivity of the listeners to critical allusions in times of extreme political stress.

In all epochs of history repressive regimes have encountered the allusive power of criticism contained in older literature. Although censors may attempt and be able to suppress the contemporary expression of dissent, they cannot possibly prevent associations of suppressed criticism that classical works of the past may evoke in a contemporary audience. For example, in the times of the Roman Empire, theater audiences applauded certain lines in ancient plays that seemed applicable to current abuses as well as to past practices chided by the author.[36] Schematically, such communications may at first be represented as follows:

Schema 7a $\quad C \leftarrow m \longrightarrow M_o \rightarrow R_i$
$\qquad\qquad\qquad\qquad\qquad\qquad M_c \leftarrow R_u$

Upon reflection, however, this schema is not always fitting. To begin with, while R_u, the present audience, was *unknown* to C, the past author, it cannot be said to have been *unwanted* by him. By the same token, M_c is a covert meaning only in the trivial sense that C could not possibly foresee the later contingent conditions of life that R_u was to encounter and to which —in the mind of R_u—the meaning of his message would be applied. Frequently C himself must be assumed to have written his poem, play, novel, or satire with its open meaning to apply not only within the confines of the work he created. The universal quality of the contingent conditions under which R_u lives may have been fully in C's mind. To put it differently, the meaning of C's message may be unhistorical, timeless, universal rather than contingent, no matter how timebound its form. When Marquis Posa, in Friedrich Schiller's *Don Karlos,* begs the king to permit freedom of thought, the validity of this open meaning is not confined to the historical setting of the drama —Spain under Philip II in the age of the Counter-Reformation—nor to the period in which the author wrote his work—the end of the eighteenth century in Germany. Finally, in no way did it become covert in historically later circumstances when freedom of thought was suppressed. To repeat, what has been presented in schema 7a as the covert meaning M_c may be merely the renewed timeliness of the author's original, perfectly open meaning. His message was never addressed to a historically restricted audience, but to all men who ever live under an illiberal regime and—as demand or supplication—to all those who ever suppress freedom of thought.

When in schema 7a M_c is presented as something "sought"

by unintended recipients rather than something intended by the author, we may possibly neglect Schiller's ironic admonition, which he uttered, incidentally, with reference to critics of *Don Karlos:* ". . . among his readers the author seldom is the least informed."[37] In short, schema 7a is applicable to Ernst Jünger's Chief Forester, but not to Schiller's Marquis Posa. In the case exemplified by Marquis Posa's demand for freedom of thought in *Don Karlos* and in many other instances, schema 7a might be corrected to resemble schema 1 as follows:

Schema 7b $\quad C \rightarrow m \rightarrow M_o \rightarrow R_i \cdots\cdots R_z$

R_z are recipients of m and M_o beyond the life span of C, and the added arrow pointing back from R_z to M_o is to indicate that certain recipients avidly notice the *open* meaning of an old, timeless message because their understanding of this meaning is sharpened by the dire circumstances in which they live.

It is important to realize, however, that many past events and a great deal of old literature, produced long before later-born censors do their work, are a source of intense embarrassment to contemporary guardians of prescribed thought. Hence the policy of illiberal regimes to confiscate or burn objectionable books of authors long dead, to restrict access to such books in libraries, to rewrite history, to eliminate certain plays from the repertoire of the theater, to rename cities, to dismantle public monuments, to prohibit old songs and drive musical compositions out of concert halls.

After the Decembrist Revolution in Russia in 1825, the chair of philosophy at Petersburg University was abolished because the government decided that "it was impossible to draw any distinction between dangerous and not-dangerous thought." All lectures at the university were read from carefully censored books, and "the students were expected to take them down and repeat them verbatim because to answer 'in their own words' was considered 'subversive free thinking.' "[38]

In 1874 Czech progressive circles cited Shakespeare against Habsburg suppression. Ninety years later, in 1964, this fact was recalled by Czech anticommunists when the communists tried to exploit Shakespeare in their cultural propaganda. Schiller's *Wilhelm Tell* was removed by the Nazis from the list of required readings in schools and banished from the stage because of the antityrannical verses the play contained.[39]

Truly covert meaning, that has been recalled quite often in
dire political circumstances, is contained in Tacitus' works. As a
senator under the reign of Domitian (A.D. +96), whom he regarded as a worse tyrant than Nero, Tacitus witnessed the expulsion of philosophers, book burnings, and death penalties executed upon command of the emperor. Later, he wrote,
". . . as previous ages saw the utmost of liberty, so we saw the
utmost of servitude, since we were robbed by spying of speech
and hearing. With our voices we would have lost memory itself,
if it were as much in our power to forget as it was to be silent.''[40]
And again, "How few are we who have survived not only others
but, as it were, ourselves. . . .''[41] When the good emperor Ner-
va was chosen to succeed Domitian, Tacitus began to publish
his history of the emperors. Long after his death, the Attic brev-
ity and simplicity of his style were associated with unorthodoxy
"and even libertinism" in many ages, whereas Cicero's ornate
style became that of the church, the universities, the Jesuits, the
foreign offices: in general, of orthodoxy.[42]

Interestingly enough, as late as the eighteenth and the early
nineteenth centuries, Tacitus was regarded "as a dangerously
subversive writer," particularly "under the dictatorships both
of the Jacobins and of Napoleon.''[43] Similarly, in this century,
three years after Hitler had assumed power, the Phaidon Publishing House issued a German translation of Tacitus' works. In
a brief note at the conclusion of the volume, signed by the publisher, the reader learned that Tacitus had awaited the end of
the arbitrary rule of tyranny in "embittered silence" and that
its long duration had made him cautious. ". . . He did not
always want to be understood, not always easily, not always by
everybody; many of his sentences are dark as hiding places and
brief as riddles. It is remarkable that precisely in such times of
anxiety, rather than in times when the press is free, the strongest statements are made and the most intricate thought becomes expressible: severe constraint produces the greatest
stylists.''[44] Evidently the German publisher hoped that some
readers of the book would discover and cherish in Tacitus' work
certain timely critical views of tyranny.

The more widely acknowledged the fame and the more deeply rooted the admiration for an old author, the more difficult it
is for censors to punish contemporary readers for attributing to
his work a timely, subversive, meaning. Sometimes even old

poetry may defy the censors despite the fierce criticism that contemporary readers and listeners suddenly read into the stanzas
whose political meaning has lain dormant for a very long time.
An especially pertinent instance is a poem written by Gottfried
Keller, which became very popular in the Third Reich. To Germans critical of Hitler the poem seemed to display uncanny
foresight of their political plight. It conjured up a thoroughly
evil state of affairs with the people living in shame. The poem
continued that some time in the future, when this misery will
have come to an end, people will speak of it as of the Black
Death, but on the heather, children will build a strawman and
put the torch to it so as to bring "joy out of suffering and light
out of ancient horror." In November 1939, Fritz Reck-
Malleczewen, who was twice arrested by the Gestapo and finally
murdered in Dachau, wrote in his posthumously published
diary that "everybody" knew this poem. "One reads it to the
other. I recently witnessed in Steinicke's restaurant in Schwab-
ing that old Steinicke read it out loud to his astonished guests.
The Gestapo is furious about these stanzas, which it can neither
render unwritten nor restrain: after all, we have not reached the
point where we could be forbidden to read a poem by
Keller. . . ."[45]

Similarly, Rudolf Pechel, for nine years until his arrest in
1942 the courageous editor of *Deutsche Rundschau,* published
in his magazine not only many essays that were obliquely critical of the regime but also excerpts from the writings of old
authors whom the readers could suddenly recognize as famous
champions of ideas opposed by the Nazis. The authors, whose
writings were excerpted under the heading "The Living Past,"
included Erasmus, Francis Bacon, Balthasar Gracian, Boetius,
Marcus Aurelius, Lao-tse, Montesquieu, Vauvenargues, Man-
zoni, Kant, Jacob Burckhardt, and Jonathan Swift.

Sacred literature that embodies "eternal" values is relatively
safe from political censors. Victor Klemperer, distinguished observer of the deterioration of morality and language in the Nazi
era, noted triumphantly that sermons that took the authorities
and their policies to task, if only by implication, were "quite
unassailably timeless."[46] But even sacred literature is not always
exempt from political persecution. When the Chinese communists decided in 1974 to label all resistance to revolutionary

values as Confucian, it became necessary to instruct Chinese youth on a mass scale what abominable "reactionaries" Confucius and Mencius had been. Now Mencius had generally been credited with advocating the right to slay those despised for having outraged humanity and righteousness. But according to a Chinese broadcast in 1974, a meeting of "poor and lower-middle class peasants" was held in Tsouhsien County in the eastern province of Shantung, where Mencius had been born more than two thousand years ago. At this meeting it was recalled that a certain Meng Fan-chi, said to be a "Mencius descendant of the seventy-fourth generation," gave a banquet for Japanese army officers during World War II. "This," the broadcast said, "shows the hypocrisy of Mencius."[47]

This instance surpasses in delay of censure other cases, such as that of Hobbes's *De Cive,* published in 1642, put on the Roman Index in 1654, and burned at Oxford in 1683; that of Copernicus's *De Revolutionibus,* quickly denounced by Luther, but kept off the Roman Index for almost a century; or the condemnation of John Scot Erigena's heresy by Honorius III in 1225, nearly four centuries after its publication.

FUTILE OBLIQUITY AND MENTAL RESERVATION

Cautious behavior in consideration of personal safety and in disregard of one's true convictions is demoralizing if the spurned virtues include candor and courage. The hypocrite reproaches himself in this case for untruthfulness and cowardice. He suffers discomfort not only because he is dishonest but also because dishonesty and diminished self-respect follow from the lack of his power to be honest. Cautious concealment of one's true opinions is possible without loss of self-respect only for those whose secretiveness or mendacity protects persons or values they love and respect. Similarly, simulation or dissimulation to advance or protect a cause that is regarded worthier than that pursued by the persecutor, is not felt to be dishonorable; the superior cause may join righteous conspirators in their design to seize power or prudent philosophers who secretly recognize the deficiencies of the political conventions with which they comply in order to pursue their studies.

In modern totalitarian regimes there are certain professions that are especially vulnerable to demoralization. Different from ancient tyrannies, modern dictators rule with the help of ideologies and beliefs which the masses of the population are supposed to share.

Professional writers and talkers are chosen, organized, and supervised to convey in public the "language regulations" on prescribed and proscribed subjects. Journalists in totalitarian regimes thus become persons who publish what is not in their minds but is in the minds of others who are more powerful than they are. Although in liberal society authors can perform a critical function in public, in totalitarian societies this function can be performed only by the audience without the guidance of professional communicators.

As a totalitarian regime entrenches itself in power, the journalists comprise two groups, the zealots and the secret critics of the regime. The former have no moral problems, as their own zeal impels them to comply and overcomply with the orders they receive. They do as they are told to do because they welcome the orders, and they do more than necessary because they identify with those in control. They believe in the ideology they spread.

The critics have the choice to leave their profession or to become hypocrites, as in this profession everybody is forced to *appear* as a zealot whether he is one or not. The critics who do not abandon their work must behave in public like zealots, for the nature of their work, unlike that of dissenters in most other walks of life, compels them to *advocate* rather than merely tolerate beliefs they do not share. Writing between the lines then serves not only the objective purpose of spreading criticism obliquely but also the subjective need to gain a respite from pretended zeal for false causes.

The moral stress to which critical journalists are exposed in totalitarian regimes may find release in cynicism and, in the last resort, in the illusion that their esoteric dissent will be detected in their exoteric production. Reck-Malleczewen observed in 1939 that "the same journalists who only yesterday were up to their neck in their twaddle, crack cynical jokes at their own Byzantine behavior as soon as one speaks to them in the street."[48]

Alternatively, after prolonged compliance with official regulations of language that conflict with reality or after entertaining for a long time prohibited secret views, the journalist may attribute to his readers an understanding of meanings hidden in his writings that they either no longer possess or have ceased to be interested in; or else the hidden meaning may be so faint as to pass unnoticed. Such illusions indicate that, through habituation to fear, the subjective need for moral rehabilitation may be stronger than the weak effort or the small opportunity to attain it.

Bruno E. Werner's *Die Galeere,* a novel with an evidently broad autobiographical base, conveys many insights into the moral problems of journalists in the Nazi era. Toward the end of the war, a journalist in the book says to one of his colleagues, "By the way, some people assert that my editorials contain quite a bit between the lines; I have already twice been warned officially." And the author comments that the speaker "belonged to those journalists who did not notice at all that the readers had lost the habit of finding anything in these articles but the official vocabulary. . . ."[49] Schematically, this futile act of incomplete communication may be represented as follows:

Schema 8

Finally, still another schema involving M_c must be presented. The communicator may wish to include in his message a meaning that, though hidden from *all* recipients, is to modify the overt meaning in his own mind. This is the case of statements made with a "mental reservation," which the communicator expresses in a secret (and possibly magical) way intelligible only to himself. Thus, committing perjury may be avoided in the mind of the perjurer, if not in the eyes of the law, by a publicly imperceptible gesture to which the perjurer attributes redeeming power, because to him it annuls the validity of the oath.

A student of mine once told me of a related instance from his own experience. Having recently moved to town, he had applied for a credit card at a bank. When he was asked questions regarding his wife's employment, he replied, "My wife is *presently* employed at . . ." As his wife was planning to quit her job very soon because of her pregnancy, he used the word "presently" as an oblique hint at the fact that he was withholding some information. He did so realizing that a completely truthful, open answer might result in the rejection of his application for the credit card. In analyzing his behavior, the student explained, "Had I merely said, 'My wife is employed at . . .' I would have felt a sense of guilt in not disclosing by way of a hint that her employment would end in the near future." He explained further that had the word "presently" in his reply been noticed by the interviewer and had he been asked to explain it, he had "planned in advance" to answer, "She is thinking of leaving her job for another." The "other job," of course, also had a covert meaning, which was "the job of raising a newborn infant."

In this case, then, the intended recipient of the covert meaning was the communicator himself, not in his role of transmitting the overt meaning but in that of addressing at the same time his moral self. The inconspicuous word or gesture is not, and is not meant to be, addressed to anyone but himself: it is to safeguard secretly his moral integrity, while being engaged in mundane affairs that tax this integrity. His moral standard demanded of him that he tell the whole truth—he realized, incidentally, that this demand was rooted in his religious upbringing—so that it is appropriate to consider "the common bond" between communicator and the intended recipient (his moral self) of the covert meaning to be that of a religious-moral community as distinguished from the pragmatic relationship of the interview at the bank. Of course, the student applied, as it were, a double standard in that he excluded the interrogator momentarily from that community by withholding from him what he disclosed obliquely to himself in order to assuage his qualms. Whatever moral unease remained nonetheless was removed (as he fully explained) by his intention not to abuse the privileges of the credit card, which he needed primarily for paying the costs of his wife's expected confinement and by the paramount importance of caring for his wife and family.

Schematically, such communication may be presented as

Schema 9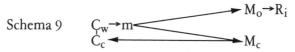

C_w signifies the communicator in his role "in the world," and C_c as a person in dialogue with his conscience.

THE FEAR OF DEATH AND THE LOVE OF TRUTH

Of the various schemata that have been presented, schema 6

is the most important one in investigating the communication of hidden meaning. The schema has been applied first to erotic bonds between C and R_i, for example, Lucien and Countess Chasteller. Miss Bérard (R_u) was viewed with apprehension by both of them, because she could intrude upon, and desecrate by gossip or laughter, the love between Lucien and the countess; she might even have destroyed their love. Now, it has already been indicated but still needs to be amplified that the erotic relationship is only one of many possible contexts in which esoteric communication occurs.

For one thing, fear of ridicule is not confined to lovers. It is a ubiquitous emotion. Theodore Agrippa d'Aubigné (1552–1630) concluded the preface to his memoirs, which first appeared as *Histoire Secrète* in 1729, with an order to his children that they not keep "more than two copies of this book," that these should be closely guarded, and that neither copy should leave the house. Otherwise those who are envious of the children will punish them by laughing at the divine miracles by which his life had been saved.[50] Nor is the unwanted recipient always feared merely because he is a gossip who may bring on the social sanctions of ridicule, defamation, social rejection, and the like; instead he may inspire political or religious fear. Although the fear of social sanctions is a strong motive of cautious behavior, political and religious fear are even more potent, as they are rooted in the fear of death.

The hunter, fisherman, or sailor in preliterate society who imagines himself to be overheard or understood by animals, spirits, demons, and the like, uses "guarded speech" because he is afraid that open discourse would arouse the envy or wrath of uncontrollable powers and entail evil consequences for him. "In place of the forbidden word it is therefore necessary to use some kind of figurative paraphrase, to dig up an otherwise obsolete term, or to disguise the real world so as to render it more innocent."[51] Taboos are observed also with reference to ominous and mysterious physiological functions, events of nature, and in respect of powers that are held in awe, like God. They must not be named; substitute appellations are used.[52]

But man fears not only supernatural powers, but also the power of man over man. Like God, great human power as well can inspire awe. If in communicating with a heterogeneous audience, the recipients include persons of great power or their agents, the urge to abstain from open expression of skeptical or aggressive opinions is very strong. Rivals are mistrusted, because they might use the candor of others to further their own ends. The patron is feared because if openly criticized he may not only withdraw favors but ruin his client. The fact that it is dangerous to tell the truth to powerful masters is known from the folklore of many lands and is commonplace in the literature dealing with political counseling. Trusted counselors know they must speak cautiously to their prince.[53] Plautus has one of his characters say quite simply, "It's foolish for you to be disagreeable to a person who has more power."[54]

Even the life of satirical entertainers is hazardous in illiberal times. They may be ruthlessly punished for as little as a hint in their work, although their subversive intent may be doubtful. At the time of the ruthless emperor Domitian ". . . the young Stoic nobleman Helvidius Priscus produced a farce about Paris —not the dancer, but the mythical Trojan prince—deserting the nymph Oenone. Domitian took this as an allusion to his own divorce, and executed Helvidius. It did not matter whether the allusion was intentional or not. It was sufficient if it was likely to be noticed and enjoyed by the public."[55]

But disclosing the truth is particularly dangerous if it finds fault with authoritative doctrines and sacred beliefs. This is so because even in the absence of a church and a priesthood with their vested interests in guarding the sacred against heresy, the believers do not tolerate any trifling with their gods and their worship. The mere expression of doubt may be intolerable. According to Cicero, Protagoras of Abdera opened a book with the statement "About the gods I am unable to affirm either how they exist or how they do not exist."[56] The Athenian Assembly banished him from the city and had his books burnt in the marketplace.

However distant the believers may be from the exercise of political power, the rulers themselves must reckon with the religious predispositions of their subjects. Should they not share the communal faith or the deeply ingrained superstitions of their subjects, they had yet better feign respect for them. It is therefore erroneous to equate ''the vulgar'' with those who have no power. This, of course, has been known to philosophers through the ages. As a rather modern observer, Pierre Bayle, remarked:

> If what is most falsely said by impious Men were true, viz. That Religion is a mere human invention, set up by the Sovereigns to keep their Subjects within the Bounds of Obedience, may we not assert, that Princes are the first who have been taken in their own Snares? For Religion is so far from making them Masters of their Subjects, that, on the contrary, it gives their Subjects a Power over them, since they are obliged to profess the Religion of their People, and not That, which seems to them the best: And if they are resolved to profess a Religion different from that of their Subjects, their Crowns will fit loose upon their Heads.[57]

Under certain conditions, then, the powerful must resort to exoteric—religious, orthodox—speech, for fear of their subjects, and withhold from them esoteric views that are religiously heterodox or irreligious.

The rulers share the need for such prudence with philosophers who put reason above faith, although philosophers are not hungry for power. They want to be able to pursue the truth without having to drink poison. Although they do not need to manipulate the superstitions of the vulgar, as statesmen and generals sometimes must do in order to achieve their ends,[58] they may have reason to fear being deprived of liberty and life in retaliation for questioning powerful popular beliefs. They may also feel obliged not to cause moral and social disorder in consequence of fully disclosing what is on their minds. The wise, therefore, avoid speaking rashly of God in a manner that may be misunderstood and abused by the vulgar, be they powerful or not.

Finally, teaching philosophy requires well-measured communication: acquiring any skill, like that of playing a musical instrument or that of carving a stone, demands practice of the student. No good teacher wishes to instruct the inept, nor does he expect the difficult to be mastered before the simple. There is a *gradus ad parnassum*. The teacher may be said to speak to a homogeneous group when he has students who are eager to learn, and yet without courting failure he cannot disclose at once everything he knows. Measured discourse, in which something may be withheld, shows more love of the truth and greater respect for the students than does instant, complete disclosure.

URBANE DISSIMULATION

Covert meaning occurs in communication to "insiders." It excludes unwanted recipients, no matter whether they are in earshot of the communicator or are part of an outside world that is considered to be vulgar, profane, hostile, or dangerous. Often the transmission of hidden meaning is associated with consciousness of superiority over those excluded from the communication. It has been said that cultists and sectaries who teach hidden doctrines have a common failing, "the desire to feel superior to others by virtue of esoteric knowledge."[59] Although it may be an open question whether they have "a desire" to feel superior, the "feeling" itself is indeed common.

It must still be noted that something similar to covert meaning may appear in the absence of unwanted recipients, that is to say, in entirely homogeneous groups. This is the *urbane dissimulation* employed in toning down a painful evocation among civilized people or in softening bad, saddening news. "Among civilized peoples and especially in refined circles," as Eric Partridge put it in an essay on euphemism,[60] talk about death, sickness, madness, idiocy, ruin, and similarly disturbing subjects is "toned down," if it cannot be altogether avoided. The relative who has died is said to have "departed," and the person who is very ill may be characterized as *"bien fatigué"*—very tired.[61] Conversely, unrestrained, direct talk among mourners is heartless, as is chillingly shown in Leo Tolstoy's short story "The Death of Ivan Ilyich." Talk about low physical functions and processes as well is avoided in "polite society"; or euphemism, allusions, and abbreviations are employed instead. She "powders her nose"; "he spends the night with her"; somebody has "TB," and so on. Such unpragmatic patterns of speech are capable of extraordinary elaboration and refinement.

The standards of propriety and decorum are not immutable. Although Martial used many euphemisms in political discourse, he was "indecent" on sexual topics; the opposite was true of the Western middle classes in the nineteenth and twentieth centuries until fairly recently. Similarly, the sense of sexual shame is not immutable. Even today, it manifests itself with some in allusions to conceal intimate desires, while others use allusions to reveal them and still others are past shame.

All upper classes tend to develop a vocabulary of refined speech, the mastery of which identifies its members. "Correct" pronunciation as well as the "proper" choice of words and, under certain conditions, calligraphy may be indispensable for a successful claim to upper-class status.[62] The understanding of literary allusions may become a mark of distinction. Sei Shōnagon, a lady at court, relates in her tenth-century Japanese *Pillow-Book* a conversation with a gentleman in which she tells him "that it is often a good thing to act according to circumstances, instead of making for oneself these hard-and-fast rules. But he said it came natural to him to live according to rule, and 'one can't change one's nature.' 'Don't stand on ceremony,' I answered. He did not see the allusion. . . ."[63] Instead he thought that Shōnagon was inviting him to take liberties with her. The allusion, explained by Arthur Waley, the twentieth-century translator of the *Pillow-Book,* not by its tenth-century author, is to the Analects of Confucius: "If you are wrong, don't stand on ceremony with yourself, but change!"

Similar to allusive discourse in socially exclusive circles is the use of learned allusions by poets in order to display their erudition (to other poets) rather than to please the multitude. In Camoëns' *The Lusiads* (1572), "the bird whose song the Phaetonian death wailed loud and long" is the swan; "the glowing amourist who won fair faithless Larissaea's love" is Apollo, and so on. Renaissance poets were much concerned with showing their familiarity with the world of Virgil and Ovid; they referred to "the gods and heroes of antiquity by allusion or association rather than directly."[64] Similarly, in the Italian Renaissance, prose composition required the ornate style as the mark distinguishing the learned from the unlearned. Authors had to study the rigid rules of the *artes dictandi;*[65] the contempt for the unlettered found in Medieval Latin poetry had not subsided. Disdain for general popularity survived among serious writers and composers well into the Baroque and Classicist eras.[66] In English poetry the late seventeenth and early eighteenth centuries were the great age of allusion. Only thereafter do allusions of great poets sometimes take on the air of labored futility.[67]

As the beautiful must not show the effort it takes to produce it, negligence and carelessness in communication may be regarded as attributes of high standing, if speech or writing otherwise clearly meets the required standards. For example, in Lady Murasaki's *Tale of Genji,* it is said about a poem written on a fan: "It was written with a deliberate negligence which seemed to aim at concealing the writer's status and identity. But for all that the hand showed breeding and distinction. . . ."[68]

Schematically, the hidden meaning appearing in courteous discourse within homogeneous groups may be represented as follows,

Schema 10 $C \rightarrow m \rightarrow M_o \rightarrow M_c \rightarrow R_i$

A social class that places a high value on courtesy and good manners observes many verbal taboos; it dreads the emphatic. That which is felt to offend, disturb, or frighten man is hidden behind a veil of politeness. Outsiders may be inclined to scorn the artificiality of such convention, which can indeed degenerate into fastidious niceties indistinguishable from silliness. It should be noted, however, that polite speech and conduct not only are attributes of social distinction but also serve to render life bearable and light in defiance of its dark terrors.

NOTES

An excerpt from this chapter was published in *Social Research* 44 (Autumn 1977).

1. Cicero, *De Oratore,* II, LXIV-LXV.

2. See Richard Broxton Onians, *The Origin of European Thought* (Cambridge: Cambridge University Press, 1954), pt. 3, Chaps. 4–5, pp. 349–377.

3. See Hans Speier, "Grimmelshausen's Laughter," in *Force and Folly* (Cambridge, Mass.: M.I.T. Press, 1969), pp. 307–313. It should be noted that the hidden truth may also be regarded as sweet, not bitter; this was the view held, for example, by St. Augustine.

4. Lali Horstman, *Nothing for Tears* (London, 1953), pp. 39, 62, 67, 73.

Similar references to impromptu codes can be found in Margret Boveri, *Tage des Überlebens* (Munich, 1968), p. 199; and in Rudolf Pechel, *Zwischen den Zeilen* (Wientheid, 1948), p. 343. An older illustration from eighteenth-century France: "Nicolas Boindin, a man of letters . . . was usually 'at home' at the Café Procope, and was a recognized freethinker there. He had a jargon all his own, and a plentiful assortment of nick-names. Liberty he called Jeanneton, Religion was Jacotte, and God M. de l'Être. 'May I venture to ask,' said a detective who was listening, 'who this M. de l'Être may be who so often misbehaves himself, and with whom you seem to have so much fault to find?' 'Yes, Monsieur; he's a police spy' " (Paul Hazard, *European Thought in the Eighteenth Century* [New Haven: Yale University Press, 1954], p. 95).

5. *The Presidential Transcripts* (New York, 1974), pp. 133–134.

6. *Entsiklopedicheskii Slovar* (Petersburg, 1903), vol. 37, pp. 955ff. For Aesopic language in *Pravda* prior to the October Revolution, see Whitman Bassow, "The Pre-revolutionary *Pravda* and Tsarist Censorship," *The American Slavic and East European Review* 13 (1954):47–65.

7. Nathan Leites and Elsa Bernaut, *Ritual of Liquidation* (Glencoe, Ill.: The Free Press, 1954).

8. Myron Rush, *The Rise of Khrushchev* (Washington, D.C., 1958); Myron Rush, "Esoteric Communication in Soviet Politics," *World Politics* 11 (1959):614–620; Robert Conquest, *Power and Policy in the USSR* (New York, 1961); Donald S. Zagoria, *The Sino-Soviet Conflict 1956–1961* (Princeton, 1962), pp. 24–35; William E. Griffith, *Communist Esoteric Communications: Explication de Texte* (Cambridge, Mass.: Massachusetts Institute of Technology, Center for International Studies, 1967); Leites and Bernaut, pp. 277–349.

9. Leo Strauss, *Persecution and the Art of Writing* (Glencoe, Ill.: The Free Press, 1952), pp. 33–34. (The paper from which the quotation is taken was first published in 1941.) The wise avoid speaking rashly of God not only for fear of persecution. As late as 1784, Moses Mendelssohn pointed out in his essay *"Ueber die Frage: was heisst aufklären?"* that the enlightening philosopher will not spread certain truths if they tear down principles of religion and morality. Cf. Norbert Hinske, ed., *Was ist Aufklärung? Beiträge aus der Berliner Monatsschrift,* 2nd ed., (Darmstadt, 1977), pp. 449–450.

10. Freud referred in this connection to Goethe's Faust: "Das Beste was Du wissen kannst darfst Du den Buben doch nicht sagen." It may be questioned, however, that Goethe regarded "the most intimate things" as "the best one can know." Leo Strauss, too, refers to Goethe in connection with self-imposed silence; see *Thoughts on Machiavelli* (Glencoe, Ill.: The Free Press, 1958), p. 174. On the silence of the wise, see also G. E. Lessing's *Ernst und Falk,* Second Dialogue.

11. Sigmund Freud, *Collected Papers,* 7th ed. (London, 1950), vol. 2, p. 18.

12. Freud, pp. 19–21.

13. *Eleven Letters,* ed. G. R. Carpenter (Boston and New York, 1892), pp. 194–195.

14. See "Allegory," *Hastings' Encyclopedia of Religion and Ethics* (1908); F. W. Farrar, *History of Interpretation* (London, 1886); H. A. Wolfson, *Philo,* 2 vols. (Cambridge, Mass.: Harvard University Press, 1947), esp. vol. 1, pp. 115–163.

15. See J. Tate, "The Beginnings of Greek Allegory," *The Classical Review* 41 (1927).

16. Wolfson, p. 134.

17. Farrar, p. 249.

18. Wolfson, p. 116. Cf. "Therefore speak I to them in parables: because they seeing see not; and hearing they hear not, neither do they understand" (Matthew 13:13).

19. Farrar, p. 237.

20. U.S. Atomic Energy Commission, *In the Matter of J. Robert Oppenheimer. Transcript of Hearing before Personnel Security Board,* Washington, D.C., 12 April 1954 through 6 May 1954 (Government Printing Office, 1954), p. 87.

21. For two illustrations, see Strauss, pp. 30–31.

22. Hugo von Hofmannsthal, *Der Schwierige* (1921), act 3, sc. 13; *Gesammelte Werke* (Berlin, 1934), vol. 1, pt. 2, p. 446. Similarly, ". . . it happens to me that I say quite out loud what I am thinking—what an impossible situation if one goes out to meet people." (Vol. 1, pt. 2, p. 273.) Cf. also the essays by George Steiner, "Der Rückzug aus dem Wort" and "Der Dichter und das Schweigen," in *Sprache und Schweigen* (Frankfurt, 1969), pp. 44–97; and the play by Robert Bolt, *A Man For All Seasons.*

23. G. W. F. Hegel, *Phänomenologie des Geistes,* ed. Georg Lasson, Philosophische Bibliothek, 2d. ed. (Leipzig, 1921), vol. 114, p. 8.

24. *New York Times,* 13 March 1974.

25. Edward Gibbon, *Decline and Fall of the Roman Empire,* chap. 40.

26. See J. Vendryes, *Language,* trans. Paul Radin (New York, 1925), pt. 4, chap. 2 ("Dialects and Specialized Languages").

27. Otto Jespersen, *Language* (New York, 1922), p. 242.

28. Vendryes, p. 255.

29. Stendhal, *Lucien Leuwen,* pt. 1, chap. 24.

30. Molière, *The School for Husbands,* II, 14.

31. *Chin P'ing Mei,* with an introduction by Arthur Waley (New York: Putnam, 1940), p. 678.

32. See Georg Schneider, *Die Schlüsselliteratur,* 3 vols. (Stuttgart, 1951–1953).

33. Ernst Jünger, *Strahlungen III* (Munich, 1966), p. 147.

34. Werner Bergengruen, "Foreword" to Rudolf Pechel's, *Zwischen den Zeilen,* pp. 8–9.

35. Helmut Thielicke, *Das Gebet, das die Welt umspannt* (Stuttgart, 1953).

36. Moses Hadas, *Ancilla to Classical Reading* (New York, 1954), p. 76.

37. "Briefe über Don Karlos," in *Schillers sämtliche Werke,* ed. Karl Goedecke (Stuttgart, n.d.), vol. 12, p. 194.

38. David Margashak, *Turgenev: A Life* (New York, 1954), p. 54.

39. Theodor Heuss, *Dank und Bekenntnis. Gedenkrede zum 20. Juli 1944* (Tübingen, 1954), p. 23. The opposition of the Nazis to Schiller's *Don Karlos* has a precedent in the removal of the play from the repertoire of the theater in Graz by the Austrian police in 1830. The incident inspired Joh. Nestroy the following day to an extraordinarily effective satirical demonstration on the stage. Cf. Hans Speier, *Witz und Politik. Essay über die Macht und das Lachen* (Zurich, 1975), pp. 30–31.

40. Tacitus, *Agricola,* 2.

41. *Agricola,* 3

42. Gilbert Highet, *The Classical Tradition* (New York, 1949), chap. 18. As a certain parallel it may be mentioned that Stendhal wrote *Lucien Leuwen* in 1836 for "the happy few" who would understand his meaning and appreciate his style fifty years later. He wrote eschewing the popular romanticism of his day and while reading the Code Napoleon in order to avoid in his own prose the stylistic frills he detested. His novel, which was devastatingly critical of politics in the Second Empire, was published posthumously.

43. Lionel Trilling, "Tacitus Now," in *The Liberal Imagination* (New York, 1953), p. 194. In the United States, Tacitus' aristocratic values have kept liberals from admiring him. On Tacitus, cf. also Ronald Syme, *Tacitus,* 2 vols. (London, 1958).

44. "Nachwort" to Tacitus' *Sämtliche Werke* (Vienna: Phaidon-Verlag, 1935), p. 800.

45. Friedrich Percival Reck-Malleczewen, *Tagebuch eines Verzweifelten* (Lorch/Württemberg-Stuttgart: Bürger-Verlag, 1947), p. 97.

46. Victor Klemperer, *LIT* [*Lingua Tertii Imperii,* Language of the Third Reich] (Berlin: Aufbau Verlag, 1949), p. 279.

47. *New York Times,* 4 April 1974.

48. Reck-Malleczewen, p. 92.

49. Bruno E. Werner, *Die Galeere* (Frankfurt, 1949), p. 494.

50. *Thomas and Felix Platters and Theodor Agrippa d'Aubignés Lebensbeschreibungen,* ed. Otto Fischer. (Munich: Otto Moericke Verlag, 1911), p. 294.

51. Jespersen, p. 289.

52. Heinz Werner in his important investigation into the origins of metaphor advanced the opinion that fear is prior to awe: "*Furcht ist früher als Ehrfurcht.*" See H. Werner, *Die Ursprünge der Metapher* (Leipzig, 1919), p. 43.

53. Cf. Thomas More's "Dialogue of Counsel" in his *Utopia,* book 1.

54. Plautus, *Casina*, II, 4.

55. Gilbert Highet, *Juvenal the Satirist* (Oxford, 1954), p. 26.

56. Cicero, *De natura deorum*, I, XXIII.

57. *Selections from Bayle's Dictionary*, ed. E. A. Beller and M. du P. Lee, Jr. (Princeton: Princeton University Press, 1952), p. 4.

58. Machiavelli, *The Discourses*, I, 14–15.

59. Jeffrey Burton Russell, *Dissent and Reform in the Early Middle Ages* (Berkeley: University of California Press, 1965), p. 12.

60. Eric Partridge, "Euphemism and Euphemisms," republished in *Here, There and Everywhere* (London, 1950), pp. 39–49.

61. Laurence Wylie, *Village in the Vaucluse* (Cambridge, Mass.: Harvard University Press, 1957), p. 188. Cf. *abire ad plures* for *mori* in Latin. On euphemisms in Latin, see Otto Keller, *Zur lateinischen Sprachgeschichte, 2. Teil. Gesammelte Aufsätze* (Leipzig, 1895).

62. Introduction to *The Pillow-Book for Sei Shōnagon*, trans. by Arthur Waley, 3rd ed. (Woking: Unwin Brothers, 1949). For the high esteem in which calligraphy was held in Islam, see Ernst Robert Curtius, *European Literature and the Latin Middle Ages* (New York, 1953), p. 341.

63. *Pillow-Book*, p. 65.

64. William C. Atkinson, "Introduction" to his translation of Camoëns's *The Lusiads* (London: Penguin Classics, 1952), p. 34.

65. Michele Barbi, *Life of Dante*, trans. and ed. Paul L. Ruggiers (Berkeley and Los Angeles, 1954), pp. 52–53.

66. See Hans Speier, "Court and Tavern in the German Baroque Novel," *Force and Folly*, p. 224.

67. See, for example, E. M. W. Tillyard's comments on Ezra Pound's "Ode pour l'élection de son sépulcre" in *Poetry Direct and Oblique* (London: Chatto & Windus, 1948), p. 35. Tillyard speaks of "bogus obliquity" and "would-be obliquity through allusion."

68. *The Tale of Genji*, trans. Arthur Waley (Boston: n.d.), vol. 1, p. 56. There are many other passages showing the importance of calligraphy.

10

THE TRUTH IN HELL: MAURICE JOLY ON MODERN DESPOTISM

Hans Speier

I

In an autobiographical account, published in 1870, Maurice Joly told the story of how he came to write his *Dialogue aux Enfers*. He was scandalized by Napoleon III's domestic and foreign policies. After Napoleon had usurped imperial power, his regime became repressive and corrupt, and his foreign policies involved the country in many wars. Joly was fiercely critical of the emperor's despotism and his vainglorious ventures abroad. Searching for an appropriate disguise that would enable him to hoodwink the censors when attacking the emperor publicly, he recalled the *Dialogues sur le commerce des blés* by the Abbé Ferdinando Galiani (1770), in which this friend of Holbach's and Mme d'Epinay's had departed souls wittily discuss tariffs and trade in grain. "While walking on the terrace along the river near Pont Royal in bad weather," Joly happened upon the idea of a fictional conversation between Montesquieu and Machiavelli in Hades. "It is Machiavelli who represents the policy of force as opposed to Montesquieu who will represent the policy of justice; and Machiavelli will be Napoleon III, who himself would describe his abominable policies."[1]

Commenting upon contemporary events in the form of such a conversation rendered Joly's attack more elegant and dramatic, but hardly less obvious. The time-honored literary device

would have been too thin a veil to conceal his thought even
from censors less experienced than the police in the Second Empire.

The *Dialogue in Hell between Machiavelli and Montesquieu
or Machiavelli's Policies in the Nineteenth Century* was published anonymously in French at Brussels in 1864. Copies of the
book, smuggled across the border for distribution in France,
were seized by the French police, and its author was easily identified. Joly was arrested and held for several months until the
court pronounced sentence on 25 April 1865. The newspaper *Le
Droit* published a lengthy excerpt from the decision:

> . . . in a dialogue between Machiavelli and Montesquieu the
> author begins by opposing the political principles developed in the
> writings of these famous men, then establishes a general thesis that
> the dreadful despotism taught by Machiavelli in his treatise, *The
> Prince,* has succeeded, by artifice and evil ways, in imposing itself
> on modern society. . . . The author charges the French government
> with having, through shameful means, hypocritical ways, and per-
> fidious contrivances, led the public astray, degraded the character
> of the nation, and corrupted its morals. . . . For these reasons Mau-
> rice Joly, having committed the crime of inciting hatred and con-
> tempt against the Government, is sentenced to fifteen months im-
> prisonment, 300 francs fine, and confiscation of the copies of the
> *Dialogue in Hell.*[2]

Joly's account of 1870 did not do full justice to his intellectual achievement, for he had done more than set forth
Napoleon's misrule: the resort to a plebiscite in order to legitimize his coup d'etat, the corruption of parliament and the
courts, the perversion of the freedom of the press, the fraudu-
lent handling of public finances, the ubiquitous employment
of political informers, the Saint-Simonian policy of public
works, the cynical use of all available symbolic means of power,
and the distraction of public attention from domestic affairs by
waging wars. Concealing his indignation Joly exposed all this
with chilling detachment. But it should not be overlooked that
in the preface to the *Dialogue in Hell* he claimed that his book
was a serious undertaking and neither a lampoon nor a political
pamphlet. Like all serious writing, he said, it ought to be read
slowly.

The very first sentence of Joly's preface claims that the work contains fancies applicable to *all* governments, and early in the conversation Machiavelli protests to his adversary that Machiavellism is older than Machiavelli. It seems to follow that Machiavelli cannot be regarded as the architect of Machiavellism nor can Napoleon III be held solely responsible for his despotic regime. Indeed, in the plebiscite of 21 December 1851 more than 90 percent of about eight million French voters had legitimized his rule.[3] Joly's book deals with the legacy of the French Revolution inherited by modern industrial society and perverted by a modern Caesar. It is for this reason that all serious students of his book have commented not only upon Joly's intellectual brilliance, which matches his moral passion, but also upon his startling foresight, which anticipates political developments in the twentieth century.

Maurice Joly was born of Catholic parents in 1821. His father, married to an Italian woman, was councillor-general of the Jura. Maurice Joly studied law. After serving as secretary to Princess Mathilde, a cousin of Napoleon III, he became a barrister in Paris and published several political and literary studies of advocates under the title *Le Barreau de Paris.*

After his release from prison in 1867 Joly was denounced by the defenders of the empire and treated with reserve by the republicans. Perhaps his friends did not consider him politically adroit enough or he may have offended them by his uncompromising sternness, as moralists sometimes do. In any event, his failure to spare the people for their support of the emperor must have alienated him from radicals.

While the emperor was still in power, Joly embarked upon a new venture as editor of the journal *Le Palais,* but this activity ended in a duel with his principal collaborator. After the collapse of the empire, in October 1870, Joly sought to obtain a government post through Jules Grévy who was to become president of the National Assembly in 1871. He failed and joined the radical resistance under the leadership of Louis Auguste Blanqui and Louis Charles Deslescluze. In November he was arrested again and freed only a few months later by the Council of War. Joly considered himself at that time a "revolutionary," but he opposed communism.

In 1872 he was offered an important position on the journal

La Liberté. In 1878, before Jules Grévy succeeded General Mac-
Mahon as president of the Republic, Joly attacked Grévy in
public. Thereupon not only Gambetta but whatever other supporters or friends Joly still had turned against him. The list of
public figures Joly attacked in his life is long indeed and com-
prises persons of very different political persuasion: Napoleon
III, Victor Hugo, Gambetta, Grévy. In addition, he had many
feuds in his professional life. He was a lonely man, devoted to
moral principles and apparently never forgiving of anyone who
did not live up to his standards. Perhaps his keen insight into
politics and society was sharpened by a passionate desire to remain pure and morally inviolate. If so, he paid for his rigor with
his life. On 16 July 1878 he shot himself. He left the manuscript of a novel, *Les Affamés,* dealing with French society of his
time.

II

If Maurice Joly did not receive during his life the recognition
which his intellectual achievements deserved, posterity has
treated him more capriciously than any other writer of distinction. His *Dialogue in Hell* became the source of the most momentous fraud in the history of political propaganda. In many
lands across Europe it was plagiarized by opportunists, common
criminals, terrorists, police agents, paranoid priests, and reactionary fanatics. Many of Machiavelli's observations in Joly's
book about the practices and principles of statecraft in the Second Empire were attributed by the plagiarists to a fictitious
group of Jewish leaders plotting the corruption of the prevailing
political and moral order so as to bring about Jewish world
domination. Some liberal ideas of Montesquieu as well were exploited by the forgers in order to document alleged stratagems
of the Jews in their efforts to enfeeble their victims' will and
ability to resist.

   The history of this notorious case of plagiarism began in 1868
when a German writer published a novel, *To Sedan,* under the
pseudonym Sir John Retcliffe. His true name was Hermann
Goedsche. After having been dishonorably discharged, at age
thirty-four, as a petty official of the Prussian Postal Service, he
became a staff member of a conservative newspaper, the
Preussische Kreutz Zeitung, and a popular author of sensational

fiction. His novel *To Sedan* contains the weird story "The Jewish Cemetery in Prague," in which the heads of the twelve Jewish tribes keep a centennial appointment in the presence of
Satan to report on their plans for the enslavement of the world.
The speeches of the Jewish leaders deal with topics discussed
and ideas propounded by Machiavelli in Joly's book.

It is not known for a fact that Goedsche read one of the rare
copies of the first edition of the *Dialogue in Hell.* Nor is it certain that he knew French. It would have been easy for him,
however, to get access to Joly's book through the first German
translation published anonymously by Otto Wigand at Leipzig
in 1865.[4]

The sinister proposals made by the twelve fictional Jewish
leaders at the cemetery in Prague were consolidated in a single
pronouncement that became known among anti-Semites
everywhere as *The Rabbi's Speech.* It was printed many times,
beginning in the 1870s, in France, Germany, Russia, Austria,
and later in other countries as well, always with the claim that
the speech was not fiction but fact. The rabbi soon acquired a
name, and it was stated that he had revealed actual secret plans
of Jewish leaders to corrupt the world and seize power. Joly's
analysis of existing conditions in the second empire had been
turned into an evil design of the future. *The Rabbi's Speech*
helped in provoking the pogrom at Kishinev in Bessarabia in
1903. In this century it became intertwined with the crowning
forgery, *The Protocols of the Elders of Zion,* many editions of
which also contain *The Rabbi's Speech.*[5] The *Protocols* consist
of a series of fabricated minutes of an alleged council meeting
of Jewish leaders discussing their ruthless and cunning measures
to reach the goal of world domination.

The framework for the *Protocols,* a meeting of a council of
Elders, was perhaps set by Osman-Bey in his book *World Conquest by the Jews.* The author of this fantasy was of Jewish
origin; his real name was Millinger. Before trying to make a living through anti-Semitic writings, he had been an international
swindler with a history of several arrests.[6]

The fabricators of the *Protocols* wrote in French and drew inspiration also from writings in the French anti-Semitic tradition, in particular *La France Juive* (1886) by Edouard Drumont
who in turn had plagiarized Gougenot des Mourreaux's *Le Juif,*

le judaisme et le judaisation des peuples chrétiens (1869), and
La Franc-Maçonnerie, Synagogue de Satan (1893) by Msgr.
Meurin, archbishop of Port-Louis, Mauritius. The main source
of the plagiarists, however, was Joly's *Dialogue in Hell*. "In all,
over 160 passages in the Protocols, totalling two-fifths of the entire text, are clearly based on passages in Joly; in nine of the
chapters the borrowings amount to more than half the text, in
some they amount to three quarters, in one (Protocol VII) to
almost the entire text."[7]

Although the first version of the *Protocols* seems to have been
fabricated in French at the time of the Dreyfus affair, probably
in 1897, the form in which the forgery was launched upon its
career throughout the world was as an insertion in the third edition of a Russian book by the eccentric priest Sergey Nilus, *The
Great and the Small,* published in 1905. In a conversation with
Count A. M. du Chayla, a Frenchman who spent many years in
Russia and had accepted the orthodox faith, Nilus referred to
the *Protocols* as "the charter of the Kingdom of Anti-Christ."[8]
No doubt, Nilus believed that the Jews were secretly at work to
enslave and inherit the world. Nilus was a former landowner,
who after the loss of his fortune abroad had turned from being a
believer in anarchism and Nietzschean teachings into a priest in
the orthodox church; as such he continued to reject modern civilization. A mystic with worldly ambitions, his mind bordering
on madness, he lived with three women, one of whom was a
former court lady who maintained his menage.

The *Protocols* became a worldwide best seller after 1917. The
Bolshevik Revolution, the collapse of the Austro-Hungarian
Empire, and the defeat of Germany in World War I left the
West with shattered political institutions and disrupted traditions, with dashed hopes among the vanquished and an appetite among the victors for sweeter fruits of victory than history
had granted them. War propaganda had fomented national
self-righteousness and hatred of others. The political and economic upheavals of the struggle and its aftermath created fear
and resentment of other nations and social classes. The results
were intellectual disorientation, moral weakness, slackened re-
straints of the forces destroying civility, and an atmosphere of
civil war that seemed to engulf the international community.

In these circumstances, the *Protocols* offered a conspiratorial theory of history to those who could not, or would not, cope with the vicissitudes of life, and an appealing invitation to hatred and aggression. They enabled large masses to blame innocent victims who were nearer at hand than enlightenment or courage: the Jews and their "tools," liberals, freemasons, socialists, communists, and unpopular statesmen. The Nazis in Germany and, in the thirties, Nazi organizations abroad were most active in using the *Protocols* to foment anti-Semitism throughout the world. At the trial of Ernst Techow, the driver of the car from which two young assassins fired the shots that killed Walter Rathenau, the German foreign minister, on 24 June 1922, the following exchange occurred. "President (of the Court): Rathenau is supposed to have confessed that he was himself one of the three hundred Elders of Zion. The three hundred Elders of Zion come from a pamphlet. Have you read it? Techow: Yes."[9] In Germany, the forgery became required reading in the schools. But had it not been for latent hostility everywhere it would not have been possible for the *Protocols* to become, in this century, the most widely read book next to the Bible. Today, it is available in any language: Russian, English, Polish, Portuguese, Norwegian, Spanish, Japanese, Flemish, Latvian, Dutch, Rumanian, Czech, Walloon, Arabic, Bulgarian, Chinese, Yugoslav, Greek. And new editions are still being published.

In the United States, the *Protocols* were launched by full editions published in New York and Boston and, in 1920, by Henry Ford's newspaper, the *Dearborn Independent.* This last edition, prepared by a German, August Müller, and a Russian refugee, Boris Bracol, was republished as a book under the title *The International Jew,* which in Norman Cohn's opinion did more than any other publication to make the *Protocols* worldfamous. Although Henry Ford finally disclaimed all responsibility for the book in 1927, it was translated into sixteen languages, and still advertised in Germany at the beginning of World War II. Hitler sported a photograph of "Heinrich Ford" in his study for years.

Thus Joly's ideas became effective in history by way of a monstrous distortion. Joly's concern with liberty was perverted beyond recognition. Against his will and unknown to him his words helped to incite persecution of liberal reformers in Czarist

Russia. He exposed political repression in his homeland, and half a century later his words helped reactionary White Russians abroad to foment hatred of the Bolshevik leaders. Like Montesquieu in the *Dialogue in Hell,* Joly hoped that constitutional government would ensure civil order and restrict violence in the streets; yet his book became instrumental in instigating pogroms culminating in the mass murders of five to six million Jews by the Nazis.

III

The *Protocols* contain many obvious discrepancies. In addition, the various editors have given conflicting accounts of both the alleged authorship and the ways in which the text had allegedly come to light. Today, it is hard to understand that it should have been necessary to prove painstakingly that the *Protocols* were put together by literary counterfeiters. And yet, tracing the history and the precise nature of the forgery took years of effort by many publicists, historians, and lawyers.

The American diplomat Herman Bernstein in his book *The History of a Lie,* published in February 1921, was the first to trace the content of the *Protocols* to Goedsche's tale, *The Jewish Cemetery in Prague.* Bernstein also showed the transformation of the speeches by Jewish leaders in that short story into *The Rabbi's Speech.*

At about the same time, Philip Graves, a British correspondent in Istanbul, acquired by chance a rare copy of the first edition of the *Dialogue aux enfers* from a White Russian émigré. Graves was the first to notice that many passages in this obscure book coincided with statements in the *Protocols.* In August 1921, he published a series of three articles in the *Times* exposing the plagiarism. It was a jolt to many who had been duped by the forgery. Only a year earlier, two English-language editions of the *Protocols* had been published, one under the title *The Jewish Peril.* The *Morning Post* had endorsed the main theme in a series of articles; the *Spectator,* in its issue of 15 May 1920, had considered the *Protocols* "brilliant in [their] moral perversity and intellectual depravity." A *Times* editorial of 8 May 1920 had raised the question "Have we by straining every fibre of our national body escaped a 'Pax Germanica' only to fall into a 'Pax Judaica'?" and had advocated an investigation of the charges! Now that Graves had uncovered the forgery, the *Times* stood up for the truth, endorsing Graves's findings in an editorial.

The next major step in tracing the history of the forgery was taken in 1934–1935 in Bern, when Swiss Jews brought a lawsuit against two Swiss Nazis charging them with violating the Bern law against *Schundliteratur,* improper literature, by circulating the *Protocols.* The trial, which attracted international attention, was remarkable for the array of distinguished witnesses—including Baron du Chalay, Philip Graves, Paul Miliukow, S. G. Svatikov, Boris Nikolaevsky, and Vladimir Burtsev—all of whom denied the authenticity of the *Protocols.* The defendants did not meet this issue, but argued their case on narrow legal grounds, trying to prove that the *Protocols* were not "improper" according to Swiss law.[10] Two of the Russian witnesses gave testimony pointing to the involvement of Pyotr Ivanovich Rachkovsky in the forgery.

Rachkovsky, like Goedsche in Germany, had started out as a minor civil servant. In 1879 he avoided banishment to Siberia by joining the ranks of the secret police that had arrested him. He had a spectacular career. From 1894 to 1903, he was the head of the Okhrana outside Russia, and in 1905 he became assistant director of the police in Russia. Rachkovsky's career abounds with ingenious political intrigues and accomplished forgeries. He was responsible for the arrest of many Russian liberals and radicals in Russia and abroad, for pogroms in his country, for assassinations of politicians standing in his way, for various bomb plots and other acts of violence perpetrated by his agents and attributed to political opponents he wanted to destroy. He was a reactionary, a ruthless anti-Semite, and the founder of a terrorist organization in his homeland.

The Bern trial established once more that the *Protocols* were a fabrication based to a large extent on Joly's *Dialogue aux enfers,* but it did not ascertain beyond doubt the identity of the original forger or forgers. Most recent research supports the views of Boris Nikolaevsky, expressed in a personal communication to Norman Cohn, and of Henri Rollin in *L'Apocalypse de notre temps,* to the effect that the *Dialogue aux enfers* was first used for polemical purposes against the Russian minister of finance, Count Sergei Witte, by a Russian expatriate named Elie de

Cyon (Ilya Tsion). He was of Jewish origin, and his published writings testify to the fact that he was not an anti-Semite. But he plagiarized Joly's book in writing a political satire against Witte. Witte introduced the gold standard in Russia and, by promoting the modernization of Russian industry and transportation, set forces into motion that led to the revolution in 1905. Upon orders from Witte, the Okhrana burglarized de Cyon's villa in Switzerland and obtained his unpublished manuscript attacking the Russian minister. According to Norman Cohn, "All in all, the most likely hypothesis is that Joly's satire on Napoleon III was transformed by de Cyon into a satire on Witte which was then transformed under Rachkovsky's guidance into the *Protocols of the Elders of Zion.* . . . There is also good reason for thinking that Rachkovsky had some contact either with Nilus or with Nilus' copy of the *Protocols.* "[11]

IV

In histories of political thought, Joly's *Dialogue in Hell* has generally been overlooked. Historians who know the work as the most important source of the *Protocols* have used it to prove plagiarism: many studies contain page after page of parallel columns from the two publications in order to demonstrate the extent of the fabrication. In this procedure, Joly's originality has been lost sight of, although Norman Cohn, who refers to Joly's book as a "pamphlet"—as does the *Grande Encyclopédie*—and consistently misquotes its title, acknowledges Joly's brilliance. Even the dates of Joly's birth and death vary widely in the literature.[12]

On the other end of the spectrum are admirers who deny that Joly wrote the *Dialogue in Hell* for any specific political purpose —despite the author's own explicit statement to the contrary. As though satirical skill and polemical fervor diminish intellectual merit, Hans Leisegang shuts his eyes to Joly's polemical intent. He considers the *Dialogue in Hell* an elegantly written masterpiece of modern political philosophy and compares its importance for understanding the history of European politics with that of Dostoevsky's chapter "The Grand Inquisitor" in *The Brothers Karamazov* for understanding the history of Christianity.

Fair appraisal of Joly's contribution to political thought lies somewhere between these two extreme views: the polemic against Napoleon III is at the same time a masterful statement on the preservation of despotic political power in modern industrialized society. Precisely for this reason, Joly's book gave a shock of recognition to generations of readers living under very different political conditions. Each of them felt that the *Dialogue in Hell* stated the principles of statecraft practiced by the regime they knew best from bitter personal experience. In 1864, the French printer whom Joly tried to persuade that his manuscript was the translation of a work by an English author named McPherson, recognized Napoleon III at the end of the third dialogue. He refused to continue the printing. The German philosopher Hans Leisegang, who translated Joly's book when Hitler was ruling Germany, quoted in his introduction one of Machiavelli's predictions, which he thought had come true in the present. The latest French edition of the *Dialogue aux enfers* was published in 1968. In the preface, Jean-Francois Revel ascribed to Joly "a prophetic view" of the manipulation of public opinion by modern governments, referring in particular to DeGaulle's use of the electronic media. And who can read Joly today without thinking of contemporary American political scandals as apt illustrations of Machiavelli's teaching in Joly's book? Nor is the bitter freshness of the *Dialogue* confined to the discussion of public opinion and its manipulation. Much of what Joly had to say about the secret police, the invasion of privacy by informers, political apathy, the abuse of the courts for political ends, the debasement of patriotic rhetoric, the corruption of moral standards in modern political life, the cult of personality—much of all this applies to Bismarck's Prussia, Hitler's Germany, Stalin's Russia, and other illiberal modern regimes as well as to Napoleon III's despotism.

Ironically enough, the only trait of modern totalitarianism that Joly did not foresee was precisely that which his book—perverted by forgers—helped so much to promote: genocidal anti-Semitism. In many other respects, however, the work invites reflection on the lesson it holds for the fashionable concern with "futurology." The contemporary reader may be led to compare the power of Joly's foresight with that of Alexis de Tocqueville or Jacob Burckhardt, and his satirical sharpness with that of George Orwell's *1984*. How was it possible, then, for a French liberal lawyer in the sixties of the past century to have such keenly predictive powers? Joly's method was neither that of extrapolation, as in predicting future developments from statistical data showing past trends, nor that of a historicist philosophy such as Marxism. Instead, it was derived from certain firmly held views of human nature in combination with very close, analytical observation of the political scene. Sensitized by his liberal predilections to the hazards of liberty in the industrialized society of nineteenth-century France, he described Bonapartism as though it were a prototype of twentieth-century totalitarianism.

Joly sympathised with Montesquieu's views on liberty, but through Machiavelli refuted Montesquieu's belief in progress toward the perfection of man and his social order. In the *Dialogue* Montesquieu holds that institutional inventions of the modern enlightened age have erected a bulwark against repressive political forces of the past. To the extent that the principles of enlightenment have spread in Europe and the principles of modern political science have become known, law has replaced force in theory as well as practice. Machiavelli counters with what he regards as an "eternal truth": Man's "evil instinct" is more potent than are his good intentions, and force, fear, and greed hold sway over him. Montesquieu contends that his teaching has promoted order and liberty; Machiavelli answers with the charge that by giving the nations the right to choose their political institutions, Montesquieu had introduced "the infinite era of revolutions." According to Joly's Machiavelli, the people lack the virtues that must sustain a liberal social order; they live instead "without God and faith," dedicated to the pursuit of their subjective interests and of a high standard of living. Furthermore, they easily turn from their admiration of a powerful man to violent rebellion, unless they are manipulated without moral squeamishness. Thus despotism can save the great modern states from revolution and anarchy.

Although Joly was a liberal, his pessimistic view of the corruptibility of the masses matched his moral condemnation of the unscrupulous use of force and cunning in ruling them. Joly was no democrat. Like many other nineteenth-century European liberals, he had the fear of Jacobinism in his bones. His *Dialogue in Hell* reverberates with distrust not only of plebiscitarian despotism but also of the "novel ideas" of Napoleon I, the "testamentary executor of the Revolution" of 1789. Prince Napoleon-Louis Bonaparte, the later emperor, had characterized Napoleon I, his uncle, as such in a political manifesto published as early as 1839. Trying to capitalize on the growing legend of Napoleon I, the nephew had depicted him as the founder of peace in Europe, serving the idea of a solid European association, and as the harbinger of domestic freedom and order. Prince Napoleon-Louis Bonaparte had claimed that the interests of the sovereign and the people were identical. "The Napoleonic idea," he had written, "is by no means an idea of war, but a social, industrial, commercial, humanitarian idea." If Machiavelli in Joly's *Dialogue* sometimes appears to speak of the Nazi regime when satirizing the statecraft of Napoleon III, it may be observed in passing that this manifesto of 1839 adumbrates appeals and claims made by totalitarian leaders in twentieth-century politics. As one of the liberals, whose political perception was bounded neither by a blind faith in progress nor by the Napoleon-worship of the French bourgeoisie, Joly foresaw a great deal of the future because he stood between the political fronts, perceiving the hazards of popular sovereignty as well as abuse of power by social engineers. In looking at France under Napoleon III he detected political forces that can be activated at any time in modern society. They result from the interplay of egalitarianism as an ideology with increasing efficiency in all spheres of life—whether in the modes of peacetime production or the methods of destruction in war, whether in the techniques of communication or the technology employed in the invasion of privacy.

Joly did not peer into the future but looked piercingly at the political and social forces of his time. Or to put it more precisely, only Montesquieu in the *Dialogue* viewed political life in historical perspective, whereas Machiavelli discovered unchanging political principles in contemporary conditions. Montesquieu's delusion about progress in human affairs is predicated, moreover, on his *ignorance* of the present. In the netherworld he has learned of what has been happening on earth only until the year 1847, whereas Machiavelli's information is up to date so that, ironically enough, Montesquieu's historical view is faulted by lack of information on the latest happenings, whereas Machiavelli's unhistorical view, which does not really need this information, is vindicated by it. In this regard, Joly is in the good company of political philosophers prior to the rise of positivism and historicism. Although critics have often pointed out that Joly's sympathies are on the side of Montesquieu, it would be more correct to stress that in the *Dialogue* he shared Montesquieu's moral preferences but regarded Machiavelli's knowledge of politics as superior to that of his adversary. The explanation of Joly's power of prediction, then, can be reduced to the paradox that, strictly speaking, his foresight was insight.

This paradox also applies to Joly's contribution in the field of mass communication. At first glance, it is quite extraordinary that seventy years prior to the rise of Hitler and Goebbels and long before the emergence of the electronic media Joly described in considerable detail the political manipulation of public opinion, which we associate today with totalitarianism. Nobody who studies political propaganda in the twentieth century can afford to neglect its most eminent nineteenth-century analyst. Considerably more can be learned about Hitler's propaganda techniques from Joly's two *Dialogues* about censorship and the management of public opinion than from the famous passages dealing with this subject in Hitler's *Mein Kampf.* Interestingly enough, there are a few close parallels, for example, the importance both Hitler and Joly's Machiavelli attribute to the spoken word in swaying the masses, or the power both of them attribute to the media in creating and destroying what we now term public "images." But the early analyst of modern propaganda techniques was more articulate, specific, and incisive than were its latter-day practitioners. Again, this paradox will startle the historian more than the political philosopher. It ought to caution the contemporary reader not to underestimate the analytical power of a mind familiar only with a prototype of modern totalitarianism.

Joly's insight into the politics of modern mass communication could have been buttressed by a more detailed description of the interplay between power and economic gain in the Second Empire. For example, DeMorny, a half-brother of the emperor, invested one hundred thousand francs in a journalistic enterprise and sold his interest later for half a million. Another newspaper felt obliged to protest that it was not involved in speculations on the stock exchange. Similarly, it was true enough, as Joly mentioned, that the emperor spent regularly as well as on special occasions large sums of money to buy journalistic services and that he gave honorific positions in his government and decorations to obliging press servants. Joly did not mention, however, that quite apart from Napoleon's techniques it was sometimes difficult to decide whether it was lucrativeness of journalism or enthusiasm for causes believed to be righteous that drew some of the most distinguished minds of the nation to writing for newspapers: men like Ernest Renan, Hippolyte Taine, Alexander Dumas, Theophile Gautier, Prosper Merimée.[13]

Unlike his novel *Les Affamés,* Joly's *Dialogue aux enfers* does not focus on a sociological analysis of the conditions of life prevailing at the time of Napoleon III. The *Dialogue* is a political work concerned with the anatomy of power. Nor did Joly buttress his findings by comparative studies as he might well have done. When Joly wrote his book, neither press censorship nor the use of domestic and foreign newspapers by the government was a uniquely French phenomenon. After 1848, Prokesch-Osten, the Austrian ambassador in Berlin, took up contact with the press of the opposition and furnished it with material. He was careless enough to let his drafts fall into the hands of the Prussian authorities. Bismarck, who despised public opinion when it criticized him, had highly-paid, talented henchmen like Lothar Bucher and Moritz Busch write for the press and influence it according to his instructions. Although the French emperor had even fewer scruples than Bismarck in using the media for his political ends, he was by no means the only European statesman to manipulate public opinion at the time Joly wrote his book. Maurice Joly did not need the comparative method to make his point. He showed for a span of time far exceeding that of his life and for many countries other than France the precariousness of liberty in modern society.

The excerpts from Joly's *Dialogue aux enfers* presented in the next chapter of this volume cannot do justice to the masterful development of Joly's main argument concerning the conflict between liberty and power in modern society. They were selected with a view to showing above all Joly's understanding of the symbolic dimension of power.

NOTES

This chapter was published in *Polity* 10 (Fall 1977).

1. Quoted in Herman Bernstein, *The Truth About "The Protocols of Zion"* (New York, 1935), pp. 16–17.

2. Ibid.

3. The margin of electoral support of Napoleon dropped steadily during the emperor's reign from 6.9 million in 1851 to 4.8 million in 1857, 3.3 million in 1863, and 1.1 million in 1869. See S. C. Burchell, *Imperial Masquerade* (New York, 1971), pp. 36, 345.

4. The existence of this translation has been widely overlooked in the literature. Even Hans Leisegang in the preface to his own, excellent modern translation of Joly's books into German (Hamburg, 1948) does not mention the first translation of 1865. Hans Barth does, in his valuable essay "Maurice Joly, der plebiszitäre Cäsarismus und die 'Protokolle der Weisen von Zion,' " *Neue Zürcher Zeitung,* 31 March, 1962.

5. For English translations of "The Jewish Cemetery in Prague," "The Rabbi's Speech," and *The Protocols of the Elders of Zion,* see exhibits C, D, and E in Herman Bernstein.

6. On Osman-Bey, see Walter Laqueur, *Russia and Germany* (London, 1965), p. 96.

7. Norman Cohn, *Warrant for Genocide* (New York, 1969), pp. 74–75. Cohn's books contains the most recent scholarly research on *The Protocols of the Elders of Zion.*

8. Quoted by Cohn, p. 91.

9. Quoted by Cohn, p. 146.

10. For a description of the Bern Trial, see John S. Curtis, *An Appraisal of the Protocols of Zion* (New York, 1942), chap. 5.

11. Cohn, pp. 106–107.

12. The article on Joly in *Grande Encyclopédie,* Leisegang, and Barth state that Maurice Joly lived from 1821 to 1878; Herman Bernstein gives the dates 1831–1878; Cohn has 1829–1879; finally, Henri Rollin, in his "Avant-Propos" to Maurice Joly, *Dialogue aux enfers entre Machiavel et Montesquieu* (Paris, 1968), states that Joly was born in 1829 and died on 17 July 1877.

13. For a comparison of Napoleon III's and Bismarck's manipulation of public opinion, see Wilhelm Bauer, *Die Öffentliche Meinung in der Weltgeschichte* (Wildpark-Potsdam, 1929), pp. 326–347.

11

SELECTIONS FROM *DIALOGUE IN HELL BETWEEN MACHIAVELLI AND MONTESQUIEU*

MAURICE JOLY

MACHIAVELLI ABOUT HIMSELF

MACHIAVELLI. My single crime was to say the truth to the people as to the kings; not the moral truth, but the political truth; not truth such as it should have been, but such as it is, such as it will always be. It is not I who am the founder of the doctrine the paternity of which is attributed to me; it is the human heart. *Machiavellism preceded Machiavelli. . . .* (1)

ON THE NATURE OF CONTEMPORARY SOCIETY

MACHIAVELLI. I am in the heart of voluptuous societies which ally the fury of pleasures to that of arms, the transports of force to those of the senses, which no longer desire divine authority, paternal authority, religious restraint. Is it I who have created the world in the midst of which I live? I am such because it is such. Would I have the power to stop its inclination? No, I can only prolong its life because it would dissolve still more quickly

The complete text of Joly's *Dialogue aux enfers entre Machiavel et Montesquieu ou La Politique de Machiavel au XIXe siècle* (1864) was translated by Dorothy Nash and David Bernstein and published as "Exhibit A" in Herman Bernstein, *The Truth about "The Protocols of Zion"* (New York: Covici Friede, 1935), pp. 75–258. The subtitles in the following selections have been added. The numbers in parentheses at the end of each selection refer to the number of the *Dialogue*.

tages, emit line.

if it were left to itself. I take this society by its vices because it presents only vices to me; if it had virtues, I should take it by its virtues.

But if austere principles can affront my power, can they disregard the real services that I render, my genius and even my grandeur?

I am the arm, I am the sword of the revolutions which the harbinger breath of final destruction is leading astray. I contain insane forces which have no other motive power, at bottom, than the brutality of the instincts, which hunt plunder under the veil of principles. If I discipline these forces, if I arrest their expansion in my country, even for only a century, have I not deserved well of it? Can I not even claim the gratitude of the European states which turn their eyes toward me as toward Osiris who alone has the power to captivate these trembling crowds? Raise your eyes higher and bow before one who bears on his brow the fatal sign of human predestination.

MONTESQUIEU. Exterminating angel, grandson of Tamerlane, reduce the people to slavery, yet you will not prevent that somewhere there will be free souls who will brave you, and their disdain will suffice to safeguard the rights of the human conscience rendered imperceptible by God.

MACHIAVELLI. God protects the strong. . . . (23)

ON ENFEEBLING THE PUBLIC SPIRIT

MACHIAVELLI. The principal secret of government consists in enfeebling the public spirit to the point of disinteresting it entirely in the ideas and the principles with which revolutions are made nowadays. In all times, peoples, like individuals, have been paid in words. Appearances nearly always are sufficient for them; they demand no more. One can, then, establish artificial institutions which correspond to a language and to ideas equally artificial; it is necessary to have the talent to strip the parties of *that liberal phraseology* with which they arm themselves against the government. It is necessary to satiate the people with it until they are weary, until they are disgusted. One speaks often today of the power of public opinion. I shall show you that it is made to express whatever one wants when one knows well the hidden resources of power. But before thinking of directing it, one must benumb it, strike it with uncertainty by astounding contradictions, work on it with incessant diversions, dazzle it with all sorts of different actions, mislead it imperceptibly in its pathways. One of the great secrets of the day is to know how to take possession of popular prejudices and passions, in such a way as to introduce a confusion of principles which makes impossible all understanding between those who speak the same language and have the same interests.

MONTESQUIEU. Where are you going with these words whose obscurity has in it something sinister?

MACHIAVELLI. If the wise Montesquieu means to put sentiment in the place of politics, I should perhaps stop here; I have not pretended to place myself on the terrain of morals. You have defied me to stop the progress in your societies unendingly tormented by the spirit of anarchy and revolt. Do you wish to let me say how I would solve the problem? You can put aside your scruples in accepting this thesis as a question of pure curiosity.

MONTESQUIEU. So be it.

MACHIAVELLI. I understand moreover that you would demand more precise information of me; I will arrive at that. But permit me to tell you first under what essential conditions the prince can hope today to consolidate his power. He will have to endeavor above all to destroy the parties, to dissolve the collective forces wherever they exist, to paralyze in all its manifestations individual initiative; then the level of character would descend to himself, and all knees will soon bend in servitude. Absolute power will no longer be an accident, it will become a need. These political precepts are not entirely new, but, as I said to you, it is the processes that must be new. A large number of these results can be obtained by simple regulations of the police and the administration. In your societies, so fine and so well organized, in the place of absolute monarchies you have put a *monster which is called the State,* a new Briareus whose arms extend everywhere, a colossal organism of tyranny in whose shadow despotism is always reborn. Well, under the invocation of the state, nothing will be easier than to consummate the occult work of which I spoke to you just now, and the most powerful methods of action will perhaps be precisely those that one will have the talent to borrow from this very industrial regime which calls forth your admiration. . . .

Head of the government, all my edicts, all my ordinances

would constantly tend toward the same goal: to annihilate collective and individual forces; to develop excessively the preponderance of the state, to make of it the sovereign protector, promoter and remunerator. . . .

Here is another scheme borrowed from the industrial order: In modern times, the aristocracy, as a political force, has disappeared; but the landed bourgeoisie is still an element of dangerous resistance to governments, because it is independent in itself; it may be necessary to impoverish it or even to ruin it completely. It is enough, for this, to increase the charges which weigh on landed property, to maintain agriculture in a state of relative inferiority, to favor commerce and industry excessively, but speculation principally; for too great prosperity in industry can itself become a danger, in creating too large a number of independent fortunes.

The great industrialists and manufacturers will be reacted against advantageously by stimulation to a disproportionate luxury, by the elevation of taxes on salaries, by deep blows ably struck at the sources of production. I need not develop these ideas, you can readily understand in what circumstances and under what pretexts all this can be done. The interests of the people, and even a sort of zeal for liberty, for the great economic principles, will easily cover the true goal, if it is desired. It is useless to add that the perpetual upkeep of a large army continually exercised by foreign wars must be the indispensable complement of this system; it is necessary to arrive at the existence in the state only of proletarians, several millionaires, and soldiers. . . . (7)

ON LANGUAGE IN POLITICS AND ON CHOOSING THE MEN TO HOLD SUBORDINATE POWER

MACHIAVELLI. You have been able to see in my institutions and my acts what attention I have always given to the creating of appearances; words are as necessary as actions. The height of cleverness is to create a belief in franchise, when one has a Punic faith. Not only will my aims be impenetrable, but my words will nearly always signify the opposite of what they will seem to indicate. Only the initiated will be able to penetrate the sense of the characteristic phrases that I will drop from the heights of my throne: when I will say: *My reign means peace,* it means there will be war; when I will say that I call upon *moral means,* it means I will use methods of force. Do you hear me?

MONTESQUIEU. Yes. . . . (24)

MACHIAVELLI. Since in politics words must never be in accord with deeds, it is necessary that, in these various crises, the prince be able enough to disguise his real designs under contrary design; he must always give the impression of acceding to public opinion while he does what his hands have secretly prepared.

To sum up the whole system in a word, revolution in the state is restrained on the one hand by the terror of anarchy, on the other, by bankruptcy, and, all things considered, by general war.

You have already been able to see, by means of the rapid outline I have just given you, what an important role the art of language is called upon to play in modern politics. I am far from disdaining the press, as you can see, and I would be able in time of need to use the rostrum; what is essential is the use against one's enemies of all the arms they could employ against you. Not content with relying on the violent force of democracy, I would borrow of the subtleties of justice their most learned resources. When one makes decisions that could seem unjust or rash, it is essential to know how to express them in fine terms, to give them the highest reasons of morality and justice.

The power of which I dream, far, as you can see, from having barbarian customs, must draw to itself all the forces and all the talents of the civilization in the heart of which it lives. It must surround itself with publicists, lawyers, jurisconsults, practical men and administrators, men who know thoroughly all the secrets, all the strength of social life, who speak all languages, who have studied man in all circles. They must be taken from anywhere and everywhere, for these men give surprising service through the ingenious procedures they apply to politics. With that, a whole world of economists is necessary, of bankers, of industrialists, of capitalists, of men of vision, of men with millions, for all fundamentally resolves itself into a question of figures.

As for the principal dignities, the principal dismemberment of power, one must so arrange as to give them to men whose antecedents and character place a gulf between them and other men, every one of whom has only to expect death or exile in case of a change in government and is in need of defending until his last breath all that exists.

Imagine for a moment that I have at my disposal the different moral and material resources which I have just sketched for you, and now give me any nation, do you hear! You regard it as a capital point, in the *Esprit des Lois, not to change the character of a nation* [*Esprit des Lois,* book XIX, chap. V] when one wishes it to conserve its original vigor. Well, I do not ask you twenty years to transform in the most complete way the most untamable European character and to make it as docile under tyranny as the smallest nation in Asia. . . . (7)

ON THE PRESS

MACHIAVELLI. I dare say that no government, up to the present, has had a bolder conception than the one of which I am going to speak to you. In parliamentary countries, it is almost always because of the press that the governments fail; well, I foresee the possibility of counteracting the press by the press itself. Since journalism is such a great force, do you know what my government would do? It would turn journalist, it would become journalism incarnate.

MONTESQUIEU. Truly, you treat me to strange surprises! It is a panorama of infinite variety that you spread out before me; I am very curious, I must admit, to see how you will go about putting into effect this new program.

MACHIAVELLI. Much less effort of imagination is necessary than you think. I shall count the number of newspapers which represent what you call the opposition. If there are ten for the opposition, I shall have twenty for the government; if there are twenty, I shall have forty; if there are forty, I shall have eighty. You can readily understand now to what use I will put the faculty which I reserved for myself to authorize the creation of new political papers.

MONTESQUIEU. Really, that is very simple.

MACHIAVELLI. Not quite as simple as you think, though, because the masses must have no suspicion of these tactics; the scheme would lose its point, public opinion would shy at newspapers which openly defended my policies.

I shall divide in three or four categories the papers devoted to my power. In first rank I shall put a certain number of newspapers whose tone will be frankly official and which, at any encounter, will defend my deeds to the death. I tell you right from the start, these will not be the ones which will have the greatest influence on public opinion. In the second rank I shall place another series of newspapers the character of which will be no more than officious and the purposes of which will be to rally to my power that mass of lukewarm and indifferent persons who accept without scruple what is established but who do not go beyond that in their political faith.

It is the newspaper categories which follow that will be found the most powerful supporters of my power. Here, the official or officious tone is completely dropped, in appearance, that is, for the newspapers of which I am going to speak will all be attached by the same chain to my government, a chain visible for some, invisible for others. I shall not attempt to tell you how many of them there will be, for I shall count on a devoted organ in each opinion, in each party; I shall have an aristocratic organ in the aristocratic party, a republican organ in the republican party, a revolutionary organ in the revolutionary party, an anarchist organ, if necessary, in the anarchist party. Like the god Vishnu my press will have a hundred arms, and these arms will stretch out their hands to all the possible shades of opinion over the whole surface of the country. Everyone will be of my party whether he knows it or not. Those who think they are speaking their own language will be speaking mine, those who think they are agitating their own party will be agitating mine, those who think they are marching under their own flag will be marching under mine.

MONTESQUIEU. Are these conceptions realizable or merely phantasmagoria? It is enough to make one dizzy.

MACHIAVELLI. Spare your strength, for you have not yet come to the end.

MONTESQUIEU. I am only wondering how you will be able to direct and rally all these military forces of publicity secretly hired by your government.

MACHIAVELLI. That is only a question of organization, you must understand; I shall institute, for instance, under the title of division of printing and the press, a center of operation to which one will come for orders. So, for those who will be only half in on the secret of this scheme, it will be a strange spectacle: they

will see sheets, devoted to my government, which will attack
me, which will shout, which will stir up a turmoil of confusion.
MONTESQUIEU. This is beyond me; I no longer follow.
MACHIAVELLI. And yet it is not too difficult to understand; you
will notice that the foundation and the principles of my government will never be attacked by the newspapers of which I am
speaking; they will never go in for anything more than a polemic skirmish, a dynastic opposition within the narrowest limits.
MONTESQUIEU. And what advantage do you find in that?
MACHIAVELLI. Your question is rather ingenuous. The result,
considerable enough, will be to make the greatest number say:
"But you see, one is free, one may speak under this regime, it is
unjustly attacked; instead of repressing, as it might do, it toler-
ates these things!" Another result, not less important, will be to
provoke, for instance, such observations as these: "You see to
what point the foundations and principles of this government
command the respect of all; here are newspapers which allow
themselves the greatest freedom of speech; well, they never attack the established institutions. They must be above the injustices of human passions, since the very enemies of the government cannot help rendering homage to them."
MONTESQUIEU. That, I confess, is truly machiavellian.
MACHIAVELLI. You do me a great honor, but something better
is yet to come: With the aid of the secret loyalty of these public
papers, I may say that I can direct at will the general opinion in
all questions of internal or external politics. I arouse or lull the
minds, I reassure or disturb them, I plead for and against, true
and false. I have a fact announced and I have it refuted, according to the circumstances; in this way I plumb public thought, I
gather the impression produced. I try combinations, projects,
sudden decisions; in other words, I send out what you call in
France feelers. I fight my enemies as I please without ever compromising my power, since, after having the papers make certain statements, I may, when necessary, deny them most ener-
getically; I solicit opinion on certain resolutions, I urge it on or
hold it back, I always have my finger on its pulse; it reflects,
without knowing it, my personal impressions, and it occasionally is astonished at being so constantly in accord with its sovereign. Then they say that I have the feeling for the people, that
there is a secret and mysterious sympathy which unites me to
the movements of my people.

MONTESQUIEU. These various projects seem to be ideally perfect. Nevertheless I should like to comment on something, but very timidly this time: If you depart from the silence of China, if you permit, for the furthering of your designs, the provisional opposition which you have just spoken of on the part of your army of newspapers, I really do not understand how you can prevent the non-affiliated newspapers from answering, by overwhelming thrusts, the provocations the source of which they will guess. Do you not think that they will finally succeed in raising some of the veils which cover so many mysterious forces? When they will learn the secret of this comedy, will you be able to stop them from laughing at it? The game seems to me a little dangerous.

MACHIAVELLI. Not at all; I must tell you that I have spent a good part of my time at this point to examine the strength and the weakness of these schemes; I am well informed on all that has to do with the conditions of existence of the press in parliamentary countries. You must know that journalism is a sort of freemasonry; those who live by it are all more or less attached to one another by the bonds of professional discretion; like the ancient soothsayers, they do not readily divulge the secret of their oracles. They would gain nothing by betraying one another, for the majority of them have some more or less shameful secrets. It is quite probable, I agree, that at the heart of the capital, within a certain radius of people, these things will be no mystery; but, everywhere else, no one will suspect, and the great majority of the nation will follow, with the utmost confidence, the trail of the leaders which I have given them.

What does it matter to me that, in the capital, a certain set will be aware of the tricks of my journalism? It is in the provinces that the greatest part of its influence will be felt. There I shall always have the barometer of opinion which is necessary for me, and there every one of my strokes will have the desired effect. The provincial press will belong to me entirely, there can be no contradiction nor discussion as to that; from the center of the administration where I shall hold court, they will transmit regularly to the governor of each province the order to have the newspapers speak in such and such a way, so that at the same moment, all over the country, such and such an influence will be produced, such and such an impulse will be given, often even before the capital becomes cognizant of it. You see by this that the opinion of the capital is not enough to preoccupy me. When necessary, it will learn too late about the external movement which would surround it without its knowledge.

MONTESQUIEU. The chain of your ideas carries everything away with such force that you make me lose the consciousness of a last objection which I wanted to refer to you. The fact still remains, in spite of all you have just said, that there still is in the capital a certain number of independent newspapers. It will be practically impossible for them to talk politics, that is certain, but they may still wage a war of details. Your administration will not be perfect; the development of absolute power brings with it a quantity of grievances of which even the sovereign is not the cause; for all the acts of your representatives which will touch private interests, you will be held guilty; they will complain, they will attack your representatives, you will necessarily be considered responsible for them, and esteem for you will decrease gradually.

MACHIAVELLI. I am not afraid of that.

MONTESQUIEU. It is true that you have increased to such an extent the means of repression that you have but to choose your method.

MACHIAVELLI. That is not what I was going to say; I do not even wish to be obliged to have ceaseless recourse to repression: I wish, through a simple injunction, to make it possible to put an end to any discussion on a subject concerning the administration.

MONTESQUIEU. And how do you expect to go about that?

MACHIAVELLI. I shall oblige the newspapers to put at the head of their columns the corrections which the government will impart to them; the representatives of the administration will give them notes in which they will be told categorically: "You have asserted such and such a fact, it is not exact; you made such and such a criticism, you were unjust, you were improper, you were wrong, do not forget it." That will be, as you see, a loyal and open censure.

MONTESQUIEU. To which, of course, there will be no reply.

MACHIAVELLI. Obviously not; discussion will be closed.

MONTESQUIEU. In this way you will always have the last word, and you will have it without the use of violence—it is very ingenious. You put it very well a short time ago when you said your government is journalism incarnate.

MACHIAVELLI. Just as I do not wish the country to be disturbed by rumors from abroad, so I do not wish it to be so by rumors from within, even the simplest private news. When there will be some extraordinary suicide, some big money question a little too suspicious, some misdeed by a public official, I shall forbid the papers to write of it. Silence about these things shows more respect for public honesty than does scandal.

MONTESQUIEU. And during this time you yourself will be a journalist with a vengeance?

MACHIAVELLI. I must. To make use of the press, to make use of it in all its forms: such is, today, the law of the powers which wish to exist. It is very singular, but it is so. And I shall engage in it to a much greater extent than you can imagine.

In order to understand the breadth of my system, it is necessary to see how the language of my press is called to cooperate with the official acts of my politics: I wish, suppose, to bring to light the solution to a certain external or internal complication; this solution, recommended by my newspapers which for several months have been guiding public opinion each in its own way, is brought forth one fine day as an official event. You know with what discretion and what ingenious consideration authoritative documents must be drawn up on important matters: the problem to be solved in such a case is to give a certain amount of satisfaction to each party. Well, then, every one of my newspapers, according to its tendency, will strive to persuade its party that the resolution that has been made is the one which favors itself most. That which will not be written in an official document, will be brought to light by means of interpretation; that which is only indicated, the officious newspapers will construe more openly, and the democratic and revolutionary papers will shout from the housetops; and while they are disputing and giving the most varied interpretations to my acts, my government will always be able to answer to one and all: ''You are mistaken about my intentions, you have misconstrued my declarations; I only meant this or that.'' The main thing is never to be found in contradiction with oneself.

MONTESQUIEU. What! After what you have just told me, you make such a claim?

MACHIAVELLI. Certainly, and your astonishment proves that you did not understand me. It is necessary to make words, rather than deeds, harmonize. How do you expect the masses of the

328 Dialogue in Hell

people to judge if it is reason which rules its government? It is sufficient to tell it to them. I wish, then, that the various phases of my policies be presented as the development of a single thought clinging to an unchanging goal. Every event, foreseen or unforeseen, will be a result wisely brought about, the deviations of direction will only be the different facets of the same question, the various roads which lead to the same goal, the diversified means to an identical solution pursued unceasingly in the face of obstacles. The most recent event will be given as the logical conclusion to the previous ones.

MONTESQUIEU. In truth, you are admirable! What strength of mind! What activity!

MACHIAVELLI. Every day my newspapers will be filled with official speeches, with accountings, with references to the ministers and references to the sovereign. I shall not forget that I am living in a period where it is believed that all social problems may be settled by industry, and where the amelioration of the fate of the working classes is constantly being sought. I shall interest myself all the more in these questions inasmuch as they are a very fortunate counter-irritant to absorption in internal politics. When it comes to the peoples of the south, the governments must appear to be unceasingly occupied; the masses are satisfied to be inactive on condition that those who govern them give them the spectacle of a continual activity, a sort of fever; that they constantly attract their attention by novelties, surprises, theatrical strokes. That is strange, perhaps, but, once more, it is so.

I would comply with these indications, point by point; consequently, I would, in matters of commerce, industry, arts, and even administration, look into all sorts of projects, plans, combinations, changes, alterations, and improvements the fame of which in the press would cover the voices of the most numerous and most prolific publicists. Political economy has, it is said, made a fortune in France; well, I should leave to your theorists, to your utopians, to the most impassioned declaimers of your schools nothing to invent, nothing to publish, nothing even to say. The good of the people would be the sole and unchanging object of my public confidences. Whether I speak myself, or whether I have my ministers or my writers speak, one would never exhaust the subject of the grandeur of the country, of its prosperity, of the majesty of its purpose and of its destiny; one would never cease to support it for its great principles of modern law, for the great problems which arouse humanity. The most enthusiastic, the most universal liberalism would breathe through my writings. The people of the occident love the oriental style, and so the style of all official speeches, of all official manifestoes should always be adorned with images, always pompous, full of loftiness and reflections. The people do not like atheistic governments; in my communications with the public I should not fail to put my acts under the invocation of the Divinity, while tactfully associating my own star with that of the nation.

I should like the acts of my reign to be compared at every moment with those of past governments. It would be the best way to bring out my good deeds and to arouse the gratitude which they deserve.

It would be very important to place in relief the mistakes of those who preceded me, to show that I have always known how to avoid those mistakes. In this way, people would entertain toward the regimes which preceded my power a sort of antipathy, aversion even, which would end by becoming irreparable as an atonement.

Not only would I give to a certain number of newspapers the mission of continually exalting the glory of my reign, of throwing back upon governments other than mine the responsibility for the errors of European politics, but I should like most of these eulogies to appear to be echoes of foreign papers from which articles would be reproduced, true or false, which would render striking homage to my own policies. Besides, I would have, abroad, some paid newspapers whose support would be all the more efficacious since I would give them an appearance of opposition on several points of detail.

My principles, my ideas, my acts would be represented with the halo of youth, with the prestige of the new law in contrast to the decrepitude and decay of ancient institutions.

I realize that safety valves are necessary for public spirit, that intellectual activity, driven back at one point, is necessarily carried over to another. That is why I would not be afraid to throw the nation into all sorts of theoretical and practical speculations about the industrial regime.

Outside of politics, moreover, I assure you that I would be a very good prince, that I would peacefully allow the people to stir up philosophical or religious questions. Concerning religion, the doctrine of free examination has become a sort of monomania. One must not oppose this tendency, in fact, it would not be done without danger. In those countries of Europe which are furthest advanced in civilization, the invention of printing ended by giving birth to a literature that is insane, furious, unrestrained, almost unclean—it is a great misfortune. Well, it is sad to say, but, to satisfy this rage of writing which possesses your parliamentary countries, it is almost enough merely not to thwart it.

This pestiferous literature, the course of which cannot be obstructed, and the platitude of writers and political men who would be at the head of journalism, would not fail to form a shocking contrast to the dignity of the language which would fall from the steps of the throne, with the vivacious and colorful dialectic upon which care would be taken to rest all the manifestations of power. You understand, now, why I wished to surround the prince with this host of publicists, administrators, lawyers, businessmen and attorneys who are essential to the drawing up of this quantity of official communications of which I have spoken to you, and the impression of which on public opinion would always be very strong.

Such, in brief, is the general disposition of my regime concerning the press. . . . (12)

ON THE POLICE

MACHIAVELLI. I shall begin by creating a ministry of police which will be the most important of my ministries and which will centralize, as much for the exterior as for the interior, the numerous functions which I give over to that part of my administration.

MONTESQUIEU. But if you do that, your subjects will see immediately that they are caught in a prodigious net.

MACHIAVELLI. If this ministry incurs displeasure, I shall abolish it and I shall call it, if that pleases you better, the ministry of state. Besides, I shall organize in other ministries corresponding functions the greater part of which will be quietly blended in with what you call nowadays the ministry of the interior and the ministry of foreign affairs. You understand perfectly that here I am not interested in diplomacy but only in the proper means to assure my security against factions, foreign as well as domestic. . . .

In addition, I expect that my police will be interspersed in all ranks of society. There will be no secret meeting, no committee, no salon, no intimate hearth where there will not be an ear to hear what is said in every place, at every hour. Alas, for those who have wielded power it is an astonishing phenomenon with what facility men denounce one another. What is still more astonishing is the faculty of observation and of analysis which is developed in those who make up the political police; you have no idea of their ruses, their disguises, their instincts, the passion which they bring to their researches, their patience, their impenetrability; there are men of all ranks who go in for this profession through—how shall I say it?—a sort of love of the art. . . . (17)

ON CRIMINAL JUSTICE

MACHIAVELLI. Is the one who undertakes something against the government not as guilty as, if not more so than, the one who commits an ordinary crime or misdemeanor? Passion or misery mitigates many faults, but who forces people to busy themselves with politics? So I wish no distinction between the misdemeanors of common law and the political misdemeanors. Where, then, is the mentality of modern governments, to set up a sort of criminal court of justice for their slanderers? In my kingdom, the insolent journalist will mingle in the prisons with the plain thief and will appear at his side before the correctional jurisdiction. The conspirator will be seated before the criminal jury, side by side with the counterfeiter and the murderer. That is an excellent legislative modification, you must notice, for public opinion, seeing the conspirator treated as the equal of the ordinary criminal, will end up by confusing the two types in the same scorn.

MONTESQUIEU. You are ruining the very foundation of moral sense; but what does that matter to you? What surprises me is that you are keeping a criminal jury.

MACHIAVELLI. In those states which are centralized like mine, the public officials are the ones who appoint the members of the jury. In a question of a simple political misdemeanor, my minister of justice can always, when necessary, compose the chamber of judges who are well versed in such things. . . . (17)

ON TALKING ABOUT THE PUBLIC DEBT

MACHIAVELLI. Sometimes, you know, in finance there are words ready made, stereotyped phrases, which have a great effect on the public, calming and reassuring the people.

Thus, in artfully presenting such and such a debt, one says: *this figure is not at all exorbitant—it is normal, it conforms to previous budgets—the figure of the floating debt is very reassuring.* There is a host of similar locutions which I shall not mention because there are other more important practical stratagems to which I wish to call your attention.

First, in all official documents it is necessary to insist upon the development of prosperity, of commercial activity and of *the ever increasing progress of consumption.*

The taxpayer is less aroused by the disproportion of the budget when these things are repeated to him, and they may be repeated to satiety without his ever becoming suspicious, to such an extent do authentic accounts produce a magic effect upon the mind of bourgeois fools. When the budget can no longer be balanced and one wishes to prepare public spirit for some disappointment for the following year, one says in advance, in a report, *next year the deficit will only be so and so much.*

If the deficit is less than the estimate, it is a veritable triumph; if it is greater, one says: *"the deficit was greater than was estimated, but it was still higher last year;* altogether the situation is better, because less has been spent and yet we have gone through exceptionally difficult circumstances: war, poverty, epidemics, unforeseen subsistence crises, etc.

"But next year, the increase of revenues will, in all probability, permit the attainment of a balance which has been so long sought: the debt will be reduced, the budget *suitably balanced.* This progress will continue, it may be hoped, and, save for extraordinary events, balance will become the custom of our finances, as it is the rule."

MONTESQUIEU. That is high comedy; the custom will be like the rule, it will never work, for I imagine that, under your reign, there will always be some extraordinary circumstance, a war, a crisis.

MACHIAVELLI. I do not know whether there will be subsistence crises; one thing is certain and that is that I shall hold the banner of national dignity very high.

MONTESQUIEU. That is the very least you could do. If you gather glory, one need not be grateful to you, for in your hands it is only a means of government; it is not that which will liquidate the debts of your state. (20)

ON PUBLIC BUILDING PROGRAMS, DECORATIONS, AND OTHER SYMBOLIC INSTRUMENTS OF POWER

MACHIAVELLI. The fertility of resources that my government must have suggests an idea to me; that would be to build for the people huge cities where the rent would be very low and where the masses would find themselves reunited by bonds as in great families.

MONTESQUIEU. Mousetraps!

MACHIAVELLI. Oh! the spirit of disparagement, the unbridled hatred of the parties will not fail to vilify my institutions. They will say what you say. That matters little to me; if this method does not succeed another will be found.

I must not leave the chapter on constructions without mentioning a detail insignificant in appearance, but what is insignificant in politics? The innumerable edifices that I shall construct must be marked with my name, they must contain attributes, bas-reliefs, groups, which recall a theme of my history. My arms, my monogram, must be woven in everywhere. In one place, there will be angels who support my crown, in another, statues of justice and wisdom which bear my initials. These points are of the utmost importance, I consider them essentials.

It is by these signs, by these emblems that the person of the sovereign is always present; one lives with him, with his memory, with his thought. The feeling of his absolute sovereignty enters into the most rebellious spirits as the drop of water which falls unceasingly from the rock hollows out even granite. For the same reason I want my statue, my bust, my portraits to be in every public establishment, especially in the auditorium of the courts; I would be represented in royal costume or on horseback.

MONTESQUIEU. Beside the image of Christ.

MACHIAVELLI. Not at all, but opposite it; for sovereign power is

an image of divine power. My image is thus allied with that of
Providence and of justice.

MONTESQUIEU. Justice itself should wear your livery. You are
not a Christian, you are a Greek emperor of the Lower Empire.

MACHIAVELLI. I am a Catholic, Apostolic and Roman emperor.
For the same reasons as these which I have just pointed out to
you, I wish my name, the name Royal, to be given to every public establishment. Royal Tribunal, royal Court, royal Academy,
royal Legislative Body, royal Senate, royal Council of State; as
often as possible this same term will be given to the officials,
the agents, the official personnel which surrounds the government. Lieutenant of the king, archbishop of the king, comedi-
an of the king, judge of the king, attorney of the king. In short,
the name of royal will be imprinted on whatever will represent a
sign of power, whether it be men or things. Only my birthday
will be a national holiday and not a royal one. I must add that,
whenever possible, streets, public places, squares, must bear
names which recall historic memories of my reign. If one carefully follows these indications, whether he be Caligula or Nero,
he is certain to impress himself forever upon the memory of the
people and to transmit his prestige to the most distant posterity.
How many things I have yet to add! I must limit myself.

For who could say everything without a mortal tedium?

Here I am at petty means; I regret it, for these things are perhaps not worthy of your attention, but, for me, they are vital.

Bureaucracy is, they say, an evil of monarchic governments; I
do not believe that. They are thousands of servants who are naturally attached to the order of existing things. I have an army of
soldiers, an army of judges, an army of workers, I desire an army
of employees.

MONTESQUIEU. You no longer take the pains to justify anything.

MACHIAVELLI. Have I time for that?

MONTESQUIEU. No, go on.

MACHIAVELLI. In the states which have been monarchic, and
they all have been at least once, I have observed that there is a
veritable frenzy for decorations, for ribbons. These things cost
the prince scarcely anything and he can make happy people,
and, even better, loyal ones, by means of some pieces of stuff,
some baubles in silver or gold. In truth, I would need little per-

suasion to decorate without exception those who would ask it of me. A man decorated is a man bought. I would make of these marks of distinction a rallying sign for devoted subjects; I really believe I would have, at this price, nine-tenths of my kingdom. In this way I realize, as far as possible, the instincts of equality of the nation. Note carefully: the more a nation in general sticks to equality, the more the individual has a passion for distinctions. Here, then, is a means of action which it would be too stupid to deprive oneself of. Therefore far from giving up titles, as you advise me, I would multiply them around me as often as I would the dignities. In my court I want the etiquette of Louis XIV, the domestic hierarchy of Constantine, a severe diplomatic formalism, an imposing ceremonial; these are the infallible methods of government upon the spirit of the masses. Against all that, the sovereign appears like a God. (23)

ON THE DESTRUCTION OF MORAL CONSCIENCE

MACHIAVELLI. I have destroyed as many organized forces as was necessary so that nothing could proceed without me, so that even the enemies of my power would tremble at the thought of overthrowing it.

All that now remains for me to do consists only in the development of the moral methods which are sprouting in my institutions. My reign is a reign of pleasures; you will not forbid me to cheer my people by games, by festivals; that is how I expect to modify the customs. One cannot conceal that this century is a century of money; needs have doubled, luxury is ruining families; on every hand people aspire to material pleasures; a sovereign would have to be not of his times not to know how to turn to his profit this universal passion for money and this sensual ardor which consumes men nowadays. Misery clamps them as in a vice, luxury crushes them; ambition devours them, they are mine. But when I speak thus, at bottom it is the interest of my people which guides me. Yes, I shall call forth good from evil; I shall exploit materialism to the profit of concord and civilization; I shall extinguish the political passions of men by satisfying their ambitions, their desires and their needs. I claim to have as servants of my reign those who, under previous governments, will have made the most noise in the name of liberty. The most austere virtues are like that of the wife of Giocondo;

all that is necessary is always to double the price of defeat. Those who resist money will not resist honors; those who resist honors will not resist money. In seeing those whom it believes the purest fall in their turn, public opinion will weaken so much that it will end up by abdicating completely. How could one complain after all? I shall not be severe except for that which has reference to politics; I shall persecute only this passion; I shall even secretly favor the others by the thousand underground ways which absolute power has at its disposal.

MONTESQUIEU. After having destroyed political conscience, you ought to undertake to destroy moral conscience; you have killed society, now you are killing man. May it please God that your words should resound to the very earth; never could a more striking refutation of your own doctrines strike human ears. . . . (23)

ON "THE LITTLE MACHIAVELLIS" IN GOVERNMENT AND THE DESTRUCTION OF LIBERTY

MACHIAVELLI. I will even go so far as to satisfy the monomania of liberty. The wars which will be waged during my reign will be undertaken in the name of the liberty of men and the independence of nations, and, while the people acclaim me on my travels, I will whisper secretly into the ears of the absolute monarchs: Fear nothing, I am with you, I wear a crown like you and I intend to conserve it: *I embrace European liberty, but only to strangle it.*

One thing alone could perhaps compromise my fortune at some moment; that will be the day when it is realized on every side that my policies are not honest, that my every act is marked by the stamp of cunning.

MONTESQUIEU. Who will be the blind who will not see that?

MACHIAVELLI. My entire people, excepting several groups of which I fear little. I have moreover formed about me a school of politicians of a very great relative strength. You cannot believe to what point Machiavellism is contagious, and how easy its precepts are to follow. In every branch of government there will be men of no consequence, or of very little consequence, who will be veritable Machiavellis in miniature who will scheme, who will dissimulate, who will lie with an imperturbable cold-bloodedness; truth will not be able to see light anywhere.

MONTESQUIEU. If you have not done anything but jest from one end to the other of this conversation, as I think you have, Machiavelli, I regard this irony as your most magnificent work.

MACHIAVELLI. Irony! You are deceiving yourself if you think that. Do you not understand that I have spoken without veiling my meaning, and that it is the terrible violence of truth that gives my words the color you think you see! . . .

MONTESQUIEU. Here is a citation that I can guarantee you: it will revenge through eternity the people you libel:

"The habits of the Prince contribute as much to liberty as the laws. He can, like them, make men beasts, and beasts men; if he loves free souls, he will have subjects, if he loves boors, he will have slaves."

That is my reply, and if I had to add something to this quotation today, I would say:

"When public honesty is banished from the heart of the courts, when corruption spreads there without shame, yet it will never penetrate save in the hearts of those who have access to a bad Prince; love of virtue still lives in the hearts of the people, and the power of this principle is so great that the bad Prince has only to disappear in order that, by the very force of things, honesty will return in the practice of government at the same time as liberty."

MACHIAVELLI. That is very well written, in a very simple manner. There is only one thing wrong in what you have just said, that, in the mind as in the soul of my people, I personify virtue, and more, I personify *liberty,* do you hear, as I personify revolution, progress, the modern spirit, all that is good at the bottom of modern civilization. I do not say that I am respected, I do not say that I am loved, I say that I am venerated, I say that the people adore me; that if I wished it, I could have altars erected to me, for, explain it as you wish, I have the fatal gifts that work upon the masses. . . .

The soul of the people expands when I pass; it runs drunkenly in my footsteps; I am an object of idolatry; the father points me out to his son, the mother invokes my name in her prayers, the maiden looks at me with sighs and dreams that if my glance fell upon her by chance, she could perhaps lie for a moment on my couch. When the unhappy is oppressed, he says: *If the king but knew;* when someone desires revenge, when he hopes for help, he says, *The king will know.* Besides, I will never be approached without being found with my hands filled with gold. Those who surround me, it is true, are hard, violent, they deserve the stick at times, but it is necessary to have things thus; for their hateful despicable character, their cheap cupidity, their dissoluteness, their shameful wastefulness, their crass avarice make a contrast with the sweetness of my character, my simple bearing, my inexhaustible generosity. They will invoke my name, I tell you, like that of a god; in storms, in periods of want, in great fires, I hasten to them, the people throw themselves at my feet, they would carry me to the heavens in their arms, if God gave them wings.

MONTESQUIEU. All of which would not stop you from crushing it with cannonshot at the least sign of resistance.

MACHIAVELLI. That is true, but love does not exist without fear.

MONTESQUIEU. Has this frightful vision ended?

MACHIAVELLI. Vision! Ah! Montesquieu! you will shed tears for a long time: tear up the *Esprit des Lois,* beg God to give you forgetfulness for your part in heaven; for here is the terrible truth of which you already have the foreboding; there was no vision in what I have just told you.

MONTESQUIEU. What are you telling me?

MACHIAVELLI. What I have just described, this gathering of monstrous things before which the mind recoils in fright, this work that only hell itself could accomplish, all this is fact, all this exists, all this prospers in the face of the sun, at this very moment, in a part of the globe which we have left. . . . (25)

12

DECEPTION—ITS DECLINE AND REVIVAL IN INTERNATIONAL CONFLICT

BARTON WHALEY

Although deception is a common and often important means of influence, it is a neglected topic of study. This essay explores one aspect of how, as Machiavelli put it, certain groups rise to or hold power by clever fraud rather than brute force. I will focus on the relationship between deception and force in the context only of international conflict, with particular reference to their place in diplomacy and war, while recognizing that political power can be expressed both in other ways and in most other sociopolitical settings. Although thus restricting my topic, I will range both through the two most recent centuries and across four major national cultures. Several specific factors—cultural, institutional, and psychological—will be suggested to account for the recent marked variations through time and across nations in the prevalence of guile.[1]

Propaganda, when applied to the international arena, goes by many other terms: psychological warfare, political warfare, international political communication, or, most recently, public diplomacy. By whatever name, it is one means by which various groups (usually a nation's foreign policy elite) seek to influence the behavior of one or more foreign groups, ranging from the general public to particular elites. Deception is an often important and sometimes dominant element of such efforts to control or influence. This essay further limits itself to the use of deception in the struggle for control between the strategic foreign policy leaderships of nations.

I treat deception as information designed to manipulate the behavior of others by inducing them to accept a false or distorted presentation of their environment—physical, social, or political. So defined, deception is a special psychological mode of both communication and power. In terms of communication it is disinformation, that is, information *intended* to mislead. Disinformation is thus distinct from "misinformation," which describes only the truth value of the information and not its intention.[2] Although, in practice, disinformation is usually misinformation, it is not necessarily always so, for even true information can be used to deceive, as in the familiar Minsk-Pinsk paradox. Disinformation is also distinct from the "noise" of information theory and intelligence analysts. Unlike either misinformation or "noise," disinformation does not merely inadvertently confuse its recipient, it deliberately misleads. By stratagem I mean the planned coordination of separate ruses in a deception campaign.[3]

Power here is taken in Max Weber's sense as the ability of an individual or group to control or modify the behavior of others, even against their resistance. And *political* power is defined, in Fred Frey's terms, as the power to allocate power, "power over power, as distinguished from power over the allocation of . . . prestige and other values."[4] With one addition and one caveat, I also accept Hans Morgenthau's definition of political power as "a psychological relation between those who exercise it and those over whom it is exercised [that] gives the former control over certain actions of the latter through the influence which the former exert over the latter's minds." Morgenthau notes that such influence "may be exerted through orders, threats, persuasion, the authority or charisma of a man or of an office, or a combination of any of these."[5] He should, perhaps, have added a more explicit recognition that political power is itself only a means for controlling one's social, physical, or even psychic environment.

Also, I suggest caution in accepting Morgenthau's categorical distinction between political power and force. While accepting the *threat* of physical violence as "an intrinsic element of politics," he argues that the actual exercise of physical violence excludes the psychological aspect that is an essential element of all political relationships. Thus Morgenthau (with Bernard Crick and Hannah Arendt among others) sees politics and diplomacy ending when war begins. Even Clausewitz, by viewing war as an extension of politics by other means, saw discontinuity between means if not ends. However, I find it more useful to stress the continuity between political, diplomatic, and martial behavior. All three are activities intended to secure political power, and all involve the use (in various and shifting mixes) of the several expressions of power, including both force and guile. Admittedly, the outbreak of war usually does represent a catastrophic failure of diplomacy (and often also of national politics) by at least one of the antagonists (and, as in World War I, of all). But this failure does not necessarily prevent political or diplomatic processes from reasserting themselves during the conduct of the war. Seldom does a war become the private plaything of generals and even then, as with Caesar, the warpath is simply an alternate route to high political office. Politics and diplomacy can (and commonly do) intrude themselves in wartime: in the search for allies, the detachment of the antagonist's allies, selective collaboration when that is mutually convenient,[6] threats of further escalation,[7] and the negotiations over conditions of surrender.[8] Moreover, even in battle, politics enters wherever the outcome is influenced by such institutionalized rituals as rules of chivalry, the duel between heroes, the solicitation of treason, or the negotiation of surrender. All such rituals are as much political processes as is an election; and like elections all are subject to influence by either force or guile or both.

THE PREVALENCE OF DECEPTION

Deception is one way of life. In internal or domestic politics it is common enough at the local, state, and national levels to warrant serious study.[9] For example, at the national level, it is sufficient to note that, for the conspiratorial coup d'etat alone, between 1946 and 1964 there were 88 attempted coups (62 of which succeeded) in 37 countries, that is, in nearly a third of the world's then approximately 118 nations.[10] Nor is the coup d'etat a purely modern political technique: for example, three of the first twelve "Caesars" (Nero, Galba, and Otho) were deposed by army coups. Nor is the coup a Western monopoly: the nine Liao dynasty emperors of China (907–1125) had to fight off 19 "rebellions" by their own closest relatives.[11] And the coup is, of course, often enough the preferred means of covert international action or the welcome consequence of subversive "destabilization."

Assassination—or, rather, its planning—is another nominally covert and usually deceptive technique to gain (or hold) power. It was quite commonly practiced and with considerable flair in the Roman and Byzantine empires, at times in China, during the Indian Maurya dynasty and the Italian Renaissance, in the medieval Arab world, in early twentieth-century Japan, and intermittently in the contemporary West. During the 50 years since 1918 there were (at least) 218 assassination attempts (68 successful) directed against chief executives in 36 countries.[12] As with the coup, assassination may be national, international, or a mix of both.

In his more-or-less systematic survey of 280 "campaigns" in 30 European wars during the period from 490 B.C. to A.D. 1913, Liddell Hart found that the strategically "direct approach" was the usual one, while a purposefully "indirect approach" involving deception was the rare exception. Moreover, he discovered a direct relationship between the degree of military success and the degree of strategic indirectness. Thus of the 32 campaigns that produced "decisive" victories, only 6 succeeded by a direct approach while the 26 others (81 percent) were credited by him to use of an indirect strategy.[13]

My own close study of 217 major battles in 21 wars from 1914 to 1974 confirmed and extended Liddell Hart. I found 33 victories that greatly exceeded their planners' expectations. Of these, only 5 involved a direct approach whereas the 28 others (85 percent) involved at least some calculated effort to deceive. Furthermore, success correlates with surprise through stratagem. That is, the more sophisticated the deception, the better the chance for major surprise (as perceived by the victim) and, consequently, the greater the degree of success (as measured by the deceiver's expectations).

Nor, finally, is deception the sole prerogative of just large states. So-called primitive war, as practiced by the majority of tribal communities of old Europe and among modern Amerindian, African, Melanesian, and some other cultures, often involves rather high levels of guile. American anthropologist Turney-High stresses the sophistication of these groups in surprise tactics achieved through effective intelligence and security systems and their relatively developed ability to avoid surprise.[14]

DISCONTINUITY: "PROGRESS" AND ROMANTICISM IN THE NINETEENTH CENTURY

Napoleon, Jomini, and Clausewitz mark a watershed in which stratagem, having reached and held a high level from 1732 to 1806, suddenly and mysteriously disappears from European military practice and theory. How could this remarkable—yet almost unnoticed—discontinuity occur? Paradoxically, for all their own appreciation of stratagem, these three men contributed unwittingly to the sudden eclipse of their own hard-earned insights about surprise through deception.

The shift away from strategic indirection and tactical deception begins intriguingly enough with Napoleon Bonaparte himself. From 1793 to 1804, as Colonel and then General Bonaparte, he was a master deceiver, adroitly and successfully maneuvering his small armies against much larger ones. Then in 1804 he becomes Emperor Napoleon and soon (beginning at Friedland in 1807) comes to rely on number—big battalions and massed artillery. Maneuver gives way to ponderous and costly assault by main force; initiative yields to mere precipitateness; and victory soon becomes defeat.

On his part, Jomini, despite his stress on surprise and diversion, gives no guide as to how to achieve them. He leaves their realization to the ineffable psychological realms of intuition and "opportunity."

Similarly, Clausewitz was unable to integrate his concepts of surprise, stratagem, and diversion into a general theory. Consequently his disciples were able to shop freely among his notions—accepting some, rejecting others. In this competition for attention, it is understandable that his stratagemic principles were bypassed in favor of the more readily applied ones. But in doing this his successors ignored his injuction that without surprise "preponderance at the decisive point is not properly conceivable." Clausewitz also followed Frederick the Great in stressing its pervasive role: "Surprise lies at the foundation of all undertakings without exception." He added that "there is a degree of stratagem, be it ever so small, which lies at the foundation of every attempt to surprise.'' In developing these maxims Clausewitz produced some worthy contributions toward a theory of surprise that have been almost entirely overlooked by his followers.

The essence of this problem is that deception is a psychological notion. As such it falls within the set of military ''principles'' that includes surprise, determination or morale, endurance, and—in part—security. It closely relates to concepts such as deterrence and psychological warfare. Conversely, it falls outside the set of ''principles'' that includes objective, mass, direction, offensive, economy of force, concentration, rapidity, mobility, and distribution. These latter concepts of military theory are conventionally defined in terms of Euclidian geometry or Newtonian physics. Being geometrical and physical, they are mappable and measurable. They readily fit the broad academic subjects of ballistics, logistics, topography, and tactical evolutions. Consequently they can be and are successfully taught in all military schools and barracks, analyzed by operations research techniques, and presented in organizational charts, vectored maps, tables of equipment, and similar quantitative or representational models. The polished products of such education are engineers and administrators and only rarely, and then inadvertently, a ''Great Captain.''

One rather accurate indicator of the relative place of deception in the military doctrine of a given period is obtained by arraying chronologically the rank-ordered ''principles of war'' laid down by the various official manuals and influential writers. Thus a survey of thirty military theorists and manuals found six that simply do not consider deception (or surprise) to have any relevance to war. All six were written in the period 1837–1920. Moreover, while surprise is acknowledged by the four other works surveyed in that same period, all but one give it a low priority.[15]

Granting that the students of Napoleon, Jomini, and Clausewitz disregarded the stratagemic elements in their masters' practice and writings and chose instead the mechanical (physical-geometrical) ones, we must still somehow account for that one-sided choice. It is not enough to argue as I once did that it was a biased or forced choice merely because these three

strategists had failed to integrate fully their psychological principles into their theories or because their followers were too
stupid to perfect that promising line of theoretical development. The masters' failure to develop integrated theories and
their students' intellectual impoverishment are true enough.
But this does not explain why, given a seemingly clear set of options, the nineteenth-century doctrinalists *selected* the "scientific" principles over the "psychological" ones and then pro-
ceeded to build upon those particular ones.

I am rather sure there is one sufficient explanation. Moreover,
I suggest that it also satisfactorily accounts for the persisting
celebration of force over cunning in American, Russian, Japanese, and most other modern military doctrines. This overriding factor is the notion of Progress, specifically technological
progress.

During the eighteenth century, the innovative philosophers
of the Enlightenment raised Progress to the position of main
concept. Rationalism and natural philosophy (science) reigned.
Then, from 1830 to 1842, Auguste Comte published his *The
Positive Philosophy* that explicitly linked *technology* to progress.[16] Henceforward the notion of technological progress has
been the central paradigm of our age, embracing the Industrial
Revolution, Darwinian evolution, *and* "scientific" (technologically oriented) military doctrine. It is surely no accident that
Clausewitz and Jomini were published at the same time as
Comte. Writing when they did, they were still free to rummage
the past and select *both* psychological and mechanical principles. But their followers, already thinking and writing in the
Machine Age, were conditioned to perceive and select only the
new mechanical principles.

This modern Western tendency away from guilefulness was
strongly reinforced by that other contemporary Great Idea of
the Western World: Romanticism. Prideful heroic display as a
necessary proof of manliness is an old Western tradition quite at
odds with the survival instinct. A clear complaint against this
romantic sentiment was put by a wise mid–nineteenth-century
British soldier: "As a nation we are bred up to feel it is a disgrace even to succeed by falsehood; the word spy conveys something as repulsive as slave; we will keep hammering along with
the conviction that 'honesty is the best policy,' and that truth

always wins in the long run. These pretty little sentences do well
for a child's copy-book, but the man who acts upon them in war
had better sheathe his sword forever.''[17]

Despite such occasional warnings, romantic gestures multiply
throughout the nineteenth and twentieth centuries: Lord Byron
swims the Hellespont in 1810 and, as every schoolboy knows,
singlehandedly frees Greece from the Terrible Turk. In 1854,
the Light Brigade blunders into the Valley of Death and General Bosquet backhandedly compliments their heroism: ''It is
magnificent, but it is not war.'' At Tanga in 1914, Royal Navy
Captain F. W. Caulfield courteously notifies the off-guard German garrison of the impending British landing; the British attack fails disastrously and Caulfield is promoted.

Those military writers and practitioners who held this attitude of romantic heroism were quick to emphasize Clausewitz's
notions about force and ''will.'' This combination was thought
to guarantee delivery of a physically and psychologically overwhelming force at the decisive point, breaking the enemy army's morale and then his ranks. Rigid discipline, élan, quality-
over-quantity were stressed. But the ''psychological'' element
was only a metaphor for physical struggle in which one breaks
the other's morale not indirectly through insightful, empathic
understanding but directly by sheer ''willpower.'' This romantic doctrine is responsible for the single most costly and usually
self-defeating type of military order sloganized as ''They shall
not pass!'' and ''Fight to the last man!'' that senselessly cost
France 377,000 men at Verdun and Germany 400,000 at Stalin-
grad.

In the Romantic mythology heroes and heroines are good and
God-fearing, truthful, patient in adversity, naive, impulsive,
and often just a bit stupid. The Romantic villain is evil and godless (or satanic), a weaver of lies, quick to revenge, cynical, calculating, and always astute. Westerners are most effectively so-
cialized to accept these simplistic bad guy–good guy models of
shrewd villains and gullible heroes, the very opposite of those
models inculcated, as we shall see, in Chinese folklore and literature.

When labeled as evil, disreputable, or cowardly, it is understandable that officers nurtured on the nineteenth-century code
of the gentleman would feel uneasy in using deception on the

field of battle. Certainly the tendency in the nineteenth and twentieth centuries has been for the great majority of professional soldiers either to reject stratagem entirely or to avoid it by passing such an "unsoldierly" task to the limbo of the secret services along with psychological warfare, covert operations, and such other sinister arts. Although there are some rational if moot arguments for placing deception planning and, particularly, operations under the intelligence (or counterespionage) staffs, I suspect that this psychological factor has been at least as effective in ensuring that placement. Moreover, it has almost certainly inhibited the effective integration of stratagem with routine operations planning. For example, this might well prove to be an unconscious contributing factor in the slow and still incomplete adoption of stratagem in U.S. military doctrine.

This predominantly negative attitude toward deception was a concomitant of the fashionable new style of big battalions with technologized weaponry. Military power and the national prestige and the ability for imperial expansion or defensive deterrence that follow from it was believed to depend on possession of this fashionable military doctrine. As its recent revival proves, deception is not necessarily inconsistent with the deployment of large technologized military forces. But, in adopting this style, the officer corps of France, Germany, and Britain did initially omit deception for the reasons discussed. And it was precisely these officer corps that the world's other armies had to employ as teachers to master the new complicated engineering and weapons. Thus did the world's officer corps come to resemble an international fraternity as virtually all officers soon became the products of French, German, or British military education by on-the-job service in their armies, study in their academies, or by local instruction from their military advisers. By the mid-nineteenth century the new style had spread to all European nations. The far-flung empires of these states guaranteed a quick worldwide diffusion. The few independent nations of Latin America, the Near East, and Asia soon followed the trend.

We will now look briefly at this remarkable case of cultural diffusion and acculturaton as it occurred in Japan and China. These two nations are specially relevant not just because they were the most important independent countries at the time but, more significantly, because both had their own strong non-Western traditions of deception.

THE JAPANESE STYLE

The slow development of feudal society in Japan through the tenth century into the twelfth bred a provincial warrior class, the *samurai*. Like the early European knights, they fought strictly individualistic duels by rigid rules: open challenges, careful pairing-off of equals, rewards according to number of *(samurai)* heads fetched back to one's lord, and so on. They did differ in one main respect from Western chivalry: lacking the Western custom of either ransom or *wergild* (payment of death damages), *samurai* combat ended in death that bred an unrelieved cyclical pressure for vendetta. This otherwise chivalrous style persisted until the fourteenth century, when more or less regular armies were first formed and mass tactics introduced.[18]

Texts of Sun Tzu, the ancient Chinese advocate of military deception, circulated and were taught in Japan from at least as early as the eighth century; and by the end of the twelfth century this Chinese stratagemic doctrine had been fully adopted by the *samurai*. From then, for nearly six hundred years, until the mid-seventeenth century, Sun Tzu and stratagem dominated Japanese military theory and, to greater or lesser extent, practice.[19] Even the new, popular, late seventeenth-century Genroku literary style reflected the new ethos, replacing the former moralistic writings with a stress on the daily life of money, cunning, and gullibility.

But from this point on in Japan, stratagem met two countervailing influences that gradually eroded its practical and theoretical roles. These were, first, the rise of the indigenous code of *Bushidō* from the mid-seventeenth century and, then, two centuries later, the importation of European military doctrine.[20]

For two and a quarter centuries, from 1638 until 1863, the *samurai* were unable to practice their trade in battle—it was a period entirely free of internal or external warfare. While retaining their class status, the *samurai* transformed themselves from warriors into educated bureaucrats. Their military training began to stress such character-building martial arts as *jūdō*. And their martial ethos gradually forgot strategy and tactics, to stress instead the ethical principles of loyalty, honor, and mindless bravery codified in *Bushidō,* the "Way of the Warrior." Sun Tzu remained the main required text, but was reinterpreted to emphasize those points coinciding with the ethics of *Bushidō*—the rest became empty maxims.[21]

This was the state of the art in the mid-nineteenth century when European military doctrine was imported wholesale, displacing and largely eclipsing the already failing stratagemic tradition of Sun Tzu, as it would almost succeed in doing in China, a quarter century later. Thus, in 1867, after five years of dabbling on its own with Western fighting techniques, Japan received its first contingent of Western military instructors—fifteen Frenchmen selected by the French war ministry. The Shōgun had picked the world's then most prestigious military doctrine. But the Franco-Prussian War soon ended French pre-eminence. The Prussian general staff theoretician, Klemens Wilhelm Jacob Meckel, arrived in 1885 and henceforward German doctrine prevailed. Major Meckel was typically the advocate of the massed infantry assault, which by weight, organization, discipline, and sheer courage would sweep all before it.[22]

Japan acquired a truly modern army in equipment, training, and doctrine. But by adopting the contemporary European model, it was an army without guile. Thenceforward, victories or defeats were a simple function of which side had the advantage in élan, matériel, and organization. Japan's victories and defeats both carried inordinately expensive butcher's bills. The self-sacrificing spirit of *Bushidō* meshed nicely with the demands of the German Field Service Regulations.

In the small Sino-Japanese War of 1894–1895, Meckel's students proved their mastery of the entire curriculum of modern war, including the costly massed frontal assault tactics by which they took Port Arthur from a Chinese force one-third their size. Their only concession to guile was that units were permitted to use ground cover—when available. Otherwise, strictly up-and-at-'em. These tactics prevailed once more in winning (but just barely) the Russo-Japanese War of 1904–1905. Again Port Arthur was taken by direct assault—and 59,000 casualties. Only at Mukden did the Japanese, by improvising less packed-mass assault tactics, manage to sustain fewer casualties than their defeated enemy.[23]

Their indecisive campaigning throughout the protracted

Sino-Japanese War (1937–1945) earned the contempt of Mao Tse-tung who, in 1938, listed among Japan's "many mistakes" her inflexible persistence in reinforcing lost battles and stubbornly defending untenable areas.

A brief flurry of probing border warfare with Russia ended in 1939 with Japan's crushing defeat at Khalkhin-Gol at the hands of a young general named Zhukov, who used a crude World War I–type deception plan to take the Japanese quite by surprise.[24]

We all remember Japan's magnificently successful surprise strikes at Pearl Harbor and in Malaya. Both operations did, in fact, hinge upon deception planning. This was true also of the naval battles of Midway (1942) and Leyte Gulf (1944), which, intended as lures for the U.S. fleet, ended in catastrophe for the Japanese. These four cases represent the total Japanese stratagemic effort throughout World War II, aside from some minor tactical achievements in night attack and camouflage. It was their opponents, MacArthur and Halsey, and Wavell and Slim, and Mao, who consistently used coordinated deception planning.[25]

THE CHINESE WAY

Deception in war and politics has been practiced in Chinese civilization in its purest historical form, less adulterated than elsewhere by countervailing ethical, religious, or sociopolitical constraints. However, I cannot agree with Scott Boorman that this Chinese tradition represents a higher or more sophisticated understanding of stratagem than was ever reached in the West.[26] Indeed, by Boorman's own criteria, I find the same high quality, albeit less consistently, in Western tradition.

Moreover, the stratagemic tradition in China, although more secure there than in the West, is not, as Griffith and Boorman imply, a perfect lineage. There were at least five major perturbations or even discontinuities. First, stratagem did not arise full blush with the dawning of Chinese civilization but developed only in the politico-military hothouse environment of the fourth century B.C. Second, it apparently underwent a dramatic if only very brief total eclipse two centuries later. Third and fourth, it briefly but sharply declined in both the tenth and late thirteenth centuries. And, fifth and most recently, it declined during the nineteenth and early twentieth centuries as a consequence of bureaucratic policy and the importation of the then fashionable nonstratagemic Western military doctrines.[27] The reintroduction of stratagem occurred only after 1930, and then only among the Chinese Communist armies.

China entered its most recent period of decline in stratagem around 1800. This decline started as a direct consequence of the Manchu regime's official scholastic policy that increasingly emphasized a rigidly formalistic training in which stereotyped forms became the rule at the expense of practical content, professional skill, and original thought.[28] As this empty formalism was effectively enforced through the state-monopolized civil service examination system, the texts and the training for military officers were soon reduced to the overall amateurish scholastic level. The dynasty was moribund, prey to both rebel and foreign armies.

There is an additional factor that helps explain the frequent failure of Chinese imperial armies to apply stratagem to battle despite the dominant Sun Tzu tradition. This is the political tradition of civilian command of the military. As with Roman warfare, most major (that is, politically important) military operations against both "bandits" (rebels) and "barbarians" (foreigners) were the direct responsibility of civilian bureaucrats appointed specially for each operation. These commands were either assigned to high court officials or made the personal responsibility of the local provincial governor. Obviously such commands often fell to (or were actively sought by) men whose competence lay elsewhere than in military affairs.

The emperor's martial nakedness soon revealed itself in the bizarre Taiping Rebellion of 1851–1864. Then it was the rebels who employed much guile to sustain their prolonged (although eventually unsuccessful) challenge to the empire. Similarly with the more mobile Nien rebels of the same period.[29]

In the Sino-Japanese War of 1894–1895, the new, modern, German-trained Imperial Japanese Army soundly thumped the traditional armies of the Manchus, as described in the preceding section. Although the moribund Manchu regime was visibly disintegrating, many provincial leaders began to build their own modern, that is, "European," armies. The training and doctrine was exclusively German: the several new Chinese military academies were staffed with either German or German-trained officers and the Japanese Military Academy had by 1910 graduated 620 Chinese, all thoroughly indoctrinated with the German Field Service Regulations. The "New Armies" were modern in every sense, including that utter disregard for strata-gem which then characterized European doctrine. Revolution brought the final collapse of the Manchu dynasty in 1911. Within a year, a third of the thirty-four revolutionary provincial governors were graduates of either the Japanese Military Academy (eight) or the new Chinese military academies (three).[30]

The Chinese military academies gradually replaced their ex-pensive German (and other European) instructors with cheaper Japanese models and the still cheaper returned Chinese student-officers. But the training remained German. By 1922 the main school, the Paoting Military Academy, had its nine thousand graduates spread among the many warlord armies of China.

The Nationalist-Communist united front regime began from Canton its drive north to seize all China. Their justly famed Whampoa Military Academy (which graduated two regiments of cadets) was now, from 1924 to 1927, staffed by Soviet Rus-sian instructors who also served as advisers to the coalition army. But Soviet military doctrine, while imbued with Marxist-Leninist notions of the dialectic and conspiratorial deception and incorporating the principle of surprise, was itself too much a mirror image of contemporary Western military doctrine to stress stratagem.[31]

When, in 1927, the Nationalists and Communists parted mortal enemies, their military doctrines also diverged. General Chiang K'ai-shek trained originally in the Japanese and Paoting military academies, reverted to the revered German model. Reinforced by a parade of 137 German military advisers, from 1927 to 1938, Germanic style dominated Nationalist doctrine until the arrival of American advisers in the 1940s. While it is not likely that any purely *military* doctrine could have saved the Nationalists, their stubborn adherence to an inappropriate doc-trine rendered them the too-easy dupes of the highly flexible and stratagemic Chinese Communists and certainly hastened their expulsion in 1949.

On their part the Communists continued after 1927 to cling

to Soviet Russian military doctrine. Key senior officers were sent for further training in Russia from 1928 to 1934 and again during World War II, and a few Soviet military advisers served the Chinese Red Armies in the 1930s. After the final victory of the Communists over the Nationalists, Soviet-style military academies were founded at Nanking (in 1951) and Peking (1958), and numerous Russian military advisers and technicians helped modernize and professionalize the People's Liberation Army until in 1960 they were withdrawn at the beginning of the Sino-Soviet split.

Although the nonstratagemic Western doctrines predominated in China from 1894, the native tradition of Sun Tzu did not die. It was only dormant. All literate Chinese (and many of the illiterate) knew of it through literature and folklore, which preserved and lauded the trickeries of the crafty heroes of *The Romance of the Three Kingdoms,* the *Shui Hu Chuan,* and the Taiping Rebellion.[32] Although the new Chinese officers, enamored of "modernization" and technology, scoffed at the lessons of Sun Tzu, even Chiang K'ai-shek once complained that too many of his generals were blind to China's own military traditions.

The restoration of stratagem to Chinese military practice and doctrine is due mainly to Mao Tse-tung. He had studied Sun Tzu and the rebels of Chinese folklore as well as Clausewitz. Since 1928, when with Chu Teh he formed the Communist Chu-Mao Army in the Kiangsi Soviet, the principles of deception and surprise came to predominate—at least in those operations over which Mao had direct control or influence. Otherwise, as Colonel Whitson argues, the history of the Chinese Communist high command has involved a never-resolved tension among the European ("warlord"), Soviet Marxist ("Russian"), and Maoist ("peasant") doctrines.[33]

A characteristic feature of the Chinese style in warfare is the cautious avoidance of battle. Ideally, every effort to gain victory without battle is exhausted before battle is joined, and even then only if the odds are overwhelmingly favorable. The object of this Chinese "tradition of victory through nonviolence," as Whitson calls it, is to induce the enemy to capitulate before battle by bribery, treachery, or tricking him into a position that he perceives is hopeless. The modern Western (and Japanese) fight-to-the-last-man syndrome is not congenial to Chinese soldiers, generals, or politicians.[34] But this traditional unwillingness to risk an uncertain battle is not a monopoly of Chinese culture. It is found among all other major political cultures at one time or other. For example, Byzantium and Imperial Victorian England employed effective "divide-and-rule" diplomacies to avoid unnecessary wars. Once war was declared, bribery, treachery, assassination, and Fabian tactics were preferred to battle by the Italian Renaissance states. And collaboration with the declared enemy has been a significant component in the wartime politics of many governments.

TWENTIETH-CENTURY LIMITED

After being moribund if not quite dead for a century after Napoleon and Wellington, military deception began its still fitful revival in World War I. It has done so despite continuing psychological, institutional, and psychocultural constraints. Given the oppressive burden of these constraints, how is this modern revival of stratagem possible?

Necessity encourages invention. Even the guileless ethos of the atomistic, mechanistic, Romantic nineteenth century could not prevent a very occasional commander from rediscovering stratagem to his own advantage. These exceptions are almost entirely limited to the American Civil War (1861–1865). Although it was war characterized more by the pompous by-the-manual McClellans, the flamboyant "Jeb" Stuarts, and the abysmally stupid Burnsides, two stratagemic champions did emerge: Jackson for the South and Sherman for the North. And Lee and even Grant showed flair.

The intermittently successful effort through the first half of the present century to incorporate strategic deception in professional military doctrine was the result almost entirely of a fragile chain of transmission from one teacher to another. Only after 1941 did it begin to diffuse through a few military staff networks.

The tenuous tradition of military deception returned to Britain from America. Lieutenant-Colonel G. F. R. Henderson was Britain's most unorthodox military scholar in the nineteenth century. His classic study of the American Civil War, published in 1898, identified a whole range of strategic (and tactical) ruses used by the Confederates, particularly the highly unorthodox General "Stonewall" Jackson, and to which Henderson explicitly attributed their frequent attainment of surprise. Henderson received the very rare opportunity to apply his purely academic theories to war when two years later he accompanied Lord Roberts into the hitherto disastrous quagmire of the Boer War. As head of Robert's intelligence service, Colonel Henderson devised the carefully coordinated plan of feint-and-deception that in 1900 relieved Kimberley and permitted the move against Bloemfontein. It is significant for the future of deception that a twenty-nine-year-old major named Allenby was present and that an even younger second lieutenant named Wavell soon joined this fated company.

At the outbreak of the Great War, the imaginative and innovative Captain Archibald Wavell was placed in charge of M.O.5, the key staff section of the Military Operations Directorate concerned with security, the secret service, ciphers, and general military intelligence. One of Wavell's many odd jobs was the "last-minute improvisation" of a field intelligence service. This brand-new Intelligence Corps virtually monopolized the keen advocates of stratagem during the Great War. However, for two very costly years its superiors rejected deception as fit only for "comic opera," as one put it during the instructive butchery at the Somme in 1916.[35]

Then, in 1917, on another bogged front, General Allenby unloosed a full bag of tricks—tactical and strategic—on the German and Turkish commanders in Palestine. There, on 31 October, he launched his famed feint-cum-deception Third Battle of Gaza that thoroughly surprised General Falkenhayn and routed the off-guard and off-balance Turkish army, breaking an eight-month stalemate and going on to take Jerusalem as trophy. Allenby himself had learned some of these tricks in the Boer War from Roberts and Henderson. Now, at Third Gaza, his own brilliantly innovative intelligence officer, Major Richard Meinertzhagen, was to design his stratagems. "After the Meinertzhagen success," as T. E. Lawrence wrote, "deceptions, which for the ordinary general were just witty hors d'oeuvres before battle, became for Allenby a main point of strategy." Thus Allenby repeated the initial success a year later, on 19 September 1918, at Megiddo. This time he used a similar pattern of feint-cum-deception but reversed the real line of operations to the coast. Coordinated with this were a series of feints and ruses by Intelligence Major T. E. Lawrence to divert enemy attention inland to his trans-Jordan desert front. This strategy succeeded in unbalancing the Turkish-German force and precipitated it into headlong flight. Seven days later all Palestine had fallen.

Meanwhile, on the Western Front, 1918 saw a revival of deception planning by the British, French, Americans, and, independently, the Germans. Even Field-Marshal Haig had at last recognized the bankruptcy of the old methods and encouraged his staff to experiment with new ones.

Captain B. H. Liddell Hart and many other soldiers returned with deep-felt revulsion from the monstrous slaughter of the Western Front. While many intellectuals adopted such noble pacifisms as the Oxford Movement to forestall the predicted horrors of another Great War, Liddell Hart—like Fuller, Lawrence, Wavell, von Seeckt, Marshall, and MacArthur—believed that, as further war was probable if not inevitable, the wise course was to reform it. Accordingly, these men sought fervently to harness the modern technological means of war, making those means once again responsive to the political goals that unleash them.

Liddell Hart achieved the first comprehensive formulation of his general theory with the publication in 1929 of *The Decisive Wars of History,* in which he introduced and vigorously advocated his central concept of the "indirect approach." As codified by Liddell Hart, this theory has found wide acceptance in military doctrine (particularly the Nazi German and Israeli) and with most individual practitioners of surprise through deception.[36] However, it is curious that it has not been refined, much less enlarged, by any subsequent military theoreticians.

Liddell Hart concluded from his survey that "the indirect is by far the most hopeful and economic form of strategy."[37] Moreover, he found that the relationship of ineffectiveness/effectiveness to direct/indirect strategies matched so closely along their scales that it was almost a general rule that *whatever the attendant circumstances* the direct approach should be avoided and a deceptively indirect approach sought. He also largely succeeded in integrating into his theory one other finding stressed by his intellectual forebears, by showing that the essence of the indirect approach is psychological, quoting Lenin with approval to the effect that: "The soundest strategy in war is to postpone operations until the moral disintegration of the enemy renders the delivery of the mortal blow both possible and easy."[38]

Although the British had become the acknowledged masters of deception during the Great War, they had lost this technique by the beginning of World War II. The sole repository of such wisdom in a position of command was General Wavell, then in the quiescent Middle East. He had learned deception under Allenby in Palestine during the Great War and had perfected its theory in his highly unorthodox interwar training maneuvers. After the fall of France, Wavell put theory to effective practice in his rearguard defense against the overcautious, semicompetent, but far stronger Italian army in the Western Desert. Finally, in December 1940, he proved its value by gaining the first British strategic surprise and victory of the war. Then, early in 1941 he sent his principal deception planning officer, Colonel Dudley Clarke, to London to argue the need for centralized intertheater planning and coordination of strategic deception. The dreary failures of previous half-hearted cover plans were vivid reminders of the need to improve such operations.

It seems likely that Wavell's revolutionary recommendation to upgrade and centralize deception was accepted because of the fortuitous circumstance that Churchill was then prime minister. Churchill was himself a quite unorthodox military thinker, always ready to consider (and sometimes overly willing to approve) the most outrageous innovations—such as tanks, amphibious warfare, guerrilla warfare—anything that might strengthen Britain's weak hand against the Axis. Moreover, Churchill had himself successfully practiced military stratagem in the Great War. Lawrence and Liddell Hart had once had his ear and he was an early advocate of the "indirect approach"; indeed he had independently conceived the outlines of this strategic doctrine as early as 1915.[39] Moreover, during the extensive reorganization of the proliferated British secret services in late 1941, Churchill was known fully to endorse deception, favoring it over even psychological warfare, of whose utility he was skeptical. Following acceptance of Wavell's 1941 proposal on deception planning, Churchill was quick to use it and to recommend its use to others, including both Roosevelt and Stalin.

In any case, the combined Chiefs of Staff adopted Wavell's proposal. Thenceforward, strategic deception planning became institutionalized as a regular staff function. Centralized in the so-called London Controlling Section headed by Colonel J. H. "Johnny" Bevan, small deception staffs appeared among all British military echelons from theater down to corps level. The British then taught their model to the Americans (and, in part, the Russians).[40] I suspect that one reason the U.S. military so readily adopted "special plans" (as the British called it) was that its chairman of the Joint Chiefs of Staff was General George C. Marshall, who as one of Pershing's successful deception planners in 1918 had designed the famed "Belfort Ruse."

However, deception planning would continue until today to meet with skepticism and rejection. For example, the JCS's favorable attitude was not in general shared by its navy member nor by the U.S. Navy. Thus the chief of naval operations, Admiral Ernest J. King, penciled in on his rejection in 1943 of a study recommending that the United States build midget surprise-attack submarines the remark: "The element of surprise has been dissipated. —EJK."[41] At that point, U.S. Navy policy on surprise was felt to be fulfilled by a large-scale harbor defense program, while its potential in offensive operations was overlooked in a confident reliance on sheer numbers. Surprise and its tools were deemed "weapons of despair of the have-not nations, . . . not for us."[42] For some, only a display of naked force could avenge the wounded pride of the Pearl Harbor "sneak attack." This negative attitude toward surprise and deception, connected with a simple misunderstanding of their nature and interrelationship, permeates the magnificent fifteen-volume, semiofficial history of U.S. naval operations in World War II by Rear Admiral Samuel Eliot Morison. For him, deception is seldom more than a comic interlude before the real business of battle.

Although theoretically there is no reason why small nations in the post–World War II period should not have integrated stratagem with their military doctrine, I am aware of no case except Israel. Moreover, Israel has emerged as one of the modern masters of this technique—indeed, perhaps, *the* master, despite the momentary reversal of roles in the October War.

The early years of the current revival in the West of military

TABLE I: *Frequency of Use and Sophistication of Deception in Battles 1914–1974*

Period	Percent Involving Some Deception	Percent Involving Moderate or High Deception[a]	Number of Battles Studied
1914–19	43	23	56
1920–29	50	25	4
1930–39	46	27	11
1940–49	73	37	114
1950–59	57	33	21
1960–69	67	67	6
1970–74	100	80	5
			217

[a]That is, with an index of 3 or more on a 0-to-12 scale that indicates the number of possible types of "channels" used to communicate disinformation.

stratagem coincide with the rise of the modern Machiavellian political theorists. Henderson, Maurice, T. E. Lawrence, and Liddell Hart published their major military theses from 1898 to 1929; and the political realists Mosca, Sorel, Michels, Pareto, and Meinecke issued theirs between 1883 and 1925. Theories of political and military realism were very much "in the air" and have remained so to this day. I rather think that the body of theory on deception that has been developing among a small number of scholars from Liddell Hart through R. V. Jones to the present generation owes much more than we suspect to this prevalent atmosphere, particularly as most of our initial work on *military* deception was done independently of each other.

Since its reinvention in World War I, deception in warfare has been generally increasing in both relative frequency of its use and in sophistication, as shown in table 1.

SOVIET DOCTRINE

Although czarist Russia had produced the occasional mildly stratagemic commander such as Suvorov and Brusilov, it bequeathed to its Bolshevik successors the disastrous "scientific" doctrines of Lloyd, Clausewitz, Jomini, and von Moltke. As in Japan and China, Russia's dire need to "modernize" its army was learned in the mid-nineteenth century—in this case in the Crimean War in 1855—and this policy dominated Russian military doctrine from 1851 through World War I.[43] It would plague the czar's miserable generals and infect the tacticians of the Red Army from Trotsky through Frunze, Tuchachevsky, Shaposhnikov, and Zhukov to the current officer corps. Moreover, this military "science" blended nicely with traditional Russian views about manpower to yield the self-fulfilling prophesy that victories were necessarily bloody. Soviet history is an extraordinarily interesting case because it shows how both ideology and power politics can first encourage and then inhibit the development of political and military doctrine on stratagem.[44]

In 1917, Red October suddenly fused the two major contemporary intellectual traditions that explicitly, frankly, and realistically understood deception or hypocrisy to be a veritable way of life. It brought together the cosmopolitan Marxist and the Russian national literary intellectual. Both recognized deception to be a major weapon for defense or attack, by self or foe, and in politics and diplomacy equally as in war.[45]

The Soviet Union made deception a part of its military doctrine well before World War II. Indeed, as early as 1918, Stalin himself had raised the concept of surprise to the status of a major "factor" in war.[46] Nevertheless, later Soviet military theory has suffered from a curious inhibition regarding the concept of surprise. This is the direct and immediate and still operative consequence of the German invasion on 22 June 1941. That was a strategic and tactical surprise whose shock was felt throughout the country—even Stalin suffered a temporary nervous collapse —and neither the appalling lack of defenses nor the utter failure of the leader's vaunted omniscience could be concealed.[47] Stalin therefore adjusted the concept of surprise by simultaneously downgrading and separating it from the other "factors" or principles of war. The others became "permanently operating factors," while surprise was immediately relegated to a specifically created lower class of *nonpermanently* operating factors. The hasty improvisation involved and the embarrassed avoidance of this problem are evident from the fact that Stalin never specified the *other* factors that fell into this supposedly secondary class. This intimate linkage of Stalin's name and role with the topic of surprise made any critical reappraisal of the subject taboo during his lifetime.[48] Similarly, it has remained one of the more sensitive topics since his death in 1953, because it is one of the central questions involved in any reappraisals connected with the wavering struggle over de-Stalinization. This unique circumstance has deeply inhibited Soviet restatements of military *doctrine,* although it remains a moot point to what degree it has degraded or calcified their *practice* of stratagem.

From 1941 through early 1944 the level of Soviet stratagemic art shows no advance over that of the czarist Russian army in World War I,[49] except in the extensive use of double agents for radio "games." Then, as an integral part of their vast summer 1944 offensive in conjunction with the Allied invasion of Normandy, the Russians suddenly displayed a more sophisticated flair for deception. Despite the implied Soviet claims that this was an indigenous advance in strategic art, it seems most likely that it was the result of the lecturing on strategic deception that Stalin and his military intelligence chiefs received directly from Churchill at Teheran in 1943 and from Colonel John Bevan, the chief British deception planner, in Moscow from January to March 1944.[50]

Their summer 1944 offensive marks the high-water mark of Russian art in stratagem in World War II. Yet it merely shows how far behind the British and Germans the Russians then were in understanding this technique.[51] For example, Colonel Shimansky proudly discloses that among several otherwise unidentified innovations was the use of: "reconnaissance in force not only in front areas involved in the offensive, but also in other contiguous strategic directions." But this "new element" in Soviet stratagem had already been standard practice in British, U.S., and German military deception operations in the *First* World War. Moreover, Shimansky uses this rather primitive historical case study explicitly to illustrate *future* means: "why in order to achieve strategic surprise it [is] necessary to carry out a whole system of measures aimed at strategic camouflage and disinformation." Thus, Shimansky unwittingly implies that current (1968) Soviet thinking on surprise and deception still lags behind that in, at least, the British and Israeli armies. Incidentally, this article cannot be dismissed as the idiosyncratic view of some uninformed minor officer. Colonel A. N. Shimansky, as a Candidate of Historical Sciences and one of the fifteen members of the committee chaired by Marshal Sokolovsky that coauthored *Military Strategy* in 1962, would have full access to his subject. Soviet naivete about stratagem is even more recently seen in an otherwise excellent study of Anglo-American amphibious operations.[52]

If the Russians are indeed still as weak at stratagem as the limited public evidence indicates, this is seemingly a direct consequence of the dead hand of Stalin, which still restrains comprehensive rethinking about the broader topic of military surprise. At the beginning of this section it was noted that Stalin's solution to the intolerable embarrassment of the surprise of the German invasion in 1941 was the mindless evasion of recategorizing surprise as a transitory factor. By making military doctrine a cosmetic mask for his "cult of personality," Stalin imposed a political barrier that prevented any reevaluation of doctrine during his life and has inhibited pragmatic or empirical reassessment since his death in 1953. Even the urgent Soviet search for doctrines appropriate to the unprecedented opportunities opened by missile-nuclear technology for surprise and preemption has had to proceed with wary attention to the day-to-day political vagaries of de-Stalinization.

The first attack on Stalin's doctrine of permanent-versus-transitory factors appeared six months after Stalin's death in the chief theoretical journal of the Soviet Ministry of Defense. It was an article by that confidential journal's editor, Major General Talensky.[53] Although this piece opened the debate in mild terms that merely qualified rather than overthrew Stalin's doctrine, it was an immediate sensation both because of its high-level sponsorship and because it presented the first original thoughts on Communist military theory to have come from any writer other than Stalin himself in the previous twenty-five years. Because of the very way in which Stalin had formulated his doctrine, the entire subsequent debate has necessarily involved a reassessment of the role of surprise. This was true even in Talensky's very general original piece. The ensuing internal debate—conducted in limited-circulation journals—soon erupted in public view through a series of articles in *Red Star,* the official army newspaper. Subsequently, with much disputatious vacillation, the debate progressed from modifications of this Stalin doctrine to its eventual overthrow in 1955.[54] The landmark article supporting and enhancing the rediscovery of surprise was by Tank Marshal Rotmistrov.[55] Khrushchev's "Secret Speech" of 1956 merely dealt the coup de grace and brought this specific issue before the entire Communist party membership. Since then the occasional Soviet books and articles on surprise show an increasing sophistication but still fall short of British or Israeli writings in their grasp of the relationship between surprise and deception. Moreover, to a greater extent than even American writers, they continue to be obsessed with the false notion that "security"—in its narrow sense of secrecy—is the crucial factor in surprise.[56]

The general quality of Soviet psychological warfare in World War II was rather crude, being geared more to postwar political power considerations in the recaptured Russian lands and the newly taken Eastern European states.[57] The first decade of the cold war saw a gradual rise in both the volume and sophistication of psychological operations applied to international politics. Then, in 1959, Soviet psychological warfare and political deception planning and operations were combined and coordinated in the KGB's newly created Disinformation Department under the clever and imaginative Major General Ivan Agayants. Even so, as the former deputy director of the Czechoslovak Department D, Major Ladislav Bittman, admits, these operations were marked by a very high proportion of aborts, failures, backfires, and expensive yet trivial practical jokes.[58]

My conclusion that the Russians still have much to learn about the subtleties of stratagem is reinforced by the abject failure of their military advisory mission in any way to prepare their Egyptian clients to anticipate much less even understand the stratagems played upon them by Israel in 1956, 1967, and 1973. Even their successful surprise-through-deception in Czechoslovakia in 1968 proves only that they can do an adequate job of strategic deception when strongly favored by circumstances.[59] A recent article by the commander of the Leningrad Military District does show, however, that Soviet military doctrine has finally begun to understand that technological advances open up new opportunities for surprise and, by implication, deception.[60]

CONCLUSIONS

The differences in styles of deception between nations are more an accident of timing than of differences in so-called national character. There are usually very real differences in the relative use of fraud (and of force) between different nations and, indeed, whole cultural areas *at any given time.*[61] In other words, each separate culture seems capable of generating various levels of guilefulness (and forcefulness) at different periods in its history. These fluctuations are a consequence of a complex variety and ever-changing mix of internal and international constraints or limitations.

The only nearly total exception is the roughly half-century period before World War I when the then current West European nonstratagemic military doctrine diffused to *all* national armies.

NOTES

1. An extended discussion covering eight cultures over the past twenty-eight centuries and incorporating political as well as diplomatic and military deception appears in my forthcoming *On the Prevalence of Guile.*

2. See Robert Jervis, "Hypotheses on Misperception," *World Politics* 20 (1967– 1968):454–479.

3. See my *Stratagem: Deception and Surprise in Modern Warfare* (Syracuse: Syracuse University Press, 1975). See also my *Research Guide to Propaganda, Psychological Warfare, and Deception* (Detroit: Gale Research Corp., 1976).

4. A convenient survey of power concepts is F[rederick] W. F[rey], "Political Power," *Encyclopaedia Britannica,* 15th ed. (1974), *Macropaedia,* chap. 14, pp. 697–702.

5. Hans J. Morgenthau, *Politics among Nations,* 4th ed. (New York: Knopf, 1967), pp. 26–27.

6. See especially John Hunter Boyle, *China and Japan at War, 1937–1945: The Politics of Collaboration* (Stanford: Stanford University Press, 1972).

7. Thomas C. Schelling, *Arms and Influence* (New Haven: Yale University Press, 1966), chap. 1 ("The Diplomacy of Violence"), pp. 1–34.

8. Paul Kecskemeti, *Strategic Surrender: The Politics of Victory and Defeat* (Stanford: Stanford University Press, 1958), pp. 1–27.

9. See the pioneering Ph.D. dissertation done at Harvard by A. George Gitter, "Hypocrisy as a Way of Life," 2 vols., multilithed (1963). A useful but moralistic general study is Carl J. Friedrich, *The Pathology of Politics: Violence, Betrayal, Corruption, Secrecy, and Propaganda* (New York: Harper & Row, 1972). A popular history of political chicanery in America is Bruce L. Felknor, *Dirty Politics* (New York: Norton, 1966).

10. Edward Luttwak, *Coup d'Etat* (London: Lane, 1968), and statistics based on my secondary analysis of Luttwak's somewhat recalcitrant data in Tables 2 and 3, pp. 184–188.

11. Karl Wittfogel and Fêng Chia-shêng, *History of Chinese Society: Liao (907- 1125)* (New York: Macmillan, 1949), pp. 400–404.

12. Murray Clark Havens, Carl Leiden, and Karl M. Schmitt, *The Politics of Assassination* (Englewood Cliffs, N.J.: Prentice-Hall, 1970), Appendix A.

13. B. H. Liddell Hart, *Strategy: The Indirect Approach* (London: Faber and Faber, 1954), pp. 161–162.

14. Harry Holbert Turney-High, *Primitive War: Its Practice and Concepts* (Columbia: University of South Carolina Press, 1949), esp. pp. 107–122.

15. Whaley, *Stratagem,* pp. 122–126, plus six additions.

16. See especially J. B. Bury, *The Idea of Progress: An Inquiry into Its Origin and Growth* (London: Macmillan, 1920).

17. Garnet J. Wolseley, *The Soldier's Pocket-Book for Field Service* (London: Macmillan, 1869), section on "Intelligence."

18. Paul Varley, *Samurai* (London: Weidenfeld & Nicolson, 1970).

19. Samuel B. Griffith, trans., *Sun Tzu: The Art of War* (London: Oxford University Press, 1963), pp. 169–178, gives a useful preliminary survey of "Sun Tzu's Influence on Japanese Military Thought" but tends to mistake theory for practice.

20. By entirely overlooking these two new factors, Griffith, pp. 175–178, incorrectly sees the stratagemic influence of Sun Tzu continuing as the preeminent doctrine right down into World War II.

21. As Griffith, pp. 174–176, unconsciously shows.

22. Ernst L. Presseisen, *Before Aggression: Europeans Prepare the Japanese Army* (Tucson: University of Arizona Press, 1965). Presseisen makes the opposite omission from that of Griffith by totally overlooking Sun Tzu and giving only passing attention to traditional Japanese training and doctrine.

23. Presseisen, pp. 139–149.

24. Whaley, *Stratagem,* case 70.

25. Ibid., cases 99, 100, 105, 156.

26. Scott A. Boorman, "Deception in Chinese Strategy," in William W. Whitson, ed., *The Military and Political Power in China in the 1970s* (New York: Praeger, 1972), pp. 313–337. Another, general assessment is John King Fairbank, "Varieties of the Chinese Military Experience," in Frank A. Kierman, Jr., and John King Fairbank, eds., *Chinese Ways in Warfare* (Cambridge: Harvard University Press, 1974), pp. 1 et seq.

27. See my *On the Prevalence of Guile.*

28. See, for example, Joseph R. Levenson, *Confucian China and Its Modern Fate* (Berkeley: University of California Press, 1958).

29. Teng Ssu-yü, *New Light on the History of the Taiping Rebellion* (Cambridge: Harvard University Press, 1950), p. 65; Siang-tseh Chiang, *The Nien Rebellion* (Seattle: University of Washington Press, 1954), pp. 71–74; S. Y. Teng, *The Nien Army and Their Guerrilla Warfare: 1851-1868* (The Hague: Mouton, 1960), chap. 6.

30. Mary Clabaugh Wright, ed., *China in Revolution: The First Phase,*

1900-1913 (New Haven: Yale University Press, 1968), pp. 27, 314–317, 370–375, 426; Ralph L. Powell, *The Rise of Chinese Military Power, 1895–1912* (Princeton: Princeton University Press, 1955); and F. F. Liu, *A Military History of Modern China, 1924-1949* (Princeton: Princeton University Press, 1956).

31. William W. Whitson, *The Chinese High Command: A History of Communist Chinese Military Politics, 1927-71* (New York: Praeger, 1973), pp. 7–23, 472–479.

32. See Robert Ruhlmann, "Traditional Heroes in Chinese Popular Fiction," in Arthur F. Wright, ed., *The Confucian Persuasion* (Stanford: Stanford University Press, 1960), pp. 141–176.

33. Griffith, pp. 44–56; and Whitson, pp. 8, 18–22. Mao's main discussions of deception and surprise appear in his booklets *On the Protracted War* (1938), para. 83; and, to a lesser extent, *Strategic Problems of China's Revolutionary War* (1936).

34. Whitson, pp. 470–472.

35. Ferdinand Tuohy, *The Secret Corps* (London: Murray, 1920), pp. 213–215.

36. Jay Luvaas, *The Education of an Army: British Military Thought 1815–1940* (Chicago: University of Chicago Press, 1964), pp. 376–424; and Robin Higham, *The Military Intellectuals in Britain, 1918-1939* (New Brunswick: Rutgers University Press, 1966), pp. 46–49, 82–116.

37. B. H. Liddell Hart, *The Decisive Wars of History: A Study in Strategy* (London: Bell, 1929), p. 143.

38. Ibid., p. 146.

39. Winston S. Churchill, *The World Crisis, 1915* (London: Butterworth, 1923), pp. 49–50.

40. Sir Ronald Wingate, *Not in the Limelight* (London: Hutchinson, 1959), pp. 189–204; J. C. Masterman, *The Double-Cross System* (New Haven: Yale University Press, 1972); and Sefton Delmer, *The Counterfeit Spy* (New York: Harper & Row, 1971).

41. Burke Wilkinson, *By Sea and by Stealth* (New York: Coward-McCann, 1956), p. 204.

42. Wilkinson, pp. 205–212,

43. Charles Shelton Curtiss, *The Russian Army under Nicholas I, 1825–1855* (Durham: Duke University Press, 1965), pp. 96–151; and Peter von Wahlde, "A Pioneer of Russian Strategic Thought: G. A. Leer, 1829–1904," *Military Affairs* 35 (1971):148–153.

44. For a detailed history of Soviet military deception, see Whaley, *Stratagem,* esp. pp. 62–76.

45. Some one hundred examples of Russian views on deceptiveness are collected and rather inductively analyzed in Nathan Leites, *A Study of Bolshevism* (Glencoe, Ill.: The Free Press, 1953), chap. 13, pp. 324–340.

46. Raymond L. Garthoff, *Soviet Military Doctrines* (Glencoe, Ill.: The Free Press, 1953), pp. 34, 265–275.

47. Barton Whaley, *Codeword BARBAROSSA* (Cambridge, Mass.: The M.I.T. Press, 1973).

48. H. S. Dinerstein, *War and the Soviet Union* (New York: Praeger, 1959), pp. 6–9; and Garthoff, p. 34.

49. As unwittingly revealed by "Sovetskie organy gosudarstvennoi bezopasnosti v godu velikoi otechestvennoi voiny" (Soviet state security organ in the years of the Great Patriotic War), *Voprosy Istorii* 5 (May 1965):20–39, 219–220.

50. John R. Deane, *The Strange Alliance* (New York: Viking, 1947), pp. 146–151, giving the only (inadvertently) unclassified account of Bevan's mission to Moscow.

51. A. Shimansky, "O dostizhenii strategicheskoi vnezapnosti pri podgotovke letne-osennei kampanii 1944 goda" (About the achievement of strategic surprise in the preparation for the summer-fall campaign of 1944), *Voenno-Istoricheskiy Zhurnal* 6 (1968):17–28.

52. N. Gordeyev, "Operational Camouflage in Naval Landing Operations" (original in Russian), *Voenno-Istoricheskiy Zhurnal* (April 1969): 41–51.

53. N. Talensky, "On the Question of the Character of the Laws of Military Science" (original in Russian), *Voennaya Mysl* 9 (September 1953), as described in Dinerstein, pp. 9, 36–47, 168.

54. Dinerstein, pp. 49–51, 180–212.

55. P. Rotmistrov, "On the Role of Surprise in Contemporary War" (original in Russian), *Voennaya Mysl* 2 (February 1955), as described in Dinerstein, pp. 181, 184–188.

56. For a detailed critique of this common myth, see Whaley, *Stratagem,* pp. 194–200.

57. John A. Armstrong, *Soviet Partisans in World War II* (Madison: University of Wisconsin Press, 1964), pp. 39–42, 48–49.

58. Ladislav Bittman, *The Deception Game: Czechoslovak Intelligence in Soviet Political Warfare* (Syracuse: Syracuse University Research Corp., 1972). See also John Barron, *KGB: The Secret Work of Soviet Secret Agents* (New York: Reader's Digest Press, 1974), pp. 164–186.

59. S. W. Barton [pseud. of Barton Whaley] and Lawrence M. Martin, "Public Diplomacy and the Soviet Invasion of Czechoslovakia in 1969," in G. Henderson, ed., *Public Diplomacy and Political Change* (New York: Praeger, 1973), pp. 241–314.

60. A. Gribnov, "Surprise in Combat" (original in Russian), *Krasnaya Zvezda* 11 (January 1974):2.

61. The empirical evidence is summarized in Charts A and B and Table 10 in my *On the Prevalence of Guile.*

MOBILIZATION FOR GLOBAL
DEVELOPMENT AND SECURITY

13

THE REVOLUTIONARY ELITES
AND WORLD SYMBOLISM

DANIEL LERNER

This volume on the emergence of public opinion has stressed the "enlarging symbolic" of the modern West. The symbolic expansion of "reality" is the tie that binds the Renaissance, the Reformation, and the Enlightenment into the historical sequence of rising identifications, expectations, and demands. This enlargement of Western man's psychic domain in turn nurtured the revolutionary processes that, stimulated by the French and American Revolutions, continued through the nineteenth century into our own times. Until the end of World War I, which was justified in terms of making the world safe for democracy, the movement of history seemed to be unidirectional: moving constantly toward the goals of *liberté, égalité, fraternité* by enhancing life, liberty, and the pursuit of happiness.

The Great War shattered this Western dream of social progress and human perfectibility. High expectations produced deep frustrations; optimism curdled into cynicism. A transformation of morals and mores accompanied the evaporation of institutions and ideologies on which the European tradition had been built.[1] Gone in a twinkling were the great dynasties of the Old Continent: Hapsburg and Hohenzollern, Ottoman and Romanov, followed shortly by the House of Savoy. In their wake came the foundering of the great empires based on these dynasties.[2] The New World was not far behind.[3] Indeed, in terms of stateways and folkways, it was far ahead as witnessed by the rapid interwar "Americanization of Europe."[4] The rest of the earth's surface—what we nowadays call the "third world" —was, in historical perspective, set afloat.[5]

The aftermath of World War I was a quarter century of unprecedented turbulence—the "crisis politics" designated in the title of the previous part of this volume. As the traditional structures of European political life crumbled, new forces took shape in contending for the seats of power. The epochal event was the Bolshevik Revolution of 1918, which seemed for a time to be the sole claimant to world dominion under a new dispensation. Its claim was soon disputed throughout Europe by rival "totalitarians," coercive ideologues who adapted its techniques of coercion but restyled its ideology of world communism into variant forms of national socialism. Fascism in Italy, Nazism in Germany, Falangism in Spain—these were the counterblows to Bolshevik claims upon world attention and obeisance. Everywhere in the West, and beyond, the crisis politics of the interbellum decades framed itself as a struggle for supremacy between "communism and fascism."[6]

The "collision course" set by these new claimants to power —and the challenges they posed to the more stable democratic regimes of the West, by both internal subversion and external threat—eventuated in World War II. More global and more "total" than War I, War II completed several processes activated in 1914–1918 and initiated several new processes that have shaped crisis politics since 1945. Chief among these have been: (1) the displacement of Europe as the world power center;[7] (2) the bipolarization of the world arena between two "superpowers";[8] (3) the nuclear instrumentation of bipolar conflict;[9] (4) the efforts to delineate a "third world";[10] and (5) the quest for a viable world order.[11]

These processes are dealt with more fully in the three chapters and the colloquy that follow. Our task here is to trace the historical sequence from World War I through World War II in ways that will clarify the "continuing spread of crisis politics" with special reference to its impact upon "symbol management." Our purpose is to discern the symbolic components of contemporary world history, to construe political processes as communication processes. In this sense, the fall of the great European dynasties was a historic transformation of political institutions expressed in the symbols of majesty. The "crowned heads of Europe" who symbolized political authority have all but vanished from the world scene; the few crowns that remain, from Britain to Japan, are tokens of tradition rather than symbols of power. The crumbled empires over which they once reigned have emerged in the world arena as "new nations." The symbolism of Nation, for good and ill, has taken primacy in the language of power.[12]

SYMBOL TRANSFORMATIONS

This transformation of vocabulary—from crown to nation—has transformed political action as well as political discourse. The two nations that possess nuclear arsenals become "superpowers" and the other nations of the world are "bipolarized" between their respective camps. Even those nations that wish to challenge or evade bipolarity feel obliged to speak and act in terms of a "third" world—whether it be as a *troisième force* in developed Europe or as a "nonaligned" presence in underdeveloped Afro-Asia. The very organization created to lead the quest for a transnational world order is named United *Nations*.

The symbolism of nation has been liberating to those former colonies of the European dynasties for whom it represented political independence in a world of "equals." But de jure equivalence of title does not guarantee de facto equality of power. Witness the efforts to find a working title for those poor new nations, comprising most of the world's area and population, that would be descriptive without seeming pejorative—that would represent their actual condition without belittling their aspiration. In rapid succession their appellation changed from "underdeveloped" to "less developed" to "developing." Although some economists still refer to them as "LDCs," in the vain hope that the initials obviate the words for which they stand (Less Developed Countries), others more sensitive to symbolism have floated such trial balloons as "the reviving civilizations." Many have abandoned the semantic struggle and nowadays refer to them simply as "new nations" or "poor countries."

Along with the symbolism of Nation, primacy in world communication has been given to the symbolism of Class. But the sense of this key symbol has been transmuted from its usage in the Marxist lexicon, which dominated political discourse among intellectuals (that is, symbol managers) over the past century. No longer does it mean "class conflict" that pits Class *against* Nation (and against the State conceived as "the agency of the ruling class"). Rather, through the melding of Nation and Class—de facto under Stalin as world communism became "socialism in one state" (and the USSR became the "workers' fatherland"), in "theory" as Mussolini's Fascism and Hitler's Nazism diffused the idea of "national socialism"—there has emerged a version of socialism that incorporates nationalism and builds upon it.

This tendency has been evident in post–World War II Europe, where one socialist party after another has disavowed Marxism in Britain, France, Germany. The "Socialist Internationals" (all four of them) are defunct. European socialists now speak in terms of a "mixed economy"—in which the old ideal of public ownership is replaced by a productivity-oriented mixture of private and public sectors—that operates on a strictly national basis. The resonant slogan of *The Communist Manifesto,* "Workers of the world, unite!" has been stilled. The non-Marxist "scientific socialism" of the Western world today considers it more important that the input to output components of the mixed economy should sustain rising coefficients of GNP.

A parallel tendency has marked the evolving symbolism of the "communist" world in the post–World War II period. There, where consumers still have a much longer road to equity than in the capitalist West, concern for productivity (output per head) is much more intense than concern for distribution (income per head). This has led to the theory of "convergence," which alleges that highly industrialized nations tend to face the same problems and converge on the same solutions. Without entering into the highly ambiguous and often polemical terms of the convergence controversy, we note here that "demystification" of economic life (which often means reformulating policy issues in technical terms) has deprived political discourse of some key symbols and—in communist as well as capitalist countries—has given a historic new turn to the problems and practices of symbol management.

The merging of Nation and Class into an ideology of national socialism, buttressed by an ethic of Growth or Development (GNP-oriented social change), has produced some conspicuous effects in the symbolic life of the new nations. In the past Marxist century, when the poor took over the assets of the rich (whether of their own or other nations), the cry rang out: "Expropriate the expropriators!" At the present time, when the British and French are relieved of their assets in the Suez Canal, the process is called "Egyptianization." This version of national socialism appears to be beyond dispute, even beyond question —at least to the symbol managers of the new nations. This righteous sense of recovering what is only one's due is strengthened when the expropriated cannot even fight back as the British and French vainly did at Suez. Examples of such expropriation—from the Portuguese at Goa to the Indians in East Africa —have multiplied over the past decade.

The version of national socialism now diffused by symbol managers in the new nations is a variant of historical populism. This has deep roots in the major religions of the world and a strong base in the value goals (*liberté, égalité, fraternité* et seq.) evolved during the modernization of the West. It is a tradition that bespeaks the shaping and sharing of all values—power, wealth, enlightenment, and so on—among all mankind by reason only of their humanity. Occasionally, the universality of these value goals has been proclaimed to the world at large, as in the Declaration of the Rights of Man and in the Nuremberg Trials' conception of "crimes against humanity." More often, the populist spirit has been parochialized—as in the modernizing nations of Western history and the emergent new nations today—to focus upon that segment of humanity living within the boundaries of a single political jurisdiction, that is, a nation.

The spread of populism in the historical West as in the contemporary new nations coincided with the rise of public opinion and the growth of communication networks. In the interbellum years of crisis politics that are our primary concern here, populism construed as national socialism took a dramatic turn in the direction of ethnocentrism and even xenophobia. The most strident voice was Hitler's and the most unabashed ideology was Nazism (itself a German acronym for national socialism). Under the key slogan of "Ein Reich, ein Volk" (one state, one people) Nazism unified disparate regions and religions under a regime centralized beyond Bismarck's ambitions.

The word *Volk* (the people) was central to Nazi propaganda, which declared Germans to be a *Herrenvolk* (master race). The Third Reich conferred this honored status upon selected neighbors by *Gleichschaltung* (assimilation). Those who were annexed, like the Austrians, became *Reichsdeutsch*. Those who were merely overrun, from Sudetenland to the Volga, received the less exalted but still honorific title of *Volksdeutsch*— allegedly clamoring to come "home" *(Heim ins Reich)*. The populist label became the emblem of shared values: the new mass-produced automobile was named *Volkswagen;* the cops on the beat were *Volkspolizei;* the last-ditch resistance to Allied victory was baptized *Volkssturm*. This transformation of symbols has aptly been labeled *"Nazideutsch."*[13] Echoes resound today in such slogans as "Egyptianization."

But the diffusion of populism required more than a new set of key symbols. Our paradigm of any communication process requires attention to a set of variables that includes source, content, audience, channel, effect: "Who says what to whom, through what channel, with what effects?" The foregoing review of transformed key symbols has sketched the changing *contents* of communication in the contemporary context of crisis politics. Let us turn next to the *channels,* with special attention to the technology that transformed Western communication so dramatically and continues to operate throughout the world today.

CHANNEL TRANSFORMATION

The modern world has witnessed five major "communication revolutions" based on technology, all of which were initiated or incorporated primarily in the West. Each of these revolutions grew out of a technological invention and stimulated a profound transformation of sociopolitical behavior and institutions. We shall deal later with the sociopolitical consequences. Here we briefly review the technological components and consequences of the five revolutions: print, film, radio, television, and satellites.

The print "revolution" in the West was a long, slow process.

It dates conventionally from Gutenberg's invention of movable type in the mid-fifteenth century. It is useful to recall that print antedated by a half-century another important process in modern Western history—the development of maritime exploration, which initiated European colonization of the globe, conventionally dated from Columbus's landing in the New World in 1492. Maritime technology produced more rapid and spectacular results, largely because of its beneficent effects upon royal coffers and national treasuries, but the question merits empirical inquiry whether the technology of print has not produced deeper and more lasting consequences for world society. The spread of print via national languages undermined the Holy Roman Empire and the Universal Church on which it was based, broke the monopoly of enlightenment by the tiny elite who communicated exclusively in medieval Latin, and instrumented the reshaping of Western history by the Reformation and its aftermath.

Though the effects of print were genuinely revolutionary in this sense, it is important to note that its emergence as a social institution did not occur until four hundred years after the technology was invented. The "penny press"—the first of the "mass media"—became a social force only in the nineteenth century. The impact of print in Britain, which led the way, was noted by Samuel Johnson: "Every Englishman, nowadays, expects to be promptly and accurately informed upon the condition of public affairs." The continental nations of Europe did not lag far behind the British in creating a press and a public opinion. The work of Tocqueville bears eloquent witness to the diffusion of information and opinion under the ancien régime and in the New World. The French and American revolutions, as the eighteenth century moved toward its turbulent end, provide the testimony of events to its revolutionary consequences.

But the question arises why the Western nations took about four hundred years to incorporate the relatively simple technology of print into their social institutions. The post–World War II nations-in-a-hurry may well ask: What were the Europeans doing all this time? It is with no lack of respect to the complex interplay of events (what Lasswell's conclusion to these volumes calls the "zig-zag course" of historical experience) that we offer a simple answer to this hard question. Our own forays into the works of more learned historians indicate that it took the Europeans four centuries to build a penny press because the viability of this institution required a sufficiently large class of people who: (1) knew how to read their national language; (2) had an extra penny to spend; (3) were motivated to spend this penny on news and views rather than cakes and ale. The creation of this literate class with disposable income and a sense of participation in public affairs was a momentous achievement—perhaps the most distinctive achievement of modern Western society. Small wonder that it took four hundred years!

Once the print revolution was achieved, however, the acceleration of history that beguiled European scholars of the nineteenth century was under way. Once the technology of print production became operative it functioned as a "breeder reactor" for subsequent invention of new communication technologies. Once the sociology of print consumption was established it provided the base for innovation and transformation of communication institutions. The next four communication revolutions occurred at a rapid, indeed accelerating, tempo. It was in the course of these transformations that the West, educated via print technology and expanded via maritime technology, established its primacy over the rest of the world.

The second communication revolution, for example, was visual. Based on the new technology of the camera and film, it enabled Western men to reproduce the sights of their world mechanically and massively. For the first time in human history, people could build visual archives of their past, representations of their present, and projections of their possible futures. These visual records of human experience became "available" to most people, including those who could not read print. It brought a large new segment of the illiterate periphery of public affairs into a participant relationship with *la chose publique*. Yet this great historical transformation is only a century old. Most Americans date it from Matthew Brady's celebrated photographs of the Civil War, which first enabled them to "see" what was happening on distant battlefields and "share" the experience of strange persons in remote places. Visual communication became, in this sense, the great historical teacher of empathy and the multiplier of mobility—especially of what we have called "psychic mobility."[14]

The third communication revolution is only a half-century old, that is, it occurred within the lifetime of most of the contributors of this book. This was the audial transformation of communication, based on the technology of sound transmission and the vacuum tube, which was accelerated during World War I. It was institutionalized in Western lifeways as "the radio" only during the 1920s. This brought the sound as well as the sight of human experience, however strange and remote, within the sensory range of living men. This was followed rapidly by the integration of sound and sight in cinema—first "the movies," then "the talkies." It seemed as if these new wonders of communication would never cease, as Aldous Huxley in *Brave New World* projected "the feelies." Indeed, the impact of cinema upon the human psyche (for the first time exposed to the "naturalistic" representation of human beings in action and interaction) was so great as to merit separate status in the succession of communication revolutions.

Let us reserve this fourth place, however, for television. Utilizing the new technology of the picture tube, with a strong recent assist from transistors, television brought cinema's "naturalistic" representation of reality into the homes of people and thereby into their daily lives. No communication medium of the past has operated so continuously, and so profoundly, in the transformation of lifeways among so many hundreds of millions of contemporaneous people. Nor had any of the earlier mass media worked its transformation of human lifeways so rapidly. Television as we know it today is less than a quarter century old —which means that its entire history has been incorporated in the biography of most people now living. So recent is television that, despite valiant efforts by communication researchers in many countries, we have only rudimentary knowledge of its effects upon those it reaches.

This is true a fortiori of the fifth communication revolution —that of communication satellites—which is less than a decade old. What satellites have done, by adapting the extant technology of the mass media to the new technology of space, is to create the first *operational* "world communication network" in human history. This phrase has been used for years and in fact the earlier media of print, sight, and sound did operate, in some respects, on a transnational basis. But not until the IN-

TELSAT system positioned satellites over the Atlantic, Pacific, and Indian Oceans 22,300 miles above the equator did there ever exist a technological capability for instantaneous, simultaneous, and continuous transmissions of messages to every part of planet Earth.

We have briefly reviewed the communication revolutions that, with increasing celerity, brought the world communication network to its current condition. It may make the acceleration of history more vivid if we represent the transformation of communication channels schematically as follows:

Communication channel	Approximate age in 1975
Print	500 years
Film	100 years
Radio	50 years
Television	20 years
Satellite	10 years

Clearly, technology has not yet run its course and wonders did not cease in 1975. Such spin-offs from extant technology information processing continue to multiply communication channels at an exponential rate. Even if there should be a deceleration of "revolutionary" innovation in communication technology over the decades ahead, it is reasonable to expect that channels will continue to increase at a high rate.

It is therefore reasonable to foresee that mankind will have to deal seriously with communication effects that contemporary Cassandras now merely decry as "media saturation" and "information overload." It may be useful, as we face the great efforts of inquiry that will be needed, to review some communication effects upon human lifeways in the past and present.

AUDIENCE TRANSFORMATIONS

To speak of audience transformations is to focus attention upon those changes in human lifeways effected by communication, changes worked in people by reason of their exposure to "mediated" ideas and information, news and views. The role of audience in the "mass media" drama is neither passive spectator nor active player, but an integration of both in the mode of participant-observers sharing a vicarious experience with others who enact the drama. This is the passive-active mode we have called "psychic mobility" and its mechanism is empathy: the ability to see *oneself* in the other fellow's shoes, to imagine *oneself* in new and strange situations other than one's "real-life" situation. It is the creative world of poetry characterized by Marianne Moore as "imaginary gardens with real toads in them"; it is what media analysts, in the apt phrase of Herta Hertzog, have called "the world of the daytime serial."

Empathy is activated by the dimension of personality labeled *identity,* the sense of oneself in relation to others who may be "incorporated" (or rejected). Identification is thus a highly personal process, which every individual operates by himself and for himself. As such, identification is as old as human experience of the external world. What modern communication has done is to present individuals with a population of relevant "others" much larger than any person could experience directly in his real life—a plenitude (often, as the king of Siam told Anna, a "puzzlement") of roles with which he can identify and incorporate. The "mass media" distinctively, as their name suggests, have made this great gallery of alternative "roles" available to masses of individuals at the same time. What occurred in the transformation of Western personality and conceptions of personality has been delineated in Lancelot Whyte's study of the unconscious before Freud:

> The general conception of unconscious mental processes, in a different context, is implicit in many ancient traditions. The development of the idea in Europe—prior to the relatively precise theories of our time—occupied some two centuries, say 1680–1880, and was the work of many countries and schools of thought. The idea was forced on them as a response to facts; it was necessary to correct an overemphasis, c. 1600–1700, on the consciousness of the individual.[15]

The central point is that these new perspectives on human personality were working through "many countries and schools of thought" upon many millions of people. This is what makes it necessary, in dealing historically with audience transformations, to deal "aggregatively" with so individual a process as empathy. The changes of personal life-style induced by the mass media have, historically and sociologically, been effected in many individuals living in the same place at the same time. It is the vicarious sharing of private experiences via mediated communication that provides the data base of modern social psychology and cultural anthropology. It is this data base in turn that enables modern scholars, without necessarily endorsing old legends or creating new stereotypes, to deal with typologies such as national character, culture traits, or even the systematic differentiation between "traditional" and "modern" lifestyles that transcend particular time-place constraints.

Moreover, psychosocial processes lead to sociopolitical consequences. Changing identifications lead to changing expectations and demands. And, as Lasswell taught us long ago, expectations and demands are the stuff of which political tapestries are woven and unraveled. In this process the identities implanted by communication media in their audiences bear the fruit of demands upon the polity by their citizens. It is what Gabriel Almond admonished political scientists to study under the headings of "interest-articulation" and "interest-aggregation." In the homelier vocabulary of David Riesman, it is the historical sequence whereby the newspaper reader became the cash customer and the opinion giver and the sovereign voter.

In the transition of Riesman's "modal personality" from tradition-direction to other-direction—and we here extend his synopsis of the American historical experience to include the modern Western world—audience transformation in our sense was a prime mover. The identifications, expectations, and demands of Western men were vastly enlarged over the past five centuries by print; the process thus initiated was accelerated, over the past century, by film and radio. Enlargement of the psychic world was accompanied (or followed upon effective demand) by real-life expansion of: (1) *mobility*—physical, social, psychic; (2) *participation*—economic, cultural, political; (3) *decision making*—information, opinion, choice. Vicarious private experience increasingly influenced the domain of public policy.

Where the public domain yielded too little too late—where popular expectations were frustrated or popular demands were ignored—"revolutionary conditions" in the Leninist sense were created and crisis politics was instigated. These were the wellsprings of Bolshevik revolution in czarist Russia, of Fascist insurrection in royalist Italy, even of Nazi takeover in republican

Germany—with the global resonance that perpetuated politics as a mode of public attitude and action. This was the sort of populism that mobilized much of social change, often violent and disruptive, in the modernizing West. It has since spread into the new nations of the developing world.

For the new nations, in the brief quarter century of their independent national life, have faced drastically altered conditions of tempo and balance. The Western quest for dynamic equilibrium in its own modernization stretched, in what now seems a leisurely fashion, over five hundred years. Even so, popular Western demands for dynamism often subverted the need for equilibrium, as testified by the record of recurrent riots, rebellions, revolutions—to say nothing of its massively organized internal and external wars. The post–World War II nations-in-a-hurry have been involved in modernization for only twenty-five years or so. Small wonder, then, that their problems of tempo and balance have been extreme, that dynamic equilibrium has not been achieved, that disruptive disequilibria have been recurrent or chronic. The new nations have not been able to "catch up" with the modernized West. More important still, they have not been able to "keep up" with the rising tide of identification, expectation, and demand among their own peoples.

Development efforts in the "third world" started out, a quarter century ago, with great expectations of the future. The catchphrase was the "revolution of rising expectations," and this was generally thought to be a Good Thing. Observers mindful of the benefits that rising expectations had brought to the Western nations over the centuries—better health, longer life, greater prosperity, broader enlightenment, shared freedoms—assumed that this beneficent sequence would recur in the Third World, possibly even (profiting from the Western experience) at lower cost in human suffering. Their optimism was shared by the peoples of the new nations. Riding the crest of the wartime wave of independence movements, they formed the expectation that nationhood would obliterate their dark past and ensure their bright future. As independent and sovereign nations, they would expropriate the expropriators and enjoy the fruits of their own soil and toil.

Leaders of the independence movements encouraged these

great expectations. As they took over the reins of power in their new nations, charismatic leaders like Nasser, Nkrumah, Sukarno called in the mass media to help them spread the good news. They were restricted mainly to radio as the extension of their voices, for print was "unavailable" to their illiterate peoples and film (such as it was) was mainly produced on a commercial basis in the private sector of foreign countries. But they made a virtue of necessity and invested heavily in developing radio networks under government management. Nasser's Egypt, for example, allocated a huge fraction of its scarce resources to the expansion of Egyptian State Broadcasting, the diffusion of "Voice of the Arabs" among its neighbors, and the distribution of cheap or free community receivers among the fellaheen at home. This policy seemed to contain within itself a self-fulfilling prophecy. As Nasser put it:

> It is true that most of our people are still illiterate. But politically that counts far less than it did twenty years ago. . . . Radio has changed everything. . . . Today people in the most remote villages hear of what is happening everywhere and form their opinions. Leaders cannot govern as they once did. We live in a new world.[16]

The great expectations that pervaded the new world by radio waves turned out, however, to be abortive. Within a decade of their independence, the new nations learned about what Lucian Pye has called "the uncertain magic of charisma" and about the dysphoria that often follows "the euphoria of revolution."[17] If the new optimism did not die a-borning, its growth was certainly stunted as soon as the new nations faced the problems laid upon them by independence.[18]

From the abortive revolution of rising expectations has grown the ominous "revolution of rising frustrations," which has spread crisis politics throughout the Third World and contains a latent threat to the stability of world public order as we have known it. The psychosocial sources and sociopolitical consequences of rising frustrations have been described elsewhere in substantial detail.[19] It derives from the postulate established by psychologists that great expectations long unfulfilled lead to great frustrations. Frustration has only two issues: regression or aggression. Regression occurs, for example, when a new literate finds no use for his acquired skill and "forgets" how to read (that is, regresses to his former state of illiteracy). Aggression occurs when a person who fails to attain his desires displaces his frustration onto an alternate object or objective (that is, seeks a substitute gratification for his expectations). In the developing world, aggression usually is expressed by the displacement of economic desires into political demands, usually with dire consequences for the developing polity.

Neither regression nor aggression typically produces constructive outcomes for development. Frustration is, in this sense, counterproductive in the development process. Rising frustrations are, a fortiori, an increasing threat to the dynamic equilibrium that is the optimal condition for rapid development. It therefore poses a grave set of problems for the Third World in the remaining decades of this century, and possibly for decades beyond. As the spread of frustration was largely the doing of mass communication, which diffused rising expectations and demands more rapidly and widely than the real world of the new nations could satisfy, so the reduction of frustration and the attainment of dynamic equilibrium in the future is, in large measure, a responsibility of symbol management. To this we now turn.

MANAGEMENT TRANSFORMATIONS

Symbol management is a function of political management. We do not blandly swallow the bromide that the pen is mightier than the sword. What is certain is that the pen can be a mighty ally of the sword, a bit of philosophic wisdom that dates at least from Plato's anointment of philosopher-kings in *The Republic*. What is desirable, in the pluralist context of democratic values, is that the pen should be used so effectively as to reduce or obviate the need for the sword. Where the Word is the Way, over a long run of historical time, the cause of human dignity usually is enhanced.

This is not invariably the case. Indeed, it is rarely the case where long-term projections of human values seek short-run benefits for those who speak the words and bear the swords. The preceding chapters on millenarianism by Guenter Lewy and on communist propaganda by William Griffith show this plainly. So does the abortive history of Hitler's *tausendjährige Reich*, which came to its desperate end in a dozen years. Crisis politics does not lend itself readily to the long-run evolution of pluralist values and political symbols via a propaganda Strategy of Truth, upon which the stable consensus needed for a democratic polity must rely.

For words and the ways they bespeak are not easily sundered —or, in any case, not for long. There is abiding democratic wisdom in Abraham Lincoln's homely aphorism: "You can't fool all of the people all of the time." What is said, and believed, becomes integral to what is done. This is more than a matter of personal honesty. Truth, in the life of any social order, is a matter of strategy as well. If its counsel is to tell no lies that can be found out, the corollary is that in the long run every lie can be found out. The Strategy of Truth relies not only on the slender reed of individual virtue but also on the tougher stuff of collective living, of which communication is the warp and woof.[20]

This perspective has been articulated and elaborated since the enlarging symbolic of the modern West taught men of the sword to watch their words in public. It made the interaction between men of power and men of knowledge more continuous and intimate. Indeed, it made feasible the emergence of symbol managers as a distinctive subset of the intelligentsia concerned with political management. The Renaissance prince was not typically a philosopher-king, but he was well advised in the minimum requirements of a Strategy of Truth by Nicolo Machiavelli. In *The Prince* and in *The Discourses,* and perhaps most vividly in *The History of Florence,* Machiavelli never tired of defining and illustrating the limits of mendacity for men of great power.

The lessons of Machiavelli were incorporated in the political and propaganda styles of later centuries. Thanks to the perceptive historical eye of Hans Speier, we are able to trace the lineage of Machiavelli directly to the crisis politics of our own time via the person of Maurice Joly, author of the extraordinary *Dialogue in Hell Between Machiavelli and Montesquieu.*[21] Joly not only foresaw the potential for media management under a modern totalitarian regime, but became the unwitting source of the greatest hoax in the history of modern political propaganda —the alleged *Protocols of the Elders of Zion.* This hoax became the "basis" of Nazi anti-Semitism and, by extension to all lesser breeds, of Nazi racist policy and propaganda practice.

Thanks again to Speier, we have been shown the operation of the Strategy of Truth at a particularly poignant moment in Western modernization. When Jacques Necker was called in as finance minister by the ancien régime to bolster the royal treasury, he proposed to do so by publishing the national budget, thus sharing with French taxpayers information about the amounts of money needed and the purposes it would serve. The perspicacious Count Vergennes, in a confidential memorandum, advised the king against Necker's propaganda strategy on the ground that it would lead those who now obey to command and those who now command to obey.[22] To share royal information, in Vergennes's view, was a first step to sharing royal power. Although Vergennes may himself have derived a faulty inference from it, his basic insight was historically sound.

It was the insight that shaped the Strategy of Truth in allied propaganda against Nazi Germany in World War II. A basic tenet was that the strategic objectives of allied policy be truthfully told even at the possible cost of failing to score "propaganda points" in various tactical situations. Thus, the war aim of unconditional surrender was publicized plainly among the German public, despite protests from some psychological warriors. As the touchstone of *credibility* became axiomatic in allied propaganda technique, some true stories were not told because they would not be believed. For example, photographs of German prisoners eating oranges in allied POW camps were eliminated from propaganda leaflets on the ground that disbelief among German soldiers (who had not seen an orange in years) would compromise the credibility of the leaflets as a whole. Indeed, in his postwar evaluation of the allied propaganda effort, one propaganda policy advisor concluded that even the disagreements and divergencies in allied communications received by the Germans contributed to the Strategy of Truth: "Our psychological warfare was credible because it was *not* uniform." Credibility, in the long run, was more valuable than the "dirty tricks" conjured up by "infantile Machiavellianism."[23]

By the end of World War II, Western symbol managers had learned many valuable lessons of crisis politics from the war and revolutions of their history. Indeed, it was the propaganda focus, as much as any other single element of that history, that shaped crisis politics in the contemporary world. Our studies of coercive ideological movements have demonstrated that world revolutionary elites have comprised symbol managers in their front ranks, at least in their initial eruptive phase. The propagandists of Communism, Fascism, Nazism—that segment of their elites specializing in the persuasive management of symbol transformations—prepared the way for their seizure of power and codification of ideology. "It was just this factor of ideology as a mode of social control, and specifically its coordination with systematic coercion, that produced the distinctive political methodology of the European totalitarians of the interwar period."[24]

The interwar lessons taught by the Western totalitarians were learned rapidly in the postwar Third World. The Chinese Communists surged to power by coordinating persuasion with coercion, and began to purge their symbol managers soon after power was theirs.[25] Elsewhere, in the new nations of Africa and Asia, a distinctive sequence evolved within a decade or so of their independence. These nations-in-a-hurry hitched their wagon to the charismatic stars—symbol-managers who swiftly adopted the available communication technology of the West in their propaganda campaign to create a "revolution of rising expectations." We have seen the high hopes, exemplified by Nasser's Egypt, that motivated and justified the heavy investment (psychopolitical as well as socioeconomic) in radio as the chosen instrument for symbolic transformation of traditional lifeways in the "new world."

We have seen as well that the charismatic conception of symbol management was faulty from the start. The sounds of laughter do not guarantee joy, nor do the sights of plenty provide better food, clothing, shelter. As rising expectations were increasingly transformed into rising frustrations, charismatic affect was alienated and the quest for dynamic equilibrium was disrupted. The symbol managers who, as in the revolutionary West of an earlier generation, were also the political managers became alarmed by their failures. They perceived that their "communication revolution" was not an adequate surrogate for popular hopes of social and economic transformation. Often they displaced frustration by projecting it onto the insidious influence of Western media in their own countries. An example was the heavy charge laid upon Hollywood by Sukarno, himself a charismatic symbol manager of great agility, that its moviemakers were unwitting revolutionaries because they taught his transformed audience in Indonesia to demand Good Things they could not have. Said Sukarno: "A refrigerator is a revolutionary symbol in a hot country like mine."[26]

Sukarno's charge against Hollywood can be extended to all Western media that have infiltrated the Third World with sights and sounds they never knew, with expectations that could not be fulfilled. To indict Western media, however, is not to exonerate indigenous symbol managers. The revolution of rising frustrations now under way in the new nations is largely home-grown, the product of charismatic leadership seeking political benefits without regard to human costs. They have injected transformed symbols via transformed channels and thereby transformed effects that must be expected when such "revolutionary conditions" are created. The charismatic leaders have harvested the bitter fruits of the wild seeds they planted.

In one new nation after another, the charismatic symbol managers have been displaced from the seats of power. From Nkrumah's Ghana in West Africa to Sukarno's Indonesia in Southeast Asia, the charismatics are out.

Throughout the Third World, the phenomenon of military takeover has recurred as shock treatment for the disequilibrium and disruption occasioned by the revolution of rising frustrations. Much of Africa, most of the Middle East, and virtually all of Asia are today under some form of military regime or martial law. Let us, in conclusion, consider the problems and prospects this raises for the world community.

PROBLEMS AND PROSPECTS

Crisis politics is still the way of the world today. Ours has been called "the age of anxiety." Such hyperbole, even by a reputable historian, may be justified by the elements of danger that daily confront the world's population. The technology of destruction has, for the first time in history, put in human hands the capability of damaging the planet beyond repair by nuclear holocaust. That this awesome military potential has thus far led to a nuclear stalemate between the superpowers is not reassuring to humanity, least of all to that portion of it which lives on either scale of the so-called balance of terror. The recurrent threats of "nuclear blackmail," at least since Suez, often have brought crisis to fever pitch over the past two decades. During the Cuban missile crisis of 1963, when the Kremlin and the White House appeared to balance the fate of the planet for several days, the world seemed to stand still.

Less agonizing, but certainly anxiety producing, is the impact of space exploration. Communication analysts who recall the panic created by Orson Welles's radio broadcast of a fictitious "invasion from Mars" in 1937, when the earth's "space barriers" had not yet been breached, will not be surprised at the fears engendered by human penetraton of heaven's eternal mysteries.[27] Such fears, whether fanciful or reasoned, are very real to those who suffer them. Like all fears, in every time and place, they provide a fertile field for political propagandists.[28]

The bipolar structure itself, in addition to the cataclysmic fears associated with nuclear and space technology, has been a source of chronic anxiety in the cold war—which has been a sustained exercise in symbol management to achieve conflicting political purposes. Berlin was for many years a key symbol, from the western Airlift to the communist Wall. The Middle East has become the current key symbol. The point is that any spot on earth, however remote, can be made into a key symbol by the rival symbol managers if policy makers choose to associate it with the bipolar conflict.

It is for these reasons that the post–World War I arena, which produced the great interbellum crises of "personal insecurity" associated with the ideological totalitarians, has been exacerbated into an age of anxiety in the post–World War II bipolar arena.[29] The historical threat of war is increased by several orders of magnitude when it involves a nuclear "balance of terror." The fear of economic and political upheaval on a global scale, already foreshadowed by the European aftermath of America's Great Depression of 1929, is magnified by the world communication network that exists today and will grow tomorrow.[30]

The propagandists of threat and fear have taken full advantage of world anxiety (while the communicators of enlightenment, as we shall see in a moment, have languished and lagged). For the afflictions of our contemporary world, the historian Barbara Tuchman tells us, we may go back to the Four Horsemen of the Apocalypse—famine, plague, war, and death—that terrified the fourteenth century. She continues: "The more important parallel lies in the decay of our governing institutions as the fourteenth-century public lost confidence in the Church."[31] A more recent historical illustration is the "Great Fear of 1789" in which it was demonstrated, as a cardinal point of communication and propaganda theory, that "in times of crisis what people believe is true is more crucial than what is true."[32]

In our anxiety-laden time all the elements of apocalyptic fear —war and death, even famine and pestilence—are still present. There is a deep heritage from the air warfare of World War II exemplified by the German *Wunderwaffen* (V-1 and V-2) over Britain; the Allied "strategic bombing" of German cities (which they called *Terrorangriffe* or terror attacks); the atomic destruction of Hiroshima and Nagasaki.[33] The antipersonnel and defoliation weaponry used in Vietnam, as well as the random violence used by Palestinian guerrillas in the Munich Oympics and Lod Airport and skyjacking murders, have kept "fear and trembling" current in our world. Nor, as military takeovers around the world and the Watergate drama in America have shown, do we lack those crises of confidence in our governing institutions of which Tuchman speaks.

While the propagandists of fear have distressed the world over these decades, the communicators of enlightenment have languished and lagged. Only in recent years has the development of communication theory and research begun to convey systematic insight into possible antidotes for Great Fears. A great step forward was taken by the research team gathered around Carl Hovland at Yale, when Irving Janis concluded from his experiments on fear-arousing appeals that the *optimal dosage* appears to be far below the level of the strongest fear appeals that a communicator could use if he chose to do so.[34] These studies have been extended to show, in language dear to behavioral scientists, "that there is a non-monotonic relationship between the intensity of the fear aroused in a message and its persuasive effectiveness"; on the contrary, an "inverted U-shaped relationship" may occur.[35] What this means is that threat propaganda seeking to arouse fears may go too far and in doing so may produce a boomerang effect upon its audience— one important version of a "credibility gap."

Applied researchers, seeking to put these basic findings to use for individual and societal behavior, have begun to create fear-reducing institutions. There is a network of Peace Research

Institutes throughout the nations of the Western world today. In the United States there is a *Journal of Conflict Resolution.* In Britain there is an Institute for the Study of Conflict, which publishes an *Annual of Power and Conflict.* A recent issue states: "Revolutionary violence continues to spread throughout the world. Its exponents operate under a bewildering variety of names. A reliable guide to their identity [is] badly needed.[36]

Such fear-reducing institutions must grow and, as the bipolar balance of terror is transformed into a more creative mode of dynamic equilibrium, they must become global. They must become sociopolitical and psychocultural as well as economic-military. Thus far, efforts in this direction have produced only feeble results. Polycentrism—whether identified as *troisième force* or *tiers monde,* whether activated as Maoism or Gaullism —has provided only tenuous alternatives to bipolarity. So, too, has the projection of a new universal symbolism embodied in the United Nations.

The failure to diffuse a persuasive universal symbolism in a political arena that has become technologically global contains ominous problems for the future of humanity. The gap between rich and poor nations is wide and, as a choir of economists with Gunnar Myrdal as lead tenor and Barbara Ward as coloratura soprano have intoned, is growing wider. As this disparity in distribution of the world's wealth (and associated values) increases, such futurists as Bertrand de Jouvenel have projected global "housing wars" as poor and populous countries determine that it is cheaper for them to take over others' housing than it is to build their own. Similar fears and anxieties can be projected about virtually every aspect of the world's present economic and ecological disequilibrium.

To avert these catastrophic dangers, there is a clear and present need for a positive politics of preventive therapy. This requires a flow of information that is relevant and reliable—information of the sort that can be produced by the policy sciences in the service of democratic development. Such information, while it is most urgently needed by policy advisers and decision makers, cannot be confined to these elites. Indeed, such information can support political therapy of appropriate scope only if it is diffused on an adequate scale to shape a new global consensus on the desirable way of the world.

The technology needed is already in place. We already have the first world communication network in operation and the channels opened via INTELSAT are sure to be broadened and deepened by the technologies still to come. The world audience is being formed by the global sharing of such vicarious experiences as the Olympic Games and man's first landing on the moon—a sharing of experience that will also be widened and deepened as the common interests of humanity are articulated and aggregated. Needed are a resonant transformation of world symbolism and a transformed cadre of symbol managers to make them resonate among all men. We now have the technological capacity to develop a world communication network that will operate with "a decent respect for the opinions of mankind" and help build a world commonwealth of human dignity.

NOTES

1. Karl Polanyi, *The Great Transformation* (Boston: Beacon Press, 1963).

2. Edmond Taylor, *The Fall of the Dynasties* (Garden City, N.Y.: Doubleday, 1963).

3. Fredrick Allen, *Only Yesterday* (New York: Harper, 1931), and *The Big Change* (New York: Harper, 1952).

4. Daniel Lerner, "Berufung zur Fuhrungsmacht," in *Amerika deutet sich selbst* (Hamburg: Hoffmann and Campe, 1965). See also the French perspectives of André Siegfried on "America's Coming of Age."

5. Rupert Emerson, *From Empire to Nation* (Boston: Beacon Press, 1964).

6. Harold D. Lasswell and Daniel Lerner, *World Revolutionary Elites* (Cambridge, Mass.: M.I.T. Press, 1966).

7. Daniel Lerner and Morton Gorden, *Euratlantica* (Cambridge, Mass.: M.I.T. Press, 1969).

8. Harold D. Lasswell, *World Politics Faces Economics* (New York: McGraw-Hill, 1945); William T. R. Fox, *The Superpowers* (New York: Harcourt, Brace & Co., 1944).

9. See chapters 17 through 19 of this volume.

10. See Lucian Pye, chapter 15, this volume.

11. See Oscar Schachter, chapter 16.

12. Harold D. Lasswell, *The Language of Power* (Cambridge, Mass.: M.I.T. Press, 1970); Ithiel de Sola Pool, *The Prestige Press* (Cambridge, Mass.: M.I.T. Press, 1970).

13. Heinz (also listed as Henry M.) Paechter, *Nazideutsch* (no publication data given).

14. Daniel Lerner, *The Passing of Traditional Society: Modernizing the Middle East* (Glencoe, Ill.: The Free Press, 1958).

15. Lancelot L. Whyte, *The Unconscious before Freud* (New York: Doubleday, Anchor Books, 1962), p. 11.

16. Gamal Abdul Nasser, quoted in Daniel Lerner, *Passing of Traditional Society*, p. 214.

17. Lucian W. Pye, "Communication, Institution Building, and the Reach of Authority," in Daniel Lerner and W. Schramm, eds., *Communication and Change in the Developing Countries* (Honolulu: The University Press of Hawaii, paperback, 1972) pp. 51–53.

18. Ibid., p. 54.

19. Daniel Lerner, "Toward a Communication Theory of Modernization," in Lucian W. Pye, ed., *Communications and Political Development* (Princeton: Princeton University Press, 1963), pp. 327–350.

20. For a more extended discussion of the Strategy of Truth, in the context of World War II, see Daniel Lerner, *Psychological Warfare Against Nazi Germany* (Cambridge, Mass.: M.I.T. Press, 1971), pp. 26–32.

21. See excerpts from M. Joly, chapter 11.

22. See Hans Speier, chapter 10.

23. Richard H. S. Crossman, in Lerner, *Psychological Warfare*, p. 337.

24. Lasswell and Lerner, *World Revolutionary Elites*, p. 467.

25. Ibid., chap. 6.

26. Sukarno, quoted in Marshall McLuhan, *The Medium Is the Message* (New York: Random House, 1967).

27. Hadley A. Cantril, *The Invasion from Mars* (Princeton: Princeton University Press, 1947).

28. Daniel Lerner, *Propaganda in War and Crisis* (New York: G. W. Stewart, 1951).

29. For the interbellum world situation, see Harold D. Lasswell, *World Politics and Personal Insecurity* (New York: Free Press, 1965).

30. For the technological basis of this forecast, see the chapters by Herbert Goldhamer and Wilbur Schramm in volume III of this work.

31. Harvard-Radcliffe Phi Beta Kappa Oration, 1973.

32. George Lefebvre, *The Great Fear of 1789: Rural Panic in Revolutionary France* (New York: Pantheon, 1973).

33. For an evaluation of World War II air warfare, see the United States Strategic Bombing Surveys; and Irving L. Janis, *Air War and Emotional Stress* (New York: McGraw-Hill, 1951).

34. Carl I. Hovland et al., *Communication and Persuasion* (New Haven: Yale University Press, 1953), p. 83.

35. Gardner Lindzey and Elliot Aronson, *The Handbook of Social Psychology* (Reading, Mass.: Addison-Wesley, 1969), vol. 3, p. 204.

36. *Annual of Power and Conflict, 1972-1973* (London).

14

CHANGING ARENAS AND IDENTITIES IN WORLD AFFAIRS

HAROLD R. ISAACS

I

Recurring intertribal tensions in the new politics of Kenya bring on episodes of new oath taking by members of the dominant Kikuyu tribe during which each oath taker swears: *"I will never leave the House of Muumbi."* Muumbi is the mother of all Kikuyu, wife of Gikuyu, legendary progenitor of the tribe. By this oath, the Kikuyu rebinds himself into the circle of the tribe, recommits himself to his tribal loyalties, and helps maintain the Kikuyu position against that of all the other tribes in the government and politics of their recently regained land. Not only in Kenya but everywhere now in the many houses of Muumbi, people who dwell in them are huddling together more closely than ever before, people who had left are looking for the way back in, and others who still seek more open and more spacious living places are halted and confused, not sure where they are going, or where there is to go. On all sides, houses of Muumbi that had begun to fall apart are being shored up or being rebuilt in new settings, and people are swarming to them, driven by their fears and by the new political pressures that need, encourage, or exploit their tribal separatenesses. We are experiencing on a massively universal scale a convulsive ingathering of men in their numberless groupings of kind—tribal, racial, ethnic, religious, national. It is a great clustering into separatenesses that will, people think, improve, assure, or extend the group's power or place, or keep it safe or safer from the power, threat, and hostility of all other groups similarly engaged.

Obviously this is no new condition, only the latest and by far the most inclusive chapter of the oft-told human story in which, after failing again to find how they can live in sight of each other without tearing each other limb from limb, Isaac and Ishmael clash and part in panic and retreat once more into their caves. This fragmentation of human society is a pervasive fact of contemporary human affairs and forms part of one of our many pervasive great paradoxes: the more global our science and technology, the more tribal our politics; the more we see of the other planets, the less we see of each other. The more it becomes apparent that man cannot decently survive with his separatenesses, the more separate he becomes. Most of the television light that showed nearly a billion people the live picture of men from earth reaching the moon flickered on the walls of the houses of Muumbi. Today's tribal caves are wired for sight and sound. Everything that goes on in or around them takes place with maximum possible electronic amplification and diffusion. The world presses hard into every retreat with the message that there is neither isolation nor escape, that no group can live alone. And for their part, all groups, asserting or reasserting themselves or—especially—when they collide with each other, must try to catch the world's eye and ear by using every available resource of global communication and propaganda.

One result is that this process of fragmentation and refragmention can be examined in every day's news, indefinitely multiplied now any day, any week, anywhere in the world, whether in East Bengal or East St. Louis, South Africa or South Bronx, northern Luzon or northern New Jersey, Alaska or Ceylon, Belgium or Biafra, Scotland or Israel, Wales or the Sudan, Uganda or Cyprus, Malaysia or Guyana, in Kiev or in Cleveland, in Bombay or in Belfast. Most of this news is about conflict, for bloody as this kind of history has always been, the present chapter has been bloodier still. The mutual massacring has taken place on a grand scale, given the unprecendented spread and scope of these collisions and the greater death-dealing capacity provided by progress. It is a somber catalogue: tribal civil wars in Nigeria, the Congo; Muslim-pagan or "black-and-tan" wars in Chad and the Sudan; irredentist killings across the new borders of Ethiopia, Somalia, and Kenya; Indians killing Nagas in northeastern Assam, Malays killing Chinese in Malaysia, Indonesians killing Chinese in Indonesia, Chinese killing Tibetans in Tibet, Catholics and Protestants killing each other in Ulster, Turks and Greeks in Cyprus, Kurds and Iraqis; Papuans fighting Indonesians in New Guinea, Israelis and Arabs in permanent conflict, Telenganas and Andhras killing each other in southeastern India, dozens of other such groups doing likewise intermittently elsewhere in that country; Filipino Christians and Filipino Muslims, and so on and on and on. One attempt to count the "ethnic-cultural fatalities" in such clashes between 1945 and 1967 listed thirty-four "major" bloodlettings and hundreds of lesser collisions and came up with an estimated total of 7,480,000 deaths.[1]

Hardly any of the situations that produced this total have been resolved or relaxed since this count was made. To almost every total, five more annual totals would have to be added by now—somewhere between fifty thousand and one hundred thousand freshly massacred, for example, in Burundi in 1972—and some wholly new entries have to be made: between one and two million dead in Biafra, more than half a million dark-skinned Bengalis killed by light-skinned Punjabis and Pathans in Bangladesh, and scatters of other thousands, like the Vietnamese killed by Cambodians at the time of the U.S.-Vietnamese invasion of Cambodia in June 1970, and the Cambodians killed by South Vietnamese thereafter. If we take the matter down in scale from open warfare or large-scale killing to ethnic-cultural conflicts marked by sporadic riots, bombings, and other collisions and clashes, the list swells from scores into hundreds. If we add those situations around the world where tension and strain exists between and among groups producing acts of violence in new political settings, the number could hardly be guessed, for here we would have to include every country in which a changing political order has to strike new balances among contending tribal, racial, ethnic, religious, and (or) national groups. And this now means virtually every country on every continent.

This enormous shaking out of all power and group relations is global in extent. It has come about as a result of the collapse or weakening of power systems—the larger coherences—that for periods of time managed to hold clusters of separate groups under the control of a single dominant group or coalition of groups. These systems created a certain coherence in which differences and divisions were not so much submerged as held in their orbits by the gravity of the center. The force of this gravity was physical, economic, cultural, and—most heavily—psychological. The rules of the game were incorporated into mystiques and mythologies of belief and behavior—all the assumptions of cultural and racial superiority-inferiority—which were internalized and accepted by all, rulers and ruled, victimizers and victims, and built into the system's institutions to keep it working. Such systems could work for given periods, producing not only selectively profitable economic well-being for the rulers and their chosen instruments among the lower orders, but occasionally even significant art and literature. But they could keep on working only so long as both the realities and mystiques of power were maintained, both externally and internally. They could work only so long as they could overcome or stay in balance with challenging rivals outside and only so long as each dominated group inside not only knew its place but accepted it. The record shows that there could be all kinds of lags, that declines could take a long time and falls run long overdue, but that these conditions could never be indefinitely maintained. From external or internal impetus—usually both—authority eroded, legitimacy was challenged, and in wars, collapse, and revolution, the system of power redrawn. Such, with all their differences, were the Ottoman, Hapsburg, and Romanov empires that ruled most of eastern and central Europe, western Asia, and most of North Africa for upwards of five hundred years, and such too were the European empires in Asia and Africa, controlling most of the world for periods lasting from not quite one to nearly three centuries.

Ottoman rule, which lasted from 1453, when the Turks took Constantinople, to 1918, when the "sick man of Europe" finally died, extended at its peak from the Adriatic to the Persian Gulf, from the western Mediterranean to the Red Sea. Its center was in what used to be loosely called "Asia Minor" and it included all of what is now loosely called the "Middle East." It governed at one time or another all the multitudes of distinct tribes, nations, peoples, races, and kinds who lived between Algeria and the borders of Iran. It extended into southeastern Europe from the Bosphorus and the shores of the Black Sea across Greece, the Balkans, Hungary, and nearly to Vienna.

Much of the European realm of the Ottoman Empire passed in time to the Hapsburg, later known as the Austro-Hungarian Empire, which, at its peak in the half century before 1918, ruled a domain that included Germans, Hungarians, Czechs, Slovaks, Poles, Ruthenians, Ukrainians, Serbs, Croats, Slovenes, Bosnians, Macedonians, Rumanians, Italians, and scores, if not hundreds, of smaller but no less distinct groups and subgroups.

To the east of the Hapsburg and north of the Ottoman, the Russian Empire had grown over some four hundred of these years, expanding westward and southwestward into Europe and gradually eastward into Asia. It became, by that same fatal year 1918, a system that included at least twenty linguistic groups of over a million each, and a much larger number of smaller groups. Its successor, the Soviet Union, liked to call itself a union of "a hundred nationalities," one source citing a count of 189 made in the 1920s.

Moving down other, swifter historical currents meanwhile, western Europeans were carrying trade and power into Asia and later into Africa. As Grover Clark graphically summed it up in his charts (in *A Place in the Sun,* New York, 1936), Europeans who ruled 9 percent of the earth in 1492 had come to rule a third of it by 1801, another third by 1880, nearly another fifth by 1913 on the eve of the First World War, 85 percent in all by 1935, on the eve of the Second. By that time, just under 70 percent of the world's population lived under the control of Western governments. The British alone held a quarter of the world's land and ruled a quarter of its people, and more people than lived in China, or in Russia, the United States, France, and Japan all put together. There had been Spain in the southern Americas until the 1820s and latecoming Germany with the pieces of Asia and Africa it had been able to seize at that century's end and hold but briefly until 1918; there was still, until World War II, in addition to the British Empire, Holland in the East Indies, the United States in the Philippines, Belgium in the Congo, France in Southeast Asia and heavily, along with Britain and Portugal, in Africa. This remarkable European takeover of the world was smaller in extent than only the conquests of the Mongols but infinitely greater in effect.

Like the Roman and Hellenic and some other great power systems of the remoter past, the longer lasting of these various empires laid much more than a political imprint on the peoples they ruled. The mystiques by which they governed for so long included whole cultural systems that survived in many shapes and measures of their real or assumed superiorities, or by the sheer transforming power of what they brought with them. Their legacies included styles of life as well as of governance, often of language, art, religion, and philosophy, of the spirit and much of the practice of bureaucratic and legal systems. In many cases, a great deal of this influence affected only the elites of the governed peoples. Much of it survived only fleetingly; the old imperial aristocracies of Europe are gone for good. But some of it survives ineradicably, like the Spanish and Catholic mark on Latin America. No one can predict its future with certainty, but English remains the lingua franca of multilingual India. Without English and French, the African emergence could not take place. In Israel, the political and bureaucratic style and much else was brought along intact from eastern Europe by the Zionist pioneers, while the position of the religious authorities in the country, with power over most matters of *etat civil*—anomalous in a regime dominated by European socialist norms—is an explicit legacy from the Ottoman system, left intact by the British during their brief post-Ottoman interregnum, while many more Ottoman legacies came with the great masses of so-called Oriental Jews to confront those brought from Europe. It will take more time than has yet passed to know what the transmutations of these many cultures will bring. But no more time is needed to verify that all the major wars, all the great convulsive revolutions of this century, whether socialist or democratic, all the European, Asian, and African nationalist movements that have transformed the power picture across the entire globe in the last century or so are rooted in the political and philosophic evolution of Europe during the last two centuries. Indeed, *all* this development, in all its scenes and varieties, comes out of the transforming ideas and technologies of industrialization, modernization, and communication that were carried, more blindly and more fatefully than anything else, by these moving, spreading, contending power systems across the continents. The impacts changed all these nations and societies beyond all chance of returning to the shapes of their past.

The collapse and disappearance of these power systems, after 1918 and after 1945, threw the peoples of most of the world into the political centrifuge in which they still spin. Since the empires fell, no new, larger coherences have effectively taken their place—only new power blocs that have failed so far to establish and sustain a decently long-lived balance between themselves, much less a balancing control over all the peoples who have fallen restlessly into their orbits. None of the proffered new coherences have worked. Neither the feeble European capitalist-victor coalition represented by the Versailles settlement and the League of Nations, nor its broader-based successor, the United Nations, could create a political system in which the power struggle of the major powers—in effect reduced to two—could be contained, much less the conflicts of the enormously increased number of smaller nations, with all their external and internal abrasions and collisions over national, ethnic, racial, tribal, and religious differences. Indeed the Soviet and American power blocs that emerged after 1945 remained fragile and uneasy combinations precisely because of the revived strength of old nationalisms and the vitality of new drives to self-assertion and self-esteem. Despite bulging nuclear muscle, neither bloc could firmly count on keeping its client states in anything resembling the older forms of proper subservience.

The superpowers have found, on the contrary, that they have been unable either at home or in the world arena to go very far in pursuit of their national-strategic interests without being pressed, decently or otherwise, to respect the opinions of this or that hitherto ignorable segment of mankind. The American system has had to give up white supremacy. The Soviet system has had to pull back from the bloodier extremes of Stalinist mass terror. In the world arena, where they had to seek a global solution, they both found the globe disconcertingly unmanageable. They could compete in space and try to avoid mutual disaster by searching for ways to limit their escalating weaponry, which in any case they dared not use. They have had to play their twentieth-century power game by nineteenth-century rules, but they have had to do it without achieving nineteenth-century results. Their fleets bump and buzz each other in all the oceans, enough for a hundred Agadirs, while electronic eyes and ears nervously guard against more fateful collisions. Both suffer the political ineffectualness of puppet-clients in the style of Nasser and Thieu, while their own resorts to marginal force, whether brief and "successful" in the Russian manner (as in Czechoslovakia and Hungary) or prolonged and disastrous, in the American style, fail to justify their cost. No stable spheres take shape, no docile dependents, no securely pliant tools, no permanently passive victims, not in Eastern Europe, not in Cuba, not in India, and not, spectacularly, in China; and not in Western Europe, not in Japan, and not, spectacularly, in Vietnam. Clearly, the new crises in human society are churning too hard to let anything settle again for long—even for any moderately extended period of time—into the old patterns of power and conquest, submission and passivity.

It took only a few years for the bipolar power system that emerged in 1945 to be pulled into new shapes, misshapen triangles and twisted quadrangles, as Western Europe recovered from the loss of its empires, Germany and Japan rose from their ashes faster than anyone dreamed possible, and China came to life like a long-extinct volcano—or, should one say, like thunder across the bay. The durability of alliances, such as it ever was in those good old days of the last century, has gone. The process of rearrangement of power in the world is the stuff itself of the inherent instability that has already filled most of the years of this century and surely will fill all of the reasonably foreseeable future. Successful establishment of new world power systems, even in semi-hemispheres, may be one of the ways in which new larger coherences may be created. Given all the circumstances, it is not easy to be hopeful about the possibilities.

If new structures based on naked force are unpromising, neither has any of the major ideas or belief systems offered much evidence of working any better. In the so-called Middle East (that is, western and southwestern Asia and northern Africa) over these decades, the cement of Islam proved to be much too thin to hold together any viable political structure or alliance in which the various Arab and related Muslim peoples could share

an effective allegiance. Not even the reentry of the Jews to re-
claim their piece of the land in the region has provided the unifying spur that the common religion failed to provide. As
events in Bangladesh showed again, Islam, like Christianity,
may make men brothers sometime somewhere else, but not
now, and not on earth. In the present context, the Roman Catholic church, the nearest thing to a universal institution the
Christian religion has produced, offers one of the most striking
of all contemporary examples of the breakup of another kind of
larger coherence no longer able to hold its parts together or
keep its belief system intact. Neither has realization come in
this half century out of the secular dream of a new revolutionary
socialist internationalism, foregone by the European social democracy in the war crisis of 1914, raised anew by the October
revolution in Russia, and betrayed again when the rubbing of
the Bolshevik lamp produced the old-new genie of Russian
national-communism. Nor, finally, did the American model of
a larger coherence prove in this time that it might still work.
Profoundly different from all the others and still far from a failure, it was only after after 1945 that it entered its testing time,
still in progress.

The task of sorting out and describing—not to say prescribing
for—all the new situations is obviously going to be a full-time
occupation for scholars and practitioners of politics for some
time to come. Many are already hard at it. If only because it may
help summarize and illustrate the truly global dimensions of
the matter, here is one way of beginning to distinguish some of
the larger features of this vast and varied landscape:

Postcolonial

The ex-empires in Asia and Africa have been carved into about
seventy-five new states since 1945, from huge India to tiny
Oman to tiniest Nauru. These new states came into being partly
because the foreign rulers could no longer sustain their rule,
partly because the ruled would no longer submit. In a few
places, independence crowned decades of sustained nationalist
struggle, as in Congress-led India or Communist-led North
Vietnam. In many more places, as in most of Africa, it came as a
result of the precipitous departure of the imperialists, as in the

Congo, or even—as in the case of most of French Africa—the cynical recognition by the foreign ruler that the name, if not the game, had to be changed at last. In British Africa, as in Ghana, Kenya, and a few other places, there was some history of nationalist politics, but most of the parties and institutions that figured in the new states created after 1957 had only been brought into being after 1948. In any case, the victory of nationalism came in Asia and Africa long after the nation-state had largely exhausted whatever utility it had in the past in Europe as an instrument for economic development and social progress. This was one of the many costly paradoxes of what used to be called the law of uneven development. Throwing off the foreign yoke —or having it drop away—could and did, however, meet a real emotional-psychological need, the need for some minimum self-respecting self-esteem. At this minimum, the new nationalists could at least replace the foreign scoundrels with local scoundrels and do away with the most egregious symbols of foreign cultural and racial superiority that had been at the core of the mystique of imperial power.

The removal of the overarching mantle of foreign rule did not, unfortunately, uncover oppressed colonial masses panting for fraternity as well as liberty. Rather the contrary. Only a few of these new nation-states had ever existed as nation-states before. All but a very few insular places were formed in boundaries inherited not from their own remoter past but from the colonial era, when boundaries were usually drawn without regard for what people lived where. The result was colonies set up as political-administrative units governing dozens to scores to hundreds of distinct and—as a rule—mutually antagonistic peoples divided along many lines, regional, racial, religious, linguistic, tribal. With only one or two exceptions, these units were carried over intact in the transfer from colonial to sovereign status. This fact has dominated most of the politics and generated most of the conflict that has taken place in these countries during recent decades. What had been the holy grail of self-determination in anticolonial politics became the poison potion of group conflict, secession, rebellion, and repression in the postcolonial era.

There are few real exemptions from this condition, even among those countries that experienced the period of Western dominance in a different way. Japan, no ex-colony, is nearly homogeneous, though not without its minorities. Reemergent China, on the other hand, has a lively "national question" of its own, with no less than half its territory—all the wide border regions along the southern mountains, through Tibet (which the Communists took and hold by armed force), Sinkiang, Mongolia—occupied by some sixty non-Chinese minorities that make up no less than 10 percent of China's population. For Communist China, no less than for Kuomintang China or imperial China before it, these minorities present important internal political problems. China's minorities have the Greater Han outlook of their Chinese rulers to deal with; in the present state of China's relations with Russia, the northern and western border peoples become a particularly pressing and even critical factor in external affairs as well.

In the ex-colonial countries, however, the populations are most generally mixed in more kinds and in larger proportions, indeed in almost every possible arrangement of majorities and minorities and mutually offsetting or unevenly grouped pluralisms, every variety producing its own kind and degree of conflict.

Thus India-Pakistan, to take a highly visible major example. It divided initially along the line of its largest division, India's Hindu majority and its Muslim minority, breaking apart amid massive slaughter and flights of populations in 1947–1948, and clashing in three wars since. India was left with a Muslim minority of 45 million, smaller numbers of Sikhs, Jains, Christians, but with other even greater and deeper sources of internal tension, division, and conflict: its dozen or so strong regionalisms, its fifteen major and some fifty minor language groups, its scores of major castes and thousands of subcastes, its 70 million Untouchables outside the caste system altogether. And then, West Pakistan: itself made up of mutually tense or hostile Punjabis, Pathans, Sindis, and others; brutally imposing itself on its own Bengali East; ending in wanton massacres, rebellion, the third war with India. It had taken rivers of blood to mark new boundaries separating the Muslim brothers from the Hindus; it has taken new rivers of blood to separate the Muslim brothers from each other. The process is obviously nowhere near its end.

These conditions, varying elsewhere almost infinitely in their mixes and their kinds, have in the first twenty-five years after the end of World War II brought on civil wars (for example, in Burma, Nigeria, Congo, Sudan, Chad, Bangladesh); uprisings and repressions (for example, Indonesia, Pakistan, Uganda, Zanzibar); intercommunal killings (for example, India, Pakistan, Cyprus, Philippines, Morocco, Ceylon, Syria, Iraq); language riots (for example, in India, Pakistan, Ceylon); tribally rooted coups and countercoups (for example, Nigeria, Congo, Uganda, and at least a dozen other African countries). Boundaries laid across the living spaces of some peoples have led to irredentist struggles (as in Somalia-Ethiopia-Kenya or Ghana-Togo), or to continuing pressure for separation (for example, the Nagas in northeast India, the Kurds in Iraq and Iran).

Most of these divisions survive from the precolonial past, patterns of conflict and oppression with a long history. Others, however, were fabricated in the colonial period by migrations—voluntary, manipulated, forced—including the massive transport of Africans into slavery; the movement of indentured or contract labor, especially from India; and the migrations, both old and new, of Chinese and Indians and Levantines to Southeast Asia, Africa, and island countries in both the Atlantic and Pacific. From these movements came a whole group of new population mixes, for example, Sinhalese-Tamil in Ceylon; Amerindian-African-European in Latin America; Malay-Chinese-Indian in Malaysia; East Indian and sometimes Chinese combinations with Africans, as in Guyana, Trinidad, Jamaica, or with Melanesians or Polynesians, as in Fiji; and the presence of Chinese minorities, large and small, in Southeast Asia and the Caribbean.

In some cases, this has produced so-called pariah communities of traders and laborers who—like the Chinese in Indonesia and the Philippines and Indians in Burma and East Africa—have often become the helpless scapegoat victims of other intergroup tensions. In others, however, they have produced wholly new ethnographic situations, as in Malaysia, where Chinese comprise nearly 40 percent of the population and challenge the politically dominant Malays for equality of status, or in Guyana where Indians, a numerical majority, are in a similar position in relation to the Afro-Guyanese. In both Malaysia and Guyana this has led to mob violence and bloodshed and remains the substance of unresolved political tensions.

All of these new states, large and small, confront the formidable problems of economic development and improved wellbeing. They all have to accommodate themselves in one way or another to the larger world power struggle that impinges on them all. And they have to do all this while internally facing the issues of power and pluralism created by their insistent and persistent separatenesses.

Postimperial

In western Europe, which used to be the center of the world, the place from which the East was Near, Middle, and Far, and where, at Greenwich, time and longitude began, the postimperial era did not bring on the collapse and revolution the Marxists had always predicted and the imperialists had always feared. Reduced again to living on a peninsula on the western end of Eurasia, the ex-imperialists with American help recovered their local balance of power and pelf, less so in Britain than in France, Holland, and Belgium. They found they could still play with profit in part of the world game—as in oil and in the ex-colonies—while being relieved of the burdens of directly wielding power in the old, no longer tenable manner. They were able to go back to worrying primarily, like good Europeans, about being swallowed up by Russia or dominated by Germany—or, now, by America. They could leave the issues of power in the rest of the world—with some postimperial lag of France in Indochina, Algeria, and West Africa, and for Britain, trailing a few threads east of Suez—for the new big powers to worry about. The wax figure of de Gaulle made up to look like French grandeur did not change the scene, although it did manage to slow down the slow progress toward the possible emergence of a new ''Europe''—a new larger coherence—to contain that continent's strongly surviving national separatenesses.

But a somewhat more insensible consequence of the end of empire and world power is the way in which it has weakened the fabric of consent, assent, or submission which had kept some subgroups in western European societies in a condition of more or less passive subordination, or less visible discontent, for centuries. The result has been the resurfacing of hoary old separatism, new ''national'' movements or drives for regaining long-lost measures of regional, linguistic, or political autonomy, or simply in militant new movements for cultural reassertion, none of these major, but none insignificant either. Thus, in varying scopes and degrees of intensity and reappearance, in Great Britain the Welsh, the Scots, the Manx, and the reopening of Catholic-Protestant hostilities in Ulster; the Flemish-Walloon conflict in Belgium; the stirrings of the Basques in Spain, the Bretons in France, even the Jurassians in Switzerland; and, by extension in North America, the militant emergence of the separatist Quebeckers in Canada.

Another fallout of the postimperial experience has been the migration to the former mother countries of sizable numbers of their ex-children—Indians, Pakistanis, Africans, and West Indians to Great Britain, Algerians to France, and ousted Indonesian Eurasians and Ambonese to Holland. These are not, as in the past, small numbers of selected individuals come for schooling in the process of being co-opted by the colonial system, but large numbers of poor working people come to make their way down those gold-paved streets to some better condition of life. The collapse of the old authority relationship in which the lesser breeds knew their place, the class of the newcomers and their status as permanent immigrants instead of tolerated visitors, and their larger numbers have led to new internal tensions, conflicts, riots in the streets. Old pretensions of the ex-metropolitan upper classes (usually aimed with polite sneers in the direction of American racial boorishness) have popped like pricked balloons as the blunter racialism at all levels in these societies is activated, more and more often to the point of violence. Blotchier European faces have appeared as the smooth old self-images have been washed—hogwashed?—off by the streams of change, and much has been devalued—such as the value of British passports so proudly held by so many unfortunate non-British British subjects or Commonwealth citizens, like West Indians or East African Asians, or the belief of some North Africans that the transplant had taken and they were indeed *Frenchmen*. These experiences have raised new questions and new problems for these ex-spreaders of the higher civilization and higher culture about the character of their own societies and the shapes of *their* pluralisms.

Postrevolutionary

Marxist socialist doctrine promised a new international socialist world order to replace capitalist anarchy, imperialist oppression, and nationalist rivalries leading to wars. In Russia the Bolsheviks promised a model of this kind of society, a political structure in which some of the hundred-odd nationalities in the country would enjoy territorial separateness and all would enjoy cultural and linguistic autonomy while sharing in some adequate fashion in the central power. These promises were broken, precisely on the rock of the "national question" that never ceased to be a central issue in Communist theory and Communist politics.

Almost involuntarily from the beginning and then deliberately under Stalin, Russia became a national-Communist power. It subverted revolutionary movements elsewhere to its own national-strategic goals and policies. This took place with especially crushing consequences in Germany, China, and Spain, aborting events that might have radically altered the course of world history in the critical decades between 1920 and 1940 had they been able to run their course independent of Russian intervention. This is a history whose threads lead directly to the subsequent cleavage between national-Communist Russia and national-Communist China, each with the device of a new socialist world order still inscribed on its banner, each readily reviving racial myths—the "yellow peril" is more vivid in Russia today than it ever was in America or in Hohenzollern Germany—and each making ready to annihilate the other in pursuit of its own national power interests.

Inside the Communist countries, the promised new order has proved equally elusive. After fifty years of more or less monolithic Communist power in Russia and twenty-five years of the same in Eastern Europe, both the internal and intrabloc politics still revolve—and constantly erupt or threaten to erupt—around unresolved issues of relations between and among the scores of tribes that make up the populations of these countries. The structure of separate republics and other nationality-centered institutions has been set up and a charade of national political-cultural autonomy continues to be played in it. But the doctrinal line of respect for national-cultural differences keeps getting tangled with the lines of authoritarian central power. Nowhere have they fallen into a design that meets the needs either of the wielders of power or of the stubborn keepers of all the many primordial bonds. The problem was not resolved in Russia, not even in the thirty-year era of the totally monolithic rule of

Stalin—a prime theoretician on the "national question"—
when whole peoples were uprooted and deported by fiat and literally millions condemned to die at the hands of the regime.
Nor, since 1945, when it gained suzerainty over eastern and
southeastern Europe, has Russian power been able to keep the
added nationalities of its extended empire under effective control. Neither, for that matter, have the Communist regimes inside any of these countries. The politics of Czechoslovakia still
revolve around being Czech and being Slovak—Russia's armed
assertion of its power in the country in 1965 made full use of
this communal division. In Yugoslavia the aging Tito vainly
struggles in his waning years to keep that country from explod-
ing again into its Serbian, Croatian, Montenegran, Bosnian,
and other assorted parts. Rumania and Hungary still tussle over
Transylvania, and every country uses the presence of national
minorites in every other one—Albanian, Macedonian, Hungarian, or whatever—as a weapon in external pressures and coun-
terpressures. This is the pattern not only on Russia's western
frontiers but equally on the eastern, where Mongolian-Chinese
antipathies are manipulated, and where, for another example, a
"free Turkestan" movement has been set up to make use of the
separatist restiveness of Turkic peoples under Chinese rule in
Sinkiang.

   Neither visionary beliefs, then, nor large-scale industrialization and urbanization, nor the passage of generations, nor concentrated centralized power, nor massive repression, nor elaborate theories, nor structural schemes have apparently been able
to check the survival and the persistence of the distinctive separateness of the many nationalities or tribes of people who live
under the Communist system. Socialist internationalism, like
Christian brotherhood, remains an elusive myth mocked by the
actualities. Resistance to Great Russian (or Great Serb or Great
Czech, or Great Hungarian or Great Rumanian, and, to be
sure, Great Han, and so on) still fuels conflicts and patterns of
behavior scarcely any different from what they were in all the
generations before the Communist era. There is something
plaintively ironic in the scolding remonstrances of Tito among
his lieutenants, or in the report that *Pravda,* as recently as 18 July 1971, "warned local officials against giving jobs to people on
the basis of their ethnic origin," a warning, the *New York
Times* report adds, "apparently directed both at Russians who

discriminate against Soviet minorities and at non-Russian local officials who favor members of their own nationality.'' The Russian effort has been under way, after all, only a little over fifty years, the American for nearly two hundred.

Postillusionary

In the United States, the breakdown of the worldwide white supremacy system after 1945 brought on the collapse of a whole set of illusions about the nature of American society and has raised in new ways and on a new scale the question of the character of the ''American'' identity. It has opened up a time of wrenching change in all group relations within the society, and within every group the beginning of a hardly less wrenching reexamination of itself. This condition has been triggered primarily by the fact that black Americans stopped accepting, stopped submitting to the old rules of the game, or the pace at which the society appeared ready to change them. They won the fifty-year-old battle to break down the legal barriers that had excluded them from the common civil rights nominally open to all. They then went on, in a veritable explosion of self-reassertion, to challenge the consequences of their long subjection, to beat at the still-standing walls of customary rejection and exclusion. Most painfully and confusedly of all, they also went on to seek to rediscover and redefine themselves, a process that has led some black Americans to go looking for their own houses of Muumbi while others, the great bulk, seek in the new and unfamiliar circumstances to discover what it might still mean to be ''American'' after all. They have thus raised in the sharpest possible way the issue of whether the American society, finally opening after 1945 to include groups long kept wholly or partially outside, would open enough to include its blacks on the same basis as it was at last coming to include everyone else, Catholics, Jews, Chinese, Japanese, and so on, in the enjoyment of rights, status, and opportunities common to all.

This crisis of ''black'' and ''American'' identity would by itself be crisis enough. But its effect has been to shake up all the other groups in the society located at various stations along the road from being ''out'' to moving ''in,'' including the ''group'' always seen by the others as ''in,'' the group now so commonly and so loosely labeled ''the Wasps.'' In other non-white groups—the Mexican-Americans, the various other

"Spanish-speaking" groups, the American Indians, and the "Orientals"—the current black syndrome is reproduced, militant radical fringe groups reflecting—and momentarily speaking for—the much more widely felt and deeply laid feelings of whole populations that their status must change.

In the groups of the white population, these lines are blurrier, the response more ambivalent and more ambiguous, and our knowledge of their present states of mind more limited. This great turning of circumstance finds the Irish Catholics the farthest "in"—they made it to the White House in this period. But with the opening of the church to the winds of change, the turmoil in Catholic education, and the emergence of Catholic priests and nuns as leaders and symbolic figures at almost every point along the spectrum of "left" or dissenting politics, we have much to learn about how the Irish Catholic population sorts itself out in relation to all these matters affecting their status and their view of themselves. The Jews—who are not likely to make it to the White House any time soon, certainly not sooner than the Poles—have made it through most of the barriers that still stood high against them as recently as 1945. This degree of inclusion has made some Jews fear for the preservation of *their* house of Muumbi, and there is much exhortation, much effort to get Jews to renew *their* vows never to leave. On the other hand, the felt limits—for example, the appearance of virulent anti-Semitism among militant blacks and of anti-Zionism in the New Left and the many ambiguities about attitudes toward Israel on all sides—allow no one to think that old ghosts have been laid, and leave Jews in general still suffering from what Kurt Lewin called "the uncertainty of belongingness." The uncertainty of what it means to be "American" leaves most Jews with the need, more than ever, to keep on being Jewish.

In the other much larger sections of the white American population—second- and third-generation European Catholic immigrant stock, the great "middle" or "blue-collar" or "white ethnic" population—the impact of these shock waves is less easy to see. Much is written now about the disaffection of this major segment of America, starting with the almost automatic backlash that the new black agressiveness has ignited across occupational and neighborhood lines in the great industrial centers of the Northeast. But no one has yet reported in any adequate way on how salient their ethnicity is in their present states of mind. The tensions have produced ethnic caucuses in some big unions and brought into being new organizations, as in Pittsburgh, designed to bring the ethnic association into the new picture of abrasive group relations. There is much assertion of newly proud ethnic identification that goes far beyond the old Hansen third-generation syndrome. Italo-Americans, Polish-Americans, Czechs and Slavs and Slovenians and Armenians are all clearly, however, going through new exposures. There can be hardly any doubt, now that the present situation in the society has forced on all kinds of people the realization that American society is not as melted as many thought it to be, that the question of what is "American" has become painfully unclear, that the task of self-redefinition still faces them.

This onset of what for some is a true identity crisis, as in the case of the blacks, or at least identity confusion for many others, comes upon us as part of a whole series of other climaxing contradictions in American life, having to do with persisting poverty, rotting central cities, drugs, polluted environments, and, in the Vietnam morass, the nature and exercise of American power in the world. In all these rather major compartments of life, old illusions have died or are dying hard—illusions about the "melting pot," and about freedom and democracy, about the virtue of ever-advancing technological progress, and the virtue of American behavior in relation to the rest of the world. The disaffection that appeared for a time in its more extreme form among the most radical or most disaffected youth in fact cuts much more deeply and much more widely among people of all ages and of every kind who thought they knew but now do not know what it does mean to be "American." It will be no wonder, as we stumble our way toward the new shapes of some new American pluralism if many people in many groups besides the blacks begin to think their only real security may lie after all in the closer circle of their own tribal kin, in their own Houses of Muumbi, American style.

II

These conditions raise new questions and new orders of questions, demand many kinds of fresh inquiry. They call us down paths either too heedlessly traveled before, or not noticed as we went down what we thought were the main roads. The force of this nearly universal self-reassertion is leading to all kinds of second thoughts—scholarly and otherwise—about the impact of modernization—or development—on communally divided societies, about the problems of assimilation, acculturation, and integration. The discussion, never marvellously clear, has become even murkier in recent years when certain long-held assumptions began to be shaken, for example, that modernization, industrialization, and "progress" were good, desirable, and necessary, and would inevitably iron out the more brutish effects of backwardness or superannuated traditionalism. Now it appears that we had better worry more than we used to about the even more brutish effects of growth and modernization. Nehru thought the caste system would have to be abolished before India could become a modern democratic, not to say socialist, nation. But political scientists now argue whether the reinforced caste system is good or bad for Indian national politics, whether modernization should—much less can—erase communal divisions, in Nigeria, for example, or whether a viable state can be created out of multiple regional-tribal-linguistic units separately ruled.

The evidence of current human affairs seems to suggest that the House of Muumbi is where man really lives, that his essential tribalism is so deeply rooted in the conditions of his existence that it will keep cropping out of whatever is laid over it, like trees forcing their way through rocks on mountainsides a mile high. This may be why the various universal dreams have either remained dreams of heaven where all human beings would finally become one before God—that is, when they are no longer human beings—or have been transmuted into power systems in which tribal differences are contained under the dominance of some particular tribe that reaches the top—that is, when human beings are held in thrall.

Those who have aspired to some higher estate for human society have generally seen man's stubborn tribalism as a function of his backwardness. Indeed, following Paul McClean's "schizophysiology," Arthur Koestler has recently suggested that the gap between man's intellectual and emotional behavior, between his technological achievements and his social-human failures, is the result of an evolutionary "mistake," that is, the survival of the phylogenetically older reptilian or lower mammalian parts of the brain after the development of the neocortex, the uniquely human "thinking cap" that in the last half million years or so has brought man to where he is now. The two have never been integrated, hence all our bewildering contradictions. This is why man knows he must die but still rejects the idea, peopling his universe with demons, ghosts, witches, and other more respectable invisible presences. Coupled with the uniquely prolonged dependence of the human on his elders and his kin for safety in a world filled with faster and stronger enemies, this is what has produced the quality and power of man's tribal solidarity, "his overwhelming urge to belong, to identify himself with tribe or nation and above all with his system of beliefs."

It could not be, of course, because these matters are lodged in the old limbic system of the brain rather than in the neocortex—everybody knows there can be nothing reptilian or mammalian about scientists and intellectuals—but it is a fact that scientists and intellectuals who have uncovered and so precisely defined so much about nature have been remarkably vague and imprecise about this aspect of human experience. Definitions, even at the simplest level, are elusive, loose, varied. From the dictionaries to the encyclopedias to all the works of scholarship, words like *tribe, clan, nation, nationality, race, ethnic group,* or *ethnicity* remain notably blurred to this day. Each writer has cast his definitions to suit his particular taste, bent, or discipline, or, one might venture, in terms of his own life's experience with his own house of Muumbi.

By now, to be sure, a considerable volume of multidisciplinary literature has grown up about problems of multiethnic societies. Much of this has to do with the problems of politics, development, and pluralism in the "new" ex-colonial countries. The surfacing of the same set of issues and confusions in the "old" states of both Western and Eastern Europe and, even more turbulently, in the American society, has widened the field of awareness and scrutiny. There must be dozens of American academic safaris tracking the snowman of "ethnicity," everyone sure now that it exists and is important, more important than most thought, but no one sure what it looks like, or whether it is abominable. The effort to get sharper about matters long left vague, to seek for some new terms of order among these old confusions, is at least under way.

Almost the first encounter on this shadowy path is with *iden-*

tity, and here too the shapes are many, the meanings numerous, the usages innumerable. Among them all, moreover, the linkage between *identity* and *group identity* remains the murkiest of all, the term *group* generally serving as a blur or amalgam for all the many kinds of groups in which people appear and sort themselves. This blurring continues all the way from Charles Cooley's "primary group" to Parsons' "collectivities" or what Ali Mazrui has more recently called "total identities." In anthropology, the seizing upon the concept of identity and its all-purpose use is well illustrated in some of the current writing in that field. In social psychology, what Gordon Allport nearly twenty years ago called "the venerable riddle of the group mind" has been getting more and more venerable despite the great increase in the volume of literature on the subject from so many different points of view.[2] In psychoanalysis, Freud never—except for some fleeting autobiographical allusions—let himself get much closer to the group than the idea of a mob or a hypnotized mass following a leader. Erikson undertook to relate "society" or "history" to the shaping of the individual ego identity and studied leaders to this end, but when it came to the specifics of group identity, he never let himself get much past seeing ethnic groups simply as "pseudospecies" blocking the way to man's achievement of some ultimate oneness.[3] The historians' thirst "for explanation in terms of group psychology and group behavior" remains unsatisfied, as one of them has unhappily remarked, "the stern and demanding challenge of group psychology and its relation to history still confronts us, unsmilingly."[4]

The need is for a fresh look at the inwardness of basic group identity and the process of its interaction with politics. The seeker is not, however, left entirely dependent on the artists and the poets, and not entirely without threads to pick up among the intellectual disciplines. It was a psychoanalyst (Erich Fromm) who noted that these "primary ties," for all their negative effects, persisted because they provided man with almost his only refuge against aloneness and powerlessness, with "an unquestionable place . . . genuine security and the knowledge of where he belongs." It was a sociologist (Edward Shils) who called these ties "primordial affinities" with their "ineffable significance" and their peculiarly coercive powers. And it was an anthropologist (Clifford Geertz) who noted that these ties differ from all other group identifications because they are the ones that uniquely make a group of people a "candidate for nationhood." What we need to do is to look more closely at what this basic group identity is made of: *name, color and physical characteristics, history and origins, nationality, language, religion, aesthetic and ethical value systems.* These are the holdings a person acquires at birth. They are the features by which groups of people have seen themselves as "unique" or "chosen" and it is around these features that the relative power or powerlessness of groups has been established, maintained, or overcome, producing so much of the blood and pain—and so much of the great art—of human history. These elements of group identity combine in different ways in different cases and much waits to be learned from examining them in their many varieties. But in all cases, I suggest, the functioning—and the great power—of this basic group identity has to do with two key ingredients in every individual's personality: his sense of *belongingness* and the quality of his *self-esteem.* These turn up in many degrees of plus-ness and minus-ness and determine thereby the behavior of the group and of its members.

These needs can be—and often have been—satisfied in one or more of the many other multiple group identities men acquire in the course of their lives in all the different collectivities to which they come to belong—social, educational, occupational, professional, even recreational. But these secondary sources of belongingness and self-esteem serve only where the conditions created by the basic group identity do not get in the way. This can occur, up to some point, in heterogeneous groupings where the community of interest is commanding. The unusual example given in this connection is that of the small group of combat soldiers confronting the foe, or the team on the athletic field. It can happen in homogeneous groupings where the basic group identity is given, shared by all, and relationship and status are determined by quite another criteria, for example, in a ghetto, inside a Knights of Columbus group, a Jewish Masonic Lodge—or a Protestant one—or any other such tightly homogeneous group. But the "outside" is nearby. Just outside the door, or over the wall, is everyone else. Out there that "uncertainty of belongingness" and the challenge to self-esteem have to be met in dealing with others who are more powerful or less powerful. Here, once more, the basic group identity and the relations between groups govern how far these needs are met or not met in some adequate fashion.

An individual *belongs* to his basic group in the deepest and most literal sense that here he is not only not alone—no small plus for most human beings—but here, as long as he chooses to remain in and of it, he cannot be denied or rejected. It is an identity he might want to abandon, but it is the identity that no one can take away from him. One thinks of Frost's line about home being the place where, when you've got to go there, they've got to take you in—the house of Muumbi. This obviously rolls inward and outward in the many layers of belongingness. The house of Muumbi is the womb to which everyone at one time or another yearns to return. It is where childhood fixed whatever emotional certainties became the handhold—life preserver, towline, shackle, anchor—to which so many people of so many different kinds seek to cling for the rest of their lives. It is the place, the physical place, high or low, wet or dry, green or yellow, where the roots were deeply laid and to which so many people remain attached by the unbreakable bonds of memory and association that seem to survive in all the senses. Or in this age of massive migration, for great numbers uprooted and transported great physical and cultural and social distances, it is the ark they carry with them, the temple of whatever rules of the game one's forebears lived by, the ''tradition'' or ''morality'' or whatever form of creed or belief in a given set of answers to all the unanswerables. Indeed, it can be said, I think, that one core of the crisis of American identity lies in whether, how, and in what form the American identity can finally become as primordial as all the others that have bonded men together. This will have to do more than anything else with how far and how deeply *all* who are American come to feel that they *belong,* beyond any chance of rejection or exclusion, together with all other Americans.

With this *belongingness* there goes, all but inseparably, the matter of self-esteem, the supporting measure of self-acceptance, or pride in self that every individual has to find from somewhere to live a tolerable existence. There are people, of course, who can derive a sufficient self-esteem out of the stuff of their individual personalities, above, beyond, or often despite the character or situation of their group. Others have to depend heavily on their group identities to supply what their own individualities may too often deny them. Most people, let us say, living intolerable existences, need all they can get from both sources.

Again, like health or money, group identity presents no problem when it is an assured given, when the self-acceptance it generates is an unquestioned premise of life and is not a source of conflict. This, once more, is the situation that can exist in a tightly homogeneous society or group, or in a stable society in which all groups, from top to bottom in the pecking order, not only know their place but accept it. All, including the master groups at the top and the lowest at the bottom—for example, the Untouchables in the Hindu caste system—accept themselves as they are told they are and fully accept the belief system that determines the conditions of their lives. Such frozen pecking orders have persisted for prolonged periods in preindustrial societies, and even modernizing or industrialized societies have experienced it, though more fleetingly and more limitedly, as perhaps in late Victorian England or post-Meiji Japan.

But it is precisely this element of self-esteem, of the need to acquire it and feel it and assert it, that upset all such orders and became one of the major drives behind all our volcanic politics. The drive to self-assertion, to group pride, is what fueled all the nationalist movements that eventually broke the rule of the empires. It is a principal element in the national and racial chauvinisms that have characterized both the Russian and the Chinese revolutions. It is above and beyond all the fuel for the power that broke the system of white supremacy. The themes of *somebodiness* as against *nobodiness* dominated the whole long history of the struggle of black men in America to regain a self-respecting status. We have grown familiar with the phenomenon of identification with the aggressor, with the patterns of self-rejection and self-hate coming out of negative group identities successfully imposed by stronger on weaker groups. But it is precisely when members of such groups stop submitting to this condition, as we have already remarked, that group identity becomes a problem, to both victimizers and victims, and, as our current affairs show, sooner or later a matter of crisis. This is the point at which group identity and politics meet. It has been the starting point of many notable lives, much notable history, and hardly any more notable than the history of our own present time and of the time that lies just ahead.

The questions persist: how long is the retribalizing spasm—if it is a spasm—likely to last? As we tribalize or retribalize, what are the effects of all the ongoing pressure on human society to globalize? What is—and what is to be—the relation between communal separateness and modernization? (And what now, indeed, in the light of our new awareness of some of the outcomes of advancing technology, *is* modernization?) What happens meanwhile to all the detribalized of the earth who have nothing to lose but their lostness in a retribalizing world? There is an immense reportorial task to be done—we still know much too little about the actualities in all these settings. With what fresh perceptions must we relate these aspects of current social change and politics to all the other large impinging factors: geography and resources, production and development and trade, power blocs outside and classes inside? There are all the heavy pressures and problems that weigh upon us all—and not only as inquirers—about where these circumstances might, can, or should lead us.

As some of the world scene already suggests, for example, in parts of Africa, the politics of fragmentation could lead to a condition that would make the Balkans seem like a marvel of coherent order by comparison. As Biafra, Tibet, Hungary, Czechoslovakia, Sudan, Bangladesh and, in many different ways, Vietnam show, the time of forcible imposition of one group on others is still very much with us. The larger coherences of the future—if they do not take the form of a postnuclear quiet—can yet appear as new systems of concentrated power imposed by bloody force. Our wars have accustomed us to death of people by the millions. Since Hitler, the reality of genocide as an option in human affairs has become very palpable, and the image of it rises swiftly out of much of the violence around us. On the other hand, there is the demand—the challenge, perhaps even the chance—to shape new pluralisms that somehow will better meet the needs of these new circumstances, somehow make human existence more humane. And as this is going to require above all confronting the more-than-ever universal demand for mutual respect and self-respect among the multitudes of ethnic, racial, national, tribal, and religious groups of human beings, there is a peculiarly pressing need to take a fresh look at the nature and functioning of these group identities. As we can so plainly see, they keep forever sprouting out of the ruins of empires, reappearing in the interstices of every kind of new culture and new politics, and continuing to frustrate the idealists and rationalists who stubbornly go on thinking that there must be some better way than this to carry on the human story.

On the one hand, we see all around us the process of fragmentation, which deepens in its own self-reinforcing way with all its ugly abrasions and its dehumanizing intergroup conflict. From many directions—whether the breakup of old power systems or the atomization of industrial society—comes the onset of turmoil and instability for all people in *all* their relationships, quickly bringing on conflict and crisis. When even the "order" achieved in an oppressive society is wrenched away, fear and confusion and a veritable identity panic overtake great masses of individuals caught out in the storms of change. There is either a fierce holding on to vestiges of the more secure past, or a search for what has somewhere somehow been lost. So for many, "liberation" becomes a lunge back to the tribal caves, back to the houses of Muumbi, a desperate effort to regain that condition of life in which certain key needs were met, to build walls to enclose them once more, if only in their minds, in a place where they can feel they belong, and where, grouped with their kind, they can regain some measure of both physical and emotional safety. A decade or more ago, James Baldwin bleakly warned American Negroes that they would have to learn how to get along without "the crutch of their blackness." He meant, of course, the powerful negative identity that had become crusted around the image of blackness. But in this time, the crutch has been refashioned into a wand, waving blacks into angry self-reassertion, but also into frightened withdrawal. In much more concrete—and usually much less poignant—ways, the prime elements of group identity become the poles around which people can rally, or be brought to rally, whether to seek a change in their status or to defend whatever security they think they may already have. This is growing more visible in the "new ethnic politics" in America. In the new politics in the postcolonial world it has produced numberless examples of the dynamics of this process, as Selig Harrison pointed out about caste in India and as Aristide Zolberg and others have remarked on the strengthening of weakened tribal connections in Africa. It has led to what Ali Mazrui has called the "retribalization of politics," not only in Africa but similarly in all its various Asian, European, and American forms.

On the other hand, the universal spread of this group self-assertion promotes in an unprecedented way the hitherto utopian notion that *all* groups of men—indeed, all men—are entitled to an adequate basis for self-esteem, that is, to a respected and therefore self-respecting status in both the social and political systems. There will be those who—with good cause—fear for what happens in all this to the free-seeking, free-thinking individual. There will be those who will not count too heavily on men ceasing to do what comes to them most naturally.

But if the drive to self-assertion and self-esteem *is* joined by all groups in a given society and if we have in fact moved out of the era of winner-takes-all, then it is at least barely possible that we can move through the ensuing chaos into the era of all-win-a-little.

Along the way lie formidable riddles: the shapes of world power, the course of development and population growth, the fate of the environment—all these, and the question too: what kind of balance can be struck between all that demands greater community among men and all that keeps them apart? What institutions and what political system will correspond to the global dimensions of technology and development and yet assure the pluralism demanded by the separatenesses that men insist on preserving? Can we have our separate ethnic joys and a tolerable human community too? This will require holding on to the civilizing and enhancing qualities of our differences, while somehow getting rid of whatever it is about them that makes us tear each other limb from limb, literally or psychically, in their name. There are no encouraging precedents.

NOTES

The material in this chapter appeared in somewhat different form in the author's *Idols of the Tribe: Group Identity and Political Change* (New York: Harper & Row, 1975).

1. Some of the items:

2,000,000 killed in the Hindu-Muslim holocaust during the partition of India and the creation of Pakistan;

500,000 Sudanese blacks killed in their ongoing war against the ruling Sudanese Arabs;

200,000 Watusi and Bahutu mutually slaughtered during the breakup of Burundi and Rwanda;

150,000 Kurds killed in their wars against the Iraqis;

100,000 Nagas, Mizos, and Ahams killed in Assam in their effort to separate from India;

100,000 Karens, Shans, and Kachins killed in their wars against the ruling Burmese in Burma;

100,000 Chinese killed by Indonesians in communal attacks;

35,000 Khambas killed by the Chinese in Tibet;

30,000 Somalis killed by Kenyans and Ethiopians;

10,000 Arabs eliminated by black Africans in Zanzibar;

10,000 Berbers killed by Arabs in Morocco and Algeria;

5,000 East Indians, Negroes, and Amerindians killed in communal clashes in Guyana.

See Robert D. Crane, "Post war Ethnic Cultural Conflicts: Some Quantitative and Other Considerations," manuscript, Hudson Institute, New York, March 1968.

2. William L. Eilers, "The Uses of Identity," M.S. thesis, Massachusetts Institute of Technology, 1966; Leonard Broom and Philip Selznick, "Primary Groups," in *Sociology: A Text with Adapted Readings* (New York, 1963), pp. 135–175; Talcott Parsons and Edward Shils, eds., *Toward a General Theory of Action* (Cambridge, 1951), pp. 192–195; Ward Goodenough, *Cooperation in Change* (New York, 1963), chaps. 8, 9; Ali A. Mazrui, "Pluralism and National Integration," in Leo Kuper and M. G. Smith, eds., *Pluralism in Africa* (Berkeley, 1969); Gordon Allport, "The Historical Background of Modern Social Psychology," in Gardner Lindzey, ed., *Handbook of Social Psychology* (Cambridge, 1954), vol. 1, pp. 31–40.

3. Erik Erikson, "Identity and the Life Cycle: Selected Papers," and "The Problem of Ego Identity," *Psychological Issues* 1 (1959):18–49, 101–164.

4. Bruce Mazlish, "Group Psychology and the Problems of Contemporary History," *Journal of Contemporary History* 3 (1968):163.

15

COMMUNICATION, DEVELOPMENT, AND POWER

LUCIAN W. PYE

In the exhilarating atmosphere that briefly enlivened the newly independent states of Asia and Africa of the 1950s, the commonly articulated faith was that all would soon fall into a constructive state of harmony: increased communication would inspire and guide social and economic development, and the consequent modernization would bring national power and benefits to all. When the end was coming to European empires there was much rhetoric about birth pains for the new era of nationalism, but few appreciated how acute and contradictory the problems of the new rulers were going to be.

In subsequent years when development proved to be more intractable than expected, it was easy to level the blame at the door of the first generation of national heroes who had championed the cause of nationalism. All could point to the obvious failings of Nkrumah, Sukarno, and even Nehru in achieving economic development and institution building. But despite more than a decade of problems, the basic assumption remained intact: with proper management, it should be reasonably possible for modern means of communication to provide the necessary stimulus for development, and thus the realization of respectable national power still lay in the realm of the technically feasible. Yet, there are grounds for doubts; so it is appropriate to pay special heed to the factors which, greater than just the normal human failings of rulers, constitute obstacles to more rapid progress in the Third World.[1]

THE AMBIGUOUS HERITAGE OF COLONIALISM

The linkage between mass communication and development would seem to have been established during the period of colonial rule, for both the technology of the mass media and the concept of planned economic development and political modernization were products of Western civilization. Indeed, precisely because it was during the colonial era that the diffusion of modern communication and the idea of the modern state occurred, the view that the two processes were mutually supportive seems plausible.[2]

But a careful historical view of what took place in the various Asian and African colonies reveals that from the very outset of Western domination there was little connection between the introduction of modern mass communication and the processes of economic and political development. The initial establishment of European rule in traditional societies involves surprisingly little use of any form of mass communication. The spread of colonial authority generally preceded the introduction of more advanced communication facilities.

True, the building of harbors and the remarkably early introduction of the railroad did ease the task of governing.[3] Improvements in communication and transportation did make it possible for colonial governments to rule effectively, but this was not in the main the conscious goal of the European authorities. Indeed, it is strange to contemplate how little concern colonial rulers initially had over the possible advantages of more effective means of communication. Instead of seeking to introduce new channels of communication and bypass the old ones, colonial governments generally went to great lengths in striving to use precolonial institutions of authority and communication.

The first introduction of newspapers and printed journals in the Asian and African colonies did not awaken the European officials to the possibility that continuous and extensive communication between rulers and subjects might be desirable in facilitating their rule. The various colonial administrations did establish official publications or gazettes, but the purpose of such publications was almost exclusively to inform lesser officials of important decisions and to provide them with important administrative guidelines—a reflection on the internal growth of government—and not to be a means of reaching the general public.

The first Western-language newpapers of a public nature generally had the European trading communities as their principal audience, and they clearly belonged outside of officialdom. As traders and other civilians frequently felt the colonial authorities were less than satisfactorily responsive to their special interests, the first English-language papers in Bombay, Calcutta, Hong Kong, and Singapore tended to be critical of their respective colonial governments. Thus, very interestingly, from the outset the European-language papers were adversaries of the European colonial governments. In the French and Dutch colonies they were usually both semiofficial and advisory papers, but all strived for the pretense of being independent.[4] The normal reaction of colonial governments to any early forms of press criticism was to retreat into arrogant isolation and secrecy. Few governments have appreciated more, or more persistently overestimated, the advantages of privacy in thinking through and carrying out policies. This may also in part explain why colonial governments tended to spin out for themselves some of the most convoluted and elaborately designed rationales for their policies.

As far as the development of the Western-language press was concerned, the early tradition of being critical of government continued right into the period of rising nationalist criticism of foreign rule. In time, some of the Western-language papers found themselves caught between the rising nationalist cries for independence and the lingering colonial authorities who had been their traditional targets. In the final stages of colonialism some of the Western-language papers became stalwart champions of the old order and outright defenders of the colonial authorities. Others maintained their criticism of government, but largely on the basis that government policies were likely to speed the end of the era of colonial government.

Yet, what is more significant, a far larger proportion of the Western-language papers were surprisingly successful in navigating the narrows that carried them from being the Western trader-oriented critic of government to becoming the educated nationalist's critic of government.[5] Such are the powers of the customer that papers that were once sharp critics of colonial administrators successfully transformed themselves into, first, anticolonial forums and later into apologists for the newly independent authorities. Indeed in nearly every ex-colony, the standard process of change has seen the principal foreign-language paper, which in colonial days was a demanding critic of authority, become a docile defender of the new government. The obvious explanation for this decline in critical instincts is that as a visibly "foreign" element in the postindependence environment, the survival of Western-language papers, often with expatriate staffs, was most tenuous, and therefore they have had little choice but to be nationalizers for the new authorities.

But in speaking of this postcolonial paradox we are getting ahead of our analysis. A more profound paradox generally took shape as the inevitable mobilization of nationalism, led by Westernized elites who utilized mass communication, began to challenge colonial authority and force European rulers to reply publicly. As the European authorities created the form and structure of the modern nation-state in their colonial administrations, the colonial subjects in time inevitably asserted claims of nationalism and a right to manage their own affairs. The stage was set for a great debate, a debate that greatly speeded the spread of communication media as more people sought ways to give voice to their sentiments.[6]

The final issue of colonialism was in essence a crisis of legitimacy. By what right did foreigners claim jurisdiction over alien cultures? The one rationale of legitimacy available to colonial authorities which had any sense of respectability was that they possessed superior knowledge and, hence, could provide a better, more just, and more progressive form of government for the masses of the people. In other times, other bases of legitimacy had been advanced by colonial regimes, but in the terminal stages the universal justification was that development and modernization could be more effectively realized by a continuation of European colonial rule rather than a premature shift to self-government. Indeed, as the European empires receded they vigorously disseminated the idea that the legitimacy of all governments depended above all on their ability to bring economic development and social progress. Thus a heritage of colonialism was the concept that only governments that could advance development were, in fact, legitimate.[7]

Nationalist leaders, while generally arguing that inferior colonial rule involved "exploitation" of their peoples, were to accept this understandably hesitant colonial reasoning about the ultimate source of legitimacy. Nationalist leaders often asserted the contrary view that "misrule by our own leaders was better than efficient rule by foreigners." Therefore legitimacy was not linked in any way with substantive policies, but rather with the identity of the policy makers. Out of this final clash between colonial authorities and nationalist spokesmen a tragic contradiction was established that has plagued the continuing modernization of several Asian and African societies.

The harder the nationalists pressed for the justice of independence and self-rule, regardless of economic consequences, the more colonial governments pressed the concept that development was the only proper goal of legitimate government. A vicious circle was established and the debate planted the seeds of deep ambivalence as to what should or should not be the proper objectives of independent regimes. The more the issue of development was identified with the colonial administrations, the harder it was for the subsequent nationalist governments to champion economic development as an ultimate goal.

Let there be no mistake: the final policies of most colonial administrations were heavily oriented toward development, whatever they might have been in prior decades, and many of the policies, whether wise or not, were exceedingly costly. In Ceylon it was the British authorities during World War II who introduced the plan to provide the quota of two pounds of free rice to all in order to prevent labor unrest, but ever since, all Ceylonese governments have had to maintain that unreasonably costly policy even though it has nearly driven the country into bankruptcy.[8] In Burma, in the late 1930s, the British introduced a system of health care and hospitalization that exceeded anything in England at the time, and that has left the Burmese government with a commitment in this field that strains the limited tax resources of the country.[9] In the last days of British rule in West Africa, expenditures for education dramatically rose and set the base for growing expenditures that could not be easily met in the years ahead without foreign assistance. Indeed, implicit appreciation of what took place was acknowledged by the British in their continuing support for education even after their legal responsibilities ended with independence.

When formal colonial policy did not give substance to the concept that legitimacy was linked to development, the West in a variety of other and more indirect ways still contributed to spreading such a theory. The Keynesian revolution in economics, which was initially designed to achieve economic stability and growth in advanced economies, contributed also to strengthening the earlier socialist vision that economic planning could raise the lot of all people, including those in the most retarded parts of the world. As has so often been mentioned, the London School of Economics preached to a generation of Africans and Asians that policies existed which could bring development and modernization to even the most benighted lands.

Thus Asian and African intellectuals, trained at the same institutions that produced development-minded colonial officials, also came to accept development as the proper goal for their societies. However, they assumed that their deeper commitment to economic planning and various versions of socialism should make it possible for them to achieve what colonial officials had not. Returning to their home countries, they often found themselves torn between their intellectual fascination with development by way of socialism and their appreciation that the bulk of their countrymen were attracted to a nationalism that contained little of Western modernization and hence development in it.

Thus, one of the important sources of ambivalence among Afro-Asian intellectuals, which they were pleased to articulate, was that their particular disease was being "rootless," of belonging neither to their traditional nor to the modern world. In some respects it was a pleasant ambivalence that asserted on the one hand that they were capable of appreciating all that Western intellectuals knew, but that they "knew" something more —the spirit of their own cultures; while on the other hand it suggested that, contrary to the normal alienation of intellectuals, they would have been easily capable of being in touch with their own cultures, if only the West hadn't contaminated them. The sum effect was that the intellectuals of the new states, much as their compatriot politicians, learned to speak the language of development and modernization, but they were also left profoundly unsure of what it should mean or how committed they should be to achieving it. This latter was so because, given the circumstances of the colonial era, development seemed to be the same as becoming Westernized instead of learning how to participate in a worldwide process based on exploiting scientific knowledge.

Although not as troubled as nationalist politicians or Westernized intellectuals, the commercial and business elements that emerged under colonialism participated in much the same process of communication which constantly informed them that the practices of the metropole were the most advanced and, therefore, development meant cooperating either with companies of the colonial country or with other Western companies. Progress in the private sector meant above all staying in close communication with developments in the West, and thus in a slightly different manner the emerging entrepreneurs in the new states sensed a peculiar linkage between communication and development that in general was based upon reactions to the Western impact.

The sum effect of the colonial heritage in communication and development was highly ambiguous. The very phenomenon of colonialism was in part an extraordinary historical communication process as Western ideas and practices were diffused throughout much of the non-European world. The process did result in many features of Western culture becoming the ideals of non-Western peoples.

Yet at the same time the introduction of such Western technologies for mass communication as newspapers and journals raised serious questions as to what should be communicated. Should the mass media perform the same roles, particularly in relationship to governmental processes, as the media were accustomed to do in the mother countries? The question was unanswerable because it was submerged under the far larger and more perplexing question of what should be the goals of independent governments in the postcolonial era? When colonial authorities introduced the concepts of economic and social development, could independent governments merely continue in the same directions, or was there not an obligation to find new directions? And what should these be? The basic uncertainty and ambivalence over the meaning of development in the postcolonial context created an ambiguous situation for the mass media.

As long as the struggle was for the relatively unambiguous goal of independence, the media did have a clear-cut function, that of mobilizing sentiment either for or against independence. Once the political objectives had been realized, all the media had to come to terms with the new authorities. But this was generally not easy, for the authorities themselves often were unsure of priorities, except for the immediate need to maintain power. The insecurity of new rulers stemmed in part from the novelty of holding power and hating the prospect of losing it, but even more it stemmed from the crippling fact that they possessed more the forms than the reality of power. Weak societies have weak governments.

The historic problem of what should be the goals of development in non-European societies then became linked in the postcolonial period with the more fundamental problem of building effective power in order actually to rule.

THE DELAYED EMERGENCE OF POWER AS A REALITY OF POLITICS

Although the ending of European colonialism was almost universally accompanied by exhortation of the "struggles for independence," actual tests of power were more the exception than the rule. World War II, which left Europe in a shambles, had set the stage for the nationalists to champion the inherent human right of men to rule themselves. The concept that legitimacy should be based on the efficiency of government evaporated as soon as European governments had to devote more resources to their domestic rehabilitation than to progress in overseas lands. The future seemed to belong to the articulators of nationalism. Yet, history was not so kind to them, for it left them as holders of offices that commanded little power.

There were, of course, many reasons why the leaders of the new states did not command significant power. Yet what is not so obvious is why it was not generally recognized that the new nationalist leaders were likely to have problems because of inadequate power in their societies. In part this was the result of the fact that Western thought on the matter of political power has always tended to assume the automatic or "natural" existence of power in any society, and that the problem for political theory is how power should be controlled, balanced, checked, and generally regulated. Western thought was so addicted to the idea that power was a relative phenomenon that it did not take seriously the question of the absolute levels of power in different systems and what can happen when a society has little capacity to generate effective power.

Another reason why the problem of power was overlooked at the phase of early independence was that the nationalist leaders were seen as merely stepping into the administrative structure that the colonial authorities had built, and as these situations had been adequate for colonial rule it was easily assumed that they should be sufficient for the new leaders. What was not asked was what kind of sound basis of power the new leaders might have outside of the formal structures of government.

Political development in most of the new states was seen as proceeding from state building to nation building in the sense that those who controlled the state apparatus were expected to be able to reshape their societies to create a sense of nationhood. This is quite contrary to the historical pattern in Europe in which the sense of nationhood often preceded the creation of binding state structures. The difference is most dramatic when we compare the end of empires after World War I with what happened after World War II. At Versailles the notion of nation-state started with the belief that legitimacy rested with phenomena of common culture, language, and ethnic identity, and upon this sense of "nation" should be erected the more legalistic and adaptable structure of the state. In contrast, legitimacy in Asia and Africa stemmed from continuity with colonial administrative structures, and ethnic divisions were expected to accommodate to the supremacy of legal identities. With the end of the Hapsburg and Ottoman empires, the great concern was self-determination, which was universally defined as requiring the identification of collective power. The boundaries of the new states were seen as readily adjustable to ensure maximum regard for ethnic or national homogeneity. With the end of the overseas empires after World War II, it was the other way around, and the boundaries of the colonially administered territories were taken as being rigidly fixed (with the sole exception of the division of India), and it was assured that ethnic power, regardless of how sharply divided, would readily conform to the administrative divisions of territory and hence produce national power.

In a sense, the nation-states that were carved out of collapsing empires on the European continent gave emphasis to the realities of ethnic differences and the assumption that nations should be the bases of states. In Asia and Africa the basic assumption was that the state, as defined by colonial administration, should provide the basis for the nation and ethnic differences should be down-played as much as possible as mere holdovers from a traditional order that was about to disappear in a rising tide of modernization.

Thus a strange irony underlay the emergence of postindependence politics in many Afro-Asian states. The new nationalist leaders soon were claiming their "legitimacy" as stemming from the colonial administrations who were once their declared adversaries. In their initial assertions of independence, it was essential for the founders of the new states to claim all the powers that had once belonged to the colonial rulers. Continuity with their colonial domain and with a continuing sense of the legitimacy of government was more important than the communication of natural or ethnic identities. The sense of "nationalism" that was popularized was thus defined more in terms of reactions to colonial administrations than to expression of historical ethnic sentiments.

In terms of communication processes, this meant that the nationalism propaganda came closer to projecting a "public" that was homogeneous, which the colonial authorities had assumed, than to the expression of ethnic distinctiveness, which might only have divided the ethnically heterogeneous population of the new states. Consequently, in many newly independent countries there was a brief period during which the nationalist leadership articulated development programs that seemed entirely consistent with the terminal colonial regimes' efforts in the accelerated modernization period. The initial outcome of struggle between nationalist politicians and colonial-trained administrators was thus often one in which powers evolved to the politicians, but they in turn accepted the administration's definition of development as the appropriate national goal. The result was that many Western observers, particularly those who wished the new states well, came to believe that there was a "natural" coincidence between nationalist goals and technically oriented economic and political development.

The effect of this brief period was to suggest that the dominant theme of the postcolonial era was to be state building and that the strengthening of administrative capabilities of government would produce in its wake the consolidation of nationalism. The universal assumption was that the ethnic and linguistic differences would soon be ironed out as the new nationalisms of those who commanded the state became diffused.

The new leaders were quick to identify themselves as the only legitimate articulators of the new national interests. Yet the new states often seemed unduly fragile precisely because the new leaders lacked solid bases of power in the natural communities, and the new national identity was often severely compromised by the linguistic and ethnic diversity that often made a mockery of the very idea of a new common nationalism.

During this period several national leaders were successful in giving dignity to the concept that nationalism and the striving for economic development were identical sentiments throughout the Third World. Proceeding from such a premise it is understandable that advocates of foreign aid in the late 1950s and 1960s presumed that this assistance would be seen as consistent with the support of nationalism in the Afro-Asian countries.

In time, however, the realities of power in most of the new states forced leaders to acknowledge that ethnic divisions could fragment any sense of national community. Moreover, many programs of development contained issues that could intensify such divisions, as some community might benefit more than another, and some might even be disadvantaged by proposed changes. Communication policies that initially had been severely directed toward mobilizing the entire population indiscriminately had to be adjusted to appeal to, or publicly attack, particular segments of the nation. Communal, which really meant ethnic or linguistic, divisions threatened country after country, and increasingly the realities of these ethnic and linguistic groupings became the basis of political competition. National leaders who presumed to speak for the whole nation often were seen as being the de facto spokesmen of more limited segments of the society who were seeking to make their subculture the only legitimate expression of nationalism. In other countries the noncommunal leaders have remained as nationalist figures because there is no alternative among the ethnically divided populations. The result, however, has not been the building of greater national strength, but rather a standoff situation in which all can politically benefit from a general state of mutual weakness but the society as a whole is denied forceful leadership. Accommodation of differences has a higher priority than accomplishing national development.

By the mid-1960s the realities of power had asserted themselves against the continuing legitimacy of colonially inspired institutions in most of the new states. Increasingly the realities of power relationships forced potential conflicts into the open. Leaders were trapped between championing the initial goals of modernization and the imperatives of accommodating ethnic and other communal differences. The competing pulls were made more acute by the generally low level of power in these political systems, which meant that there was not the necessary prerequisite for effective and dynamic leadership.

GENERAL SOCIAL CHANGE AND PARTICULAR THEORIES

While these general historical trends were first building up and then letting down the potentialities of political leadership in the new states, other more general social processes were taking place that affected the role of communication in national development. Just as colonial governments could not exclude the dissemination of new and challenging ideas, the new governments have not been able to check deep social and economic processes that over time have affected the bases of government. At the same time, however, governments as themselves actors in these processes have had some influence on trends.

In the immediate postcolonial period these processes of industrial development, urban growth, the rise in levels of education, and the spread of communications seemed to fit together with some reasonable degree of coherence so that it was possible to think of a general process of modernization and development.

It was under these conditions that possibly the most power-ful, and testable, theory of development was formulated by Daniel Lerner.[10] Specifically, the theory describes the modern-ization process in terms of four basic variables: urbanization, literacy, mass media exposure, and political participation. Mod-ernization itself involves moving along the continuum from tra-ditional to modern society, which is characterized by a high level of social and political participation and by citizens who have a psychic sense of "empathy." This quality of "psychic mobility" of the individual, which makes it possible for him to imagine himself in the place of many others, is developed out of the sense of social and physical mobility that occurs as a result of greater urbanization, literacy, mass media exposure, and op-portunities for social participation. The theory is thus remark-able in that it deals equally with the individual and the whole society, and is thus both psychologically and sociologically oriented.

Moreover, the theory does not suggest just a random relation-ship of the basic variables, but rather suggests that there is an inherent sequence that causally relates the variables into an in-tegrated process of modernization. The process in Lerner's words is that "everywhere . . . increasing urbanization has tended to raise literacy; rising literacy has tended to increase media exposure; increasing media exposure has 'gone with' wider economic participation (per capita income) and political participation (voting)."[11] Lerner also suggests that the rise in media exposure works to increase literacy in "a supply and de-mand reciprocal in the communications market."[12] According to Lerner's empirical work, the urbanization variable triggers the process of modernization when about 10 percent of the pop-ulation is in cities, and then, after 25 percent is reached, changes in this variable are no longer significant. The effects of literacy become highly significant when about 40 percent of the population can read. Lerner's concept of participation is a broad one involving both economic and political activities, but it is also susceptible to the interpretation of democratic develop-ment.

The precision of Lerner's theory has inspired others to test it against other bodies of data. Hayward Alker found that it stood up well when tested by the techniques of causal inference.[13]

Another highly elaborate analysis based on aggregate indicators for seventy-six nations and causal modeling techniques essentially supported Lerner's theory in the following conclusions:

1. Democratic political development occurs when mass communications permeates society.

Education affects democratic political development by contributing to the growth of mass communications, therefore:

2. Mass communication occurs when literacy and educational levels rise in a society.

Urbanization affects democratic political development primarily by increasing educational levels, which then increase mass communications, therefore:

3. Education and literacy development occur in urbanizing societies.[14]

The evidence is thus very strong that Lerner's theory does describe a basic historical process. It is significant that the theory is stronger when the data are for the years prior to 1960, and that for more recent years the evidence is more confused. In testing the model Schramm and Ruggels discovered that literacy was not always so closely linked to urbanization and exposure to mass media was not as dependent upon literacy as the theory would suggest. They conclude: "The last decade has seen the great growth of radio (a medium that does not depend so heavily on an urban concentration), of fast transportation, of primary schools spread through rural areas. Is it not possible, therefore, that literacy is not so dependent on urbanization in 1961–64 as it was in 1951–54?"[15]

Certain basic processes, sometimes facilitated by governmental policies, have been making more complicated the essential coherence of the modernization process. In some situations it is probably safe to say that the process has indeed "broken down" in that the social order has been weakened by developments that undermine rather than strengthen the effects of governmental policy. In short, political power has been further weakened by the developmental process.

On the other hand, there is considerable evidence that the less orderly patterns of development may not be entirely detrimental to the ultimate growth of a society. Accelerated development in some areas may in time compel the society to advance in others and thus ultimately arrive at a new level of coherence. The fact that it is so difficult to judge the probable outcomes of different patterns of change among even the most gross social variables indicates that there must be considerable uncertainty as to the appropriateness of different governmental policies with respect to communications development.

The one thing, however, that is clear is that it is easier to effect communications development than most other aspects of the modernization process. With respect to the Third World in general, it is striking how little governmental or state investment there has been in communication facilities and the mass media. In India and Turkey less than one-half of one percent of investment outlays for the early five-year plan was committed to communications media.[16] In spite of this low investment, it is striking that the mass media appear to be having an increasingly important effect on developments in the Third World.

THE GROWTH OF THE MEDIA

In area after area comparisons between the developing and the developed worlds seem to suggest that during the last two decades the gap between the rich and the poor seems to be growing. It is therefore extremely significant that the figures on the number of radio sets per capita reveal that there has been extraordinary growth in the last few years in the Third World and that the gap seems to be narrowing with respect to this particular indicator. At present, radios reach more people than any other medium and on a worldwide basis there is one radio for every five persons. The spectacular rise in the number of radio receivers in Africa and South Asia reflects in part the declining cost of sets, but also the fact that the radio has become an increasingly indispensable and, in some cases, sole source of critical information.

The picture with respect to newspapers, the second most important medium in the world, suggests a much more static situation. In fact, the per capita consumption of newspapers in Latin America has dropped from 1950 to 1970. There has been no appreciable rise in the figures for South Asia and Southeast Asia. On a worldwide scale it is interesting that there is possibly a greater difference in the exposure to newspapers than to any other medium. The countries with low per capita consumption show only two or three copies per thousand people, whereas those with high levels show over five hundred copies per thousand people. The fact that the countries at the top of the scale for newspaper consumption do not show any change over the last twenty years suggests that the gap possibly can be reduced in the future. On the other hand, the comparative popularity of radio over newspapers at the present time indicates how difficult it will be economically to increase the numbers of newspapers in the poorer societies. At present the worldwide average of newspapers is one for every eight persons.

The third most important medium of communication in the world is television, and this also is a very dynamically growing medium in parts of the developing world. Indeed, the spread of television may be one of the most sensitive indicators as to the differences among developing countries. Whereas with radios we find that the pattern is pretty uniform among all the developing countries and therefore it is possible to talk in general terms of trends in the Third World, with respect to television the picture is much more differentiated and we find that in those countries where television has made rapid advances, a rise in general economic and social levels has been closely associated with that development. The most dynamically changing societies in the Third World are those that have had the sharpest rise in television consumption: Thailand, Taiwan, South Korea, Iran, and Nigeria. The more static countries such as India, Ceylon, and the poorer countries of black Africa show very little rise in the use of television.

DILEMMAS OF COMMUNICATION POLICIES

With this historical background and a review of the theories about the relationship of communication to modernization, it is appropriate now to turn to the question of public policies toward the media in the Third World. It should be apparent that policies of communication for national development usually face some awkward dilemmas. The most basic dilemma is whether the policies should concentrate on supporting the administratively oriented plans for economic development which the new elites associate with their expression of a new nationalism, or whether communication policy should be sensitive to the diversity of subnational cultures and to the need to allow all significant segments in the new state to give expression to their historical claims of identity. The first alternative would emphasize the need to reduce any gap between the more Westernized elite and the more traditional masses by using technologies of modern mass communication to assimilate the traditional into a synthetic national and quasi–middle-class culture. The second choice would give priority to offering subnational communities the opportunity to strengthen their historical distinctiveness and give them a sense of genuine participation in the larger task of nation building even at the risk of encouraging the development of separatists and new nationalist movements.

Posed in these most general terms the dilemma in the minds of national leaders has often been seen as a choice between publicizing the merits of their own policies and the dangers of allowing others to advance their parochial views. It is therefore not surprising that to the extent that governments in the Third World have communication policies, the emphasis is generally one of providing (latent) propaganda in support of governmental policies.

The development of effective communication policies is further complicated by considerable doubt over the efficiency of the mass media in changing attitudes and values. Over the last two decades there has been an extensive debate about the power of the mass media to change the thinking of people. The question of the utility of the mass media in changing traditional attitudes blends into the larger question of the relationship of mass communication and personality changes. This is an issue, of course, that has been raised in terms of the effects of television on children and the efficacy of advertising in the developed world. Unquestionably the media do have the capacity of influencing choices when a previous predisposition exists, as in the case of advertising, or when there are other social processes at work that would support the same tendencies. Thus, the mass media can have a strong effect when there is a two-step flow of communication in which the second step involves face-to-face communication that reinforces what the media are disseminating. In terms of political development, it is quite clear that in some of the Communist states, and particularly in China, the mass media probably have a high degree of effectiveness because they are constantly being reinforced through the activities of party cadres who on a face-to-face basis reinforce the larger messages of the media.

The real question in the developing world is whether the

media will have much effect when operating on their own. In the early 1950s there was some hope that the media might provide a cheap and efficient way of changing attitudes and mobilizing support for the policies of the government. The lack of any reinforcement, however, from the social context of the messages that came through the mass media tended to bring disenchantment. It is now clear that public information programs designed to teach new skills and impart new attitudes need both the mass media and more direct contacts between officials and citizens.[17]

Communication policies that start on a modest basis and seek only to support governmental policies have tended generally to run into some very complex cultural issues. The government may start off with the assumption that it will try to communicate in the same voice to all its citizens and merely make adjustments as to the language in which the common message is disseminated. Yet, the requirement to speak in different languages does inevitably bring up cultural issues. Are those who speak minority languages also to be treated as members of a cultural minority? What is to be the culture of the majority? All communication policies tend in the end also to become part of the state's cultural policy. This means that in the new states, which have been formed largely on an administrative basis rather than on the ethnic-cultural basis, some very complex issues emerge. Should the culture of the new state have an historical orientation, or should it be focused largely on the future? If it is to be on the future, what concept of modernization will guide it and how is this to be different from the concept of Westernization?

Confronted with this dilemma, most states have tried to find some basis in history that would reach beyond the colonial era and provide a new sense of national identity and a source of legitimacy. Some of the new states have had rather thin histories and therefore the attempt to look back has not been easy. In other cases, the societies have had rich histories and the problem becomes one of selecting an appropriate period for the basis of the new nationalism. In India, for example, Prime Minister Nehru greatly admired the seventeenth-century emperor Akbar who sought to create a Hindu-Moslem political and religious synthesis. Yet appeals to the Akbar tradition would not only offend India's Moslems who regard him as a heretic, but also Hindus and Sikhs who recall the Moguls as alien conquerors and despots.[18] An alternative possibility in finding a neutral tradition to appeal to was that of the Buddhist Asoka, who reigned about 269–232 B.C. and was the greatest Buddhist leader. Attempts to identify India with the history of Buddhism were useful in India's foreign relations, particularly with the Buddhist countries of Southeast Asia and with China, but any effort to revive memories of Buddhism within India was quite futile.

Another major dilemma that arises in new states attempting to develop historical traditions to strengthen their communication policies is the necessity to compromise between seeking to reach a broad audience, which requires the search for a prestigious and remote level of culture, and the need to motivate a particular audience in terms of meaningful loyalties, which requires that the appeal be in terms of local and immediate cultures. This classic dilemma was most acute in the case of Pakistan, where the general appeal to Islam was not enough strongly to motivate all segments of the society, and where, if there was to be an appeal to more parochial cultures, the problems of divisiveness would arise. Eventually in Pakistan, the realities of the more vital subcultures proved to be superior to the abstract appeal to Islam and to the fear of India.

Here we seem to have the heart of the problem: to create real power and to motivate and affect the behavior of people, it has been necessary to communicate in terms of local cultures and the living strength of those ethnic groupings that tend to emphasize the plural nature of states which were created out of administrative boundaries rather than cultural ones. To avoid this pitfall, spokesmen have sought to appeal to a nationalism based either upon a history that is not vital or upon concepts of modernization that tend to suggest the very weakness of states which have come out of a colonial experience. Most people in Burma know that the "Burmese way to socialism" has to be an ineffectual approach because in their experiences with all things related to the modern world, anything imported is superior to domestic products. So it has been in many other parts of the world.

THE GROPING FOR A NEW SYNTHESIS

As the nationalisms that were built out of the anticolonial experience begin to wear thin with the passing of generations, the inevitable process in the Third World has been a trend toward more explicit and open recognition of the ethnic divisions and the reality of subcultures. The result has been a considerable confusion over the basis of legitimacy of the state and the appropriate direction of social policies. On the other hand, the result has also been the opening up of politics to the competitive clashes of different ethnic or communal groupings. In the case of Pakistan, the result was the dissolving of the state and the creation of a new one. Elsewhere the strain has not been as severe but the authority of governments has generally been greatly weakened.

The new era that seems to be approaching in many of the Third World societies will be characterized by new and more explicit modes of accommodation among the different ethnic groups. The need to recognize that they live in highly pluralistic societies is now increasingly accepted. Pretensions that a homogeneous sense of nationalism pervades the entire society have to be abandoned. The result will be more complex patterns of public policy as questions of equity and mutual understanding become central rather than the claims of an impersonal technology and the imperatives of efficiency.

It is conceivable that in this new phase communication policies will become far more important than they were in the past. Control of the media and the creative use of the media will become central features in the establishment of the appropriate sense of ethnic identity. At the same time the communication processes will be vital also in governing the degree to which these ethnic identities are effectively related to the new sense of national identity. Although the balance between the separate communities and the nation will be important in areas of economic, social, and educational policies, it is likely that whatever is communicated through the mass media will prove to be a more immediate and more sensitive variable in affecting the balance between nation and community and any sense of injustice.

NOTES

1. There is a danger today in overstating the extent to which changing public moods about the prospects of the developing world were reflected in the writings of scholars. The basic tone of Max F. Millikan and Donald L. M.

Blackmer, eds., *The Emerging Nations* (Boston: Little, Brown & Co., 1961) is far more qualified and restrained than subsequent characterization might suggest, and Samuel P. Huntington, *Political Order in Changing Societies* (New Haven: Yale University Press, 1968) is not as pessimistic as it has been made out to be.

2. See, for example, Joseph T. Klapper, "What We Know About the Effects of Mass Communications: The Brink of Hope," *Public Opinion Quarterly* 16 (Winter 1957–1958):453–474; V. B. Damle, "Communications of Modern Ideas and Knowledge in Indian Villages," *Public Opinion Quarterly* 20 (Spring 1956):257–270.

3. The lag in time between the invention and application of a new technology in Europe and its appearance in the colonial world was in some respects shorter than the contemporary pace of technological diffusion. Within a decade after the first commercially successful railroads were established in England and Holland, more extensive operations were planned for India and Java. A comparison of the general rate of diffusion of railroads with, say, the current spread in the use of computers dramatizes the increasing unevenness in the distribution of the most advanced technologies.

4. The advisory tradition of press and government in some colonies has possibly affected the writing of history in that where historians have press accounts critical of government policies, they have been less inclined to accept government intentions on face value. Note, for example, how the reliance upon newspaper records provides for sharp criticism in John F. Cady, *A History of Burma* (Ithaca: Cornell University Press, 1959).

5. Asad Husain, "The Future of English Language Newspapers in India," *Journalism Quarterly* 33 (Spring 1956):213–219.

6. A review of the issues in this debate is to be found in Rupert Emerson, *From Empire to Nation* (Cambridge: Harvard University Press, 1959).

7. David Apter, *Ghana in Transition* (New York: Atheneum, 1963).

8. W. Howard Wiggins, *Ceylon: The Dilemmas of a Nation* (Princeton: Princeton University Press, 1960).

9. Hugh Tinker, *The Union of Burma* (London: Oxford University Press, 1957).

10. *The Passing of Traditional Society* (Glencoe, Ill.: The Free Press, 1958).

11. Ibid., p. 46.

12. Ibid., p. 60.

13. Hayward R. Alker, Jr., "Causal Inference and Political Analysis," in Joseph Bernd, ed., *Mathematical Applications in Political Science* (Dallas: Southern Methodist University Press, 1966), pp. 7–43.

14. Donald J. McCrone and Charles F. Cnudde, "Toward a Communications Theory of Democratic Development: A Causal Model," *American Political Science Review* 61 (March 1967):78.

15. Wilbur Schramm and W. Lee Ruggels, "How Mass Media Systems Grow," in Daniel Lerner and Wilbur Schramm, eds., *Communication and Change in The Developing Countries* (Honolulu: East-West Center Press, 1967), p. 66.

16. Ithiel de Sola Pool, "The Mass Media and Politics in the Modernization Process," in Lucian W. Pye, ed., *Communications and Political Development* (Princeton: Princeton University Press, 1963), p. 231; Frederick W. Frey, *The Mass Media and Rural Development in Turkey,* Rural Development Research Project Report no. 3 (Cambridge: M.I.T. Center for International Studies, 1966), p. 201.

17. Ithiel de Sola Pool, pp. 234–253.

18. McKim Marriott, "Cultural Policies in the New States," in Clifford Geertz, *Old Societies and New States* (New York: The Free Press, 1963), p. 34.

16

RHETORIC AND LAW
IN INTERNATIONAL
POLITICAL ORGANS

OSCAR SCHACHTER

This chapter is an exploratory essay on the role of legal language and argumentation in international political bodies such as the General Assembly and the Security Council of the United Nations. It starts from the premise—which is well supported by observation—that legal categories (concepts, norms, rules) constitute a significant part of the common terminology, the *code,* with which the diverse participants in international political bodies communicate with each other and assimilate the flow of information into that organ. A cognitive filter is thereby established with special characteristics derived from the juridical features of the code. This chapter explores some of the implications of this and suggests how it affects the demands and expectations of the participants, the aspects of an issue that receive attention, the perceptions of common interests, and the solutions proposed for collective action. I hasten to add that this may promise too much, as I shall do little more than open up a large subject and make a modest attempt to throw new light on the link between language, law, and political decision making. This has been done as an armchair exercise based mainly on impressions gathered over some thirty years as a ''participant-observer'' in United Nations political organs. I hope it will encourage others to undertake more systematic empirical research, directed toward better understanding of how normative language and structures can contribute to more rational and effective decision processes on the international level.

I

As in the case of any organization, the political bodies in the international realm require a set of categories—accepted by all the participants—with which to organize and assimilate the flow of information into that system. Such information includes demands, claims, expectations, descriptions of events, predictions, and various other inputs into the decision processes of the organ. The categories used to organize and assimilate those informational inputs constitute (in the parlance of information theory) a code that is employed by the participants as a common language to formulate the issues and their solutions. That code is used also in the retention or accumulation of information (the "memory" of the organ) and therefore determines what are regarded as precedents and prevailing practice. The encoding process is continuous and may go on without explicit recognition by the participants. Those who participate in the organ—delegates and secretariat—learn the code, more or less naturally; if they did not, they would be unable to communicate in a common language and would find it impossible to negotiate and reach agreements on the decisions sought.

It is not difficult to demonstrate that the code used to assimilate the flow of information into the organ contains a significant number of legal categories. To put it in another way, the assertions and positions of the governments commonly refer to rights, obligations, competence, and authority. This is particularly the case for political organs dealing with what are regarded as political matters, in contrast to technical issues. The reason for this is that such issues tend to be perceived in terms of the authority or "discretion" of a state to deal with a matter unilaterally and of the right of the collective body to take up the matter and to adopt decisions affecting the state in question. In addition to this basic issue of competence or jurisdiction, there are likely to be references to principles or rules of conduct that are regarded or asserted as binding on individual states. It therefore tends to be a common and characteristic feature of collective political organs to categorize in legal concepts the facts and information that flow into the organ.

When a question is raised as to an act of a government, that act must be characterized (or "qualified") in terms that are accepted as legal grounds for international competence if the matter is to be discussed at all. And, on the other side, those objecting to such discussion will tend to characterize the governmental action in question as falling outside of categories recognized as conferring jurisdiction. Clearly it is not enough for a state that brings a matter to the organ to assert its own interest —as, for example, that it has been injured or threatened with injury or that it will profit from a proposed action. In the present state system, the international organ would not regard individual interest as sufficient without support in international norms that permit the organ to take up that matter and take other action. The boundary between the "reserved domain" of domestic jurisdiction and international competence is largely and necessarily delineated by reference to rights, duties, and the related categories of law.

What are the consequences of this in the organ? What are the effects of "coding" the information inputs into legal categories? One is that the facts and the demands will be analyzed and categorized in terms of criteria that have to be justified by their basis in legal authority or "sources." In effect, this means that the criteria are expected to be derived from such sources as international agreements or custom or general principles accepted as law. The issues and the debate then require specific support in past decisions and in spelling out through lexical and semantic analyses the meaning of formulations in the text. This can result, and undoubtedly has done so in many cases, in shifting the attention of the organ away from the "merits" of the particular case into an inevitable consequence. It is also apparent that the political organs can apply the legal categories so as to focus attention on the basic goals and values of the participants and on the procedures for bringing about a reconciliation of conflicting positions.

We should bear in mind, in this connection, that each political organ, like other complex systems, must maintain a measure of compatibility between its diverse activities and its multiple goals and subgoals. Moreover, it is essential to keep the expectations and motivations of its participants compatible with the roles they have to play. Their activities have to be perceived by them as fitting together in a meaningful way; there must be an understandable relationship between means and ends and a sense that there is not an insoluble clash between conflicting goals. These requirements (which may be characterized as a need for cognitive consonance) impose on each political organ continuing tasks of legitimization and integration. Both tasks are characteristically performed by the code references to authoritative doctrine—that is, to the charters and constitutional instruments and their principles, rules, and procedures that confer legitimacy and express accepted common goals. Hence the appeal to law is not only an indispensable feature of the rhetoric of political debate; it is deeply bound up with the fundamental needs (one might say the systemic needs) of political organs, especially organs composed of highly diverse members with conflicting interests and diverse outlooks.

II

An interesting consequence of assimilating the informational input of such organs through legal categories is that it gives rise to an expectation among participants that the categories will be applied on an objective basis or at least that they can be so applied. More precisely, this means that it is understood that the question of "obligation" or "right" can be and properly should be determined by reference to criteria that are to be applied independently of the preference of the states concerned and that the participants must look to the generally recognized tests of legal validity. Is this—one might ask—an actual expectation, or is it only a manifestation of a rhetorical attempt to conceal political motives? This broad question needs to be considered on different levels of analysis.

One such level is that of the overt behavior of the participants in the organs. One cannot, to begin with, dismiss as unimportant the fact that governments actually devote a good deal of time and effort to legal argumentation. If they are themselves parties to a controversy, they would not go to great lengths to demonstrate the legal validity of their position unless they felt a need to do so. Moreover, the other governments—those to whom the arguments are addressed (especially those whose positions have not been predetermined by ties of alliance or dependence)—will respond in most cases on the basis of the legal issue. It is indeed rare in a political organ—such as the General Assembly or the Security Council—that a noncommitted state would assert that its attitude is determined by its own interest or political preference. It will normally regard itself as obliged to base its position on its understanding of the charter principle or rule involved. It will be aware that deviations from principle in particular cases can be used to validate similar deviations in the future with the effect of weakening the whole structure. Moreover, many governments will be concerned with demonstrating to their own constituencies (as well as to some segments of foreign communities) that they have supported commitments and lived up to expectations engendered by their acceptance of rules of international order. This is not to say, of course, that their judgments are reached in the same way as those of the ideal judge. In a political context, it is inescapable that national sympathies and calculations of advantage will enter into the process of decision. But I believe this does not vitiate the conclusion that most such states when acting within the United Nations forum normally will seek to arrive at a judgment that can be explained and justified as based upon (or at least consistent with) the obligation of the charter and the rules of international law.

But this brings us to another level of analysis. Assuming that governments seek to arrive at judgments based on legal concepts, is it possible for them to do so "objectively"? We must remember that in many cases the issues in political bodies revolve around norms with a high degree of generality and ambiguity; frequently these norms appear to be contradictory, pointing to opposite conclusions; rarely are the facts agreed upon or the circumstances regarded as governed by precedent. In such situations, is it possible intellectually for a supposedly "impartial" government (or, for that matter, a disinterested observer) to determine its choice on grounds that are legally proper and objective—that is, in terms of criteria which are based upon the charter and accepted principles and which therefore transcend individual preferences and interests?

If we look back at some of the specific controversies debated in the United Nations—say, those relating to Cuba, Katanga, Goa, and Bangladesh—the difficulties of such decisions become more apparent. In all of these cases, the issues were framed and argued in terms of conflicting principles of the charter. Even if the issues were drastically simplified, they would still present sharp choices as to the priority or importance of one governing norm over another (which in many cases may be viewed as variations on the recurrent antimony of "peace" versus "justice"). In actual fact, the cases could not be reduced to that kind of choice alone, for they also involved conflicting assessments of facts—the political, economic, and psychological conditions— as well as varying estimates of the aims of the principal participants. It is evident that cases of this kind cannot be decided solely by looking at the words of the charter or by a logical analysis of the relations of its propositions or, for that matter, by seeking the intentions of the drafters at San Francisco. These may all be relevant and perhaps helpful but rarely will they provide the answers to the complex and novel issues raised in the specific cases mentioned or in most other political disputes. To find the answers within the limits of an impartial "legal" inquiry, it seems essential to broaden considerably the frame of relevance and to apply criteria that go beyond the dictionary meanings and other simple-minded means of interpretation, criteria that are, nonetheless, objective in the sense that they can be validated in terms of generally accepted principles rather than on the basis of individual or group preferences.

What are examples of such objective criteria of interpretation? Before attempting to suggest some, I should make it clear that I am not proposing any novel task. The function of interpretation is essentially to fulfill the intentions and expectations shared by the parties to the international agreement in question; this task can be carried out only through inferences from their words and conduct and, as required, by reference to principles that can be established as authoritative and controlling for them. To carry out this task in regard to political controversies of the kind mentioned above, the problem may become extraordinarily complex, involving a large number of variables, including, as a rule, "subjective" factors (such as intentions and expectations), estimates of future consequences, and conflicting versions of past events. Such criteria as may be suggested would serve essentially as guides to the variables and to the priorities that rationally should be taken into account in resolving the issue.

Obviously one set of such guiding principles would direct attention to those elements of the negotiation or drafting conference (the *travaux préparatoires*) that bear upon the intentions of the parties at that time. Examples of relevant elements would include statements of objectives and expectations, anticipated and rejected solutions of problems foreseen, the relative importance of particular parties (for example, sponsors, major powers) in asserting intentions, and so on. A second set of criteria would focus on the expression and formulation of the terms of the agreement. It would point to such elements as consistency of terminology, usage of terms, special meanings, logical structure. One might also include in this context evidence of intentions of the parties manifested by subsequent conduct that has been generally accepted.

These are all principles of interpretation that are recognized in international usage. However, they constitute only a part of the methods of inquiry that would be necessary to resolve particular controversies. A further set of criteria would be required to focus attention on those elements that relate to the fulfillment of the fundamental objectives of the agreement. For both common sense and judicial experience demonstrate that interpretation requires more than looking backward to certain predetermined results; it must include as well an assessment of the consequences of a decision in relation to the major purposes sought by the parties. In international law this is sometimes described as the "principle of effectiveness," and it is regarded as especially pertinent in the interpretation of constitutional instruments that are designed and expected to meet changing circumstances for an undefined future. It is perhaps within the ambit of this set of principles that one would include consideration of the postulates that lie beyond or beneath the words of constitutional provisions, for these, too, as many jurists have recognized, are implicitly part of the compact itself and may properly be given weight in resolving the conflicts between explicit rules.

Some will say, at this point, that we have now left the realm of objective legal interpretation and moved into that of political principles and social values. The suggestion that one must look to the "consequences of a decision in the light of its relation to major purposes" or to the "postulates that lie beneath a text"

will be regarded as another way of introducing political considerations and "subjective" preferences. However, it can be that
the criteria themselves and the process of choice should be validated by reference to principles that are ascertained and applied
objectively, that is, independently of particular individual preferences. In fact, the principles of interpretation we have already
suggested are indications of such objective standards. I would
emphasize that there is an important difference between political communication which seeks to base choice on agreed principle and that in which there is an assertion of will or fiat, resting
on nothing more than a particular interest without sanction in
agreement or community policy.

What is perhaps the most difficult point for many is reconcil-
ing the procedures of impartial, reasoned analysis with the ultimate act of choice that must, in the end, be made. For no matter how many standards may be employed and how many facts
established, the element of human choice would not be eliminated; in that sense the process of interpretation could not be
"depersonalized" and mechanized. But an essential point is
that the act of choice by a state of a collective body need not be
arbitrary. It is not arbitrary when it has been decided—or can be
justified—on the ground of its conformity to authoritative principles and rules that are themselves verifiable through objective
procedures and empirical evidence. Thus, while it may seem
that the assertion of claims in legal terms emphasizes the self-
interest of the individual state, the process of dealing with competing legal claims in a multipartisan organ leads away from expressions of individual interests to a search for accepted norms.
It is for this reason that the rhetoric of law—the debate and
framing of issues in legal phraseology—goes beyond rhetoric
and encourages a process of ascertaining authoritative norms
and, through that process, of identifying common interests and
preferences. This is so even though the process remains political
without any reference to an objective third party for determination of the legal issues.

III

This last observation suggests that the appeal to law in political
organs does not imply that there will be "adjudicative" decisions—that is, decisions that involve responding in affirmative

or negative terms to the question of whether the "law" has been complied with. Many of the problems that come before the international political bodies are simply not susceptible to such adjudicative procedures. In these situations, the function of legal concepts is to facilitate a legislative solution (rather than an adjudication) by providing a normative basis for ordering relations and creating stability of expectations.

The use of legal categories also arises from the need for organizing coalitions in the political organ concerned. Such coalitions, which are required to bring about majority decisions, often will depend on the acceptance of a common principle by states having divergent interests and ideologies. This is not to say that considerations based on ties of alliance or on political bargaining are excluded; clearly they play an important role. However, in the present heterogeneous international community, the building of majorities necessitates a wide range of support by states with divergent interests and ties. For this reason, it is important for those who seek a majority to build their case on principles that are widely shared. The juridical expression of such principles, as formulated in the basic instruments and doctrines, may serve as an essential element in the construction of the political coalition.

This can be seen in the efforts made in the United Nations as well as in meetings of the Third World to put forward political and economic demands on the basis of such principles and concepts as "sovereignty over natural resources" and the right of self-determination. A not insignificant aspect of the political strategy is to seek an elaboration of declarations and charters framed in the language of rights and duties of states that then can be utilized in specific cases to organize support among the large majorities that have subscribed to the declarations and charters, even though their precise legal effect may be uncertain. The repetition of authoritative norms thus serves to create or reaffirm a solidarity of interest.

Somewhat related to this is still another dimension that is affected by the use of legal categories in international political organs. It must be remembered that such organs do more than pass upon claims of states engaged in disputes. They are also sources of authority for institutional action by or in the name of the international organization. That may include peacekeeping or international regulatory and operational functions. When such collective actions are instituted or authorized by the international political organs, such as the General Assembly of the United Nations, there is a determination of the common interest of member states that often finds expression in a legal concept or principle. This may range from broad concepts such as *res communis* to specific concepts of state responsibility on which are based rules of restraint or arrangements for multinational regulatory or management operations in the common interest. By employing such legal concepts, the governments are able to express in a succinct and understandable way how conflicting claims may be resolved in an institutional context. It also enables them to specify by the juridical categorization how resources may be managed (or distributed) through an enterprise that supersedes the laissez-faire system of a decentralized legal order. I do not intend to suggest that conflicts are necessarily eliminated in this way. It may well be that a new collective institution will sharpen the demands of a particular group and possibly result in an increased benefit to them. The principal point for the present discussion is that an international political organ will have devised a new arrangement for dealing with conflicting claims through a conception that enables (and compels) governments to see the problems in a different way. Illustrations of this can be found in a wide range of international arrangements, as, for example, in regard to the common resources of the seas or the regulation of international telecommunications.

We should not completely overlook the situations in which legal rhetoric does stimulate adjudicative decisions (in contrast to legislative solutions) in political bodies. It must be remembered that the assertion of a legal right or grievance is often an essential condition of bringing a matter before an international political body. This is notably true in cases affecting international peace and human rights. In these situations, the issue concerns the conduct of a specific state (or group of states) that is challenged or complained of by others. For an international organ to have the right to concern itself with the case, it is essential that the conduct should not be within the exclusively national competence (the "domestic" jurisdiction of the state) or the recognized sovereign prerogatives of the state. It is for this reason that a challenge to the conduct of a state in matters of peace or human rights is normally put forward on the basis of an alleged violation of a rule of law, whether based on treaty or custom. This reflects the underlying conception that the prerogatives of national states to act as they please are rooted in basic principles of law and that any questioning of the exercise of those prerogatives must be predicated similarly on legal prescriptions. The consequence is that political bodies perform an adjudicatory function of passing upon compliance with legal rules and determining rights and obligations in concrete situations. As we have already seen, this gives rise to a demand for objective determination and to problems of validation and interpretation discussed in the preceding section.

We should observe that it also involves a legislative or norm-creating activity in that the application of general rules to concrete cases implies as a matter of logic the assertion of a rule of a more specific character than the general rule applied. This is so even though the participants in the political organ disclaim any intention to legislate and declare they do not intend to create a precedent. The question whether a particular decision will be regarded in actual practice as asserting a new rule for future cases does not depend entirely on the intent of the members of the organ at the time they adopted that decision. Whether they like it or not, a decision rendered by an authoritative body (even if it is political and not judicial) enters into the body of decisions that will be looked to in the future as a source of law. The consequence is that when similar cases arise in the future, one side or another will argue that the earlier decision is a precedent and persuasive, if not controlling, for the new case. In this way, the introduction of legal categories in a controversial case may not only lead to an authoritative decision but also may contribute to the creation and development of new rules of law. This would not be the case if the issues were treated purely as political questions without reference to the concepts of law and to the explicit or implied assertions of legal obligation.

In conclusion, it can be said that the use of legal categories and legal argumentation in international political organs involves more than rhetoric to cover up the play of power and interest. In a variety of ways, often subtle, it has profound con-

sequences for the political process and for institutional developments. As I have indicated, the common code through which
the participants communicate and the categories through which
information is assimilated are, to a marked degree, juridical,
and this significantly affects the demands, expectations, and responses of the participants and the collective functioning of the
organ. This chapter has noted in particular the relation between
legal rhetoric and the requirements of cognitive consonance and
legitimization of diverse activities; it has suggested how legal
concepts give rise to expectations of objective appraisal and influence perceptions of common interests; and it has pointed to
the effect of juridical language on the building of political coalitions, the development of collective action, and the process
of norm creation. All of this demonstrates that even in the
highly political context of international bodies, law has a pervasive influence, an influence that does not flow so much from
formal authority as from the processes of communication and
conceptualization in those bodies. It is to be hoped that scholars
will look more closely into these processes and seek to relate
them particularly to the policy goals and effective functioning
of the international organs dedicated to world order and justice.

NUCLEAR POWER: A COLLOQUY

INTRODUCTION

The United States achieved the first atomic explosion at Los Alamos in July 1945 and a month later ended the war against Japan with the two atomic bombs dropped on Hiroshima and Nagasaki. Some five years later the Soviet Union achieved a nuclear explosion. This initiated the nuclear bipolarization of the world and intensified the cold war, which in one form or another has shaped world politics and propaganda over the past quarter century. Although no nuclear bombs have been used in war since the fateful two in 1945, the omnipresent menace of nuclear annihilation has affected every phase of international political life—as expressed in such phrases as "balance of terror" and "nuclear blackmail." It seems appropriate that this volume on the evolution of modern Western communication should conclude with a colloquy on the dominant communication topic of our recent past and proximate future.

The colloquy opens with the "War Department Release on New Mexico Test, 16 July 1945," the day of the first atomic explosion. Unlike most military communications, it conveys a sense of the time and place. One shares the excitement at the historic achievement as well as the undercurrent of anxiety about what this "breakthrough" would do to the world in the years ahead. Those familiar with the *Bulletin of the Atomic Scientists* are aware that, after Hiroshima, the anxiety rapidly overtook the enthusiasm at Los Alamos. Those with a taste for historical analogies will see a parallel between the subsequent afflictions of J. R. Oppenheimer in the United States and A. D. Sakharov in the Soviet Union.

It is with Sakharov, indeed, that our colloquy continues. This great nuclear physicist and deeply thoughtful citizen of the world produced in 1968 an essay which, taking a broad view of the past quarter century as the context, focuses on two problem-sets for the present and future: "Dangers" and "The Basis for Hope." He derives a "Four-Stage Plan for Cooperation" that richly merits study by everyone in the world concerned about our common future. Sakharov is a "controversial" figure in the Soviet Union, as Oppenheimer was in the United States. If the reader leaves aside their personal backgrounds and concentrates on the policy issues they both have faced, he will better appreciate the issues of communication that confront our world today and tomorrow.

The colloquy concludes with a chapter by Hans Speier, a co-editor of these three volumes. Speier, a social scientist born in Germany, has been an interpreter of world events over the past forty years in U.S. academic, governmental, and public service institutions. He was the first to explicate the meaning of nuclear blackmail, and his books—I mention only *German Rearmament and Atomic War, Social Order and the Risks of War,* and *Force and Folly*—have been contributions to the subject of this colloquy. Though Hans Speier suggested the inclusion of the first two components of the colloquy, Harold D. Lasswell and I chose Speier's paper on "The Chances for Peace" for its conclusion. The editors can hope only that these three chapters will be read with as much attention as has been given to selecting them.

D. L.

17

WAR DEPARTMENT RELEASE ON
NEW MEXICO TEST, 16 JULY 1945

Mankind's successful transition to a new age, the Atomic Age, was ushered in July 16, 1945, before the eyes of a tense group of renowned scientists and military men gathered in the desert-lands of New Mexico to witness the first end results of their $2,000,000,000 effort. Here in a remote section of the Alamo-gordo Air Base 120 miles southeast of Albuquerque the first man-made atomic explosion, the outstanding achievement of nuclear science, was achieved at 5:30 A.M. of that day. Darkening heavens, pouring forth rain and lightning immediately up to the zero hour, heightened the drama.

Mounted on a steel tower, a revolutionary weapon destined to change war as we know it, or which may even be the instrumentality to end all wars, was set off with an impact which signalized man's entrance into a new physical world. Success was greater than the most ambitious estimates. A small amount of matter, the product of a chain of huge specially constructed industrial plants, was made to release the energy of the universe locked up within the atom from the beginning of time. A fabulous achievement had been reached. Speculative theory, barely established in pre-war laboratories, had been projected into practicality.

This phase of the Atomic Bomb Project, which is headed by Major General Leslie R. Groves, was under the direction of Dr. J. R. Oppenheimer, theoretical physicist of the University of

California. He is to be credited with achieving the implementation of atomic energy for military purposes.

Tension before the actual detonation was at a tremendous pitch. Failure was an ever-present possibility. Too great a success, envisioned by some of those present, might have meant an uncontrollable, unusable weapon.

Final assembly of the atomic bomb began on the night of July 12 in an old ranch house. As various component assemblies arrived from distant points, tension among the scientists rose to an increasing pitch. Coolest of all was the man charged with the actual assembly of the vital core, Dr. R. F. Bacher, in normal times a professor at Cornell University.

The entire cost of the project, representing the erection of whole cities and radically new plants spread over many miles of countryside, plus unprecedented experimentation, was represented in the pilot bomb and its parts. Here was the focal point of the venture. No other country in the world had been capable of such an outlay in brains and technical effort.

The full significance of these closing moments before the final factual test was *not* lost on these men of science. They fully knew their position as pioneers into another age. They also knew that one false move would blast them and their entire effort into eternity. Before the assembly started a receipt for the vital matter was signed by Brigadier General Thomas F. Farrell, General Groves' deputy. This signalized the formal transfer of the irreplaceable material from the scientists to the Army.

During final preliminary assembly, a bad few minutes developed when the assembly of an important section of the bomb was delayed. The entire unit was machine-tooled to the finest measurement. The insertion was partially completed when it apparently wedged tightly and would go no farther. Dr. Bacher, however, was undismayed and reassured the group that time would solve the problem. In three minutes' time, Dr. Bacher's statement was verified and basic assembly was completed without further incident.

Specialty teams, comprised of the top men on specific phases of science, all of which were bound up in the whole, took over their specialized parts of the assembly. In each group was centralized months and even years of channelized endeavor.

On Saturday, July 14, the unit which was to determine the success or failure of the entire project was elevated to the top of the steel tower. All that day and the next, the job of preparation went on. In addition to the apparatus necessary to cause the detonation, complete instrumentation to determine the pulse beat and all reactions of the bomb was rigged on the tower.

The ominous weather which had dogged the assembly of the bomb had a very sobering affect on the assembled experts whose work was accomplished amid lightning flashes and peals of thunder. The weather, unusual and upsetting, blocked out aerial observation of the test. It even held up the actual explosion scheduled at 4:00 A.M. for an hour and a half. For many months the approximate date and time had been set and had been one of the high-level secrets of the best kept secret of the entire war.

Nearest observation point was set up 10,000 yards south of the tower where in a timber and earth shelter the controls for the test were located. At a point 17,000 yards from the tower at a point which would give the best observation the key figures in the atomic bomb project took their posts. These included General Groves, Dr. Vannevar Bush, head of the Office of Scientific Research and Development, and Dr. James B. Conant, president of Harvard University.

Actual detonation was in charge of Dr. K. T. Bainbridge of Massachusetts Institute of Technology. He and Lieutenant Bush, in charge of the Military Police Detachment, were the last men to inspect the tower with its cosmic bomb.

At three o'clock in the morning the party moved forward to the control station. General Groves and Dr. Oppenheimer consulted with the weathermen. The decision was made to go ahead with the test despite the lack of assurance of favorable weather. The time was set for 5:30 A.M.

General Groves rejoined Dr. Conant and Dr. Bush, and just before the test time they joined the many scientists gathered at the Base Camp. Here all present were ordered to lie on the ground, face downward, heads away from the blast direction.

Tension reached a tremendous pitch in the control room as the deadline approached. The several observation points in the area were tied in to the control room by radio and with twenty minutes to go, Dr. S. K. Allison of Chicago University took over the radio net and made periodic time announcements.

The time signals, ''minus twenty minutes, minus fifteen minutes,'' and on and on increased the tension to the breaking

point as the group in the control room, including Dr. Oppenheimer and General Farrell, held their breaths, all praying with
the intensity of the moment which will live forever with each
man who was there. At "minus 45 seconds," robot mechanism
took over and from that point on the whole great complicated
mass of intricate mechanism was in operation without human
control. Stationed at a reserve switch, however, was a soldier
scientist ready to attempt to stop the explosion should the order
be issued. The order never came.

At the appointed time there was a blinding flash lighting up
the whole area brighter than the brightest daylight. A mountain range three miles from the observation point stood out in
bold relief. Then came a tremendous sustained roar and a heavy
pressure wave which knocked down two men outside the control
center. Immediately thereafter, a huge multi-colored surging
cloud boiled to an altitude of over 40,000 feet. Clouds in its
path disappeared. Soon the shifting substratosphere winds dis-
persed the now grey mass.

The test was over, the project a success.

The steel tower had been entirely vaporized. Where the tower
had stood, there was a huge sloping crater. Dazed but relieved
at the success of their tests, the scientists promptly marshalled
their forces to estimate the strength of America's new weapon.
To examine the nature of the crater, specially equipped tanks
were wheeled into the area, one of which carried Dr. Enrico Fer-
mi, noted nuclear scientist. Answer to their findings rests in the
destruction effected in Japan today in the first military use of
the atomic bomb.

Had it not been for the desolated area were the test was held
and for the cooperation of the press in the area, it is certain that
the test itself would have attracted far-reaching attention. As it
was, many people in that area are still discussing the effect of
the smash. A significant aspect, recorded by the press, was the
experience of a blind girl near Albuquerque many miles from
the scene, who, when the flash of the test lighted the sky before
the explosion could be heard, exclaimed, "What was that?"

Interviews of General Groves and General Farrell give the following on-the-scene versions of the test. General Groves said:
"My impressions of the night's high points follow: After about
an hour's sleep I got up at 0100 and from that time on until
about five I was with Dr. Oppenheimer constantly. Naturally he

was tense, although his mind was working at its usual extraordinary efficiency. I attempted to shield him from the evident concern shown by many of his assistants who were disturbed by the uncertain weather conditions. By 0330 we decided that we could probably fire at 0530. By 0400 the rain had stopped but the sky was heavily overcast. Our decision became firmer as time went on.

"During most of these hours the two of us journeyed from the control house out into the darkness to look at the stars and to assure each other that the one or two visible stars were becoming brighter. At 0510 I left Dr. Oppenheimer and returned to the main observation point which was 17,000 yards from the point of explosion. In accordance with our orders I found all personnel not otherwise occupied massed on a bit of high ground.

"Two minutes before the scheduled firing time, all persons lay face down with their feet pointing towards the explosion. As the remaining time was called from the loud speaker from the 10,000-yard control station there was complete awesome silence. Dr. Conant said he had never imagined seconds could be so long. Most of the individuals in accordance with orders shielded their eyes in one way or another.

"First came the burst of light of a brilliance beyond any comparison. We all rolled over and looked through dark glasses at the ball of fire. About forty seconds later came the shock wave followed by the sound, neither of which seemed startling after our complete astonishment at the extraordinary lighting intensity.

"A massive cloud was formed which surged and billowed upward with tremendous power, reaching the substratosphere in about five minutes.

"Two supplementary explosions of minor effect other than the lighting occurred in the cloud shortly after the main explosion.

"The cloud traveled to a great height first in the form of a ball, then mushroomed, then changed into a long trailing chimney-shaped column and finally was sent in several directions by the variable winds at the different elevations.

"Dr. Conant reached over and we shook hands in mutual congratulations. Dr. Bush, who was on the other side of me, did likewise. The feeling of the entire assembly, even the uninitiated, was of profound awe. Drs. Conant and Bush and myself were struck by an even stronger feeling that the faith of those who had been responsible for the initiation and the carrying on of this Herculean project had been justified.''

General Farrell's impressions are: ''The scene inside the shelter was dramatic beyond words. In and around the shelter were some twenty-odd people concerned with last-minute arrangements. Included were Dr. Oppenheimer, the director who had borne the great scientific burden of developing the weapon from the raw materials made in Tennessee and Washington, and a dozen of his key assistants, Dr. Kistiakowsky, Dr. Bainbridge, who supervised all the detailed arrangements for the test; the weather expert, and several others. Besides those, there were a handful of soldiers, two or three Army officers and one Naval Officer. The shelter was filled with a great variety of instruments and radios.

''For some hectic two hours preceding the blast, General Groves stayed with the director. Twenty minutes before the zero hour, General Groves left for his station at the base camp, first because it provided a better observation point and second, because of our rule that he and I must not be together in situations where there is an element of danger which existed at both points.

''Just after General Groves left, announcements began to be broadcast of the interval remaining before the blast to the other groups participating in and observing the test. As the time interval grew smaller and changed from minutes to seconds, the tension increased by leaps and bounds. Everyone in that room knew the awful potentialities of the thing that they thought was about to happen. The scientists felt that their figuring must be right and that the bomb had to go off but there was in everyone's mind a strong measure of doubt.

''We were reaching into the unknown and we did not know what might come of it. It can safely be said that most of those present were praying—and praying harder than they had ever prayed before. If the shot were successful, it was a justification of the several years of intensive effort of tens of thousands of people—statesmen, scientists, engineers, manufacturers, soldiers, and many others in every walk of life.

''In that brief instant in the remote New Mexico desert, the tremendous effort of the brains and brawn of all these people came suddenly and startlingly to the fullest fruition. Dr. Oppenheimer, on whom had rested a very heavy burden, grew tenser as the last seconds ticked off. He scarcely breathed. He held on to a post to steady himself. For the last few seconds, he stared directly ahead and then when the announcer shouted 'Now!' and there came this tremendous burst of light followed shortly thereafter by the deep growling roar of the explosion, his face relaxed into an expression of tremendous relief. Several of the observers standing back of the shelter to watch the lighting effects were knocked flat by the blast.

"The tension in the room let up and all started congratulating each other. Everyone sensed 'This is it!' No matter what might happen now all knew that the impossible scientific job had been done. Atomic fission would no longer be hidden in the cloisters of the theoretical physicists' dreams. It was almost full grown at birth. It was a great new force to be used for good or for evil. There was a feeling in that shelter that those concerned with its nativity should dedicate their lives to the mission that it would always be used for good and never for evil.

"Dr. Kistiakowsky threw his arms around Dr. Oppenheimer and embraced him with shouts of glee. Others were equally enthusiastic. All the pent-up emotions were released in those few minutes and all seemed to sense immediately that the explosion had far exceeded the most optimistic expectations and wildest hopes of the scientists. All seemed to feel that they had been present at the birth of a new age—The Age of Atomic Energy—and felt their profound responsibility to help in guiding into right channels the tremendous forces which had been unlocked for the first time in history.

"As to the present war, there was a feeling that no matter what else might happen, we now had the means to insure its speedy conclusion and save thousands of American lives. As to the future, there had been brought into being something big and something new that would prove to be immeasurably more important than the discovery of electricity or any of the other great discoveries which have so affected our existence.

"The effects could well be called unprecedented, magnificent, beautiful, stupendous and terrifying. No man-made phenomenon of such tremendous power had ever occurred before.

The lighting effects beggared description. The whole country was lighted by a searing light with the intensity many times that of the midday sun. It was golden, purple, violet, gray and blue. It lighted every peak, crevasse and ridge of the nearby mountain range with a clarity and beauty that cannot be described but must be seen to be imagined. It was that beauty the great poets dream about but describe most poorly and inadequately. Thirty seconds after, the explosion came first, the air blast pressing hard against the people and things, to be followed almost immediately by the strong, sustained, awesome roar which warned of doomsday and made us feel that we puny things were blasphemous to dare tamper with the forces heretofore reserved to the Almighty. Words are inadequate tools for the job of acquainting those not present with the physical, mental and psychological effects. It had to be witnessed to be realized.''

18

THOUGHTS ON PROGRESS, PEACEFUL COEXISTENCE AND INTELLECTUAL FREEDOM

Andrei D. Sakharov

The views of the author were formed in the milieu of the scientific and scientific-technological intelligentsia, which manifests much anxiety over the principles and specific aspects of foreign and domestic policy and over the future of mankind. This anxiety is nourished, in particular, by a realization that the scientific method of directing policy, the economy, arts, education, and military affairs still has not become a reality.

We regard as "scientific" a method based on deep analysis of facts, theories and views, presupposing unprejudiced, unfearing open discussion and conclusions. The complexity and diversity of all the phenomena of modern life, the great possibilities and dangers linked with the scientific-technical revolution and with a number of social tendencies demand precisely such an approach, as has been acknowledged in a number of official statements.

In this pamphlet, advanced for discussion by its readers, the author has set himself the goal to present, with the greatest conviction and frankness, two theses that are supported by many people in the world. The theses are:

1. The division of mankind threatens it with destruction. Civilization is imperiled by: a universal thermonuclear war,

Reprinted from *The New York Times*, 22 July 1968.

catastrophic hunger for most of mankind, stupefaction from the narcotic of "mass culture" and bureaucratized dogmatism, a spreading of mass myths that put entire peoples and continents under the power of cruel and treacherous demagogues, and destruction or degeneration from the unforeseeable consequences of swift changes in the conditions of life on our planet.

In the face of these perils, any action increasing the division of mankind, any preaching of the incompatibility of world ideologies and nations is madness and a crime. Only universal cooperation under conditions of intellectual freedom and the lofty moral ideals of socialism and labor, accompanied by the elimination of dogmatism and pressures of the concealed interests of ruling classes, will preserve civilization.

The reader will understand that ideological collaboration cannot apply to those fanatical, sectarian, and extremist ideologies that reject all possibility of rapprochement, discussion, and compromise, for example, the ideologies of Fascist, racist, militaristic, and Maoist demagogy.

Millions of people throughout the world are striving to put an end to poverty. They despise oppression, dogmatism, and demagogy (and their more extreme manifestations—racism, Fascism, Stalinism, and Maoism). They believe in progress based on the use, under conditions of social justice and intellectual freedom, of all the positive experience accumulated by mankind.

2. The second basic thesis is that intellectual freedom is essential to human society—freedom to obtain and distribute information, freedom for open-minded and unfearing debate, and freedom from pressure by officialdom and prejudices. Such a trinity of freedom of thought is the only guarantee against an infection of people by mass myths, which, in the hands of treacherous hypocrites and demagogues, can be transformed into bloody dictatorship. Freedom of thought is the only guarantee of the feasibility of a scientific democratic approach to politics, economy, and culture.

But freedom of thought is under a triple threat in modern society—from the opium of mass culture, from cowardly, egotistic, and narrow-minded ideologies, and from the ossified dogmatism of a bureaucratic oligarchy and its favorite weapon, ideological censorship. Therefore, freedom of thought requires the defense of all thinking and honest people. This is a mission not only for the intelligentsia but for all strata of society, particularly its most active and organized stratum, the working class. The worldwide dangers of war, famine, cults of personality, and bureaucracy—these are perils for all of mankind.

Recognition by the working class and the intelligentsia of their common interests has been a striking phenomenon of the present day. The most progressive, internationalist, and dedicated element of the intelligentsia is, in essence, part of the working class, and the most advanced, educated, internationalist, and broad-minded part of the working class is part of the intelligentsia.

This position of the intelligentsia in society renders senseless any loud demands that the intelligentsia subordinate its strivings to the will and interests of the working class (in the Soviet Union, Poland, and other socialist countries). What these demands really mean is subordination to the will of the party or, even more specifically, to the party's central apparatus and its officials. Who will guarantee that these officials always express the genuine interests of the working class as a whole and the genuine interests of progress rather than their own caste interests?

We will divide this pamphlet into two parts. The first we will title "Dangers," and the second, "The Basis of Hope."

DANGERS
The Threat of Nuclear War

Three technical aspects of thermonuclear weapons have made thermonuclear war a peril to the very existence of humanity. These aspects are the enormous destructive power of a thermonuclear explosion, the relative cheapness of rocket-thermonuclear weapons, and the impossibility of an effective defense against a massive rocket-nuclear attack.

Today one can consider a three-megaton nuclear warhead as "typical" (this is somewhere between the warhead of a Minuteman and of a Titan II). The area of fires from the explosion of such a warhead is 150 times greater than from the Hiroshima bomb and the area of destruction is 30 times greater. The detonation of such a warhead over a city would create a 100-square-kilometer [40-square-mile] area of total destruction and fire. Tens of millions of square meters of living space would be destroyed. No fewer than a million people would perish under the ruins of buildings, from fire and radiation, suffocate in the dust and smoke, or die in shelters buried under debris. In the event of a ground-level explosion, the fallout of radioactive dust would create a danger of fatal exposure in an area of tens of thousands of square kilometers.

A few words about the cost and the possible number of explosions. After the stage of research and development has been passed, mass production of thermonuclear weapons and carrier rockets is no more complex and expensive than, for example, the production of military aircraft, which were produced by the tens of thousands during the war. The annual production of plutonium in the world now is in the tens of thousands of tons. If one assumes that half this output goes for military purposes and that an average of several kilograms of plutonium goes into one warhead, then enough warheads have already been accumulated to destroy mankind many times over.

The third aspect of thermonuclear peril (along with the power and cheapness of warheads) is what we term the practical impossibility of preventing a massive rocket attack. This situation is well known to specialists. In the popular scientific literature, for example, one can read this in an article by Richard L. Garwin and Hans A. Bethe in the *Scientific American* of March 1968. The technology and tactics of attack have now far surpassed the technology of defense despite the development of highly maneuverable and powerful antimissiles with nuclear warheads and despite other technical ideas, such as the use of laser rays and so forth. Improvements in the resistance of warheads to shock waves and to the radiation effects of neutron and X-ray exposure, the possibility of mass use of relatively light and inexpensive decoys that are virtually indistinguishable from warheads and exhaust the capabilities of an antimissile defense system, a perfection of tactics of massed and concentrated attacks, in time and space, that overstrain the defense detection centers, the use of orbital and fractional-orbital attacks, the use of active and passive jamming and other methods not disclosed in the press—all this has created technical and economic obstacles to an effective missile defense that, at the present time, are virtually insurmountable.

The experience of past wars shows that the first use of a new technical or tactical method of attack is usually highly effective even if a simple antidote can soon be developed. But in a thermonuclear war the first blow may be the decisive one and render null and void years of work and billions spent on creation of an antimissile system.

An exception to this would be the case of a great technical and economic difference in the potentials of two enemies. In such a case, the stronger side, creating an antimissile defense system with a multiple reserve, would face the temptation of ending the dangerous and unstable balance once and for all by embarking on a pre-emptive adventure, expending part of its attack potential on destruction of most of the enemy's launching bases and counting on impunity for the last stage of escalation, that is, the destruction of the cities and industry of the enemy.

Fortunately for the stability of the world, the difference between the technical-economic potentials of the Soviet Union and the United States is not so great that one of the sides could undertake a "preventive aggression" without an almost inevitable risk of a destructive retaliatory blow. This situation would not be changed by a broadening of the arms race through the development of antimissile defenses.

In the opinion of many people, an opinion shared by the author, a diplomatic formulation of this mutually comprehended situation, for example, in the form of a moratorium on the construction of antimissile systems, would be a useful demonstration of a desire of the Soviet Union and the United States to preserve the status quo and not to widen the arms race for senselessly expensive antimissile systems. It would be a demonstration of a desire to cooperate, not to fight.

A thermonuclear war cannot be considered a continuation of politics by other means (according to the formula of Clausewitz). It would be a means of universal suicide.

Two kinds of attempts are being made to portray thermonuclear war as an "ordinary" political act in the eyes of public opinion. One is the concept of the "paper tiger," the concept of the irresponsible Maoist adventurists. The other is the strategic doctrine of escalation, worked out by scientific and militarist circles in the United States. Without minimizing the seriousness of the challenge inherent in that doctrine, we will just note that the political strategy of peaceful coexistence is an effective counterweight to the doctrine.

A complete destruction of cities, industry, transport, and sys-

tems of education; a poisoning of fields, water, and air by ra-
dioactivity; a physical destruction of the larger part of mankind,
poverty, barbarism, a return to savagery, and a genetic degener-
acy of the survivors under the impact of radiation; a destruction
of the material and information basis of civilization—this is a
measure of the peril that threatens the world as a result of the
estrangement of the world's two superpowers.

Every rational creature, finding itself on the brink of a disaster, first tries to get away from the brink and only then does it
think about the satisfaction of its other needs. If mankind is to
get away from the brink, it must overcome its divisions.

A vital step would be a review of the traditional method of
international affairs, which may be termed "empirical-
competitive." In the simplest definition, this is a method aim-
ing at maximum improvement of one's position everywhere
possible and, simultaneously, a method of causing maximum
unpleasantness to opposing forces without consideration of
common welfare and common interests.

If politics were a game of two gamblers, then this would be
the only possible method. But where does such a method lead
in the present unprecedented situation?

In Vietnam, the forces of reaction, lacking hope for an expression of national will in their favor, are using the force of
military pressure. They are violating all legal and moral norms
and are carrying out flagrant crimes against humanity. An entire people is being sacrificed to the proclaimed goal of stopping
the "Communist tide."

They strive to conceal from the American people considerations of personal and party prestige, the cynicism and cruelty,
the hopelessness and ineffectiveness of the anti-Communist
tasks of American policy in Vietnam, as well as the harm this
war is doing to the true goals of the American people, which
coincide with the universal tasks of bolstering peaceful coexistence.

To end the war in Vietnam would first of all save the people
perishing there. But it also is a matter of saving peace in all the
world. Nothing undermines the possibilities of peaceful coexistence more than a continuation of the war in Vietnam.

Another tragic example is the Middle East. If direct responsibility on Vietnam rests with the United States, in the Middle

East direct responsibility rests not with the United States but with the Soviet Union (and with Britain in 1948 and 1956).

On one hand, there was an irresponsible encouragement of so-called Arab unity (which in no way has a socialist character—look at Jordan—but was purely nationalist and anti-Israel). It was said that the struggle of the Arabs had an essentially anti-imperialist character. On the other hand, there was an equally irresponsible encouragement of Israeli extremists.

We cannot here analyze the entire contradictory and tragic history of the events of the last twenty years, in the course of which the Arabs and Israel, along with historically justified actions, carried out reprehensible deeds, often brought about by the actions of external forces.

Thus in 1948, Israel waged a defensive war. But in 1956, the actions of Israel appeared reprehensible. The preventive six-day war in the face of threats of destruction by merciless, numerically vastly superior forces of the Arab coalition could have been justifiable. But the cruelty to refugees and prisoners of war and the striving to settle territorial questions by military means must be condemned. Despite this condemnation, the breaking of relations with Israel appears a mistake, complicating a peaceful settlement in this region and complicating a necessary diplomatic recognition of Israel by the Arab governments.

In our opinion, certain changes must be made in the conduct of international affairs, systematically subordinating all concrete aims and local tasks to the basic task of actively preventing an aggravation of the international situation, of actively pursuing and expanding peaceful coexistence to the level of cooperation, of making policy in such a way that its immediate and long-range effects will in no way sharpen international tensions and will not create difficulties for either side that would strengthen the forces of reaction, militarism, nationalism, Fascism, and revanchism.

International affairs must be completely permeated with scientific methodology and a democratic spirit, with a fearless weighing of all facts, views and theories, with maximum publicity of ultimate and intermediate goals, and with a consistency of principles.

The international policies of the world's two leading superpowers (the United States and the Soviet Union) must be based on a universal acceptance of unified and general principles, which we initially would formulate as follows:

All peoples have the right to decide their own fate with a free expression of will. This right is guaranteed by international control over observance by all governments of the "Declaration of the Rights of Man." International control presupposes the use of economic sanctions as well as the use of military forces of the United Nations in defense of "the rights of man."

All military and military-economic forms of export of revolution and counterrevolution are illegal and are tantamount to aggression.

All countries strive toward mutual help in economic, cultural and general-organizational problems with the aim of eliminating painlessly all domestic and international difficulties and preventing a sharpening of international tensions and a strengthening of the forces of reaction.

International policy does not aim at exploiting local, specific conditions to widen zones of influence and create difficulties for another country. The goal of international policy is to insure universal fulfillment of the "Declaration of the Rights of Man" and to prevent a sharpening of international tensions and a strengthening of militarist and nationalist tendencies.

Such a set of principles would in no way be a betrayal of the revolutionary and national liberation struggle, the struggle against reaction and counterrevolution. On the contrary, with the elimination of all doubtful cases, it would be easier to take decisive action in those extreme cases of reaction, racism, and militarism that allow no course other than armed struggle. A strengthening of peaceful coexistence would create an opportunity to avert such tragic events as those in Greece and Indonesia.

Such a set of principles would present the Soviet armed forces with a precisely defined defensive mission, a mission of defending our country and our allies from aggression. As history has shown, our people and their armed forces are unconquerable when they are defending their homeland and its great social and cultural achievements.

Hunger and Overpopulation

Specialists are paying attention to a growing threat of hunger in the poorer half of the world. Although the 50 percent increase of the world's population in the last thirty years has been accompanied by a 70 percent increase in food production, the balance in the poorer half of the world has been unfavorable. The situation in India, Indonesia, in a number of countries of Latin America, and in a large number of countries of other underdeveloped countries—the absence of technical-economic reserves, competent officials, and cultural skills; social backwardness, a high birth rate—all this systematically worsens the food balance and without doubt will continue to worsen it in the coming years.

The answer would be a wide application of fertilizers, an improvement of irrigation systems, better farm technology, wider use of the resources of the oceans, and a gradual perfection of the production already technically feasible, of synthetic foods, primarily amino acids. However, this is all fine for the rich nations. In the more backward countries, it is apparent from an analysis of the situation and existing trends that an improvement cannot be achieved in the near future, before the expected date of tragedy, 1975–1980.

What is involved is a prognosticated deterioration of the average food balance in which localized food crises merge into a sea of hunger, intolerable suffering and desperation, the grief and fury of millions of people. This is a tragic threat to all mankind. A catastrophe of such dimension cannot but have profound consequences for the entire world and for every human being. It will provoke a wave of wars and hatred, a decline of standards of living throughout the world and will leave a tragic, cynical, and anti-Communist mark on the life of future generations.

The first reaction of a Philistine in hearing about the problem is that "they" are responsible for their plight because "they reproduce so rapidly." Unquestionably, control of the birth rate is important and the people in India, for example, are taking steps in this direction. But these steps remain largely ineffective under social and economic backwardness, surviving traditions of large families, an absence of old-age benefits, a high infant mortality rate, until quite recently, and a continuing threat of death from starvation.

It is apparently futile only to insist that the more backward countries restrict their birth rates. What is needed most of all is economic and technical assistance to these countries. This assistance must be of such scale and generosity that it is absolutely impossible before the estrangement in the world and the egotistical, narrow-minded approach to relations between nations and races is eliminated. It is impossible as long as the United States and the Soviet Union, the world's two great superpowers, look upon each other as rivals and opponents.

Social factors play an important role in the tragic present situation and the still more tragic future of the poor regions. It must be clearly understood that if a threat of hunger is, along with a striving toward national independence, the main cause of "agrarian" revolution, the "agrarian" revolution in itself will not eliminate the threat of hunger, at least not in the immediate future. The threat of hunger cannot be eliminated without the assistance of the developed countries, and this requires significant changes in their foreign and domestic policies.

At this time, the white citizens of the United States are unwilling to accept even minimum sacrifices to eliminate the unequal economic and cultural position of the country's black citizens, who make up 10 percent of the population, It is necessary to change the psychology of the American citizens so that they will voluntarily and generously support their government and worldwide efforts to change the economy, technology, and level of living of billions of people. This, of course, would entail a serious decline in the United States rate of economic growth. The Americans should be willing to do this solely for the sake of lofty and distant goals, for the sake of preserving civilization and mankind on our planet.

Similar changes in the psychology of people and practical activities of governments must be achieved in the Soviet Union and other developed countries. In the opinion of the author, a fifteen-year tax equal to 20 percent of national incomes must be imposed on developed nations. The imposition of such a tax would automatically lead to a significant reduction in expenditures for weapons. Such common assistance would have an important effect of stabilizing and improving the situation in the most underdeveloped countries, restricting the influence of extremists of all types.

Changes in the economic situation of underdeveloped countries would solve the problem of high birth rates with relative ease, as has been shown by the experience of developed countries, without the barbaric method of sterilization. Certain changes in the policies, viewpoints, and traditions on this delicate question are inescapable in the advanced countries as well. Mankind can develop smoothly only if it looks upon itself in a demographic sense as a unit, a single family without divisions into nations other than in matters of history and traditions. Therefore, government policy, legislation on the family and marriage, and propaganda should not encourage an increase in the birth rates of advanced countries while demanding that it be curtailed in underdeveloped countries that are receiving assistance. Such a two-faced game would produce nothing but bitterness and nationalism.

In conclusion on that point, I want to emphasize that the question of regulating birth rates is highly complex and that any standardized, dogmatic solution "for all time and all peoples" would be wrong. All the foregoing, incidentally, should be accepted with the reservation that it is somewhat of a simplification.

Pollution of Environment

We live in a swiftly changing world. Industrial and water-engineering projects, cutting of forests, plowing up of virgin lands, the use of poisonous chemicals—all this is changing the face of the earth, our "habitat." Scientific study of all the interrelationships in nature and the consequences of our interference clearly lag behind the changes. Large amounts of harmful wastes of industry and transport are being dumped into the air and water, including cancer-inducing substances. Will the safe limit be passed everywhere, as has already happened in a number of places?

Carbon dioxide from the burning of coal is altering the heat-reflecting qualities of the atmosphere. Sooner or later, this will reach a dangerous level. But we do not know when. Poisonous chemicals used in agriculture are penetrating into the body of man and animals directly and in more dangerous modified compounds, causing serious damage to the brain, the nervous system, blood-forming organs, the liver, and other organs. Here, too, the safe limit can be easily crossed, but the question has not been fully studied and it is difficult to control all these processes.

The use of antibiotics in poultry raising has led to the development of new disease-causing microbes that are resistant to antibiotics. I could also mention the problems of dumping detergents and radioactive wastes, erosion and salinization of soils, the flooding of meadows, the cutting of forests on mountain slopes and in watersheds, the destruction of birds and other useful wildlife like toads and frogs, and many other examples of senseless despoliation caused by local, temporary, bureaucratic, and egotistical interest and sometimes simply by questions of bureaucratic prestige, as in the sad fate of Lake Baikal.

The problem of geohygiene (earth hygiene) is highly complex and closely tied to economic and social problems. This problem can therefore not be solved on a national and especially not on a local basis. The salvation of our environment requires that we overcome our divisions and the pressure of temporary, local interests. Otherwise, the Soviet Union will poison the United States with its wastes and vice versa. At present, this is a hyperbole. But with a 10 percent annual increase of wastes, the increase over one hundred years will be twenty thousand times.

Police Dictatorships

An extreme reflection of the dangers confronting modern social development is the growth of racism, nationalism, and militarism and, in particular, the rise of demagogic, hypocritical, and monstrously cruel dictatorial police regimes. Foremost are the regimes of Stalin, Hitler, and Mao Tse-tung, and a number of extremely reactionary regimes in smaller countries: Spain, Portugal, South Africa, Greece, Albania, Haiti, and other Latin-American countries.

These tragic developments have always derived from the struggle of egotistical and group interests, the struggle for unlimited power, suppression of intellectual freedom, a spread of intellectually simplified, narrow-minded mass myths (the myth of race, of land and blood, the myth about the Jewish danger, anti-intellectualism, the concept of *lebensraum* in Germany, the myth about the sharpening of the class struggle and proletarian infallibility bolstered by the cult of Stalin and by exaggeration of the contradictions with capitalism in the Soviet Union, the myth about Mao Tse-tung, extreme Chinese nationalism and the resurrection of the *lebensraum* concept, of anti-intellectualism, extreme antihumanism, and certain prejudices of peasant socialism in China.) The usual practice is the use of demagogy, storm troopers, and Red Guards in the first stage and terrorist bureaucracy with reliable cadres of the type of Eichmann, Himmler, Yezhov, and Beria at the summit of the deification of unlimited power.

The world will never forget the burning of books in the squares of German cities, the hysterical, cannibalistic speeches of the Fascist "fuehrers," and their even more cannibalistic plans for the destruction of entire peoples, including the Russians. Fascism began a partial realization of these plans during the war they unleashed, annihilating prisoners of war and hostages, burning villages, carrying out a criminal policy of genocide (during the war, the main blow of genocide was aimed at the Jews, a policy that apparently was also meant to be provocative, especially in the Ukraine and Poland).

We shall never forget the kilometer-long trenches filled with bodies, the gas chambers, the SS dogs, the fanatical doctors, the piles of women's hair, suitcases with gold teeth, and fertilizer from the factories of death.

Analyzing the causes of Hitler's coming to power, we will never forget the role of German and international monopolist capital. We also will not forget the criminally sectarian and dogmatically narrow policies of Stalin and his associates, setting Socialists and Communists against one another (this has been well related in the famous letter to Ilya Ehrenburg by Ernst Henri).

Fascism lasted twelve years in Germany. Stalinism lasted twice as long in the Soviet Union. There are many common features but also certain differences. Stalinism exhibited a much more subtle kind of hypocrisy and demagogy, with reliance not on an openly cannibalistic program like Hitler's but on a progressive, scientific, and popular socialist ideology.

This served as a convenient screen for deceiving the working class and weakening the vigilance of the intellectuals and other rivals in the struggle for power, with the treacherous and sudden use of the machinery of torture, execution, and informants, intimidating and making fools of millions of people, the majority of whom were neither cowards nor fools. As a consequence of this "specific feature" of Stalinism, it was the Soviet people, its most active, talented, and honest representatives, who suffered the most terrible blow.

At least ten to fifteen million people perished in the torture

chambers of the N.K.V.D. [secret police] from torture and execution, in camps for exiled kulaks [rich peasants] and so-called
semikulaks and members of their families, and in camps "without the right of correspondence" (which were in fact the proto-
types of the Fascist death camps where, for example, thousands
of prisoners were machine-gunned because of "overcrowding"
or as a result of "special orders").

People perished in the mines of Norilsk and Vorkuta from
freezing, starvation, and exhausting labor; at countless construction projects; in timber cutting, building of canals, or simply during transportation in prison trains; in the overcrowded
holds of "death ships" in the Sea of Okhotsk; and during the
resettlement of entire peoples, the Crimean Tatars, the Volga
Germans, the Kalmyks and other Caucasus peoples. Readers of
the literary journal *Novy Mir* recently could read for themselves
a description of the "road of death" between Norilsk and Igar-
ka [in northern Siberia].

Temporary masters were replaced (Yagoda, Molotov, Yezhov, Zhdanov, Malenkov, Beria), but the antipeople's regime
of Stalin remained equally cruel and at the same time dogmatically narrow and blind in its cruelty. The killing of military and
engineering officials before the war, the blind faith in the "rea-
sonableness" of the colleague in crime, Hitler, and the other
reasons for the national tragedy of 1941 have been well described in the book by Nekrich, in the notes of Major General
Grigorenko and other publications—these are far from the only
examples of the combination of crime, narrow-mindedness,
and short-sightedness.

Stalinist dogmatism and isolation from real life was demonstrated particularly in the countryside, in the policy of unlimited exploitation and the predatory forced deliveries at
"symbolic" prices, in the almost serf-like enslavement of the
peasantry, the depriving of peasants of the most simple means
of mechanization, and the appointment of collective-farm
chairmen on the basis of their cunning and obsequiousness. The
results are evident—a profound and hard-to-correct destruction
of the economy and way of life in the countryside, which, by the
law of interconnected vessels, damaged industry as well.

The inhuman character of Stalinism was demonstrated by the
repression of prisoners of war who survived Fascist camps and

then were thrown into Stalinist camps, the antiworker "decrees," the criminal exile of entire peoples condemned to slow death, the unenlightened zoological kind of anti-Semitism that was characteristic of Stalinist bureaucracy and the N.K.V.D. (and Stalin personally), the Ukrainophobia characteristic of Stalin, and the draconian laws for the protection of socialist property (five years' imprisonment for stealing some grain from the fields and so forth) that served mainly as a means of fulfilling the demands of the "slave market."

A profound analysis of the origin and development of Stalinism is contained in the one thousand-page monograph of R. Medvedev. This was written from a socialist, Marxist point of view and is a successful work, but unfortunately it has not yet been published. The present author is not likely to receive such a compliment from Comrade Medvedev, who finds elements of "Westernism" in his views. Well, there is nothing like controversy! Actually the views of the present author are profoundly socialist and he hopes that the attentive reader will understand this.

The author is quite aware of the monstrous relations in human and international affairs brought forth by the egotistical principle of capital when it is not under pressure from socialist and progressive forces. He also thinks however, that progressives in the West understand this better than he does and are waging a struggle against these manifestations. The author is concentrating his attention on what is before his eyes and on what is obstructing, from his point of view, a worldwide overcoming of estrangement, obstructing the struggle for democracy, social progress, and intellectual freedom.

Our country has started on the path of cleansing away the foulness of Stalinism. "We are squeezing the slave out of ourselves drop by drop" (an expression of Anton Chekhov). We are learning to express our opinions, without taking the lead from the bosses and without fearing for our lives.

The beginning of this arduous and far-from-straight path evidently dates from the report of Nikita S. Khrushchev to the twentieth congress of the Soviet Communist party. This bold speech, which came as a surprise to Stalin's accomplices in crime, and a number of associated measures—the release of hundreds of thousands of political prisoners and their rehabilitation, steps toward a revival of the principles of peaceful coexistence and toward a revival of democracy—oblige us to value highly the historic role of Khrushchev despite his regrettable mistakes of a voluntarist character in subsequent years and despite the fact that Khrushchev, while Stalin was alive, was one of his collaborators in crime, occupying a number of influential posts.

The exposure of Stalinism in our country still has a long way to go. It is imperative, of course, that we publish all authentic documents, including the archives of the N.K.V.D., and conduct nationwide investigations. It would be highly useful for the international authority of the Soviet Communist party and the ideals of socialism if, as was planned in 1964 but never carried out, the party were to announce the "symbolic" expulsion of Stalin, murderer of millions of party members, and at the same time the political rehabilitation of the victims of Stalinism.

In 1936–1939 alone more than 1.2 million party members, half of the total membership, were arrested. Only 50,000 regained freedom; the others were tortured during interrogation or were shot (600,000) or died in camps. Only in isolated cases were the rehabilitated allowed to assume responsible posts; even fewer were permitted to take part in the investigation of crimes of which they had been witnesses or victims.

We are often told lately not to "rub salt into wounds." This is usually being said by people who suffered no wounds. Actually only the most meticulous analysis of the past and of its consequences will now enable us to wash off the blood and dirt that befouled our banner.

It is sometimes suggested in the literature that the political manifestations of Stalinism represented a sort of superstructure over the economic basis of an anti-Leninist pseudosocialism that led to the formation in the Soviet Union of a distinct class—a bureaucratic elite from which all key positions are filled and which is rewarded for its work through open and concealed privileges. I cannot deny that there is some (but not the whole) truth in such an interpretation, which would help explain the vitality of neo-Stalinism, but a full analysis of this issue would go beyond the scope of this article, which focuses on another aspect of the problem.

It is imperative that we restrict in every possible way the influence of neo-Stalinists in our political life. Here we are compelled to mention a specific person. One of the most influential representatives of neo-Stalinism at the present time is the director of the Science Department of the Communist party's Central Committee, Sergei P. Trapeznikov. The leadership of our country and our people should know that the views of this unquestionably intelligent, shrewd, and highly consistent man are basically Stalinist (from our point of view, they reflect the interests of the bureaucratic elite).

His views differ fundamentally from the dreams and aspirations of the majority and most active section of the intelligentsia, which, in our opinion, reflect the true interests of all our people and progressive mankind. The leadership of our country should understand that as long as such a man (if I correctly understand the nature of his views) exercises influence, it is impossible to hope for a strengthening of the party's position among scientific and artistic intellectuals. An indication of this was given at the last elections in the Academy of Sciences when S. P. Trapeznikov was rejected by a substantial majority of votes, but this hint was not "understood" by the leadership.

The issue does not involve the professional or personal qualities of Trapeznikov, about which I know little. The issue involves his political views. I have based the foregoing on word-of-mouth evidence. Therefore, I cannot in principle exclude the possibility (although it is unlikely) that in reality everything is quite the opposite. In that pleasant event, I would beg forgiveness and retract what I have written.

In recent years, demagogy, violence, cruelty, and vileness have seized a great country that had embarked on the path of socialist development. I refer, of course, to China. It is impossible without horror and pain to read about the mass contagion of antihumanism being spread by "the great helmsman" and his accomplices, about the Red Guards who, according to the Chinese radio, "jumped with joy" during public executions of "ideological enemies" of Chairman Mao.

The idiocy of the cult of personality has assumed in China monstrous, grotesquely tragicomic forms, carrying to the point of absurdity many of the traits of Stalinism and Hitlerism. But this absurdity has proved effective in making fools of tens of millions of people and in destroying and humiliating millions of more honest and more intelligent people.

The full picture of the tragedy in China is unclear. But in any case, it is impossible to look at it in isolation from the internal economic difficulties of China after the collapse of the adventure of "the great leap forward," in isolation from the struggle by various groups for power, or in isolation from the foreign political situation—the war in Vietnam, the estrangement in the world, and the inadequate and lagging struggle against Stalinism in the Soviet Union.

The greatest damage from Maoism is often seen in the split of the world Communist movement. That is, of course, not so. The split is the result of a disease and to some extent represents the way to treat that disease. In the presence of the disease a formal unity would have been a dangerous, unprincipled compromise that would have led the world Communist movement into a blind alley once and for all.

Actually the crimes of the Maoists against human rights have gone much too far, and the Chinese people are now in much greater need of help from the world's democratic forces to defend their rights than in need of the unity of the world's Communist forces, in the Maoist sense, for the purpose of combatting the so-called imperialist peril somewhere in Africa or in Latin America or in the Middle East.

The Threat to Intellectual Freedom

This is a threat to the independence and worth of the human personality, a threat to the meaning of human life. Nothing threatens freedom of the personality and the meaning of life like war, poverty, terror. But there are also indirect and only slightly more remote dangers.

One of these is the stupefaction of man (the "gray mass," to use the cynical term of bourgeois prognosticators) by mass culture with its intentional or commercially motivated lowering of intellectual level and content, with its stress on entertainment or utilitarianism, and with its carefully protective censorship.

Another example is related to the question of education. A system of education under government control, separation of school and church, universal free education—all these are great achievements of social progress. But everything has a reverse side. In this case it is excessive standardization, extending to the teaching process itself, to the curriculum, especially in literature, history, civics, geography, and to the system of examinations.

One cannot but see a danger in excessive reference to authority and in the limitation of discussion and intellectual boldness at an age when personal convictions are beginning to be formed. In the old China, the system of examinations for official positions led to mental stagnation and to the canonizing of the reactionary aspects of Confucianism. It is highly undesirable to have anything like that in modern society.

Modern technology and mass psychology constantly suggest new possibilities of managing the norms of behavior, the strivings and convictions of masses of people. This involves not only management through information based on the theory of advertising and mass psychology, but also more technical methods that are widely discussed in the press abroad. Examples are biochemical control of the birth rate, biochemical control of psychic processes, and electronic control of such processes.

It seems to me that we cannot completely ignore these new methods or prohibit the progress of science and technology, but we must be clearly aware of the awesome danger to basic human values and to the meaning of life that may be concealed in the misuse of technical and biochemical methods and the methods of mass psychology.

Man must not be turned into a chicken or a rat as in the well-known experiments in which elation is induced electrically through electrodes inserted into the brain. Related to this is the question of the ever-increasing use of tranquilizers and antidepressants, legal and illegal narcotics, and so forth.

We also must not forget the very real danger mentioned by Norbert Wiener in his book *Cybernetics,* namely the absence in cybernetic machines of stable human norms of behavior. The tempting, unprecedented power that mankind, or, even worse, a particular group in a divided mankind, may derive from the wise counsels of its future intellectual aides, the artificial "thinking" automata, may become, as Wiener warned, a fatal trap; the counsels may turn out to be incredibly insidious and, instead of pursuing human objectives, may pursue completely abstract problems that had been transformed in an unforeseen manner in the artificial brain. Such a danger will become quite real in a few decades if human values, particularly freedom of thought, are not strengthened, if alienation is not eliminated.

Let us now return to the dangers of today, to the need for intellectual freedom, which will enable the public at large and the intelligentsia to control and assess all acts, designs, and decisions of the ruling group.

Marx once wrote that the illusion that the "bosses know everything best" and "only the higher circles familiar with the official nature of things can pass judgment" was held by officials who equate the public weal with governmental authority. Both Marx and Lenin always stressed the viciousness of a bureaucratic system as the opposite of a democratic system. Lenin used to say that every cook should learn how to govern. Now the diversity and complexity of social phenomena and the dangers facing mankind have become immeasurably greater; and it is therefore all the more important that mankind be protected against the danger of dogmatic and voluntaristic errors, which are inevitable when decisions are reached in a closed circle of secret advisers or shadow cabinets.

It is no wonder that the problem of censorship (in the broadest sense of the word) has been one of the central issues in the ideological struggle of the last few years. Here is what a progressive American sociologist, Lewis A. Coser, has to say on this point:

> It would be absurd to attribute the alienation of many avant-garde authors solely to the battle with the censors, yet one may well maintain that those battles contributed in no mean measure to such alienation. To these authors, the censor came to be the very symbol of the Philistinism, hypocrisy, and meanness of bourgeois society.
>
> Many an author who was initially apolitical was drawn to the political left in the United States because the left was in the forefront of the battle against censorship. The close alliance of avant-garde art with avant-garde political and social radicalism can be accounted for, at least in part, by the fact that they came to be merged in the mind of many as a single battle for freedom against all repression. (I quote from an article by Igor Kon, published in *Novy Mir* in January 1968).

We are all familiar with the passionate and closely argued appeal against censorship by the outstanding Soviet writer A. Solzhenitsyn. He as well as G. Vladimov, G. Svirsky, and other writers who have spoken out on the subject have clearly shown how incompetent censorship destroys the living soul of Soviet literature; but the same applies, of course, to all other manifestations of social thought, causing stagnation and dullness and preventing fresh and deep ideas.

Such ideas, after all, can arise only in discussion, in the face of objections, only if there is a potential possibility of expressing not only true, but also dubious ideas. This was clear to the philosophers of ancient Greece and hardly anyone nowadays would have any doubts on that score. But after fifty years of complete domination over the minds of an entire nation, our leaders seem to fear even allusions to such a discussion.

At this point we must touch on some disgraceful tendencies that have become evident in the last few years. We will cite only a few isolated examples without trying to create a whole picture. The crippling censorship of Soviet artistic and political literature has again been intensified. Dozens of brilliant writings cannot see the light of day. They include some of the best of Solzhenitsyn's works, executed with great artistic and moral force and containing profound artistic and philosophical generalizations. Is this not a disgrace?

Wide indignation has been aroused by the recent decree adopted by the Supreme Soviet of the Russian Republic, amending the Criminal Code in direct contravention of the civil rights proclaimed by our Constitution. [The decree included literary protests among acts punishable under Article 190, which deals with failure to report crimes.]

The Daniel-Sinyavsky trial, which has been condemned by the progressive public in the Soviet Union and abroad (from Louis Aragon to Graham Greene) and has compromised the Communist system, has still not been reviewed. The two writers languish in a camp with a strict regime and are being subjected (especially Daniel) to harsh humiliations and ordeals.

Most political prisoners are now kept in a group of camps in the Mordvinian Republic, where the total number of prisoners, including criminals, is about fifty thousand. According to available information, the regime has become increasingly severe in these camps, with personnel left over from Stalinist times playing an increasing role. It should be said, in all fairness, that a certain improvement has been noted very recently; it is to be hoped that this turn of events will continue.

The restoration of Leninist principles of public control over places of imprisonment would undoubtedly be a healthy development. Equally important would be a complete amnesty of political prisoners, and not just the recent limited amnesty, which was proclaimed on the fiftieth anniversary of the October Revolution as a result of a temporary victory of rightist tendencies in our leadership. There should also be a review of all political trials that are still raising doubts among the progressive public.

Was it not disgraceful to allow the arrest, twelve-month detention without trial, and then the conviction and sentencing to terms of five to seven years of Ginzburg, Galanskov, and others for activities that actually amounted to a defense of civil liberties and (partly as an example) of Daniel and Sinyavsky personally. The author of these lines sent an appeal to the party's Central Committee on February 11, 1967, asking that the Ginzburg-Galanskov case be closed. He received no reply and no explanations on the substance of the case. It was only later that he heard that there had been an attempt (apparently inspired by Semichastny, the former chairman of the K.G.B.) to slander the present writer and several other persons on the basis of inspired false testimony by one of the accused in the Galanskov-Ginzburg case. Subsequently the testimony of that person—Dobrovolsky—was used at the trial as evidence to show that Ginzburg and Galanskov had ties with a foreign anti-Soviet organization, which one cannot help but doubt. [The reference here is to evidence given by Dobrovolsky in the pretrial investigation of the case of Vladimir Bukovsky, Vadim Delone, and Yevgeny Kushev in early 1967. Dobrovolsky said there allegedly existed "a single anti-Communist front ranging from Academicians Sakharov and Leontovich to SMOG," an illegal group of young writers and artists.]

Was it not disgraceful to permit the conviction and sentencing (to three years in camps) of Khaustov and Bukovsky for participation in a meeting in defense of their comrades? Was it not disgraceful to allow persecution, in the best witchhunt tradition, of dozens of members of the Soviet intelligentsia who spoke out against the arbitrariness of judicial and psychiatric agencies, to attempt to force honorable people to sign false, hypocritical "retractions," to dismiss and blacklist people, to deprive young writers, editors, and other members of the intelligentsia of all means of existence?

Here is a typical example of this kind of activity.

Comrade B., a woman editor of books on motion pictures, was summoned to the party's district committee. The first question was, Who gave you the letter in defense of Ginzburg to sign? Allow me not to reply to that question, she answered. All right, you can go, we want to talk this over, she was told. The decision was to expel the woman from the party and to recommend that she be dismissed from her job and barred from working anywhere else in the field of culture.

With such methods of persuasion and indoctrination the party can hardly expect to claim the role of spiritual leader of mankind.

Was it not disgraceful to have the speech at the Moscow party conference by the president of the Academy of Sciences [Mstislav V. Keldvsh], who is evidently either too intimidated or too dogmatic in his views? Is it not disgraceful to allow another backsliding into anti-Semitism in our appointments policy (incidentally, in the highest bureaucratic elite of our government, the spirit of anti-Semitism was never fully dispelled after the nineteen thirties)?

Was it not disgraceful to continue to restrict the civil rights of the Crimean Tatars, who lost about 46 percent of their numbers (mainly children and old people) in the Stalinist repressions? Nationality problems will continue to be a reason for unrest and dissatisfaction unless all departures from Leninist principles are acknowledged and analyzed and firm steps are taken to correct mistakes.

Is it not highly disgraceful and dangerous to make increasingly frequent attempts, either directly or indirectly (through silence), to publicly rehabilitate Stalin, his associates and his policy, his pseudosocialism of terroristic bureaucracy, a socialism of hypocrisy and ostentatious growth that was at best a quantitative and one-sided growth involving the loss of many qualitative features? (This is a reference to the basic tendencies and consequences of Stalin's policy, or Stalinism, rather than a comprehensive assessment of the entire diversified situation in a huge country with 200 million people.)

Although all these disgraceful phenomena are still far from the monstrous scale of the crimes of Stalinism and rather resemble in scope the sadly famous McCarthyism of the cold war era, the Soviet public cannot but be highly disturbed and indignant and display vigilance even in the face of insignificant manifestations of neo-Stalinism in our country.

We are convinced that the world's Communists will also view negatively any attempts to revive Stalinism in our country, which would, after all, be an awful blow to the attractive force of Communist ideas throughout the world.

Today the key to a progressive restructuring of the system of government in the interests of mankind lies in intellectual freedom. This has been understood, in particular, by the Czechoslovaks and there can be no doubt that we should support their bold initiative, which is so valuable for the future of socialism and all mankind. That support should be political and, in the early stages, include increased economic aid.

The situation involving censorship in our country is such that it can hardly be corrected for any length of time simply by ''liberalized'' directives. Major organizational and legislative measures are required, for example, adoption of a special law on press and information that would clearly and convincingly define what can and what cannot be printed and would place the responsibility on competent people who would be under public control. It is essential that the exchange of information on an international scale (press, tourism, and so forth) be expanded in every way, that to get to know ourselves better we not try to save on sociological, political, and economic research and surveys, which should not be conducted only according to government-controlled programs (otherwise we might be tempted to avoid ''unpleasant'' subjects and questions).

THE BASIS FOR HOPE

The prospects of socialism now depend on whether socialism can be made attractive, whether the moral attractiveness of the ideas of socialism and the glorification of labor, compared with the egotistical ideas of private ownership and the glorification of capital, will be the decisive factors that people will bear in mind when comparing socialism and capitalism, or whether people will remember mainly the limitations of intellectual freedom under socialism or, even worse, the Fascistic regimes of the cult [of personality].

I am placing the accent on the moral aspect because, when it comes to achieving a high productivity of social labor or developing all productive forces or insuring a high standard of living for most of the population, capitalism and socialism seem to have "played to a tie." Let us examine this question in detail.

Imagine two skiers racing through deep snow. At the start of the race, one of them, in striped jacket, was many kilometers ahead, but now the skier in the red jacket is catching up to the leader. What can he say about their relative strength? Not very much since each skier is racing under different conditions. The striped one broke the snow, and the red one did not have to. (The reader will understand that this ski race symbolizes the burden of research and development costs that the country leading in technology has to bear.) All one can say about the race is that there is not much difference in strength between the two skiers. (The parable does not, of course, reflect the whole complexity of comparing economic and technological progress in the United States and the Soviet Union, the relative vitality of RRS and American Efficiency.) We cannot forget that during much of the period in question the Soviet Union waged a hard war and then healed its wounds; we cannot forget that some absurdities in our development were not an inherent aspect of the socialist course of development, but a tragic accident, a serious, though not inevitable, disease.

On the other hand, any comparison must take account of the fact that we are now catching up with the United States only in some of the old, traditional industries, which are no longer as important as they used to be for the United States (for example, coal and steel). In some of the newer fields, for example, automation, computers, petrochemicals, and especially in industrial research and development, we are not only lagging behind but are also growing more slowly, so that a complete victory of our economy in the next few decades is unlikely.

It must also be borne in mind that our nation is endowed

with vast natural resources, from fertile black earth to coal and forest, from oil to manganese and diamonds. It must be borne in mind that during the period under review our people worked to the limit of its capacity, which resulted in a certain depletion of resources.

We must also bear in mind the ski-track effect, in which the Soviet Union adopted principles of industrial organization and technological and development previously tested in the United States. Examples are the method of calculating the national fuel budget, assembly-line techniques, antibiotics, nuclear power, oxygen converters in steel making, hybrid corn, self-propelled harvester combines, strip mining of coal, rotary excavators, semiconductors in electronics, the shift from steam to diesel locomotives, and much more.

There is only one justifiable conclusion and it can be formulated cautiously as follows:

1. We have demonstrated the vitality of the socialist course, which has done a great deal for the people materially, culturally, and socially and, like no other system, has glorified the moral significance of labor.

2. There are no grounds for asserting, as is often done in the dogmatic vein, that the capitalist mode of production leads the economy into a blind alley or that it is obviously inferior to the socialist mode in labor productivity, and there are certainly no grounds for asserting that capitalism always leads to absolute impoverishment of the working class.

The continuing economic progress being achieved under capitalism should be a fact of great theoretical significance for any nondogmatic Marxist. It is precisely this fact that lies at the basis of peaceful coexistence and it suggests, in principle, that if capitalism ever runs into an economic blind alley it will not necessarily have to leap into a desperate military adventure. Both capitalism and socialism are capable of long-term development, borrowing positive elements from each other in a number of essential aspects.

I can just hear the outcries about revisionism and blunting of the class approach to this issue; I can just see the smirks about political naiveté and immaturity. But the facts suggest that there is real economic progress in the United States and other capitalist countries, that the capitalists are actually using the social principles of socialism, and that there has been real improvement of the position of the working people. More important, the facts suggest that on any other course except ever-increasing coexistence and collaboration between the two systems and the two superpowers, with a smoothing of contradictions and with mutual assistance, on any other course annihilation awaits mankind. There is no other way out.

We will now compare the distribution of personal income and consumption for various social groups in the United States and the Soviet Union. Our propaganda materials usually assert that there is crying inequality in the United States, while the Soviet Union has something entirely just, entirely in the interests of the working people. Actually both statements contain half-truths and a fair amount of hypocritical evasion.

I have no intention of minimizing the tragic aspects of the poverty, lack of rights, and humiliation of the twenty-two million American Negroes. But we must clearly understand that this problem is not primarily a class problem, but a racial problem, involving the racism and egotism of white workers, and that the ruling group in the United States is interested in solving this problem. To be sure the government has not been as active as it should be; this may be related to fears of an electoral character and to fears of upsetting the unstable equilibrium in the country and thus activating extreme leftist and especially extreme rightist parties. It seems to me that we in the socialist camp should be interested in letting the ruling group in the United States settle the Negro problem without aggravating the situation in the country.

At the other extreme, the presence of millionaires in the United States is not a serious economic burden in view of their small number. The total consumption of the rich is less than 20 percent, that is, less than the total rise of national consumption over a five-year period. From this point of view, a revolution, which would be likely to halt economic progress for more than five years, does not appear to be an economically advantageous move for the working people. And I am not even talking of the blood-letting that is inevitable in a revolution. And I am not talking of the danger of the "irony of history," about which Friedrich Engels wrote so well in his famous letter to V. Zasulich, the "irony" that took the form of Stalinism in our country.

There are, of course, situations where revolution is the only way out. This applies especially to national uprisings. But that is not the case in the United States and other developed capitalist countries, as suggested, incidentally, in the programs of the Communist parties of these countries.

As far as our country is concerned, here, too, we should avoid painting an idyllic picture. There is still great inequality in property between the city and the countryside, especially in rural areas that lack a transport outlet to the private market or do not produce any goods in demand in private trade. There are great differences between cities with some of the new, privileged industries and those with older, antiquated industries. As a result 40 percent of the Soviet population is in difficult economic circumstances. In the United States about 25 percent of the population is on the verge of poverty. On the other hand the 5 percent of the Soviet population that belong to the managerial group is as privileged as its counterpart in the United States.

The development of modern society in both the Soviet Union and the United States is now following the same course of increasing complexity of structure and of industrial management, giving rise in both countries to managerial groups that are similar in social character. We must therefore acknowledge that there is no qualitative difference in the structure of society of the two countries in terms of distribution of consumption. Unfortunately the effectiveness of the managerial group in the Soviet Union (and, to a lesser extent, in the United States) is measured not only in purely economic or productive terms. This group also performs a concealed protective function that is rewarded in the sphere of consumption by concealed privileges. Few people are aware of the practice under Stalin of paying salaries in sealed envelopes, of the constantly recurring concealed distribution of scarce foods and goods for various services, privileges in vacation resorts, and so forth.

I want to emphasize that I am not opposed to the socialist principle of payment based on the amount and quality of labor. Relatively higher wages for better administrators, for highly skilled workers, teachers, and physicians, for workers in dangerous or harmful occupations, for workers in science, culture, and the arts, all of whom account for a relatively small part of the total wage bill, do not threaten society if they are not accompanied by concealed privileges; moreover, higher wages benefit society if they are deserved.

The point is that every wasted minute of a leading administrator represents a major material loss for the economy and every wasted minute of a leading figure in the arts means a loss in the emotional, philosophical, and artistic wealth of society. But when something is done in secret, the suspicion inevitably arises that things are not clean, that loyal servants of the existing system are being bribed.

It seems to me that the rational way of solving this touchy problem would be not the setting of income ceilings for party members or some such measure, but simply the prohibition of all privileges and the establishment of unified wage rates based on the social value of labor and an economic market approach to the wage problem.

I consider that further advances in our economic reform and a greater role for economic and market factors accompanied by increased public control over the managerial group (which, incidentally, is also essential in capitalist countries) will help eliminate all the roughness in our present distribution pattern.

An even more important aspect of the economic reform for the regulation and stimulation of production is the establishment of a correct system of market prices, proper allocation and rapid utilization of investment funds, and proper use of natural and human resources based on appropriate rents in the interest of our society. A number of socialist countries, including the Soviet Union, Yugoslavia, and Czechoslovakia, are now experimenting with basic economic problems of the role of planning and of the market, government and cooperative ownership, and so forth. These experiments are of great significance.

Summing up, we now come to our basic conclusion about the moral and ethical character of the advantages of the socialist course of development of human society. In our view, this does not in any way minimize the significance of socialism. Without socialism, bourgeois practicism and the egotistical principle of private ownership gave rise to the "people of the abyss" described by Jack London and earlier by Engels.

Only the competition with socialism and the pressure of the working class made possible the social progress of the twentieth century and, all the more, will insure the now inevitable process of rapprochement of the two systems. It took socialism to raise the meaning of labor to the heights of a moral feat. Before the advent of socialism, national egotism gave rise to colonial oppression, nationalism, and racism. By now it has become clear that victory is on the side of the humanistic, international approach.

The capitalist world could not help giving birth to the socialist, but now the socialist world should not seek to destroy by force the ground from which it grew. Under the present conditions this would be tantamount to suicide of mankind. Socialism should ennoble that ground by its example and other indirect forms of pressure and then merge with it.

The rapprochement with the capitalist world should not be an unprincipled, antipopular plot between ruling groups, as happened in the extreme case [of the Soviet-Nazi rapprochement] of 1939–1940. Such a rapprochement must rest not only on a socialist, but on a popular, democratic foundation, under the control of public opinion as expressed through publicity, elections, and so forth.

Such a rapprochement implies not only wide social reforms in the capitalist countries, but also substantial changes in the structure of ownership, with a greater role played by government and cooperative ownership, and the preservation of the basic present features of ownership of the means of production in the socialist countries.

Our allies along this road are not only the working class and the progressive intelligentsia, which are interested in peaceful coexistence and social progress and in a democratic, peaceful transition to socialism (as reflected in the programs of the Communist parties of the developed countries), but also the reformist part of the bourgeoisie, which supports such a program of "convergence." (Although I am using this term, taken from the Western literature, it is clear from the foregoing that I have given it a socialist and democratic meaning.)

Typical representatives of the reformist bourgeoisie are Cyrus Eaton, President Franklin D. Roosevelt, and, especially, President John F. Kennedy. Without wishing to cast a stone in the direction of Comrade N. S. Khrushchev (our high esteem of his services was expressed earlier), I cannot help recalling one of his statements, which may have been more typical of his entourage than of him personally.

On July 10, 1961, in speaking at a reception of specialists about his meeting with Kennedy in Vienna, Comrade Khrushchev recalled Kennedy's request that the Soviet Union, in conducting policy and making demands, consider the actual possibilities and the difficulties of the new Kennedy Administration and refrain from demanding more than it could grant without courting the danger of being defeated in elections and being replaced by rightist forces. At that time, Khrushchev did not give Kennedy's unprecedented request the proper attention, to put it mildly, and began to rail. And now, after the shots in Dallas, who can say what auspicious opportunities in world history have been, if not destroyed, at any rate set back because of a lack of understanding.

Bertrand Russell once told a peace congress in Moscow that ''the world will be saved from thermonuclear annihilation if the leaders of each of the two systems prefer complete victory of the other system to a thermonuclear war'' (I am quoting from memory). It seems to me that such a solution would be acceptable to the majority of people in any country, whether capitalist or socialist. I consider that the leaders of the capitalist and socialist systems by the very nature of things will gradually be forced to adopt the point of view of the majority of mankind.

Intellectual freedom of society will facilitate and smooth the way for this trend toward patience, flexibility, and a security from dogmatism, fear, and adventurism. All mankind, including its best organized and active forces, the working class and the intelligentsia, is interested in freedom and security.

Four-Stage Plan for Cooperation

Having examined in the first part of this essay the development of mankind according to the worse alternative, leading to annihilation, we must now attempt, even schematically, to suggest the better alternative. (The author concedes the primitiveness of his attempts at prognostication, which requires the joint efforts of many specialists, and here, even more than elsewhere, invites positive criticism.)

In the first stage, a growing ideological struggle in the socialist countries between Stalinist and Maoist forces, on the one hand, and the realistic forces of leftist Leninist Communists (and leftist Westerners), on the other, will lead to a deep ideological split on an international, national, and intraparty scale.

In the Soviet Union and other socialist countries, this process will lead first to a multiparty system (here and there) and to acute ideological struggle and discussions, and then to the ideological victory of the realists, affirming the policy of increasing peaceful coexistence, strengthening democracy, and expanding economic reforms (1960–1980). The dates reflect the most optimistic unrolling of events.

The author, incidentally, is not one of those who consider the multiparty system to be an essential stage in the development of the socialist system or, even less, a panacea for all ills, but he assumes that in some cases a multiparty system may be an inevitable consequence of the course of events when a ruling Communist party refuses for one reason or another to rule by the scientific democratic method required by history.

In the second stage, persistent demands for social progress and peaceful coexistence in the United States and other capitalist countries, and pressure exerted by the example of the socialist countries and by internal progressive forces (the working class and the intelligentsia) will lead to the victory of the leftist reformist wing of the bourgeoisie, which will begin to implement a program of rapprochement (convergence) with socialism, that is, social progress, peaceful coexistence, and collaboration with socialism on a world scale and changes in the structure of ownership. This phase includes an expanded role for the intelligentsia and an attack on the forces of racism and militarism (1972–1985). (The various stages overlap.)

In the third stage, the Soviet Union and the United States, having overcome their alienation, solve the problem of saving the poorer half of the world. The above-mentioned 20-percent tax on the national income of developed countries is applied. Gigantic fertilizer factories and irrigation systems using atomic power will be built [in the developing countries], the resources of the sea will be used to a vastly greater extent, indigenous personnel will be trained, and industrialization will be carried out. Gigantic factories will produce synthetic amino acids, and synthesize proteins, fats, and carbohydrates. At the same time disarmament will proceed (1972–1990).

In the fourth stage, the socialist convergence will reduce differences in social structure, promote intellectual freedom, scientific and economic progress, and lead to creation of a world government and the smoothing of national contradictions

(1980–2000). During this period decisive progress can be expected in the field of nuclear power, on the basis of both uranium and thorium and, probably, deuterium and lithium. Some authors consider it likely that explosive breeding (the reproduction of active materials such as plutonium, uranium 233 and tritium) may be used in subterranean or other enclosed explosions.

During this period the expansion of space exploration will require thousands of people to work and live continuously on other planets and on the moon, on artificial satellites and on asteroids whose orbits will have been changed by nuclear explosions.

The synthesis of materials that are superconductors at room temperature may completely revolutionize electrical technology, cybernetics, transportation, and communications. Progress in biology (in this and subsequent periods) will make possible effective control and direction of all life processes at the levels of the cell, organism, ecology, and society, from fertility and aging to psychic processes and heredity.

If such an all-encompassing scientific and technological revolution, promising uncounted benefits for mankind, is to be possible and safe, it will require the greatest possible scientific foresight and care and concern for human values of a moral, ethical, and personal character. (I touched briefly on the danger of a thoughtless bureaucratic use of the scientific and technological revolution in a divided world in the section on "Dangers," but could add a great deal more.) Such a revolution will be possible and safe only under highly intelligent worldwide guidance.

The foregoing program presumes: (a) worldwide interest in overcoming the present divisions; (b) the expectation that modifications in both the socialist and capitalist countries will tend to reduce contradictions and differences; (c) worldwide interest of the intelligentsia, the working class, and other progressive forces in a scientific democratic approach to politics, economics, and culture; (d) the absence of unsurmountable obstacles to economic development in both world economic systems that might otherwise lead inevitably into a blind alley, despair, and adventurism.

Every honorable and thinking person who has not been poisoned by narrowminded indifference will seek to insure that future development will be along the lines of the better alternative. However only broad, open discussion without the pressure of fear and prejudice will help the majority to adopt the correct and best course of action.

In conclusion, I will sum up some of the concrete proposals of varying degrees of importance that have been discussed in the text. These proposals, addressed to the leadership of the country, do not exhaust the content of the article.

The strategy of peaceful coexistence and collaboration must be deepened in every way. Scientific methods and principles of international policy will have to be worked out, based on scientific prediction of the immediate and more distant consequences.

The initiative must be seized in working out a broad program of struggle against hunger.

A law on press and information must be drafted, widely discussed, and adopted, with the aim not only of ending irresponsible and irrational censorship, but of encouraging self-study in our society, fearless discussion, and the search for truth. The law must provide for the material resources of freedom of thought.

All anticonstitutional laws and decrees violating human rights must be abrogated.

Political prisoners must be amnestied and some of the recent political trials must be reviewed (for example, the Daniel-Sinyavsky and Galanskov-Ginzburg cases). The camp regime of political prisoners must be promptly relaxed.

The exposure of Stalin must be carried through to the end, to the complete truth, and not just to the carefully weighed half-truth dictated by caste considerations. The influence of neo-Stalinists in our political life must be restricted in every way (the text mentioned, as an example, the case of S. Trapeznikov, who enjoys too much influence).

The economic reform must be deepened in every way and the area of experimentation expanded, with conclusions based on the results.

A law on geohygiene must be adopted after broad discussion, and ultimately become part of world efforts in this area.

With this article the author addresses the leadership of our country and all its citizens as well as all people of goodwill throughout the world. The author is aware of the controversial character of many of his statements. His purpose is open, frank discussion under conditions of publicity.

In conclusion, a textological comment. In the process of discussion of previous drafts of this article, some incomplete and in some respects one-sided texts have been circulated. Some of them contained certain passages that were inept in form and tact and were included through oversight. The author asks readers to bear this in mind. The author is deeply grateful to readers of preliminary drafts who communicated their friendly comments and thus helped improve the article and refine a number of basic statements.

APPENDIX: PEOPLE MENTIONED

ARAGON, LOUIS (born 1895): French Communist writer, who protested Soviet literary trials.

BERIA, LAVRENTI P. (1899–1953): Stalin's chief of secret police; executed by Stalin's successors.

BUKOVSKY, VLADIMIR: young Soviet writer; sentenced in September 1967 to three years' imprisonment for participation in an unauthorized demonstration.

CLAUSEWITZ, KARL VON (1780–1831): Prussian general and military writer.

CRIMEAN TATARS: Soviet ethnic minority, exiled in World War II for alleged collaboration with the Germans; fully cleared of accusation in July 1967.

DANIEL, YULI M.: Soviet writer, sentenced in February 1966 to five years' imprisonment on charges of having slandered the Soviet Union in books published abroad under the pen name Nikolai Arzhak.

DELONE, VADIM: young Soviet poet; sentenced with Bukovsky to one year's imprisonment.

EHRENBURG, ILYA: the Soviet novelist, who died last August at the age of 76.

DOBROVOLSKY, ALEKSEI: contributor to Soviet underground magazine *Phoenix* 1966; arrested January 1967 with Ginzburg and Galanskov; turned state's evidence; sentenced in January 1968 to two years.

EICHMANN, ADOLF: SS colonel who headed Gestapo's Jewish section; arrested by Israel in May 1960; tried and executed in May 1962.

GALANSKOV, YURI: editor of Soviet underground magazine *Phoenix* 1966; sentenced in January 1968 to seven years' imprisonment for anti-Soviet activity.

GINZBURG, ALEKSANDR: author of a book on the Sinyavsky-Daniel case that was published abroad; sentenced in January 1968 to five years' imprisonment for anti-Soviet activity.

GLAVLIT: the Soviet censorship agency.

GREENE, GRAHAM: the British novelist, who protested Soviet literary trials.

GRIGORENKO, PYOTR G.: former major general in World War II; cashiered in 1964 on charges of anti-Soviet activity.

HENRI, ERNST: pseudonym for a Soviet commentator, Semyon Rostovsky, who contributes frequently to the weekly *Literaturnaya Gazeta.*

HIMMLER, HEINRICH: Hitler's secret police chief; suicide in 1945.

KHAUSTOV, VIKTOR: sentenced in February 1967 to three years' imprisonment for organizing demonstration on behalf of arrested writers.

KUSHEV, YEVGENY: young Soviet poet; sentenced in September 1967 to one year's imprisonment for participation in protest demonstration.

LEONTOVICH, MIKHAIL A. (born 1903): Soviet nuclear physicist; an associate of Andrei D. Sakharov.

MALENKOV, GEORGI M. (born 1902): a close associate of Stalin; expelled from the Soviet leadership by Nikita S. Khrushchev in 1957.

MOLOTOV, VYACHESLAV M. (born 1890): a close associate of Stalin; expelled from the Soviet leadership by Nikita S. Khrushchev in 1957.

NEKRICH, ALEKSANDR M.: Soviet historian, author of book on the German attack on the Soviet Union in 1941; ousted from Communist party in 1967.

SEMICHASTNY, VLADIMIR Y.: chairman of the K.G.B., Soviet secret police from 1961 until relieved of his post in May 1967.

SINYAVSKY, ANDREI D.: Soviet writer, sentenced in February 1966 to seven years' imprisonment on charges of having slandered the Soviet Union in books published abroad under the pen name of Abram Tertz.

SOLZHENITSYN, ALEKSANDR I.: Soviet writer; author of *One Day in the Life of Ivan Denisovich;* in official disfavor and unpublished in recent years [subsequently emigrated to the West, where *The Gulag Archipelago* was published].

WIENER, NORBERT (1894–1964): American mathematician; founder of the science of cybernetics, which laid the basis for computer technology.

YAGODA, GENRIKH G.: Stalin's chief of secret police from 1934 to 1936; supervised early phase of great purges; was himself purged and executed in 1938.

YEZHOV, NIKOLAI I.: Stalin's chief of secret police from 1936 to 1938; supervised the main phase of great purges; disappeared in 1939.

ZASULICH, VERA I. (1851–1919): early Russian Marxist who had correspondence with Marx and Engels; she opposed terrorism as a revolutionary tactic and joined Menshevik faction against Lenin.

ZHDANOV, ANDREI A. (1896–1948): a close associate of Stalin, in charge of artistic and scientific policies at height of his career from 1945 to 1948.

19

THE CHANCES FOR PEACE

HANS SPEIER

Statesmen frequently declare that they want to preserve peace. Such declarations are both popular and useful. For one thing, we associate peace with life and the expectation that tomorrow's calamities will not be worse than the misfortunes we survived yesterday. For another, existing international conflicts appear less disturbing to us when we are not urged to view them in the light of national interests but hear that men who deal full time with the conflicts want to resolve them amicably. Clearly, professions of peace are preferable to warnings that war is inevitable or imminent, as we have heard them in recent times primarily from Chinese and Arab leaders.

Of course, when statesmen and diplomats publicly talk of peace or war they usually have certain political objectives in mind, so it would be naive to consider their pronouncements to be the historical or philosophical truth. It takes at least two to make peace, but only one to disturb it. Often in the past declarations of peace did not halt the outbreak of war, and sometimes talk of peace has been rhetoric that statesmen indulged in to deceive others or themselves.

Neville Chamberlain proclaimed "peace in our time" after reaching an agreement with Hitler in Munich; the invasion of Poland was not far off. Throughout the period of the so-called cold war, the leaders of Communist nations claimed to speak and act in the interest of peace-loving people everywhere, but they rejected the Baruch Plan and they denounced the Marshall Plan. Under John F. Kennedy, "peace as a process" became an oft-repeated slogan; the president insisted on it, among other things, in order to disabuse people of the notion that peace had been firmly established by the beginnings of détente with the Soviet Union so that costly security efforts could be relaxed. Lately, we have heard a great deal in the United States about "peace with honor," the "structure of a lasting peace," and, with reference to China, even about "the long march toward peace." Brezhnev, on his part, and the Soviet press welcome the recognition of existing boundaries in Europe as the foundation of peace.

PEACE NOT INDIVISIBLE

As the era of negotiation allegedly has replaced that of confrontation, and as "relaxation of tension," "peaceful coexistence," "détente," and "renunciation of force" have become favored terms in the political vocabulary, peace research has become fashionable in Western academic circles. Some now hold it to be more respectable than research on war and to be different from, if not morally superior to, the study of international relations.

In my opinion, a generalized conception of peace is not very helpful in understanding the problems of war and peace because there are many different kinds of peace as well as war. Unless we specify more exactly what we are talking about, our talk will be empty.

Let us start with the observation that peace is not indivisible. At least four reasons can be adduced to support this proposition.

First, as Hobbes observed, the climate in the relations between states is not confined to the extremes of foul and fair weather. There are many kinds of weather, that is, many kinds of war and peace. Just as not all wars are total wars, so not all peaceful relations represent a state of full harmony of interests or perfect concord. Relations between states may be regarded as a continuum bounded by the extremes of total peace and total war. Peace itself is a continuum ranging from total peace to the point of severe crisis that marks the transition to war. Put differently, it is possible and useful to apply the notion of escalation not only to the means of violence when a limited war develops into total war but to international conflict as such, which can be more or less intense in times of peace. This means that but for the marginal, utopian, and lifeless condition of perfect concord, peace includes international conflict—more or less severe, more or less easily resolved, and representing risks of varying magnitude that resort to war will occur. Similarly, domestic peace includes domestic conflict of all sorts short of civil war. Peace is not indivisible because the peaceful relations that exist in various parts of the globe involve conflicts of different magnitude and intensity.

Second, just as we distinguish between localized and global war, so we must recognize that peace has a territorial dimension. There may be areas of war within larger areas of peace. A war may be extremely intense—when measured by the number of casualties in relation to the total population—and yet be confined to a certain locale, so that, as in the case of a tornado, devastation may be terribly intense at the center while large surrounding areas are not affected.

A notable case in point was the war between Paraguay on the one hand and Brazil, Argentina, and Uruguay on the other; it lasted from 1864 to 1870. In those few years, the total population of Paraguay was reduced from 525,000 to 221,000, with only one-tenth of the survivors being men. Clearly, this was war catastrophically total, but neither its impact on world peace at the time nor its long-range consequences for international relations were as momentous as the wars against Denmark, Austria, and France waged for German unification at about the same time. And these three wars taken together were relatively less bloody than was the fighting that decimated the population of Paraguay.

The third reason why peace is not indivisible is extremely painful to contemplate and perhaps for this reason frequently neglected. We regard peace around us as more important than peace elsewhere. Far-away war disturbs us less than war nearby, just as a quarrel in our family upsets us more than a case of wife-beating down the street. Is it too harsh to suggest that, generally speaking, the magnitude of bloodletting in the aftermath of decolonization in Africa and Asia since the end of the Second

World War has remained a matter of indifference in Europe and America; or if this *is* too harsh, a matter of lesser concern than, say, the uprising in East Germany in 1953, the invasion of Hungary in 1956, of Czechoslovakia in 1968, not to mention the wars in Vietnam and the war in Korea? Yet measured in numbers of people killed, the record demands a different assessment. An effort to count the fatalities in Asia and Africa in the twenty-two years from 1945 to 1967, when Europe was virtually at peace, came up with the estimate of 7.5 million deaths.[1] By this time, the figure is likely to exceed 10 million dead. The count until 1967 includes 2 million killed during the partitioning of India and the creation of Pakistan; 500,000 Sudanese blacks killed (until 1967 only!) in their war against the ruling Sudanese Arabs; 200,000 Watusi and Bahutu mutually killed in the breakup of Burundi and Rwanda; 150,000 Kurds killed in warring against the Iraqis; 100,000 Nagas, Mizos, and Ahams killed in Assam in their efforts to separate from India; 100,000 minority people killed in fighting the ruling Burmese in Burma; 100,000 Chinese killed by Indonesians.

If we were to include in our search for peace local, far-away wars of this kind, clearly our discussion would be considerably extended beyond the limits within which Western considerations of "a lasting peace" are usually conducted. Nor is it possible to discuss the subject with the facile and surprisingly vulgar Marxist expectation that continued or increased economic aid to the new states will bring peace to them.

Thus one of the reasons why peace is not indivisible may be termed a matter of political perception. We pay considerably more attention to our own domestic and international security problems than to bloody conflicts that occur far away. Nor is this ethnocentric orientation confined to matters of war. All nations tend to consider their own immediate interests of paramount importance. They often do so at considerable long-range risk to themselves and, of course, without moral qualms. Recent illustrations include the disjointed responses of NATO governments to the October War in the Middle East and to the economic warfare against countries dependent on oil imports.

The final reason why peace is not indivisible resides in the modern technology of destruction. We fear certain types of war more than others. In the period between the two World Wars, it was the devastation of cities by air attack, outlined at the time by General Giulio Douhet, and the use of poison gas as a personnel weapon, that terrified the West. In the crisis of 1938, when Czechoslovakia was dismembered, the U.S. War Department was "besieged with requests from towns all over the country, including some far inland, for antiaircraft protection."[2] Poison gas was not used in World War II, as it was after World War I by Italy against the Ethiopians and more recently by Egypt in Yemen. And contrary to Douhet's predictions, the awesome devastation of cities from the air did not suffice to achieve victory in World War II. But now we live in the age of nuclear and missile technologies, so when we hope for peace we fear above all, at least in the West, *nuclear* war.

Feelings of dread and intense indignation at new weapons have been common phenomena throughout history from the invention of gunpowder to the building of dreadnoughts, from the first feeble use of air power in the form of observation balloons in the eighteenth century to the invention of submersible ships. Unfortunately, these feelings have very rarely led to restraint in war. Instead, as science and technology have spectacularly improved our standard of living, they have also potently pushed the corresponding means of destruction to higher levels of efficiency. But this time civilization itself appears to have reached the crossroads: nuclear war, the experts tell us, would mean the end of civilization, and the laymen trust that it will not break out, or erroneously think that it cannot possibly occur.

What we may refer to as "nuclear peace" is very widely and rightly regarded as something much more important than the avoidance of "conventional war." It is probably no exaggeration to say that the Cuban missile crisis or the confrontation of Soviet and American tanks in Berlin after the erection of the Wall caused more apprehension in the Western nations than did most of the many conventional wars in the rest of the world that have occurred since the end of World War II. Fear of nuclear war also inspired the American efforts to conclude the treaty that is to prevent the proliferation of nuclear weapons among nuclear have-not powers. To Senator Robert Kennedy no domestic issue and no armed conflict abroad equalled in urgency and importance that of erecting a safeguard in the form of an international treaty against the further spread of nuclear technology. On the floor of the Senate, he made a truly astounding statement on 13 October 1965 about the problem of nonproliferation. He said:

> *I do not care* what progress we make, whether it be in education or poverty or housing, or even in South East Asia, in our relations with Laos and Vietnam, or in the Middle East; if we do not find an answer to this problem, *nothing else means anything.*[3]

TOTAL WAR

The most urgent task of a policy for peace is the avoidance of the "most total" war, if I may use that phrase—that is, of global, nuclear war. Reducing the incidence of limited, localized, or far-away war is, by comparison at least, a less urgent task. It becomes more urgent, however, to the extent that limited, localized, or far-away wars may develop into nuclear war. The probability of escalation is never zero, but in certain wars it is evidently higher than in others. For example, war in the Middle East is more dangerous in this regard than an armed conflict in South America or Central Africa. By the same token, political conflict involving West and East Germany is potentially more dangerous than one between Canada and the United States.

The trouble with this proposition, which seems to be almost a truism, is the different meaning it assumes depending on the national vantage point from which it is viewed. From a global point of view a violent conflict may appear local and limited, while in the experience of the population living and dying in the delimited locale it is well-nigh total. This statement hardly needs amplification. Particularly in the center of Europe it has long been understood and often resented that any limited World War III would in all likelihood be a total war for Europeans; after the war people would be unable to tell the elation of victory from the grief of defeat. A conventional global war may well be won in the end after the loss of a campaign at the beginning, but unlike earlier times, an ill-fated campaign in a future limited world war—in which the use of nuclear warheads was restricted by size, target, or in some other way—might well involve not the provisional loss of a province but the devastation of a country or indeed of several countries. I recall hearing this observation for the first time shortly after the formation of NATO in a conversation with the late General von Sodenstern.

He added a comment to the effect that this prospect would not readily be accepted in Europe.

To cite another illustration, in an interesting essay titled "Does War Have a Future?"[4] Louis J. Halle has recently come to the conclusion, which I regard as controversial, that "the time has probably gone, perhaps forever, when the formal resort of war . . . was an accepted practice among organized societies" and that "except for the acute danger entailed in the sudden internal collapse of some power . . . the day of general wars, directly involving great powers on both sides, may also be past." To reach the first conclusion, Halle makes light of the wars in Africa and Asia that have occurred so frequently since 1945 and have taken such an appalling toll. He comments on the war of 1972 between India and Pakistan over the secession of what had been East Pakistan by saying, in parentheses, that "it may be considered at least a peripheral case, for it concerned the settlement of an unworkable arrangement in the provisions made for the succession of a colonial empire that had been dissolved in the crucible of World War II."

Now wars usually do not break out over workable arrangements, nor are unworkable political arrangements in the wake of a war by any means uncommon. Even from the viewpoint of the victorious Indians the enormous cost of the relatively short war and the influx of 10 million refugees from Bangladesh made this minor war of 1972 a disaster, particularly if added to the economic consequences of the subsequent droughts and the suffering caused by the recent increase in the oil bill from 20 to 50 percent of India's export earnings. Thus again, from a global point of view or from far away, a war may appear as an exception on the fringes of world peace, while to the more than 500 million people directly involved it is a major calamity. Hence it ought to be with a sense of proportion and more than a touch of melancholy that we agree to regard the control of limited or localized war as a relatively unimportant task.

The circumstances in which total war—that is, war involving the depletion of nuclear arsenals—may develop can not, of course, be foreseen. And there is little sense in assuming that insight into the outbreak and course of such a war can be gained by way of war games and sophisticated calculations. Elsewhere I have called attention to the fact that in 1780 the prince of Ligne proposed the opening of an international War Academy in the belief that by studying and teaching military science with topography and geometry providing the basic analytical tools it would be possible to abolish war.[5] War would be recognized as so calculable an enterprise that no reasonable man would want to wage it in the knowledge that he would lose. By present standards, the prince of Ligne's optimism was unsophisticated. To sustain it he had neither research teams of experts nor computers at his disposal. But we who do use "think tanks" and computers should, if anything, be less optimistic than the prince was. For the most frightful war, nuclear war, which we must study in order to avoid it or to control its development, is a war without historical precedent. The experts who study nuclear war are literally studying irreality. Unable to learn from history —and usually unwilling to try—they must establish and proceed on assumptions. Nevertheless, such studies of defense analysts do contribute to the search for peace in a few principal ways.

First, they result in critical evaluations of existing or preferred defense postures on the basis of specified assumptions and assessments of probabilities. This is a more intelligent procedure than recommending defense expenditures on grounds of political preference. If we grant that an adversary may disturb the peace by the use of overwhelming force or pervert the value of peace by successful nuclear blackmail, deterrence is an important safeguard of peace, and an analytical effort that helps to shape an adequate deterrent posture is a contribution to peace.

Second, such studies consider scenarios of nuclear war and inquire into sophisticated weapons systems and strategies with the object of maximizing the likelihood of intrawar deterrence. Efforts in this regard are based on the assumption that tacit or explicit agreements with the adversary are possible during the war which will prevent escalation of the conflict to a full-scale nuclear holocaust. Restraint, for example, in the selection of certain targets or the use of certain weapons may be mutually advantageous. Personally, I am quite skeptical about many of the assumptions regarding "signals," "pauses" in which to arrive at tacit or explicit agreements, and, generally, the possibility of reaching rational decisions under conditions of unprecedented confusion and stress. It is true, however, that restraint in the use of violence is a phenomenon well known from past conventional wars at virtually all levels of technological development.

Third, such studies impress upon us the so-called irrationality of general nuclear war. They teach us that as long as the risks of an unsuccessful surprise attack are staggeringly high, it is counterproductive to embark upon nuclear war, as it will end in catastrophe. "Unsuccessful" is an attack that despite severe damage inflicted upon the enemy fails to destroy his capability of striking back. Responsible studies of nuclear war increase the awareness of the unprecedented calamity its occurrence would constitute for combatants and noncombatants alike, for neutral as well as belligerent states, and possibly even for unborn generations. To the extent that this awesome understanding does not entail a process of unilateral renunciation of power favoring the state with the stronger will and greater indifference toward the deprivations and indulgences of its citizens, a peace of submission may be avoided and the way to the search for a worthier peace may remain open.

Finally, then, analysts of the historically unprecedented nuclear war can attempt to state reasonable priorities for political efforts to establish a balance of terror on a lower technological level by means of arms control and disarmament agreements.

Belittling such analytical and political contributions would be about as foolish as turning against the research and cure of certain types of cancer for the reason that modern medicine is unable to prevent and cure all forms of that disease.

It remains a fact, however, that many so-called experts on nuclear war have little use for history. Perhaps they disdain the goddess Fortuna, and almost certainly they are disturbed by the disorderliness of the human condition. And yet history and the humanities can offer us important insights. Above all, it is possible to assert quite confidently that unrestricted wars are not the result of technology but of unmitigated hatred and horror of the enemy.

Wars tend to be unrestricted especially when the enemy is viewed as a threatening incarnation of evil or as something subhuman—vermin, dogs, snakes, beasts of prey. Such total wars, in which the enemy is satanized or monsterized and is felt to pose a horrible, existential threat, occur in preliterate societies, on very low levels of technology, as well as at more advanced stages of human development. In such conflicts, the enemy can never be bargained with. Nor is it the object to defeat him. He must be destroyed. The aim is not to gain an advantage over him, be it in territory, human or natural resources, privilege, power, or standard of living; the aim is rather to wipe him off the face of the earth.

Now wars in which few, if any, restrictions are placed on the use of violence, on cruelty, fanatical rage, and on horror felt and inflicted, occur under certain typical conditions. I shall not describe and illustrate them in detail, but confine myself to saying that total warfare tends to occur in racial wars, in wars of religion (so-called holy wars), in "ideological wars," to use de Jomini's term, and in class or civil wars. Unrestricted warfare also occurs in violent attempts at liberation from foreign rule, particularly when the subdued population is driven to magnify its power by terror. The technologically superior enemy, in turn, feels justified to lift all restraint in striking back. Guerrilla war, therefore, is characteristically merciless and, unless it ends in exhaustion, may rage until the last opponent is killed. Perhaps the most extraordinary account of guerrilla warfare in its pristine form, comparable in grandeur to Tolstoy's *War and Peace,* is Euclides da Cunha's *Rebellion in the Backlands,* telling the incredible story of the resistance offered by religiously inspired, semibarbaric natives against Brazilian government forces in 1896–1897.

Any possibility of compromise and hence of restriction of violence tends to diminish when in such ethnic, cultural, or religious clashes one side has a monopoly of superior weapons and is not interested in exploiting the manpower of the defeated enemy. As Adam Smith observed in 1776, "In ancient times the opulent and civilized found it difficult to defend themselves against the poor and barbarous nations. In modern times the poor and barbarous find it difficult to defend themselves against the opulent and civilized." Adam Smith attributed this change to the industrialization of weaponry in modern times. His observation still is pertinent, although especially the recent case of the military involvement of the United States in Indochina seems to disprove his contention. Without suggesting that North Vietnam was barbarous, it certainly was poor compared with the United States against which it scored a political victory in the end.

Adam Smith took account neither of the military assistance poor countries can receive in their wars from nations not participating in fighting nor the ideological and emotional force of public opinion that may impinge upon the conduct of the war. At the time American forces were engaged in the wasteful, non-nuclear war in Vietnam, dissatisfaction at home with the military draft and with the persistent lack of success overseas, coupled with the absence of strong moral and material incentives to win, made it possible for public opinion in the United States to rally in favor of extricating American forces. When this was accomplished the government dubbed it "Peace with honor," although no communist regarded it as anything but a victory for his cause. Bloody struggle continued as a civil war without American participation, and public opinion no longer appeared to be concerned with the moral issue of peace in what had become a far-away war.

Compared with the orgies of cruelty, death, and destruction to be found in the total wars of history at all levels of technology, limited war contains elements of civilization—the observance of conventional and legal rules, political and economic reasoning, conscience. Or, simply, limited war contains an element of peace. Again, the specific conditions giving rise to limited wars can be stated in detail, and it would be an appropriate subject of peace research to do so more systematically and more fully than has been done in the past. It must be noted that if under present conditions war does break out, preventing such a war from turning nuclear means keeping the war limited and preserving an element of peace.

Having given the analytical futurologists of thermonuclear war their due, let us now list a few simple historical or humanistic reservations with which their rational efforts must be treated.

1. Fear of violent retaliation to the use of violence deters war only if the aggressor calculates that he will suffer defeat in the end. Since the aggressor may miscalculate, however, and since the attacked—motivated by honor or outrage or simply hoping for an unforeseeable turn of events—may fight against all odds, the fear of war is no firm, reliable bulwark against its outbreak or its escalation.

2. Nor is the calculated prediction of the human and material costs of war a firm, reliable safeguard of peace, no matter how staggering and awe-inspiring these predictions are. This is so because man is capable of recklessness and self-destruction. To repeat, while rational deliberations and calculations, which in-

crease the fear of war and its consequences, help to preserve the peace, we cannot be so assured as to turn away from the problem of war in our time.

3. The control of escalation in a grave political crisis may be easier for dictatorial regimes than for democratic ones, as the former are less subject to pressure by public opinion.

4. In a grave political crisis, established bureaucratic procedures may be suspended in favor of action by small, secretive bodies of decision makers, created ad hoc, or indeed by the supreme decision maker assuming responsibility for the smallest detail. (Incidentally, in view of this phenomenon, exemplified by Churchill in World War II and John F. Kennedy during the Berlin and Cuban missile crises, it is necessary to qualify Max Weber's teaching that modern life is inexorably engulfed by ever-increasing bureaucratization.)

5. Several serious confrontations of the nuclear superpowers were resolved peacefully—for example, in Berlin, in Cuba, and, to a lesser extent, in the Arab-Israeli war of October 1973. Similarly, limited wars involving a nuclear power in the period following World War II—for example, in Korea and Vietnam— did not lead to the employment of nuclear weapons. This record holds no firm promise that such restraint will necessarily be exercised in comparable future situations. Conversely, President Kennedy once said "without vindictiveness that he felt the country was lucky that Nixon had not been president during the Cuban missile crisis."[6]

6. If history is any guide, the most nightmarish scenario of future armed conflict would be an engagement of nuclear powers in which differences in political ideology were exacerbated by racial antagonisms.

7. I do not think it likely, however, that sometime in the future the advanced countries may be subjected to nuclear blackmail and sabotage by terrorists acting for desperately starving millions of the Third World. This specter has recently been conjured up by Robert Heilbroner. In my view, increased violence in the large areas of despair is more likely to occur than terrorist warfare against the outside world. Nor do I consider it probable that the advanced contries would react meekly, should they be so challenged. Their response to the economic-warfare measures against the oil-importing countries of the world provides no precedent for response to international nuclear terror. Finally, I

do not think that attempts at such terror could count on Soviet support, as the risks would be infinitely greater than have been the risks of supporting the oil embargo.

8. At the time when the Soviet leaders were still under the spell of Stalin's doctrine that socialism would emerge victoriously from the inevitable clash between so-called imperialist and socialist powers, Western leaders advocating détente hoped that in time the Soviet leaders might understand that there could be no victor in nuclear war. That is to say, the great hope of détente policy in the West was that, in time, the Soviet leaders might prove to be capable of learning the truth about nuclear war despite their adherence to party doctrine. Khrushchev did indeed sanction this revision of Stalin's reckless and unenlightened teaching on war. Today, it is only the Chinese school of Communist ideology that still adheres to the doctrine of the inevitability of war between imperialism and socialism. Nor has the world received word from the Chinese as yet on the irrationality of nuclear war. Neither the pedagogy of détente nor the influence of conscience-stricken students of nuclear weapons has thus far had any moderating influence on the Chinese doctrine. And in this case it is likely that Russians rather than Americans would have to be the educators, but the Russians are not likely to perform that role. Of course, this doctrinal intransigence need not have any influence on policy. Just as Chinese foreign policy has been remarkably cautious despite its aggressive rhetoric, so the Chinese may exercise restraint in a major war, should they be embroiled in it. One would feel more comfortable, however, if the mounting body of professional opinion on the catastrophic consequences of nuclear war contained contributions from China.

9. As to disarmament agreements, the historical record prior to World War II does not encourage optimism for the future. But perhaps the outcome of SALT II or SALT III will break the historical pattern and set a new precedent. The consequences of failure would be much more ominous than past failures ever were.

DETERRENCE

Neither the work of the defense analysts nor the qualifying observations that a historical orientation may suggest provide very powerful reassurance for peace. On the whole, fear and caution seem to pervade responsible discourse on the chances for peace. And deterrence, itself inspired by caution and fear, emerges as a continued need.[7]

We must add that deterrence may fail not only because of unforeseeable qualitative and quantitative changes in the balance of strategic power but also by virtue of its continued success. Prolonged avoidance of nuclear war may undermine the domestic and Allied consensus without which the defense policy of the West will be enfeebled. Since the individual citizen tends to regard his personal well-being as more important than national security, the free expression of public opinion tends to favor the pursuit of social rather than national goals of policy. There are exceptions to this rule, however: armaments are economically profitable to certain interest-groups; the costs of deterrence appear bearable in times of prosperity; national pride may be aroused by defeat in the arms race; and in times of economic crisis the production of arms for international sale is easily reconciled with public professions of the value of peace. In any event, those who deny the need for deterrence may be encouraged to spread the idea that the adversary's intentions have always been peaceful and that those who insist on guarding the ramparts of peace are obsessed with war—erroneously, neurotically, or maliciously. This paradoxical result of successful deterrence may be reinforced by clamor for disengagement, isolationism, or neutralism and by demands that the government correct shortcomings of its domestic policy. Since deterrence works upon the mind and is a matter of will as well as capability, domestic denials of the need for deterrents are in fact antideterrents.

In Western Europe, such antideterrent moods have been deepened not only by prosperity at home, the Sino-Soviet conflict, and Soviet interest in Western technology and trade, but also by two other specific developments: the success of West German *Ostpolitik* and the shift in Soviet pressure from Central Europe to the Middle East and the Mediterranean. Nobody will deny that *Ostpolitik* has been a contribution to peace, whether or not he may be inclined to argue that the price paid for it has been too high. Massive Soviet support of Arab military and economic warfare and the Soviet naval buildup in the Mediterranean may be viewed as an attempt to outflank NATO after direct political attacks and threats were unproductive. In addition, these Soviet efforts probably were prompted by logistical considerations of Soviet policy toward countries bordering on the Indian Ocean. Although all direct political assaults on the Western alliance failed in the past, the October War of 1973 in conjunction with the Arab oil embargo succeeded for a while in shaking Allied solidarity more severely than any other Soviet initiative. In Europe, the October War was perhaps considered a far-away war, while in the United States at least some observers were concerned lest the war escalate into something worse than Vietnam and more dangerous to world peace than the Cuban missile crisis.[8]

Clearly, this is a matter of judgment and controversy, as is the whole broad topic of the changes for peace. I am also aware of the fact that certain aspects of the problem have been neglected in this chapter.[9]

DÉTENTE

Détente is no alternative to deterrence because the balance of power may shift at the expense of the adversary who neglects his deterrents. His opponent, if given the chance, is not likely to miss the opportunity of expanding his influence by political or military means under the umbrella of détente. He may not have to do much toward that end, as the allies of the nation that neglects the maintenance of its deterrents will drift toward the adversary that does not. A realistic policy of détente must therefore proceed from the assumption that it is designed to supplement rather than replace the policy of deterring the adversary.

The "hard" policy of deterrence has often been attributed to John Foster Dulles, but it must not be forgotten that many developments in Soviet-American relations preceded his becoming secretary of state: the rejection of the Baruch Plan, the Berlin Blockade, the Communist takeover in Czechoslovakia, the war in Korea, and the Communist rejection of aid under the Marshall Plan. Even "the spirit of Geneva" in 1955 and somewhat later "the spirit of Camp David," widely heralded as signs of a relaxation of tension, were conjured up during the Eisenhower administration with Mr. Dulles as secretary of state. But any effort at a "peaceful engagement" was indeed preempted

by the ominous rhetoric of "massive retaliation" in which
Dulles indulged at a time when the American monopoly of nuclear power had been lost forever and when according to President Eisenhower general nuclear war would mean the end of
civilization.

The new American policy of détente began only when President Kennedy assumed office. From the beginning of the Kennedy administration the Communists ceased to be regarded as
irreconcilable enemies of the United States. In a phrase in his
inaugural address, to which McGeorge Bundy called special attention, President Kennedy no longer referred to "the enemy"
or "the potential enemy," but "used a circumlocution whose
unaccustomed clumsiness was proof that it was carefully chosen:
'those nations who would make themselves our adversary.' [10]

The changed function of the American deterrent under the
Kennedy administration was expressed by McGeorge Bundy in
the statement "The President is keeping the peace as long as he
keeps his own nuclear power in check, and with it the nuclear
power of others."[11] The striking novelty of this formulation
consisted in the implied admission that U.S. defense policy
might "provoke" the Soviet Union, whereas earlier the charge
that Western policies were provocative had been left to leaders
of the Soviet bloc; indeed, they made it very often and continued to make it whenever it appeared to serve their purposes.[12]
Bundy, in explaining President Kennedy's quest for peace,
mentioned three broad categories of such provocative American
actions: (1) the deployment of nuclear weapons "which could
be used effectively only in a first strike"; (2) the deployment of
a weapon system "which required a base abroad and evoked a
real or pretended charge of encirclement from Moscow"; and
(3) "the arms race."

On the first item Bundy observed that the president "always
preferred a system which would survive an attack, as against the
systems which might provoke one"; on the second item, that
"for related reasons he preferred the system which was on the
high seas or at home to that which required a base
abroad . . . "; and on the third, that "in the United States only a strong Commander-in-Chief with a strong Secretary of Defense is in a position to press steadily for recognition that the
arms race itself is now a threat to national security."[13]

After the successful resolution of the Cuban missile crisis President Kennedy tried to keep a balance between efforts to reach limited agreements with the Soviet Union and efforts to maintain vigilance against renewed aggression. The terms he employed to describe this stance in November 1963 were "a pause in the cold war"—not its "end"—and "a change in atmosphere" in Soviet-American relations—"not a reversal of [Soviet] purpose." Ideological differences between the two superpowers as well as Soviet "views" of the so-called wars of liberation and Soviet use of subversion set limits to the possibilities of agreement. But he defended many détente measures as being in the national interest: the nuclear test ban treaty, the first wheat deal with the Soviet Union, the effort to keep weapons of mass destruction out of outer space, the emergency communication link between Washington and Moscow, the efforts "to substitute joint and peaceful exploration in the Antarctic and in outer space for cold war exploitation." The reason for this policy was the fear of nuclear war, the specter of 300 million Americans, Russians, and Europeans being wiped out in an hour's nuclear exchange, with the survivors asking, "How did it all happen?" only "to receive the incredible reply" that Bethmann-Hollweg after the outbreak of World War I in 1914 gave to Prince Bülow, the former German chancellor, "Ah, if only one knew."[14]

Shortly before the president spoke at the University of Maine on 9 November 1963, Soviet authorities had once more chosen to interfere with the free movement of Western military traffic on the autobahn in Berlin. Kennedy explicitly referred to it when mentioning the possibility of "less friendly" Soviet actions in the future. He insisted that such actions should not "cause us to regret the steps we have taken" toward limited agreement with the Soviet Union.[15] Thus, while Kennedy implicitly warned that "the pause in the cold war" might come to an end—as the term he employed suggests much more strongly than does the term "détente"—he was bent on trying patiently to extend it, perhaps even at the price of interpreting renewed Soviet political acts of aggression—like blocking the autobahn —with extraordinary magnanimity.

The policy of détente was continued by President Johnson even after the invasion of Czechoslovakia by Soviet and Satellite forces, and it was further extended by Presidents Nixon and Ford. Willy Brandt as chancellor of the Federal Republic contributed to the aims of the policy by his *Ostpolitik,* which for all intents and purposes removed the reunification of Germany from the international agenda; only West Berlin remained, in a weakened position, outside the Communist orbit. Perhaps the two most important extensions of the policy of détente since its beginning under President Kennedy have been the efforts to limit by agreement American and Soviet strategic arms capable of carrying nuclear warheads and the efforts to follow the example set by other NATO powers of reestablishing diplomatic relations with Communist China.

Under the umbrella of détente, the Soviet Union has made important advances. It has succeeded in obtaining international recognition of the existing boundaries in Europe; it has vastly improved its position in the Mediterranean and Africa; imports of American grain have compensated for shortfalls of its agricultural production; and it has increased its military and naval power relative to that of the United States. By contrast, American defense expenditures have decreased during the period of détente in consequence of various developments: the depreciation of the dollar, defeat in Vietnam, the national preoccupation with social services including economic benefits for veterans—at a time of a high rate of unemployment—and finally, rising expectations of assured peace.

Thus, like successful deterrence, détente involves costs as well as benefits. The benefits—brighter prospects for peace—are evident. The costs or risks may be summarized as follows. First, in democratic countries efforts to reach a détente may foster the illusion that the international struggle for power has ceased so that deterrence will be relaxed. Second, there is no guarantee that agreements on the limitations of strategic arms, for example, SALT, and other political agreements between the United States and the Soviet Union will be kept; yet neither side can put up with violations. Third, "preemptive concessions"[16] must never be granted to Soviet negotiators in order to advance on the road to further détente. Neither side must be allowed to use détente as "a subterfuge for unilateral advantage"—a phrase Secretary Kissinger employed in November 1975 to criticize Soviet and Cuban military support of the communist faction in Angola. The cumulative effect of costs in these four respects can be loss of political influence as well as military power.

The fifth risk, while more elusive, is no less grave: it pertains to the compromising of principles. Many such compromises are inevitable in international politics. For example, during the cold war as well as in the era of détente, the U.S. government professed American dedication to the value of liberty but failed to assist minorities in Communist countries struggling for their liberty. The United States let the outcome of such struggles be determined by Soviet armored tanks: 1953 in East Germany, 1956 in Hungary, 1968 in Czechoslovakia. This was done for the sake of peace.

In 1975, however, when President Ford refused to receive Alexander Solzhenitsyn, peace was not in jeopardy. It is difficult to fathom the considerations that prompted this act of discourtesy toward one of the most distinguished victims and critics of Communist oppression. Was it to reassure the men who had forced Solzhenitsyn into exile that the United States would not interfere in Soviet internal affairs? But Solzhenitsyn was, involutarily, on *American* soil. Was it the author's public warnings that the West should be wary of the Russians when pursuing détente? Surely, the president and his secretary of state would have been able to honor the man and respect his views without necessarily sharing them. Was the act of discourtesy possibly committed for the sake of détente? Since the Kremlin does not expect American policy to be swayed by novelists but may be assumed to view with disdain Washington's accommodation to the Kremlin's displeasure with Solzhenitsyn, the president's decision was probably counterproductive in Moscow. In any event, the president and his advisers overlooked the major symbolic significance in the United States of this minor incident. When a political leader in a free society appears not to honor distinctive devotion to liberty and extraordinary manliness of spirit, he fails the people who cherish these values and expect their leaders to uphold them.

Let me say in conclusion that I know of only one major contribution coming from the Soviet Union that has broken out of the circle of deterrence, fear, and cautious détente in which the chances for peace are otherwise confined. This is Andrei D. Sakharov's ''Thoughts on Progress, Peaceful Coexistence and Intellectual Freedom" of 1968,[17] to the effect that the nuclear powers must join in an effort to attack common problems—problems that transcend their rivalry and face all of mankind. But Sakharov, like Solzhenitsyn, is a critic of the Soviet regime.

NOTES

This chapter is an enlarged version of a paper presented at an international conference on the theme "Is Peace Possible? Can we Plan for Peace?" at Bad Godesberg, Germany, on 20–21 June 1974, and published in *Social Research* 42 (Spring 1975).

1. Robert D. Crane, "Postwar Ethnic Cultural Conflicts: Some Quantitative and Other Considerations," manuscript, Hudson Institute, New York, 1968, cited by Harold R. Isaacs in chapter 14 of this volume.

2. *New York Times,* 23 October 1938.

3. *Congressional Record,* 89th Cong., 13 October 1965, p. 25900; emphasis added. For a discussion of this statement, see Hans Speier, *Force and Folly* (Cambridge: M.I.T. Press, 1969), pp. 126ff.

4. *Foreign Affairs* 52 (October 1973):28–34.

5. Hans Speier, *Social Order and the Risks of War* (Cambridge: M.I.T. Press, 1969), p. 240.

6. Benjamin C. Bradlee, *Conversations with Kennedy* (New York: Norton, 1975), p. 133.

7. On deterrence, see Alexander L. George and Richard Smoke, *Deterrence in American Foreign Policy: Theory and Practice* (New York: Columbia University Press, 1974).

8. See Eugene V. Rostow, "America, Europe and the Middle East," *Commentary* 58 (February 1974):40–55.

9. I regret especially that my selective treatment does not include a discussion of Harold D. Lasswell's notion of "the expectation of violence" introduced into the literature more than forty years ago in "The Balancing of Power; the Expectation of Violence," in *World Politics and Personal Insecurity* (New York: McGraw-Hill, 1935).

10. McGeorge Bundy, "The President and the Peace," *Foreign Affairs* 43 (April 1964):358.

11. Ibid.

12. For example, when in April 1965 East German and Soviet authorities tried to prevent the West German Bundestag from exercising its right to hold a one-day meeting with Allied permission in Berlin, some members of the Bundestag, unable to proceed on the blocked roads, used civilian and military aircraft flying from West Germany to West Berlin. On 7 April, *Pravda* described this situation as follows: "A whole crowd of provocateurs with Deputy's credentials, including 12 Bonn ministers, has already gathered on the

banks of the Spree. All this contraband freight, so to speak, has been delivered aboard American military planes'' (*Current Digest of the Soviet Press,* 28 April 1965, p. 20).

13. McGeorge Bundy, pp. 356–362.

14. President Kennedy's address at the University of Maine, 9 November 1963; see *The New York Times,* 20 November 1963.

15. Ibid.

16. The term was reported in 1975 to have been used by James Schlesinger before he resigned as secretary of defense.

17. See chapter 18 of this volume.

CONTRIBUTORS

ZEV BARBU has taught social psychology and sociology in the United States and Scotland and in his native Romania, where he also held important diplomatic posts. He is the author of *Democracy and Dictatorship* (1956), *Problems of Historical Psychology* (1960), and *Society, Culture and Personality* (1971).

WILLIAM BOUWSMA received his Ph.D. in history from Harvard and has taught at the University of Illinois and the University of California at Berkeley, where he is Sather Professor of History. His works include *Concordia Mundi: The Career and Thought of Guillaume Postel* (1957), *Venice and the Defense of Republican Liberty* (1968), and *The Culture of Renaissance Humanism* (1973).

PETER GAY was born in Berlin, in 1923, and received his Ph.D. in government from Columbia University. He has taught at Columbia and at Yale University, where he is Durfee Professor of History. His many publications include *Voltaire's Politics: The Poet as Realist* (1959), *The Enlightenment: An Interpretation* (1966, 1969), *Style in History* (1974), and *Art and Act: On Causes in History* (1976).

WILLIAM E. GRIFFITH received a Ph.D. in history from Harvard and from 1951 to 1958 was political advisor to Radio Free Europe, Munich. He has taught at the Fletcher School of Law and Diplomacy, Tufts University, and at the Massachusetts Institute of Technology, where he is Ford Professor of Political Science. His works include *Albania and the Sino-Soviet Rift* (1963) and *The Sino-Soviet Rift* (1964).

HAROLD R. ISAACS worked as a reporter, editor, and foreign correspondent for more than twenty years. In 1953 he joined MIT's Center for International Studies as a research associate, and in 1965 became a professor of political science. He is the author of *The Tragedy of the Chinese* (1938, rev. 1961), *Scratches on Our Minds* (1958), *The New World of Negro Americans* (1963), *India's Ex-*

Untouchables (1965), *American Jews in Israel* (1967), and *Idols of the Tribe: Group Identity and Political Change* (1975).

MAURICE JOLY (1821–1878), French barrister and publicist, was the author of *Dialogue in Hell between Machiavelli and Montesquieu or Machiavelli's Policies in the Nineteenth Century*. This treatise, published anonymously in Brussels in 1864, was an imperfectly disguised attack on the policies of Napoleon III, but at the same time a brilliant exposition of modern plebiscitarian despotism. The book was later plagiarized by the fabricators of the *Protocols of the Elders of Zion*.

DANIEL LERNER received his Ph.D. from New York University and taught at Stanford University, where he also served as research director of the International Studies project, Hoover Library. In 1953 he joined the faculty of MIT, becoming Ford Professor of Sociology in 1958. His works include the classic *Passing of Traditional Society* (1958).

GUENTER LEWY received his Ph.D. from Columbia University and has taught at Columbia, Smith College, and the University of Massachusetts, Amherst, where he is professor of political science. He is the author of *Religion and Revolution* (1974) and other books and articles in the field of religion and politics.

SAUL K. PADOVER received his Ph.D. from the University of Chicago and joined the graduate faculty of the New School for Social Research as professor of political science in 1948. In 1970 he became Distinguished Service Professor. His works include *Jefferson: A Biography* (1942), *The Genius of America* (1960), *The Meaning of Democracy* (1963), and several volumes of the writings of Karl Marx which he edited for the Karl Marx Library.

LUCIAN W. PYE has been professor of political science at MIT since 1960. He received his Ph.D. in political science from Yale and worked as a research associate at the Center for International Studies at Princeton from 1952 to 1956, when he joined the MIT faculty. Among his works are *Guerrilla Communism in Malaya* (1956); *Politics, Personality and Nation-Building* (1961); *Aspects of Political Development* (1966); *Spirit of Chinese Politics* (1968); *China: An Introduction* (1972); and *Mao Tse-Tung: The Man in the Leader* (1976).

NANCY L. ROELKER received a Ph.D. in history from Harvard and has taught at Tufts University and Boston University, where she is professor of history. She is the author of *In Search of France* (1963) and *Queen of Navarre: Jeanne d'Albret, 1528-1572* (1968).

ANDREI D. SAKHAROV, following graduation from Moscow University in 1942, joined the Lebedev Institute of Physics in Moscow, where he received his doctorate in physics in 1947. In 1953, at age 32, he was elected a full member of the Soviet Academy of Sciences for his work on theoretical aspects of controlled thermonuclear fusion—the harnessing of nuclear power for the generation of electricity for peaceful purposes. In recent years Dr. Sakharov has continued to voice his views on public affairs.

OSCAR SCHACHTER has combined a scholarly and a practical career in international affairs for more than thirty years. He has been a State Department official, a director of the Legal Division of the United Nations, a representative of the Secretary-General at international conferences, a teacher of international law at Yale and Columbia, and the author of numerous publications on international law and institutions. He is currently professor of international law at Columbia University and editor-in-chief of the *American Journal of International Law*.

HANS SPEIER received his Ph.D. from the University of Heidelberg and was a member of the graduate faculty of the New School for Social Research from 1933 to 1942. He joined the Rand Corporation in 1948, serving as chief of the Social Sciences Division until 1960 and as a member of the research council from 1961 to 1969. He is now Robert M. MacIver Professor Emeritus in Political Science and Sociology at the University of Massachusetts, Amherst. Among his works are *Social Order and the Risks of War* (1952) and *Force and Folly* (1969).

BARTON WHALEY received his Ph.D. from MIT and is a Fellow of the Royal Asiatic Society. He has been a member of the Joint Harvard–MIT Arms Control Seminar since 1967. Among his publications are *Stratagem: Deception and Surprise in War* (1970) and *Operation Barbarossa* (1973).

INDEX

180, 196; Sabbatean movement, 171; thought, 35; tradition in interpretation of scripture, 267
Jews: pogroms of, 308; reentry of, in Middle East, 403; Swiss, 309; in U.S., 411, 412
John, St., 269
John of Leyden, 172, 191, 193
John of Salisbury, 268
Johnson, President Lyndon, 523
Johnson, Samuel, 101–102, 377
Jokes and ambiguity, 261–262
Joly, Maurice, 301–316, 386, 394n; biography of, 303–304; contribution of, to political thought, 310–311, 312–314; *Dialogue* of, 306, 307–308, 309, 310, 317–338; predictive powers of, 311–312, 314
Jomini, Baron Henri, 159, 343, 344–345, 359, 516
Jones, R. V., 359
Joseph of Arimethea, 74
Journal de Trévoux, 104
Journal of Conflict Resolution, 392
Journalism: European, 211; as a freemasonry, 325; Kierkegaard on, 164; Marx in, 210–211, 214, 215, 234n; and Napoleon III, 315; in totalitarian regimes, 288–289
Journals, 155, 425
Jouvenel, Bertrand de, 392
Judaism: idea of new world in, 184–185; teleological conception of history, 185, 186
Jünger, Ernst, 281–282, 284, 298n
Juridical categories, 455, 457
Jurisdiction, issues of, 447, 448
Justice, theme of, in Protestant propaganda, 75–76
Justification by faith, doctrine of, 63

Kant, Immanuel, 91, 92, 94, 96, 97, 98, 99, 286; on Enlightenment, 85, 100, 101, 109
Katanga, U.N. controversy on, 450
Keldvsh, Mstislav V., 493
Keller, Gottfried, 286
Kempis, Thomas à, 22
Kennedy, President John F., 500–501, 508, 518, 522–523, 524, 527n
Kennedy, Senator Robert, 511–512
Kenya, 395, 396–397, 404, 406
KGB, 363, 492, 506a
Khalkhin-Gol, 350
Khaustov, Viktor, 492, 506a
Khrushchev, Nikita S., 246, 247–248, 500–501, 506a; destalinization by, 362–363, 485–486, 519
Kierkegaard, Sören, 154, 164, 165n, 167n

Kimbangu, Simon, 174, 199; cult of, 199
King: Burmese notion of Future, 207n; as enemy, 130; as future Buddha, 187; trial of French, 123, 124
King, Admiral Ernest J., 358
Kingdom of God, 169, 172, 179, 182, 185, 198, 203
Kirk of Scotland, 69, 72
Kishinev, Bessarabia, 305
Kissinger, Secretary of State Henry, 276, 524
Kistiakowsky, Dr., 468, 469
Klemperer, Victor, 286, 299n
Klings, Carl, 224–225
Klopstock, Friedrich Gottlieb, 93
Knowledge, 78–79, 239; accumulation of, 32–33
Koestler, Arthur, 414
Kon, Igor, 490
Korea, war in, 510, 518, 521
Kosygin, Aleksei N., 248
Kovalevsky, Maxim, 213, 235n
Kugelmann, Dr. Ludwig, 225–226, 228, 229, 230
Kurds, 397, 406, 510
Kushev, Yevgeny, 492, 506a

Labor, 217, 219; camps, Stalinist, 484; glorification of, 494–495, 496; indentured, 406; physical, 250; social value of, 498–499; unions, 413
Laclos, Chaderlos de, 135
Language, 25; aesthetic uses of, 20, 262; everyday, 274–275; groups, 405, 433, 434, 441; humanist view of, 18; metaphorical, 262; orders, aristocratic, 156; playful uses of, 262; of the press, 327, 330; in public communication, 28; regulation, 286, 288, 289; riots, 406; secret, 277, 278; special and exclusive, 277–278
Languages: ancient, 25, 27, 78; of great empires, 400; liturgical, 278; national, 377. *See also* Vernacular
Lao Tzu, 188, 286
Lassalle, Ferdinand, 221, 222
Lasswell, Harold D., xii, 377, 382, 393n, 394n, 462, 526n
Latimer, Hugh, 51, 54, 60, 63
Latin, 9, 11, 17, 20, 29; euphemisms, 300n; fathers, 80n; literature, 9, 10, 17, 28, 29; medieval, 16, 20; medieval as elite communication, xi, 28, 35, 278, 295, 377; translations, 16, 20, 26
Latin America, 488, 512; Castro and revolution in, 252, 253; food balance in, 479; military doctrine in, 347; newspaper consumption in, 438; population mixes in, 406; reactionary

✸ Production Notes

This book was designed by Roger J. Eggers and
typeset on the Unified Composing System by the
design and production staff of The University
Press of Hawaii.

The text and display typeface is Garamond No. 49.

Offset presswork and binding were done by Halliday
Lithograph. Text paper is Glatfelter P & S Offset,
basis 55.